REVISED EDITION

MONEY
MATTERS

ENGLISCH FÜR BANKKAUFLEUTE

SUSAN LAU

Cornelsen
& OXFORD

Money Matters wurde geplant und entwickelt von der
Verlagsredaktion der Cornelsen & Oxford University Press
GmbH & Co., Berlin

Verfasserin:	Susan Lau
Verlagsredaktion:	James Austin
Redaktionelle Mitarbeit:	Christine House, Leah Williams
Berater:	Wilfried Ramacher, Berliner Bank, Berlin
Design / Herstellung:	Oxford Designers & Illustrators
Bildredaktion:	Uta Hübner

Erhältlich sind auch:
Audio CD (Best.-Nr.) 23044
Lehrerhandbuch (Best.-Nr.) 23036

Cornelsen online www.cornelsen.de

1. Auflage €

5	4.	3.	2.	Die letzten Ziffern bezeichnen Zahl
05	04	03	02	und Jahr des Druckes.

Alle Drucke dieser Auflage können, weil untereinander unverändert, im Unterricht nebeneinander verwendet werden.

Bestellnummer 23028

Druck & Weiterverarbeitung: Freiburger Graphische Betriebe
Gedruckt auf chlorfrei gebleichtem Papier ohne Dioxinbelastung der Gewässer.

ISBN 3-8109-2302-8

Vertrieb: Cornelsen Verlag, Berlin

Vorwort

Money Matters ist ein Lehrwerk für angehende und erfahrene Bank- und Sparkassenkaufleute, die am Berufsschulunterricht oder an betrieblichen Fortbildungsmaßnahmen teilnehmen. Es richtet sich an Lernende, deren allgemeine Englischkenntnisse dem Niveau eines soliden mittleren Bildungsabschlusses bzw. dem eines durchschnittlichen gymnasialen Grundkursabschlusses entsprechen, bietet aber zusätzlich in allen Einheiten fakultative *Advanced Materials*, um Fortgeschrittene, die Englisch als Leistungsfach betrieben oder Erfahrung im englischsprachigen Ausland gewonnen haben, gezielt zu fördern. Kenntnisse in Wirtschaftsenglisch werden nicht vorausgesetzt.

Money Matters lehrt in erster Linie die sprachlich korrekte und angemessene Bedienung und Beratung von englischsprachigen Privat- und Firmenkunden in allen wichtigen Bereichen des deutschen Bankgeschäfts. Es setzt Grundkenntnisse der deutschen Bankbetriebslehre aus Schule und Praxis voraus und erarbeitet die fremdsprachlichen Kompetenzen, die am Arbeitsplatz erforderlich sind. Banktypische Dialoge, auch am Telefon, mit Gesprächspartnern unterschiedlicher Nationalität schulen das Hörverständnis; realistische Rollenspiele und *case studies* aktivieren die Bereitschaft zur mündlichen Kommunikation; praxisrelevante Auszüge aus Presseartikeln und Bankbroschüren sowie authentische Formulare und Dokumente fördern das Leseverständnis und bieten zusammen mit Zahlen- (Börsenkursen Bilanzzahlen, Grafiken) und Bildmaterial (Fotos und Cartoons), eine Vielzahl weiterer Sprechanlässe. Mit den *Advanced Materials* wird neben dem Vertiefen des Fachvokabulars eine in Wort und Schrift differenzierte Ausdrucksweise angestrebt.

Das Kreditwesen – besonders in Deutschland – befindet sich in einer Phase starken Wandels. In dieser neuen Ausgabe von *Money Matters* wird den teils positiven, teils problematischen Veränderungen Rechnung getragen, z.B. der wachsenden Konkurrenz im Finanzdienstleistungssektor, dem Internet-Banking, der Notwendigkeit der privaten Altersvorsorge, dem gestiegenen Interesse an Börsengeschäften, dem Neuen Markt, der Globalisierung und Innovationen in der Kundenbetreuung wie Bank-Shops. Im Bankenbereich werden sich nur die stärksten Unternehmen durchsetzen: Dies gilt auch für Bankkaufleute, die aber durch Qualifizierung ihre Chancen auf dem Arbeitsmarkt verbessern können. *Money Matters* will einen Beitrag dazu leisten, dieses Ziel zu erreichen.

Susan Lau
Hamburg, im Juni 2001

🎧 Dieses Symbol weist darauf hin, dass sich der Text bzw. Dialog auf der CD befindet.

Contents

Danksagung

Wir bedanken uns bei folgenden Firmen, die uns freundlicherweise Material für dieses Lehrwerk zur Verfügung gestellt haben.

Alfru Industriefrucht GmbH
American Express Inc.
Association of British Insurers
Barclays Bank plc
Berliner Bank Niederlassung der Bankgesellschaft Berlin AG
Boone County National Bank
Business Channel / RKD
Commerzbank AG
Deutsche Bank AG
Deutsches Institut für Altersvorsorge
Hamburger Sparkasse
Institute of Financial Services
Kreissparkasse Pinneberg
Lloyds TSB plc
National Westminster Bank plc
Tesco Personal Finance Ltd.
Vereins- und Westbank AG
Washington Mutual Inc.

Ferner gilt unser herzlicher Dank den Herausgebern folgender Presseerzeugnisse.

Connectis
Frankfurter Allgemeine Zeitung
Hamburger Abendblatt
The Economist
The Financial Times
The Times
Time Magazine

Money Matters wird von dem *British Swiss Chamber of Commerce* (BSCC) und dem *Institute of Financial Services* (ifs) – dies ist die offizielle Kennzeichnung des *Chartered Institute of Bankers* (CIB) – zur Vorbereitung auf die Prüfungen *Certificate in English for Banking and Finance* und *Diploma in English for Banking and Finance* als geeignetes Lehr- und Lernmaterial empfohlen.

Diese Prüfungen werden von dem *Chartered Institute of Bankers* und dem *British Swiss Chamber of Commerce* gemeinsam erstellt, bewertet und zertifiziert.

UNIT 1

Introducing banking

Lead-in

Describe the picture above. What trend does it show? In your opinion, could banks look like this in the future? Is personal service still important in banking today?

1 *Shopping*

A British customer in a large department store in Germany asks a sales assistant for help.

CUSTOMER	Excuse me ... Excuse me! ... EXCUSE ME! ... Could you help me, please? Do you speak English?
SALES ASSISTANT	Sure. What can I do for you?
CUSTOMER	That portable CD player over there – the one on the top shelf ... Could I have a closer look at it, please?
SALES ASSISTANT	This one? Just a minute ... Here you are.
CUSTOMER	Thanks.
SALES ASSISTANT	It's the last one we've got in stock at the moment. I'll put a disc in so you can hear what it sounds like.
CUSTOMER	No, don't bother. It's just what I'm looking for. How much is it?
SALES ASSISTANT	Let me see ... 59 euros – that's including VAT.

CUSTOMER That's a bargain. I'd have to pay a lot more than that to get one as good as this in England.

SALES ASSISTANT They usually cost more here, too. It's on special offer this month.

CUSTOMER Great. I'll take it.

SALES ASSISTANT Anything else I can do for you?

CUSTOMER No, that's all, thanks. ... Oh dear, I'm running out of cash. You wouldn't accept a Barclays cheque, would you? I've got a cheque card.

SALES ASSISTANT May I see? Is it a Eurocheque card? ... No, sorry, we don't accept any other cheque cards. But we take all the usual credit cards: American Express, VISA, Eurocard.

CUSTOMER Hang on a second. I think I can just about manage to pay for it in cash after all. I've got a note here somewhere – and I want to get rid of all these coins before I leave the country.

SALES ASSISTANT I'll just make out your bill. Then if you take it to the till over there on the left, my colleague will give you the CD player and your receipt. ... Here you are. Are you going back to Britain soon then?

CUSTOMER Yes, I'm flying back tonight. I'm playing a concert in London tomorrow evening.

SALES ASSISTANT Really? What do you play?

CUSTOMER The drums.

SALES ASSISTANT So do I! In a group?

CUSTOMER Well, yes, you could say so.

SALES ASSISTANT I hope your concert goes well. What's your group called, by the way?

CUSTOMER The BBC Symphony Orchestra.

Answer these questions.

1 Why is the CD player a bargain?
2 What means of payment are mentioned?
3 Which method of payment does the customer prefer? Why?
4 The sales assistant speaks of the bill and the receipt. What is the difference?
5 What is the customer planning to do later?

2 *Role play I*

With a partner play the roles of a customer and a sales assistant. The customer may buy any kind of goods he or she likes. Use these words in your dialogue.

bill • *cash* • *cheque card* • *coin* • *credit card* • *note* • *receipt* • *till*

LOOKING AT LANGUAGE

THE PRESENT

1 We **take** all the usual credit cards.
2 What **do** you **play**? – I **play** the drums.
3 **I'm running out** of cash.
4 **Are** you **going** back to Britain soon? – Yes, **I'm playing** in a concert tomorrow.

- The **present tense** is used in two forms in the dialogue.
- The **simple present** is used for actions which are generally true *(1)* or which occur from time to time *(2)*.
- The **present progressive** is used for actions which are happening at the moment *(3)* or which are planned for the future *(4)*.

3 *Practice*

Use the simple present or the present progressive to answer the following questions.

1 What foreign languages do you speak?
2 Why are you learning English?
3 What are you wearing at the moment?
4 What sort of clothes do you normally wear at home?
5 Where do you live?
6 How do you usually travel to work?
7 What are you doing after work this evening?
8 How do you like to spend your holidays?
9 Where are you spending your next holiday?
10 How do you usually spend Christmas?
11 What are you doing this weekend?
12 What sort of books do you enjoy reading?

4 *Interview your neighbour*

Ask the person sitting next to you questions about his or her place of work, home, family, hobbies, etc. Take notes and use them to introduce your neighbour to your fellow students. Start like this:

May I introduce you to …

She He	works as a	trainee clerk	with at	the … Bank. the … Savings Bank.

She He	lives … enjoys … likes …

5 *At work*

Julia Weber is a trainee with a German bank. She works at a large branch in the city centre. Here are some of her colleagues. Look at the layout of the branch below and say who usually works where.

Ilona Albrecht
– branch manager

Anne Kleinschmidt
– customer service officer

Hans Petersen
– investment consultant

Ali Özcan
– personal loan adviser

Dieter Holm
– corporate business manager

Jane Kaminsky
– cashier + counter clerk

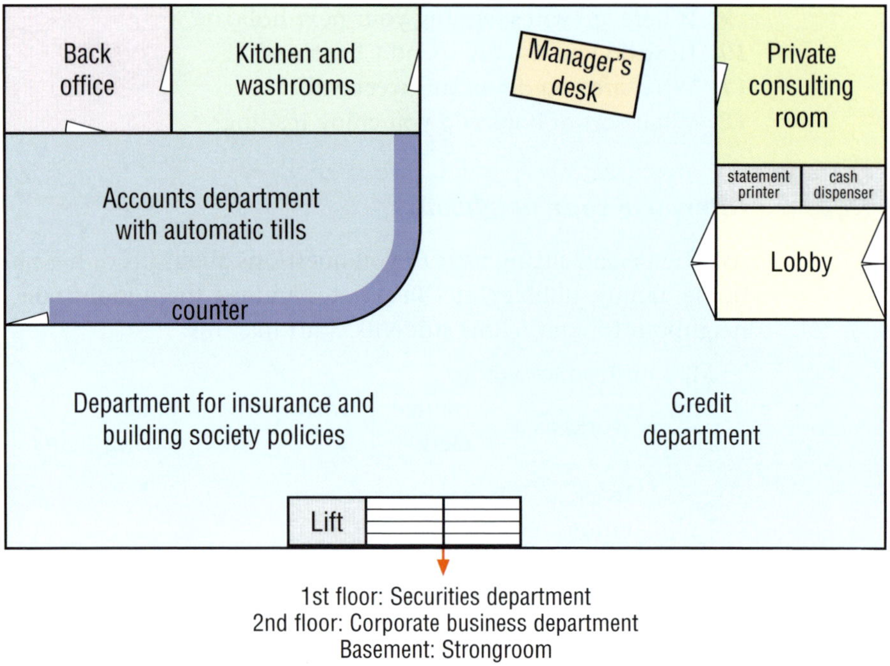

6 *At the counter*

During Julia's first week at the branch five English-speaking customers come in. Listen and take notes about what each person wants and how Julia serves him or her. Then report to the other members of the group.

7 *Serving customers*

Listen to the dialogues from exercise 6 again (or read them on page 125) and do the following.

1 Write down the expressions Julia Weber uses:
   a to greet each customer,
   b to offer the customer a seat or some coffee,
   c to arrange for a customer to see a colleague.

2 Compare what you have written with the expressions below to see if your lists are complete.

HOW TO

– greet a customer

Good | morning. / afternoon. | Nice to see you again. / How are you today?

Can / May | I help you?

What can I do for you?

– offer a customer a seat / coffee

Would you come this way?
Take a seat, please.
Would you like to sit down for a moment?
Would you like to wait in the office?
Can I offer you a cup of coffee while you're waiting?

– arrange for a customer to see a colleague

I'll just call our customer service officer. She'll be able to help you.
I'll ring through to our … department and see if … is free.
Would you please go over to the till? My colleague there will be able to help you.
Would you like to have an appointment with …?
Would … o'clock be convenient?
I'm afraid … is in a meeting. Would you like to speak to … instead?

8 A mind map

Look at this mind map which shows the main financial services that banks offer and do the following.

1 Find the services mentioned in exercise 6 on the map.
2 Say which other services personal customers use.
3 Name the services which are often used by corporate clients.

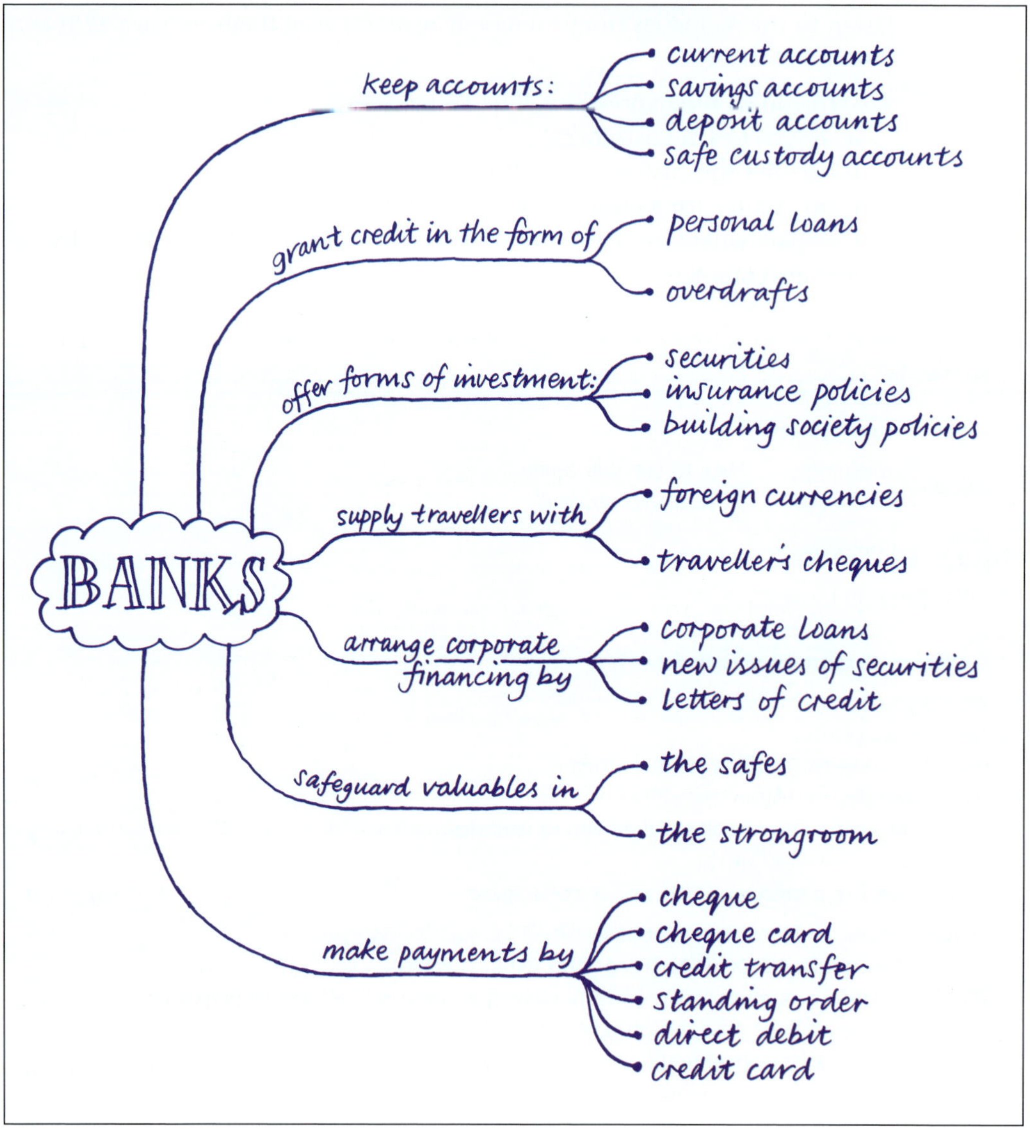

9 Your bank

Write a short text about the branch where you work. Describe what types of customers come in and what services are offered.

10 *Role play II*

With a partner taking the part of the customer, play the role of the trainee at the counter. Serve the customer as far as you can* using expressions from the box on page 11 and vocabulary from the mind map. Keep changing the roles.

** If you cannot serve a customer yourself, you should arrange for him or her to see a colleague in the appropriate department.*

Here are some suggestions for the customers' roles. Use them or think up ideas of your own.

1 You want to transfer some money to Canada.
2 You are going on holiday to Australia and want advice on how to take your money with you.
3 You want an account for your son, aged six, for his pocket money.
4 You are going away for three months and don't want to leave your collection of gold coins at home.
5 You have inherited some capital and want to invest it.
6 You want to know about using bank services outside banking hours.
7 You need a loan to buy a new computer for your business.
8 You are planning to buy a house in three years' time.
9 You need extra money to pay for some driving lessons.
10 Your company is starting to export and you need advice.

11 *Working with words*

Use expressions from this unit to complete these sentences.

1 A person who is training to become a bank clerk is a … .
2 A person who works together with me at my work-place is a … .
3 The money which people earn monthly is their … .
4 Most people keep their money in a … … .
5 Dollars, euros and yen are three types of … .
6 If a customer wants to invest money, he or she can arrange some life … at the bank.
7 If a customer plans to build or buy a house in the future, it is advisable to open a … … policy now.
8 The place at the branch where the cash is kept is the … .
9 Bank clerks who give specialist advice on investments or loans are called investment … or loan … .
10 If a customer wishes to speak to the branch manager, it is best to make an … .
11 Companies are granted loans in the … … department.
12 Outside banking hours customers can use the … … to obtain cash.
13 Customers who need to borrow money will be granted a … .
14 Customers wishing to invest can buy … .
15 Valuables can be placed in a safe in the bank's … .

12 *A brochure*

Customers do not have to come into the branch to use banking services. This brochure from NatWest in Britain describes two other ways to contact the bank. Answer these questions.

1. What advantages do both services offer customers?
2. What can customers do if they use these services?
3. How can customers arrange to join these services?
4. What home banking services does your bank offer?

Put yourself in

contact

24 hours a day with telephone and PC banking

Telephone banking

With NatWest's telephone banking service, you can keep in touch with your bank account 24 hours a day, 365 days of the year. This means you have the convenience of doing your banking by phone at any time of day or night – from home, from where you work or from abroad.

You can do everyday things, such as checking your balance or finding out what's gone in or out of your account. You have much greater access to your account, too.

You can ask for our telephone banking service when you open your account. Or, if you already have a NatWest account, simply call **0345 77 77 66** and we'll send you full details about joining.

We also offer a person-to-person telephone banking service called Primeline which gives you the option of having your own Personal Banking Manager to help you with more complicated financial matters. Ask at any branch or call **0800 00 44 00** for more details.

PC banking

NatWest On-Line, our PC banking service, gives you 24-hour access to your account from your PC, at home or in the office.

You can check your balance on-screen, view recent transactions and see what's gone in and out of your account in seconds (including any NatWest credit card accounts). What's more, you can order chequebooks and paying-in books, set up and pay all your regular bills and transfer money between your accounts – all at the touch of a button.

NatWest On-Line is easy to set up and simple to use. Your calls to the service are charged at a local rate. And you have the full support of our 24-hour freephone help desk.

To apply to join NatWest On-Line, simply ask at your local branch. Or call us on **0800 281 292** from 8am to 8pm Monday to Friday, 9am to 6pm Saturday. We're also on the internet at **www.natwest.co.uk**

13 *Creative writing*

Your bank is preparing a brochure to inform its English-speaking customers about new ways of doing their banking business. Write a short text to inform readers about either telephone banking or PC banking. Include the following points in any order you like.

1. Say what the customer needs to use the service.
2. Explain what the service can be used for.
3. Point out two advantages for the user.
4. Mention how the reader can apply for this service.

Advanced materials

Internet banking

14 *Banking: past, present and future*

Describe these three pictures. Explain what development they show.

Banking, 1990

Banking, 1998

Banking, 2001

15 *Group work*

Form five groups. Each group should discuss one of these topics. Use the text on the next page as a starting point and add ideas of your own. Then choose a speaker to present your group's results to the other students.

1. What are the advantages of Internet banking for banks and their customers? Present them in order of importance.

2. Does Internet banking have any disadvantages, risks or problems from the user's or the bank's point of view? Make suggestions how they can be overcome.

3. Do banks want to attract a particular type of customer with Internet banking? Draw up a customer profile. Suggest marketing strategies to attract these people.

4. "Quality of service, rather than products or technology, will decide who survives in the banking sector." How far do you agree? Support your group's opinion with examples.

5. Could Internet banking replace branch banking? Describe how you see banks twenty years from now. Look at the consequences for the bank, its customers and its staff.

@ The Bank

The rapid growth of the Internet as a service delivery option presents banks with perhaps the greatest dilemma in their long history.

More and more high net-worth clients are choosing to do their banking via their personal computer. Market analysis has shown that Internet banking is most popular among educated professionals in the 25–45 age group. These are the cash-rich, time-starved folk who rarely have time to visit their local branch and who value the extra control of their finances that direct online access offers. They see the value in investing in computer technology at home for the potential lifestyle enhancement that it brings, as well as giving their children an educational headstart in life. The Internet thus gives banks an opportunity to capture the next generation of account holders at an early age. It also offers a means of marketing products to consumer groups who find it physically difficult to visit a branch or use a call-centre: the disabled, the deaf and people on shift work.

One aspect which will ultimately increase the growth of Internet banking services is that of economics. Research has shown that exceptional cost savings can be achieved by processing traditional bank transactions online, compared with branch or telephone operations. Even the cost of setting up and maintaining an Internet banking service compares favourably with the expense of running bank branches.

Despite these advantages, however, banks are having to consider a number of problems. First, how will Internet banking affect their relationship with their customers? Will it be weakened if customers never deal with a "warm body" in the bank's organization. In the longer term, what will it mean if fewer and fewer customers need to go into, or even need, a bank branch? Additionally the installation of ATMs at garages, supermarkets and other locations means that customers no longer have to visit a branch to withdraw cash. Electronic means of payment further reduce the need even for ATM visits.

While banks have to provide Internet services to avoid losing valued clients, what about the rest of their customers – those that cannot afford the outlay of £1,000 for a computer to get online? The majority of the population can probably think of nothing worse than spending their leisure time staring at a computer screen and tinkering around with their personal finances. But to be viable, Internet banking has to find ways of appealing to the mass market. Digital TV could become a powerful delivery channel – after all, many spend hours looking at their television screens every day.

In Internet banking, the USA leads the way. But is the US situation applicable to Europe? In a country where the average citizen spends 24 hours a year writing and posting cheques to pay bills, there is obviously a need for electronic bill presentment. In Europe, however, direct debits and standing orders are popular and convenient payment systems. Consumers are also nervous about the question of security. The argument that "security which is good enough for the US military is good enough for the banks" carries little weight in Europe. People would prefer to see banks acting as guarantors for Internet transactions in the same way as credit card organizations do for fraudulent misuse.

For banks, competition in the market for financial services is increasing daily. Any provider with data that gives an accurate consumer profile can, in fact, offer banking transactions. Competitors range from supermarkets offering banking to pure online banks. In the past customers stayed with their bank from the age of 18 till their death; today they can switch to a competitor with a mouse-click. To be successful, banks must offer more than the standard account enquiry and bill payment options. Loans, forex purchase, share-dealing or access to e-commerce virtual shopping malls have a broader appeal.

In the end, quality of service, rather than products or technology, will decide who survives in the banking sector. Customers who have extra cash at the end of the month want to know if it is better to pay off their loan or their credit card debt. If someone is looking for a mortgage, information on the area they would like to live in – what the rail service is like, which schools are the best and a brief history of the area – could be provided on the website. Banks need vision and capital to beat the competition and become pan-European providers. Less successful ones will have to submit to the dominance of a brand leader, which might not even be a bank at all.

(adapted from an article by Roger Issott of Compaq in *Financial World*, the Chartered Institute of Bankers Magazine)

UNIT
2 Types of account

Lead-in

Describe the cartoon and explain the development it shows.

1 Current accounts

Sally Lawson from Britain enters a branch of a German bank and approaches Mark Richter, the clerk at the counter.

SALLY LAWSON Hello. I was wondering if you could help me.

MARK RICHTER Sure. What can I do for you?

SALLY LAWSON I'd like some information about the current accounts you offer. I'm from Scotland, but I'll be staying in Germany for a year.

MARK RICHTER Are you working here?

SALLY LAWSON Yes, I'm learning hotel management at the Interconti, so I'll need an account for getting my salary.

MARK RICHTER Of course. Would you like to take a look at our brochure about current accounts? Just a minute. ... Here you are. Sorry we haven't got any English ones.

SALLY LAWSON That doesn't matter. I'm sure British banks don't have any brochures in German!

MARK RICHTER Probably not. Now I'd suggest our Student Account. You'll get all our basic services completely free of charge while you're training ...

SALLY LAWSON Actually I don't think I'd be eligible for that. I'm not a trainee any more. I'm here on a one-year contract.

MARK RICHTER Oh, sorry. In that case our Classic Account would be suitable for you. It's for receiving and withdrawing money and of course for transferring sums to other accounts as well.

SALLY LAWSON In Britain we often pay regular bills by standing order or direct debit. Will I be able to do that here, too?

MARK RICHTER Yes, you can use all the various means of payment.

SALLY LAWSON Will I get a cheque book, as well then? I pay for lots of things by cheque in Britain.

MARK RICHTER Most people don't write cheques any more in Germany. They just use the Eurocheque card on its own – in shops for example.

SALLY LAWSON I see. Will I get one with this account?

MARK RICHTER Yes, you will. You'll need it to operate the statement printer and the ATM as well.

SALLY LAWSON By the way, is there any period of notice for withdrawals from this account?

MARK RICHTER No, you needn't give notice at all. You have access to all the money in your account at any time.

SALLY LAWSON That's good, but what about overdrafts?

MARK RICHTER When your salary has been paid into your account, we'll arrange an overdraft facility for you so there won't be any problems if you overdraw the account. Of course interest will be charged on any debit balance you have.

SALLY LAWSON Really? In Britain you mustn't go into the red at all. If you do, it usually means an expensive letter from the bank manager and a penalty fee.

MARK RICHTER I didn't know that. That can't happen to you here.

SALLY LAWSON That's great. Is any interest paid on this account?

MARK RICHTER No, I'm afraid we don't pay any interest at all on a Classic Account. Our Gold Account pays interest on credit balances of 5,000 euros or more and includes a free credit card as well. The rate of interest you get depends on how much ...

SALLY LAWSON I think we can skip that one. I'm not likely to have that much money in my account. What about this Classic Account? Does it include a credit card, too?

MARK RICHTER I'm afraid it doesn't. I'm sure that we could arrange for you to have a Eurocard, but there would be an extra annual charge for it. All the other services I've mentioned are included in the basic monthly fee for our Classic Account. Oh, I nearly forgot to ask – are you interested in telephone or online banking?

SALLY LAWSON Definitely. I'd be lost without my notebook.

MARK RICHTER The Classic Account includes both telephone banking and online banking. It's all described in the brochure.

SALLY LAWSON Hmm. I'd like to have a closer look at it at home. I can probably manage with a dictionary.

MARK RICHTER Of course. Here's my card with the branch phone number and opening hours. Just give me a ring or call in if there's anything else you'd like to ask.

SALLY LAWSON I will. Thanks for your help.

MARK RICHTER You're welcome. Goodbye.

Answer these questions.

1 Why does Sally Lawson need a bank account in Germany?
2 Which means of payment does a Classic Account offer?
3 What does Mark Richter tell Sally Lawson about withdrawals?
4 What is the difference between banking in Britain and in Germany, as regards overdrawing the account?
5 How is a Classic Account different from a Gold Account?
6 Which account is Sally Lawson interested in? Why?

2 *A presentation*

What current accounts does your bank offer? List their main features. Then use your notes to give a short presentation that makes the differences clear.

3 *Working with words*

Find banking terms in the dialogue in exercise 1 for the following.

1 a machine that gives out money round the clock
2 the times when the bank is open
3 a system for paying fixed sums regularly
4 a system for paying varying sums regularly or irregularly
5 a paper which the account holder prints to see details about the account
6 a yearly fee, eg for a credit card
7 a sum that the bank charges every month for keeping the account
8 the action of taking money out of an account
9 the amount of money in an account
10 the amount by which an account is overdrawn
11 the permission given to an account holder to overdraw the account
12 money that banks pay on savings
13 the time when a customer must inform the bank before withdrawing money from an account
14 two different types of home banking
15 a booklet giving information about bank services

4 *Prepositions*

Fill in the missing prepositions.

1 We pay interest ... credit balances of 5,000 euros or more.
2 Are you interested ... online banking?
3 Would you like to have a look ... our brochure?
4 The rate of interest depends ... how much you save.
5 You can pay regular bills ... standing order.
6 In Britain people pay ... things in shops ... cheque or credit card.
7 You have access to all the money ... your current account.
8 Your employer can transfer your salary ... your account.
9 Interest is paid ... a savings account.
10 Why not open an account ... our bank?

5 *Serving customers*

Read the opening dialogue again and write down the expressions Mark Richter uses to offer the customer a brochure and to offer her further help.

6 *Role play*

These people come into the branch where you work. With a partner taking a customer's role, play the role of the clerk. Using expressions from exercise 5, give the customer the information and help he or she needs. Then change roles.

PETER RADLEY, single, aged 19, has started a traineeship in catering. His employer has told him to open an account. Peter plans to rent a flat with friends and buy some inexpensive furniture. He is not sure which account he needs.

MARY-JO BARNES, single, aged 22, is an office clerk with a US firm. She loves shopping and would like to know more about making payments in Germany. She often runs short of money towards the end of the month.

JANET MILLS, divorced, aged 44, is thinking of transferring her current account to your bank. She works long hours as a nurse, so she is especially interested in the opening hours and ways of using banking services at other times.

FRANK FILTON, widowed, a retired English teacher, always transfers all his pension from his current account to his savings account to earn interest. Then he sometimes forgets to pay important bills. He is angry that Telekom has just disconnected his telephone.

LOOKING AT LANGUAGE

NEGATIVE FORMS

1 British banks **don't** have brochures in German.
2 That **doesn't** matter.
3 I **didn't** know that.
4 There **won't** be any problems.
5 I'm **not** a trainee any more.
6 We haven**'t** got any English ones.
7 That can**'t** happen here.
8 You must **not** go into the red.
9 You need **not** give notice at all.

- The verb *do* + *not* is used to make a negative sentence in the simple present *(1, 2)* and the simple past *(3)*.
- The verb *do* is not used with any other tenses, eg the future *(4)*, with the verbs *be (5)* and *have got (6)* or with modal verbs *(7–9)*.
- The negative form *must not (8)* means "it is wrong to ..." (= *nicht dürfen*).
- The negative form *need not (9)* means "it is not necessary to ..." (= *nicht müssen*).

7 *Practice I*

Use a negative and a positive sentence to correct these statements.

EXAMPLE: Banks pay interest on current accounts.
Banks don't pay interest on current accounts.
They pay interest on savings accounts.

1 Customers can make withdrawals at the counter round the clock.
2 Account holders need a computer to find out their account balance.
3 You must have a PIN to operate the statement printer.
4 The bank charges high fees for student accounts.
5 Most people receive their salaries in cash.
6 Customers may overdraw as much as they wish.

8 *Practice II*

Fill in "must not" or "need not" in the following sentences.

1 If you have an overdraft facility, you ... ask for permission to overdraw when you are short of money.
2 When you pay money into your account you ... lose your receipt.
3 People who have standing orders ... remember to pay their regular bills themselves.
4 Students, trainees and people doing military or community service ... pay any charges for their current accounts.
5 If you have a cheque card, you ... make withdrawals at the counter, but you ... tell anyone your PIN.
6 People who use online banking ... go to their branch so often and they ... pay so much for transferring money.

9 *Savings accounts*

Read this extract from a brochure about the Barclays 60 Day Savings Account and then answer the questions below.

Barclays
60 DAY SAVINGS ACCOUNT

The *longer* you leave it – the *harder* it will work for you

In financial matters, it always pays to look longer-term if you can. So, when it comes to savings, our 60 Day Savings Account could make sound financial sense. By leaving your savings with us longer, the account will work harder to make even more of your money. You can choose to take your interest each month, or once a year.

Remember, if you need your money in a hurry you can withdraw it subject to a charge. 50p per £100 withdrawn for each 30 day period (or part thereof) for which notice is not given. Minimum charge £15.

Your interest rate *rises* as your *savings grow*

This account offers the best interest rates of all our notice accounts as you can see...

Balance	Gross*/ AER**	Gross Interest earned at Current Rates £ p.a.
£1,000+	2.65%	£26.50
£10,000+	3.95%	£395.00
£100,000+	4.60%	£4,600.00

**Gross Rate: Annual interest option is quoted. Interest is payable gross to non-taxpayers subject to the required certification. Otherwise income tax will be deducted at the lower rate, but may be reclaimed by non-tax payers. **Annual Equivalent Rate (AER): Illustrates what the interest rate would be if interest was paid and compounded each year.*

These rates may vary. Rates correct as at 12th July 1999.

As before, the more you save the more you'll earn and of course, if you give us 60 days notice, you can withdraw your savings without charge or restrictions.

1 Why does this account pay different rates of interest?
2 How often is the interest paid?
3 What are the conditions for withdrawals?
4 What does the picture show? Why do you think it was chosen to advertise this account?
5 Does your bank offer an account similar to this one? If so, describe its terms.

HOW TO

– describe entries to accounts

When money is taken out of an account:

the bank **debits** | the account with the sum.
the sum to the account.

When money is paid into an account:

the bank **credits** | the account with the sum.
the sum to the account.

Often the passive is used:

The account The sum	**is** **was** **will be**	**debited.** **credited.**

The entries shown on the account holder's statement are **debits** and **credits.**

10 *A bank statement*

Statements of account help account holders keep track of their money. Look at this statement and then do the tasks below.

Bitte beachten Sie die Hinweise auf der Rückseite

VL 180 199 130

Kontonummer [redacted] | KREISSPARKASSE PINNEBERG | Bankleitzahl 221 514 10

Buchungstag	Tag der Wertstellung	Verwendungszweck/Buchungstext	Buchungsnummer	alter Kontostand EUR 149,32 –
2109	2109	KONTOFÜHRUNGSGEBÜHR 210600-200900	999116	20,00 –
2109	2109	SOLLZINSEN	999116	2,67 –
2809	2809	LOHN/GEHALT	999001	1.460,50 +
0210	0910	DA: HAUSVERWALTUNG BECK MIETER-NR. 69210	999101	450,00 –
0310	0310	ÜBERWEISUNG	041002	100,00 –
1010	1310	SCHECK E.V.	420002	200,00 +
1010	1010	DAS MODELÄDCHEN EC54037145	999008	149,00 –
				EUR 789,51 + neuer Kontostand

IHR DISPOSITIONSKREDIT BETRÄGT EUR 4.000,00 | 12.10.00 Kontoauszug vom | 32 Auszug | 1 Blatt

1 Explain the entries on this statement to a new account holder. Use the words "debited" and "credited".

EXAMPLE: *On September 21st the fee for keeping the account was debited.*

2 Point out the difference between the two balances.

3 Explain the following terms.

- Buchungstag
- Tag der Wertstellung
- Dispositionskredit
- Bankleitzahl

11 *Project work*

1 Luke O'Brien from Toronto is on a three-year course at a Berlin college of art.

2 Willem Hokker from Amsterdam works for an oil company in the Ruhr area. Anna, his wife, is a part-time teacher. They have two children.

3 Dr Shakira Ghandi, a computer scientist from Calcutta, has come to work for a software company in Leipzig.

4 Lars and Hanna Anderssen have sold their farm near Copenhagen and come to live near their son in Bavaria on their retirement.

Divide your class into four groups. Each group should choose one of the customers shown above and do the following.

1. Analyse the lifestyle of the type of customer shown in the photo. Examine the needs of this target group as regards a bank account.
2. Invent a new bank account to suit this target group. Choose the features it will have and give the account a name.
3. Create a brochure about the new account. Decide on the use of colour, pictures, graphics, etc. Write the text for the brochure.
4. Discuss how to market the new account. Work out which marketing methods would be most effective to attract your target group.
5. Imagine that your fellow students are your colleagues at the bank who will be selling the new account you have created. Present your group's results to them. Use visual aids, eg pin boards, overhead projectors, flip charts, mind maps, handouts, etc.

Advanced materials

Financial supermarkets

12 ***Banking with Tesco***

Tesco, one of Britain's largest supermarkets, also offers a range of banking services. Using this extract from one of their brochures, point out what makes a Tesco account attractive.

HOW TO

– express your opinion

In my opinion, …
In my view, …
To my mind, …
From my point of view, …
The way I see it, …
I would like to point out that …

I feel (very strongly) that …
I (definitely) believe that …
It is important to | see that … / remember that …
You / One | must not | forget that … / overlook the fact that …

13 *Express your opinion*

Use expressions from the box above to discuss the following statement with one student writing the points made on the overhead projector. Then weigh up the pros and cons to see which side has the most support.

"Supermarkets will become serious competitors for banks."

14 *Banks in supermarkets?*

Some banks, like the one in this photo, are trying to beat the supermarkets at their own game. Explain how. Then express your opinion about this development. Consider the bank's customers, the bank itself and the bank staff.

Durchbruch am Sonnabend

Im Winterhuder Toom-Markt hat die Hamburger Sparkasse (Haspa) ihren Banking-Shop eingerichtet. Er hat länger geöffnet als jede normale Filiale. Die Haspa ist zufrieden, das Geschäft läuft. Auch andere Geldinstitute setzen auf solche Banking-Shops.

UNIT 3

Opening an account

Lead-in

Describe the picture above. Why are banks keen to attract young customers? What marketing methods do they use to do this?

1 *On the phone*

Joe Forster, an American computer scientist who has come to work in Germany, has already enquired about current accounts. A day later he phones the bank.

SONIA KLEIN Klein. Guten Morgen.

JOE FORSTER Good morning. This is Joe Forster. Could I speak to Herr Richter, please?

SONIA KLEIN Hold the line please, Mr Forster. I'll put you through. ... I'm afraid Herr Richter's line is engaged at the moment. Would you like to leave a message for him to call you back?

JOE FORSTER No, it's all right, thanks. It's not urgent. It's just that ... you see, I'm from the States and my German's not that great. There's a point in the brochure he gave me about current accounts that I don't quite understand.

SONIA KLEIN In that case perhaps I can help you. What exactly would you like to know?

JOE FORSTER Could you tell me what the word "Vollmacht" means, please?

SONIA KLEIN I think the legal term is "power of attorney". In banking we also say "authority for per pro signatory". That means that you can authorize another person to use your account – to make withdrawals, transfer money, receive your statements or even overdraw it.

JOE FORSTER Does that person become an account holder as well, then?

SONIA KLEIN No, you're still the sole account holder. Nobody but you can grant authority to anyone else and you are the only person who is allowed to close the account. An account with two or more holders who have equal rights is called a joint account. Husbands and wives often have one. If you're interested, we could arrange one for ...

JOE FORSTER Good Lord, no. I'm in the middle of getting a divorce! Look, I'd like to open a current account. What time do you close in the evening?

SONIA KLEIN Normally at four in the afternoon except on Thursdays when we're open till six. Just come in whenever it suits you. Oh, by the way, we'll need proof of your identity and legal residence in Germany for opening the account. Did you say you're from the USA?

JOE FORSTER That's right.

SONIA KLEIN In that case, would you bring your passport with you, please, and have you got a certificate from the residents' registration office as well?

JOE FORSTER Sure, no problem. Anything else?

SONIA KLEIN No, I just have to enter your personal details into the computer, then all you have to do is sign the application form so that we've got a specimen signature.

JOE FORSTER What's a specimen signature for?

SONIA KLEIN It's for comparison. Every time we receive a credit transfer or any other order you've written, we have to examine your signature on it to make sure it's genuine. That way the bank can prevent an unauthorized person from withdrawing money from your account. It's really for your own protection.

JOE FORSTER I get it. I'll look in tomorrow then. Thanks for the information.

SONIA KLEIN You're welcome. Goodbye, Mr Forster. Have a nice day.

JOE FORSTER Thanks, you too. Bye.

Use information and expressions from the call to deal with these enquiries.

1. Can I speak to the branch manager, please?
2. What is a person who has authority for per pro signatory allowed to do?
3. Can you tell me what a joint account is, please?

4. How long is the bank open?
5. What do I have to bring with me to open a current account?
6. Why do I have to give a specimen signature?

2 *Working with words I*

Find nouns used in exercise 1 that correspond to these verbs.

to apply ◆ *to authorize* ◆ *to compare* ◆ *to enquire* ◆ *to inform* ◆ *to protect* ◆ *to prove* ◆ *to sign* ◆ *to transfer* ◆ *to withdraw*

3 *Working with words II*

Choose the correct word or expression to complete these sentences.

1 *say / tell*
Please can you … me your full name?
Most people … they are acting on their own account.

2 *check / prove*
Please take a seat while I … your passport.
If you want to open an account, you have to … your identity.

3 *look after / look at / look for*
The bank has to … its account holders' money.
I can't find my passport. I must … it.
Please … the form and ask me if there is anything you don't understand.

4 *prevent / protect*
Banks have to … unauthorized people from withdrawing money.
Security systems … the bank at night.

5 *advice / advise*
Bank clerks give … on banking services.
We can … you how to invest your savings.

LOOKING AT LANGUAGE

INTERROGATIVE FORMS

1 What time **do** you close in the evening?
2 **Does** that person become an account holder as well?
3 **Did** you say you're from the USA?
4 **Would** you like to leave a message?
5 What **can** I do for you?
6 What **is** a specimen signature for?
7 **Have** you got a certificate from the residents' registration office?

- Questions in the simple present are formed using *do (1)*, except for the third person singular which uses *does (2)*.
- Questions in the simple past are formed using *did (3)*.
- In sentences with auxiliary verbs, questions are formed by reversing the subject and the auxiliary. This is the case for all other tenses *(4)*, modal verbs *(5)*, the verb *be (6)* and the verb *have got (7)*.

4 *Practice I*

You are opening an account for a customer and need some information. Ask him or her questions. You have to find out:

1 ... what the customer's full name is.
2 ... where he/she lives.
3 ... how long he/she has been living there.
4 ... where he/she lived previously.
5 ... where he/she works.
6 ... whether he/she is married.
7 ... when he/she was born.
8 ... whether he/she would like to grant anyone power of attorney.
9 ... where he/she can be reached by phone during the day.
10 ... whether he/she has got any questions about the application form.

5 *Practice II*

It is often necessary to ask customers questions before you can help them. What questions would you ask people who come into your branch and say the following?

1 "I've lost my credit card!"
2 "I'm going on holiday and I'd like to change some money."
3 "I want to change one of my standing orders."
4 "I need a loan."
5 "I'd like to have some advice on investing some capital."
6 "I paid in a British cheque but it isn't shown on my statement."
7 "I need a higher overdraft limit on my current account."
8 "This statement can't be right. I never withdrew all that money!"

6 *What goes wrong?*

The dialogue you will hear does not go very well. Listen and take notes about what goes wrong.

CUSTOMER Good afternoon, I was hoping that you could help me.
CLERK Schon wieder einer, der kein Deutsch kann! Mein Gott! Immer kommen sie zu mir! ... Well, what do you want?
CUSTOMER I'd like to open a current account, but there are just one or two points I'm not clear on ...
CLERK Haven't you read our brochure?
CUSTOMER Perhaps you could tell me what "Vollmacht" means?
CLERK That means "power of attorney".
CUSTOMER Power of what?
CLERK AT–TOR–NEY! That person is authorized to sign in your name, pay in money, transfer money, make withdrawals, make standing orders, operate the cash dispenser, overdraw the account and collect your statements.
CUSTOMER I see. Can you tell me what I have to do to open an account, please?
CLERK I need your passport first and then I want a certificate from the residents' registration office.
CUSTOMER Here you are. Is that all?
CLERK Of course it isn't! You have to tell me your personal details so that I can fill in your application on the computer. Then you have to give me a specimen signature.
CUSTOMER Sorry, I don't quite understand. What's a specimen signature?
CLERK Well we have to have something to compare with other things you've signed, don't we? How do you expect us to know whether your signature's genuine or not?
CUSTOMER Where do I have to sign?
CLERK There! At the bottom! Now sit down over there and read the application form while I check your passport!
CUSTOMER I hope I can understand it.
CLERK So do I. We close in ten minutes.

7 *Serving customers*

Do these tasks to practise serving customers politely.

1 Write down as many expressions as you can for asking someone to do something politely (eg to show his/her passport). The opening dialogue of this unit will be helpful.
2 Compare the polite phrases that you have written with the ones in the box on the next page to see if your list is complete.
3 Take over the clerk's role in the dialogue in the last exercise and serve the customer politely this time.

HOW TO

– ask politely

May I see your passport, please?
Could | you sign here, please?
Would |
Just sign here, please.
All you have to do is fill in the form, please.
Would you like to fill the form in now or later?*
Would you mind waiting a moment, please?**
Would you be so kind as to ring back later, please?**

* Used only if the customer has a choice.
** Very polite. Used when asking someone to do something inconvenient.

8 *Ask politely*

Use suitable expressions for asking politely in the following situations.

1 A customer speaks too fast for you to understand.
2 You cannot understand a customer's name.
3 You don't know how to spell a customer's name.
4 You have to see a customer's passport.
5 A customer has forgotten to sign a transfer form.
6 A customer cashes a traveller's cheque. You want to know if he wants the money in large or small notes.
7 You need to know the name of the customer's wife.
8 You want a customer to ask his wife to come to the bank and give her specimen signature, too.
9 A customer wants to speak to the branch manager, who will be busy for the next ten minutes.
10 The manager is ill so you have to phone a customer and postpone her appointment with him till next week.

9 *Authority for per pro signatory*

In a group of three play the roles of the bank clerk, the account holder and the person who would like to sign per pro. The clerk should ask politely for the necessary information and signatures. Use this form from Lloyds TSB.

Authority for per pro signatory

Lloyds TSB

To Lloyds Bank Plc

Until further notice in writing from me/any one of us, please accept the signature of

Full name of person who will sign 'per pro'

Signature of person who will sign 'per pro'

Date

as authorised on my/our behalf:

1 To draw, sign, accept or endorse cheques, drafts, bills of exchange, promissory notes, or other orders (including standing orders and direct debits) for the payment of or receipts for money. You may honour and debit the amounts concerned to my/our account(s) as detailed below.

*This applies whether the account(s) is/are in credit or overdrawn or become overdrawn as a result of debiting such amounts.

2 This authority applies to *(delete as applicable):*

(a) All accounts in my name

(b) All accounts in our names

(c) The following account(s) only

or as they may be re-designated or re-numbered from time to time.

3 **To sign generally for me/us in all matters relating to my/our account(s).

4 **To withdraw and deal with any of my/our property or securities which you may hold from time to time and to sign on my/our behalf any indemnities which you may require from time to time.

You may act on instructions as above without making any enquiries about the circumstances of the instructions.

Signature(s) of Customer(s)
(In Scotland each signatory must write the words 'Adopted as holograph' in his or her own handwriting before the signature)

Date

NOTES
*Delete if Per Pro signatory is not to have authority to overdraw the account.
**Delete if not required.

All customers must sign the form **and** initial alterations

10 *Checking identification*

Look at this page of a British passport and say which details on it are important for opening an account.

11 *An application form*

This application form (see opposite) is used by a German bank for its English-speaking customers. Answer the questions below about it.

1 What personal details does the form ask for which are not shown in the customer's passport?
2 What is money laundering?
3 What does the bank need to know under the Money Laundering Act?
4 What sort of information can the bank pass on to the Schufa, the German banks' credit reference agency? Give examples.
5 Who may receive information from the Schufa?
6 With his or her signature the applicant accepts the bank's General Business Conditions. What do they govern? Give examples.

12 *Role play*

Get an application form in German from your bank and use it to open a current account with a partner taking the customer's role. Use expressions for asking politely and include the points below. Then change roles.

1 Ask for proof of identity and legal residence in Germany.
2 Find out any details required for the application form which are not in the passport or identity card.
3 Explain what the bank needs to know under the Money Laundering Act.
4 Make sure that the applicant understands the Schufa declaration.
5 Offer help if the customer has any questions about the General Business Conditions.
6 Ask the applicant to sign the application form.
7 Find out whether the applicant wishes to grant anyone authority for per pro signatory.

Account/safe custody account opening form

Account holder (Account name)		Branch No.	Customer master No.
Specimen signature(s) *Please repeat below*			

Personal details

Dr Mr Ms Mrs/First name/Surname		Date of birth
Street, Number, Postal code, Country (registered address)		
Place of birth	Maiden name	
Residential status (owner occupied, rent, parents)	Marital status	Telephone (home)
Nationality	Telephone (work)	Fax

Job details

Industry		
Position	Professional qualifications	
Current employer	Self-employed as (occupation)	Self-employed since (year)

Information pursuant to § 8 Money Laundering Act:

☐ I am acting on my own account	I am acting for *(Name and address of person for whose account the account/safe custody account is maintained):*

I hereby open an account/safe custody account with Deutsche Bank 24 AG under the above customer master number and subject to the following terms and conditions:

1. Type of settlement for Personal Account

☐ Online-account 24 ☐ Service-account 24

2. Account statement printers

The account statement printer service is to be made available to all suitable accounts opened under the above customer master number, unless I agree otherwise with you.

3. Current account agreement, accounting period

The accounts are maintained on a current basis, unless otherwise agreed. In the case of current accounts, the bank - unless otherwise agreed - will issue a periodic balance statement at the end of each calendar quarter. The legal effect of a periodic balance statement and the duty to check its contents and, if necessary, to raise objections are regulated by No. 7 of the General Business Conditions.

4. Agreement to transmission of data to SCHUFA *(only applies to current accounts)*

I agree to the bank passing on to the office of the SCHUFA (Protective Association for General Safeguarding of Credit) responsible for my place of residence the data concerning the application for, establishment and termination of this account relationship.
Irrespective of this, the bank will also notify SCHUFA about any conduct not according with the terms of the contract (e.g. eurocheque card abuse by the rightful cardholder, cheques returned due to lack of cover, bills protested, formal debt notices filed on undisputed claims and distraint measures). In accordance with the Federal Data Protection Act, such reports may only be made insofar as they are required to protect the legitimate interests of the bank, of a contractual partner of SCHUFA or of the general public, and provided such reports do not damage those of my interests which merit protection.

For notifications fulfilling these conditions, I also release the bank from its duty of banking secrecy.

SCHUFA stores the data so that it can supply information needed for the assessment of a customer's creditworthiness to member banks, leasing firms, retailers, mail-order houses and other companies which, in the course of their business, provide consumers with cash advances or trade credit. To help locate debtors, address data may be given to companies whose business is to collect debts and which are contractual partners of SCHUFA. This information is only supplied to contractual partners if they can plausibly substantiate a legitimate interest in the transmission of data. SCHUFA only passes on objective data, without disclosing the account-keeping bank; subjective value judgements and details of personal income and assets are not contained in SCHUFA reports. I can obtain information from SCHUFA about the data it has stored concerning me.

The address of the competent SCHUFA office is as follows:

If my place of residence changes, I agree to my data being transferred by the above SCHUFA office to the office then responsible. A leaflet giving further details about the SCHUFA system is available on request.

X

Signature of account holder

Deutsche Bank 24

1 E576 01 01 *Ausfertigung für die Bank* D

Advanced materials

Banking in Britain

13 ### *Banking in Britain*

Compare the British bank shown in this photo with the branch where you work. Point out the advantages and disadvantages of each one.

14 ### *An interview*

Dave Butler, the manager of a branch of Lloyds TSB, one of the largest British high street banks, gave *Money Matters* an interview about his work. Listen and take notes under these headings.

Internal Structure	Customer Service Organization	Range of Services	Procedure for Opening Accounts	Accounts Offered	Staff & Training

15 ### *Make comparisons*

Use your notes from the last exercise to compare Lloyds TSB with the bank where you work. Point out the similarities and the differences.

16 *Lloyds TSB looks to the future*

This review by the Chief Executive describes Lloyds TSB Group's three strategic aims for beating the keen competition in the market for financial services. Say what these aims are and how the Group plans to achieve them.

World class...

Achieving our three strategic aims

We continue to pursue our governing objective of maximising shareholder value over time, and our three strategic aims. In 1999 a great deal of progress was made towards meeting these aims.

Our first strategic aim is to be a leader in our chosen markets. In June 1999, we announced the purchase of Scottish Widows in a transaction that greatly enhances our market position in the life assurance business. The combined business will immediately make Lloyds TSB the second largest life assurance and pensions provider in the UK.

Our second strategic aim is to be first choice for our customers. We have a product range which is more competitive than ever before and, augmenting our comprehensive branch network, we have continued to extend our telephone banking and internet banking operations during the year. We aim to offer our customers the widest possible choice of when, where and how they want to transact their financial business, be it at the branch, over the telephone or through the internet. The extent and range of ways by which we serve our customers is second to none.

We need constantly to improve our understanding of our customers' needs and to be able to respond to those needs. We have invested heavily in systems which help us to do this and we have put this information to good use in 1999. Our aim is to become world class in the management of our relationships with our customers. It is only by satisfying our customers' needs and earning their trust by offering first class products and excellent service that we will gain the privilege of looking after more of their business.

Strong revenue generation remains at the heart of our strategies, but being the lowest cost provider of services and products is also a key measure of a company's ability to obtain and sustain competitive advantage. That is why our third strategic aim is to drive down our day-to-day operating costs so that we will have more resources to reinvest in the business to improve our services and products. 1999 saw the successful attainment of the £400 million per annum cost saving target we promised as a result of the merger of Lloyds Bank and TSB Group and the integration of Lloyds Abbey Life. This is a significant achievement. We are committed to build on past success and to bring about further reductions in the early years of the new millennium, whilst at the same time investing heavily in business growth.

Accordingly, we have now commenced a major new efficiency programme that will aim to reduce further our cost base and in 2000 we expect to incur a restructuring charge of up to £200 million. The cost reductions from this programme are such that by 2002 we expect the Group's efficiency ratio will be below 35 per cent, with further improvements to come in subsequent years. The programme, which is primarily focused on non-customer facing activities, will result in the centralisation of large scale processing activities and the further rationalisation of support functions, and will facilitate additional investment in lower cost delivery channels such as telephone banking and internet operations, and the development of our e-commerce activities.

Looking ahead

No organisation can successfully manage change without the support and commitment of its staff. The pace and scope of change will not diminish as competition in the financial services market continues to increase. One of our greatest competitive advantages is the ability of our people to adapt to rapid and far reaching change.

As competition intensifies we will continue to focus on our governing objective and our strategic aims in order to maximise organic growth. At the same time we will continue to explore opportunities of mergers and acquisitions in the UK and overseas. We go into the new millennium with a restless pursuit of perfection. It is the staff of this organisation who have delivered the company's success and I thank them most warmly for their hard work and great effort.

Peter Ellwood
Group Chief Executive

UNIT 4

Transferring money

Zero tolerance

From Mr Robert Brooks

Sir, Today I have received two communications from the Inland Revenue. The first provides details of a refund for the amount of £0.00. A cheque for £0.00 is attached.

The second provides details of the amount I owe – again £0.00. With this the Revenue has kindly provided a Freepost envelope in which I should send the money.

Yours faithfully,
BOB BROOKS,
47 Fairclough Road,
Worthing, West Sussex BN13 6XH

Lead-in

Why do you think Mr Brooks wrote the above letter to *The Times*? Why are cheques seldom used in Germany? What other means of non-cash payment are used instead?

1 *A what?*

Peter Bingham is a retired British army colonel who rents a house in Germany for six months every summer. Christian Falk is at the counter when the colonel comes into the branch.

PETER BINGHAM Afternoon, young man. I've come about this form. I applied to join the golf club recently, and now they've sent me this ...

CHRISTIAN FALK May I have a look? ... Ah, yes, it's an Einzugsermächtigung.

PETER BINGHAM A what? I can't even pronounce it, let alone understand the damn thing.

CHRISTIAN FALK It's a direct debit authorization.

PETER BINGHAM Well I knew it had something to do with paying the membership dues.

CHRISTIAN FALK That's right. The system works quite simply really. All you have to do is fill this form in and forward it to the payee, in your case the golf club. With your signature you authorize them to debit your account for a particular purpose. So the club needn't ask for permission every time payments are due.

PETER BINGHAM Just a minute. I can't let other people start helping themselves to the money in my account.

CHRISTIAN FALK There's no need to worry about that. You can see all the entries on your statements and revoke a debit immediately if you see that it isn't correct.

PETER BINGHAM Why bother? I'd prefer a standing order like the one I have for the rent.

CHRISTIAN FALK Most large organizations like sports clubs prefer direct debit these days. It's more flexible for them because they can vary the sums or change the dates if necessary. Standing orders are for paying fixed sums regularly ...

PETER BINGHAM But my membership fee *is* a fixed monthly sum!

CHRISTIAN FALK Yes, but direct debit allows the payees to claim the sums directly, which means they don't have to rely on people paying punctually and they needn't send off reminders to people who don't. They save a lot of money that way and can just run all the data through their computer ...

PETER BINGHAM That's it! Computers! Those things rule the world nowadays. Since they were invented, life has become more complicated and expensive all the time.

CHRISTIAN FALK I wouldn't worry about that. After all, the golf club pays the charges for every direct debit, not you. In return they can be sure of getting punctual payment. And it's not complicated either. In fact, if we go through the form together, you'll see it's quite simple, really.

PETER BINGHAM I suppose you're right. Well, if you can help me to fill this thing in correctly, the only difficult question will be how to get my handicap down.

CHRISTIAN FALK I'm sorry, sir. That's one problem we can't help you to solve.

Answer these questions.

1 How does a customer arrange a direct debit? Compare this with setting up a standing order.
2 What happens when payment is due? Compare this with the standing order system.
3 Is there any risk in signing a direct debit authorization?
4 Why is direct debiting more flexible than the standing order system?
5 How do large organizations save money when using direct debiting?
6 What advantages of direct debiting convince Mr Bingham in the end?

HOW TO

– work with forms

These expressions are useful for helping customers to fill in forms.

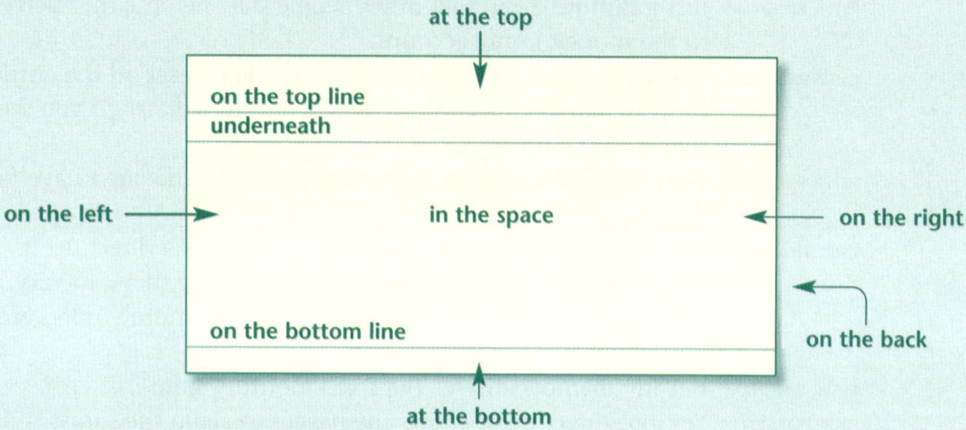

2 *A direct debit authorization*

Take over Christian Falk's role and help Mr Bingham to understand and fill in the authorization form below. Use the expressions above. The following words may also be useful.

quarterly ◆ *half-yearly* ◆ *annually* ◆ *admission fee* ◆ *club subscription*

GOLF-PARK STEINBACHER HOF

EINZUGSERMÄCHTIGUNG

Hiermit ermächtige ich den Golf-Park Steinbacher Hof e.V., die einmalige Aufnahmegebühr sowie den Vereinsbeitrag

vierteljährlich ☐ halbjährlich ☐ jährlich ☐ *

bei Fälligkeit von meinem nachstehenden Konto durch Lastschrift einzuziehen.

Name des Kontoinhabers: ______________________

Anschrift: ______________________

Bank / Sparkasse: ______________________

Kontonummer: ______________ BLZ: ______________

Unterschrift des Kontoinhabers: ______________________

Ort, Datum: ______________

* Gewünschtes bitte ankreuzen.

3 *A credit transfer form*

Look at the form below and explain the points numbered 1–10. Customers may also make credit transfers online at self-service terminals. Describe how the system works.

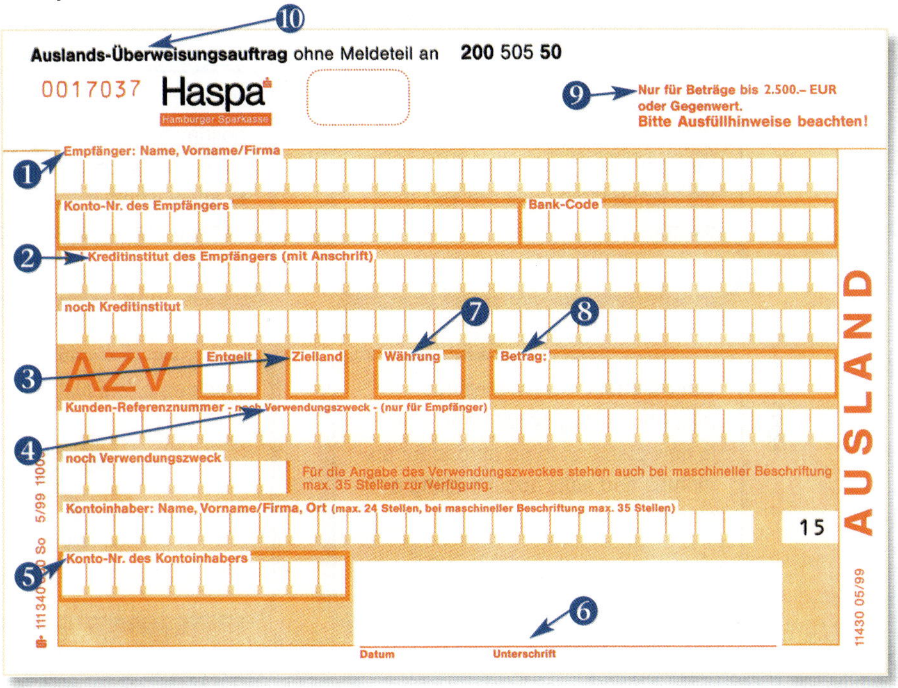

4 *A standing order form*

Look at the computer printout below and do the following tasks.

1 Say what data the bank clerk enters into the computer that is not required for a credit transfer.
2 Point out the main advantages of payment by standing order.
3 Give examples of payments that customers often make in this way.

Dauerauftrag
Eröffnung

Ausführung	Erstmals am	Letztmals am	Betrag
Empfänger		Empfänger-Konto-Nr.	
Konto bei		Bankleitzahl	
Verwendungszweck			
Konto-Nr.	Auftraggeber		

Ich bitte Sie, den vorstehenden Dauerauftrag vorzumerken.

Unterschrift

E878 01 01 Ausfertigung für die Bank

5 Role play

With a partner, take turns to play the roles of the bank clerk and one of these customers. The clerk should advise the customer on the most suitable way to pay and arrange payment using the direct debit authorization (p 40), the credit transfer form or the standing order (p 41).

COLIN EVERTON comes in to make a credit transfer. He has just joined a fitness centre and his membership dues are €80 a month.

MARIE PERCIER wants to book a holiday flat in Cannes for three weeks in the summer. She wants to know whether it is advisable to send the owner a cheque for €2,200.

SEAN O'BRIEN always pays his telephone bill by credit transfer. He is now planning to go abroad for six months and asks about making a standing order.

Think up a role play yourself.

?

LOOKING AT LANGUAGE

ADJECTIVES AND ADVERBS

1 The system works quite **simply**.
2 They don't have to rely on people paying **punctually**.
3 You can help me to fill this thing in **correctly**.
4 You'll see it's quite **simple**.
5 They can be sure of getting **punctual** payment.
6 You can revoke the debit if it isn't **correct**.

- Adverbs describe verbs or adjectives *(1–3)*.
- Adjectives describe nouns or pronouns *(4–6)*. The verbs *be, seem, look* and *appear* are followed by an adjective *(4, 6)*.
- Adverbs usually end in *-ly (1–3)*, but a small number of adjectives do not have adverbs ending in *-ly*.

He speaks **good** English.	He speaks English **well**.
It is a **fast** train.	It travels **fast**.
She is a **hard** worker.	She works **hard**. (hardly = *kaum*)
He is **late** for work.	He arrives **late**. (lately = *in letzter Zeit*)
She is **friendly**.	She behaves **in a friendly way**.

6 *Practice I*

Use adjectives or adverbs in these sentences.

1 It is ... *(difficult)* to pronounce this word ... *(correct).*
2 Most people cannot understand forms ... *(easy).*
3 The new trainee does not write very ... *(clear).*
4 She is trying ... *(hard)* to improve her English.
5 Account holders should check their statements ... *(careful).*
6 Direct debit is a way of paying bills ... *(convenient).*
7 It does not matter if the dates of payment are ... *(irregular).*
8 Jane works ... *(good)* but she is not very ... *(punctual).*
9 The post ... *(regular)* arrives ... *(late).*
10 The bank will debit your account ... *(automatic).*

7 *Practice II*

Rewrite the following sentences using adverbs instead of adjectives.

EXAMPLE: The instructions on the cash dispenser are *easy* for customers to understand.
Customers can *easily understand the instructions on the cash dispenser.*

1 Be *careful* when inserting your cheque card into the slot.
Insert your ...
2 You can make *regular* payments by standing order.
Payments can ...
3 Her spoken English is *good* but her written work is often *incorrect.*
She speaks ...
4 There is a *simple* solution to this problem.
This problem can ...
5 Credit transfer is a *safe* way of paying bills.
You can pay ...
6 Firms using direct debit have an *efficient* means of claiming payments.
Firms can ...
7 It is *convenient* for companies in Europe to do business in euros.
Firms in Europe can ...
8 The ECB* in Frankfurt has strict control over monetary policy.
The ECB in Frankfurt controls ...

*European Central Bank

8 *A cheque*

In Britain and in the USA, cheques are still widely used. Match the red letters (a–g) on the cheque below with the terms 1–7.

1 date of issue
2 drawer's/payer's signature
3 sum in figures
4 sum in words
5 currency
6 drawee
7 beneficiary's name

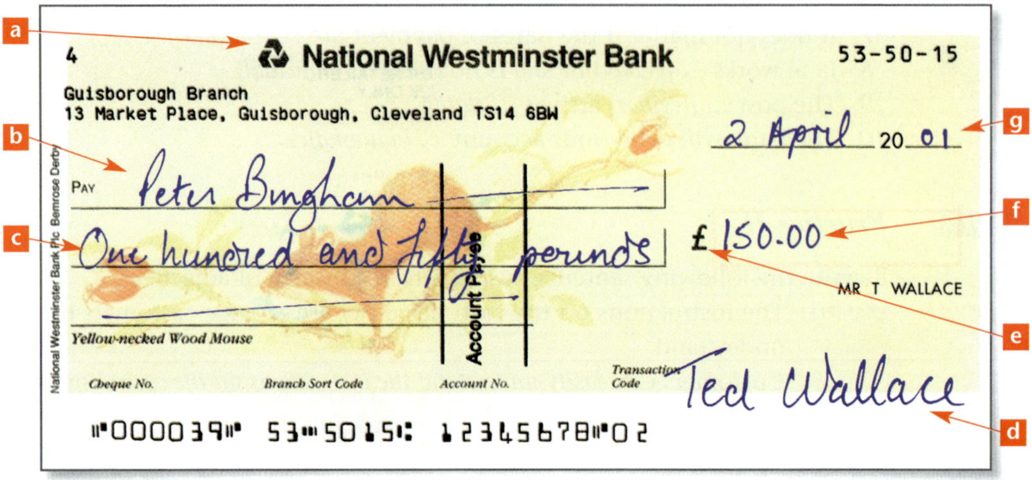

9 *Types of cheque*

Look at the cheque above again. The two parallel lines on the face of the cheque mean that it is **a crossed cheque**. In Britain account holders get books of cheques which are already crossed by the bank.

It is not normally possible to cash a cheque at a bank. To receive the sum, the beneficiary has to pay the cheque into his or her account. The words "Account Payee" between the lines mean that the cheque may only be credited to the payee's account.

Using a crossed cheque is safer – especially if the cheque is sent by post. If a crossed cheque is lost or stolen, the bank can trace the bank, branch and account where it was presented. A cheque that is not crossed is **an open cheque**. This is not as safe to use because it may be cashed by the drawee.

The above cheque is also **an order cheque**. If the payee wishes to give it to another person rather than pay it into an account, he or she must transfer the rights to the new recipient by endorsement. (This is not normally possible if the cheque bears the words "Account Payee".) The payee endorses the cheque by signing it on the back. Now another person is authorized to receive the sum.

Not all cheques are order cheques. **A bearer cheque** has the words "Pay … or bearer" on the face. It can be passed on to another person without endorsement because anyone who holds it is authorized to receive the sum.

Make meaningful sentences from this table about the different types of cheque – at least two sentences for each type.

A crossed cheque An open cheque An order cheque A bearer cheque	may be can be need not be cannot be must be must not be	sent by post safely. cashed by the drawee. traced if it is stolen. paid into a bank account. transferred by endorsement. endorsed on the back. credited to the payee named.

10 *Dialogue-writing*

Use the information from the last exercise to serve Mr Bingham when he comes into his branch with his NatWest cheque for £150. Write or play your part in the dialogue. Be as polite and helpful as possible.

MR BINGHAM Good afternoon.

YOU ...

MR BINGHAM I'd like to cash this cheque, please. I've just received it from a friend of mine in England.

YOU ...

MR BINGHAM Certainly, here it is.

YOU ...

MR BINGHAM Not cash it? Good Lord, why not? It's a perfectly good cheque from a highly-recognized British bank!

YOU ...

MR BINGHAM So how can I receive the money then?

YOU ...

MR BINGHAM Hmm! What exactly do I have to do?

YOU ...

MR BINGHAM Peter Bingham. 5677324. Look here, I need this money pretty urgently. My friend wants me to buy him a new putter. How long will it take?

YOU ...

MR BINGHAM And how will I know when it's been cleared?

YOU ...

MR BINGHAM All right. Though it seems to me like a lot of unnecessary bureaucracy!

YOU ...

MR BINGHAM I suppose you're right. After all, we can't have every Tom, Dick or Harry cashing other people's cheques, can we? Thanks for your help.

YOU ...

Point of sale

11 *Payment at point of sale*

Look at this NatWest brochure about their payments system called "Switch" and then answer the questions below about it.

NatWest SERVICECARD – WORKING FOR YOU IN MORE WAYS THAN ONE

The NatWest Servicecard is a very convenient way to make the most of your NatWest current account.

THE KEY TO YOUR CURRENT ACCOUNT

Combining three cards in one, it allows you to:

- pay directly for goods and services through the Switch Card Scheme without having to write a cheque
- obtain cash 24 hours a day, 7 days a week
- guarantee cheques up to £50.

SWITCH – THE CONVENIENT WAY TO PAY

The front of the NatWest Servicecard carries the 'Switch' symbol. This means that wherever you see this sign in shops, petrol stations or any of the increasing number of outlets which accept Switch, you can use your Servicecard instead of cash or a cheque to pay for goods and services.

All you have to do is hand your Servicecard to the cashier and then sign a sales receipt. In a very few outlets, you may have the option to use your Personal Number at the sales point. It's as simple and quick as that.
When you use Switch, your current account is debited in about three working days, just as if you had written a cheque. Your Servicecard therefore acts as a debit card, not a credit card.

1 What are the different functions of a NatWest Servicecard?
2 What does the customer do when using Switch to pay in a shop?
3 Why is the NatWest Servicecard a debit card, not a credit card?
4 What advantages does POS payment offer the customer?

12 Creative writing

Your bank has decided to produce a brochure to inform English-speaking customers about the German system, Electronic Cash. You have been asked to write the brochure text and given these instructions.

NOTE: this is not a translation exercise. You may change the order of the points.

1. Erklären Sie, wo man mit Electronic Cash bezahlen kann.
2. Erwähnen Sie, welche Karte man benötigt, um mit diesem System zu zahlen.
3. Erläutern Sie, wie Electronic Cash funktioniert. Machen Sie den Unterschied zwischen dem POS- und dem POZ-System deutlich.
4. Weisen Sie auf einen wichtigen Vorteil dieser Zahlungsweise hin.
5. Informieren Sie den Leser / die Leserin, wie er / sie weitere Informationen zu diesem Thema erhalten kann.

13 Prepositions

Fill in the missing prepositions.

1. Mr Bingham received a cheque ... £150.
2. The cheque was drawn ... NatWest bank.
3. Mr Bingham paid the cheque ... his account.
4. You have to sign a credit transfer form ... the bottom.
5. The money was transferred ... April 1st.
6. The sum will be debited ... your account.
7. The amount will be credited ... the payee's account.
8. The sum will be ... your account by the end of the week.
9. Most people find payment ... direct debit very convenient.
10. Perhaps I can help you to fill ... the form?

14 Working with words

Add a prefix to the following adjectives to give them the opposite meaning. You may need to use a dictionary.

1	convenient	6	regular
2	correct	7	punctual
3	expensive	8	secure
4	possible	9	safe
5	effective	10	efficient

Advanced materials

E-money

15 *Internet shopping: a survey*

Find out the attitudes within your group towards Internet shopping, eg how many of you shop on the web, why, how often, what you order and how you pay. Alternatively find out who seldom or never shops online and why. See what conclusions you can draw about e-shopping.

16 *Cybercash*

Use this article to explain how beenz work and point out their function.

Beenz Counters

E★EUROPE

IF YOU DON'T HAVE A BEENZ IN YOUR VIRTUAL pocket, maybe you should. beenz (the trademarked word is both singular and plural) are a new kind of money that circulates exclusively on the Internet. There are no beenz coins or beenz bills. The only place you can earn beenz is on the Web, and, until now, the Web was the only place you could spend them. beenz are the product of a company called Beenz.com that hopes to make them the currency of the Internet, and they may be the future of cash as we know it. In five years, says Beenz.com founder Charles Cohen, "I believe we'll start to see beenz listed against other major currencies." This vision moved closer to reality this month with the launch of a debit card which will allow consumers to convert beenz for local currency – spendable in real or online stores.

beenz aren't a currency in the strictest sense. But beenz are one of the more successful attempts to solve a problem that's as old as the Web – that of finding an easy and safe way for people to spend money online in small amounts. "Right now there isn't really a viable way for consumers to pay for something that costs 50¢, because that's about how much a credit-card transaction costs the merchant," says Ken Cassar, an analyst with the e-commerce research firm Jupiter Communications. Early attempts to create a practical alternative to credit cards for online financial transactions have been slow to gain consumer confidence.

Here's how beenz work. First, you open a free account with Beenz.com, a New York-based outfit that's been in business since 1998. You earn beenz by visiting certain websites that give beenz away to reward customer loyalty, in exchange for personal information or as a reward to surfers for just showing up. Hence the name – "You get something for just having 'been' there," explains Beenz.com chairman and CEO Philip Letts. Among the sites that offer beenz are Excite UK, Dash and Fortune City. Then, once your virtual wallet is bulging, you can spend beenz at any of some 200 e-commerce sites that accept beenz as a form of payment, including Flooz, ishop, Jellybeenz Gifts and MP3.com.

Alternatively you could use your beenz rewardzcard MasterCard to spend your credit on- or off-line in any store or restaurant worldwide which accepts MasterCard, giving customers the choice which previously limited the service. The card will be issued by Columbus Bank and Trust and will be available in the U.S. this month and the U.K. and Australia later this year. This deal is not exclusive and Beenz.com could issue co-branded cards with other banks.

Cohen founded Beenz.com because he was fed up with existing customer-incentive programs. He saw an opportunity to give consumers more of a choice in how companies rewarded them for purchases, and to grease the wheels of the burgeoning Internet economy. Beenz.com launched in March 1999, and by August 159 companies were signed up to accept the new tokens.

beenz is now a global operation, with offices from New York to Stockholm to Sydney to Hong Kong. And it's getting to be a significant business: its technology partners include Oracle, Sun Microsystems and Web-hosting giant Exodus. Almost 750 million beenz are in circulation – roughly equivalent to the currency float of a small country.

(*TIME*, 5 June 2000, shortened)

HOW TO

– express agreement and disagreement

If you agree with someone:

I entirely / absolutely agree with you.
I think so, too.
I second that.
I think you're right.
That's just what I was thinking.
I couldn't agree more.

If you partially agree:

I agree with you up to a point, but …
I see what you mean, but …
That's true, but on the other hand …

If you disagree:

I don't agree at all.
That's not the way I see it.
I see things differently.
I (totally) disagree.
That's just not true. / correct. / the case.
Definitely not!

17 *The future of money?*

"Real-time pricing and exchange of goods and services across the Internet could bypass the need for traditional currencies issued by a central bank. Without a settlement role, central banks in their present form would no longer exist; nor would money. The successors to Bill Gates could put the successors to Alan Greenspan* out of business."

(Mervyn King, deputy governor of the Bank of England, in a speech at the turn of the millennium.)

**Chairman of the US Federal Reserve Board, which is responsible for monetary policy in the USA.*

Express your agreement or disagreement with Mr King's views.

UNIT 5

Credit cards and traveller's cheques

Lead-in

How can travellers make payments in foreign countries? List the different ways. Which means did you use on your last holiday abroad? Give your reasons for doing so.

1 On Her Majesty's Service

The scene is London, Whitehall, the Centre of British Intelligence. M, the head of the British Secret Service, is at his desk when a buzzer goes off on his intercom.

MONEYPENNY Commander James Bond to see you, sir.
M Send him in, Miss Moneypenny.
MONEYPENNY M will see you now, James.
JAMES BOND It's all right, Moneypenny. I know the way. ... *(Now in M's office.)* You wanted to see me, sir.
M Come in, 007. Take a seat. I wouldn't have called you back from the Bahamas if the situation hadn't been so serious.
JAMES BOND What's up, sir?
M The microprocessors for the British space defence mechanism have been stolen. We know they have been smuggled to Istanbul.

JAMES BOND Isn't 006 already in Istanbul, sir?

M His body was fished out of the Bosporus last night. I want you to take over the mission. It's deadly dangerous and could lead you anywhere – South America, Central Asia even. I've discussed the matter with the PM and her Majesty. Your country is depending on you, 007.

JAMES BOND Is everything prepared?

M You'll find everything you need in this case. ... A Beretta with a silencer and ammunition, this watch with a hidden satellite transmitter so that you can report back wherever you are, these pills – take one and you can survive without food and water for a week – and here, most important of all, a credit card!

JAMES BOND The gold one!

M What else? Here you are, 007. Miss Moneypenny will give you the other details you need. Goodbye – and good luck!

JAMES BOND Thank you, sir. ... *(Returns to Miss Moneypenny's office.)* Moneypenny, there's one thing I want you to do for me before I leave.

MONEYPENNY Oh yes, James ... anything!

JAMES BOND Get me one of those brochures on credit cards, will you please?

Say why Mr Bond is going to need a credit card – especially a gold one!

2 *Group work*

Work out the clerk's role in the dialogue. These expressions will help you.

insurance ◆ recipient ◆ replacement ◆ sales receipt ◆ stop the card

CUSTOMER Good afternoon. I've read your brochure about credit cards but there are one or two things I'm not sure about.

YOU ... ?

CUSTOMER What exactly must I do if I want to use my credit card in a shop?

YOU ...

CUSTOMER I see, and what if I buy something on the Internet? I can't sign anything if I'm online.

YOU ...

CUSTOMER Will my account be debited every time I pay for something?

YOU ...

CUSTOMER But how can I check that my account has been debited correctly?

YOU ...

CUSTOMER But what if I lose the card or somebody steals it?

YOU ...

CUSTOMER In that case I'd like you to order one for me right away.

3 *A US credit card*

You don't have to be James Bond to find out about credit cards. All you need is a brochure like this one from the Boone County National Bank in the USA. Read it and answer the questions below.

For All The Right Reasons

Right Card.

Does your credit card give you three choices of rates? Do you earn travel dollars that you can apply to *any* airline, cruise package, hotel, rental car or other travel benefits? And do you have a credit card with no annual fee? If not ... you have the wrong credit card!

Our credit card offers more benefits than cards offered by other Missouri banks and more than most national credit cards or frequent flyer programs. Plus, you can select either a MasterCard or Visa to fit the way you live and travel. It's time you got the right card with the right benefits.

Right Benefits.

- **Earn Travel Dollars**
  Finally, the credit card that makes travel easier and more affordable. Every time you use our MasterCard or Visa, you'll earn 1% of all your purchases in travel dollars. You can then apply those travel dollars to any airline to go anywhere, anytime without the restrictions of a frequent flyer program. Or use travel dollars to reduce the cost of a cruise vacation, hotel room, rental car or any other travel choice.
- **Low Monthly Payments**
  If you choose the variable-rate option, your rate adjusts with Prime Rate, keeping your payments as low as possible.
- **Over 12 Million Locations**
  MasterCard and Visa are accepted at merchants worldwide.
- **Worldwide Quick Cash Advances via ATM**
  You can obtain cash advances anywhere in the world through Cirrus network ATMs. In the United States, get advances at not only Cirrus ATMs but BankMate machines in the Midwest. And look for our 24-Hour Bank ATMs at our banks in Missouri.
- **Fast Credit Card Replacement**
  Call the 1-800 number on the back of the credit card toll-free, 24 hours a day for fast card replacement.

Right Rate.

Our credit cards offer you the choice of *three* different low annual percentage rates. Choose from two fixed-rate options or the variable-rate selection for your credit needs.

Fixed Rate

17.4% ... APR — with no annual fee and a 25-day grace period.

or

15.9% ... APR — with a $20 annual fee and 25-day grace period or no annual fee if you maintain a primary, non-business checking account at our bank.

Variable Rate

or

16.4% ... APR — our variable rate is based on the fluctuations of Prime Rate plus 7.9%* and offers a 25-day grace period. The $20 annual fee is waived if you maintain a primary, non-business checking account at our bank.

Right Now.

What are you waiting for? Cut up your other credit cards. Complete, sign and mail this application for the best travel rewards credit card with three great rate choices!

Boone County National Bank

*As of April 15, 1997 the variable rate was 16.4%. Rate is determined by adding 7.9% to the highest Prime Rate as reported in the *Wall Street Journal* on the 15th of every month. Your annual percentage rate may change monthly.

1. How does this credit card make travel easier and more affordable?
2. What uses of a credit card are mentioned in the brochure?
3. What should the holder do if the credit card gets lost?
4. What are the "three choices of rates"? Explain the main difference between them.
5. Who is this brochure aimed at: existing card holders or people who have never had a card before?

4 *The US credit card v the Eurocard*

Compare the US credit card with the Eurocard to see which one offers the better conditions. Compare:

- the annual fee
- the grace period
- the interest rate
- the acceptability
- the extra benefits

5 *Role play I*

Using this application form or a credit card application form from your bank, work with a partner who takes the customer's role and help her or him to apply for a credit card.

Antrag für die Berliner Bank Kreditkarten

Bitte geben Sie den Antrag bei Ihrer Berliner Bank Filiale ab oder kleben Sie ihn zu und senden ihn kostenfrei an die Berliner Bank.

☐ **Kreditkarten-Doppel VISA & EUROCARD** ☐ **VISA Card** ☐ **EUROCARD**
☐ Ich wünsche, daß die Kontoführung in Euro erfolgt.

1. Meine persönlichen Angaben

☐ Frau ☐ Herr

Name, Vorname

Straße, Hausnummer

Postleitzahl | Wohnort

Wohnhaft seit: Monat | Jahr

Telefon-Nummer, privat | Telefon-Nummer, Geschäft

Geburtsdatum | Geburtsort | Staatsangehörigkeit

Familienstand: ☐ ledig ☐ verheiratet ☐ geschieden/getrennt lebend ☐ verwitwet

Anzahl der unterhaltspflichtigen Kinder ☐ | Immobilienbesitz vorhanden? ☐ ja ☐ nein

2. Meine Bankverbindung

Ich ermächtige hiermit widerruflich die Berliner Bank, meine Monatsrechnung per Lastschrift von meinem angegebenen Konto einzuziehen.

Name der Bank | Kto.-Verbindung seit:

Postleitzahl | Anschrift der Bank (Ort)

Kontonummer | Bankleitzahl

Ich verfüge über andere Kreditkarten ☐ nein ☐ ja, welche ....

Ich verfüge über eine eurocheque-Karte ☐ nein ☐ ja

3. Berufliche Angaben

Arbeitgeber/Firmenname | Öffentlicher Dienst ☐ nein ☐ ja

beschäftigt/selbständ. seit | Monat | Jahr | bei Selbständigen bitte Branche eintragen:

Beruf ☐ Arbeiter ☐ Angestellter ☐ Beamter ☐ Rentner/Pensionär ☐ selbständig ☐ Sonstiges ....

Ihr monatliches Nettoeinkommen:

☐ **unter 2.000,– DM** / 1.000 EUR
☐ **über 2.000,– DM** / 1.000 EUR
☐ **über 3.000,– DM** / 1.500 EUR
☐ **über 4.000,– DM** / 2.000 EUR
☐ **über 5.000,– DM** / 2.500 EUR
☐ **über 6.000,– DM** / 3.000 EUR
☐ **über 8.000,– DM** / 4.000 EUR

Bitte zusätzlich angeben: Gesamt-Haushalts-Nettoeinkommen ________ ☐DM ☐EUR

4. Fotoservice

☐ Ja, ich möchte meine Kreditkarten mit Foto. Aufpreis für Fotokarte 6,– DM / 3,07 EUR p.a. Foto beim Kartendoppel im Preis enthalten.

5. Zahlungsmöglichkeiten

☐ Meine Monatsrechnung zahle ich in voller Höhe des Rechnungsbetrages.

☐ Ich möchte die Monatsabrechnung in Teilbeträgen von 10 % des Gesamtrechnungsbetrages, mindestens jedoch 50,– DM/25,56 EUR bei einem effektiven Jahreszins von derzeit 12,68 % (Stand Februar 1999) begleichen. Bitte übersenden Sie mir eine entsprechende Teilzahlungsvereinbarung. Diese ist vom Kartenvertrag unabhängig und kommt erst dann zustande, wenn sie der Berliner Bank unterschrieben zugegangen ist. Bis dahin zahle ich die Monatsrechnung in voller Höhe des Rechnungsbetrages.

Persönliche Geheimzahl (PIN) erwünscht: ja ☐ nein ☐

6. Versicherung

☐ Die Versicherungsmöglichkeit möchte ich **nicht** wahrnehmen und zahle daher nur eine Jahresgebühr von 39,– DM / 19,94 EUR für eine Einzelkarte.

Schufa-Klausel:

Ich willige ein, daß die Berliner Bank der für meinen Wohnsitz zuständigen SCHUFA-Gesellschaft (Schutzgemeinschaft für allgemeine Kreditsicherung) Daten über die Beantragung, den Abschluß und die Beendigung dieses Kreditkartenvertrages übermittelt. Unabhängig davon wird die Berliner Bank der SCHUFA auch Daten aufgrund nicht vertragsgemäßen Verhaltens (z.B. Einziehung der Kreditkarte wegen mißbräuchlicher Verwendung durch den Karteninhaber, beantragter Mahnbescheid bei unbestrittener Forderung sowie Zwangsvollstreckungsmaßnahmen) melden. Diese Meldungen dürfen nach dem Bundesdatenschutzgesetz nur erfolgen, soweit dies zur Wahrung der berechtigten Interessen der Berliner Bank, eines Vertragspartners der SCHUFA oder der Allgemeinheit erforderlich ist und dadurch meine schutzwürdigen Belange nicht beeinträchtigt werden. Soweit hiernach eine Übermittlung erfolgen kann, befreie ich die Berliner Bank zugleich vom Bankgeheimnis.
Die SCHUFA speichert Daten, um den ihr angeschlossenen Kreditinstituten, Leasinggesellschaften, Einzelhandels-, Versandhandels- und sonstigen Unternehmen, die gewerbsmäßig Geld- oder Warenkredite an Konsumenten geben, Informationen zur Beurteilung der Kreditwürdigkeit von Kunden geben zu können. Sie stellt diese Daten ihren Vertragspartnern zur Verfügung, wenn diese ein berechtigtes Interesse an der Datenübermittlung glaubhaft darlegen. Die SCHUFA übermittelt nur objektive Daten ohne Angabe des Kreditgebers. Subjektive Werturteile, persönliche Einkommens- und Vermögensverhältnisse sind in SCHUFA-Auskünften nicht enthalten. Ich kann Auskunft bei der SCHUFA über die mich betreffenden Daten erhalten. Die Adresse der SCHUFA wird mir zusammen mit der Übersendung meiner Karte bekanntgegeben. Ich willige ein, daß im Falle eines Wohnsitzwechsels die Daten an die dann zuständige SCHUFA übermittelt werden. Weitere Informationen über das SCHUFA-Verfahren enthält ein Merkblatt, das auf Wunsch zugesandt wird.

Rechtsverbindliche Erklärungen:

Die Berliner Bank wird ermächtigt, die erforderlichen banküblichen Auskünfte bei meiner angegebenen Bank oder einer Kreditauskunftei einzuholen. Diese werden zur Auskunftserteilung ermächtigt.

Mit der Übermittlung und Speicherung meines Fotos und der zur Erstellung der Fotokarte notwendigen Daten an die GEMPLUS-MIDS GmbH, Forellstraße 120, 44653 Herne bin ich einverstanden.

Auf die Frage nach §8 Geldwäschegesetz, ob ich für eigene oder fremde Rechnung handele, erkläre ich, daß ich für eigene Rechnung handele.

Es gelten die umseitig abgedruckten Bedingungen der Berliner Bank Kreditkarten.

Der Jahreskartenpreis beträgt derzeit 70,– DM / 35,79 EUR für das Kartendoppel (inkl. Fotoservice) bzw. 40– DM / 20,45 EUR für eine Einzelkarte inkl. Reiseunfallversicherung. Mit Foto jährlicher Aufpreis 6,– DM / 3,07 EUR.

Datum X Unterschrift des Antragstellers

Filial-Nr. ☐ DM ☐ EUR Limit:

Händler-Nr. / BB: BST

genehmigt: ________

6 *Marketing credit cards*

These are the covers of brochures used by Barclays and Lloyds TSB to advertise their credit cards. Answer the questions below to compare them.

1 Describe the picture, text and layout of each brochure cover.
2 What is the message behind each one?
3 What sort of customer is each brochure trying to attract?
4 Which brochure cover do you find more effective? Why?

7 *Creative writing*

Your bank has decided to launch a new credit card for persons aged 18 to 30 onto the market. Write a suitable text for the advertising brochure. Include the following points.

1 Give the new credit card a name.
2 Point out its two main advantages.
3 Describe an innovative feature which only this card has got.
4 Draw the readers' attention to a current special offer in connection with this card.
5 Tell the readers how they can get more information.

8 *A tourist from Tokyo*

Kiyoko Mori from Japan is on holiday in Europe. She goes to a German bank because she needs some cash.

KIYOKO MORI Hi.
PIA BRANDT Hello. Can I help you?
KIYOKO MORI Could you tell me whether that ATM outside takes American Express cards, please? I need some cash, you see.
PIA BRANDT I'm afraid it doesn't. Have you got any traveller's cheques that you could change instead?
KIYOKO MORI Sure, but they're in US dollars so I was going to use them for paying in stores. I want to do some shopping while I'm here.
PIA BRANDT Actually, you may find that most shops don't want to accept your dollar traveller's cheques ...
KIYOKO MORI Oh dear, I knew I should have got them in euros instead!
PIA BRANDT Even with traveller's cheques in euros you could still have problems. Traveller's cheques have fixed denominations and if the item you're buying costs less than the value of the cheque, the shop is going to have to pay you the difference in cash, and they might refuse to do that.
KIYOKO MORI But they'd take my American Express card?
PIA BRANDT Yes. Credit cards are much more convenient for them because they don't have to check your identity – you just sign, that's all. You'll find that most big stores in the city centre accept American Express.
KIYOKO MORI Well in that case, can I cash three cheques for 100 dollars, please?
PIA BRANDT Of course. Would you please countersign each cheque? And may I see your passport, as well?
KIYOKO MORI Yes ... here it is.
PIA BRANDT Thanks. I'll just make out your receipt, Ms Mori.
KIYOKO MORI Do you charge anything for cashing traveller's cheques?
PIA BRANDT Yes, we do. There's a commission of 0.5% on cheques for sums up to 1,000 euros or the equivalent in another currency, minimum

5 euros, plus an additional handling charge of 5 euros per cheque.

KIYOKO MORI Hmm, that's still not as much as they charge in Japan. Could you tell me what the exchange rate is at the moment?

PIA BRANDT I'll just check. ... Here we are. ... The euro is standing at 0.9265 dollars today.

KIYOKO MORI That's a bit higher than it was in Venice yesterday.

PIA BRANDT You're visiting other places in Europe as well, then?

KIYOKO MORI Oh yes. I want to see as much as possible. I'm going to Vienna tomorrow, Paris the day after, London on Friday and home at the weekend.

PIA BRANDT Then you haven't got much time to lose, have you? Here's your cash and here's your receipt, Ms Mori. I hope you enjoy your stay here.

KIYOKO MORI I'm sure I will. I'd like to come to Germany again. Maybe I can even stay for a couple of days next time!

Answer these questions.

1 Why will the Japanese visitor not be able to get cash from the ATM?
2 Why might she have difficulty paying with traveller's cheques in shops?
3 What is the procedure for cashing traveller's cheques?
4 What are the charges for cashing traveller's cheques at this bank?
5 Why do many people prefer taking traveller's cheques rather than large sums in cash on trips abroad?

9 *A traveller's cheque*

Name the points numbered on this traveller's cheque.

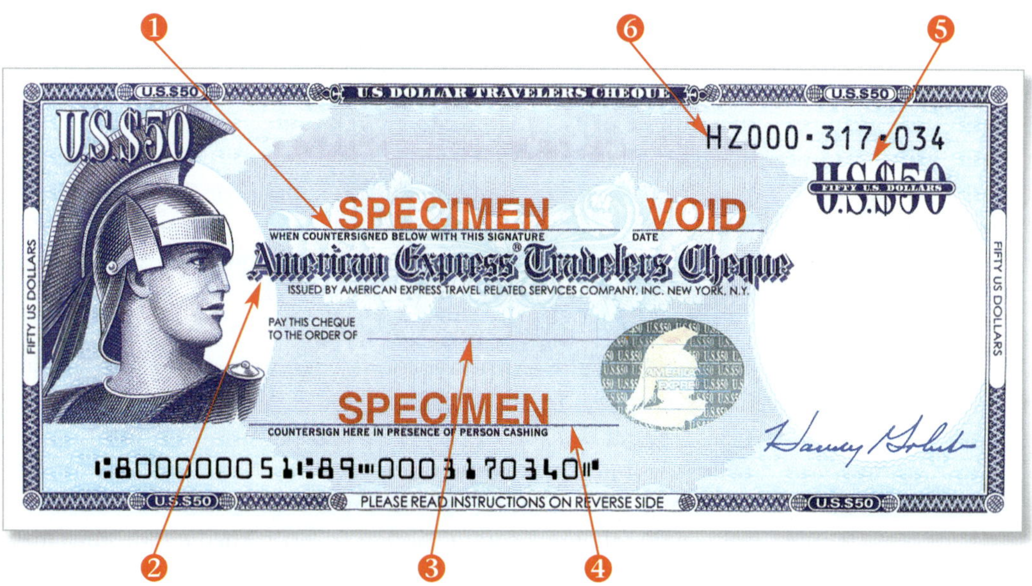

10 *Role play II*

Find out the current exchange rates for the Canadian dollar, the US dollar, the Swiss franc and the Australian dollar against the euro. With a partner taking the customer's role, play one of these situations. Then change the roles.

YVONNE LIVINGSTONE from Sydney has got a VISA card and 1,500 Australian dollars' worth of traveller's cheques. She asks about ways of getting cash, the charges, the exchange rate and whether she can use traveller's cheques in shops in Germany. She wants to buy a camera here.

MARCEL MERCIER wants to change 500 Swiss francs and asks about the exchange rate. He would also like to cash two traveller's cheques for 200 Swiss francs each. He countersigned them while waiting in the queue to be served.

RASCHID SHARIF has an account and a credit card at your bank. He is going on a tour of California soon and wants to change 5,000 euros into US dollars to take with him. Advise him against this.

MIRIAM ELVESTROM comes to collect traveller's cheques for 800 Canadian dollars that she has ordered for a trip to Canada. She has never used traveller's cheques before and asks how to use them. She would like to take 300 dollars in Canadian currency as well.

11 *Working with words*

Fill in the missing words to complete this brochure about the safety precautions for traveller's cheques.

Ten tips to remember if you go abroad:

1 Keep your traveller's cheques and your foreign … in a safe place!

2 Always keep your cheques … from your passport!

3 Order several cheques in small … rather than just one or two large ones!

4 Don't lose the … which you got when you bought the cheques!

5 Never … a cheque until you are in the presence of the recipient!

6 Record the … number of every cheque you cash!

7 Inform us immediately if you think a cheque is missing so that it can be … !

8 Inform the local police, too, if you think that your cheques have been stolen. Then you will be insured against … !

9 If you follow these safety precautions, we will arrange a refund or a … of your lost cheques!

10 Last but not least: now you have no money worries, … your holiday!

LOOKING AT LANGUAGE

COMPARATIVE AND SUPERLATIVE FORMS

1 The rate is a bit **higher than** it was in Venice yesterday.
2 Credit cards are much **more convenient** ...
3 I want to see **as much as** possible.
4 That's **not as much as** they charge in Japan.
5 ... if the item you are buying costs **less than** the value of the cheque ...
6 **Most** big stores in the city centre will accept American Express.

- There are four ways of making comparisons:

...er than	For words of one syllable *(1)* and some words of two syllables, especially those ending in *-y*, eg *happy – happier.*
more than	For most words of two syllables and all words of three syllables or more *(2)*.
as ... as	For two things that are equal *(3)*.
not as ... as / not so ... as	For two things that are not equal *(4)*.

- Some adjectives have irregular comparative *(5)* and superlative *(6)* forms.
  NOTE: *die meisten* = **most**, not ~~the most~~.

good	better	best
bad	worse	worst
much/many	more	most
little (= *wenig*)	less	least

12 *Practice I*

Use a comparison with "than" to make sentences that mean the same as the sentences given.

EXAMPLE: Stolen traveller's cheques can be stopped. Stolen cash is gone for good.
*Using traveller's cheques is **safer than** carrying cash around.*

1 Withdrawals at the ATM take only a minute. Cashing traveller's cheques takes several minutes.
2 The only country I have visited is Denmark. My friend has travelled through the States and Canada.
3 My colleague speaks very good English because he used to live in the USA. My English is not as good as his.
4 Peter is a hard worker. Jack hardly does a thing.
5 Serving at the counter is interesting because you have personal contact with customers. When working at the till you do not have time to talk to customers.
6 A trainee earns a salary of about 500 euros a month. A qualified bank clerk earns twice as much.
7 Exclusive shops sell expensive goods. Department stores do not charge such high prices.
8 I bought the securities for 200 euros each and sold them for 250.

13 *Practice II*

Make comparisons between the photos in each of the following pairs. Use any adjectives that you find suitable.

1

2

3

4

14 *Case studies*

Explain which of these means of payment – a Eurocheque card, a credit card, traveller's cheques or currency – would be advisable for the following customers. Use superlatives: *the most suitable, the simplest, the cheapest, the safest, the most convenient*, etc.

1 Kris and Karen Karlsson and their two children are planning a four-week cycling and fishing tour of the west coast of the USA.

2 Toby Forrester, 25, is going to drive overland to India. He has no idea how long it will take him.

3 Janice Berry, 17, intends to travel all over Europe for six weeks on an Interrail ticket.

4 Lawrence van Damm has a new job which means that he will have to fly to Asia regularly to promote sales and entertain clients there.

15 *Memo-writing*

Listen to these three phone calls and write a memo about each one. Include all the relevant information. Then report to the class.

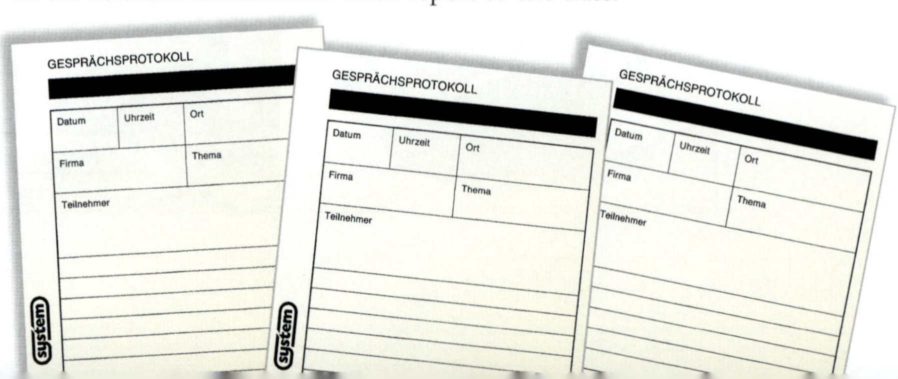

Advanced materials

E-commerce

16 *Paying for online purchases*

Describe the methods of payment shown in the picture below and point out their advantages or disadvantages for the user.

(*Connectis*, July 2000)

17 *Security on the web*

A customer who is worried about using a credit card to pay for online purchases asks your advice. Use this text to tell him or her about the steps taken so far to improve security in e-commerce.

The concept of electronic payment is not a new one. Credit cards paved the way towards e-commerce as long as three decades ago and, for 90% of consumers who shop on the web today, they are still the most convenient payment option. On the other hand, there are many people who are tempted to go e-shopping but who do not do so because they are reluctant to give their credit card number. Reports of hackers who exploit the anonymity of online transactions to steal data and order goods and services at the expense of others make would-be shoppers worried about the security of Internet-based electronic payment. Credit card companies, banks, software producers and manufacturers of electronic payments systems are urgently trying to find ways of solving this problem.

SSL (secure socket layer) and SET (secure electronic transaction) are two of the best-known applications for secure Internet operations. SSL encrypts data entered from the user's browser before transferring it to the merchant's site. SSL is widely used but has the disadvantage of not identifying the user. The SET security system goes further: it authenticates the identity of both customer and merchant as well as guaranteeing data privacy and non-cancellation of the transaction. While the consumer can easily obtain the free software, the e-merchant requires a special electronic infrastructure, which many have been slow to install.

Europay, Mastercard and Visa have set standards for "smart" credit cards, fitted with tamper-proof microchips instead of the usual magnetic strips. The POS terminal interprets the card data on each transaction and updates the user information on the chip. Michael Behringer, consultant of Cisco Systems, the world's leading supplier of Internet-capable payment solutions, says, "The new smartcards offer a high degree of security because the user has to enter a personal code on each transaction."

Other solutions for would-be shoppers worried about giving their credit card numbers are offered by companies which allow customers to pay by credit card on delivery of goods or which open free online accounts for customers: the online purchases are charged to the monthy bill sent by their Internet service provider or phone company.

The greatest danger, however, lies in e-suppliers storing customers' credit card details on non-secure servers. Standard browsers keep the user informed on a site's security: the padlock in the bottom right of the Netscape window closes when the computer connects to a secure site and Explorer activates a cookie to warn the user if a site is insecure.

"The web will never be a totally secure environment," says Michael Behringer, "but then traditional transactions are not totally secure either."

(based on an article in *Connectis*, July 2000)

18 *Go online*

Find out more about security of e-payments by visiting one of these websites. Report your findings.

www.berliner-bank.de
(for information about SET)
www.visa.com
www.mastercard.com
www.americanexpress.com
www.europay.com

UNIT 6

Personal borrowing

Lead-in

Why do personal customers need to borrow money from banks? In what different ways can they do so?

1 *A familiar face*

Stephen Radcliffe is a British actor who is working in Germany. He enters the branch of his bank where Jürgen Bahr is working at the counter. Mr Radcliffe has not been in since he opened his account nearly a year ago.

STEPHEN RADCLIFFE	Excuse me. Could you or one of your colleagues help me, please?
JÜRGEN BAHR	Certainly, sir. In fact, I believe we spoke once before when you opened your account. It's Mr Radcliffe, isn't it?
STEPHEN RADCLIFFE	I say! You should be an actor with a memory like that!
JÜRGEN BAHR	Well, it helps in this job, too. Did you have a successful tour with your play?
STEPHEN RADCLIFFE	Great, thanks. We've been on tour all over Germany for eleven months now, and audiences have been so good that we've arranged to play the winter season at the theatre here. We open on December 1st.
JÜRGEN BAHR	Congratulations. I'll try to come and see it.
STEPHEN RADCLIFFE	If you do, I hope you enjoy it. Now, what I wanted to ask you about is this: I've just found a small flat to rent here from December onwards. I've been living out of a suitcase since last year and I can't stand it any longer. The only snag is that the landlord wants a deposit – but I gather that's normal in Germany. At any rate, I wanted to check whether I could overdraw my account to pay it.
JÜRGEN BAHR	I see. ... How long have you had your account with us, Mr Radcliffe?
STEPHEN RADCLIFFE	For about a year now, I should say.

JÜRGEN BAHR And you've been earning a regular salary for the same period, haven't you? ... Yes, here we are. I see that you have an overdraft facility of 3,000 euros at your disposal. Would that be enough to cover the deposit for the flat?

STEPHEN RADCLIFFE Yes, more than enough, but there's one other thing I wanted to ask about. The flat is miles out of town, and there's no way of getting back there in the evenings after the performance. I'm going to have to buy a car – something cheap, second-hand of course, that I can sell again when I leave the country.

JÜRGEN BAHR How much do you have in mind?

STEPHEN RADCLIFFE Perhaps you could extend my overdraft facility to say 8,000 euros? Then I could pay the deposit for the flat and use the rest to buy the car ...

JÜRGEN BAHR I suggest that we leave the overdraft facility as it is and arrange a personal loan for the car.

STEPHEN RADCLIFFE That sounds a bit complicated.

JÜRGEN BAHR Not really. In fact, it's simpler because a loan has fixed instalments so you can decide in advance exactly how much you can afford to repay each month and what term will suit you best. It works out cheaper, too, because the interest charged on loans is lower than the rate for overdrafts. This brochure explains our lending terms for both types of credit.

STEPHEN RADCLIFFE Hmm. I'd better read the small print first.

JÜRGEN BAHR Of course. Would you like to make an appointment with our adviser to discuss the details?

STEPHEN RADCLIFFE All right. What about some time on Thursday afternoon?

JÜRGEN BAHR That would be fine. Would half past three be convenient?

STEPHEN RADCLIFFE Yes, three thirty on Thursday, but while I'm here I'd like to use my overdraft facility to pay the deposit right away.

JÜRGEN BAHR Good idea. Better make sure you get that flat before anyone else does!

Answer these questions.

1 Why does Mr Radcliffe want to borrow from the bank?
2 Why does he already have an overdraft facility at his disposal?
3 How does Mr Radcliffe plan to borrow the money he needs?
4 What alternative method of borrowing does the clerk suggest? What are the reasons for this?
5 What does the customer decide to do in the end?

2 *Comparing personal loans and overdrafts*

The brochure which Mr Radcliffe received may have been similar to this one from Lloyds Bank. Use information from it and your own ideas to compare personal loans and overdrafts in Germany. Write parallel sentences, following the example below.

Lloyds Bank Personal Loans from £500

Most suitable:

- For any higher value purchase – normally up to £10,000.
- Where repayment can be made comfortably within five years or less.
- When a set monthly payment is preferable to repaying varying amounts.
- When the borrower wants protection against future changes in interest rates.

Not suitable:

- For short-term credit (less than six months).

You can use a Lloyds Bank Personal Loan for almost any purpose. Particularly recommended for major purchases like a car, home furnishing and all but the largest home improvements.

Quite unlike retail credit schemes, your loan is tailored to suit you. You can repay over the period of your choice from 12 months to 5 years.

You can repay early, if you wish, without penalty. And the interest rate is guaranteed not to change during the whole period of your loan, so you can plan the finance with confidence.

Lloyds Bank Personal Overdrafts

Most suitable:

- To take advantage of special bargains and as a standby for unexpected expenses.
- For short-term credit, especially under 6 months.
- To smooth out fluctuations between income and expenditure.

Not suitable:

- For longer-term credit.
- For larger purchases.

Special advice

Usually, the level of your overdraft is related to your normal monthly salary and reviewed regularly.

While it is very useful to have an overdraft facility, the full benefit of your facility can be lost if you are using it up to your limit on a continuous basis. It is comforting to know that once your overdraft has been arranged, you have the flexibility to cope with an emergency without further formalities.

If you are thinking of applying for an overdraft, do bear in mind that, when you use it, it can trigger bank charges that you might otherwise not have to pay.

When you apply, we will advise you in writing of your agreed borrowing facility and include details of the interest rate, how it is charged, and what fees, if any, are payable.

Personal loans	Personal overdrafts
• are granted for a fixed sum.	• are allowed for any sum within the overdraft facility.
• …	• …

3 *Prepositions*

Fill in the missing prepositions.

1 Mr Radcliffe applies ... a loan ... 5,000 euros.
2 He already has an overdraft facility ... 3,000 euros ... his disposal.
3 He is going to see the loan adviser ... Thursday ... three thirty.
4 The interest charged ... loans is lower ... the rate ... overdrafts.
5 Lloyds Bank loans have to be repaid ... five years or less.
6 Overdrafts enable borrowers to cope ... emergencies.
7 Borrowers should bear ... mind that overdrawing can be expensive.
8 Customers may use overdrafts to take advantage ... special bargains.

LOOKING AT LANGUAGE

THE PRESENT PERFECT AND THE SIMPLE PAST

1 Mr Radcliffe **has not been** in since the day he opened his account.
2 We**'ve arranged** to play the winter season at the theatre.
3 I**'ve** just **found** a small flat to rent.
4 How long **have** you **had** your account with us?
5 You**'ve been earning** a regular salary for the same period.
6 I**'ve been living** out of a suitcase since last year.
7 Audiences **have been** so good.
8 Mr Radcliffe **opened** his account one year ago.
9 We **spoke** once before when you opened your account.
10 **Did** you **have** a successful tour with your play?

- If an action began in the past and continues up to the moment of speaking, we use the present perfect *(1)*. It is also used when no particular time is mentioned but when there is a connection to the present *(2)*, especially in sentences with words like *just (3), always, often, never, sometimes* and *yet.*
- In questions with *how long* the present perfect is used to ask about an action or situation which began in the past and continues until the present *(4).*
- The present perfect may be used in the progressive form when an action has been happening without interruption during the whole period up to the moment of speaking *(5)*, or when an action has been taking place repeatedly up to the moment of speaking *(6).*

  NOTE: For the German word "seit", both *since* and *for* are used: *since* = from a point in time *(1, 6)*; *for* = over a period of time *(5).*
- The progressive form is not normally used with these verbs:
  be (7) ◆ *believe* ◆ *belong* ◆ *forget* ◆ *have* ◆ *know* ◆ *like* ◆ *own* ◆ *prefer* ◆ *realize* ◆ *remember* ◆ *seem* ◆ *suppose* ◆ *understand,* etc.
- The simple past is used when an action was completed at a named *(8)* or known *(9)* time in the past. It is also used in questions, especially those beginning with *when*, if we are asking about an action or situation completed in the past *(10).*

4 Practice I

Use the present perfect simple or the present perfect progressive and "since" or "for" to complete these sentences.

1 That customer ... *(wait)* ... *(since/for)* over half an hour!
2 I ... *(know)* Mr Bailey ... *(since/for)* he came to live in Germany.
3 They ... *(work)* with the new software ... *(since/for)* last year.
4 That old lady ... *(come)* into the branch every day ... *(since/for)* years.
5 That customer's account ... *(be overdrawn)* ... *(since/for)* nine months now.
6 Ms Forster ... *(own)* the business ... *(since/for)* her father died.
7 House prices ... *(rise)* constantly ... *(since/for)* the last year.
8 Our customers ... *(use)* online banking ... *(since/for)* 1998.
9 The ATM ... *(be)* out of order ... *(since/for)* this morning.
10 The phone ... *(ring)* ... *(since/for)* hours.

5 Practice II

Make the sentences in exercise 4 into questions beginning "How long".
EXAMPLE: *How long has that customer been waiting?*

6 Practice III

Answer these questions using the simple past or the present perfect.
EXAMPLES: Have you read the report yet? – Yes / yesterday
Yes, I have. I read it yesterday.
Have you seen the report yet? – Yes, / already
Yes, I have already seen it.

1 Have you seen the new cheque cards? – Yes / when they arrived
2 Has that client rung up yet? – Yes / ten minutes ago
3 Has the dollar risen recently? – Yes / last Thursday
4 Has the company ever done business with Japan? – Yes / frequently
5 Have you worked in the loan department? – Yes / in July
6 Have you ever spent a holiday in London? – Yes / several times
7 Has the cheque been paid in yet? – Yes / just
8 Has the bank opened a branch in Prague? – Yes / in 1999
9 Has the company started to make a profit? – Yes / already
10 Has the manager left yet? – Yes / at half past eight

7 Practice IV

Change the questions in exercise 6 so that they begin with "when".
EXAMPLE: Have you read the report yet?
When did you read the report?

HOW TO

– ask for personal information

It is important to ask a customer for his or her personal details politely. Sometimes it is necessary to ask questions beginning with *what*:

What nationality are you?
What is your current occupation?

Try to avoid using *what*-questions too often. Vary your language by using other question words:

Where have you lived during the last two years?
When were you born?
Why do you need a loan?
How long have you been living in Germany?
How much rent do you pay a month?
How many people are there in your household?
How are you and your partner assessed for tax purposes?

Sometimes no question word is necessary:
Do you have community of property or separation of property?
Have you done military or community service?

Questions with or without question words can sound very abrupt. It is sometimes more polite to use an introductory phrase. Introduce some of your questions like this:

Could you tell me | whether you have any other sources of income?
| what other regular expenses you have, please?

NOTE: When an introductory phrase is used, the second verb in the sentence is not in the question form. Compare:
How much **do you earn**?
and
Could you tell me how much **you earn**?

8 *An application for a loan*

Use the form for the voluntary disclosure of confidential information shown on the opposite page to do the following tasks.

1 Match these expressions with German ones printed on the form.

a	purpose	*g*	civil servant
b	co-applicant	*h*	annual turnover
c	residence permit	*i*	income from property
d	system of marital property	*j*	monthly disposable income
e	employment status	*k*	total expenditure
f	self-employed	*l*	surplus

2 Use expressions from the box above to ask a customer for personal information for filling in the disclosure form.
EXAMPLE: *Could you tell me your surname, first name and name at birth?*

COMMERZBANK

Filial-Nr.	Kunden-Nr.

☐ Vertrauliche Selbstauskunft

☐ Bearbeitungsblatt zur Bürgschaft / zum Kredit-Vertrag vom ______________

Der Antragsteller / Mitantragsteller / Bürge gibt gegenüber der COMMERZBANK AG die Angaben zur vertraulichen Selbstauskunft zu den nachstehend aufgeführten Bedingungen ab. Die Selbstauskunft wird in ☐ DM ☐ Euro vorgenommen. Alle Beträge sind in dieser Währungseinheit (WE) angegeben. Wird keine Regelung über die Währungseinheit getroffen, wird die Selbstauskunft solange dies rechtlich möglich ist, als in DM abgegeben betrachtet.

Kreditwunsch: WE ______________ Rate: WE ______________ Laufzeit: ___/___ (Jahre/Monate) Zahlungsform: ______________

Verwendungszweck: ☐ privat ☐ gewerblich Nähere Angaben: ______________

Commerzbank-Kunde: ☐ nein ☐ ja: ______________

Kreditlebensversicherung wird vom Kreditantragsteller gewünscht: ☐ mit ☐ ohne Arbeitsunfähigkeits-Zusatzversicherung

Persönliche Angaben	Kreditantragsteller	Mitantragsteller / Bürge
Name, Vorname (Geburtsname) Straße, Haus-Nr. PLZ, Ort Telefon (privat/geschäftl./mobil)		
Aktuelle Anschrift seit		
Wohnstatus	☐ Eigentümer ☐ Mieter/Untermieter ☐ bei den Eltern	☐ Eigentümer ☐ Mieter/Untermieter ☐ bei den Eltern
vorherige Anschrift(en) innerhalb der letzten zwei Jahre		
Geburtsdatum, -ort Nationalität	☐ deutsch ☐ sonstige ______	☐ deutsch ☐ sonstige ______
Zusätzliche Angaben bei ausländischen Staatsangehörigen	in Deutschland seit ______ Arbeitserlaubnis bis ______ Aufenthaltsgenehmigung/-erlaubnis bis ______	in Deutschland seit ______ Arbeitserlaubnis bis ______ Aufenthaltsgenehmigung/-erlaubnis bis ______
Familienstand Haushaltsgröße	☐ ledig ☐ verh. ☐ zus.leb. ☐ verw. ☐ gesch. ☐ getr.leb. insges. ______ davon Kinder (Alter) ______	☐ ledig ☐ verh. ☐ zus.leb. ☐ verw. ☐ gesch. ☐ getr.leb insges. ______ davon Kinder (Alter) ______
Güterstand	☐ gesetzlich ☐ Gütertrennung ☐ Gütergemeinschaft	☐ gesetzlich ☐ Gütertrennung ☐ Gütergemeinschaft
Wehr-/Zivildienst abgeleistet	☐ ja ☐ nein ☐ entfällt	☐ ja ☐ nein ☐ entfällt
Beschäftigungsverhältnis	☐ selbständig ☐ angestellt ☐ Auszubildender/Student ☐ Arbeiter ☐ Beamter ☐ Rentner seit ______	☐ selbständig ☐ angestellt ☐ Auszubildender/Student ☐ Arbeiter ☐ Beamter ☐ Rentner seit ______
Branche / ausgeübter Beruf		
Firma PLZ, Ort		
Bei Selbständigen	Jahresumsatz TSD ______ Anzahl Mitarbeiter ______	Jahresumsatz TSD ______ Anzahl Mitarbeiter ______

Einnahmen- / Ausgaben-Rechnung **Monatliche Netto-Einnahmen (Nachweise bitte beifügen)**	**Kreditantragsteller in WE**	**Mitantragsteller**/Bürge in WE**	**Summe in WE**
Nettoeinkommen aus Lohn / Gehalt / Pension*			
Einkünfte aus selbständiger Tätigkeit *			
Einkünfte aus Vermietung und Verpachtung			
Einkünfte aus Kapitalvermögen (Zinsen / Dividenden)			
Sonstige regelmäßige Einkünfte:			
abzüglich Steuern:	%	%	
Summe Einnahmen			
Monatliche Ausgaben			
Lebenshaltungskosten (inkl. Kfz, Sachversicherungen)			
Miete inkl. Nebenkosten			
Hausnebenkosten (soweit Haus- bzw. Wohnungseigentümer)			
Rate(n) für Sparvertrag (WE ______), Bausparvertrag (WE ______)			
Lebens-/Rentenversicherung (WE ______)			
Rate(n) für andere(n) Kredit(e) / Baufinanzierung über WE ______			
Sonstige regelmäßige Ausgaben für ______			
Summe Ausgaben			
frei verfügbares Monatseinkommen = Summe Einnahmen ./. Ausgaben			
Monatliche Rate bzw. Belastung für diesen Kredit			
Überschuss			

* nach Abzug von Vorsorgeaufwendungen, falls direkt vom Kreditantragsteller / Mitantragsteller zu tragen (z. B. Kranken-/Rentenversicherung).
** separate Überschussermittlung nur bei getrenntem Haushalt.

2/3

Ausfertigung für die Bank

341/11/21 HD0700

9 *Explain the chart*

Explain the information given on this chart to a customer who asks about the cost and repayment of personal loans.

Kosten und Tilgungspläne für Darlehen ab €10.000,– mit Laufzeitzinssatz (regelmäßige Tilgung)

Monatlicher Zinssatz: 0,44%
Bearbeitungsentgelt: 2% vom Kapitalbetrag

Kreditbetrag	Laufzeit	Effektiver Jahreszins*	1. Rate	Monatliche Rate
€10.000,–	24 Monate	12,65%	€448,–	23 × €471,–
	36 Monate	11,80%	€294,–	35 × €329,–
	60 Monate	10,95%	€180,–	59 × €215,–
€15.000,–	24 Monate	12,56%	€694,–	23 × €704,–
	36 Monate	11,75%	€481,–	35 × €492,–
	60 Monate	10,92%	€287,–	59 × €322,–
€20.000,–	24 Monate	12,52%	€917,–	23 × €940,–
	36 Monate	11,72%	€633,–	35 × €656,–
	60 Monate	10,90%	€394,–	59 × €429,–
€30.000,–	24 Monate	12,48%	€1.386,–	23 × €1.409,–
	36 Monate	11,69%	€972,–	35 × €983,–
	60 Monate	10,89%	€608,–	59 × €643,–

**Effektiver Jahreszins = true annual rate of interest*

10 *Role play*

Working with a partner, play these roles. Reach a loan agreement using the form from exercise 8 and the above chart. Then reverse the roles.

You are the loan adviser. Find out the customer's intentions. Ask for the necessary details to fill in the form on p 69. Then, using the chart from the last exercise, help the applicant choose a suitable repayment method. Finish by asking him or her to sign the application form and the SCHUFA declaration.

You are the customer. Ask for a loan of between 10,000 and 30,000 euros for any purpose you like. Give the loan adviser all the information he or she asks for. Find out how much a loan will cost you and how you can pay it back. Ask questions, eg about what the SCHUFA declaration is for. Finish by signing the necessary forms.

11 *Note-taking*

Listen to these extracts from four discussions in the loan department of the bank. Note the main details about each case, eg disposable income, occupation, loan amount, purpose, term, etc.

12 *Case studies*

Working in a small group, study one of the cases from the last exercise. Discuss whether you approve the application and, if so, which type of borrowing – loan or overdraft – is suitable. Report your group's decision.

13 *Working with words I*

Use words from this unit to complete these sentences.

1. The person who applies for a loan is the … .
2. If a second person applies too, he or she is the … .
3. The reason why a loan is needed is the … .
4. The period for which a loan runs is the … .
5. The service fee charged by the bank for arranging a loan is the … .
6. The monthly repayments of a loan are the … .
7. The amount that a borrower spends every month on rent, food, etc is his or her monthly … .
8. The amount of the borrower's income left after the regular costs have been deducted is the … .
9. The percentage of interest charged yearly, including all the costs, is the … .
10. The contract between the borrower and the bank is the loan … .
11. The statement which a borrower has to sign regarding the SCHUFA is the SCHUFA … .
12. The conditions of a loan are the lending … .

14 *Working with words II*

Use words from the box to complete these sentences.

credit ◆ *instalments* ◆ *loan* ◆ *rates*

1. Mr Radcliffe needed a … to buy a car.
2. He arranged to pay the sum in monthy … .
3. If interest … are high, borrowing is expensive.
4. With a Eurocard you can buy goods on … .
5. If the bank grants a …, the … include interest and repayment of the sum.

15 *Working with pictures*

The captions and the pictures below should warn people about the dangers of unwise borrowing. Match each caption with one of the pictures. Then describe each picture and explain what the danger for the borrower is.

- *Do not overcommit yourself.*
- *Read the small print.*
- *It can be expensive to repay a loan early.*
- *The most tempting offer is not always the best.*
- *Do not underestimate your monthly expenditure.*
- *Your home can be at risk if you do not keep up your mortgage payments.*

Advanced materials

Dealing with debt

16 *Credit card debt*

Statistics show that credit card debt per capita is lower in Germany than in Britain or the USA. Suggest reasons why.

17 *A true story*

List as many reasons as you can why private borrowers sometimes get heavily into debt. This report from TIME, 17 January 2000, may give you some ideas.

Sliding Down the Slippery Slope of Consumer Credit

The answer to personal debt problems, says Professor Steve Worthington of England's Staffordshire University, is to "increase our financial literacy". He thinks schools should be teaching how to look after money and avoid unmanageable debt. "Some people take the view of revolving credit that so long as they can afford the minimum payment each month, they're okay."

Tom Martin, 57, has learned how untrue that can be. That's not his real name; like most people who have succumbed to debt and who are trying to get back on their feet, he requests anonymity. An information technology consultant in the north of England, Martin has been on a slow slide since he borrowed $350 on a Barclaycard in 1972. He says the company kept raising his limit without him asking, but he managed well until 1985, when he started his own computer-aided design business. At the same time he continued working as a salesman, using his credit card for his expenses, which his employer was slow to reimburse.

"If the credit limit is too high," says Martin, "and you find ways of getting up to that limit – which is human nature – it's not easy to control." In 1989 he acquired another card, rapidly reaching his limit on that too. He was just able to meet his minimum repayments. Then his business failed. He stumbled along and increased his house mortgage to start another business. Eventually he and his wife had about eight credit cards between them. Their revolving debt climbed to about $417,500 – and that didn't count the checking account overdraft for his business. All he could do was drip feed repayments, based on who screamed loudest. "In the end you're inundated with mail, and you fall into the trap of just not opening the bills."

Martin finally approached the Consumer Credit Counselling Service, a charity which helps people with debt problems. As he would probably be able to pay off his debts if they were rescheduled over several years, the CCCS agreed to intercede with his creditors. He now pays a set monthly sum that is distributed among them. He has had to sell his house to pay off his business debts, and obtaining another mortgage will be difficult until he can clear his credit rating. His advice to young people thinking of plastic? "Look at the interest rates on the cards. They're diabolical. We have the lowest bank rates for years, and they're around 20%." He hopes to start over again, which is not easy as he approaches 60. "The legacy of debt is a very long one," he warns.

18 *Credit scoring*

Banks try to prevent customers from taking on more borrowing than they can repay. NatWest uses the system of credit scoring, described in this brochure. Read the brochure and answer the questions below.

CREDIT SCORING?

Credit scoring is a process used by banks and other financial organisations to help them assess applications to open accounts or borrow money.

Why does NatWest use credit scoring?

We are committed to helping you make financial decisions that best suit your circumstances. We want to make sure that you do not take on too much or put yourself in financial difficulty when you apply to open an account or borrow money. We use credit scoring to help us decide whether it is sensible for customers to take on the financial commitments they have asked for.

Credit scoring is established as a fair method of assessing applications.

How will I know that you will credit score my application?

All our application forms clearly state whether we will use credit scoring in assessing the application.

You must fill in forms as fully as possible so that we have enough details to assess your application.

How does it work?

Each piece of information that you give us on your application form, such as your age and occupation, has a score. These scores are based on the way that previous customers with similar details handle their money. In many cases we also use information from a credit reference agency. We then add up the scores and your application is either approved or refused depending on your total score.

If you have had an account with us before, or already hold an account, we will consider any relevant information.

What information does NatWest get from a credit reference agency?

Credit reference agencies keep records about people to help financial organisations assess applications.

The records include:

- county court judgements
- electoral roll
- bankruptcies and insolvencies
- credit agreements in arrears
- previous credit searches by other organisations

1 What is credit scoring?
2 Why is credit scoring necessary?
3 How does NatWest credit score a loan application? Compare this with the method used at the bank where you work.
4 NatWest describes credit scoring as "a fair method of assessing applications". How far do you agree?
5 In what other ways can banks protect themselves from customers who are unable to repay borrowed money?

UNIT 7

Corporate loans

Lead-in

How is lending to corporate clients different from lending to personal customers? What additional information does the bank need?

1 Restoring old links (I)

Annika Born works in the corporate loan department of the German subsidiary of a British bank. One day she gets a call from her opposite number in London, Jim Woodall.

ANNIKA BORN Born. Guten Tag.

JIM WOODALL Hi, Annika. Jim here.

ANNIKA BORN Hi, Jim. How are things in London?

JIM WOODALL Not too bad at all, thanks. The weather could be better.

ANNIKA BORN Same here. What can I do for you today?

JIM WOODALL We've got a client who's planning to set up a branch of his company in Germany and wants to apply for a loan from the Kreditanstalt für Wiederaufbau. I'm not absolutely sure that we've got the latest KfW conditions over here, so I just thought I'd ring you and check.

ANNIKA BORN No problem. I suppose it's the Kreditanstalt's Mittelstands-programm you mean. The one for privately-owned companies?

JIM WOODALL That's right. There's a limit how high a company's annual turnover can be, isn't there? What's the limit at the moment?

ANNIKA BORN For a company to be eligible for a KfW loan, its annual turnover must not exceed 500 million euros. The other conditions are that the loan has to be invested in Germany, of course, and it mustn't be used for repaying other loans or as additional finance for existing investments.

JIM WOODALL How much can companies actually borrow?

ANNIKA BORN That depends on their annual turnover. If it's less than 50 million euros, the maximum loan is 5 million euros, but they have to contribute at least a quarter of the total investment sum themselves. Companies with an annual turnover of over 50 million euros can borrow larger sums, but have to contribute at least one third of the total amount they need.

JIM WOODALL And what about the term? These loans are granted for terms of up to ten years, aren't they?

ANNIKA BORN Yes, but in certain cases – for financing real estate or building costs, for example – terms of up to 20 years can be arranged.

JIM WOODALL I see. I've told our customer that these loans have very favourable conditions because they're subsidized by the German state. Can you tell me what the current interest rate on them is?

ANNIKA BORN At the moment[1] it's 5.25% on loans of up to ten years. 96% of the loan amount will be paid out, so the true interest rate is 6.18%. On loans of up to twenty years the interest rate is 5.85% – that's a true APR[2] of 6.52%.

JIM WOODALL There's nothing like that over here. What about repayment?

ANNIKA BORN Borrowers can pay just the interest for the first two years on ten-year loans and for the first three years on twenty-year loans. Repayment follows after that in equal, half-yearly instalments. As an alternative, the loan can be paid off in a lump sum at the end of the term.

JIM WOODALL And the interest rate is fixed for the full term, I take it?

ANNIKA BORN Generally, yes. Another advantage is that no penalty fees will be charged if the loan is repaid earlier than agreed.

JIM WOODALL Sounds excellent. I'll put that to my client right away.

ANNIKA BORN The sooner he applies, the better. We're expecting the ECB to raise interest rates shortly.

JIM WOODALL I'll tell him, but you may get the opportunity of discussing the matter with him yourself. He has to go over to Germany and I believe he intends to make the application with you.

ANNIKA BORN Really? Then I'd better brush up my English. What's the name of the company?

JIM WOODALL Freeman & Sons. They do light engineering. Michael Freeman, the managing director, is the person you'll be dealing with. Well, that's it for now, Annika. Thanks for all the information.

ANNIKA BORN You're welcome, Jim. I'll let you know how I get on with Mr Freeman. Bye for now.

JIM WOODALL Bye.

[1] = as on 4/2001 [2] = annual percentage rate of interest

Copy this table into your exercise book and use information from the dialogue to complete it.

General conditions of KfW loans
1 Criteria for eligibility: ...
2 Purpose of the loan: ...
3 Maximum loan amount: ...
4 Applicant's own contribution: ...
5 Maximum term: ...
6 Interest rate: ...
7 Repayment methods for ten-year loans: ...

2 *Restoring old links (II)*

Michael Freeman of Freeman & Sons Limited has made an appointment with Annika Born in the bank's corporate loan department in Germany. Listen to their conversation and write down all the details about Mr Freeman's company and its plans.

MICHAEL FREEMAN Good morning, Ms Born. How do you do? I'm Michael Freeman.

ANNIKA BORN How do you do, Mr Freeman? Pleased to meet you. Do take a seat.

MICHAEL FREEMAN Thank you.

ANNIKA BORN I hope you had a good journey. You must have had to leave London very early this morning.

MICHAEL FREEMAN I flew out on Friday, actually, and spent the weekend in Potsdam. Our business was founded by my grandfather there in 1922. Then, in the thirties, my parents emigrated to England. So you see we have strong links with Germany.

ANNIKA BORN Is the company still in the hands of your family?

MICHAEL FREEMAN Yes. Since my father's death my brother and I have been managing the business. Together with our mother and two uncles we own all the shares. I've brought the articles of association which show that I'm authorized to act on their behalf.

ANNIKA BORN I understand from my colleague in London that you intend setting up a branch of your business in Germany again?

MICHAEL FREEMAN Yes. We specialize in restoring antique metal-work. We've got contracts for reconstruction work which the states of Mecklenburg-Vorpommern and Brandenburg are planning on various historic buildings over here.

ANNIKA BORN Well, there's still a lot of work to be done. Have you found premises in Germany yet?

MICHAEL FREEMAN Yes. We're planning to buy a small engineering plant just outside Schwerin. For that we'll need 2,400,000 euros plus another 600,000 for alterations and a further 1,800,000 which will be spent on machinery and vehicles.

ANNIKA BORN So all in all the total sum you'll be investing will be 4,800,000 euros ...

MICHAEL FREEMAN We can contribute 1,200,000 euros towards that ourselves, so the actual sum we'd apply for would be 3,600,000 euros.

ANNIKA BORN I see. And what term do you have in mind?

MICHAEL FREEMAN This file contains a detailed breakdown of how we plan to invest the sum and when the investment should start to pay for itself. On the basis of that, we estimate that we can repay the loan over a ten-year period – perhaps even earlier. I understand from Mr Woodall that we have to secure the loan with the bank, not with the Kreditanstalt itself?

ANNIKA BORN That's right. You apply to the Kreditanstalt through us and we then become liable for repayment of the loan. The security that we agree on has to be specified in the KfW loan application form.

MICHAEL FREEMAN I see. How are these loans usually secured?

ANNIKA BORN We often register land-charges on property or ask for guarantees. If a loan has been granted for machinery, an assignment by bill of sale is quite common. In your case, a combination might well be the best solution. But I suggest we postpone discussing the security until our next meeting. I take it you've brought your company's balance sheets with you?

MICHAEL FREEMAN Yes, our last three are in the file with profit and loss accounts, though I'm afraid everything's in English.

ANNIKA BORN That's no problem at all. Will you be staying on in the area?

MICHAEL FREEMAN Yes, till the end of the week.

ANNIKA BORN Then I suggest meeting again on – let's say, Thursday morning?

MICHAEL FREEMAN That would be fine. Would 9.30 be convenient?

ANNIKA BORN Perfectly. Goodbye, Mr Freeman. I'll look forward to seeing you again then.

MICHAEL FREEMAN Thank you, Ms Born. Goodbye.

3 *Making a decision*

Use your notes from exercise 2 and the information from exercise 1 to decide whether Freeman & Sons meet the conditions of a KfW loan.

LOOKING AT LANGUAGE

THE PASSIVE

1 These loans **are subsidized** by the German state.
2 96% of the loan amount **will be paid out**.
3 Our family business **was founded** there in 1922.
4 If a loan **has been granted** for machinery, ...
5 Repayment in a lump sum **can also be arranged**.
6 The loan **has to be invested** in Germany.

- The passive voice is formed using a form of the verb *to be* and the past participle. The passive can be used with all tenses of the verb *to be (1–4)*, with modal verbs *(5)* and with their substitutes *(6)*.
- The passive is often used in sentences in which the person or thing taking the action is not as important as the action itself.
  NOTE: The word *by* is used if the agent is mentioned *(1)*.

4 *Practice*

Use the passive to give a customer the following information about KfW loans.

EXAMPLE: KfW loans often help small businesses.
Small businesses are often helped by KfW loans.

1 The KfW grants loans of up to 5 million euros to small companies.
2 They have to invest the money in Germany.
3 They must make the application through a bank.
4 They can use the money only for long-term investment.
5 The KfW does not allow borrowers to finance their running costs with these loans.
6 Borrowers usually make repayment in half-yearly instalments.
7 They need not pay the loan off during the first two years.
8 The KfW will fix the interest rate on a ten-year loan.
9 The KfW always requires applicants to arrange security with their bank.
10 Borrowers may repay the loan earlier than agreed without penalty.
11 The German state has always subsidized KfW loans.
12 In the early years after reunification, the KfW financed many projects in the eastern federal states.

5 *Write an e-mail*

When Freeman & Sons' KfW loan has been approved, Annika Born wants to let Jim Woodall in London know the details. Write a short e-mail that includes all the conditions. Use the passive where suitable.

6 *Looking at a balance sheet*

1 Look at the balance sheet below and decide under which headings you would find the following.

a Company premises
b Raw materials
c Computers and furniture
d Delivery trucks
e Goodwill
f Sums owed to suppliers
g Sums owed by customers
h The shareholders' money
i Retained profits
j Borrowing from outside sources

2 Which parts of the balance sheet would you examine and compare to assess the financial standing of Freeman & Sons?

BALANCE SHEET OF FREEMAN & SONS LTD
as of 31 December 2000

	2000 £1000	1999 £1000	1998 £1000
ASSETS:			
FIXED ASSETS			
Tangible assets			
Land and buildings	385	299	291
Vehicles and machinery	664	580	422
Fittings and equipment	68	88	57
Intangible assets	7	–	–
	1124	967	770
CURRENT ASSETS			
Stocks	10	9	9
Trade debtors	124	135	166
Cash at bank and in hand	203	403	574
	337	547	749
EQUITY AND LIABILITIES:			
CREDITORS: AMOUNTS FALLING DUE WITHIN ONE YEAR			
Bank loans and overdrafts	266	139	77
Trade creditors	101	224	25
Tax	36	53	255
Provisions for liabilities and charges	16	19	80
	419	435	437
CREDITORS: AMOUNTS FALLING DUE AFTER ONE YEAR			
Loans	146	232	234
CAPITAL AND RESERVES			
Share Capital	614	637	551
Reserves	282	210	297
	896	847	848

Note that some words would be different on a balance sheet in the USA.

- stocks → inventory
- trade debtors; trade debts → accounts receivable; receivables
- trade creditors → accounts payable; payables
- share capital → capital stock

7 *Securing loans*

Use this information to describe how the bank could use each of the items shown in the photos below as security for a loan.

TYPES OF SECURITY

Land-charges and mortgages:
The borrower may take out a mortgage or the bank can register a land-charge on all types of real estate.

Assignments:
The borrower can assign rights to the bank, eg the rights to an insurance policy. If the security, eg machinery, is needed for the business, the borrower can assign it by bill of sale. The bank becomes the owner, but the borrower may continue to use it.

Pledges or liens:
Goods which can be handed over to secure a loan, eg securities, may be pledged by placing them in the custody of the bank.
Large items can be pledged by handing over the title documents: a warrant is used to pledge goods in a warehouse; goods on board a ship are pledged by handing over the bill of lading.

Guarantees:
The guarantor is liable to repay if the borrower defaults on the loan.

1

2

3

4

5

6

8 *Case studies*

Which type of security would the bank prefer in these cases? Explain why.

1 The English Bookshop has applied for a four-year loan for the purchase of a new delivery van. As security the owner could:
a) assign the vehicle by bill of sale or *b)* assign outstanding trade debts.

2 Claire and Jeremy Bayswater own an art gallery. After a burglary they want to install an alarm system. As security for a two-year loan they could:
a) pledge a valuable painting or *b)* assign a life assurance policy.

3 Country Cottage Antiques has applied for a ten-year loan for the extension of its profitable antiques shop. As security the proprietor could:
a) register a land-charge on the premises or *b)* offer the bank a guarantee given by his father, a retired doctor.

9 Working with words

Find words to match these definitions.

1. This can be registered to secure a loan against buildings or land.
2. If the bank accepts this, another person becomes liable to repay the loan if the borrower defaults.
3. This document is handed over if the bank becomes the owner of a vehicle or piece of machinery, but the borrower can continue using it.
4. This arrangement gives the bank the rights to an insurance policy.
5. This document is used to pledge goods that are on board a ship.
6. This word describes all types of buildings that a company owns or rents.
7. The borrower may take this out to secure a loan against real estate.
8. On a US balance sheet, trade debts are sometimes called this.
9. On a British balance sheet, this word is used for the bank or suppliers to whom a company owes money.
10. Borrowed capital appears on the balance sheet as this.

10 Reporting

Report the main points of this article in your own words.

SMALL BUSINESSES HANG ONTO CREDIT LIFELINE

KIYOSHI IKEDA, the owner of a small light engineering factory in Kamata, a town on the outskirts of Tokyo, has been making parts for many of Japan's manufacturing giants for more than 40 years. He is convinced that the Japanese economy is still in a recession.

"It's the worst I've ever known," says Mr Ikeda. "There's been almost no work for us for the last three months. My revenues are down 50 per cent from last year. I'm in the red every month. By the time I've paid the rent and the utilities charges, there's nothing left."

His words are echoed by small business owners in Kamata, which once was the first port of call for companies like Nissan, Toshiba, Canon, Nikon and Sony looking for delicate tools and machine parts for their products. As these companies have cut back their operations in Japan, factory owners in Kamata are struggling to survive.

Since October many have been faced with extra payments on government-guaranteed loans they took out last year. Then, the government scheme seemed incredibly attractive, but a year after its launch, many small business owners are having difficulty making payments on their loans.

Mr Ikeda is nevertheless one of the lucky ones. Despite using most of the ¥100m ($970,000) loan to pay back other loans, he still manages to make small repayments on the government-guaranteed loan. But he admits it is a struggle. "I have pretty much used up the rest of the loan on day-to-day expenses. If I don't make some repayment, I won't be able to apply for any more money," he says. "And if I don't apply for a new loan, I won't be able to survive much longer."

In fact Japan's goverment loan scheme may mean that small businesses collapse in the end with a larger amount of debt than they would have had without the government's aid. Some have become easy targets for credit companies offering quick, large loans at interest rates of more than 30 per cent.

(*Financial Times*, 15 December 1999, abridged)

11 Weigh up the pros and cons

Should governments help businesses that are in financial difficulties? Working in a small group, list all the pros and cons you can think of. Then discuss the points in class and see what conclusion you reach.

Advanced materials

Venture capital

12 *The first venture capitalists?*

Could King Ferdinand and Queen Isabella of Spain who backed Christopher Columbus in the fifteenth century be described as "the first venture capitalists"? How do you view their investment?

13 *Venture capitalism in Germany*

Use this article from the *Financial Times* to find out why venture capitalism is growing in Germany. List the reasons for its development.

Germany embraces venture capitalism

The industry has mushroomed in the last few years with the help of the government but there are risks, writes Bertrand Benoit.

Once a distinctly Anglo-Saxon pursuit, venture capitalism is growing roots across Europe and few countries are embracing the change with more enthusiasm than Germany.

Long reliant on banks for financing, the country has seen an explosion in the number of funds providing increasingly aggressive entrepreneurs with a pool of capital hard to imagine only five years ago.

According to the Berlin-based German venture capital association, private equity investment has trebled over the last five years to reach DM3.3bn (€1.68bn, $1.69bn) last year, a quarter of it going into early-stage finance.

Compared with neighbouring countries and particularly the UK, Germany remains a lightweight. Total funds available for investment account for a mere 0.07 per cent of its GDP, putting the country neck-and-neck with Portugal. Yet these funds are expected to grow nearly 80 per cent this year.

The key factor behind this increase has been the simultaneous rise in demand for and supply of capital. "Low interest rates, expensive stock markets, and dismal real estate returns mean people are looking for alternative investments," says Falk Strascheg, co-founder of Technologieholding, Germany's largest venture capital fund based in Munich.

"At the same time, there is renewed confidence in entrepreneurs, who are no longer seen as evil blood-suckers but as nice job-creators."

The German government has played a central role in kick-starting the industry. The state-sponsored EXIST programme, launched in 1997, has encouraged university-based networks to come up with high-technology ventures. Once concentrated around Munich – the "laptop and Lederhosen" capital of Germany – high-tech companies are mushrooming all over the country, whether linked to universities, in the case of Freiburg, or on the rubble of older industries in the Ruhr and North-Rhine Westphalia regions.

Meanwhile, the state has also provided venture capitalists with the sort of financial support their British and US counterparts could only dream of. Federal agencies such as KfW, the development bank, and regional ones, such as Bayern Kapital in Bavaria, can provide up to two-thirds of venture capital investments in the form of loans, in addition to various guarantees protecting funds against losses.

"There is a snow-balling effect that increases the capital available to funds while considerably minimising their risks," says Alexander Wessendorff, editor of Deutsche, a private equity newsletter. The most radical transformation, however, has been the emergence of a viable exit route for funds, avoiding the disasters of the 1970s when banks bought into high-tech companies that later proved impossible to sell.

The creation in 1997 of the Neuer Markt, the Frankfurt-based high-growth/high risk market, and its strong performance have allowed funds to realise their investments through IPOs. These constituted 17 per cent of exits for private equity houses last year, against a mere 4 per cent in 1997. Trade sales, once the preferred exit route, now make up less than a third of the total. For venture capital funds, this has translated into handsome returns.

(*Financial Times* January 7, 2000, abridged)

14 *A cartoon*

Describe the cartoon. Say what point you think the artist wants to make.

(*The Financial Times Survey*, December 2, 1999)

15 *Go online*

The Kreditanstalt für Wiederaufbau and the Deutsche Börse AG cooperate in offering Venture-Management-Services, a platform where companies seeking capital and potential investors ("business angels") can meet. Look at www.venture-management-services.de to find out more.

Business angel

UNIT
8 Financing

Lead-in

Why do companies, especially young companies in the New Economy, sometimes need to raise capital? What can be an alternative to borrowing from a bank?

1 *The Infineon story (I)*

Colin Wells and Anna Klaus met on the train on their way to work on Monday, February 21, 2000.

COLIN WELLS Morning, Anna.

ANNA KLAUS Hi, Colin. You're a bit late today, aren't you? Don't you usually take an earlier train than this?

COLIN WELLS Yes, but I had to be at my bank as soon as they opened.

ANNA KLAUS Your bank? That's a funny place to go first thing on a Monday morning. Why the rush?

COLIN WELLS Ah, you see I wanted to be one of the first to get my name down ...

ANNA KLAUS Don't tell me you've subscribed to the new issue of Infineon shares!

COLIN WELLS Hasn't everybody? The bank was packed this morning. I had to queue for ages. They nearly ran out of forms.

ANNA KLAUS Colin, somehow I just can't imagine you as a shareholder. Have you ever bought any shares before?

COLIN WELLS No, I seem to be about the only person on this planet who hasn't, so it looked like a good time to start.

ANNA KLAUS But why Infineon? I've seen the ads for the IPO on ...

COLIN WELLS Er, for the what?

ANNA KLAUS IPO. That stands for "initial public offering". That's when a new company is floated and its shares are launched onto the market.

COLIN WELLS You seem to know more about the whole business than I do.

ANNA KLAUS Yes, I'm beginning to think that too. Do you have any idea what Infineon actually produces?

COLIN WELLS God knows. Something to do with computers ... or software ... or the Internet ... well, you know, that sort of stuff.

ANNA KLAUS As far as I know they used to be a division of Siemens. The new issue is to raise the capital they need to set up and expand as a plc on their own.

COLIN WELLS Er, plc?

ANNA KLAUS Public limited company – one whose shares are listed on the stock exchange. Really, Colin, I rather get the impression you've gone into this with your eyes shut.

COLIN WELLS Well, I must admit, I wasn't quite sure how to spell Infineon, but the bank clerk filled the form in for me!

ANNA KLAUS I don't believe it! Anyway, how much are you going to invest?

COLIN WELLS I've put my name down for 150 shares and ...

ANNA KLAUS What? Have you won the lottery? You and Janet have just bought a new kitchen and Janet told me that it cost you a bomb!

COLIN WELLS Janet has put her name down for 150 shares as well.

ANNA KLAUS I've read that the bookbuilding isn't finished yet, but the shares are probably going to cost 35 euros each. Frankly, I think you've both gone mad. After all, let's say you're allocated some shares – well, somehow you've got to pay for them!

COLIN WELLS Oh, of course we don't have the money but we'll sell them again as soon as they go up and just take the profit. The price is expected to hit 100 euros on the first day of trading.

ANNA KLAUS Colin, don't you think you should leave this sort of game to the professionals? It sounds like a dream but it could turn into a nightmare. These new issues don't always rise, you know, and it's not easy to get out at the right time. Oh, and speaking of getting out at the right time, this is my station coming up now. I'll see you in the office later on.

COLIN WELLS You're not getting off here to go to your bank, are you?

ANNA KLAUS Not likely! I'm going to the travel agency. Stefan and I are booking a trip to the Seychelles. That's the sort of dream I prefer to invest in!

Answer these questions.

1 What have Colin and Janet Wells done?
2 Why have they done this?
3 What does Anna Klaus tell Colin about Infineon?
4 Why does Anna say "you've both gone mad"?
5 What risk does she point out?

2 *Give your opinion*

Look at the cartoon and answer these questions.

1 What does the artist want to express in this cartoon?
2 What is the connection between the cartoon and the dialogue?
3 What advice would you give inexperienced investors who subscribe to new shares?

3 *Prepositions*

Fill in the missing prepositions.

1 Colin and Janet Wells decided to invest ... Infineon shares.
2 They both subscribed ... the new issue.
3 The clerk helped Colin fill ... the form.
4 The new shares were launched ... the market ... 13 March 2000.
5 After the IPO the shares were listed ... the stock exchange.
6 Colin and Janet expected the price to rise ... the first day of trading.
7 They were not worried about paying ... the shares they ordered.
8 The new issue was advertised ... TV and ... the press.

4 *The Infineon story (II)*

One day after her conversation with Colin Wells, Anna Klaus read this article in the *Financial Times* and decided to subscribe to Infineon shares after all. Which points in the article made Anna change her mind?

Offering could value Infineon at €20bn-plus

By Tony Barber in Frankfurt

Infineon, the semiconductor division of the German electronics and engineering group Siemens, could be valued at more than €20bn ($19.7bn) when it lists on the Frankfurt and New York stock exchanges next month in one of the largest initial public offerings of a European high-tech company.

Siemens is selling up to 29 per cent of Infineon. Based on the indicative price range of €29 to €35 a share disclosed yesterday, that values the stake at between €5bn and €6bn. The stock will begin trading on March 13.

The Infineon IPO, lead managed by Deutsche Bank and Goldman Sachs, is expected to be the largest in Germany since 1996, when Deutsche Telekom's first market issue was valued at about €10bn. It vies with Deutsche Post to be the biggest German IPO of the year.

Technology analysts expect heavy demand for Infineon shares, partly because it is enjoying strong sales growth and has returned to profit after a difficult three years in the late 1990s when semiconductor prices collapsed.

Ulrich Schumacher, Infineon chief executive, said the group would use the proceeds from its IPO to finance domestic and international acquisitions but he declined to name specific targets, saying only that Infineon was interested in "small firms with know-how".

Infineon also announced that the US computer maker Intel had agreed to invest $250m in the German company by means of a private placement. Intel and Infineon plan to co-operate on making dynamic rapid access memory (D-Ram) chip products.

The subscription period is due to last until March 10, and private investors who take up the offer by March 1 will receive €1 discount.

(*Financial Times*, February 22, 2000, abridged)

5 *Working with words I*

Replace the words in italics in these sentences with an expression from the box that has the same meaning. Use each expression once.

allocated ◆ *floated* ◆ *issued* ◆ *launched* ◆ *listed* ◆ *set up*
subscribed to ◆ *valued at*

1 A plc is a company whose shares are *registered* on the stock exchange.
2 An IPO is when the shares of a new company are *sold for the first time* on the market.
3 Infineon was a division of Siemens before it was *made into a separate company*.
4 Many investors *put their name down for* Infineon shares.
5 The shares were *given out by the company* at 35 euros each.
6 Most people were not *given* the full number of shares that they applied for.
7 The issue was estimated to be *worth* over €20bn.
8 Infineon was *established* as a public limited company in 2000.

6 *Going public*

Read the text and then explain these terms. Say why each is important.

1 an equity story (line 9)
2 a beauty contest (line 14)
3 a lead manager (line 16)
4 a syndicate (line 19)
5 a bookbuilding spread (line 20)
6 an online issuing house (line 34)

A company that goes public issues its shares on the stock market for the first time. Since the turn of the millennium, going public has become common in Germany: more and more young companies issue shares to raise capital for their development instead of borrowing from a bank. The number of IPOs – especially on the Neuer Markt – has boomed.

Companies wanting to go public do not have to approach a bank themselves. Instead, banks comb through the German "Mittelstand", especially in the high-tech sector, in search of promising candidates for an IPO. They are looking for a company with a good equity story – a past history and development that will attract investors. The company's business plan describing its strategy with a market survey and its financial plans for the coming years must also be convincing.

On the other hand, the company will take a good look at the bank: generally six banks are invited to a beauty contest in which they must each put forward their plans for the IPO. The company management decides on a lead manager, the bank under whose leadership the shares will be placed. The good name of the lead manager should give investors confidence in the issue. The lead manager will ask other banks to join a syndicate. As well as publicizing the new issue and placing the shares on the markets, the banks fix the bookbuilding spread, the price range within which investors may subscribe to the issue. Infineon, for example, had Deutsche Bank and Goldman Sachs as lead managers and seven other banks in its syndicate.

The Internet is another means of bringing issuing companies and investors together. Private investors can receive all the publicity by a mouse-click and subscribe to a new issue without going to a bank. After registering online and paying by direct debit, they can have new shares placed in their existing portfolio at their bank. Companies profit too: by going public online with the help of an online issuing house like Virtuelles Emissionshaus AG, they can reach a huge number of young, affluent investors without involving a bank at all.

(for more information go to: www.going-public.de)

A beauty contest

7 *Issuing bonds and shares*

Use this information to fill in the chart below and compare the three methods of financing to see where their advantages and disadvantages lie.

Issuing bonds

Instead of borrowing from a bank, a company can raise capital by issuing bonds. A bank acting as lead manager will assemble a syndicate of other banks to launch the new issue onto the market, where the bonds can be bought by anyone who is interested in investing in the business. Buyers of bonds grant a sort of loan to the issuing company, which, in return, gives them certain rights:

- Bond holders can rely on receiving interest, called the "coupon", paid regularly at a fixed rate.
- As nearly all bonds mature after a set term, holders can be sure of recovering the full nominal value of bonds on their redemption date.

'My name is Bond … Junk Bond.'

Long-term bonds issued by companies are also called "debentures". Debentures may not be as safe as government bonds, which are backed by the tax-revenue of the issuing country. Junk bonds are high-risk bonds: they promise excellent returns but the risk of default is greater.

Yields of debentures are often compared with yields of government bonds with the same term. The difference is called the "spread".

Issuing shares

A share issue enables a company to raise capital without borrowing at all. Shareholders are part-owners, not creditors, and as their capital is part of the company's equity, it does not have to be paid back. No interest is payable on the capital and, in times of poor business, the company avoids having to pay dividends because if profits have not been large enough, shareholders receive nothing at all.

A new issue of shares in an existing company is called a "rights issue" because shareholders have the right to buy new shares in proportion to their original holdings. Companies can issue ordinary shares (also called "equities"; US: "common stock") or preference shares (US: "preferred stock"). Ordinary shareholders are entitled to vote at the annual general meeting and so have the opportunity of influencing company policy.

Raising capital by a rights issue is complicated and expensive. To plan, publicize and place the issue successfully, companies use the services of an investment bank or issuing house.

A Bank Loan	A Rights Issue of Shares	A Bond Issue
The loan has to be repaid.	The capital …	

8 *Case study I*

Read this article from *The Times* and decide which of the following statements are correct.

Capital & Counties makes £182 million rights issue

By Cliff Feltham

Capital & Counties, the property group, is raising £182 million from shareholders to help pay for the development of three large shopping centres around London.

Capital & Counties is preparing to start work on three massive shopping centre schemes fringing the M25 – 700,000 sq ft at Watford, Hertfordshire; 400,000 sq ft at Bromley, Kent; and 1,500,000 sq ft at Thurrock, Essex, for which it is awaiting planning approval.

The project will cost more than £300 million over the next three to four years. Other developments in hand or in prospect will need a further £75 million.

Capital & Counties is sweetening the cash call with a forecast that profits for the current year will be not less than £14 million, an increase of 16 per cent. Total dividends for the full year are forecast at 8p a share, up 14.3 per cent.

Helped by a rising property market, the company now estimates net assets of 358p a share, up from 322p last December. In the stock market the shares were 5p lower at 415p.

The rights issue will raise £182 million by offering a mixture of ordinary and preference shares.

The terms are a unit of one new ordinary share and four preference shares valued at £8.10 for holders of four existing ordinary shares.

1 ***a*** Capital & Counties wants to build three shopping centres.
b Capital & Counties wants to buy three shopping centres.
c Capital & Counties owns three shopping centres.

2 ***a*** The project will cost a total of 182 million pounds.
b The project will cost a total of 300 million pounds.
c The project will cost over 375 million pounds.

3 ***a*** They hope to raise 182 million pounds by a new issue of shares.
b They hope to get a loan of 182 million pounds from their bank.
c They will have to sell land to raise the capital.

4 ***a*** The company expects good profits for the current year.
b The company is in financial difficulties at the moment.
c The company is in trouble as property prices are rising.

5 ***a*** The company will pay higher dividends than last year.
b The company cannot afford to pay out any dividends this year.
c The company will pay dividends, but lower than last year.

6 ***a*** The company's shares have risen on the stock market recently.
b The company's shares have fallen on the stock market recently.
c The price for the company's shares has not changed.

7 It is a rights issue. This means that
   a everyone has the same right to buy these shares.
   b existing shareholders have the right to increase their holdings.
   c only the directors have the right to buy the new shares.

8 *a* The company plans to issue only ordinary shares.
   b The company plans to issue preference shares and units.
   c The company plans to issue ordinary and preference shares.

9 A shareholder has a right to buy the new issue
   a if he or she pays £8.10 to the company.
   b if he or she has four existing ordinary shares.
   c if he or she has one ordinary share and four preference shares.

10 Each investor will receive
   a units based on the company's shares.
   b cheaper goods in the shopping centres.
   c one ordinary share and four preference shares.

9 *Case study II*

Look at this list of bonds and answer these questions.

1 What is the issuer of each bond obliged to pay to the holder?
2 Which bond has
   a the latest redemption date?
   b the highest interest rate?
   c the worst rating?
   d the lowest bid price?
   e the highest yield?
   f the widest spread?
3 Why is the yield on the Unilever bond lower than its coupon?
4 Why is the yield on the TEPCO bond higher than its coupon?
5 Which investors might be interested in low-coupon bonds? Why?

EURO-ZONE BONDS

MAR 29	Red date	Coupon	S&P Rating	Moody's Rating	Bid price	Bid yield	Day's chge yield	Mth's chge yield	Spread vs Govts
■ **SUPRANATIONALS**									
ADB	10/07	5.500	AAA	Aaa	99.009	5.66	+0.02	-0.11	+0.55
EIB	04/09	4.000	AAA	Aaa	88.665	5.64	+0.05	-0.14	+0.37
Eurofima	12/09	5.625	AAA	Aaa	98.111	5.88	+0.04	-0.08	+0.61
World Bank	04/05	7.125	AAA	Aaa	107.844	5.30	+0.03	-0.10	+0.36
■ **UTILITIES**									
EDF	01/09	5.000	AA+	Aaa	95.264	5.69	+0.03	-0.20	+0.42
TEPCO	05/09	4.375	AA	Aa2	89.894	5.87	+0.05	-0.18	+0.60
Hydro-Quebec	03/08	5.375	A+	A2	96.532	5.93	+0.02	-0.15	+0.74
Powergen (UK)	07/09	5.000	A	A2	90.460	6.39	+0.09	+0.04	+1.12
■ **FINANCIALS**									
Bad Wurt	02/10	5.375	AAA	Aaa	95.997	5.92	+0.05	-0.15	+0.59
OKB	04/08	5.250	AAA	Aaa	97.908	5.58	+0.04	-0.17	+0.39
Credit Local	04/09	4.750	n/a	Aa1	92.484	5.84	+0.04	-0.15	+0.57
Abbey Natl	01/09	5.000	AA-	Aa3	92.058	6.20	+0.04	-0.10	+0.93
■ **INDUSTRIALS**									
Unilever	05/04	6.500	AAA	Aaa	103.837	5.42	+0.08	-0.08	+0.55
McDonald's	03/08	5.125	AA	Aa2	96.113	5.75	+0.02	-0.13	+0.56
Philip Morris	06/08	5.625	A	A2	88.537	7.54	+0.02	+1.03	+2.35
BAT Int Fin	07/06	5.375	A	A2	91.051	7.18	+0.05	+0.89	+2.16
■ **PFANDBRIEFE**									
Rhein Hypo	12/01	5.500	AAA	Aaa	101.322	4.64	-0.01	+0.08	+0.47
Euro Hypo	01/04	5.000	AAA	Aaa	99.594	5.11	-0.02	-0.12	+0.24
Bayer Hypo	01/06	6.000	AAA	Aaa	102.886	5.40	+0.00	-0.09	+0.38
Depfa	01/10	5.500	AAA	Aaa	98.046	5.76	+0.00	-0.15	+0.43
■ **HIGH YIELD**									
Jazztel	12/09	13.250	CCC+	Caa1	103.987	12.52	-0.08	-0.35	+7.25
Konqwest	06/09	7.125	BB	Ba1	99.358	7.22	+0.10	-0.81	+1.95

Financial Times, 2000

LOOKING AT LANGUAGE

GERUNDS

1 **Going** public has become more and more common.
2 **Raising** capital by a rights issue is complicated.
3 Companies avoid **having** to pay dividends in times of poor business.
4 One of their tasks involves **fixing** the bookbuilding spread.
5 The holder can be sure of **recovering** the full nominal value of bonds.
6 The holder can rely on **receiving** interest on debentures.
7 Shareholders have the opportunity of **influencing** company policy.
8 The Internet is a means of **bringing** companies and investors together.

- The gerund is formed by using the *-ing* form of the verb. *(1–8)*
- Gerunds can be used as the subject of a sentence *(1, 2)* or as the object of a sentence after certain verbs:
  admit ◆ *advise* ◆ *avoid (3)* ◆ *consider* ◆ *deny* ◆ *dislike* ◆ *enjoy* ◆ *finish* ◆ *hate* ◆ *imagine* ◆ *involve (4)* ◆ *like* ◆ *love* ◆ *mind* ◆ *practise* ◆ *recommend* ◆ *risk* ◆ *suggest*, etc.
- Verbs used after prepositions must be in the form of the gerund. Various combinations are possible:
  - adjective + preposition + gerund *(5)*
  - verb + preposition + gerund *(6)*
  - noun + preposition + gerund *(7, 8)*
- Common expressions followed by a gerund are:
  the advantage of ◆ *advice on* ◆ *an alternative to* ◆ *the disadvantage of* ◆ *a means of* ◆ *a method of* ◆ *the possibility of* ◆ *the reason for* ◆ *the risk of* ◆ *the service of* ◆ *a way of.*

10 *Practice 1*

Replace the words in *italics* with a noun + preposition + gerund.

EXAMPLE: Capital & Counties see the advantage *the firm will have if it issues new shares.*
Capital & Counties see the advantage of issuing shares.

1 The directors ask the bank for advice on *how to arrange the issue.*
2 They need information on *how to fix the number of new shares.*
3 They want to avoid the risk *that they will lose money.*
4 They ask about the cost *they will have if they issue shares.*
5 At the annual general meeting they explain the reason *why they want to make a rights issue.*
6 The shareholders see the opportunity *they will have to increase their holdings.*
7 The new issue offers the company a way *to raise capital* without the disadvantages *they would have if they borrowed from a bank.*
8 Banks charge fees for the service *when they place a new issue.*

11 *Practice II*

Rewrite these sentences using a gerund as the subject.

EXAMPLE: It is expensive to issue new shares.
Issuing new shares is expensive.

1 One way of raising capital is to apply for a bank loan.
2 An alternative to a bank loan is to issue corporate bonds.
3 It requires experience to prepare a rights issue.
4 It is not easy to fix the share price of a new issue.
5 It is very important to have a lead manager with a good name.
6 It takes time to place a new issue of bonds.
7 It can be difficult to know when to use gerunds!

12 *Practice III*

Complete these sentences using gerunds.

1 My bank specializes in ...
2 My daily work consists mainly of ...
3 Working in a bank I particularly like ...
4 At the weekend I enjoy ...
5 During my next holidays I am looking forward to ...
6 I think a successful career in banking depends on ...
7 After my examinations I would consider ...

13 *Working with words II*

Use words from this unit to complete these sentences.

1 All types of bonds and shares are called s... .
2 Bonds issued by companies can be called d... .
3 Bonds run for a fixed term until they m... .
4 The date at the end of the term may be called the r... date.
5 "Equities" is another name for o... shares.
6 The other type of shares are called p... shares.
7 People who own shares are known as s... .
8 At the annual general meeting people are allowed to v... on matters of company policy.
9 Earnings from shares are paid out by the company in the form of d... .
10 An investor is a person who makes an i... .
11 Companies issue bonds or shares to r... capital.
12 The process of issuing shares on the stock market for the first time is known as g... p... .
13 The main bank in a syndicate is the l... ... .
14 IPO stands for ... ...
15 PLC stands for ... ...

Advanced materials

The Neuer Markt

14 ***Charts and statistics***

Look at the charts 1–4 and express the main points shown in each one in words. Go online on www.neuermarkt.com and update the information.

1

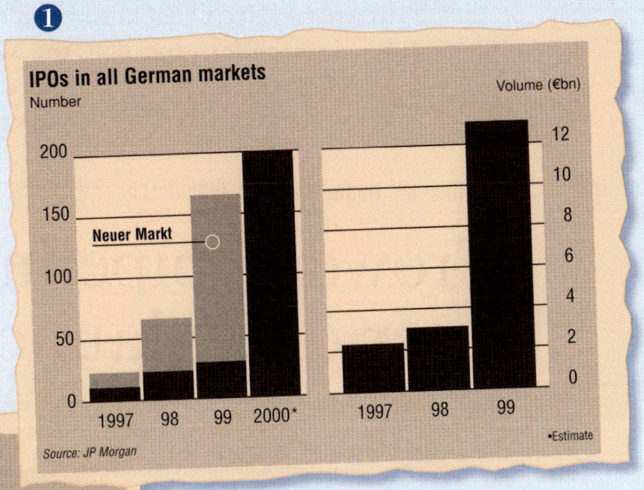

2

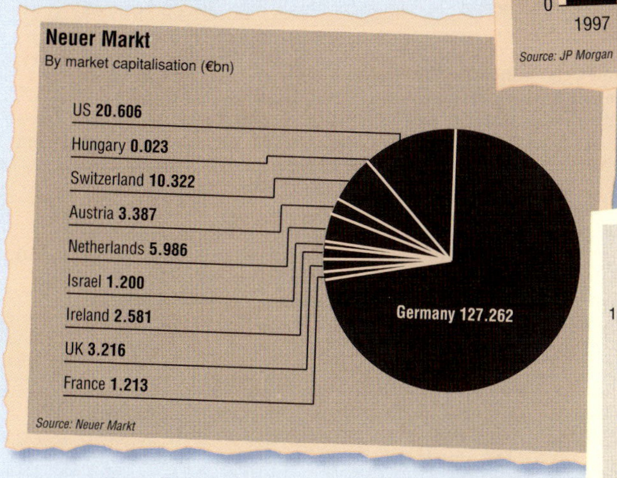

3

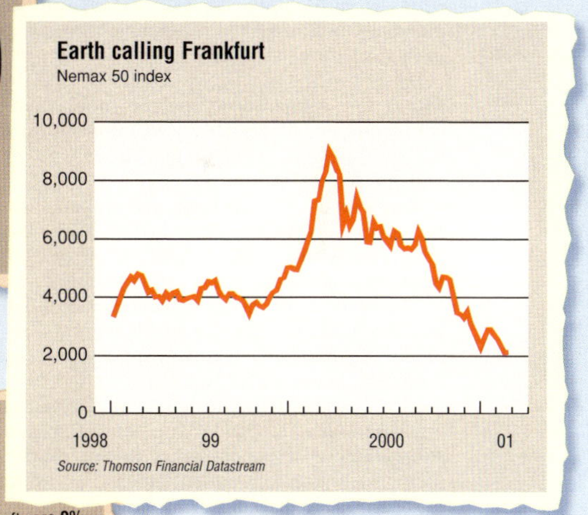

4

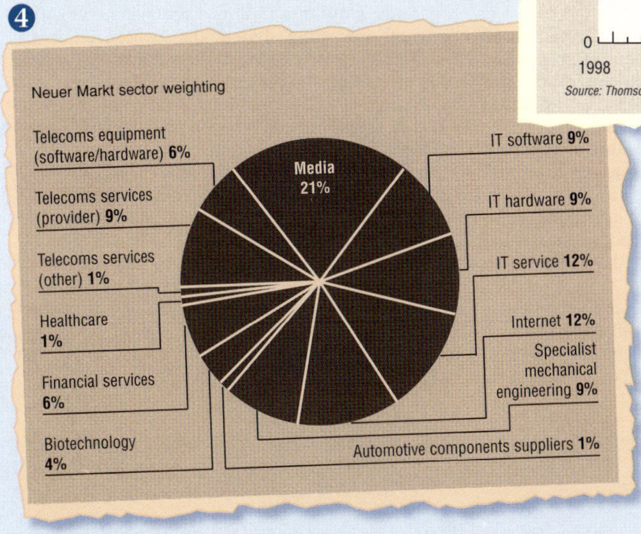

15 *New issues on the Neuer Markt*

Use information from the article below to answer these questions.

1 How has the Neuer Markt developed since its launch in 1997?
2 In what way has Edel Music profited from the Neuer Markt?
3 What sort of investors does the Neuer Markt attract?
4 How has regulation on the Neuer Markt been improved?
5 What does the writer see as the main achievement of the Neuer Markt?

Equities: the Neuer Markt by Tony Barber

Crowded pipeline after dizzy launch

The main achievement may be that it has provided access to capital for small, high-risk companies

The Neuer Markt, Germany's stock market segment for young, fast-growing companies, is entering a phase of consolidation after a dizzy launch in 1997 that saw it outperform all other markets in the world.

"The Neuer Markt will do very well in the future," says Jochen Grossmann, director of global equities and equity capital markets at Commerzbank in Frankfurt. "Companies that are good in their sector can still be placed."

Since starting up in March 1997, the Neuer Markt has expanded to include more than 160 companies, most specialising in information technology, software, telecommunications, and media and entertainment.

The Neuer Markt took an important step forward in July with the introduction of the Nemax 50, an index that reflects about 80 per cent of the market's capitalisation and trading volumes.

The Nemax 50 includes the biggest and most liquid companies in the Neuer Markt and does not contain shares from a relatively small sector such as automobile component suppliers.

Mr Grossmann says the launch of the Nemax 50 could soon lead to the development of specialised sub-indices, enabling investors to put funds in a sector such as entertainment stocks if it appeared more attractive than, for example, software.

The Neuer Markt may also see more listings next year from companies in the biotechnology and medical technology sectors, which are particularly strong in Germany. "The best performing companies are those with a growth strategy, those that invest effectively the money they get from investors," Mr Grossmann says.

One successful Neuer Markt company that is fairly typical of its sector is Edel Music, which started life in 1986 as a mail order business for film music and has grown into Europe's largest integrated music company.

Its flotation last year, followed by a capital increase this year, has enabled it to generate funds for expansion not only through internal growth but through acquisitions and partnership projects. Most notably, it has secured the licensing and marketing rights in Europe for Walt Disney film soundtracks such as *Snow White and the Seven Dwarfs* and *The Lion King*.

Although some investors complain that the large number of potential new issues results in a glut of information, making it hard to sift the wheat from the chaff, there is still strong interest in the Neuer Markt from abroad. US and UK institutional fund managers see the market as highly promising despite this year's weaker prices.

Overall, experts say institutional demand accounts for about 55 to 70 per cent of investment, with retail investors comprising 30 to 45 per cent. This stands in contrast to the Neuer Markt's early days, when investment was predominantly retail-driven.

Regulation is, however, an increasingly important issue. Until this autumn, there was no effective way of preventing shareholders whose company went public from cashing in their stocks on the first day of trading and making an instant profit.

"It was just like gambling. That's not the right way of teaching people how to be a shareholder," says Mr Grossmann.

Now, people who hold shares before their company's IPO must carry a special stock identity number, meaning that they can be traced if they try to cash in within six months of the issue's launch.

While the Neuer Markt has undoubtedly done much to stimulate popular equity culture in Germany, its main achievement may lie in the fact that it has provided access to capital for small, high-risk companies that found it hard in the old days to interest banks in their activities.

(*Financial Times* 25 October 1999, abridged)

UNIT

9 *Investment*

Lead-in

In what sense is the stock exchange a "swimming pool"? Are the opening hours shown the same as in Germany? Who are the sharks?

1 *The man from down under*

Tom Nainby, a New Zealander working in Germany, approaches Karin Schulz, an investment consultant in the securities department of his bank. Their conversation took place on January 3, 2000.

TOM NAINBY Hi. Your colleague over there told me you could help me.

KARIN SCHULZ Certainly. What can I do for you?

TOM NAINBY I'd like your advice on investing some money. I bought some bonds here about five years ago and now they have been paid out. If I don't invest the money again pretty soon, I'll probably spend it all.

KARIN SCHULZ Well, I'm sure we can find something suitable, Mr ... ?

TOM NAINBY Nainby, Tom Nainby.

KARIN SCHULZ Let's go over to my desk. ... Take a seat, please. Are you from Australia, Mr Nainby?

TOM NAINBY No, New Zealand, but most people hear my accent and think I'm Australian.

KARIN SCHULZ We don't have many people from New Zealand wanting to live in our country. It's usually the other way around. ... Now how much are you thinking of investing?

TOM NAINBY About 8,000 euros.

KARIN SCHULZ And what term do you have in mind?

TOM NAINBY Three years, till my contract runs out. Then I'll be heading back down under. This place is great, but the weather! I don't know how you folks stand it all the time!

KARIN SCHULZ I suppose we're just used to it. ... Now there are various ways in which you could save the sum – our savings accounts, for example ...

TOM NAINBY I don't know about that. Savings accounts pay a very low interest rate at the moment, don't they?

KARIN SCHULZ I'm afraid so, though you'll receive 2% or 2.5% if you save the money for a longer period in a term deposit account. We also offer certificates of deposit that pay 4% and there's a range of bonds that you could invest in as well.

TOM NAINBY Look, I've been thinking about this. All my friends at work seem to be making loads of money with shares. While I was getting 5% on those bonds, they were all doubling their money. I think it's time I bought some shares, too.

KARIN SCHULZ Of course you can buy shares if you wish, as long as you're aware of the risks involved.

TOM NAINBY Risks? Oh I would only invest in the best companies.

KARIN SCHULZ Even then there are certain things you should bear in mind. Your bonds had a fixed rate of interest that was paid to you every year. Now if you bought shares, you wouldn't have a guaranteed income. Your dividends would depend on the profits the company made.

TOM NAINBY But it's not the dividend I'm interested in. I'd sell them again when the share price rises and make a profit that way.

KARIN SCHULZ Yes, but share prices fluctuate easily and you'd make a loss if you needed the money and had to sell them for less than you paid for them. Bonds have a fixed redemption date but capital gains on shares aren't guaranteed. The markets are so volatile at the moment. You can't be sure how much you're going to get for your shares at any particular time in the future. Some of your friends may have made losses they don't talk about!

TOM NAINBY You're probably right. So what would you suggest then?

KARIN SCHULZ I'd recommend putting the money into a unit trust.

TOM NAINBY Hmm, I'm not sure.

KARIN SCHULZ This brochure tells you about several unit trusts offered by our bank. This one might be just what you're looking for ...

Answer these questions.

1. Why is Mr Nainby interested in buying securities?
2. What information does the investment consultant ask for before she can advise the customer?
3. Why is Mr Nainby not interested in saving the money?
4. The investment consultant points out two risks in buying shares. What are they?
5. Why are bonds a safer investment than shares? Give two reasons.
6. What does Frau Schulz advise Mr Nainby to do in the end?

2 *Buying shares*

Tom Nainby does not take Karin Schulz's advice. Look at this confirmation he received from his bank and answer the following questions.

1. What has he bought?
2. How much does he have to pay for the shares?
3. What other costs are there?
4. How does he pay?
5. What is the difference between accounts 4124451 and 577889?

Ihr Partner für Geldgeschäfte

K A U F

Geschäfts-Nr. **188034**
Bei Rückfragen bitte angeben

5400.0.01123

Nennwert	Wertpapierbezeichnung	Kenn-Nr.
ST 150	**VOLKSWAGEN AG ST O.N.**	**766400**

Zinstermin	Zinslauf ab	Ende der Laufzeit	nächstf. Zinsschein	Zinsvaluta	Tage	Zinssatz	
							71926

Depotkonto Nr.	DA	VA	StA	So	Lagerstalle	Zusatzdatum StA	Zusatzdatum So	VZ-Datum	Sperre EA	Besonderheit Handel
577889	**0**	**02**	**00**	**00**	**0000**					**variabler Hdl.**

Börse	Schlußtag	Wertpapierkurs	Kurswert	
FRANKFURT	**7.01.00**	**56,00**	**EUR**	**8.400,00**

Devisenkurs

Konversionskurs		**Maklergebühr**	**0,40**	**0/00**	**3,36**
DEM	**1,955830**	**Provision**	**1,00**	**0/0**	**84,25**
		Auslagen			**3,07**

Betriebsstelle	Bankleitzahl	Konto-Nr.	Wert	Endbetrag Wertpapierabrechnung		
041	**22151410**	**4124451**	**10.01.00**	**Lastschrift**	**EUR**	**8.490,68**

Kontoinhaber: Thomas Nainby

Den Gegenwert belasten wir dem o.g. Konto und erkennen das Depotkonto mit den aufgeführten Wertpapieren.

3 *A nasty shock*

Some weeks later Mr Nainby sees this information on the Internet. Describe what has happened.

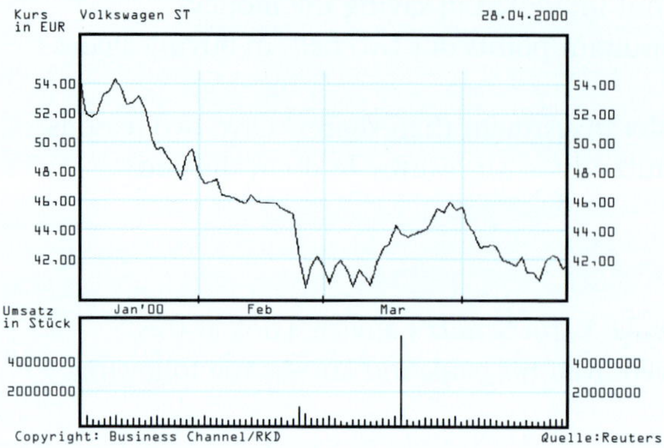

Wertpapierart	deutsche Aktie
Wertpapiername	Volkswagen ST
Wertpapierkenn-Nr.	766400
Land	Deutschland
Währung	EUR
Börsenplatz	Frankfurt
Branche	Automobil
Datum, Uhrzeit	28.4.2000, 12:29
Vortageskurs	41.50
aktueller Kurs	41.90
Tageseröffnung	42.00
Tageshoch	42.00
Tagestief	41.60
Umsatz	28813
52-Wochen-Hoch	71.60
52-Wochen-Tief	40.15

zurück zum Depot | Detailangaben

4 *If I'd known ...*

Tom Nainby visits Karin Schulz in the securities department again.

KARIN SCHULZ Hello, Mr Nainby. Nice to see you again.

TOM NAINBY Hi. You know I really should have listened to you folks.

KARIN SCHULZ I beg your pardon?

TOM NAINBY About those Volkswagen shares I bought. Have you seen what's happened to them? I can't believe it. They're supposed to be blue chips! They're in the DAX! I thought they'd be as safe as houses. If I'd known they were going to fall like that, I'd never have touched them!

KARIN SCHULZ Yes, they've fallen quite drastically, haven't they?

TOM NAINBY You can say that again. It makes me mad to think that if I'd followed your advice, I wouldn't have got into this mess.

KARIN SCHULZ Mess? You haven't got to sell them, have you? I'd suggest holding on to them. They're bound to recover sooner or later.

TOM NAINBY Fortunately I don't need to sell them right now. In fact, I wanted to ask you about those unit trusts you mentioned last time. I'm looking for a way of investing 200 euros a month.

KARIN SCHULZ Are you still intending to leave Germany in a few years' time?

TOM NAINBY No ... I might even be staying here permanently.

KARIN SCHULZ Changed your mind about the weather?

TOM NAINBY A better reason than that. I'm getting married soon.

KARIN SCHULZ Oh, congratulations!

TOM NAINBY Thanks. It seems a bit early to me to start saving for my retirement but at work they've advised me to invest part of my salary to supplement my pension.

KARIN SCHULZ We recommend all our younger customers make provision for when they retire. Unit trusts are a way of investing regularly to obtain a good yield but spread the risk at the same time.

TOM NAINBY How's that?

KARIN SCHULZ In a trust or fund many investors pool their capital which is invested on their behalf in different kinds of bonds or shares ...

TOM NAINBY No thanks! Not shares! I've lost enough money already!

KARIN SCHULZ Unit trusts are managed by experts who select securities that they expect to grow and yield profits.

TOM NAINBY You mean they might be a lot better at it than I was.

KARIN SCHULZ You could put it like that. After all, they have experience and resources that you don't have.

TOM NAINBY And what do they invest in?

KARIN SCHULZ Shares, bonds or a mixture of the two, or real estate. There are also trusts that invest in one particular sector like information technology stocks or in one particular region like the USA, for example. We've got a selection of trusts on offer, but they all have the same aim: diversifying the portfolio of investments in the trust to spread the risk but ensure a good yield.

TOM NAINBY Does that mean I'll get an income from them every year?

KARIN SCHULZ Yes, though I'd recommend reinvesting it in new units unless you need the sum. With lots of trusts this is done automatically.

TOM NAINBY But what if I need all or just part of the money?

KARIN SCHULZ You can return your units to the trust whenever you want.

TOM NAINBY Isn't all this very expensive? What about the costs?

KARIN SCHULZ Most of them have an initial charge that you pay when you buy the units. The money covers the costs of managing the trust.

TOM NAINBY Just a minute. What about tax?

KARIN SCHULZ The law requires you to declare all your earnings from securities, but they will not be subject to capital gains tax if you hold the securities for longer than one year.

TOM NAINBY It all sounds far less risky than my little flirtation with the stock market. I'd never have bothered with those shares if I'd known they would fall like that.

KARIN SCHULZ Oh, they'll recover one day, that's for sure.

TOM NAINBY Well, let's hope I don't have to wait till I retire to see it happen!

Answer these questions.

1 Why does Mr Nainby say that he should have listened to Frau Schulz's advice?

2 What advice does Frau Schulz give him about his investment in Volkswagen shares?

3 What are the customer's investment plans this time?

4 How does a unit trust work?

5 What advantages does a unit trust offer a small investor like Mr Nainby?

DekaZins-international

Profitieren Sie mit internationalen Rentenwerten von einer auf Kursstabilität ausgerichteten Anlagepolitik

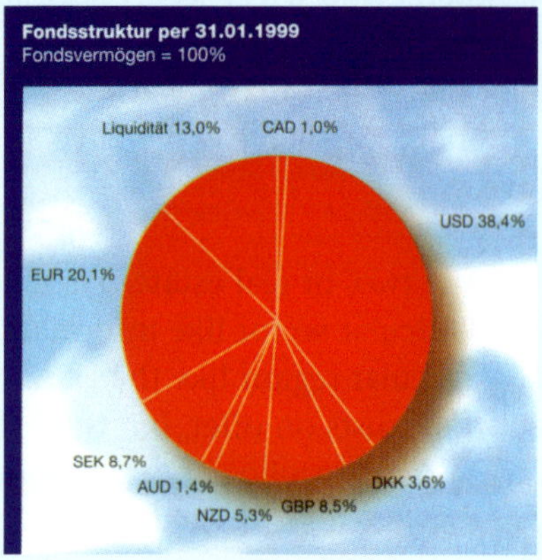

Kurzporträt:

Wertpapier-Kenn-Nummer:
848 075

Anlagegrundsätze:
DekaZins-international ist ein internationaler Rentenfonds, der überwiegend in Papiere ausländischer Aussteller mit Laufzeiten von maximal vier Jahren anlegt. In verzinslichen Wertpapieren mit längeren Laufzeiten und Aktien sowie Wandel- und Optionsanleihen dürfen insgesamt max. 20% des Fondsvermögens angelegt werden.

Ausgabeaufschlag:
2,5% vom Anteilwert = 2,44% vom Ausgabepreis

Fondswährung:
EUR

Geschäftsjahr:
1. Januar bis 31. Dezember

Ertragsthesaurierung:
keine Ausschüttung, Thesaurierung zum Geschäftsjahresende

Stückelung:
1, 10, 100, 1.000 Anteile

nordasia.com

WKN 979 217

NORDINVEST
Eine Tochtergesellschaft der Vereins-und Westbank

Internationaler Aktienfonds der NORDINVEST.
Anlageziel: Vermögensaufbau durch Wertzuwachs der in diesem Fonds enthaltenen **Internet-Aktien.**

Anlagepolitik

Der Fonds erwirbt Wertpapiere von Ausstellern, deren Firmensitz sich im asiatischen Raum befindet, und die zumindest einen Teil ihrer Umsatzerlöse und/oder Gewinne über die Schaffung von Internet-Infrastruktur oder dessen Nutzung erwirtschaften.

Der Internet-Rückstand in Asien ...

In Asien herrscht Goldgräberstimmung. So hinkt die Entwicklung des Internet in dieser Region der Welt den USA etwa fünf Jahre hinterher. Doch dieser Rückstand dürfte sehr schnell aufgeholt werden. Asiatische Aktiengesellschaften, die Internet-Infrastruktur herstellen oder die das Internet als Vertriebsweg nutzen, besitzen daher überdurchschnittliches Kurspotential.

Asiatische Internet-Aktien weisen extreme Schwankungen auf.

Asien: Erwartetes Internet-Wachstum pro Jahr *

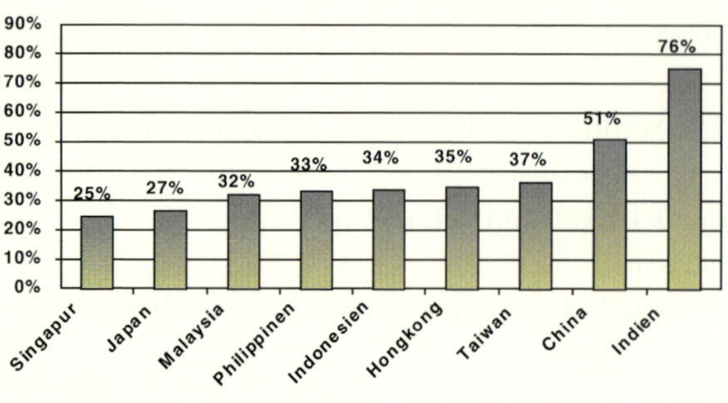

Auf einem Blick

WKN:
979 217

Fondswährung:
Euro

Ausgabeaufschlag:
5%

Ertragsverwendung:
Thesaurierung

Verwaltungsvergütung:
bis zu 1,2% p.a.

Depotbankvergütung:
bis zu 0,1% p.a.

Erstausgabepreis:
105 Euro

Auflage:
3. Januar 2000

Anlageformen:
- NORDINVEST-Anlagekonto: Einmalanlagen und Sparplan ab DM 100 monatlich
- Wertpapierdepot

Depotbank:
Vereins- und Westbank AG

Stücke:
keine effektiven Stücke

5 *Two investment trusts*

Use this chart to compare the unit trusts in the brochures opposite. Which trust would you recommend Mr Nainby to invest in?

	DekaZins-international	Nordasia.com
The type of securities included		
The region invested in		
The aim		
The risk involved		
The costs		

LOOKING AT LANGUAGE

IF-CLAUSES

1 **If** I **don't invest** the money again soon, I**'ll** probably **spend** it.
2 You**'ll receive** 2% **if** you **save** the money in a term deposit account.
3 **If** you **bought** shares, you **wouldn't have** a guaranteed income.
4 You**'d make** a loss **if** you **were forced** to sell them.
5 **If** I**'d followed** your advice, I **wouldn't have got** into this mess.
6 I**'d** never **have bothered** with those shares **if** I**'d known** they would fall like that.

- There are three types of if-clauses shown in the dialogue. If-clauses can express what is probable *(1, 2)*, what is possible *(3, 4)* and what is impossible *(5, 6)*.
- Note which tenses are used in the if-clause and in the main clause.

	if-clause	**main clause**
(1, 2)	present	future
(3, 4)	simple past	conditional
(5, 6)	past perfect	conditional perfect

Common exceptions:

7 **If** interest rates **rise**, borrowing **becomes** more expensive.
8 **If** you **could help** me, I **would be** most grateful.

- In the case of basic truths which never change, both clauses are in the present tense *(7)*. With polite requests, the conditional may be used in both clauses *(8)*.

6 *Practice I*

Make meaningful sentences from the table to give a customer advice.

If you	buy invest in bought invested in	bonds shares units	you'll you'd	receive a fixed rate of interest. know your yield in advance. let experts select the shares. run the risk of making losses. probably earn dividends. always be able to return them to the trust. have a diversified portfolio. have a safe investment.

7 *Practice II*

Put the verbs in brackets into the correct tenses.

1 If I planned to buy shares, I ... (*approach*) my bank first.
2 If you had bought bonds, you ... (*take*) less risk.
3 I would have invested in blue chips if I ... (*have*) any money.
4 Investors would do better if they ... (*take*) professional advice.
5 If you ... (*look*) on the Internet, you will get real-time prices.
6 Generally speaking, bond prices ... (*rise*) if interest rates fall.

8 *Practice III*

Make sentences with "if" to point out what mistakes these customers made.

EXAMPLE: Mrs A did not arrange a direct debit for her bills before going on a long trip, and she received a lot of reminders.
If she had arranged a direct debit for her bills, she would not have received a lot of reminders.

1 Mr B did not keep his securities for more than one year. He lost half of his capital gains in tax.
2 Mr C forgot to give his wife power of attorney. When he had to go into hospital, she was unable to make any withdrawals.
3 Mrs D countersigned her traveller's cheques before using them. When they were stolen, the bank did not refund them.
4 Ms E wrote her PIN on her cheque card. A thief withdrew a large sum from her account which was not covered by insurance.
5 Mr and Mrs F took out a mortgage which did not have a fixed interest rate. When interest rates rose, they were forced to sell their home.
6 Mr G speculated on the stock market with borrowed money. When share prices fell, he had to sell his business to pay the money back.

HOW TO

– give advice

Three useful verbs for making suggestions or recommendations are:
advise recommend suggest

Use *suggest* with a gerund:
I'd suggest investing in a unit trust.
and *advise* and *recommend* with either a gerund or an infinitive.
I'd advise you to invest in ... OR I'd advise investing in ...
I'd recommend you to invest in ... OR I'd recommend investing in ...

Alternatively:
You would be well-advised to invest in ...
In your case, it would be advisable to invest in ...

9 *Make recommendations*

Frau Schulz's bank recommends the following securities. Choose one from each category and describe it. Then say why you would recommend it. Use expressions from the box on p 104.

EXAMPLE: *I'd suggest investing in Swissmix because …*

Unsere Wertpapierabteilung empfiehlt

Aktien:

Name	*Branche*	*Land*	*Kurs am 10.4.2000*	*Kurs/Gewinn Verhältnis* *	*Dividenden-rendite* **
ABN-Amro	Bank	NL	22,84	11,36	3,50
BASF	Chemie	D	47,50	16,25	2,58
Daimler-Chrysler	Automobile	D	68,60	10,60	3,43
Metro	Einzelhandel	D	42,45	21,45	2,60
Telcom Italia	Telekommunikation	I	15,54	44,93	2,01
Unilever	Nahrungsmittel	NL	50,55	12,54	2,49
Vivendi	Versorger	F	120,70	38,94	0,83

Fonds:

Name	*Anlageschwerpunkt*	*Währung*	*Ausgabe/Rücknahme-preis*	
Hansarent	deutsche Rentenpapiere	EUR	34,38	34,03
Immobilia Europa	europ. Immobilien	EUR	47,57	45,19
Mediatel	intern. Aktien der Branchen Medien u. Telekommunikation	EUR	132,86	132,86
US-IT-Portfolio	US-Aktien des Internet-Sektors	USD	37,27	35,22
German Blue	deutsche Standardwerte	EUR	117,53	111,93
Swissmix	schweiz. Anleihen und Aktien	CHF	100,53	100,53
Emerging-Markets-Basket	ost-europ. u. asiatische Aktien	USD	19,88	18,79

Euro-Anleihen

Emittent	*Zins*	*Laufzeit*	*Ausgabekurs in %*
Caja Madrid	6,25	12	99,054
Safeway PLC	6,5	10	99,813
Allgemeine HypoBank	5,5	10	98,695
ABN Amro Bouwfond Ned.	6,0	10	99,428
Council of Europe	5,125	5	100,367
European Investment Bank	5,25	4	101,027

Sprechen Sie uns am Schalter an.
Wir laden Sie zu einem persönlichen Beratungsgespräch ein.

* = price over earnings ratio (P/E)
** = dividend yield

10 *Collecting information*

US banks use forms to find out about prospective investors. Go through this one from Washington Mutual Inc. with a partner taking the customer's role. Then compare this procedure with the method used at your bank.

WM financial services
a Washington Mutual, Inc. Company

❑ New Client ❑ Updated Acct Date:_____/_____/_____

Account Title Instructions

Account Title: ______________________________

Resident Address: ______________________________
(No P.O. Box Please) Street City State Zip

Mailing Address: ______________________________
(If Different) Street City State Zip

Primary Applicant

Last: First:

Social Security or Tax ID: Date of Birth:

Marital Status: Telephone #:

Citizenship: ❑ Non-Resident Alien ❑ Resident Alien ❑ Other/Country:__________ ❑ U.S

Occupation: __________ Employer: __________

Address:__________ Telephone #: __________

Is employer a member firm of a securities exchange, municipal securities dealer, or other securities broker or dealer? ❑ Yes ❑ No

Are you an officer, director or 10% stockholder in a public corporation? ❑ Yes ❑ No

If yes, name of company __________

Do you wish to have your name and address disclosed to the issuer of securities in which you hold a position? ❑ Yes ❑ No

Joint Applicant (If more than one, use separate sheet)

Last: First:

Social Security or Tax ID: Date of Birth:

Marital Status: Telephone #:

Citizenship: ❑ Non-Resident Alien ❑ Resident Alien ❑ Other/Country:__________ ❑ U.S

Occupation: __________ Employer: __________

Address:__________ Telephone #: __________

Is employer a member firm of a securities exchange, municipal securities dealer, or other securities broker or dealer? ❑ Yes ❑ No

Are you an officer, director or 10% stockholder in a public corporation? ❑ Yes ❑ No

If yes, name of company __________

Do you wish to have your name and address disclosed to the issuer of securities in which you hold a position? ❑ Yes ❑ No

Suitability Information

Investment Goals	Risk Tolerance	Past Investment Experience		Investment Horizon
❑ Income	❑ Stable	❑ CD's/Bank Accounts	❑ Life Insurance	❑ Less than 2 years
❑ Capital Appreciation	❑ Conservative	❑ Annuities	❑ Real Estate	❑ 2 - 5 years
❑ Tax Savings	❑ Moderate	❑ Mutual Funds	❑ Options	❑ 5 - 10 years
❑ Capital Preservation	❑ Aggressive	❑ Stocks	❑ Commodities	❑ 10 + years
❑ Other________	❑ Speculative	❑ Bonds		

Financial Information

Annual Income	Liquid Assets	Net Worth	Monthly Expenses	Tax Bracket
❑ $0- 24,999	❑ $0- 24,999	❑ $0- 24,999		
❑ $25,000- 49,999	❑ $25,000- 49,999	❑ $25,000- 49,999		
❑ $50,000- 74,999	❑ $50,000- 74,999	❑ $50,000- 74,999		
❑ $75,000- 99,999	❑ $75,000- 99,999	❑ $75,000- 99,999		
❑ $100,000-149,999	❑ $100,000-149,999	❑ $100,000-149,999	Does the client understand investments are subject to market risk and fluctuation? ❑ Yes ❑ No	
❑ $150,000-249,999	❑ $150,000-249,999	❑ $150,000-249,999		
❑ $250,000-499,999	❑ $250,000-499,999	❑ $250,000-499,999		
❑ $500,000- Above	❑ $500,000- Above	❑ $500,000- Above		

Mutual Funds / Annuities / Retirement Accounts / Life Insurance / Savings

Description	Initial Investment	Current Value	Comments

Initial Investment:

__________ Transaction Description __________ Amount ❑ Purchase ❑ Redemption

Client Initials (The above information is complete and accurate) __________ **Date** __________

11 *Role play*

With a partner taking the investor's role, play the role of the investment consultant in one of the situations below as follows.

1. Find out your customer's situation and intentions. The form on the previous page will be of help.
2. Give your customer information about the various types of securities. Use if-clauses, eg "If you buy bonds, you'll get ... ".
3. Suggest suitable investments for your customer from the list of recommended securities on p 105. Use expressions for giving advice.
4. Take the customer's order. Then change the roles.

CAROLA DE BOER is a secretary at a consulate. She has €10,000 in a term deposit account at 2.25% interest. She will not need the money until four years from now when she plans to make a long trip to her home country, South Africa. Someone told her to buy shares.

MEHMET AVCI lost a large sum investing in shares. He has got €30,000 left. He is still interested in the stock market, but feels he needs professional advice. He is more interested in capital gains than a fixed income as he has a large portfolio of bonds already.

MARIA LEE WONG is a nurse on a low income. She has inherited €45,000 which she will need to supplement her pension when she retires in ten years' time. She will be dependent on this money, as she is not married and has no family in Germany.

PER and LINA SVENSSON have sold their business in Sweden and come to live near their daughter in Germany on their retirement. After buying a house they have €250,000 left. €50,000 should be available over the next five years to finance their grandchildren's education. They would like a profitable long-term investment for the rest.

12 Working with words I

Form nouns from these verbs.

1	decide	...	*9*	invest	...
2	advise	...	*10*	retire	...
3	yield	...	*11*	save	...
4	suggest	...	*12*	provide	...
5	recommend	...	*13*	intend	...
6	lose	...	*14*	redeem	...
7	grow	...	*15*	inform	...
8	select	...			

13 Working with words II

Use nouns from the last exercise to fill the blanks in this text.

There is such a large *(1)* ... of securities on the market that it is hard for the inexperienced investor to make the right *(2)* ... which one to buy. That is why bank clerks in the securities department are specially trained in giving *(3)* ... . Before the clerk can make a suitable *(4)* ..., he or she must first find out what the customer's *(5)* ... is. If a customer wants to provide for his or her *(6)* ..., the clerk will recommend a safe *(7)* ..., for example bonds with different *(8)* ... dates. A customer who buys shares must be aware that the *(9)* ... on his or her capital will depend on the company's *(10)* ... . If a firm makes a *(11)* ..., no dividend will be paid out. In fact the capital might have been better placed in a simple *(12)* ... account!

14 Go online

Visit some of these websites to find out more.

Click here

www.iii.co.uk
Leading website for a wide range of financial advice

www.proshare.org
Non-profit starting point for information about share clubs. Good advice for the beginner

www.moneynet.co.uk
An "independent overview" of the personal finance sector

www.tipsheets.co.uk
Tips for the small investor, regulated by the Personal Investment Authority

www.uksharenet.co.uk
Provides access to resources to gather information on the London Stock Market

www.trust.co.uk
Free, updated daily charts and detailed background info on all UK unit and investment trusts

Advanced materials

Provision for the future

15 *A time bomb*

Describe the development shown by this chart. What are the reasons for it? What are the consequences for young people today? How can banks help?

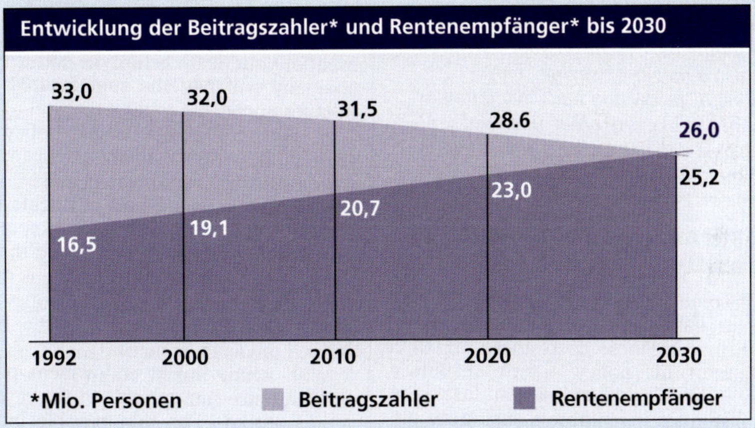

by courtesy of Deutsche Bank 24

16 *Savings in Germany*

Answer the questions below about these figures.

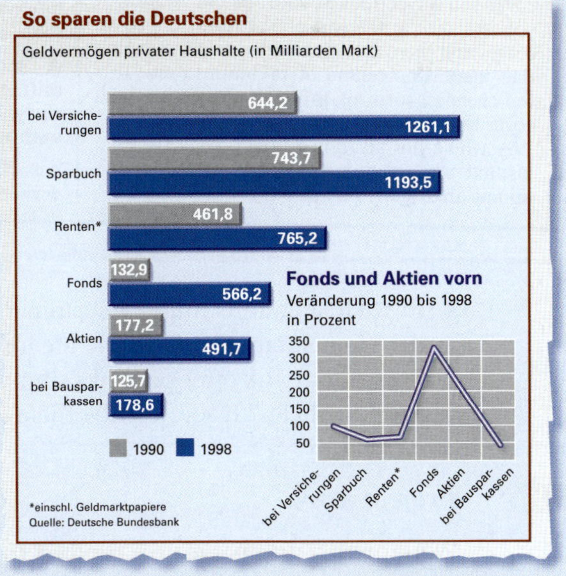

1. How do Germans save?
2. What development took place between 1990 and 1998?
3. In your opinion, have people's savings habits changed since 1998? If so, why?

17 *Life insurance*

Read this information and answer the questions below.

A Guide to Life Insurance

Life insurance offers valuable financial protection in the event of your early death if you have family dependent on your earnings. But it is also a means of saving. This combination of protection and saving makes life insurance unlike any other financial product. Some policies protect, some help to save and some do both.

Life Insurance as Protection for your Family

Loss of income and problems paying debts or meeting tax liabilities can result from loss of life. To help with these costs there are three basic types of life policy – term insurance, whole life insurance and endowment insurance.

Term insurance is temporary insurance giving you financial protection if you die within a specific period. This term can be 10, 15 or 20 years, although policies can be arranged to cover you for periods as short as one month. If you are alive at the end of the term, the cover ceases and there is no surrender value, meaning that there is no refund of premiums paid. It is the cheapest form of protection, offering high cover for a low premium.

A whole life insurance policy pays the sum insured whenever death occurs and the premiums are usually higher.

Life Insurance for Saving and Protection

The long-term nature of life insurance allows you to plan long-term saving. Endowment insurance protects your family and provides for the future. You pay premiums for an agreed number of years, say 10, 15 or 20. At the end of this time a lump sum will be paid out. In the event of your death before the maturity date the company will pay the sum insured plus any bonuses applicable so far.

A with-profits endowment policy lets you share in the profits made by the insurance company from the investment it makes, usually in the form of annual bonus payments which are added to your insurance sum. It is a means of saving with a minimum of risk and the potential for a good return, although there is no guarantee of the maturity value of the policy. Without-profits policies pay out only the basic sum insured on death or maturity.

With a unit-linked endowment policy only the insurance sum payable in the case of death is guaranteed. The sum payable on maturity depends on the investments the insurance company makes: it may be higher than with a with-profits policy, but it could be lower. There is a range of opportunities with varying degrees of risk.

A life insurance policy is a long-term commitment. It is not designed for you to cash in early. Never surrender a life insurance policy without taking expert advice.

Association of British Insurers:
www.insurance.org.uk/consumer2/consumer/htm

1 In what situations might a customer of your bank take out
a term insurance? ***b*** whole life insurance? ***c*** endowment insurance?

2 Does your bank offer products similar to with-profits policies and unit-linked policies? If so, describe them.

18 *Project work*

Working in a group, create a product to meet the needs of young employees who want to make provision for the future. It may involve a unit trust, a savings plan, a life insurance or building society policy or a combination of products. Imagine that your fellow-students are your colleagues who will have to sell this product. Present it to them using visual aids.

UNIT
10 Foreign trade

Lead-in

In the past trade was carried out by barter. What advantages did barter offer? Why is it not used in our economy today? What arrangements for securing payment have taken its place?

1 A hard bargain

Andreas Altermann, the owner of ALFRU, a company in Schleswig-Holstein that imports concentrated fruit juices, gets a call from Chris Schubert of Encore Fruit Marketing in California.

ANDREAS ALTERMANN	ALFRU Industriefrucht, Altermann. Guten Morgen.
CHRIS SCHUBERT	Hi, Andy. Chris here.
ANDREAS ALTERMANN	Hi, Chris.
CHRIS SCHUBERT	I just thought I'd get back to you as soon as possible re that inquiry you made about frozen peach juice concentrate. I wanted to let you know that basically the deal can go through on the terms you wanted.
ANDREAS ALTERMANN	Great. The only point we haven't talked about yet is the payment, isn't it?
CHRIS SCHUBERT	That's right, but I don't see any problem there. As long as

you pay us in advance, we'll ship the consignment straight off to you as soon as ...

ANDREAS ALTERMANN Payment in advance? No way. You can't be serious, Chris! Look, how long have we been doing business together? How about payment on open account instead, let's say thirty days after loading. That would give me plenty of time to sell the shipment to my customer at this end before I have to pay you. Payment on open account thirty days after the date of the bill of lading. Isn't that a fair offer?

CHRIS SCHUBERT Forget it.

ANDREAS ALTERMANN Only thirty days, Chris. Isn't it worth that for the pleasure of doing business with me?

CHRIS SCHUBERT Andy, how do I know your business is gonna be around thirty days from now? Think of the risk my firm would be taking! Hey! I got a great idea. How about a nice letter of credit? Then my boss can sleep better at night ...

ANDREAS ALTERMANN My bank manager, too. Do you know what a letter of credit costs here in Germany?

CHRIS SCHUBERT Peanuts, Andy.

ANDREAS ALTERMANN Okay, okay. A letter of credit – but only on condition that you accept deferred payment – thirty days after loading.

CHRIS SCHUBERT Deferred payment? Is this some kinda joke? Haven't you guys in Europe ever heard that time is money? It's gotta be payment at sight. My boss is allergic to anything else.

ANDREAS ALTERMANN Documents against payment if you want payment at sight.

CHRIS SCHUBERT You got a deal. Documents against payment.

ANDREAS ALTERMANN You drive a hard bargain, Chris.

CHRIS SCHUBERT You're a pretty tough guy yourself. Funny thing is, I seem to remember us having this little discussion before.

ANDREAS ALTERMANN Last time, and the time before and the time before that.

CHRIS SCHUBERT That's why it's so great doing business with you, Andy.

ANDREAS ALTERMANN I'll fax you my order right away.

CHRIS SCHUBERT Great. Then I can get along to the bank and place the collection order.

ANDREAS ALTERMANN Cheerio, Chris. Have a nice day.

CHRIS SCHUBERT You too, Andy. Bye.

Answer these questions.

1 Four terms of payment are mentioned in the dialogue. What are they?
2 Two conditions regarding the due date of payment are suggested: deferred payment (30 days after loading) and payment at sight. Who prefers payment at sight? Explain why.
3 What agreement about payment do both parties finally reach?

2 *Terms of payment*

Match each of the four terms of payment mentioned in the last exercise with one of these definitions.

1 It is an arrangement by which payment has to be made before the goods are shipped.
2 It is a guarantee given by a bank that payment will be made to a named beneficiary up to an agreed amount before a fixed expiry date against presentation of certain documents.
3 It is an arrangement between the exporter, a bank and the importer by which documents are sent to a bank with instructions to hold them until goods are paid for.
4 It means that the exporter ships the goods, sends the invoice and then waits for the importer to make payment.

3 *Make comparisons*

Copy this table and complete it to compare the four terms of payment described in exercise 2 from the payer's and beneficiary's points of view.

Term of Payment	Advantages/Disadvantages for the payer	Advantages/Disadvantages for the beneficiary
payment in advance		

4 *The documents*

The following two documents are presented to Mr Altermann by his bank. Answer these questions about them.

1 How much peach juice concentrate has Mr Altermann bought?
2 How will it be sent to him?
3 What is included in the sum of $29,124.55?
4 How will the beneficiary receive the sum?
5 When must Mr Altermann pay for the shipment?
6 Who has signed the bill of lading "clean on board"?*
7 When and where was the B/L signed?
8 What does the clean bill of lading prove?
9 Why will Mr Altermann need the bill of lading?
10 From whom and when will Mr Altermann receive the invoice and the B/L?

** Generally the B/L should be signed by the captain of the ship but he can delegate this to the shipping line.*

ENCORE FRUIT MARKETING, INC.

120 WEST BONITA AVE., SUITE 204
SAN DIMAS, CALIFORNIA 91773-3085
(909) 394-5640 • FAX: (909) 394-5646
E-MAIL: encore@ns1.com

INVOICE

BILL TO: ALFRU INDUSTRIEFRUCHT VERTIEBS GMBH
ATTN: MR A. ALTERMANN
WERKSTRASSE 4
25497 PRISDORF, GERMANY

INVOICE NUMBER: 7136

INVOICE DATE 3-08-99

DUE DATE 4-07-99

PO#: ALTERMANN
CIF ROTTERDAM

PAYMENT TERMS: D/P AT SIGHT

SALESPERSON: CHRIS SCHUBERT

QUANTITY	SIZE	PRODUCT DESCRIPTION	UNITS	PRICE	AMOUNT
65 DRUMS	52 GAL.	FROZEN PEACH JUICE CONCENTRATE 65 BRIX ESSENCE RETURNED	16,835 KG	$1.73 KG	$29,124.55

BOOKING#: BOIN 3267
SHIP VIA NYK LINE 1-20' REEFER CONTAINER ABOARD "OOCL FORTUNE"

SHIP TO: ROTTERDAM, NETHERLANDS, ETA 4-06-99

ENCORE REF: S/M# 88158
CA/98-079

WIRE FUNDS TO:

BANK OF AMERICA
135 WEST BONITA AVE.
SAN DIMAS, CALIFORNIA 91773
U.S.A.

ROUTING: 12100358 B O A U.S. 6-5
ACCOUNT: 1234-5678

TOTAL AMOUNT DUE **$29,124.55**

PLEASE NOTE: **ENCORE... INVOICES THIS PRODUCT (THESE PRODUCTS) AS SELLER, BUT IS NOT THE MANUFACTURER OF THE PRODUCT, AND MAKES NO FINAL WARRANTIES, DIRECT OR IMPLIED FOR THE PRODUCT(S). ALL CLAIMS FOR PRODUCT LIABILITY WILL BE FOR THE ACCOUNT OF THE MANUFACTURER.

NYK LINE
NIPPON YUSEN KAISHA

ORIGINAL BILL OF LADING

FORM NO. A1NYO2S93

ENCP04

SHIPPER ENCORE FRUIT MARKETING, INC. 120 WEST BONITA AVE., STE 204 SAN DIMAS, CA 91773	DOCUMENT NUMBER BOI N 3267 TAA STACASCN099-0819 EXPORT REFERENCES EECR98041
CONSIGNEE TO ORDER OF SHIPPER	FORWARDING AGENT REFERENCES O'NEILL & WHITAKER, INC. 2951 LA10 2999 PACIFIC COMMERCE DR. CHB 6431 RANCHO DOMINGUEZ CA 90221 POINT AND COUNTRY OF ORIGIN (FOR THE MERCHANT'S REFERENCE ONLY). CA
NOTIFY PARTY MENTREX & LEMAC B.V. LINSCHOTENSTRAAT 2-12 NL 3044 AT ROTTERDAM	DOMESTIC ROUTING/EXPORT INSTRUCTIONS (FOR THE MERCHANT'S REFERENCE ONLY). THESE COMMODITIES TECHNOLOGY, OR SOFTWARE WERE EXPORTED FROM THE UNITED STATES IN ACCORDANCE WITH THE EXPORT ADMINISTRATION REGULATIONS. DIVERSION CONTRARY TO U.S. LAW PROHIBITED. NLR JE
PRECARRIAGE BY * / PLACE OF RECEIPT * OAKLAND, CA	
VESSEL / VOYAGE NO. OOCL FORTUNE 082 / PORT OF LOADING OAKLAND, CA	FINAL DESTINATION (FOR THE MERCHANT'S REFERENCE ONLY)
PORT OF DISCHARGE ROTTERDAM, NETHERLANDS / PLACE OF DELIVERY ROTTERDAM, NETHERLANDS	

PARTICULARS FURNISHED BY THE MERCHANT PAGE 1

Container No., Seal No.; Marks & No's	No. of Containers or Packages	H** M	Kind of Packages; Description of Goods	Gross Weight/Code	Measurement/Code
AS ADDR NYKU7588512 63970	65		SHIPPER'S LOAD AND COUNT CY/CY FREIGHT PREPAID LADEN ON BOARD OOCL FORTUNE 082 AT OAKLAND 03/11/99 1 X 20' REEFER CONTAINER SAID TO CONTAIN: DRUMS @ 52 GALS. EACH OF FROZEN PEACH JUICE CONCENTRATE MAINTAIN TEMP AT 0 DEG F. VENTS CLOSED	18015.0KGS 39715.0LBS	

TOTAL CONTAINERS: 1

ITEM NUMBER	WEIGHT	MEASUREMENT	CUR.	RATE	BASIS	P/C	PREPAID	COLLECT

LADEN ON BOARD THE VESSEL DATE	BY	Number of Original Bills of Lading	Place of Bills of Lading Issue	Prepaid at	Payable at
03 11 99		THREE	LOS ANGELES	LOS ANGELES	ROTTERDAM, NETH

(TERMS OF BILL OF LADING CONTINUED FROM BACK HEREOF) ENLARGED VERSION OF BACK CLAUSES IS AVAILABLE UPON REQUEST FROM THE CARRIER. In witness whereof, the undersigned, on behalf of Nippon Yusen Kaisha, the Master and the owner of the Vessel, has signed the number of Bill(s) of Lading stated above, all of this tenor and date, one of which being accomplished, the others to stand void.

SERVICE RE'V	SERVICE DEL'Y	TYPE OF GOODS	
1. CY	1. CY	1. ORD.	5. LIQ.
2. CFS	2. CFS	2. REEF	6. LIV.ANI.
3. DOOR	3. DOOR	3. DANG.	7. BULK
4. DIRECT	4. DIRECT	4. AUTO	8. MAIL

PRINTED IN U.S.A.

NIPPON YUSEN KAISHA (N Y K LINE)

Dated Month 03 Day 11 Year 99 B/L No. NYKS351061276

By NYK (N.A.) INC. - WESTERN REGION AS AGENTS FOR NYK LINE CARRIER

* APPLICABLE ONLY WHEN USED FOR MULTI-MODAL BILL OF LADING
** INDICATES WHETHER ANY OF THE CARGO IS HAZARDOUS MATERIAL UNDER DOT, IMCO, OR OTHER REGULATIONS AND INDICATES CORRECT COMMODITY NUMBER IN DESCRIPTION OF GOODS.

5 *Working with words*

Find expressions on the bill of lading (p 115) which mean the following.

1 the sender of the goods
2 the recipient of the goods
3 the ship
4 the place where the goods are taken on board
5 the place where the goods are unloaded from the ship
6 the place where the goods will be handed over to the buyer
7 the place where the goods should finally arrive
8 how heavy the goods are
9 how large the goods are
10 transport costs paid in advance

6 *Documents against payment*

Use this diagram to describe how the transaction between Encore Marketing and ALFRU took place.

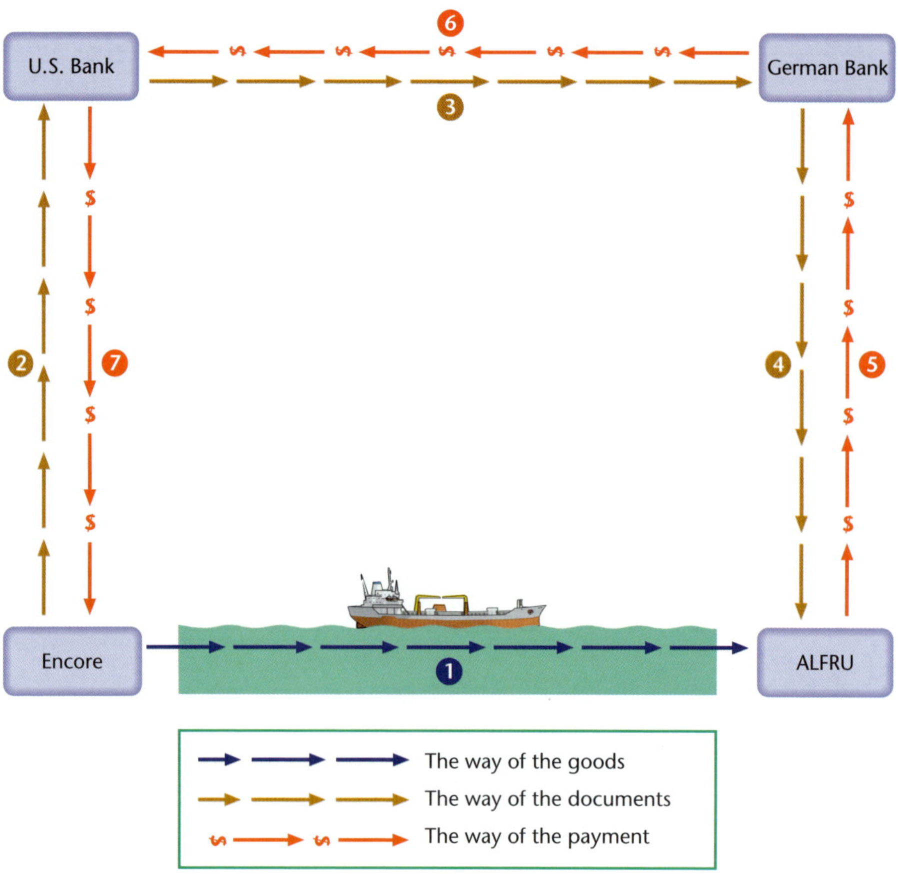

LOOKING AT LANGUAGE

REPORTED SPEECH

1 Chris Schubert: "I **cannot accept** deferred payment."
2 Chris Schubert says (that) he **cannot accept** deferred payment.
3 Chris Schubert said (that) he **could not accept** deferred payment.
4 Andy Altermann: "**Will** you **accept** payment in advance?"
5 Andy Altermann has often asked Chris Schubert if/whether he **will accept** payment in advance.
6 Andy Altermann asked Chris Schubert if/whether he **would accept** payment in advance.
7 Chris said (that) time **is** money.
8 Andy told Chris (that) they **had not talked** about the payment.

- The tense of the original sentence in direct speech *(1, 4)* does not change if speech is reported using the present tense *(2)* or present perfect tense *(5)*.
- If speech is reported using the past tense *(3, 6, 8)*, the tense of the original sentence changes as follows:

Direct Speech		**Reported Speech**
simple present	→	simple past
future	→	conditional
simple past	→	past perfect
present perfect	→	past perfect

Exception: The tense may remain unchanged if the original statement is still thought to be true at the time of reporting *(7)*.

NOTE: *tell* is used as a reporting verb only if the listener is mentioned *(8)*.

- It is good style to vary one's reporting verbs. Some possibilities are: *add* ◆ *agree* ◆ *believe* ◆ *deny* ◆ *explain* ◆ *mention* ◆ *point out* ◆ *state* ◆ *suggest*, and for reported questions: *ask* ◆ *inquire* ◆ *want to know* ◆ *wonder.*

7 *Practice I*

Your customers tell or ask you the following. Report the information to another bank. Use a reporting verb in the present or present perfect tense.

EXAMPLE: Customer: "I need the documents at once."
You: *"Our customer says he needs the documents at once."*
Or: *"Our customer has told me that he needs the documents at once."*

1 Customer: "I have agreed to documents against payment."
2 Customer: "I do not require a certificate of origin."
3 Customer: "I am expecting the shipment to arrive soon."
4 Customer: "I want to pay in US dollars."
5 Customer: "I refused to apply for a letter of credit."
6 Customer: "When will I receive the documents?"
7 Customer: "Can the documents be sent by courier?"
8 Customer: "Is the bill of lading clean?"
9 Customer: "How much does the bank charge for collection?"
10 Customer: "When did the vessel leave the port of loading?"

8 Practice II

Report the statements and questions from the last exercise again. Use a reporting verb in the past this time. Vary your reporting verbs.
EXAMPLE: *Our customer told us that he needed the documents at once.*

HOW TO

– mediate

Imagine that a colleague of yours who does not speak English has to deal with an English-speaking customer who cannot understand German. It is your task to mediate between the two. That means that you tell your colleague in German what the customer has told you in English and you tell the customer in English what your German colleague has said.

German colleague *Mediator* *English-speaking customer*

NOTE: **mediating is not the same as translating or interpreting.**

Do not try to translate exactly what someone has said. Simply pass the information on, using your own words.

EXAMPLE:

A customer says: "Why on earth did it take five days for my account to be credited?"
As mediator, you might say: *"Der Kunde möchte wissen, warum der Betrag erst nach fünf Tagen gutgeschrieben wurde."*
Or: *"Der Kunde fragt, warum die Gutschrift erst nach fünf Tagen erfolgte."*

If you use reporting verbs when you mediate, it is clear that you are mediating and not speaking on your own behalf. It can also sound more polite.
If you are mediating between two persons who are both present, use reporting verbs in the **present** tense and **do not change** the tense of the speaker's words.

EXAMPLE:

"Fragen Sie die Dame, ob sie eine Aufenthaltserlaubnis hat."
"My colleague wants to know if you have got a residence permit."

If you are mediating and only one of the parties is present, it will be necessary to contact the other party later. In this case the reporting verb may be in the **present** or **past** tense. Remember: if the reporting verb is in the **past**, the tense of the original speaker's words **changes**.

EXAMPLE:

"Sagen Sie dem Kunden, dass ihm der Betrag Montag gutgeschrieben wird."
"My colleague says the amount will be credited to you on Monday."
Or: "My colleague told me the amount would be credited to you on Monday."

Remember to vary your reporting verbs.

9 *Mediation*

Jan Nevering, a trainee at your bank who does not speak English, has to serve Mohammed Ben Saud from Kuwait. He asks you to mediate. Write down what you would say.

BEN SAUD:	MEDIATOR:	JAN NEVERING:
I'd like to place an order for cash against documents. I have an account with your bank. Could you tell me what I have to do, please?	....	Selbstverständlich. Er muss nur dieses Formular ausfüllen und zusammen mit den Dokumenten bei uns einreichen.
Can you help me fill the form in, please?	....	
	....	Kein Problem. Bitten Sie ihn, seinen Namen und seine Anschrift oben rechts einzutragen und die Daten des Käufers und dessen Bankverbindung darunter.
Of course. *(Fills in these details.)* I've got the documents here: the invoice, the bill of lading, the certificate of origin and the insurance policy.	....	
	....	Gut. Fragen Sie ihn, wer die Kosten und Spesen des Inkassoauftrags zahlen wird.
I'll pay all the costs arising in Germany but the consignee has to pay all the other costs and charges.	....	
	....	Und auf welches Konto möchte er die Gutschrift haben? Auf sein Euro-Konto oder sein Dollar-Konto?
My dollar account, please. Where do I sign?	....	
	....	Hier … unten links.
(Signs.) Thank you.	....	

10 *Mediation role play*

Working in groups of three, play the roles of the English-speaking customer, the German bank clerk who speaks no English and the mediator in the following situations. Change the roles each time. NOTE: the mediator should not ask or answer any questions directly. All the questions and information should come from the other two parties.

SAMIRA RASPINDI from India wants to transfer 1,500 euros to a cousin in Bombay. The mediator helps the clerk find out the details for arranging the transfer. Ms Raspindi wants to know the costs and how long it will take.

VIKTOR JURIN from the Ukraine wants the bank to extend his overdraft facility on his current account. The mediator helps the clerk find out whether a personal loan might be more suitable. Mr Jurin asks about the interest rates for both types of credit and whether security is needed.

AKITO FUJIMORI from Japan wants to order some shares. The mediator helps the clerk find out the details for taking the order. Mr Fujimori asks about the costs and whether tax is payable on capital gains from shares in Germany.

11 *A letter of credit*

Mr Altermann of ALFRU makes a phone call to Jugosa, a company in Chile that supplies fruit juice.

CARLA DA SILVA ¿Diga me?

ANDREAS ALTERMANN Bueños Dias. This is Andreas Altermann of ALFRU calling from Germany. Could I speak to Señora da Silva, please?

CARLA DA SILVA Da Silva speaking. Bueños Dias, Señor Altermann.

ANDREAS ALTERMANN Thank you for sending us that sample of blackberry concentrate. Sample number 9704 is excellent. Could you supply us with 12 tons of the same quality?

CARLA DA SILVA No problem at all, Señor Altermann. 12 tons of blackberry concentrate as in sample 9704.

ANDREAS ALTERMANN We paid 5,800 dollars a ton last time. Would you be able to let us have it at the same price again?

CARLA DA SILVA Yes, why not? 5,800 dollars per ton, CFR Rotterdam like last time. And can you let us have an irrevocable letter of credit again, please?

ANDREAS ALTERMANN Certainly. I'll get in touch with my bank. But in that case would you agree to deferred payment, 45 days after the date of the bill of lading?

CARLA DA SILVA Yes, that'd be fine.

ANDREAS ALTERMANN Of course my bank will need the export invoice, the certificate of origin for customs and the bill of lading.

	All these three documents should be presented at our bank counter in Hamburg within 21 days after the date of the bill of lading.
CARLA DA SILVA	No problem at all.
ANDREAS ALTERMANN	Could you arrange for the goods to be shipped to Rotterdam as soon as possible, please? We've got a Dutch customer who needs the consignment very urgently.
CARLA DA SILVA	We'll prepare everything for loading. What about transshipment or partial shipments?
ANDREAS ALTERMANN	Transshipment and partial shipments should be prohibited if that's all right with you. Just one more point, do you want the letter of credit to be confirmed?
CARLA DA SILVA	No, that won't be necessary.
ANDREAS ALTERMANN	Then I'll ask my bank to open the letter of credit right away.
CARLA DA SILVA	Good. As soon as our bank advises us that the L/C has been opened in our favour, we'll ship the goods and give the documents to our bank.
ANDREAS ALTERMANN	As soon as you do, could you e-mail me an advice of dispatch with copies of the documents in advance, please? Then I can check them before the originals are presented to my bank.
CARLA DA SILVA	Sure. Thanks for your order, Señor Altermann.
ANDREAS ALTERMANN	I'll look forward to hearing from you. Goodbye, Señora da Silva.
CARLA DA SILVA	¡Adios!

Answer these questions.

1 Who will ask a bank to open a letter of credit?
2 In whose favour will the L/C be opened?
3 On what condition does Mr Altermann agree to the L/C?
4 What documents will be named in the L/C?
5 What does Mr Altermann want Señora da Silva to send him? Why?

12 *Case study*

Working with a partner or in a small group, discuss these questions about ALFRU's import deal with Jugosa. Write down your ideas and report them to the other members of the class.

1 Who wants an L/C to be opened? Why?
2 Why does the exporter want the L/C to be irrevocable?
3 The exporter's bank in Chile will advise him of the L/C but will not confirm it. What is the difference between advising and confirming?
4 What advantages does ALFRU have from agreeing to an L/C? Are there any disadvantages?

13 *An e-mail*

Use expressions from the box to fill the gaps in this e-mail.

clean ◆ *consignment* ◆ *destination* ◆ *dispatch* ◆ *favour* ◆ *forward*
invoice ◆ *irrevocable* ◆ *lading* ◆ *origin* ◆ *order* ◆ *present* ◆ *prohibited*
shipment ◆ *terms* ◆ *vessel*

Account: Email: Carla da Silva **Priority:** Normal
To: Andreas Altermann
Cc:
Bcc:
Subject: Advice of (1) ...

20 August 20—

Dear Mr Altermann

Thank you for your (2) ... of 12 tons of blackberry concentrate.
Today our bank advised us that an (3) ... letter of credit has been opened in our (4) ... .
We are pleased to inform you that we have shipped the (5) ... on the Cap Corrientes which is due at the port of (6) ..., Rotterdam, on 30 August. Partial shipments and transshipment are (7) ... .
As requested, we are forwarding copies of the documents to you: the export (8) ..., the certificate of (9) ... and the bill of (10) ..., which was signed (11) ... on board by the captain of the (12) ... .
Under the (13) ... of the L/C we have instructed our bank to (14) ... the originals at your bank counter in Hamburg within 21 days after the date of the B/L.

We hope that the (15) ... is satisfactory and look (16) ... to doing business with you again.

Best wishes

Carla da Silva

Advanced materials

Globalisation

14 ***What is globalisation?***

The following article will help you to answer this question and find reasons why globalisation is now taking place.

What drives globalisation?

Globalisation occurs because specific managers in specific companies make decisions that result in increased cross-border flows of capital, goods and/or know-how. Managers are making such decisions at an increasing rate because globalisation is becoming both more feasible and more desirable. Four trends lie at the core of these developments.

1 An ever-increasing number of countries are embracing the free-market ideology.

The shift from a "planning" mentality to a "market" mentality by economic policy makers in industrialised and industrialising nations is well known and has been well documented.

Since the end of the second world war, the rising tide of free-market ideology that started with the developed economies has swept up South Korea, Taiwan, Hong Kong and Singapore, then the other "tigers" of south-east Asia and is now carrying along other major economies such as China, India, Latin America, parts of Africa, and central and eastern Europe including Russia.

An increasing number of countries are liberalising their investment regimes.

2 The economic centre of gravity is shifting from the developed to the developing countries.

Economic liberalisation promotes competition, efficiency, innovation, new capital investment and faster economic growth.

Not surprisingly, the embrace of market mechanisms has allowed the developing economies of the world to start catching up with the advanced economies. Taiwan, Hong Kong and Singapore, some of the world's poorest countries in the 1950s, already count among the advanced economies. Despite the short-term disruptions caused by the recent Asian financial crisis, the projections of long-term growth for the region are still valid.

Other, even larger, economies are advancing, notably China. Having sustained a better than 10 per cent annual growth rate since 1980, China has already transformed itself into the third largest economy in the world – at least on a purchasing power parity basis – and seems poised to overtake Japan in the not-too-distant future.

The world's economic centre of gravity is shifting. Virtually any company today that seeks to grow has little choice but to go where the growth is. For the vast majority of the world's top 500 industrial corporations, such growth is rarely in the home market.

3 Technological advances are constantly improving communications.

Costs of air transportation, telecommunications and computers have declined sharply since 1950. The decline in transportation costs has shrunk the cost of shipping goods.

In the case of computers and telecommunications, both the sharp cost decline and the recent widespread adoption of technologies such as video conferencing and electronic mail have made co-ordination of far-flung operations not only more feasible but also more reliable and efficient.

4 The opening of borders to trade, investment and technology transfers not only creates new market opportunities for companies but also enables competitors from abroad to enter their home markets.

As competition intensifies, it fuels the race among competitors to serve globalising customers, to capture economies of scale, to exploit the cost-reducing or quality-enhancing potential of optimal locations and to tap technological advancements wherever they may occur. The result is that globalisation has now become a self-accelerating frenzy.

Financial Times Survey:
Mastering Global Business 1999

15 *Mergers and acquisitions*

Describe what takes place in each of the four cases shown below, making the differences clear. Give examples. Then explain why the number of mergers and acquisitions is increasing.

a merger

a joint venture

a friendly takeover

a hostile takeover

16 *Banks as global players*

Discuss these four questions in groups. Then compare your group's ideas with those of the other groups. Give examples where possible.

1. Why do many German high-street banks want to become global players?
2. How can banks become global players?
3. What may be the results of globalisation for banks' customers?
4. What may be the results of globalisation for bank staff?

Transcripts

Unit 1, Exercise 6 At the counter

1

CUSTOMER Excuse me. Do you speak English?
WEBER Yes. Can I help you?
CUSTOMER Yes. I've just arrived in Germany. I'm from Ireland, you see. I've got a job here as an au pair. The family I'm working for has told me that I'll need an account so that they can pay me every month. They told me to come and arrange it here.
WEBER That's right. Did you have an account when you lived in Ireland?
CUSTOMER No. I used to work in a shop there and I always got my wages paid in cash.
WEBER I see. In this country you will need what is called a current account. Then your employers can transfer your salary into it every month.
CUSTOMER Can I open one now?
WEBER Of course, if you've got your passport with you.
CUSTOMER Yes, here it is.
WEBER That's fine. Would you come this way? ... Take a seat, please. I'll just call our customer service officer, Frau Kleinschmidt. She'll be able to open the account for you.

2

CUSTOMER Hello, Frau Weber.
WEBER Hello, Mr Shaw. Nice to see you again. How are you today?
CUSTOMER Not too bad at all, my dear. There's something I wanted to ask about.
WEBER What can I do for you?
CUSTOMER I'm not very happy about the money in my savings account. The interest rate is so low at the moment. I feel that I could get a much higher return so I'd like some advice on how to invest it. I've been reading in the papers about all the different possibilities on offer at the moment.
WEBER Certainly, Mr Shaw. Would you like to sit down over there for a moment? I'll ring through to our securities department and see if our investment consultant, Herr Petersen, is free at the moment.

3

CUSTOMER Good morning.
WEBER Good morning. May I help you?
CUSTOMER Could you tell me the rate of exchange for US dollars, please?
WEBER Of course. Do you want to change currency or cash a cheque?
CUSTOMER I'd like to cash a US dollar traveller's cheque.
WEBER Let me see ... today's rate for traveller's cheques is 2.015 euros for one dollar.
CUSTOMER And can you tell me how much you charge for cashing them?
WEBER Would you please go over to the till? My colleague there will be able to help you. He can tell you about the charges and he can cash the cheque for you as well.

4

CUSTOMER Good afternoon.
WEBER Good afternoon. What can I do for you?
CUSTOMER My wife and I are buying a flat here. We discussed the matter with your loan adviser, Herr Özcan, last week. Can we see him again, please? There are some more points we'd like to talk to him about.
WEBER I'm afraid Herr Özcan's not in today, but he'll be back tomorrow. Would you like to have an appointment for tomorrow?
CUSTOMER Yes, but in the afternoon, if possible.
WEBER Would three o'clock be convenient?
CUSTOMER Could you make that three thirty?
WEBER Three thirty, then. Could you give me your name, please?
CUSTOMER Wilson, Dennis and Kathleen Wilson.
WEBER Thank you, Mr Wilson. Herr Özcan will be expecting you and your wife at half past three.

5

CUSTOMER Good morning. I'm Jennifer Pitt of Pitt Plastics. I had an appointment with Herr Holm in the corporate credit department at 8.30. Sorry I'm so late. I got held up in the traffic.
WEBER Yes, it's always bad at this time of the morning, isn't it? One moment please. I'll just ring through and tell him you're here. Frau Pitt von Pitt Plastics ist hier für Herrn Holm. ... Danke. ... I'm afraid Herr Holm is in a meeting right now, Ms Pitt. Would you like to speak to one of our other advisers instead?
CUSTOMER I'd prefer to wait if it won't take too long.
WEBER He should be out again in about ten minutes. Would you like to wait in the office? Can I offer you a cup of coffee while you're waiting?
CUSTOMER Thank you. That would be very nice.

Unit 3, Exercise 14 An interview

MONEY MATTERS Perhaps we could start by talking about the branch that you manage, Mr Butler. Can you tell us how is it organized?
MR BUTLER Well, there are twelve front-line staff working in this branch here in Melton Mowbray. All the back-office work is done at our regional head office in Leicester – that's where they handle cheques or any orders we take over the counter. We also have a separate call centre that answers telephone enquiries and we offer Internet banking with a growing number of online accounts as well.
MONEY MATTERS So quite a lot of work is outsourced?
MR BUTLER That's right. In that way we can concentrate on our main aim which is providing customer service.
MONEY MATTERS How do you organize that?
MR BUTLER For our personal customers we offer three levels of service. We have a customer account manager who looks after the average customer, a personal choice manager for taking care of high net

worth customers and for our most affluent customers we offer private banking: they can make an appointment with our financial consultant. Oh yes, and we have a mortgage arranger who comes in twice a week.

MONEY MATTERS And what about corporate clients? Do you make the same distinctions?

MR BUTLER Yes, here again we have three levels. Our business banking manager deals with small firms with a turnover of up to about £100,000 a year. Larger companies are dealt with by our commercial service officer in our regional head office, and of course for the really big companies there's our corporate banking office in London.

MONEY MATTERS And when is the branch open?

MR BUTLER From 9 am till 5 pm, Monday to Friday only. For out-of-hours customers we have two cashpoints and a deposit box, as well.

MONEY MATTERS And what range of services is available?

MR BUTLER Basically the provision of accounts, savings and current accounts with cheque books, cheque cards, credit cards ...

MONEY MATTERS Are cheques still widely used? In Germany people use a credit transfer system for paying money into another account.

MR BUTLER Do they? We don't have anything like that here. People write cheques, backed by our own Lloyds TSB cheque guarantee card, but for recurring payments we encourage them to set up standing orders and direct debits.

MONEY MATTERS What about other services?

MR BUTLER That's where our partners come in. Lloyds has merged with Cheltenham and Gloucester, a former building society that specializes in mortgages and recently we have taken over Scottish Widows, an insurance company, offering life assurance and other types of protection. These are very strong partners.

MONEY MATTERS Let's say I wanted to open a current account with Lloyds TSB now. What would I have to do?

MR BUTLER Well, to start with, we'd need proof of your identity – a passport, driver's licence or a credit card, for example. If you didn't have that, we would ask you to name a professional person whom we would ask for a reference. After that, your application would be credit-scored. We use a credit reference agency called Experion to assess applicants. It gives them a risk indicator of nought to nine, nought being the best rating. Your score determines which type of account and which services we can offer you.

MONEY MATTERS You mean the computer decides whether I can have an account ...

MR BUTLER That's right. And I can't change its decision either! Your account would then be opened for a probationary period of three months. After four months you'd be invited to the bank for a service review – to assess how you're getting on and you might be up-graded. We try to see our customers in person every twelve months because so many people use the cashpoints, the phone and the Internet for banking these days. We call that 'activity migration'. It makes cross-selling very difficult.

MONEY MATTERS And what kind of account would you offer me?

MR BUTLER There's our Classic Account, which is a basic current account with a cheque book and costs £5 a month.

MONEY MATTERS Can I overdraw it?

MR BUTLER Yes, though each overdraft within your credit limit will cost you £5 a month plus debit interest. Unauthorized overdrafts cost £10 every time you go over the limit plus £5 plus debit interest. If you had a risk indicator of nought to three, you would be eligible for our Gold Service Account with benefits like interest on the credit balance, free travel insurance, lower debit interest – which would cost you £10 a month. We have a wide range of savings accounts as well.

MONEY MATTERS Just one point which may surprise our listeners. I notice that all the staff in the branch, including yourself, are wearing uniform – navy blue suits, with skirts for the women, and matching shirts, ties and blouses. Is the uniform provided by the bank?

MR BUTLER Yes. Nobody's forced to wear it, but everyone does. It saves wear and tear on your other clothes and I suppose it's better for our corporate identity, too.

MONEY MATTERS Perhaps you could tell our listeners something about staff training at Lloyds TSB. Do bank clerks have to attend vocational schools and take exams like they have to in Germany?

MR BUTLER Good Lord, no. They're needed here in the branch.

MONEY MATTERS So how are they trained then?

MR BUTLER Basically on the job. We take people on at the age of 17 or 18 for a probationary period in which they sit next to one of our staff and learn basic office routines. If they make out all right, they'll get a permanent contract after about a year.

MONEY MATTERS Just like that? Without taking any courses or exams?

MR BUTLER Yes. We don't run training courses as such and there are no mandatory exams. Staff can sit the Chartered Institute of Bankers examinations, but they don't have to.

MONEY MATTERS I think some of our listeners will be quite envious of their counterparts in Britain! Thank you for talking to us, Mr Butler.

Unit 5, Exercise 15 Memo-writing

CLIVE WILLIAMS Hello ... hello ... can you hear me? This line is terrible. My name is Clive Williams. I'm phoning from Egypt, from Cairo. I want to report that all my traveller's cheques have been stolen. Six cheques for 100 dollars and four for 200. I've got a record of the serial numbers here ... 977604331 to 6 and 855624963 to 6. Can you stop them at once, please? I've informed the police. Thank God I've still got my credit ca... .

AKITO YAMAMOTO Good morning. Yamamoto speaking, Akito Yamamoto. I've got to fly out to Toronto unexpectedly this evening and need the following traveller's cheques urgently: in US dollars, ten in denominations of 100 and eight in denominations of 50. Oh yes, and some Canadian currency as well ... let's say ... 300 Canadian dollars. If you can get it all ready, I'll pick everything up shortly before 4 this afternoon. By the way, my account number is 2799551.

MARIA CARPONETTI Hello ... Am I through now? I don't know if you can hear me ... I'm phoning from Morocco, from my hotel in Casablanca. I've been trying to get through all day. ... My name is Maria Carponetti. Somebody snatched my handbag and I've lost everything. All my traveller's cheques, my Eurocard, my passport, my purse, everything. I had twelve traveller's cheques in it – for 100 euros each. I don't know the numbers, but I got them from you last Friday. And my credit card has gone, too. You've just got to help me ... I don't know what to do ... I can't pay the hotel bill or anything ... Can you arrange a refund for me or something? I'm staying at the Holiday Inn on Avenue ... *(cut off)*

Unit 6, Exercise 11 Note-taking

1 *(fade in)*

LOAN ADVISER Do take a seat please, Mrs Linton.

JANE LINTON Thank you. My husband is sorry he can't be here as well. One of our driving instructors is ill and John's had to take over. That's one of the problems of being self-employed, I'm afraid.

LOAN ADVISER Yes, it must be difficult sometimes, especially for a small business like yours. You and your husband have been running your driving school for about ten years now, haven't you?

JANE LINTON Yes, that's right. We started our own business in 1992. Of course we've had our ups and downs but generally speaking we've managed quite well on our own.

LOAN ADVISER I'm pleased to hear it – though I gather from my colleague whom you spoke to on the phone that the reason for our meeting today is more personal than anything to do with the business.

JANE LINTON Absolutely. My husband and I would like to extend our home. John's father is planning to come and live with us, so we'll have to have an extra bathroom put in and make various other alterations.

LOAN ADVISER Your house is your own property isn't it? ... Yes, I've got the details here ... How much do you have in mind?

JANE LINTON Well, the builder has given us an estimate of €15,000 – but John and I think that we should apply for 18,000 – there are bound to be some extra expenses ...

LOAN ADVISER Yes, there always are, aren't they? Let's get a few figures on paper. Your net monthly income is ...

JANE LINTON Our joint income is €6000 on average. Of course sometimes – like in summer – we tend to earn less, but the winter months generally make up for it.

LOAN ADVISER And your average monthly expenditure?

JANE LINTON I've worked that out as €4,200 – on average again of course.

LOAN ADVISER Which leaves us with a disposable income averaging €1,800. Well, as I see it, Mrs Linton from the bank's point of view ...

(fade out)

2 *(fade in)*

LOAN ADVISER Sorry to have kept you waiting, Mr Gates. How do you do? Do take a seat.

ROGER GATES How do you do?

LOAN ADVISER My colleague tells me that you asked for us to meet today because you're planning to buy a computer.

ROGER GATES That's right, though the sort of equipment I need is a bit different from what you've got on your desk.

LOAN ADVISER I expect it is. You need it for your work, I take it.

ROGER GATES That's right. I'm a freelance computer scientist. I help small companies create their own websites.

LOAN ADVISER How long have you been self-employed?

ROGER GATES Oh, for nearly three years now. Obviously it's important for me to keep ahead of the competition – which is why I need a new computer – but I've been doing quite well so far.

LOAN ADVISER And how much would you require?

ROGER GATES I have some savings but I'd need a further €10,000.

LOAN ADVISER I see. Could you tell me your average monthly income and expenditure please?

ROGER GATES Sure. On average I earn €8,000 a month but I have a lot of expenses to cover. I'd put my expenditure at – 6,500 a month.

LOAN ADVISER Hmm – that means 1,500 disposable income – I see that you've had your account with us for over two years. Well, on the basis of what you have told me, Mr Gates, it seems to me that ...

(fade out)

(fade in)

LOAN ADVISER Could you tell me where you are employed, Ms McAllen?

CARRIE MCALLEN I'm a secretary at the consulate. I've been working there for five years now.

LOAN ADVISER And you've had your account with us for the same period, haven't you?

CARRIE MCALLEN That's right. That's why I wanted to ask whether I could apply for a loan. You see, my father in the States is very ill. I'd like to fly out next week and stay for two weeks with him and Mom.

LOAN ADVISER Oh, I'm sorry to hear about your father. How much were you thinking of borrowing?

CARRIE MCALLEN €600 for the flight – and then I'm going to have to take unpaid leave from my job because I've used up all my holiday for this year already. So I think I'll need another 800 just to tide me over until I'm back on my normal full salary next month.

LOAN ADVISER I see from your file here that your net salary is €1900 at present. How much of that do you need for monthly expenses?

CARRIE MCALLEN 1200 – no, 1250. The rent has just gone up.

LOAN ADVISER Well in that case, Ms McAllen, I don't see any reason why we should ... *(fade out)*

(fade in)

LOAN ADVISER Good morning, Mr Wills. How is your wife?

PHILIP WILLS I'm afraid she still hasn't recovered from the car accident. The doctor doesn't think that she'll be able to work again – and we haven't received a penny in compensation from the insurance company yet.

LOAN ADVISER I'm sorry to hear that. It must be a very difficult situation for you both.

PHILIP WILLS Well, to tell the truth Maria and I are just about coping – it's not easy – we really miss her salary of course, but mine just about covers our expenses – living costs and the mortgage payments on the house and so on, but we've been supporting Alexander, our son, at university and that's our real problem at the moment.

LOAN ADVISER How much have you been giving your son?

PHILIP WILLS €500 a month. We hoped the bank would help us to continue to support him for one more year – then he will be qualified.

LOAN ADVISER I see. Your income is ...

PHILIP WILLS 2900 euros a month, net that is, and all of that more or less goes straight out again in expenses. Perhaps if we could take out a loan of €6000 – just till Alexander passes his exams, then I'm sure that ...

(fade out)

Unit word list

Die neuen Wörter sind in der Reihenfolge des Vorkommens im Text verzeichnet.

Die Zahlen am linken Rand beziehen sich auf die Seitenzahlen.

Die neuen Wörter, die im *Transcript* bzw. in den *Advanced Materials* vorkommen, sind dementsprechend gekennzeichnet.

In den Listen werden folgende Abkürzungen verwendet:
infl. = umgangssprachlich
pl. only = nur Plural
no pl. = kein Plural
AE = Amerikanisches Englisch
BE = Britisches Englisch

UNIT 1

7	**introduce** [ˌɪntrəˈdjuːs]	vorstellen, einführen
	service [ˈsɜːvɪs]	Dienst(leistung)
	sales assistant [ˈseɪlz əsɪstənt]	Verkäufer/in
	portable [ˈpɔːtəbl]	tragbar
	shelf [ʃelf]	Regal(brett)
	have a closer look at [həv ə ˈkləʊsə lʊk ət]	genauer ansehen
	here you are [hɪə ju ˈɑː]	bitte
	in stock [ɪn ˈstɒk]	vorrätig
	don't bother [dəʊnt ˈbɒðə]	bemühen Sie sich nicht
	including [ɪnˈkluːdɪŋ]	einschließlich, inbegriffen
	VAT (= value-added tax) [ˌviː eɪ ˈtiː, ˌvæljuː ˈædɪd tæks]	Mehrwertsteuer
8	**bargain** [ˈbɑːgɪn]	Schnäppchen
	on (special) offer [ɒn ˌspeʃl ˈɒfə]	im (Sonder)angebot
	run out of [ˌrʌn ˈaʊt əv]	ausgehen, zu Ende gehen
	cheque [tʃek]	Scheck
	(euro)cheque card [ˈjʊərəʊtʃek kɑːd]	(Euro-)Scheckkarte
	credit card [ˈkredɪt kɑːd]	Kreditkarte
	hang on (infl.) [ˌhæŋ ˈɒn]	warten
	just about [dʒʌst əˈbaʊt]	gerade noch
	pay in cash [peɪ ɪn ˈkæʃ]	bar bezahlen
	note [nəʊt]	Geldschein
	get rid of [get ˈrɪd əv]	loswerden
	coin [kɔɪn]	Münze
	make out [ˌmeɪk ˈaʊt]	ausstellen
	till [tɪl]	(Laden-)Kasse
	colleague [ˈkɒliːg]	Kollege, Kollegin
	receipt [rɪˈsiːt]	Quittung, Beleg
	play the drums [ˌpleɪ ðə ˈdrʌmz]	Schlagzeug spielen
	by the way [baɪ ðə ˈweɪ]	übrigens
	means of payment [ˌmiːnz əv ˈpeɪmənt]	Zahlungsmittel
	mention [ˈmenʃn]	erwähnen, nennen
	method of payment [ˌmeθəd əv ˈpeɪmənt]	Zahlungsweise
	goods [gʊdz]	Ware(n), Güter (pl. only)
9	**occur** [əˈkɜː]	geschehen, vorkommen
	fellow student [ˌfeləʊ ˈstjuːdnt]	Kursteilnehmer/in
	trainee [treɪˈniː]	Auszubildende/r, Praktikant/in
	(bank) clerk [bæŋk klɑːk]	(Bank-)Angestellte/r
	savings bank [ˈseɪvɪŋz bæŋk]	Sparkasse
10	**branch** [brɑːntʃ]	Filiale, Zweig(stelle)
	manager [ˈmænɪdʒə]	(Filial-)Leiter/in
	customer service officer [ˌkʌstəmə ˈsɜːvɪs ɒfɪsə]	Kundenberater/in
	investment consultant [ɪnˌvestmənt kənˈsʌltənt]	Anlage-, Vermögensberater/in
	personal loan adviser [ˌpɜːsənl ˈləʊn ədvaɪzə]	Kleinkreditberater/in
	corporate business [ˌkɔːpərət ˈbɪznəs]	Firmenkunden-(geschäft)
	cashier [kæˈʃɪə]	Kassierer/in
	counter [ˈkaʊntə]	Schalter
	back office [ˌbæk ˈɒfɪs]	Büro
	account [əˈkaʊnt]	Konto
	department [dɪˈpɑːtmənt]	Abteilung
	insurance (policy) [ɪnˈʃʊərəns pɒləsi]	Versicherung(spolice)
	building society (policy) [ˌbɪldɪŋ səsaɪəti ˈpɒləsi]	Bausparkasse, -vertrag
	lift [lɪft]	Fahrstuhl, Aufzug
	securities [sɪkˈjʊərətiz]	Wertpapiere, Effekten
	strongroom [ˈstrɒŋruːm]	(Bank-)Tresor, Stahlkammer
	lobby [ˈlɒbi]	Foyer, Eingangshalle
	statement printer [ˈsteɪtmənt prɪntə]	Kontoauszugsdrucker
	cash dispenser [ˈkæʃ dɪspensə]	(Bar-)Geldautomat
	private consulting room [ˌpraɪvət kənˈsʌltɪŋ ruːm]	Beratungs-, Sprechzimmer

TRANSCRIPT

	credit (no pl.) ['kredɪt]	Kredit
11	**serve** [sɜːv]	bedienen
	used to work [ˌjuːs tə 'wɜːk]	arbeitete(n) früher
	wage(s) ['weɪdʒɪz]	Lohn
	current account ['kʌrənt əkaʊnt]	Girokonto, Kontokorrentkonto
	employer [ɪm'plɔɪə]	Arbeitgeber/in
	transfer [træns'fɜː]	überweisen
	salary ['sæləri]	Gehalt
	take a seat [teɪk ə siːt]	Platz nehmen
	savings (pl. only) ['seɪvɪŋz]	Ersparnisse
	savings account ['seɪvɪŋz əkaʊnt]	Sparkonto
	interest rate ['ɪntrəst reɪt]	Zinssatz, -rate
	return [rɪ'tɜːn]	Gewinn, Ertrag
	advice (no pl.) [əd'vaɪs]	Ratschlag, (guter) Rat
	invest [ɪn'vest]	investieren, anlegen
	rate of exchange [ˌreɪt əv ɪks'tʃeɪndʒ]	Wechselkurs
	change [tʃeɪndʒ]	(aus)wechseln, (um)tauschen
	currency ['kʌrənsi]	Währung
	cash [kæʃ]	bar einlösen
	traveller's cheque ['trævələz tʃek]	Reisescheck
	charge [tʃɑːdʒ]	berechnen
	matter ['mætə]	Angelegenheit
	afraid (I'm ~) [aɪm ə'freɪd]	leider
	appointment [ə'pɔɪntmənt]	Termin
	convenient [kən'viːniənt]	passend
	get held up [get ˌheld 'ʌp]	aufgehalten werden
	traffic ['træfɪk]	(Straßen-)Verkehr
	instead [ɪnsted]	stattdessen, anstatt
12	**personal customer** [ˌpɜːsənl 'kʌstəmə]	Privatkunde, -kundin
	corporate client [ˌkɔːpərət 'klaɪənt]	Firmenkunde, -kundin
	keep (accounts) [kiːp ə'kaʊnts]	(Konten) führen
	deposit account [dɪ'pɒzɪt əkaʊnt]	Sparkonto, Festgeldkonto
	safe custody account [seɪf 'kʌstədi əkaʊnt]	Depotkonto, Effektendepot
	grant [grɑːnt]	gewähren, bewilligen
	personal loan [ˌpɜːsənl 'ləʊn]	Privatkredit, Privatdarlehen
	overdraft ['əʊvədrɑːft]	Kontoüberziehung, Überziehungskredit
	investment [ɪn'vestmənt]	Investition, Anlage
	supply [sə'plaɪ]	(be)liefern, versorgen
	foreign currency [ˌfɒrən 'kʌrənsi]	Sorten, Fremdwährung
	financing [faɪ'nænsɪŋ]	Finanzierung
	corporate loan [ˌkɔːpərət 'ləʊn]	Firmendarlehen
	issue ['ɪʃuː]	Ausgabe, Emission
	letter of credit [ˌletər əv 'kredɪt]	Akkreditiv
	safeguard ['seɪfgɑːd]	sicher aufbewahren
	valuables ['væljuəblz]	Wertsachen
	credit transfer ['kredɪt trænsfɜː]	Überweisung
	standing order [ˌstændɪŋ 'ɔːdə]	Dauerauftrag
	direct debit [dəˌrekt 'debɪt]	Abbuchungs-, Einzugsverfahren, Lastschrift
13	**appropriate** [ə'prəʊpriət]	geeignet, passend
	suggestion [sə'dʒestʃən]	Vorschlag
	inherit [ɪn'herɪt]	erben
	outside banking hours [ˌaʊtsaɪd 'bæŋkɪŋ aʊəz]	außerhalb der Öffnungszeiten
	driving lesson ['draɪvɪŋ 'lesn]	Fahrstunde
	advisable [əd'vaɪzəbl]	ratsam
	obtain [əb'teɪn]	erhalten, erlangen
14	**brochure** ['brəʊʃə]	Broschüre, Prospekt
	contact ['kɒntækt]	Kontakt, Verbindung
	keep in touch [ˌkiːp ɪn 'tʌtʃ]	in Verbindung bleiben
	convenience [kən'viːniəns]	Komfort, Annehmlichkeit
	abroad [ə'brɔːd]	(im) Ausland
	balance ['bæləns]	Kontostand, Saldo
	access ['ækses]	Zugang, Zugriff
	complicated [kɒmplɪkeɪtɪd]	kompliziert
	on-screen [ˌɒn'skriːn]	auf dem Bildschirm
	view [vjuː]	sich ansehen
	recent ['riːsnt]	letzte(r,s), jüngst
	what is more [wɒt ɪz 'mɔː]	darüber hinaus
	chequebook ['tʃekbʊk]	Scheckbuch, -heft
	paying-in book [ˌpeɪɪŋ 'ɪn bʊk]	Einzahlungsheft
	set up [ˌset 'ʌp]	eröffnen, einrichten
	regular [regjələ]	regelmäßig
	at the touch of a button [ət ðə ˌtʌtʃ əv ə 'bʌtn]	auf Knopfdruck
	local rate [ˌləʊkəl 'reɪt]	Ortsgebühr
	support [sə'pɔːt]	Unterstützung, (technische) Hilfe
	apply (for) [ə'plaɪ fə]	beantragen
	local ['ləʊkl]	örtlich, lokal
	do business [du bɪznəs]	Geschäfte machen
	include [ɪn'kluːd]	einbeziehen

ADVANCED MATERIALS

15	**topic** ['tɒpɪk]	Thema
	overcome [ˌəʊvə'kʌm]	überwinden
	attract [ə'trækt]	anziehen, anlocken
	suggest [sə'dʒest]	vorschlagen
	sector ['sektə]	Sektor, Bereich
	staff [stɑːf]	Personal
16	**delivery** [dɪ'lɪvəri]	(Aus-)Lieferung
	high net-worth [haɪ 'netwɜːθ]	vermögend
	educated professional [ˌedʒukeɪtɪd prə'feʃənl]	Akademiker/in
	time-starved ['taɪmstɑːvd]	in Zeitnot, unter Zeitdruck
	value ['væljuː]	schätzen
	value ['væljuː]	Wert, Nutzen
	enhancement [ɪn'hɑːnsmənt]	Erhöhung, Steigerung
	educational headstart [edʒuˌkeɪʃənl 'hedstɑːt]	Bildungsvorsprung
	thus [ðʌs]	so, somit
	capture ['kæptʃə]	einfangen
	account holder [ə'kaʊnt həʊldə]	Kontoinhaber/in
	consumer [kən'sjuːmə]	Verbraucher/in
	disabled [dɪs'eɪbld]	behindert
	shift work ['ʃɪft wɜːk]	Schichtarbeit
	ultimately ['ʌltɪmətli]	schließlich, letzten Endes
	economics [ˌiːkə'nɒmɪks]	Wirtschaft(lichkeit)
	research [rɪ'sɜːtʃ]	Forschung
	achieve [ə'tʃiːv]	erreichen, erlangen
	process ['prəʊses]	bearbeiten
	maintain [meɪn'teɪn]	aufrechterhalten
	favourably ['feɪvərəbli]	vorteilhaft, günstig
	affect [ə'fekt]	sich auswirken auf, beeinflussen
	warm body [wɔːm 'bɒdi]	lebende Person
	in the long term [ɪn ðə lɒŋ 'tɜːm]	auf die Dauer
	ATM (automatic teller machine) [ˌeɪ tiː 'em]	Geldautomat
	withdraw [wɪð'drɔː]	abheben
	outlay ['aʊtleɪ]	Ausgaben, -lagen
	tinker around with [ˌtɪŋkər ə'raʊnd wɪð]	herumpfuschen mit
	viable ['vaɪəbl]	brauchbar, rentabel
	appeal to [ə'piːl tə]	zusagen, ansprechen
	applicable [ə'plɪkəbl]	anwendbar, zutreffend
	citizen ['sɪtɪzn]	(Staats-)Bürger/in
	presentment [prɪ'zentmənt]	Zustellung
	carry little weight [ˌkæri lɪtl 'weɪt]	wenig gelten
	guarantor [ˌgærən'tɔː]	Bürge, Garant
	fraudulent ['frɔːdjələnt]	betrügerisch
	accurate [ækjərət]	genau
	range from … to … [reɪndʒ frəm, tə]	reichen von … bis …
	pure [pjʊə]	rein
	enquiry [ɪn'kwaɪəri]	Abfrage
	forex = foreign exchange [ˌfɒrən ɪks'tʃeɪndʒ]	Fremdwährung(en), Devisen
	purchase ['pɜːtʃəs]	(Ein-)Kauf
	shopping mall ['ʃɒpɪŋ mæl]	Einkaufspassage
	have a broader appeal [həv ə ˌbrɔːdər ə'piːl]	größeren Anklang finden
	debt [det]	Schuld(en)
	mortgage ['mɔːgɪdʒ]	Hypothek
	area [eəriə]	Gegend, Gebiet
	pan-European [ˌpænjʊərə'piːən]	gesamteuropäisch
	submit to [səb'mɪt tə]	sich unterwerfen
	brand leader [brænd 'liːdə]	führendes Produkt am Markt

UNIT 2

17	**R.I.P.= Rest in Peace** [ˌɑːr aɪ 'piː]	Ruhe in Frieden
	approach [ə'prəʊtʃ]	sich wenden an
18	**suggest** [sə'dʒest]	vorschlagen
	basic ['beɪsɪk]	grundsätzlich, Grund-
	free of charge [friː əv 'tʃɑːdʒ]	kostenlos, gebührenfrei
	actually ['æktʃuəli]	eigentlich, tatsächlich
	be eligible ['elɪdʒəbl]	in Frage kommen, berechtigt sein
	contract ['kɒntrækt]	Vertrag
	suitable ['suːtəbl]	geeignet, passend, angemessen
	withdraw [wɪð'drɔː]	abheben
	operate ['ɒpəreɪt]	bedienen
	ATM (automatic teller machine) [ˌeɪ tiː 'em]	Geldautomat
	period of notice [ˌpɪəriəd əv 'nəʊtɪs]	Kündigungsfrist
	withdrawal [wɪð'drɔːəl]	Abhebung
	give notice [ˌgɪv 'nəʊtɪs]	kündigen
	pay in(to) ['peɪ ɪntə]	einzahlen
	overdraft facility [ˌəʊvədrɑːft fə'sɪləti]	Dispositionskredit
	overdraw [ˌəʊvə'drɔː]	überziehen
	interest (no pl.) ['ɪntrəst]	Zins(en)
	debit balance ['debɪt bæləns]	Soll(saldo)
	go into the red [ˌgəʊ ɪntə ðə 'red]	in die roten Zahlen geraten
	penalty ['penlti]	Strafe
	fee [fiː]	Gebühr

	credit balance ['kredɪt bæləns]	Habensaldo, Guthaben
	rate of interest [reɪt əv 'ɪntrəst]	Zinssatz
	depend on [dɪpend ɒn]	abhängig sein von, darauf ankommen
	skip [skip]	überspringen
	likely [laɪkli]	wahrscheinlich
	charge [tʃɑ:dʒ]	Gebühr
	definitely ['defɪnətli]	bestimmt, auf jeden Fall
19	**you're welcome** [jɔ: 'welkəm]	nichts zu danken, bitte (schön)
	as regards [əz rɪ'gɑ:dz]	bezüglich, was anbetrifft
	feature ['fi:tʃə]	Merkmal
	term [tɜ:m]	Ausdruck
	regularly [regjələli]	regelmäßig
	irregularly [ɪregjələli]	unregelmäßig
	print [prɪnt]	(aus)drucken
	amount [ə'maʊnt]	Summe, Betrag
	account holder [ə'kaʊnt həʊldə]	Kontoinhaber/in
	booklet [bʊklət]	Büchlein, Heft
20	**save** [seɪv]	(ein)sparen
	single ['sɪŋgl]	unverheiratet, ledig
	traineeship [treɪ'ni:ʃɪp]	Ausbildung- (sverhältnis)
	catering [keɪtərɪŋ]	Gastronomie
	inexpensive [ˌɪnɪk'spensɪv]	preiswert
	run short of [rʌn 'ʃɔ:t əv]	knapp werden mit
	divorced [dɪ'vɔ:st]	geschieden
	widowed ['wɪdəʊd]	verwitwet
	retired [rɪ'taɪəd]	pensioniert, im Ruhestand
	pension ['penʃn]	Rente, Pension
	earn interest [ɜ:n 'ɪntrəst]	Zinsen erhalten
	disconnect ˌdɪskə'nekt]	abschalten
21	**statement** ['steɪtmənt]	Aussage
	do military service [du 'mɪlətri sɜ:vɪs]	Militärdienst leisten
	do community service [du ˌkə'mju:nəti sɜ:vɪs]	Zivildienst leisten
22	**extract** ['ekstrækt]	Auszug
	long-term [ˌlɒŋ 'tɜ:m]	langfristig
	when it comes to … [wen ɪt 'kʌmz tə]	wenn es um … geht
	make sense [meɪk 'sens]	sinnvoll sein
	sound [saʊnd]	gesund
	subject to ['sʌbdʒekt tə]	abhängig von
	thereof [ðeər'ɒv]	davon
	rise [raɪz]	(an)steigen, anwachsen, sich erhöhen
	notice account ['nəʊtɪs əkaʊnt]	Konto mit Kündigung(sfrist)
	gross [grəʊs]	brutto
	current ['kʌrənt]	aktuell, gegenwärtig
	restriction [rɪ'strɪkʃn]	Einschränkung
	advertise ['ædvətaɪz]	werben (für)
	similar [sɪmələ]	ähnlich
	terms [tɜ:mz]	Bedingungen, Konditionen
23	**entry** ['entri]	Eintrag, Buchung
	debit ['debɪt]	belasten, abbuchen; Abbuchung
	credit [ˌkredɪt]	gutschreiben; Gutschrift
	(bank) statement ['bæŋk steɪtmənt]	Kontoauszug
	statement of account [steɪtmənt əv ə'kaʊnt]	Kontoauszug
	keep track of [ki:p 'træk əv]	verfolgen
	task [tɑ:sk]	Aufgabe
24	**retirement** [rɪ'taɪəmənt]	(Eintritt in den) Ruhestand, Pensionierung
	divide [dɪ'vaɪd]	(sich) teilen
	need [ni:d]	Bedürfnis
	target ['tɑ:gɪt]	Ziel
	invent [ɪn'vent]	erfinden
	suit [su:t]	passen (zu)
	visual aids ['vɪʒuəl eɪdz]	Visualisierungsmittel
	pin board ['pɪn bɔ:d]	Pinwand
	ADVANCED MATERIALS	
25	**a range of** [ə 'reɪndʒ əv]	eine Reihe von
	application [ˌæplɪ'keɪʃn]	Antrag
	leaflet [li:flət]	Broschüre
	instant ['ɪnstənt]	sofortig
	outstanding [aʊt'stændɪŋ]	hervorragend
	expertise [ˌekspɜ:'ti:z]	Sachkenntnis
	committed to [kə'mɪtɪd tə]	engagiert für
	value for money [ˌvælju: fə 'mʌni]	ein gutes Preis-Leistungsverhältnis
	consistently [kən'sɪstəntli]	ständig
	competitive [kəm'petətɪv]	wettbewerbs-, konkurrenzfähig
	straightforward [ˌstreɪt'fɔ:wəd]	einfach
	jargon ['dʒɑ:gən]	Fachsprache
	knowledgeable ['nɒlɪdʒəbl]	kenntnisreich
26	**to my mind** [tə maɪ 'maɪnd]	meiner Meinung nach
	weigh up the pros and cons [ˌweɪ 'ʌp ðə ˌprəʊz ənd 'kɒnz]	das Für und Wider abwägen
	serious ['sɪəriəs]	ernst(haft)
	beat sb at their own game [ˌbi:t ət ðeər əʊn 'geɪm]	jdn mit den eigenen Waffen schlagen

UNIT 3

	keen [ki:n]	interessiert
	enquire [ɪn'kwaɪə]	sich erkundigen
	hold the line [həʊld ðə 'laɪn]	bleiben Sie am Apparat
	I'll put you through [aɪl ˌpʊt ju 'θru:]	ich verbinde
	engaged [ɪn'geɪdʒd]	besetzt
28	**leave a message** [li:v ə 'mesɪdʒ]	eine Nachricht hinterlassen
	urgent ['ɜ:dʒənt]	dringend, eilig
	legal ['li:gl]	juristisch
	power of attorney [ˌpaʊər əv ə'tɜ:ni]	(Handlungs-) Vollmacht
	authority for per pro signatory [ɔ:ˌθɒrəti fə pɜ: ˌprəʊ 'sɪgnətri]	Kontovollmacht
	authorize, authorise ['ɔ:θəraɪz]	bevollmächtigen
	as well [əz wel]	auch (noch), ebenfalls
	sole [səʊl]	alleinig
	close [kləʊz]	schließen
	equal rights [ˌi:kwəl 'raɪts]	gleiche Rechte
	joint account [dʒɔɪnt ə'kaʊnt]	Gemeinschaftskonto
	get a divorce [get ə dɪ'vɔ:s]	sich scheiden lassen
	proof of identity [pru:f əv aɪ'dentəti]	Identitätsbeweis
	proof of legal residence [ˌpru:f əv ˌli:gl 'rezɪdəns]	Meldebescheinigung
	certificate [sə'tɪfɪkət]	Bescheinigung
	residents' registration office [ˌrezɪdənts ˌredʒɪ'streɪʃn ɒfɪs]	Einwohnermeldeamt
	sign [saɪn]	unterschreiben
	application form [ˌæplɪ'keɪʃn fɔ:m]	Antragsformular
	specimen signature [ˌspesɪmən 'sɪgnətʃə]	Unterschriftsprobe
	comparison [kəm'pærɪsn]	Vergleich
	examine [ɪg'zæmɪn]	prüfen
	signature ['sɪgnətʃə]	Unterschrift
	genuine ['dʒenjuɪn]	echt
	prevent [prɪ'vent]	verhindern
	unauthorized [ˌʌn'ɔ:θəraɪzd]	unbefugt
	(for your own) protection [fə jɔ:r əʊn prə'tekʃn]	(zu Ihrem eigenen) Schutz
29	**correspond to** [ˌkɒrɪ'spɒnd tə]	entsprechen
	protect [prə'tekt]	schützen
	prove [pru:v]	beweisen
	act on one's own account [ˌækt ɒn wʌnz əʊn ə'kaʊnt]	auf eigene Rechnung handeln
	advise [əd'vaɪz]	(be)raten
30	**except for** [ɪksept fə]	außer, ausgenommen
	auxiliary (verb) [ɔ:g'zɪliəri vɜ:b]	Hilfsverb
	reverse [rɪ'vɜ:s]	vertauschen
	previously ['pri:viəsli]	vorher
	change [tʃeɪndʒ]	ändern
31	**polite(ly)** [pə'laɪt]	höflich
	phrase [freɪz]	(Rede-)Wendung, Ausdruck
32	**would you mind (+ -ing form)** [wʊd ju 'maɪnd]	würden Sie bitte
	inconvenient [ˌɪnkən'vi:niənt]	unbequem
	postpone [pə'spəʊn]	verschieben
33	**in writing** [ɪn 'raɪtɪŋ]	schriftlich
	on my behalf [ɒn maɪ bɪ'hɑ:f]	in meinem Namen
	draft [drɑ:ft]	Tratte
	bill of exchange [bɪl əv ɪkstʃeɪndʒ]	Wechsel
	promissory note [prɒmɪsəri nəʊt]	Schuldschein, Solawechsel
	honour [ɒnə]	bezahlen, einlösen
	concerned [kən'sɜ:nd]	betroffen
	designated ['dezɪgneɪtɪd]	bestimmt
	numbered ['nʌmbəd]	nummeriert
	relating to [rɪ'leɪtɪŋ]	betreffend, in Zusammenhang mit
	deal with ['di:l wɪð]	sich befassen mit, umgehen mit
	property ['prɒpəti]	Eigentum, Besitz
	indemnity [ɪn'demnəti]	Verpflichtung-(serklärung)
	instruction [ɪn'strʌkʃn]	Anweisung
	circumstance ['sɜ:kəmstəns]	Umstand, Bedingung
	delete [dɪ'li:t]	durchstreichen
	require [rɪkwaɪə]	benötigen, auf-, erfordern
34	**identification** [aɪˌdentɪfɪ'keɪʃn]	Legitimation, Identifizierung
	money laundering [ˌmʌni 'lɔ:ndərɪŋ]	Geldwäsche
	Money Laundering Act [ˌmʌni 'lɔ:ndərɪŋ ækt]	Geldwäschegesetz
	credit reference agency [ˌkredɪt 'refərəns eɪdʒənsi]	Kreditauskunftei
	applicant ['æplɪkənt]	Antragsteller/in
	General Business Conditions [ˌdʒenrəl 'bɪznəs kəndɪʃnz]	Allgemeine Geschäftsbedingungen

	govern ['gʌvn]	regeln
	SCHUFA declaration [ˌʃu:fə ˌdekləˈreɪʃn]	SCHUFA-Klausel
35	**first name** ['fɜ:st neɪm]	Vorname
	surname ['sɜ:neɪm]	Nach-, Familienname
	date of birth [ˌdeɪt əv 'bɜ:θ]	Geburtsdatum
	place of birth [ˌpleɪs əv 'bɜ:θ]	Geburtsort
	maiden name ['meɪdn neɪm]	Mädchenname
	residential status [reziˌdenʃl 'steɪtəs]	Wohnverhältnis
	marital status [ˌmærɪtl 'steɪtəs]	Familienstand
	self-employed [ˌself ɪm'plɔɪd]	selbstständig
	occupation [ˌɒkju'peɪʃn]	ausgeübter Beruf
	pursuant to [pə'sju:ənt tə]	gemäß, entsprechend
	ADVANCED MATERIALS	
36	**high street bank** [ˌhaɪ stri:t 'bæŋk]	Geschäfts-, Großbank
	TRANSCRIPT	
	organize ['ɔ:gənaɪz]	organisieren
	front-line staff [ˌfrʌnt 'laɪn stɑ:f]	Kundenberater/in
	head office [ˌhed 'ɒfɪs]	Zentrale
	outsource ['aʊtsɔ:s]	auslagern
	customer account manager [ˌkʌstəmə ə'kaʊnt mænɪdʒə]	Kundenkonten-betreuer/in
	average ['ævərɪdʒ]	Durchschnitts-
	care (take ~ of) [teɪk 'keər əv]	sich kümmern um
	affluent ['æfluənt]	wohlhabend
	consultant [kən'sʌltənt]	Berater/in
	make a distinction [meɪk ə dɪ'stɪŋkʃn]	einen Unterschied machen
	turnover ['tɜ:nəʊvə]	Umsatz
	commercial officer [kə'mɜ:ʃl 'ɒfɪsə]	Handels-, Geschäfts- (leitende/r) Angestellte/r
	cashpoint ['kæʃpɔɪnt]	Geldautomat
	deposit box [dɪ'pɒzɪt]	Nachttresor
	(be) available [bi ə'veɪləbl]	zur Verfügung (stehen)
	basically ['beɪsɪkli]	im Grunde
	provision [prə'vɪʒn]	Bereitstellung
	recurring [rɪ'kɜ:rɪŋ]	wiederkehrend
	encourage [ɪn'kʌrɪdʒ]	auffordern
	merge [mɜ:dʒ]	fusionieren, sich zusammenschließen
	life assurance ['laɪf əʃʊərəns]	Lebensversicherung
	reference ['refərəns]	Referenz, Empfehlungs-schreiben
	be credit-scored [bi 'kredɪt skɔ:d]	einer Kreditprüfung unterziehen
	assess [ə'ses]	ab-, einschätzen, beurteilen
	nought [nɔ:t]	Null
	score [skɔ:]	Punktestand
	determine [dɪ'tɜ:mɪn]	bestimmen, festlegen
	probationary period [prəˌbeɪʃnri 'pɪəriəd]	Probezeit
	review [rɪ'vju:]	(Über-)Prüfung, Bericht
	TRANSCRIPT	
	upgraded [ˌʌp'greɪdɪd]	aufgewertet
	activity migration [æk'tɪvəti maɪ'greiʃn]	Verlagerung der Bankgeschäfte
	benefit ['benɪfɪt]	Vorteil, Vergünstigung
	backed by [bækt baɪ]	unterstützt von
	navy blue [ˌneɪvi 'blu:]	marineblau
	wear and tear [ˌweər ən 'teə]	Abnutzung, Verschleiß
	vocational school [vəʊˌkeɪʃənl 'sku:l]	Berufsschule
	on the job [ɒn ðə ˌdʒɒb]	im Beruf, bei der Arbeit
	mandatory ['mændətəri]	vorgeschrieben
	sit an exam [ˌsɪt ən ɪg'zæm]	eine Prüfung machen
	envious ['enviəs]	neidisch
	counterpart ['kaʊntəpɑ:t]	Gegenüber
	similarity [ˌsɪmə'lærəti]	Ähnlichkeit
37	**chief executive (officer) (CEO)** [ˌtʃi:f ɪg'zekjətɪv ɒfɪsə]	Vorstandsvorsitz-ende/r
	pursue [pə'sju:]	verfolgen
	governing ['gʌvənɪŋ]	vorrangig
	objective [əb'dʒektɪv]	Ziel, Zweck
	progress ['prəʊgres]	Fortschritt/e
	enhance [ɪn'hɑ:ns]	erhöhen, steigern
	product range ['prɒdʌkt reɪndʒ]	Produktpalette
	augment [ɔ:g'ment]	vergrößern
	comprehensive [ˌkɒmprɪ'hensɪv]	umfassend
	extend [ɪk'stend]	ausdehnen, erweitern
	extent [ɪk'stent]	(Aus-)Maß
	second to none [ˌsekənd tə 'nʌn]	unübertroffen, unerreicht
	revenue generation [ˌrevənju: ˌdʒenə'reɪʃn]	Erzielung von Erträgen
	sustain [sə'steɪn]	aufrechterhalten
	drive down ['draɪv daʊn]	verringern
	operating costs ['ɒpəreɪtɪŋ kɒsts]	Betriebskosten
	resources [rɪ'sɔ:sɪz]	Mittel, Ressourcen
	attainment [ə'teɪnmənt]	Erreichung

merger ['mɜːdʒə]	Fusion, Zusammenschluss
significant [sɪg'nɪfɪkənt]	bedeutend, wichtig
achievement [ə'tʃiːvmənt]	Leistung, Errungenschaft
accordingly [ə'kɔːdɪŋli]	(dem)entsprechend
commence [kə'mens]	beginnen
efficiency [ɪ'fɪʃnsi]	Leistungsfähigkeit
incur [ɪn'kɜː]	eingehen
ratio ['reɪʃiəʊ]	Verhältnis
subsequent ['sʌbsɪkwənt]	(nach)folgend
focus on ['fəʊkəs ɒn]	sich konzentrieren auf
large scale ['lɑːdʒ skeɪl]	groß angelegt
facilitate [fə'sɪlɪteɪt]	erleichtern
look ahead [ˌlʊk ə'hed]	vorausschauen
commitment [kə'mɪtmənt]	Einsatz, Engagement
pace [peɪs]	Tempo
scope [skəʊp]	Umfang
diminish [dɪ'mɪnɪʃ]	abnehmen, sich verringern
adapt to [ə'dæpt tə]	sich anpassen an
acquisition [ˌækwɪ'zɪʃn]	Erwerb, Zukauf
restless ['restləs]	unermüdlich
pursuit of [pə'sjuːt əv]	Streben nach, Trachten nach
effort ['efət]	Mühe, Bemühung, Anstrengung

UNIT 4

38 **communication** [kəˌmjuːnɪ'keɪʃn]	Schreiben
provide [prə'vaɪd]	liefern, bieten
refund ['riːfʌnd]	Rückzahlung, Erstattung
owe [əʊ]	schulden
freepost envelope [ˌfriːpəʊst 'envələʊp]	Freiumschlag
Yours faithfully [jɔːz 'feɪθfəli]	Mit freundlichen Grüßen, Hochachtungsvoll
army colonel [ˌɑːmi 'kɜːnl]	Armeeoberst
join a club [dʒɔɪn ə 'klʌb]	einem Klub beitreten
recently ['riːsntli]	neulich, vor kurzem
pronounce [prə'naʊns]	aussprechen
let alone [let ə'ləʊn]	geschweige denn
direct debit authorization [dəˌrekt 'debɪt ˌɔːθəraɪ'zeɪʃn]	Einzugsermächtigung
membership dues ['membəʃɪp djuːz]	Mitgliedsbeitrag
39 **forward to** ['fɔːwəd tə]	senden an
payee [ˌpeɪ'iː]	Zahlungsempfänger
purpose ['pɜːpəs]	Zweck
due [djuː]	fällig
help oneself to sth ['help wʌnself tə]	sich (einer Sache) bedienen
revoke [rɪ'vəʊk]	rückgängig machen, zurückziehen
Why bother? [waɪ 'bɒðə]	Wozu das alles?
rent [rent]	Miete
these days [ðiːz 'deɪz]	heutzutage
vary [veəri]	wechseln, variieren
claim [kleɪm]	einziehen
rely on [rɪ'laɪ ɒn]	sich verlassen auf
punctual(ly) [pʌŋktʃuəli]	pünktlich
reminder [rɪ'maɪndə]	Mahnung
rule [ruːl]	beherrschen
nowadays [na'ʊ ə deɪz]	heutzutage
solve [sɒlv]	lösen
convince [kən'vɪns]	überzeugen
40 **quarterly** ['kwɔːtəli]	vierteljährlich
half yearly [ˌhɑːf 'jɪəli]	halbjährlich
annual(ly) ['ænjuəli]	jährlich
admission fee [əd'mɪʃn fiː]	Aufnahmegebühr
subscription [səb'skrɪpʃn]	Beitrag
42 **take turns** [teɪk 'tɜːnz]	(sich) abwechseln
hardly ['hɑːdli]	kaum
lately ['leɪtli]	in letzter Zeit
behave [bɪ'heɪv]	sich benehmen
43 **irregular** [ɪ'regjələ]	unregelmäßig
insert [ɪn'sɜːt]	einführen
slot [slɒt]	Schlitz
solution [sə'luːʃn]	Lösung
efficient [ɪ'fɪʃnt]	effizient
strict [strɪkt]	streng
monetary policy [ˌmʌnɪtri 'pɒləsi]	Geldpolitik
European Central Bank (ECB) [ˌjʊərəʊˌpiːən 'sentrəl bæŋk]	Europäische Zentralbank
44 **widely used** [ˌwaɪdli 'juːzd]	weit verbreitet
match [mætʃ]	zuordnen
date of issue [ˌdeɪt əv 'ɪʃuː]	Ausstellungsdatum
drawer [drɔː]	Aussteller/in
payer ['peɪə]	Einzahler
figure ['fɪgə]	Zahl, Ziffer
drawee [ˌdrɔː'iː]	Bezogene/r, bezogene Bank
beneficiary [ˌbenɪ'fɪʃəri]	Zahlungsempfänger-/in, Begünstigte(r)
face [feɪs]	Vorderseite
crossed cheque [ˌkrɒst 'tʃek]	Verrechnungsscheck
trace [treɪs]	zurückverfolgen
open cheque [ˌəʊpən 'tʃek]	Barscheck
order cheque ['ɔːdə tʃek]	Orderscheck
recipient [rɪ'sɪpiənt]	Empfänger/in

	endorsement [ɪn'dɔ:smənt]	Indossament, Girierung
	bear [beə]	tragen
	endorse [ɪn'dɔ:s]	indossieren
	bearer cheque ['beərə tʃek]	Überbringerscheck
45	**meaningful** [mi:nɪŋfʊl]	sinnvoll
	perfectly ['pɜ:fɪktli]	völlig
	highly-recognized [ˌhaɪli 'rekəgnaɪzd]	hoch angesehen
	pretty ['prɪti]	ziemlich, recht
	urgently ['ɜ:dʒəntli]	dringend
	putter ['pʌtə]	Putter (Golfschläger)
	clear [klɪə]	abrechnen
	(al)though [ɔ:l'ðəʊ]	obwohl
	every Tom, Dick or Harry [ˌevri ˌtɒm, dɪk ɔ: 'hæri]	jeder Hinz und Kunz
46	**scheme** [ski:m]	Vorhaben, Projekt
	wherever [weə'revə]	wo (immer)
	increasing [ɪn'kri:sɪŋ]	zunehmend
	outlet ['aʊtlet]	Verkaufsstelle
	hand to ['hænd tə]	geben, aushändigen
	sales receipt [ˌseɪlz rɪ'si:t]	Quittung, Kassenbeleg
	working day [wɜ:kɪŋ deɪ]	Werktag
	act as ['ækt əz]	dienen als
	debit card ['debɪt kɑ:d]	Bankkarte, Zahlkarte
47	**draw a cheque** [drɔ: ə 'tʃek]	einen Scheck ausstellen
	prefix ['pri:fɪks]	Vorsilbe
	secure [sɪ'kjuə]	sicher
48	**survey** ['sɜ:veɪ]	Untersuchung, Analyse, Überblick
	attitude ['ætɪtju:d]	Einstellung, Haltung
	alternatively [ɔ:l'tɜ:nətɪvli]	als Alternative, alternativ
	draw conclusions [drɔ: kən'klu:ʒnz]	Schlüsse ziehen
	ADVANCED MATERIALS	
	trademark ['treɪd mɑ:k]	Warenzeichen, Handelsmarke
	circulate ['sɜ:kjəleɪt]	zirkulieren, in Umlauf sein
	founder ['faʊndə]	Gründer/in
	launch [lɔ:ntʃ]	Einführung
	convert [kən'vɜ:t]	umwandeln
	spendable ['spendəbl]	zu verwenden
	in the strictest sense [ɪn ðə ˌstrɪktɪst 'sens]	im strengsten Sinne
	attempt [ə'tempt]	Versuch
	merchant ['mɜ:tʃənt]	Verkäufer, Kaufmann/-frau
	consumer confidence [kən'sju:mə kɒnfɪdəns]	Vertrauen der Verbraucher
	outfit ['aʊtfɪt]	Unternehmen
	reward [rɪ'wɔ:d]	belohnen; Belohnung

	loyalty ['lɔɪəlti]	Treue, Loyalität
	show up [ˌʃəʊ 'ʌp]	erscheinen, auftauchen
	hence [hens]	daher
	chairman ['tʃeəmən]	Vorsitzender
	CEO (chief executive officer) [ˌtʃi:f ɪg'zekjətɪv ɒfɪsə]	Vorstandsvorsitz-ende/r
	wallet ['wɒlɪt]	Brieftasche
	bulge [bʌldʒ]	(sich) wölben, ausbeulen
	co-branded [kəʊ'brændɪd]	mit beiden Markenzeichen
	found [faʊnd]	gründen
	fed up with (be ~) [bi ˌfed 'ʌp wɪð]	es satt haben, die Nase voll haben
	incentive [ɪn'sentɪv]	Anreiz
	grease [gri:s]	schmieren
	burgeoning ['bɜ:dʒənɪŋ]	sprießend, aufkeimend
	token ['təʊkən]	Marke, Chip
	in circulation [ɪn ˌsɜ:kjə'leɪʃn]	in Umlauf
	roughly ['rʌfli]	ungefähr
	equivalent [ɪ'kwɪvələnt]	Entsprechung, entsprechend
	currency float [fləʊt]	Geldmenge
	inducement [ɪn'dju:smənt]	Anreiz
	accumulate [ə'kju:mjəleɪt]	ansammeln
	retailer ['ri:teɪlə]	Einzelhändler/in
	redeem [rɪ'di:m]	einlösen
49	**participate** [pɑ:tɪsɪpeɪt]	teilnehmen
	pricing ['praɪsɪŋ]	Preiskalkulation, -festsetzung
	bypass [baɪpɑ:s]	umgehen
	settlement ['setlmənt]	(Be-)Zahlung, Begleichung
	successor [sək'sesə]	Nachfolger/in
	responsible [rɪ'spɒnsəbl]	verantwortlich

UNIT 5

50	**on Her Majesty's service** [ɒn hə 'mædʒəstiz sɜ:vɪs]	im Dienste Ihrer Majestät
	British Intelligence [ˌbrɪtɪʃ ɪn'telɪdʒəns]	britischer Geheimdienst
	secret service [ˌsi:krət 'sɜ:vɪs]	Geheimdienst
	buzzer ['bʌzə]	Summer
	intercom ['ɪntəkɒm]	Sprechanlage
	What's up? [wɒts 'ʌp]	Was ist los?
	space defence mechanism [ˌspeɪs dɪˌfens 'mekənɪzəm]	Raketenabwehr-programm
51	**Beretta** [bə'retə]	Beretta (Revolver)
	silencer ['saɪlənsə]	Schalldämpfer
	ammunition [ˌæmju'nɪʃn]	Munition

	satellite transmitter ['sætəlaɪt trænsmɪtə]	Satellitensender
	replacement [rɪ'pleɪsmənt]	Ersatz
	stop [stɒp]	sperren (Kreditkarte)
52	**cruise package** ['kru:z pækɪdʒ]	Kreuzfahrt-Pauschalreise
	rental car ['rentl kɑ:]	Mietwagen
	benefit ['benɪfɪt]	Vergünstigung
	frequent flyer [ˌfri:kwənt 'flaɪə]	Vielflieger/in
	select [sɪ'lekt]	auswählen
	fit [fɪt]	passen (zu)
	affordable [ə'fɔ:dəbl]	erschwinglich
	benefit ['benɪfɪt]	Vorteil
	vacation [və'keɪʃn]	Urlaub, Ferien
	variable ['veəriəbl]	veränderlich
	adjust [ə'dʒʌst]	(sich) anpassen
	merchant ['mɜ:tʃənt]	Kaufmann, Kauffrau
	worldwide ['wɜ:ldwaɪd]	weltweit
	cash advance [kæʃ əd'vɑ:ns]	Barvorschuss
	toll-free [ˌtəʊl'fri:]	gebührenfrei
	selection [sɪ'lekʃn]	Auswahl, Angebot
	APR (annual percentage rate) [ˌænjuəl pə'sentɪdʒ reɪt]	Jahreszins
	percentage [pə'sentɪdʒ]	Prozentsatz
	grace period ['greɪs pɪəriəd]	Zahlungsfrist
	maintain [meɪn'teɪn]	unterhalten
	primary ['praɪməri]	primär, erst-
	checking account (AE) ['tʃekɪŋ əkaʊnt]	Scheck-, Gehalts-, Girokonto
	fluctuation [ˌflʌktʃʊ'eɪʃn]	Schwankung
	Prime Rate (AE) [ˌpraɪm 'reɪt]	Kreditzins für erste Adressen
	waive a fee [weɪv ə 'fi:]	auf eine Gebühr verzichten
	mail [meɪl]	(mit der Post) schicken
	card holder ['kɑ:d həʊldə]	Karteninhaber/in
	acceptability [ək'septə'bɪl'ət'i]	Akzeptanz
54	**cover** [kʌvə]	Umschlag, Titelseite
	message ['mesɪdʒ]	Botschaft
55	**launch** [lɔ:ntʃ]	auf den Markt bringen
	innovative ['ɪnəʊveɪtɪv]	innovativ
	attention [ə'tenʃn]	Aufmerksamkeit
	denomination [dɪˌnɒmɪ'neɪʃn]	Nennwert, Wertbezeichnung
	denominations [dɪˌnɒmɪ'neɪʃnz]	Stückelung
	item ['aɪtəm]	Artikel, Gegenstand
	value ['vælju:]	Wert
	refuse [rɪ'fju:z]	ablehnen, sich weigern
	countersign ['kaʊntəsaɪn]	gegenzeichnen
	commission [kə'mɪʃn]	Provision
	equivalent [ɪ'kwɪvələnt]	Gegenwert
56	**additional** [ə'dɪʃnl]	zusätzlich
	handling charge ['hændlɪŋ tʃɑ:dʒ]	Bearbeitungsgebühr
	exchange rate [ɪks'tʃeɪndʒ reɪt]	(Umtausch-)Kurs, Wechselkurs
	stand at ['stænd ət]	stehen bei
57	**… dollars' worth of** ['dɒləz wɜ:θ əv]	im Wert von … Dollar
	queue [kju:]	Reihe, (Warte-)Schlange
	safety precaution [ˌseɪfti prɪ'kɔ:ʃn]	Sicherheitsvorkehrung
	in the presence of [ɪn ðə 'prezns əv]	in Gegenwart
	record [rɪ'kɔ:d]	notieren
	insure [ɪn'ʃʊə]	versichern
	refund ['ri:fʌnd]	Rückzahlung, Erstattung
58	**syllable** ['sɪləbl]	Silbe
	equal ['i:kwəl]	gleich
	gone for good [ˌgɒn fə 'gʊd]	für immer verloren
	exclusive [ɪk'sklu:sɪv]	vornehm
60	**intend** [ɪntend]	vorhaben
	serial number ['sɪəriəl nʌmbə]	Seriennummer, laufende Nummer
	snatch [snætʃ]	schnappen, wegreißen
	cut off [ˌkʌt 'ɒf]	unterbrechen, abgeschnitten

TRANSCRIPT

ADVANCED MATERIALS

61	**smart card** ['smɑ:t kɑ:d]	Scheckkarte (mit Mikrochip)
	magnetic strip [mægˌnetɪk 'strɪp]	Magnetstreifen
	tamper-proof ['tæmpə pru:f]	fälschungssicher
	updatable [ʌp'deɪtəbl]	aktualisierbar
	rechargeable [ˌri:'tʃɑ:dʒəbl]	aufladbar
	divulge [daɪ'vʌldʒ]	bekannt geben
	restricted to [rɪ'strɪktɪd tə]	beschränkt auf
	promotional [prə'məʊʃənl]	Werbe-
	involved in [ɪn'vɒlvd ɪn]	beteiligt an
	postal order ['pəʊstl ɔ:də]	Postanweisung
	ISP (internet service provider) [ˌɪntənet 'sɜ:vɪs prəvaɪdə]	Internet-Provider
	reluctant [rɪ'lʌktənt]	widerwillig, ungern
62	**pave the way** [peɪv ðə 'weɪ]	den Weg ebnen

	decade ['dekeɪd]	Jahrzehnt
	tempted (to be ~) [bi 'temptɪd]	geneigt sein
	exploit [ɪk'splɔɪt]	ausnutzen
	application [ˌæplɪ'keɪʃn]	Anwendung
	encrypt [ɪn'krɪpt]	verschlüsseln
	authenticate [ɔː'θentɪkeɪt]	beglaubigen
	data privacy [ˌdeɪtə 'prɪvəsi]	Datenschutz
	cancellation [ˌkænsə'leɪʃn]	Stornierung
	update [ˌʌp'deɪt]	aktualisieren
	degree [dɪ'griː]	Grad
	padlock ['pædlɒk]	Vorhängeschloss
	insecure [ˌɪnsɪ'kjʊə]	unsicher
	environment [ɪn'vaɪrənmənt]	Umgebung

UNIT 6

63	**familiar** [fə'mɪliə]	vertraut, bekannt
	in fact [ɪn 'fækt]	tatsächlich
	audience ['ɔːdiəns]	Publikum
	season [siːzn]	Saison
	rent [rent]	mieten
	from December onwards [frɒm dɪˌsembər 'ɒnwədz]	ab Dezember
	snag [snæg]	Haken
	landlord ['lændlɔːd]	Wirt, Vermieter
	deposit [dɪ'pɒzɪt]	Anzahlung, Kaution
	I gather [aɪ 'gæðə]	ich vermute
64	**at your disposal** [ət jɔː dɪ'spəʊzl]	zur Verfügung
	extend [ɪk'stend]	erhöhen
	instalment [ɪn'stɔːlmənt]	Rate
	repay [rɪ'peɪ]	zurück-, abzahlen, tilgen
	term [tɜːm]	Laufzeit
	work out cheaper [ˌwɜːk 'aʊt tʃiːpə]	sich als billiger herausstellen
	the small print [ˌsmɔːl 'prɪnt]	das Kleingedruckte
	alternative [ɔːl'tɜːnətɪv]	alternativ
65	**repayment** [rɪ'peɪmənt]	Rückzahlung, Tilgung
	comfortably ['kʌmftəbl]	bequem
	set [set]	festgesetzt
	be preferable to [bi 'prefərəbl tə]	vorzuziehen sein
	borrower ['bɒrəʊə]	Kreditnehmer/in
	short-term [ˌʃɔːt'tɜːm]	kurzfristig
	recommend [ˌrekə'mend]	empfehlen
	home furnishing [həʊm 'fɜːnɪʃɪŋz]	Inneneinrichtung
	home improvement [həʊm ɪm'pruːvmənt]	Renovierung
	unlike [ˌʌn'laɪk]	anders als, im Gegensatz zu
	retail ['riːteɪl]	Einzelhandels-
	tailored ['teɪləd]	maßgeschneidert
	confidence ['kɒnfɪdəns]	(Selbst-)Vertrauen
	standby ['stændbaɪ]	Hilfe
	expense(s) [ɪk'spensɪz]	Ausgabe(n)
	smooth out [ˌsmuːð 'aʊt]	ausgleichen
	expenditure [ɪk'spendɪtʃə]	(Summe der) Ausgaben
	level ['levl]	Höhe
	related to [rɪ'leɪtɪd tə]	verbunden mit
	review [rɪ'vjuː]	überprüfen
	limit ['lɪmɪt]	Grenze
	on a continuous basis [ɒn ə kən'tɪnjuəs 'beɪsɪs]	kontinuierlich
	comforting ['kʌmfətɪŋ]	tröstlich
	flexibility [ˌfleksə'bɪləti]	Flexibilität
	cope (with) ['kəʊp wɪð]	fertig werden mit
	emergency [ɪ'mɜːdʒənsi]	Notfall
	formality [fɔː'mæləti]	Formalität, Förmlichkeit
	bear in mind [ˌbeər ɪn 'maɪnd]	beachten
	trigger ['trɪgə]	auslösen
	otherwise ['ʌðəwaɪz]	sonst
66	**enable** [ɪneɪbl]	ermöglichen
	interruption [ɪntərʌpʃn]	Unterbrechung
	repeatedly [rɪ'piːtɪdli]	wiederholt, mehrfach
67	**out of order** [aʊt əv 'ɔːdə]	außer Betrieb
	frequently ['friːkwəntli]	oft, häufig
	profit ['prɒfɪt]	Profit, Gewinn
68	**household** ['haʊshəʊld]	Haushalt
	assess (for tax purposes) [ə'ses]	veranlagen (steuerlich)
	community of property [kəˌmjuːnəti əv 'prɒpəti]	Gütergemeinschaft
	separation of property [sepəˌreɪʃn əv 'prɒpəti]	Gütertrennung
	abrupt [ə'brʌpt]	abrupt
	introductory [ˌɪntrə'dʌktəri]	Einführungs-
	source of income [ˌsɔːs əv 'ɪnkʌm]	Einkommensquelle
	voluntary ['vɒləntri]	freiwillig
	disclosure [dɪs'kləʊʒə]	(Selbst)auskunft
	confidential [ˌkɒnfɪ'denʃl]	vertraulich
	co-applicant [ˌkəʊ 'æplɪkənt]	Mitantragsteller/in
	residence permit [ˌrezɪdəns 'pɜːmɪt]	Aufenthaltserlaubnis
	system of marital property ['sɪstəm əv 'mærɪtl 'prɒpəti]	Güterstand

	employment status [ɪm'plɔɪmənt steɪtəs]	Beschäftigungs-verhältnis
	civil servant [ˌsɪvl 'sɜ:vənt]	Staatsbeamter, -beamtin
	annual turnover [ˌænjuəl 'tɜ:nəʊvə]	Jahresumsatz
	disposable income [dɪˌspəʊzəbl 'ɪnkʌm]	verfügbares Einkommen
	total ['təʊtl]	Gesamt-
	surplus ['sɜ:pləs]	Überschuss
	name at birth [ˌneɪm ət 'bɜ:θ]	Geburtsname
70	**chart** [tʃɑ:t]	Tabelle
	true APR [tru: ˌeɪ pi: 'ɑ:]	effektiver Jahreszins
	agreement [ə'gri:mənt]	Vertrag, Zusage Vereinbarung
71	**driving instructor** ['draɪvɪŋ instrʌktə]	Fahrlehrer/in
	TRANSCRIPT	
	driving school ['draɪvɪŋ sku:l]	Fahrschule
	ups and downs [ˌʌps ən 'daʊnz]	Höhen und Tiefen
	generally speaking ['dʒenrəli spi:kɪŋ]	im Allgemeinen
	absolutely ['æbsəlu:tli]	absolut
	extend [ɪk'stend]	vergrößern, erweitern
	alteration [ˌɔ:ltə'reɪʃn]	Änderung
	estimate ['estɪmət]	(Kosten-)Voranschlag
	bound to be ['baʊnd tə bi]	mit Sicherheit entstehen
	net [net]	Netto-
	joint income [dʒɔɪnt 'ɪnkʌm]	gemeinsames Einkommen
	on average [ɒn 'ævərɪdʒ]	durchschnittlich
	tend to ['tend tə]	tendieren zu, neigen zu
	make up for sth [meɪk ʌp fə 'sʌmθɪŋ]	etw. ausgleichen
	averaging ['ævərɪdʒɪŋ]	von durchschnittlich
	equipment [ɪ'kwɪpmənt]	Ausrüstung, Geräte
	freelance [fri:lɑ:ns]	freiberuflich
	computer scientist [kəm'pju:tə saɪəntɪst]	Informatiker/in
	obviously ['ɒbviəsli]	offensichtlich, natürlich
	ahead of [ə'hed əv]	voraus
	competition [ˌkɒmpə'tɪʃn]	Konkurrenz
	tide sb over [ˌtaɪd 'əʊvə]	über die Runden kommen
	file [faɪl]	Akte
	recover ['ri:kʌvə]	gesund werden, sich erholen
	compensation [ˌkɒmpen'seɪʃn]	Schaden(s)ersatz, Entschädigung
	living costs [ˌlɪvɪŋ 'kɒsts]	Lebenshaltungs-kosten
	TRANSCRIPT	
	mortgage payments ['mɔ:gɪdʒ peɪmənts]	Hypothekenraten
	continue [kən'tɪnju:]	fortfahren
	support [sə'pɔ:t]	unterstützen
	straight [streɪt]	direkt
	pass an exam [pɑ:s ən ɪg'zæm]	eine Prüfung bestehen
	approve [ə'pru:v]	gutheißen, genehmigen
	decision [dɪ'sɪʒn]	Entscheidung
	deduct [dɪ'dʌkt]	abziehen
	regarding [rɪ'gɑ:dɪŋ]	in Bezug auf
72	**caption** ['kæpʃn]	Bildunterschrift
	unwise [ˌʌn'waɪz]	unklug
	overcommit oneself [ˌəʊvəkə'mɪt]	sich übernehmen
	tempting ['temptɪŋ]	verführerisch
	underestimate [ˌʌndər'estɪmeɪt]	unterschätzen
	ADVANCED MATERIALS	
73	**per capita** [pə 'kæpɪtə]	pro Kopf
	slide down [ˌslaɪd 'daʊn]	hinuntergleiten
	slippery slope [ˌslɪpəri 'sləʊp]	Rutschbahn
	financial literacy [faɪˌnænʃl 'lɪtərəsi]	finanzielle Mündigkeit
	unmanageable [ʌn'mænɪdʒəbl]	unkontrollierbar
	revolving credit [rɪˌvɒlvɪŋ 'kredɪt]	wiederholte Kreditaufnahme
	succumb to sth [sə'kʌm tə]	einer Sache erliegen
	request [rɪ'kwest]	bitten (um)
	slide [slaɪd]	schiefe Ebene
	salesman ['seɪlzmən]	Vertreter
	reimburse [ˌri:ɪm'bɜ:s]	erstatten
	acquire [ə'kwaɪə]	erwerben
	fail [feɪl]	Konkurs machen
	stumble along ['stʌmbl əlɒŋ]	weitere Fehler machen
	eventually [ɪ'ventʃuəli]	zum Schluss
	drip feed [ˌdrɪp 'fi:d]	abstottern
	inundated ['ɪnʌndeɪtɪd]	überschwemmt
	trap [træp]	Falle
	counselling ['kaʊnsəlɪŋ]	Beratung
	charity ['tʃærəti]	Wohltätigkeits-organisation
	reschedule [ˌri:'ʃedju:l]	strecken
	intercede [ˌɪntə'si:d]	vermitteln
	creditor ['kredɪtə]	Gläubiger/in
	credit rating ['kredɪt reɪtɪŋ]	Kreditwürdigkeit
	diabolical [ˌdaɪə'bɒlɪkl]	teuflisch
	legacy ['legəsi]	Vermächtnis, Erbe
74	**credit scoring** ['kredɪt skɔ:rɪŋ]	Feststellung der Kreditwürdigkeit
	be committed [bi: kə'mɪtɪd]	sich verpflichten

	commitment [kə'mɪtmənt]	Verpflichtung
	county court judgement [ˌkaʊnti kɔ:t 'dʒʌdʒmənt]	Amtsgerichtsurteil
	electoral roll [ɪ'lektərəl rəʊl]	Wählerliste
	bankruptcy ['bæŋkrʌpsi]	Bankrott, Konkurs
	insolvency [ɪn'sɒlvənsi]	Zahlungsunfähigkeit, Insolvenz
	in arrears [ɪn ə'rɪəz]	im Rückstand, in Verzug
	credit score ['kredɪt skɔ:]	Kreditrahmen festlegen

UNIT 7

75	**restore** [rɪ'stɔ:]	wiederherstellen
	link [lɪŋk]	Verbindung
	subsidiary [səb'sɪdiəri]	Tochterfirma
	opposite number [ˌɒpəzɪt 'nʌmbə]	Gegenüber
	latest ['leɪtɪst]	neueste(r,s)
	privately-owned ['praɪvətli əʊnd]	im Privatbesitz
	exceed [ɪk'si:d]	übersteigen
76	**contribute** [kən'trɪbju:t]	beisteuern
	real estate ['rɪəl ɪsteɪt]	Immobilien
	favourable ['feɪvərəbl]	günstig
	subsidize ['sʌbsɪdaɪz]	subventionieren
	state [steɪt]	Staat
	in a lump sum [ɪn ə ˌlʌmp 'sʌm]	als einmalige Summe
	shortly ['ʃɔ:tli]	in Kürze
	opportunity [ˌɒpə'tju:nəti]	Gelegenheit
	brush up [ˌbrʌʃ 'ʌp]	aufpolieren
	light engineering [laɪt ˌendʒɪ'nɪərɪŋ]	Feinmechanik
	managing director [ˌmænɪdʒɪŋ də'rektə]	Geschäftsführer/in
77	**criteria for eligibility** [kraɪˌtɪəriə fər ˌelɪdʒə'bɪləti]	Auswahlkriterien
	contribution [ˌkɒntrɪ'bju:ʃn]	Beitrag, Eigengeld
	found [faʊnd]	gründen
	in the thirties [ɪn ðə 'θɜ:tiz]	in den Dreißigern
	emigrate ['emɪgrəɪt]	auswandern
	share [ʃeə]	(Geschäfts-)Anteil, Aktie
	articles of association [ˌɑ:tɪklz əv əˌsəʊsi'eɪʃn]	Gesellschaftssatzung
	specialize in ['speʃəlaɪz ɪn]	sich spezialisieren auf
	reconstruction [ˌri:kən'strʌkʃn]	Wiederaufbau
	premises (pl. only) ['premɪsɪz]	Betriebsräume
78	**plant** [plɑ:nt]	Betrieb(sanlage), Werk
	vehicle ['vi:əkl]	Fahrzeug
	actual ['æktʃuəl]	tatsächlich
	contain [kənteɪn]	enthalten
	breakdown ['breɪkdaʊn]	Auflistung
	estimate ['estɪmeɪt]	schätzen
	secure [sɪ'kjuə]	sichern
	liable ['laɪəbl]	haftbar, verpflichtet
	specified ['spesɪfaɪd]	spezifiziert
	register ['redʒɪstə]	eintragen
	land-charge ['lændtʃɑ:dʒ]	Grundschuld
	guarantee [ˌgærən'ti:]	Bürgschaft
	assignment by bill of sale [ə'saɪnmənt baɪ ˌbɪl əv 'seɪl]	Sicherungsübereignung
	common ['kɒmən]	normal, üblich
	balance (sheet) ['bæləns ʃi:t]	Bilanz
	profit and loss account [ˌprɒfɪt ən 'lɒs əkaʊnt]	Gewinn- und Verlustrechnung
	area [eəriə]	Region
	look forward to [ˌlʊk 'fɔ:wəd tə]	sich freuen auf
79	**substitute** ['sʌbstɪtju:t]	Ersatzform
	running costs [ˌrʌnɪŋ 'kɒsts]	Unterhaltskosten, Betriebskosten
	fix [fɪks]	festlegen, -setzen
	reunification [ˌri:ju:nɪfɪ'keɪʃn]	Wiedervereinigung
	project ['prɒdʒekt]	Projekt
	federal state [ˌfedərəl 'steɪt]	Bundesland
80	**heading** ['hedɪŋ]	Überschrift
	raw material [ˌrɔ: mə'tɪəriəl]	Rohstoff(e)
	delivery truck [dɪ'lɪvəri trʌk]	Lieferwagen
	supplier [sə'plaɪə]	Zulieferer
	shareholder ['ʃeəhəʊldə]	Aktionär/in
	retained profits [rɪˌteɪnd 'prɒfɪts]	nicht ausgeschüttete Gewinne
	assets ['æsets]	Aktiva, Vermögen(swerte), Guthaben
	fixed assets [fɪkst 'æsets]	(festes) Anlagevermögen
	tangible assets [ˌtændʒəbl 'æsets]	Sach(anlage)-vermögen(swerte)
	fittings ['fɪtɪŋz]	Einrichtung, Ausstattung
	intangible assets [ɪnˌtændʒəbl 'æsets]	immaterielle(s) Vermögen(swerte)
	current assets [ˌkʌrənt 'æsets]	Umlaufvermögen
	stocks [stɒks]	Lager(bestand)
	trade debtors [ˌtreɪd 'detəz]	Forderungen

	cash at bank [kæʃ ət bæŋk]	Kontobestand
	cash in hand [kæʃ ɪn hænd]	Kassenbestand
	equity (capital) ['ekwəti kæpɪtl]	Eigenkapital
	liabilities [laɪə'bɪlətiz]	Verbindlichkeiten, Passiva
	creditor ['kredɪtə]	Gläubiger/in
	creditors (pl.) ['kredɪtəz]	Verbindlichkeiten
	fall due [ˌfɔːl 'djuː]	fällig werden
	trade creditors [treɪd 'kredɪtəz]	Verbindlichkeiten aus Lieferung und Leistung
	provisions [prəˌvɪʒnz]	Rückstellungen
	reserves [rɪ'zɜːvz]	Rücklagen
	trade debts [ˌtreɪd 'detz]	Forderungen
	share capital ['ʃeə kæpɪtl]	Stammkapital, gezeichnetes Kapital
	inventory ['ɪnvəntri]	Inventar, Lagerbestände
	accounts receivable (AE) [əˌkaʊnts rɪ'siːvəbl]	Forderungen
	receivables (AE) [rɪ'siːvəblz]	Forderungen
	accounts payable (AE) [əˌkaʊnts 'peɪəbl]	Verbindlichkeiten
	payables (AE) ['peɪəblz]	Verbindlichkeiten
81	**take out a mortgage** [ˌteɪk 'aʊt ə 'mɔːɡɪdʒ]	eine Hypothek aufnehmen
	assign rights [ə'saɪn raɪts]	Rechte abtreten
	pledge [pledʒ]	Pfand
	lien ['liːən]	Pfandrecht
	pledge [pledʒ]	verpfänden
	in the custody of [ɪn ðə 'kʌstədi əv]	im Gewahrsam von
	title document [ˌtaɪtl 'dɒkjumənt]	Traditionspapier
	warrant ['wɒrənt]	Lagerschein, Warenschein
	warehouse ['weəhaʊs]	Lager(haus)
	bill of lading [ˌbɪl əv 'leɪdɪŋ]	Konnossement
	default [dɪ'fɔːlt]	in Zahlungsverzug geraten
	outstanding [aʊt'stændɪŋ]	ausstehend
	burglary ['bɜːɡləri]	Einbruch
	valuable ['væljuəbl]	wertvoll
	life assurance ['laɪf əʃʊərəns]	Lebensversicherung, Kapitalversicherung
	extension [ɪk'stenʃn]	Erweiterung, Vergrößerung
	proprietor [prə'praɪətə]	Inhaber
82	**hang onto** ['hæŋ ɒntu]	hängen an
	lifeline ['laɪflaɪn]	Rettungsleine
	factory ['fæktəri]	Fabrik
	on the outskirts of [ɒn ði 'aʊtskɜːts əv]	in den Außenbezirken von
	manufacturing giant [mænjuˌfæktʃərɪŋ 'dʒaɪənt]	Produktionsgigant
	convinced [kən'vɪnst]	überzeugt
	recession [rɪ'seʃn]	Rezession
	in the red [ɪn ðə 'red]	in den roten Zahlen
	utilities [juː'tɪlətiz]	Versorgungsbetriebe
	echo ['ekəʊ]	wiederholen
	port of call [ˌpɔːt əv 'kɔːl]	Anlaufstelle
	delicate ['delɪkət]	empfindlich
	tool [tuːl]	Werkzeug, Instrument
	struggle ['strʌɡl]	kämpfen
	be faced with [bi 'feɪst wɪð]	(sich) gegenübersehen
	incredibly [ɪn'kredəbli]	unglaublich
	nevertheless [ˌnevəðə'les]	trotzdem, dennoch
	admit [əd'mɪt]	zugeben, gestehen
	struggle ['strʌɡl]	Kampf
	collapse [kə'læps]	zusammenbrechen
	aid [eɪd]	Hilfe
	ADVANCED MATERIALS	
83	**venture capital** ['ventʃə kæpɪtl]	Risikokapital, Wagniskapital
	venture capitalist ['ventʃə kæpɪtəlɪst]	Risikokapitalist, Wagniskapitalist
	venture capitalism ['ventʃə kæpɪtəlɪzəm]	Risikokapitalismus, Wagniskapitalismus
	embrace [ɪm'breɪs]	bereitwillig annehmen
	mushroom ['mʌʃrʊm]	emporschießen
	distinctly [dɪ'stɪŋktli]	eindeutig
	pursuit [pə'sjuːt]	Betätigung
	root [ruːt]	Wurzel
	reliant on [rɪ'laɪənt ɒn]	sich stützend auf
	fund [fʌnd]	Fond
	entrepreneur [ˌɒntrəprə'nɜː]	Unternehmer/in
	pool of capital [ˌpuːl əv 'kæpɪtl]	Kapitalfonds
	according to [ə'kɔːdɪŋ tə]	zufolge, laut, nach
	association [əˌsəʊsi'eɪʃn]	Verband, Gesellschaft
	treble ['trebl]	verdreifachen
	early-stage finance [ˌɜːli steɪdʒ 'faɪnæns]	Anfangsfinanzierung, Startfinanzierung
	GDP (gross domestic product) [ˌɡrəʊs dəˌmestɪk 'prɒdʌkt]	Bruttoinlandsprodukt (BIP)
	neck and neck [ˌnek ənd 'nek]	Kopf an Kopf
	demand [dɪ'mɑːnd]	Bedarf, Nachfrage
	supply [sə'plaɪ]	Angebot
	stock market ['stɒk mɑːkɪt]	(Wertpapier-)Börse
	dismal ['dɪzməl]	düster

	renew [rɪ'nju:]	erneuern
	evil ['i:vl]	böse
	blood-sucker ['blʌdsʌkə]	Blutsauger
	job-creator ['dʒɒbkrieɪtə]	Arbeitsplatzschaffer
	venture ['ventʃə]	Wagnis
	rubble ['rʌbl]	Trümmer
	considerably [kən'sɪdərəbli]	beträchtlich
	minimise ['mɪnɪmaɪz]	verkleinern, verringern
	emergence [ɪ'mɜ:dʒəns]	Entstehen, Auftreten
	exit route ['eksɪt ru:t]	Ausweg
	realise ['rɪəlaɪz]	realisieren, verwirklichen
	IPO (initial public offering) [ɪ,nɪʃl ,pʌblɪk 'ɒfərɪŋ]	Börsengang
	constitute ['kɒnstɪtju:t]	darstellen, bilden
	private equity house [,praɪvət 'ekwəti haʊs]	Emissionshaus, Investmentbank
	mere [mɪə]	bloß
	translate [træns'leɪt]	übertragen
	handsome ['hænsəm]	ansehnlich
84	**gold rush** ['gəʊld rʌʃ]	Goldrausch

UNIT 8

85	**asset management** [,æset 'mænɪdʒmənt]	Vermögens-verwaltung
	investor [ɪn'vestə]	Investor/in, Kapitalanleger/in
	logic ['lɒdʒɪk]	Logik
	fired ['faɪəd]	entlassen
	raise capital [reɪz 'kæpɪtl]	Kapital aufbringen
	Why the rush? [waɪ ðə 'rʌʃ]	Was soll die Hetze?
	subscribe to [səb'skraɪb tə]	zeichnen
	share(s) [ʃeəz]	Aktie(n)
	packed [pækt]	voll
86	**for ages** [fər 'eɪdʒɪz]	eine Ewigkeit
	ad (advertisement) [əd'vɜ:tɪsmənt]	Werbung, Anzeige
	IPO (initial public offering) [ɪ,nɪʃl ,pʌblɪk 'ɒfərɪŋ]	Börsengang
	float a company [fləʊt ə 'kʌmpəni]	ein Unternehmen an die Börse bringen
	launch sth onto the market [,lɔ:ntʃ ɒntə ðə 'mɑ:kɪt]	etw auf den Markt bringen
	division [dɪ'vɪʒn]	(Betriebs-)Sparte, Abteilung
	expand [ɪk'spænd]	sich ausdehnen, expandieren
	plc (public limited company) [,pi: el 'si:]	(an der Börse notierte) Aktien-gesellschaft, AG
	listed on the stock exchange [,lɪstɪd ɒn ðə 'stɒk ɪkstʃeɪndʒ]	an der Börse notiert
	impression [ɪmpreʃn]	Eindruck
	put one's name down [,pʊt wʌnz ,neɪm 'daʊn]	sich eintragen
	cost a bomb [kɒst ə 'bɒm]	ein Vermögen kosten
	bookbuilding [bʊkbɪldɪŋ]	Preisfindung (bei einer neuen Emission)
	frankly ['fræŋkli]	offen (gesagt)
	allocate ['æləkeɪt]	zuteilen
	trading ['treɪdɪŋ]	Handel
	nightmare ['naɪtmeə]	Alptraum
	travel agency ['trævl eɪdʒənsi]	Reisebüro
87	**inexperienced** [,ɪnɪk'spɪəriənst]	unerfahren
	sector ['sektə]	Sektor, Bereich
88	**semiconductor** [,semikən'dʌktə]	Halbleiter
	electronics [,ɪlek'trɒnɪks]	Elektronik
	engineering [,endʒɪ'nɪərɪŋ]	Maschinenbau
	be valued at [bi 'væljud ət]	... wert sein
	indicative [ɪn'dɪkətɪv]	angezeigt
	price range ['praɪs reɪndʒ]	Preisspanne
	disclose [dɪs'kləʊz]	bekanntgeben
	stake [steɪk]	Beteiligung, Anteil
	lead manage [li:d 'mænɪdʒ]	verwalten
	vie [vaɪ]	wetteifern
	analyst ['ænəlɪst]	Analyst
	heavy ['hevi]	hoch
	demand [dɪ'mɑ:nd]	Nachfrage
	partly [pɑ:tli]	teilweise
	sales [seɪlz]	Absatz
	chief executive [,tʃi:f ɪg'zekjətɪv]	Hauptgeschäfts-führer/in, geschäfts-führende/r Direktor/in
	proceeds ['prəʊsi:dz]	Erlös
	domestic [də'mestɪk]	Inlands-
	decline [dɪ'klaɪn]	(es) ablehnen
	specific [spə'sɪfɪk]	speziell, bestimmte/r/s
	placement ['pleɪsmənt]	Plazierung
	co-operate [kəʊ'ɒpəreɪt]	zusammenarbeiten
	subscription period [səb'skrɪpʃn pɪəriəd]	Zeichnungsphase
	discount ['dɪskaʊnt]	Rabatt, Nachlass
	issue ['ɪʃu:]	emittieren, ausgeben
	separate ['seprət]	getrennt
89	**go public** [,gəʊ 'pʌblɪk]	an die Börse gehen

	equity story ['ekwəti stɔːri]	Wertpapiergeschichte
	beauty contest ['bjuːti kɒntest]	Schönheitswettbewerb
	lead manager [liːd 'mænɪdʒə]	Konsortialführer, Leadmanager
	syndicate ['sɪndɪkət]	Gruppe, Konsortium
	spread [spred]	Kursspanne
	issuing house ['ɪʃuːɪŋ haʊs]	Emissionsbank
	boom [buːm]	boomen, blühen
	comb [kəʊm]	kämmen
	promising [prɑmɪsiŋ]	vielversprechend
	convincing [kən'vɪnsɪŋ]	überzeugend
	invite [ɪn'vaɪt]	einladen
	leadership ['liːdəʃɪp]	Führung
	publicize ['pʌblɪsaɪz]	an die Öffentlichkeit bringen
	place [pleɪs]	platzieren, unterbringen
	portfolio [pɔːt'fəʊliəʊ]	Portefeuille, Bestand, Depot
	huge [hjuːdʒ]	riesig
	affluent ['æfluənt]	wohlhabend
	involve [ɪn'vɒlv]	einbeziehen
90	**bond** [bɒnd]	Anleihe(papier), Rentenpapier, Obligation
	assemble [ə'sembl]	zusammenstellen, versammeln
	coupon ['kuːpɒn]	Kupon, Verzinsung
	mature [mə'tʃʊə]	fällig werden
	recover [rɪ'kʌvə]	zurückbekommen, wieder erhalten
	nominal ['nɒmɪnl]	Nominal-, Nenn-
	redemption date [rɪ'dempʃn deɪt]	Fälligkeit(sdatum)
	debenture [dɪ'bentʃə]	Schuldverschreibung, Obligation
	government bonds ['gʌvənmənt bɒndz]	Staatsanleihen
	tax revenue ['tæks revənjuː]	Steueraufkommen, -einnahmen
	junk bonds ['dʒʌŋk bɒndz]	ungesicherte/hochriskante Schuldverschreibungen
	default [dɪ'fɔːlt]	Zahlungsverzug, -unfähigkeit
	yield [jiːld]	Ertrag, Rendite
	dividend ['dɪvɪdend]	Dividende
	rights issue ['raɪts ɪʃuː]	Bezugsrechtsemission
	in proportion to [ɪn prə'pɔːʃn tə]	im Verhältnis zu
	holdings ['həʊldɪŋz]	(Aktien-)Besitz
	ordinary share(s) ['ɔːdnri ʃeəz]	Stammaktie(n)

	equities (pl. only) ['ekwətiz]	Stammaktie(n)
	common stock (AE) [ˌkɒmən 'stɒk]	Stammaktie
	preference share(s) ['prefrəns ʃeəz]	Vorzugsaktie(n)
	preferred stock (AE) [prɪˌfɜːd 'stɒk]	Vorzugsaktie
	be entitled to [bi ɪn'taɪtld tə]	berechtigt sein zu
	vote [vəʊt]	abstimmen, wählen
	annual general meeting (AGM) [ˌænjuəl ˌdʒenrəl 'miːtɪŋ]	(Jahres-)Hauptversammlung
	influence ['ɪnfluəns]	beeinflussen
91	**massive** ['mæsɪv]	riesig
	fringe [frɪndʒ]	säumen
	await [ə'weɪt]	erwarten
	planning approval [ˌplænɪŋ ə'pruːvl]	Baugenehmigung
	in hand [ɪn 'hænd]	in Bearbeitung, im Gange
	in prospect [ɪn 'prɒspekt]	in Aussicht
	sweeten ['swiːtn]	versüßen
	forecast ['fɔːkɑːst]	Prognose, Vorhersage
	increase ['ɪŋkriːs]	Steigerung, Erhöhung
	forecast ['fɔːkɑːst]	vorhersagen
92	**unit** ['juːnɪt]	Investmentanteil, Fondsanteil
	issuer ['ɪʃuːə]	Emittent, Aussteller
	obliged [ə'blaɪdʒd]	verpflichtet
	bid price ['bɪd praɪs]	Kauf-, Geldkurs
94	**experience** [ɪk'spɪəriəns]	Erfahrung
	consist of [kən'sɪst əv]	bestehen aus
	consider [kən'sɪdə]	erwägen
	earnings ['ɜːnɪŋz]	Einkünfte

ADVANCED MATERIALS

96	**regulation** [ˌregju'leɪʃn]	Regulierung
	pipeline ['paɪplaɪn]	Pipeline
	dizzy ['dɪzi]	schwindelerregend
	consolidation [kənˌsɒlɪ'deɪʃn]	Festigung, Konsolidierung
	outperform [ˌaʊtpə'fɔːm]	(leistungsmäßig) übertreffen
	introduction [ˌɪntrə'dʌkʃn]	Einführung
	reflect [rɪ'flekt]	wiedergeben
	capitalisation [ˌkæpɪtəlaɪ'zeɪʃn]	Kapitalisierung
	component supplier [kəm'pəʊnənt səplaɪə]	Zulieferer
	sub-index, -indices [ˌsʌb 'ɪndeks, 'ɪndɪsiːz]	Unter-Index, -Indizes
	funds (pl. only) [fʌndz]	Geldmittel, Gelder, Kapital

	stocks [stɒks]	Anleihen, Aktien
	listing ['lɪstɪŋ]	Börseneinführung, Zulassung
	mail order business [ˌmeɪl 'ɔːdə bɪznəs]	Versandunternehmen
	integrated ['ɪntɪgreɪtɪd]	integriert
	flotation [fləʊ'teɪʃn]	Börsengang
	generate ['dʒenəreɪt]	erzeugen
	expansion [ɪk'spænʃn]	Erweiterung, Expansion
	notably ['nəʊtəbli]	bemerkenswert
	glut [glʌt]	Übermaß, -angebot
	sift the wheat from the chaff [ˌsɪft ðə ˌwiːt frəm ðə 'tʃɑːf]	die Spreu vom Weizen trennen
	institutional fund manager [ɪnstɪˌtjuːʃənl 'fʌnd mænɪdʒə]	institutioneller Fondsmanager/in
	overall [əʊvər'ɔːl]	(ins)gesamt
	account for [ə'kaʊnt fə]	ausmachen, verantwortlich sein
	retail investor ['riːteɪl ɪnvestə]	Privatanleger/in
	comprise [kəm'praɪz]	umfassen
	predominantly [prɪ'dɒmɪnəntli]	vorherrschend
	cash in [ˌkæʃ 'ɪn]	(Aktien) verkaufen
	gambling ['gæmblɪŋ]	Glücksspiel
	undoubtedly [ʌn'daʊtɪdli]	zweifellos, ohne (jeden) Zweifel
	stimulate ['stɪmjuleɪt]	anregen

UNIT 9

97	**at one's own risk** [ət wʌnz əʊn 'rɪsk]	auf eigenes Risiko
	beware of [bɪ'weər əv]	Vorsicht vor
	shark [ʃɑːk]	Hai
	down under (infl.) [daʊn 'ʌndə]	Australien, Neuseeland
98	**the other way around** [ði ˌʌðə weɪ ə'raʊnd]	umgekehrt
	head back [ˌhed 'bæk]	zurückkehren
	folks (infl.) [fəʊks]	Leute
	term deposit account [ˌtɜːm dɪ'pɒzɪt əkaʊnt]	Festgeldkonto
	certificates of deposit [səˌtɪfɪkəts əv dɪ'pɒzɪt]	Spar-, Kapitalbrief
	loads of ['ləʊdz əv]	eine ganze Menge
	double ['dʌbl]	verdoppeln
	be aware of [bi ə'weər əv]	sich einer Sache bewusst sein
	fluctuate ['flʌktʃueɪt]	schwanken
	capital gain [ˌkæpɪtl 'geɪn]	Kapitalgewinn
	volatile ['vɒlətaɪl]	unbeständig, schwankend
	unit trust [ˌjuːnɪt 'trʌst]	Investmentfonds
100	**nasty** ['nɑːsti]	scheußlich, unangenehm
	I beg your pardon? [aɪ ˌbeg jə 'pɑːdn]	Wie bitte?
	be supposed to be [bi sə'pəʊzd tə bi]	sollen sein
	blue chip [ˌbluː 'tʃɪp]	Standardaktie, -wert
	as safe as houses [əz ˌseɪf əz 'haʊzɪz]	todsicher
	drastic(ally) ['dræstɪkli]	drastisch
	mess [mes]	Patsche, Klemme
	be bound to do sth [bi baʊnd tə duː 'sʌmθɪŋ]	etw. bestimmt tun
	supplement ['sʌplɪment]	ergänzen, ersetzen
	make provision for [meɪk prə'vɪʒn fə]	Vorsorge treffen für
101	**retire** [rɪ'taɪə]	in den Ruhestand gehen, in Rente/Pension gehen
	fund [fʌnd]	Fond
	pool [puːl]	sammeln
	yield profits [jiːld 'prɒfɪts]	Gewinne erzielen
	resources [rɪ'sɔːsɪz]	Mittel, Ressourcen
	aim [eɪm]	Ziel, Absicht
	diversify [daɪ'vɜːsɪfaɪ]	diversifizieren
	ensure [ɪn'ʃʊə]	sicherstellen, gewährleisten
	initial charge [ɪˌnɪʃl 'tʃɑːdʒ]	Ausgabeaufschlag
	declare [dɪ'kleə]	versteuern
	subject to ['sʌbdʒekt tə]	unterworfen
	capital gains tax [ˌkæpɪtl 'geɪnz tæks]	Kapitalgewinn-, Spekulationssteuer
	flirtation [flɜː'teɪʃn]	Flirt
103	**be forced to** [bi 'fɔːst tə]	gezwungen sein zu
	exception [ɪk'sepʃn]	Ausnahme
	grateful ['greɪtfl]	dankbar
104	**speculate** ['spekjuleɪt]	spekulieren
	recommendation [ˌrekəmen'deɪʃn]	Empfehlung
105	**category** ['kætəgəri]	Kategorie, Klasse
106	**prospective** [prə'spektɪv]	(zu)künftig
	instructions [ɪn'strʌkʃnz]	Angaben
	account title [ə'kaʊnt taɪtl]	Kontobezeichnung
	resident address [ˌrezɪdənt ə'dres]	Wohnadresse
	mailing address [ˌmeɪlɪŋ ə'dres]	Postanschrift
	zip (AE) [zɪp]	Postleitzahl
	social security [ˌsəʊʃl sɪ'kjʊərəti]	Sozialversicherung
	citizenship ['sɪtɪznʃɪp]	Staatsbürgerschaft
	non-resident [ˌnɒn 'rezɪdənt]	ohne Wohnsitz (in den USA)
	alien ['eɪliən]	Ausländer/in
	suitability [ˌsuːtə'bɪləti]	Eignung

	tolerance [ˈtɒlərəns]	Toleranz
	stable [ˈsteɪbl]	stabil
	conservative [kənˈsɜːvətɪv]	konservativ
	moderate [ˈmɒdərət]	mäßig
	speculative [ˈspekjuleɪtɪv]	spekulativ
	annuities [əˈnjuːətiz]	(Kapital-)Rente
	mutual funds [ˈmjuːtʃuəl fʌndz]	Investmentfonds
	options [ˈɒpʃnz]	Optionen
	commodities [kəˈmɒdətiz]	Waren(termin-geschäfte)
	horizon [həˈraɪzn]	Horizont
	tax bracket [tæks ˈbrækɪt]	Steuerklasse
107	**intention** [ɪnˈtenʃn]	Absicht
	dependent on [dɪˈpendənt]	abhängig von
	available [əˈveɪləbl]	verfügbar
	education [ˌedʒuˈkeɪʃn]	Ausbildung
	frankincense [ˈfræŋkɪnsens]	Weihrauch
	myrrh [mɜː]	Myrrhe
	steady [ˈstedi]	fest
108	**redeem** [rɪˈdiːm]	ablösen, einlösen
	specially [ˈspeʃəli]	speziell, besonders
	independent [ˌɪndɪˈpendənt]	unabhängig
	overview [ˈəʊvəvjuː]	Überblick
	regulate [ˈregjuleɪt]	kontrollieren, regulieren
	updated [ˌʌpˈdeɪtɪd]	aktualisiert, auf dem neuesten Stand

ADVANCED MATERIALS

109	**time bomb** [ˈtaɪm bɒm]	Zeitbombe
	habit [ˈhæbɪt]	Gewohnheit
110	**guide** [gaɪd]	Führer/in, Richtlinie
	in the event of [ɪn ði ɪˈvent əv]	im Falle des
	endowment insurance [ɪnˌdaʊmənt ɪnˈʃʊərəns]	Kapitalversicherung
	temporary [ˈtemprəri]	zeitlich befristet
	cease [siːs]	enden
	surrender value [səˈrendə væljuː]	Rückkaufswert
	premium [ˈpriːmiəm]	Beitrag
	maturity [məˈtʃʊərəti]	Fälligkeit
	be designed [bi dɪˈzaɪnd]	dazu gedacht sein
	surrender [səˈrendə]	abtreten

UNIT 10

111	**carry out** [ˌkæri ˈaʊt]	durchführen
	barter [ˈbɑːtə]	Tauschhandel
	get back to sb (infl.) [ˌget ˈbæk tə]	jdn zurückrufen
	re [riː]	bezüglich
	inquiry [ɪnˈkwaɪəri]	Anfrage
	peach [piːtʃ]	Pfirsich
	basically [ˈbeɪsɪkli]	im Grunde
112	**in advance** [ɪn ədˈvɑːns]	im Voraus
	ship [ʃɪp]	(ver)senden
	consignment [kənˈsaɪnmənt]	Sendung, Lieferung, Frachtgut
	no way [ˌnəʊ ˈweɪ]	auf keinen Fall
	payment on open account [ˌpeɪmənt ɒn ˌəʊpən əˈkaʊnt]	Zahlung gegen Rechnung (mit offenem Zahlungsziel)
	loading [ˈləʊdɪŋ]	Verladung
	shipment [ˈʃɪpmənt]	Sendung, (Schiffs-)Ladung, Lieferung
	pleasure [ˈpleʒə]	Vergnügen, Freude
	peanuts [ˈpiːnʌts]	hier: fast nichts
	deferred payment [dɪˌfɜːd ˈpeɪmənt]	Stundung der Zahlung
	you guys (infl.) [ju ˈgaɪz]	Ihr Jungs
	payment at sight [ˌpeɪmənt ət ˈsaɪt]	Zahlung bei Sicht
	allergic [əˈlɜːdʒɪk]	allergisch
	documents against payment [ˌdɒkjumənts əgenst ˈpeɪmənt]	Dokumente gegen bar/Zahlung, Kassa gegen Dokumente
	drive a hard bargain [draɪv ə hɑːd ˈbɑːgən]	harte Forderungen stellen
	tough guy (infl.) [tʌf ˈgaɪ]	zäher Bursche
	place the collection order [ˌpleɪs ðə kəˈlekʃn ɔːdə]	Inkassoauftrag erteilen
	party [ˈpɑːti]	Partei
113	**expiry date** [ɪkˈspaɪəri deɪt]	Verfallsdatum
	presentation [ˌpreznˈteɪʃn]	Vorlage, Präsentation
	invoice [ˈɪnvɔɪs]	(Waren-)Rechnung
	present [prɪˈzent]	vorlegen, präsentieren
	clean on board [ˌkliːn ɒn ˈbɔːd]	reingezeichnet
	delegate [ˈdelɪgeɪt]	delegieren
	shipping line [ˈʃɪpɪŋ laɪn]	Schifffahrtslinie, Reederei
116	**unload** [ˌʌnˈləʊd]	entladen, löschen
117	**listener** [ˈlɪsnə]	Zuhörer/in
	deny [dɪˈnaɪ]	verneinen
	state [steɪt]	feststellen
	inquire [ɪnˈkwaɪə]	sich erkundigen nach, fragen nach
	certificate of origin [səˌtɪfɪkət əv ˈɒrɪdʒɪn]	Ursprungszeugnis
	vessel [ˈvesl]	Schiff
	port of loading [ˌpɔːt əv ˈləʊdɪŋ]	Verladehafen
118	**mediate** [ˈmiːdieɪt]	vermitteln
	translate [trænsˈleɪt]	übersetzen
	interpret [ɪnˈtɜːprɪt]	dolmetschen

	mediator ['mi:dieɪtə]	Vermittler/in
119	**mediation** [ˌmi:di'eɪʃn]	Vermittlung
	arise [ə'raɪz]	entstehen, sich ergeben
	consignee [ˌkɒnsaɪ'ni:]	(Waren-)Empfänger, Adressat
120	**sample** ['sɑ:mpl]	Muster, Probe
	blackberry ['blækbəri]	Brombeere
	irrevocable [ɪ'revəkəbl]	unwiderruflich
	customs (pl. only) ['kʌstəmz]	Zoll(behörde)
121	**transshipment** [træns'ʃɪpmənt]	Umladung, Umladegeschäft
	partial shipment [ˌpɑ:ʃl 'ʃɪpmənt]	Teilverschiffung
	prohibited [prə'hɪbɪtɪd]	verboten
	confirm [kən'fɜ:m]	bestätigen
	in our favour [ɪn ˌaʊə 'feɪvə]	zu unseren Gunsten
	advice of dispatch [ədˌvaɪs əv dɪ'spætʃ]	Versandanzeige
122	**gap** [gæp]	Lücke
	destination [ˌdestɪ'neɪʃn]	Bestimmungsort, (End-)Ziel
	as requested [əz rɪ'kwestɪd]	wunschgemäß
	instruct [ɪn'strʌkt]	anweisen, beauftragen
	satisfactory [ˌsætɪs'fæktəri]	zufrieden stellend

ADVANCED MATERIALS

123	**globalisation** [ˌgləʊbəlaɪ'zeɪʃn]	Globalisierung
	cross-border ['krɒs bɔ:də]	grenzüberschreitend
	feasible ['fi:zəbl]	machbar, möglich
	desirable [dɪ'zaɪərəbl]	wünschenswert
	core [kɔ:]	Kern
	free-market ideology [ˌfri: 'mɑ:kɪt ˌaɪdi'ɒlədʒi]	Idee der freien Marktwirtschaft
	shift [ʃɪft]	Wandel, Wechsel
	tide [taɪd]	Flut
	sweep up ['swi:p 'ʌp]	hinwegfegen über
	centre of gravity [ˌsentər əv 'grævəti]	Schwerpunkt
	catch up with [ˌkætʃ 'ʌp wɪð]	einholen
	disruption [dɪs'rʌpʃn]	Unterbrechung
	projection [prə'dʒekʃn]	Prognose
	valid ['vælɪd]	gültig
	purchasing power ['pɜ:tʃəsɪŋ paʊə]	Kaufkraft
	parity ['pærəti]	Parität
	poised [pɔɪzd]	bereit
	overtake [əʊvə'teɪk]	überholen
	in the not too distant future [ɪn ðə ˌnɒt tu: ˌdɪstənt 'fju:tʃə]	in nicht allzu ferner Zukunft
	virtually ['vɜ:tʃuəli]	praktisch, nahezu
	vast [vɑ:st]	riesig, gewaltig
	sharp(ly) ['ʃɑ:pli]	rasch, schnell, stark
	shrink [ʃrɪŋk]	abbauen, verringern
	far-flung [ˌfɑ: 'flʌŋ]	weit verbreitet, ausgedehnt
	reliable [rɪ'laɪəbl]	zuverlässig
	border ['bɔ:də]	Grenze
	fuel ['fju:əl]	antreiben
	globalise ['gləʊbəlaɪz]	globalisieren
	economy of scale [ɪ'kɒnəmi əv skeɪl]	Kostendegression
	tap [tæp]	erschließen, nutzbar machen
	self-accelerating [ˌself ək'seləreɪtɪŋ]	selbst beschleunig-end
	frenzy ['frenzi]	Begeisterung, Erregung
124	**joint venture** [ˌdʒɔɪnt 'ventʃə]	Gemeinschaftsunter-nehmen
	hostile takeover [ˌhɒstaɪl 'teɪkəʊvə]	feindliche Übernahme

A–Z word list

Diese Liste enthält alle Wörter in alphabetischer Reihenfolge. Hier sind jedoch die Wörter, die zum Grundwortschatz gehören, nicht aufgeführt (siehe *Basic Word List* S. 158).

Die Zahl nach dem Stichwort bezieht sich auf die Seite, auf der das Wort zum ersten Mal erscheint.
t = das Wort befindet sich im *Transcript.*

A

abroad *14* (im) Ausland
abrupt *68* abrupt
absolutely *71t* absolut
acceptability *52* Akzeptanz
access *14* Zugang, Zugriff
according to *83* zufolge, laut, nach
accordingly *37* (dem)entsprechend
account for *96* ausmachen, betragen, verantwortlich sein
account holder *16* Kontoinhaber/in
account title *106* Kontobezeichnung
account *10* Konto
accounts payable (AE) *80* Verbindlichkeiten
accounts receivable (AE) *80* Forderungen
accumulate *48* ansammeln
accurate *16* genau
achieve *16* erreichen, erlangen
achievement *37* Leistung, Errungenschaft
acquire *73* erwerben
acquisition *37* Erwerb, Zukauf
act as *46* dienen als
act on one's own account *29* auf eigene Rechnung handeln
activity migration *36t* Verlagerung der Bankgeschäfte
actual *78* tatsächlich
actually *18* eigentlich, tatsächlich
ad (advertisement) *86* Werbung, Anzeige
adapt to *37* sich anpassen an
additional *56* zusätzlich
adjust *52* (sich) anpassen
admission fee *40* Aufnahmegebühr
admit *82* zugeben, gestehen
advance (in ~) *112* im Voraus
advertise *22* werben (für)
advice (no plural) *11t* Ratschlag, (guter) Rat
advice of dispatch *121* Versandanzeige
advisable *13* ratsam
advise *29* (be)raten
affect *16* sich auswirken auf, beeinflussen
affluent *36t, 89* wohlhabend
affordable *52* erschwinglich
afraid (I'm ~) *11t* leider
agreement *70* Vertrag, Vereinbarung, Zusage
ahead of *71t* voraus
aid *82* Hilfe
aim *101* Ziel, Absicht
alien *106* Ausländer/in
allergic *112* allergisch
allocate *86* zuteilen
alteration *71t* Änderung
alternative *64* alternativ
alternatively *48* als Alternative, alternativ
(al)though *45* obwohl
ammunition *51* Munition
amount *19* Summe, Betrag
analyst *88* Analyst
annual general meeting (AGM) *90* (Jahres-)Hauptversammlung
annual turnover *68* Jahresumsatz
annual(ly) *40* jährlich
annuities *106* (Kapital-)Rente
appeal to *16* zusagen, ansprechen
applicable *16* anwendbar, zutreffend
applicant *34* Antragsteller/in
application form *28* Antragsformular
application *25* Antrag; *62* Anwendung
apply (for) *14* beantragen
appointment *11t* Termin
approach *17* sich wenden an
appropriate *13* geeignet, passend
approve *71* gutheißen, genehmigen
APR (annual percentage rate) *52* Jahreszins
area *16* Gegend, Gebiet; *78* Region
arise *119* entstehen, sich ergeben
army colonel *38* Armeeoberst
arrears (in ~) *74* im Rückstand, in Verzug
articles of association *77* Gesellschaftssatzung
as regards *19* bezüglich, was anbetrifft
as requested *122* wunschgemäß
as safe as houses *100* todsicher
as well *28* auch (noch), ebenfalls
assemble *90* zusammenstellen, versammeln
assess *36t* ab-, einschätzen, beurteilen
assess (for tax purposes) *68* veranlagen (steuerlich)
asset management *85* Vermögensverwaltung
assets *80* Aktiva, Vermögen(swerte), Guthaben
assign rights *81* Rechte abtreten
assignment by bill of sale *78* Sicherungsübereignung
association *83* Verband, Gesellschaft
at one's own risk *97* auf eigenes Risiko
at the touch of a button *14* auf Knopfdruck
at your disposal *64* zur Verfügung
ATM (automatic teller machine) *16* Geldautomat
attainment *37* Erreichung
attempt *48* Versuch
attention *55* Aufmerksamkeit
attitude *48* Einstellung, Haltung
attract *15* anziehen, anlocken
audience *63* Publikum
augment *37* vergrößern
authenticate *62* beglaubigen
authority for per pro signatory *28* Kontovollmacht
authorize, authorise *28* bevollmächtigen
auxiliary (verb) *30* Hilfsverb
available *107* verfügbar

available (be ~) *36t* zur Verfügung (stehen)
average *36t* Durchschnitts-
average (on ~) *71t* durchschnittlich
averaging *71t* von durchschnittlich
await *91* erwarten
aware (be ~ of) *98* sich einer Sache bewusst sein

B
back office *10* Büro
backed by *36t* unterstützt von
balance *14* Kontostand, Saldo
balance (sheet) *78* Bilanz
(bank) clerk *9* (Bank-) Angestellte/r
(bank) statement *23* Kontoauszug
bankruptcy *74* Bankrott, Konkurs
bargain *8* Schnäppchen
barter *111* Tauschhandel
basic *18* grundsätzlich, Grund-
basically *36t, 111* im Grunde
bear in mind *65* beachten
bear *44* tragen
bearer cheque *44* Überbringerscheck
beat sb at their own game *26* jdn mit den eigenen Waffen schlagen
beauty contest *89* Schönheitswettbewerb
behalf (on my ~) *33* in meinem Namen
behave *42* sich benehmen
beneficiary *44* Zahlungsempfänger/in, Begünstigte(r)
benefit *36t, 52* Vorteil, Vergünstigung
Beretta *51* Beretta (Revolver)
beware of *97* Vorsicht vor
bid price *92* Kauf-, Geldkurs
bill of exchange *33* Wechsel
bill of lading *81* Konnossement
blackberry *120* Brombeere
blood-sucker *83* Blutsauger
blue chip *100* Standardaktie, -wert
bond *90* Anleihe(papier), Rentenpapier, Obligation
bookbuilding *86* Preisfindung (bei einer neuen Emission)
booklet *19* Büchlein, Heft
boom *89* boomen, blühen
border *123* Grenze
borrower *65* Kreditnehmer/in
bound (be ~ to do sth) *100* etw. bestimmt tun
bound to be *71t* mit Sicherheit entstehen
branch *10* Filiale, Zweig(stelle)
brand leader *16* führendes Produkt am Markt
breakdown *78* Auflistung
British Intelligence *50* britischer Geheimdienst
brochure *14* Broschüre, Prospekt
brush up *76* aufpolieren
building society (policy) *10* Bausparkasse, -vertrag
bulge *48* (sich) wölben, ausbeulen
burgeoning *48* sprießend, aufkeimend
burglary *81* Einbruch
buzzer *50* Summer
by the way *8* übrigens
bypass *49* umgehen

C
cancellation *62* Stornierung
capital gain *98* Kapitalgewinn
capital gains tax *101* Kapitalgewinn-, Spekulationssteuer
capitalisation *96* Kapitalisierung
caption *72* Bildunterschrift
capture *16* einfangen
card holder *52* Karteninhaber/in
care (take ~ of) *36t* sich kümmern um
carry little weight *16* wenig gelten
carry out *111* durchführen
cash *11t* bar einlösen
cash advance *52* Barvorschuss
cash at bank *80* Kontobestand
cash dispenser *10* Geldautomat
cash in *96* (Aktien) verkaufen
cash in hand *80* Kassenbestand
cashier *10* Kassierer/in
cashpoint *36t* Geldautomat
catch up with *123* einholen
category *105* Kategorie, Klasse
catering *20* Gastronomie
cease *110* enden
centre of gravity *123* Schwerpunkt
CEO (chief executive officer) *48* Vorstandsvorsitzende/r
certificate *28* Bescheinigung
certificate of origin *117* Ursprungszeugnis
certificates of deposit *98* Spar-, Kapitalbrief
chairman *48* Vorsitzender
change *11t* (aus)wechseln, (um)tauschen; *30* ändern
charge *11t* berechnen
charge *18* Gebühr
charity *73* Wohltätigkeitsorganisation
chart *70* Tabelle
checking account (AE) *52* Scheck-, Gehalts-, Girokonto
cheque *8* Scheck
chequebook *14* Scheckbuch, -heft
chief executive *88* Hauptgeschäftsführer/in, geschäftsführende/r Direktor/in
chief executive (officer) (CEO) *37* Vorstandsvorsitzende/r
circulate *48* zirkulieren, in Umlauf sein
circulation (in ~) *48* in Umlauf
circumstance *33* Umstand, Bedingung
citizen *16* (Staats-)Bürger/in
citizenship *106* Staatsbürgerschaft
civil servant *68* Staatsbeamter, -beamtin
claim *39* einziehen
clean on board *113* reingezeichnet
clear *45* abrechnen
close *28* schließen
co-applicant *68* Mitantragsteller/in
co-branded *48* mit beiden Markenzeichen
coin *8* Münze
collapse *82* zusammenbrechen
colleague *8* Kollege, Kollegin
comb *89* kämmen
comfortably *65* bequem
comforting *65* tröstlich
commence *37* beginnen
commercial *36t* Handels-, Geschäfts-
commission *55* Provision
commitment *37* Einsatz, Engagement, *74* Verpflichtung
committed (be ~) *74* sich verpflichten
committed to *25* engagiert für
commodities *106* Waren(termingeschäfte)
common stock (AE) *90* Stammaktie

common *78* normal, üblich
communication *38* Mitteilung, Benachrichtigung
community of property *68* Gütergemeinschaft
comparison *28* Vergleich
compensation *71t* Schaden(s)ersatz, Entschädigung
competition *71t* Konkurrenz
competitive *25* wettbewerbs-, konkurrenzfähig
complicated *14* kompliziert
component supplier *96* Zulieferer
comprehensive *37* umfassend
comprise *96* umfassen
computer scientist *71t* Informatiker/in
concerned *33* betroffen
confidence *65* (Selbst-)Vertrauen
confidential *68* vertraulich
confirm *121* bestätigen
conservative *106* konservativ
consider *94* erwägen
considerably *83* beträchtlich
consignee *119* (Waren-) Empfänger, Adressat
consignment *112* Sendung, Lieferung, Frachtgut
consist of *94* bestehen aus
consistently *25* ständig
consolidation *96* Festigung, Konsolidierung
constitute *83* darstellen, bilden
consultant *36t* Berater/in
consumer *16* Verbraucher/in
consumer confidence *48* Vertrauen der Verbraucher
contact *14* Kontakt, Verbindung
contain *78* enthalten
continue *71t* fortfahren
contract *18* Vertrag
contribute *76* beisteuern
contribution *77* Beitrag, Eigengeld
convenience *14* Komfort, Annehmlichkeit
convenient *11t* passend
convert *48* umwandeln
convince *39* überzeugen
convinced *82* überzeugt
convincing *89* überzeugend
co-operate *88* zusammenarbeiten
cope (with) *65* fertig werden mit
core *123* Kern
corporate business *10* Firmenkunden(geschäft)
corporate client *12* Firmenkunde, -kundin
corporate loan *12* Firmendarlehen
correspond to *29* entsprechen
cost a bomb *86* ein Vermögen kosten
counselling *73* Beratung
counter *10* Schalter
counterpart *36t* Gegenüber
countersign *55* gegenzeichnen
county court judgement *74* Amtsgerichtsurteil
coupon *90* Kupon, Verzinsung
cover *54* Umschlag, Titelseite
credit *23* gutschreiben, Gutschrift
credit (no pl.) *10* Kredit
credit balance *18* Habensaldo, Guthaben
credit card *8* Kreditkarte
credit rating *73* Kreditwürdigkeit
credit reference agency *34* Kreditauskunftei
credit score *74* Kreditrahmen festlegen
credit-scored (be ~) *36t* einer Kreditprüfung unterziehen
credit scoring *74* Feststellung der Kreditwürdigkeit
credit transfer *12* Überweisung
creditor *73* Gläubiger/in
creditors (pl.) *80* Verbindlichkeiten
criteria for eligibility *77* Auswahlkriterien
cross-border *123* grenzüberschreitend
crossed cheque *44* Verrechnungsscheck
cruise package *52* Kreuzfahrt-Pauschalreise
currency 11t Währung
currency float *48* Geldmenge
current account *11t* Girokonto, Kontokorrentkonto
current *22* aktuell, gegenwärtig
current assets *80* Umlaufvermögen
custody (in the ~ of) *81* im Gewahrsam von
customer account manager *36t* Kundenkontenbetreuer/in
customer service officer *10* Kundenberater/in
customs (pl. only) *120* Zoll(behörde)
cut off *60t* unterbrechen, abgeschnitten

D

data privacy *62* Datenschutz
date of birth *35* Geburtsdatum
date of issue *44* Ausstellungsdatum
deal with *33* sich befassen mit, umgehen mit
debenture *90* Schuldverschreibung, Obligation
debit *23* Abbuchung, belasten, abbuchen
debit balance *18* Soll(saldo)
debit card *46* Bankkarte, Zahlkarte
debt *16* Schuld(en)
decade *62* Jahrzehnt
decision *71* Entscheidung
declare *101* versteuern
decline *88* (es) ablehnen
deduct *71* abziehen
default *81* in Zahlungsverzug geraten
default *90* Zahlungsverzug, -unfähigkeit
deferred payment *112* Stundung der Zahlung
definitely *18* bestimmt, auf jeden Fall
degree *62* Grad
delegate *113* delegieren
delete *33* durchstreichen
delicate *82* empfindlich
delivery *16* (Aus-)Lieferung
delivery truck *80* Lieferwagen
demand *83* Bedarf, Nachfrage
denomination *55* Nennwert, Wertbezeichnung
denominations *55* Stückelung
deny *117* verneinen
department *10* Abteilung
depend on *18* abhängig sein von, darauf ankommen
dependent on *107* abhängig von
deposit *63* Anzahlung, Kaution
deposit account *12* Sparkonto, Festgeldkonto
deposit box *36t* Nachttresor
designated *33* bestimmt
designed (be ~) *110* dazu gedacht sein
desirable *123* wünschenswert
destination *122* Bestimmungsort, (End-)Ziel
determine *36t* bestimmen, festlegen
diabolical *73* teuflisch
diminish *37* abnehmen, sich verringern

direct debit authorization *38* Einzugsermächtigung
direct debit *12* Abbuchungs-, Einzugsverfahren, Lastschrift
disabled *16* behindert
disclose *88* bekanntgeben
disclosure *68* (Selbst)auskunft
disconnect *20* abschalten
discount *88* Rabatt, Nachlass
dismal *83* düster
disposable income *68* verfügbares Einkommen
disruption *123* Unterbrechung
distinctly *83* eindeutig
diversify *101* diversifizieren
divide *24* (sich) teilen
dividend *90* Dividende
division *86* (Betriebs-)Sparte, Abteilung
divorced *20* geschieden
divulge *61* bekannt geben
dizzy *96* schwindelerregend
do business *14* Geschäfte machen
do community service *21* Zivildienst leisten
do military service *21* Militärdienst leisten
documents against payment *112* Dokumente gegen bar/Zahlung, Kassa gegen Dokumente
... dollars' worth of *57* im Wert von ... Dollar
domestic *88* Inlands-
don't bother *7* bemühen Sie sich nicht
double *98* verdoppeln
down under (infl.) *97* Australien, Neuseeland
draft *33* Tratte
drastic(ally) *100* drastisch
draw a cheque *47* einen Scheck ausstellen
draw conclusions *48* Schlüsse ziehen
drawee *44* Bezogene/r, bezogene Bank
drawer *44* Aussteller/in
drip feed *73* abstottern
drive a hard bargain *112* harte Forderungen stellen
drive down *37* verringern
driving instructor *71t* Fahrlehrer/in
driving lesson *13* Fahrstunde
driving school *71t* Fahrschule
due *39* fällig

E

early-stage finance 83 Anfangsfinanzierung, Startfinanzierung
earn interest *20* Zinsen erhalten
earnings *94* Einkünfte
echo *82* wiederholen
economics *16* Wirtschaft(lichkeit)
economy of scale *123* Kostendegression
educated professional *16* Akademiker/in
education *107* Ausbildung
educational headstart *16* Bildungsvorsprung
efficiency *37* Leistungsfähigkeit
efficient *43* effizient
effort *37* Mühe, Bemühung, Anstrengung
electoral roll *74* Wählerliste
electronics *88* Elektronik
eligible (be ~) *18* in Frage kommen, berechtigt sein
embrace *83* bereitwillig annehmen
emergence *83* Entstehen, Auftreten
emergency *65* Notfall
emigrate *77* auswandern
employer *11t* Arbeitgeber/in
employment status *68* Beschäftigungsverhältnis
enable *66* ermöglichen
encourage *36t* auffordern
encrypt *62* verschlüsseln
endorse *44* indossieren
endorsement *44* Indossament, Girierung
endowment insurance *110* Kapitalversicherung
engaged *27* besetzt
engineering *88* Maschinenbau
enhance *37* erhöhen, steigern
enhancement *16* Erhöhung, Steigerung
enquire *27* sich erkundigen
enquiry *16* Abfrage
ensure *101* sicherstellen, gewährleisten
entitled (be ~ to) *90* berechtigt sein zu
entrepreneur *83* Unternehmer/in
entry *23* Eintrag, Buchung
envious *36t* neidisch
environment *62* Umgebung
equal *58* gleich
equal rights *28* gleiche Rechte
equipment *71t* Ausrüstung, Geräte
equities (pl. only) *90* Stammaktie(n)
equity (capital) *80* Eigenkapital
equity story *89* Wertpapiergeschichte
equivalent *48* Entsprechung, entsprechend, *55* Gegenwert
estimate *71t* (Kosten-) Voranschlag; *78* schätzen
(euro)cheque card *8* (Euro-) Scheckkarte
European Central Bank (ECB) *43* Europäische Zentralbank
event (in the ~ of) *110* im Falle des
eventually *73* zum Schluss
every Tom, Dick or Harry *45* jeder Hinz und Kunz
evil *83* böse
examine *28* prüfen
exceed *75* übersteigen
except for *30* außer, ausgenommen
exception *103* Ausnahme
exchange rate *56* (Umtausch-) Kurs, Wechselkurs
exclusive *58* vornehm
exit route *83* Ausweg
expand *86* sich ausdehnen, expandieren
expansion *96* Erweiterung, Expansion
expenditure *65* (Summe der) Ausgaben
expense(s) *65* Ausgabe(n)
experience *94* Erfahrung
expertise *25* Sachkenntnis
expiry date *113* Verfallsdatum
exploit *62* ausnutzen
extend *37, 71t* vergrößern, ausdehnen, erweitern; *64* erhöhen
extension *81* Erweiterung, Vergrößerung
extent *37* (Aus-)Maß
extract *22* Auszug

F

face *44* Vorderseite
faced (be ~ with) *82* (sich) gegenübersehen
facilitate *37* erleichtern
factory *82* Fabrik
fail *73* Konkurs machen
fall due *80* fällig werden
familiar *63* vertraut, bekannt

far-flung *123* weit verbreitet, ausgedehnt
favour (in our ~) *121* zu unseren Gunsten
favourable *76* günstig
favourably *16* vorteilhaft, günstig
feasible *123* machbar, möglich
feature *19* Merkmal
fed up with (be ~) *48* es satt haben, die Nase voll haben
federal state *79* Bundesland
fee *18* Gebühr
fellow student *9* Kursteilnehmer/in
figure *44* Zahl, Ziffer
file *71t* Akte
financial literacy *73* finanzielle Mündigkeit
financing *12* Finanzierung
fired *85* entlassen
first name *35* Vorname
fit *52* passen (zu)
fittings *80* Einrichtung, Ausstattung
fix *79* festlegen, -setzen
fixed assets *80* (festes) Anlagevermögen
flexibility *65* Flexibilität
flirtation *101* Flirt
float a company *86* ein Unternehmen an die Börse bringen
flotation *96* Börsengang
fluctuate *98* schwanken
fluctuation *52* Schwankung
focus on *37* sich konzentrieren auf
folks (infl.) *98* Leute
for ages *86* eine Ewigkeit
forced (be ~ to) *103* gezwungen sein zu
forecast *91* Prognose, Vorhersage, vorhersagen
foreign currency *12* Sorten, Fremdwährung
forex = foreign exchange *16* Fremdwährung(en), Devisen
formality *65* Formalität, Förmlichkeit
forward to *39* senden an
found *48* gründen
founder *48* Gründer/in
frankincense *107* Weihrauch
frankly *86* offen (gesagt)
fraudulent *16* betrügerisch
free of charge *18* kostenlos, gebührenfrei
freelance *71t* freiberuflich
free-market ideology *123* Idee der freien Marktwirtschaft
freepost envelope *38* Freiumschlag
frenzy *123* Begeisterung, Erregung
frequent flyer *52* Vielflieger/in
frequently *67* oft, häufig
fringe *91* säumen
from December onwards *63* ab Dezember
front-line staff *36t* Kundenberater/in
fuel *123* antreiben
fund *83* Fond
funds (pl. only) *96* Geldmittel, Gelder, Kapital

G

gambling *96* Glücksspiel
gap *122* Lücke
GDP (gross domestic product) *83* Bruttoinlandsprodukt (BIP)
General Business Conditions *34* Allgemeine Geschäftsbedingungen
generally speaking *71t* im Allgemeinen
generate *96* erzeugen
genuine *28* echt
get a divorce *28* sich scheiden lassen
get back to sb (infl.) *111* jdn zurückrufen
get held up *11t* aufgehalten werden
get rid of *8* loswerden
give notice *18* kündigen
globalisation *123* Globalisierung
globalise *123* globalisieren
glut *96* Übermaß, -angebot
go into the red *18* in die roten Zahlen geraten
go public *89* an die Börse gehen
gold rush *84* Goldrausch
gone for good *58* für immer verloren
goods *8* Ware(n), Güter (pl. only)
govern *34* regeln
governing *37* vorrangig
government bonds *90* Staatsanleihen
grace period *52* Zahlungsfrist
grant *12* gewähren, bewilligen
grateful *103* dankbar
grease *48* schmieren
gross *22* brutto
guarantee *78* Bürgschaft
guarantor *16* Bürge, Garant
guide *110* Führer/in, Richtlinie

H

habit *109* Gewohnheit
half yearly *40* halbjährlich
hand (in ~) *91* in Bearbeitung, im Gange
hand to *46* geben, aushändigen
handling charge *56* Bearbeitungsgebühr
handsome *83* ansehnlich
hang on (infl.) *8* warten
hang onto *82* hängen an
hardly *42* kaum
have a broader appeal *16* größeren Anklang finden
have a closer look at *7* genauer ansehen
head back *98* zurückkehren
head office *36t* Zentrale
heading *80* Überschrift
heavy *88* hoch
help oneself to sth *39* sich (einer Sache) bedienen
hence *48* daher
here you are *7* bitte
high net-worth *16* vermögend
high street bank *36* Geschäfts-, Großbank
highly-recognized *45* hoch angesehen
hold the line *27* bleiben Sie am Apparat
holdings *90* (Aktien-)Besitz
home furnishing *65* Inneneinrichtung
home improvement *65* Renovierung
honour *33* bezahlen, einlösen
horizon *106* Horizont
hostile takeover *124* feindliche Übernahme
household *68* Haushalt
huge *89* riesig

I

I beg your pardon? *100* Wie bitte?
I gather *63* ich vermute
I'll put you through *27* ich verbinde
identification *34* Legitimation, Identifizierung
impression *86* Eindruck
in fact *63* tatsächlich
in the not too distant future *123* in nicht allzu ferner Zukunft

in the strictest sense *48* im strengsten Sinne
in the thirties *77* in den Dreißigern
incentive *48* Anreiz
include *14* einbeziehen
including *7* einschließlich, inbegriffen
inconvenient *32* unbequem
increase *91* Steigerung, Erhöhung
increasing *46* zunehmend
incredibly *82* unglaublich
incur *37* eingehen
indemnity *33* Verpflichtung(serklärung)
independent *108* unabhängig
indicative *88* angezeigt
inducement *48* Anreiz
inexpensive *20* preiswert
inexperienced *87* unerfahren
influence *90* beeinflussen
inherit *13* erben
initial charge *101* Ausgabeaufschlag
innovative *55* innovativ
inquire *117* sich erkundigen nach, fragen nach
inquiry *111* Anfrage
insecure *62* unsicher
insert *43* einführen
insolvency *74* Zahlungsunfähigkeit, Insolvenz
instalment *64* Rate
instant *25* sofortig
instead *11t* stattdessen, anstatt
institutional fund manager *96* institutioneller Fondsmanager/in
instruct *122* anweisen, beauftragen
instruction *33* Anweisung
instructions *106* Angaben
insurance (policy) *10* Versicherung(spolice)
insure *57* versichern
intangible assets *80* immaterielle(s) Vermögen(swerte)
integrated *96* integriert
intend *60* vorhaben
intention *107* Absicht
intercede *73* vermitteln
intercom *50* Sprechanlage
interest (no pl.) *18* Zins(en)
interest rate *11t* Zinssatz, -rate
interpret *118* dolmetschen
interruption *66* Unterbrechung
introduce *7* vorstellen, einführen
introduction *96* Einführung
introductory *68* Einführungs-
inundated *73* überschwemmt
invent *24* erfinden
inventory *80* Inventar, Lagerbestände
invest *11t* investieren, anlegen
investment 12 Investition, Anlage
investment consultant *10* Anlage-, Vermögensberater/in
investor *85* Investor/in, Kapitalanleger/in
invite *89* einladen
invoice *113* (Waren-)Rechnung
involve *89* einbeziehen
involved in *61* beteiligt an
IPO (initial public offering) *83* Börsengang
irregular *43* unregelmäßig
irregularly *19* unregelmäßig
irrevocable *120* unwiderruflich
ISP (internet service provider) *61* Internet-Provider
issue *12* Ausgabe, Emission, emittieren, ausgeben
issuer *92* Emittent, Aussteller
issuing house *89* Emissionsbank
item *55* Artikel, Gegenstand

J

jargon *25* Fachsprache
job (on the ~) *36t* im Beruf, bei der Arbeit
job-creator *83* Arbeitsplatzschaffer
join a club *38* einem Klub beitreten
joint account *28* Gemeinschaftskonto
joint income *71t* gemeinsames Einkommen
joint venture *124* Gemeinschaftsunternehmen
junk bonds *90* ungesicherte/hochriskante Schuldverschreibungen
just about *8* gerade noch

K

keen *27* interessiert
keep (accounts) *12* (Konten) führen
keep in touch *14* in Verbindung bleiben
keep track of *23* verfolgen
knowledgeable *25* kenntnisreich

L

land-charge *78* Grundschuld
landlord *63* Wirt, Vermieter
large scale *37* groß angelegt
lately *42* in letzter Zeit
latest *75* neueste(r,s)
launch sth onto the market *86* etw auf den Markt bringen
launch *48* Einführung; *55* auf den Markt bringen
lead manage *88* verwalten
lead manager *89* Konsortialführer, Leadmanager
leadership *89* Führung
leaflet *25* Broschüre
leave a message *28* eine Nachricht hinterlassen
legacy *73* Vermächtnis, Erbe
legal *28* juristisch
let alone *38* geschweige denn
letter of credit *12* Akkreditiv
level *65* Höhe
liabilities *80* Verbindlichkeiten, Passiva
liable *78* haftbar, verpflichtet
lien *81* Pfandrecht
life assurance *36t, 81* Lebensversicherung, Kapitalversicherung
lifeline *82* Rettungsleine
lift *10* Fahrstuhl, Aufzug
light engineering *76* Feinmechanik
likely *18* wahrscheinlich
limit *65* Grenze
link *75* Verbindung
listed on the stock exchange *86* an der Börse notiert
listener *117* Zuhörer/in
listing *96* Börseneinführung, Zulassung
living costs *71t* Lebenshaltungskosten
loading *112* Verladung
loads of *98* eine ganze Menge
lobby *10* Foyer, Eingangshalle
local *14* örtlich, lokal
local rate *14* Ortsgebühr
logic *85* Logik
long term (in the ~) *16* auf die Dauer
long-term *22* langfristig
look ahead *37* vorausschauen
look forward to *78* sich freuen auf
loyalty *48* Treue, Loyalität
lump sum (in a ~) *76* als einmalige Summe

M

magnetic strip *61* Magnetstreifen
maiden name 35 Mädchenname
mail *52* (mit der Post) schicken
mail order business *96* Versandunternehmen
mailing address *106* Postanschrift
maintain *16* aufrechterhalten; *52* unterhalten
make a distinction *36t* einen Unterschied machen
make out *8* ausstellen
make provision for *100* Vorsorge treffen für
make sense *22* sinnvoll sein
make up for sth *71t* etwas ausgleichen
manager *10* (Filial-)Leiter/in
managing director *76* Geschäftsführer/in
mandatory *36t* vorgeschrieben
manufacturing giant *82* Produktionsgigant
marital status *35* Familienstand
massive *91* riesig
match *44* zuordnen
matter *11t* Angelegenheit
mature *90* fällig werden
maturity *110* Fälligkeit
meaningful *45* sinnvoll
means of payment *8* Zahlungsmittel
mediate *118* vermitteln
mediation *119* Vermittlung
mediator *118* Vermittler/in
membership dues *38* Mitgliedsbeitrag
mention *8* erwähnen, nennen
merchant *48* Kaufmann/-frau
mere *83* bloß
merge *36t* fusionieren, sich zusammenschließen
merger *37* Fusion, Zusammenschluss
mess *100* Patsche, Klemme
message *54* Botschaft
method of payment *8* Zahlungsweise
minimise *83* verkleinern, verringern
moderate *106* mäßig
monetary policy *43* Geldpolitik
money laundering *34* Geldwäsche
Money Laundering Act *34* Geldwäschegesetz
mortgage *16* Hypothek
mortgage payments *71t* Hypothekenraten
mushroom *83* emporschießen
mutual funds *106* Investmentfonds
myrrh *107* Myrrhe

N

name at birth *68* Geburtsname
nasty *100* scheußlich, unangenehm
navy blue *36t* marineblau
neck and neck *83* Kopf an Kopf
need *24* Bedürfnis
net *71t* Netto-
nevertheless *82* trotzdem, dennoch
nightmare *86* Alptraum
no way *112* auf keinen Fall
nominal *90* Nominal-, Nenn-
non-resident *106* ohne Wohnsitz (in den USA)
notably *96* bemerkenswert
note *8* Geldschein
notice account *22* Konto mit Kündigung(sfrist)
nought *36t* Null
nowadays *39* heutzutage
numbered *33* nummeriert

O

objective *37* Ziel, Zweck
obliged *92* verpflichtet
obtain *13* erhalten, erlangen
obviously *71t* offensichtlich, natürlich
occupation *35* ausgeübter Beruf
occur *9* geschehen, vorkommen
officer *36t* (leitende/r) Angestellte/r
on a continuous basis *65* kontinuierlich
on Her Majesty's service *50* im Dienste Ihrer Majestät
on-screen *14* auf dem Bildschirm
open cheque *44* Barscheck
operate *18* bedienen
operating costs *37* Betriebskosten
opportunity *76* Gelegenheit
opposite number *75* Gegenüber
options *106* Optionen
order cheque *44* Orderscheck
ordinary share(s) *90* Stammaktie(n)
organize *36t* organisieren
otherwise *65* sonst
out of order *67* außer Betrieb
outfit *48* Unternehmen
outlay *16* Ausgaben, -lagen
outlet *46* Verkaufsstelle
outperform *96* (leistungsmäßig) übertreffen
outside banking hours *13* außerhalb der Öffnungszeiten
outskirts (on the ~ of) *82* in den Außenbezirken von
outsource *36t* auslagern
outstanding *25* hervorragend, *81* ausstehend
overall *96* (ins)gesamt
overcome *15* überwinden
overcommit oneself *72* sich übernehmen
overdraft *12* Kontoüberziehung, Überziehungskredit
overdraft facility *18* Dispositionskredit
overdraw *18* überziehen
overtake *123* überholen
overview *108* Überblick
owe *38* schulden

P

pace *37* Tempo
packed *85* voll
padlock *62* Vorhängeschloss
pan-European *16* gesamteuropäisch
parity *123* Parität
partial shipment *121* Teilverschiffung
participate *49* teilnehmen
partly *88* teilweise
party *112* Partei
pass an exam *71t* eine Prüfung bestehen
pave the way *62* den Weg ebnen
pay in cash *8* bar bezahlen
pay in(to) *18* einzahlen
payables (AE) *80* Verbindlichkeiten
payee *39* Zahlungsempfänger/in
payer *44* Einzahler
paying-in book *14* Einzahlungsheft
payment at sight *112* Zahlung bei Sicht
payment on open account *112* Zahlung gegen Rechnung (mit offenem Zahlungsziel)
peach *111* Pfirsich
peanuts *112* hier: fast nichts
penalty *18* Strafe
pension *20* Rente, Pension

per capita *73* pro Kopf
percentage *52* Prozentsatz
perfectly *45* völlig
period of notice *18* Kündigungsfrist
personal customer *12* Privatkunde, -kundin
personal loan adviser *10* Kleinkreditberater/in
personal loan *12* Privatkredit, Privatdarlehen
phrase *31* (Rede-)Wendung, Ausdruck
pin board *24* Pinwand
pipeline *96* Pipeline
place of birth *35* Geburtsort
place the collection order *112* Inkassoauftrag erteilen
place *89* platzieren, unterbringen
placement *88* Plazierung
planning approval *91* Baugenehmigung
plant *78* Werk, Betrieb(sanlage)
play the drums *8* Schlagzeug spielen
plc (public limited company) *86* (an der Börse notierte) Aktiengesellschaft, AG
pleasure *112* Vergnügen, Freude
pledge *81* Pfand, verpfänden
poised *123* bereit
polite(ly) *31* höflich
pool *101* sammeln
pool of capital *83* Kapitalfonds
port of call *82* Anlaufstelle
port of loading *117* Verladehafen
portable *7* tragbar
portfolio *89* Portefeuille, Bestand, Depot
postal order *61* Postanweisung
postpone *32* verschieben
power of attorney *28* (Handlungs-)Vollmacht
predominantly *96* vorherrschend
preferable (be ~ to) *65* vorzuziehen sein
preference share(s) *90* Vorzugsaktie(n)
preferred stock (AE) *90* Vorzugsaktie
prefix *47* Vorsilbe
premises *77* Betriebsräume
premium *110* Beitrag
presence (in the ~ of) *57* in Gegenwart
present *113* vorlegen, präsentieren
presentation *113* Vorlage, Präsentation
presentment *16* Zustellung
pretty *45* ziemlich, recht
prevent *28* verhindern
previously *30* vorher
price range *88* Preisspanne
pricing *49* Preiskalkulation, -festsetzung
primary *52* primär, erst-
Prime Rate (AE) *52* Kreditzins für erste Adressen
print *19* (aus)drucken
private consulting room *10* Beratungs-, Sprechzimmer
private equity house *83* Emissionshaus, Investmentbank
privately-owned *75* im Privatbesitz
probationary period *36t* Probezeit
proceeds *88* Erlös
process *16* bearbeiten
product range *37* Produktpalette
profit *67* Profit, Gewinn
profit and loss account *78* Gewinn- und Verlustrechnung
progress *37* Fortschritt/e
prohibited *121* verboten
project *79* Projekt
projection *123* Prognose
promising *89* vielversprechend
promissory note *33* Schuldschein, Solawechsel
promotional *61* Werbe-
pronounce *38* aussprechen
proof of identity *28* Identitätsbeweis
proof of legal residence *28* Meldebescheinigung
property *33* Eigentum, Besitz
proportion (in ~ to) *90* im Verhältnis zu
proprietor *81* Inhaber
prospect (in ~) *91* in Aussicht
prospective *106* (zu)künftig
protect *29* schützen
(for your own) protection *28* (zu Ihrem eigenen) Schutz
prove *29* beweisen
provide *38* liefern, bieten
provision *36t* Bereitstellung
provisions *80* Rückstellungen
publicize *89* an die Öffentlichkeit bringen
punctual(ly) *39* pünktlich
purchase *16* (Ein-)Kauf
purchasing power *123* Kaufkraft
pure *16* rein
purpose *39* Zweck
pursuant to *35* gemäß, entsprechend
pursue *37* verfolgen
pursuit *83* Betätigung
pursuit of *37* Streben nach, Trachten nach
put one's name down *86* sich eintragen
putter *45* Putter (Golfschläger)

Q

quarterly *40* vierteljährlich
queue *57* Reihe, (Warte-) Schlange

R

R.I.P.= Rest in Peace *17* Ruhe in Frieden
raise capital *85* Kapital aufbringen
range (a ~ of) *25* eine Reihe von
range from ... to ... *16* reichen von ... bis ...
rate of exchange *11t* Wechselkurs
rate of interest *18* Zinssatz
ratio *37* Verhältnis
raw material *80* Rohstoff(e)
re *111* bezüglich
real estate *76* Immobilien
realise *83* realisieren, verwirklichen
receipt *8* Quittung, Beleg
receivables (AE) *80* Forderungen
recent *14* letzte(r,s), jüngst
recently *38* neulich, vor kurzem
recession *82* Rezession
rechargeable *61* aufladbar
recipient *44* Empfänger/in
recommend *65* empfehlen
recommendation *104* Empfehlung
reconstruction *77* Wiederaufbau
record *57* notieren
recover *71t* gesund werden, sich erholen; *90* zurückbekommen, wieder erhalten
recurring *36t* wiederkehrend
red (in th ~) *82* in den roten Zahlen
redeem *48* ablösen, einlösen
redemption date *90* Fälligkeit(sdatum)
reference *36t* Referenz, Empfehlungsschreiben
reflect *96* wiedergeben

refund *38* Rückzahlung, Erstattung
refuse *55* ablehnen, sich weigern
regarding *71* in Bezug auf
register *78* eintragen
regular *14* regelmäßig
regularly *19* regelmäßig
regulate *108* kontrollieren, regulieren
regulation *96* Regulierung
reimburse *73* erstatten
related to *65* verbunden mit
relating to *33* betreffend, in Zusammenhang mit
reliable *123* zuverlässig
reliant on *83* sich stützend auf
reluctant *61* widerwillig, ungern
rely on *39* sich verlassen auf
reminder *39* Mahnung
renew *83* erneuern
rent *39* Miete, 63 mieten
rental car *52* Mietwagen
repay *64* zurück-, abzahlen, tilgen
repayment *65* Rückzahlung, Tilgung
repeatedly *66* wiederholt, mehrfach
replacement *51* Ersatz
request *73* bitten (um)
require *33* benötigen, auf-, erfordern
reschedule *73* strecken
research *16* Forschung
reserves *80* Rücklagen
residence permit *68* Aufenthaltserlaubnis
resident address *106* Wohnadresse
residential status *35* Wohnverhältnis
residents' registration office *28* Einwohnermeldeamt
resources *37* Mittel, Ressourcen
responsible *49* verantwortlich
restless *37* unermüdlich
restore *75* wiederherstellen
restricted to *61* beschränkt auf
restriction *22* Einschränkung
retail investor *96* Privatanleger/in
retail *65* Einzelhandels-
retailer 48 Einzelhändler/in
retained profits *80* nicht ausgeschüttete Gewinne
retire *101* in den Ruhestand gehen, in Rente/Pension gehen
retired *20* pensioniert, im Ruhestand
retirement *24* (Eintritt in den) Ruhestand, Pensionierung
return *11t* Gewinn, Ertrag
reunification *79* Wiedervereinigung
revenue generation *37* Erzielung von Erträgen
reverse *30* vertauschen
review *36t* (Über-)Prüfung, Bericht, 65 überprüfen
revoke *39* rückgängig machen, zurückziehen
revolving credit *73* wiederholte Kreditaufnahme
reward *48* belohnen; Belohnung
rights issue *90* Bezugsrechtsemission
rise *22* (an)steigen, anwachsen, sich erhöhen
root *83* Wurzel
roughly *48* ungefähr
rubble *83* Trümmer
rule *39* beherrschen
run out of *8* ausgehen, zu Ende gehen
run short of *20* knapp werden mit
running costs *79* Unterhaltskosten, Betriebskosten

S

safe custody account *12* Depotkonto, Effektendepot
safeguard *12* sicher aufbewahren
safety precaution *57* Sicherheitsvorkehrung
salary *11t* Gehalt
sales *88* Absatz
sales assistant *7* Verkäufer/in
sales receipt *46* Quittung, Kassenbeleg
salesman *73* Vertreter
sample *120* Muster, Probe
satellite transmitter *51* Satellitensender
satisfactory *122* zufrieden stellend
save *20* (ein)sparen
savings (plural only) *11t* Ersparnisse
savings account *11t* Sparkonto
savings bank *9* Sparkasse
scheme *46* Vorhaben, Projekt
SCHUFA declaration *34* SCHUFA-Klausel
scope *37* Umfang
score *36t* Punktestand
season *63* Saison
second to none *37* unübertroffen, unerreicht
secret service *50* Geheimdienst
sector *15* Sektor, Bereich
secure *47* sicher; *78* sichern
securities *10* Wertpapiere, Effekten
select *52* auswählen
selection *52* Auswahl, Angebot
self-accelerating *123* selbst beschleunigend
self-employed *35* selbstständig
semiconductor *88* Halbleiter
separate *88* getrennt
separation of property *68* Gütertrennung
serial number *60t* Seriennummer, laufende Nummer
serious *26* ernst(haft)
serve *11* bedienen
service *7* Dienst(leistung)
set *65* festgesetzt
set up *14* eröffnen, einrichten
settlement *49* (Be-)Zahlung, Begleichung
share *77* (Geschäfts-)Anteil, Aktie
share capital *80* Stammkapital, gezeichnetes Kapital
share(s) *85* Aktie(n)
shareholder *80* Aktionär/in
shark *97* Hai
sharp(ly) *123* rasch, schnell, stark
shelf *7* Regal(brett)
shift *123* Wandel, Wechsel
shift work *16* Schichtarbeit
ship *112* (ver)senden
shipment *112* Sendung, (Schiffs-) Ladung, Lieferung
shipping line *113* Schifffahrtslinie, Reederei
shopping mall *16* Einkaufspassage
shortly *76* in Kürze
short-term *65* kurzfristig
show up *48* erscheinen, auftauchen
shrink *123* abbauen, verringern
sift the wheat from the chaff *96* die Spreu vom Weizen trennen
sign *28* unterschreiben
signature *28* Unterschrift
significant *37* bedeutend, wichtig
silencer *51* Schalldämpfer
similar *22* ähnlich
similarity *36* Ähnlichkeit
single *20* unverheiratet, ledig

sit an exam *36t* eine Prüfung machen
skip *18* überspringen
slide *73* schiefe Ebene
slide down *73* hinuntergleiten
slippery slope *73* Rutschbahn
slot *43* Schlitz
smart card *61* Scheckkarte (mit Mikrochip)
smooth out *65* ausgleichen
snag *63* Haken
snatch *60t* schnappen, wegreißen
social security *106* Sozialversicherung
sole *28* alleinig
solution *43* Lösung
solve *39* lösen
sound *22* gesund
source of income *68* Einkommensquelle
space defence mechanism *50* Raketenabwehrprogramm
(special) offer (on ~) *8* im (Sonder)angebot
specialize in *77* sich spezialisieren auf
specially *108* speziell, besonders
specific *88* speziell, bestimmte/r/s
specified *78* spezifiziert
specimen signature *28* Unterschriftsprobe
speculate *104* spekulieren
speculative *106* spekulativ
spendable *48* zu verwenden
spread *89* Kursspanne
stable *106* stabil
staff *15* Personal
stake *88* Beteiligung, Anteil
stand at *56* stehen bei
standby *65* Hilfe
standing order *12* Dauerauftrag
state *76* Staat; *117* feststellen
statement *21* Aussage
statement of account *23* Kontoauszug
statement printer *10* Kontoauszugsdrucker
steady *107* fest
stimulate *96* anregen
stock (in ~) *7* vorrätig
stock market *83* (Wertpapier-) Börse
stocks *80* Lager(bestand); *96* Anleihen, Aktien
stop *51* sperren (Kreditkarte)
straight *71t* direkt
straightforward *25* einfach
strict *43* streng
strongroom *10* (Bank-)Tresor, Stahlkammer
struggle *82* Kampf, kämpfen
stumble along *73* weitere Fehler machen
sub-index, -indices *96* Unter-Index, -Indizes
subject to *22* abhängig von; *101* unterworfen
submit to *16* sich unterwerfen
subscribe to *85* zeichnen
subscription *40* Beitrag
subscription period *88* Zeichnungsphase
subsequent *37* (nach)folgend
subsidiary *75* Tochterfirma
subsidize *76* subventionieren
substitute *79* Ersatzform
successor *49* Nachfolger/in
succumb to sth *73* einer Sache erliegen
suggest *15* vorschlagen
suggestion *13* Vorschlag
suit *24* passen (zu)
suitability *106* Eignung
suitable *18* geeignet, passend, angemessen
supplement *100* ergänzen, ersetzen
supplier *80* Zulieferer
supply *12* (be)liefern, versorgen; *83* Angebot
support *14* Unterstützung, (technische) Hilfe, *71t* unterstützen
supposed (be ~ to be) *100* sollen sein
surname *35* Nach-, Familienname
surplus *68* Überschuss
surrender *110* abtreten
surrender value *110* Rückkaufswert
survey *48* Untersuchung, Analyse, Überblick
sustain *37* aufrechterhalten
sweep up *123* hinwegfegen über
sweeten *91* versüßen
syllable *58* Silbe
syndicate *89* Gruppe, Konsortium
system of marital property *68* Güterstand

T
tailored *65* maßgeschneidert
take a seat *11t* Platz nehmen
take out a mortgage *81* eine Hypothek aufnehmen
take turns *42* (sich) abwechseln
tamper-proof *61* fälschungssicher
tangible assets *80* Sach(anlage)-vermögen(swerte)
tap *123* erschließen, nutzbar machen
target *24* Ziel
task *23* Aufgabe
tax bracket *106* Steuerklasse
tax revenue *90* Steueraufkommen, -einnahmen
temporary *110* zeitlich befristet
tempted (to be ~) *62* geneigt sein
tempting *72* verführerisch
tend to *71t* tendieren zu, neigen zu
term deposit account *98* Festgeldkonto
term *19* Ausdruck, *64* Laufzeit
terms *22* Bedingungen, Konditionen
the other way around *98* umgekehrt
the small print *64* das Kleingedruckte
thereof *22* davon
these days *39* heutzutage
thus *16* so, somit
tide sb over *71t* über die Runden kommen
tide *123* Flut
till *8* (Laden-)Kasse
time bomb *109* Zeitbombe
time-starved *16* in Zeitnot, unter Zeitdruck
tinker around with *16* herumpfuschen mit
title document *81* Traditionspapier
to my mind *26* meiner Meinung nach
token *48* Marke, Chip
tolerance *106* Toleranz
toll-free *52* gebührenfrei
tool *82* Werkzeug, Instrument
topic *15* Thema
total *68* Gesamt-
tough guy (infl.) *112* zäher Bursche
trace *44* zurückverfolgen
trade creditors *80* Verbindlichkeiten aus Lieferung und Leistung
trade debtors *80* Forderungen

trade debts *80* Forderungen
trademark *48* Warenzeichen, Handelsmarke
trading *86* Handel
traffic *11t* (Straßen-)Verkehr
trainee *9* Auszubildende/r, Praktikant/in
traineeship *20* Ausbildung-(sverhältnis)
transfer *11t* überweisen
translate *83* übertragen, *118* übersetzen
transshipment *121* Umladung, Umladegeschäft
trap *73* Falle
travel agency *86* Reisebüro
traveller's cheque *11t* Reisescheck
treble *83* verdreifachen
trigger *65* auslösen
true APR *70* effektiver Jahreszins
turnover *36t* Umsatz

U

ultimately *16* schließlich, letzten Endes
unauthorized *28* unbefugt
underestimate *72* unterschätzen
undoubtedly *96* zweifellos, ohne (jeden) Zweifel
unit *92* Investmentanteil, Fondsanteil
unit trust *98* Investmentfonds
unlike *65* anders als, im Gegensatz zu
unload *116* entladen, löschen
unmanageable *73* unkontrollierbar
unwise *72* unklug
updatable *61* aktualisierbar
update *62* aktualisieren
updated *108* aktualisiert, auf dem neuesten Stand
upgraded *36t* aufgewertet
ups and downs *71t* Höhen und Tiefen
urgent *28* dringend, eilig
urgently *45* dringend
used to work *11t* arbeitete(n) früher
utilities *82* Versorgungsbetriebe

V

vacation *52* Urlaub, Ferien
valid *123* gültig
valuable *81* wertvoll
valuables *12* Wertsachen
value for money *25* ein gutes Preis-Leistungsverhältnis
value *16* schätzen, Wert, Nutzen
valued (be ~ at) *88* ... wert sein
variable *52* veränderlich
vary *39* wechseln, variieren
vast *123* riesig, gewaltig
VAT (= value-added tax) *7* Mehrwertsteuer
vehicle *78* Fahrzeug
venture *83* Wagnis
venture capital *83* Risikokapital, Wagniskapital
venture capitalism *83* Risikokapitalismus, Wagniskapitalismus
venture capitalist *83* Risikokapitalist, Wagniskapitalist
vessel *117* Schiff
viable *16* brauchbar, rentabel
vie *88* wetteifern
view *14* sich ansehen
virtually *123* praktisch, nahezu
visual aids *24* Visualisierungsmittel
vocational school *36t* Berufsschule
volatile *98* unbeständig, schwankend
voluntary *68* freiwillig
vote *90* abstimmen, wählen

W

wage(s) *11t* Lohn
waive a fee *52* auf eine Gebühr verzichten
wallet *48* Brieftasche
warehouse *81* Lager(haus)
warm body *16* lebende Person
warrant *81* Lagerschein, Warenschein
wear and tear *36t* Abnutzung, Verschleiß
weigh up the pros and cons *26* das Für und Wider abwägen
what is more *14* darüber hinaus
What's up? *50* Was ist los?
when it comes to ... *22* wenn es um ... geht
wherever *46* wo (immer)
Why bother? *39* Wozu das alles?
Why the rush? *85* Was soll die Hetze?
widely used *44* weit verbreitet
widowed *20* verwitwet
withdraw *16* abheben
withdrawal *18* Abhebung
work out cheaper *64* sich als billiger herausstellen
working day *46* Werktag
worldwide *52* weltweit
would you mind (+ -ing form) *32* würden Sie bitte
writing (in ~) *33* schriftlich

Y

yield profits *101* Gewinne erzielen
yield *90* Ertrag, Rendite
you guys (infl.) *112* Ihr Jungs
you're welcome *19* nichts zu danken, bitte (schön)
Yours faithfully *38* Mit freundlichen Grüßen, Hochachtungsvoll

Z

zip (AE) *106* Postleitzahl

Basic word list

Diese Liste enthält ca. 1000 Grundwörter, die in *Money Matters* als bekannt vorausgesetzt werden.

a bit ein wenig, etwas
a couple of ein paar
a lot viel, sehr
able fähig, in der Lage sein
about über, etwa
above über, oben
accent Akzent
accept annehmen
accident Zufall, Unfall
across hin-, herüber
action Aktion, Handlung
actor Schauspieler/in
add addieren, hinzufügen
advantage Vorteil
after nach, nachdem
after all schließlich doch
afternoon Nachmittag
again wieder
against gegen
age Zeitalter, Alter
age group Altersgruppe
aged im Alter von
ago vor
agree übereinstimmen, zustimmen
air Luft
airline Fluggesellschaft
alarm system Alarmanlage
all alle
all in all alles in allem
all right (it's ~) in Ordnung, (schon) gut
allergic allergisch
allow erlauben, gestatten
allowed to dürfen, gestattet **sein**
almost fast, beinahe
already schon, bereits
also auch, außerdem
always immer
among in(mitten), zwischen
analyse analysieren
analysis Analyse
angel Engel
angry böse, wütend, zornig
announce bekanntgeben, ankündigen
annual jährlich
another noch eine/r/s
answer Antwort; antworten
antique Antiquität
antiques shop Antiquitätenladen
any irgendetwas, irgendwelche, jede(r,s)
anybody jemand, jeder
anyone jemand, jede/r
anything else sonst noch etwas
anytime jederzeit
anyway jedenfalls
anywhere irgendwo(hin)
appear erscheinen, auftauchen
April April
around herum, ungefähr
arrange arrangieren, vereinbaren
arrangement Vereinbarung, Termin
arranger Arrangeur
arrive ankommen
art gallery Kunstgalerie
article Artikel, Gegenstand
artist Künstler/in
ask fragen, bitten, einladen
ask for fragen nach, bitten um
at least wenigstens, mindestens
at once sofort, augenblicklich
at the bottom unten
at the moment im Augenblick
attractive attraktiv, anziehend
au pair Au-pair-Mädchen
August August
automatic automatisch
automatically automatisch
autumn Herbst
avoid vermeiden
away weg, entfernt
back Rückseite; zurück; unterstützen
back (on the ~) auf der Rückseite
bad schlecht, schlimm
banking Bankwesen, Bankgeschäfte
based on basierend auf
bathroom Badezimmer
be sein
be able to können
because weil
become werden
before vor, vorher, bevor
begin anfangen, beginnen
behind hinter, hinten
believe glauben
belong gehören
below unter, unten
best beste/r/s, am besten
Best wishes Mit freundlichen Grüßen
better besser
between zwischen
big groß, kräftig
bill Rechnung
bonus Zulage, Prämie
book Buch; buchen, reservieren
bookshop Buchhandlung
born geboren
borrow (sich etw) borgen, (aus)leihen
boss Chef/in
both beide
bottom line Endergebnis
bought kaufte/n, gekauft
box Kiste, Schachtel, Kästchen
brackets Klammern
bring bringen, holen
brother Bruder
brought brachte/n, gebracht
build (auf)bauen, errichten
build on bauen auf
builder Bauunternehmer
bureaucracy Bürokratie
business Firma, Geschäft(e)
business (do ~) Geschäfte machen
business plan Geschäftsvorhaben
busy beschäftigt, besetzt, belebt
but aber, sondern, außer
buy kaufen
buyer Käufer/in, Einkäufer/in
buying price Kaufpreis
by means of mit Hilfe von
by post mit der Post
bye tschüs
call Telefongespräch, Anruf; anrufen, rufen
call back zurückrufen
call in (herbei)rufen, kommen lassen
call-centre Callcenter
called (to be ~) heißen
camera Fotoapparat, Kamera
candidate Bewerber/in, Kandidat/in
cannot nicht können
capital Kapital, Hauptstadt
captain Kapitän
car Auto
card Karte
career Karriere, Laufbahn
careful vorsichtig, sorgfältig
carry tragen, befördern
cartoon Zeichentrickfilm, Karikatur
case study Fallstudie
central zentral, mittlere/r/s
centre Mitte, Mittelpunkt, Zentrum
certainly sicherlich, gewiss
cheap billig, günstig
check Scheck, Überprüfung; (über)prüfen, kontrollieren
children Kinder
choice Wahl, Auswahl
choose (aus)wählen, (sich) aussuchen
Christmas Weihnachten
city (Groß-)Stadt
city centre (Stadt-)Zentrum
classic klassisch
clear klar; (zollamtlich) abfertigen, einlösen (Scheck)
climb klettern, (be)steigen

close (ab)schließen
clothes Kleidung, Kleider
coast Küste
coffee Kaffee
collect sammeln, abholen
collection Sammlung, Leerung, Inkasso
college of art Kunsthochschule
colour Farbe; anmalen, färben
combination Kombination, Zusammenschluss
combine zusammenfügen
come kommen
company Unternehmen, Firma, Gesellschaft
compare vergleichen
complete vollständig; vervollständigen, ergänzen
completely völlig
concentrated konzentriert
concert Konzert
condition Zustand, Bedingung
congratulations herzlichen Glückwunsch, Glückwünsche
connect verbinden
connection Verbindung, Zusammenhang
constantly ständig
consulate Konsulat
control Kontrolle; kontrollieren, beherrschen
conversation Gespräch, Unterhaltung
copy Kopie, Exemplar; kopieren
correct korrigieren, berichtigen; richtig
correct(ly) genau, richtig
cost Kosten; kosten
costs Kosten
count zählen
country Land, Staat
courier Reiseleiter/in, Kurier
cousin Cousin/e
create (er)schaffen, verursachen, erstellen
creative kreativ, schöpferisch
crowded überfüllt
culture Kultur
cup Tasse, Pokal
customer Kunde, Kundin
cut back kürzen
cut up zerschneiden, -legen
daily täglich; Tageszeitung
danger Gefahr
dangerous gefährlich
data Daten
date Datum, Termin, Verabredung
daughter Tochter
day Tag
deadly tödlich
deaf taub
deal Geschäft
death Tod
December Dezember
decide (sich) entscheiden, beschließen
definition Definition
describe beschreiben
desk (Schreib-)Tisch, Arbeitsplatz, Schalter
detail Einzelheit, Detail
detailed detailliert, ausführlich, genau
develop (sich) entwickeln
diagram grafische Darstellung, Diagramm
dialogue Dialog
dictionary Wörterbuch
difference Unterschied
different anders, verschieden, unterschiedlich
difficult schwer, schwierig
difficulty Schwierigkeit
direct direkt; leiten
directly direkt
disadvantage Nachteil, Schaden
discuss besprechen, diskutieren (über), erörtern
discussion Diskussion
doctor Arzt, Ärztin
document Dokument
down (nach) unten, hin-, herunter
draw ziehen, zeichnen,
dream Traum; träumen
drive (Auto) fahren, antreiben; Antrieb
during während
each jede(r, s)
early früh(zeitig)
earn verdienen
easily leicht, einfach
eastern östlich, Ost-
easy einfach, leicht
effective effektiv, wirksam
either entweder
electronic elektronisch
employed beschäftigt, angestellt
end Ende, Schluss; (be)enden
English-speaking englischsprachig
enjoy genießen, gefallen, gern haben/tun
enough ausreichend, genug
enter hineingehen
entertain unterhalten, amüsieren
especially besonders
etc usw.
even eben, gerade, sogar (noch)
evening Abend
ever je(mals), schon (ein)mal
every jede/r/s
everybody jede/r
everyday alltäglich
everyone jede/r/s, alle
everything alles
exactly exakt, genau
example Beispiel
excellent ausgezeichnet, hervorragend
except außer
excuse me Entschuldigung
exist existieren
expect erwarten, schätzen
expenditure Ausgabe(n), (Un-)Kosten
expensive teuer
expert Fachmann/frau, Experte/Expertin
explain erklären, erläutern
export Export; exportieren
exporter Exporteur/in
express ausdrücken
expression (Gesichts-)Ausdruck
eye Auge
fact Tatsache
fall fallen
family Familie
far weit (entfernt)
farm Bauernhof, Farm
fast schnell
father Vater
February Februar
feel (sich) fühlen, der Meinung sein
few wenig(e), ein paar
fill in ausfüllen, eintragen
finally schließlich, endlich
financial finanziell, Wirtschafts-, Finanz-
find finden, suchen
find out herausfinden
fine gut, in Ordnung
finish (be)enden, aufhören (mit)
firm Firma; fest, bestimmt
first erste(r,s), zuerst
first class erste Klasse
fish out herausholen
fixed fest(gesetzt)
flat flach, platt; Wohnung
flexible flexibel
flight Flug
fly fliegen; Fliege
follow (ver)folgen, sich ergeben aus
following folgende(s/r)
food Essen, Lebensmittel
for für
for example zum Beispiel
foreign Auslands-, ausländisch, fremd
foreign language Fremdsprache
forget vergessen
form Form, Formular; aufstellen, (sich) bilden
fortunately glücklicherweise
free kostenlos, frei
freelance freiberuflich, -schaffend
freephone gebührenfreies Telefon
Friday Freitag
friend Freund/in
friendly freundlich
from von, aus
from time to time von Zeit zu Zeit
front Vorderseite; nach vorne
frozen (tief)gefroren

fruit Obst, Früchte
full(y) völlig
funny komisch, seltsam
furniture Möbel
further weitere(s, r)
future Zukunft; (zu)künftig
game Spiel
garage (Auto-)Werkstatt, Tankstelle, Garage
general allgemein, generell
generally im Allgemeinen
get out herauskommen, aussteigen
give geben
give out ausgeben
give sb a ring jdn anrufen
go gehen, fahren
go in hineingehen
go mad verrückt werden
go out ausgehen
go over durchgehen
go through durchmachen, -gehen
go up steigen
go wrong schief gehen
golf Golf
good gut
good lord Oh Gott!
Good luck Viel Glück
good afternoon guten Tag (nachmittags)
goodbye auf Wiedersehen
good morning guten Morgen
government Regierung
grandchildren Enkel
grandfather Großvater
graphics Grafiken, grafische Darstellung
great groß(artig), toll, prima
greatly in großem Maße
greet (be)grüßen
group Konzern, Gruppe
grow wachsen, anbauen
guarantee Garantie; garantieren
half Hälfte; halb
hand over aushändigen, übergeben
handbag Handtasche
happen geschehen
happy glücklich, zufrieden, froh
hard schwer, schwierig, hart
have haben
have to müssen
head Kopf, Leiter/in
hear hören
heart Herz
heavily schwer, sehr, stark
help Hilfe; helfen
helpdesk Auskunft
helpful hilfreich, hilfsbereit
helpline Telefonseelsorge
here hier
hide (sich) verstecken
high hoch
highly äußerst
historic historische(r,s)
history Geschichte
hit schlagen, treffen
hobby Hobby
hold (fest)halten, (um)fassen, enthalten
hold onto festhalten an
holiday flat Ferienwohnung
holiday(s) Ferien, Urlaub
home Zuhause; nach/zu Hause
home banking Homebanking
home market Binnenmarkt
hope Hoffnung; hoffen
hospital Krankenhaus
hotel Hotel
hotel management Hotelleitung
hour Stunde
house Haus
how wie
how long wie lange
how much wie viel
however doch, jedoch, aber
husband (Ehe-)Mann
I can't stand it ich halte es nicht aus
idea Idee, Gedanke, Vorstellung
identity card (Personal-)Ausweis
if wenn, falls, ob
ill krank
imagine sich vorstellen, sich einbilden
immediately sofort, umgehend
import Import; importieren
important wichtig
importer Importeur/in
impossible unmöglich
improve (sich) verbessern, sich bessern
in a hurry in Eile
in that case in diesem Fall
in the end zum Schluss, schließlich
in the future zukünftig
income Einkommen
incorrect falsch, unrichtig
industrial Industrie-, industriell
industry Industrie, Gewerbe, Branche
inform informieren, benachrichtigen
information Auskunft, Information(en)
instead stattdessen, anstatt
integration Eingliederung, Integration
interested interessiert
interesting interessant
international international
January Januar
join sich anschließen, verbinden
joke Witz, Scherz; scherzen
journey Reise, Fahrt
juice Saft
July Juli
June Juni
just einfach, nur, bloß, gerade, genau
just a minute einen Moment
keep aufbewahren, (ein)halten, behalten
key Schlüssel
kind nett, freundlich; Art, Sorte
kindly freundlicherweise
kitchen Küche
know kennen, wissen
lady Dame
land Land(besitz), Grundstück
large groß, umfangreich
last letzte(r,s), zuletzt; dauern
late spät
later später
law Jura, Recht(swissenschaft), Gesetz
layout Layout, Grundriss
leader Führer/in, Anführer/in
leading führend, prominent
learn lernen, erfahren
leave (stehen, liegen) lassen, verlassen, hinterlassen
left (on the ~) auf der linken Seite
leisure time Freizeit
lend (ver)leihen, Kredit vergeben
less weniger, abzüglich
let (zu)lassen, erlauben
let me see mal sehen
letter Buchstabe, Brief
lie liegen; lügen
life Leben
lifestyle Lebensstil
like mögen, gern haben; (ähnlich) wie
line Linie, Zeile, (Telefon-)Leitung, Anschluss, (Waren-)Sortiment
list Liste; auflisten, -schreiben
listen to an-, zuhören
little klein, wenig
live leben, wohnen
long lang; sich sehnen, verlangen (nach)
look Blick, Aussehen; (aus)sehen, blicken
look after aufpassen auf, sich kümmern um
look at ansehen, betrachten
look for suchen nach
look in hereinschauen
lose verlieren
lots viel
lottery Lotterie, Lotto
loud laut
love Liebe; lieben, sehr gern mögen
low niedrig; Tief(stand)
lucky glücklich
machinery Maschinen(park)
mad wütend, wahnsinnig, verrückt
magazine Zeitschrift, Magazin, Illustrierte
mail Post, E-Mail; E-Mails schicken
main Haupt-, hauptsächlich, wichtigste/r/s
mainly hauptsächlich, vor allem

majority Mehrheit
make machen, zubereiten, verdienen; Fabrikat, Marke
make sure absichern, sicherstellen, sich vergewissern
man Mann, der Mensch
manage (es) schaffen, leiten, verwalten
management Management, (Geschäfts-)Führung
many viele
map (Stadt-)Plan, (Land-)Karte
march März
market Markt; vermarkten
married verheiratet
maximum höchste/r/s; Maximum
May Mai
may dürfen, mögen, kann (vielleicht)
maybe vielleicht
mean bedeuten, meinen
meaning Bedeutung, Sinn
meaningful bedeutsam
meet (zusammen)treffen, sich treffen (mit)
meeting Versammlung, Sitzung, Besprechung
member Mitglied, Teil
memory Gedächtnis, (Nummern-)Speicher
metalwork Werken mit Metall
middle Mitte
might könnte, könnte(n) (vielleicht)
mile Meile
military militärisch; Militär
millennium Jahrtausend
million Million
minimum Minimum; Mindest-
minute Minute
missing verschwunden, fehlend, nicht vorhanden
mission Auftrag, Mission, Einsatz
mistake Fehler, Irrtum; missverstehen, verwechseln
mixture Mischung
Monday Montag
money Geld
month Monat
monthly Monatszeitschrift; monatlich
more mehr
more and more immer mehr
morning Morgen
most beinahe, fast, am meisten
mother Mutter
mouse Maus
move Bewegung, Initiative, Maßnahme; (sich) bewegen
much viel
must müssen
my dear mein/e Liebe/r
name Name; (be)nennen
national national, National-, Staats-, Landes-; Staatsbürger/in
nationality Staatsangehörigkeit
near nahe, in der Nähe von
nearly beinahe, fast, nahezu
necessary nötig, notwendig
need Bedürfnis, Bedarf; brauchen, benötigen
negative Verneinung; negativ
neighbour Nachbar/in
nervous nervös
network Sender, Netzwerk
never nie(mals)
new neu
next nächste/r/s, danach
next to (direkt) neben
nice schön, nett, hübsch
night Nacht
nobody niemand
nor auch nicht, noch
normal normal, üblich
normally normalerweise
not nicht
note Notiz, Note; zur Kenntnis nehmen
notebook Notizbuch
nothing nichts
now nun, jetzt
nowadays heutzutage
number (Telefon-)Nummer, Zahl, Ziffer; nummerieren
nurse Krankenschwester, -pfleger/in; pflegen
October Oktober
of course natürlich, selbstverständlich
offered angeboten
office Amt, Büro
office clerk Büroangestellte/r
often oft, häufig
oh dear ach du liebe Zeit
oil company Ölfirma
old alt
on auf, an, am
on board an Bord
on condition that unter der Bedingung, dass
once einmal, einst(mals), sobald
only nur
open (sich) öffnen, gründen, eröffnen; offen
opening hours Geschäftszeiten, -zeiten
operation Operation, Betrieb, Aktion
opinion Meinung
opposite Gegenteil; entgegengesetzt
option Option, Börsentermingeschäft, Möglichkeit
or oder
order Bestellung, Auftrag; bestellen, in Auftrag geben
organisation, organization Organisation
organise, organize organisieren, arrangieren
original original, ursprünglich; Original
other andere(r,s)
out draußen, hinaus/heraus, nicht da
over über, vorbei, vorüber
overall (ins)gesamt, total, allgemein
overland über Land
overseas ausländisch, überseeisch
overtake überholen
over there da drüben, dort
own besitzen; eigene/r/s
owner Besitzer/in
page Seite
painting Gemälde
pair Paar
parallel parallel
parents Eltern
part Teil, Rolle
particularly besonders
part-time halbtags, Teilzeit-
pass on weiterreichen, -geben, -leiten
passport (Reise-)Pass
past an ... vorbei, vorüber; Vergangenheit
pay back zurückzahlen, rückvergüten, tilgen
pay for zahlen für
pay in einzahlen
pay off ab(be)zahlen, zurück-, auszahlen, tilgen
payable zahlbar, fällig
payment system Lohnsteuerverfahren
PC banking Home-, Telebanking
people Leute, Menschen, Volk
per annum jährlich, pro Jahr
per cent Prozent
performance Vorstellung, Aufführung, Leistung(en)
perhaps vielleicht, eventuell
period Zeit(raum), Zeitspanne, Periode
permanently permanent, für immer
permission Erlaubnis, Einverständnis, Genehmigung
person Mensch, Person
personal persönlich
personal computer PC, Computer
petrol station Tankstelle
phone call Anruf
phone number Telefonnummer
photo Foto
physically physisch
pick up auf-, hochheben, (mit dem Auto) abholen
picture Bild
piece of information (Einzel-) Information
pill Pille
place Stelle, Platz, Ort; setzen, stellen, legen, platzieren
place of work Arbeitsstelle

plan Plan; planen, vorhaben
planet Planet
platform Bahnsteig, Gleis, Programm
play (Theater-)Stück; (ab)spielen
please gefallen, Freude machen; bitte
pleased froh, erfreut
plenty of eine Menge, viel
pocket Tasche
pocket money Taschengeld
point Punkt; (hin)deuten, richten
point of view Standpunkt
point out hinweisen auf, erläutern
police Polizei
poor arm, schlecht, mangelhaft
popular beliebt, populär
population Bevölkerung, Einwohner(zahl)
port Hafen(stadt)
position Stelle, Position, Stellung, Lage
positive positiv, bejahend
possibility Möglichkeit
possible möglich, denkbar
post Post, Posten, Stelle; mit der Post schicken
powerful mächtig, einflussreich, leistungs(stark)
practice Praxis, Übung, Training
practise (ein)üben
prefer vorziehen, lieber mögen, bevorzugen
prepare (sich) vorbereiten, zubereiten
present anwesend
press Presse; drücken
price (Kauf-)Preis
printout (Computer-)Ausdruck
privilege Privileg
probable wahrscheinlich
probably wahrscheinlich
problem Problem
produce produzieren, herstellen, verursachen, vorlegen
producer Produzent/in, Hersteller/in, Erzeuger
product Produkt, Erzeugnis
professional Berufs-, Fach-, professionell; Profi
professor Professor/in
profitable gewinnbringend, nützlich, rentabel
programme Sendung, Programm; programmieren
promise versprechen; Versprechen
promote (be)fördern, anpreisen
provider Provider, Lieferant
publicity Publizität, Publicity
purse Portemonnaie, Geldbörse
put setzen, stellen, legen, formulieren
qualification Qualifikation, Ausbildung, Zeugnis, Befähigung
qualified qualifiziert, ausgebildet
quality Qualität
quarter Viertel, Quartal
question Frage; be-, ausfragen, in Frage stellen
quick schnell
quite ziemlich, ganz
race Rasse, (Wett-)Rennen
rail Schiene, Gleis, (Eisen-)Bahn
raise erhöhen, (er)heben, auftreiben; Gehalts-, Lohnerhöhung
rarely selten
rather ziemlich, lieber, etwas
reach greifen, erreichen
read lesen
reader Leser/in
ready fertig, bereit
real echt, wirklich, sehr
reality Wirklichkeit
realize merken, sich klar werden, verwirklichen
really wirklich, eigentlich, tatsächlich
reason Vernunft, Grund, Begründung
receive erhalten, empfangen, bekommen
reduce reduzieren, vermindern
relevant relevant, wichtig
remember sich erinnern, daran denken
report Bericht, Reportage, (Schul-)Zeugnis; berichten
respond to reagieren auf, antworten
rest Ruhe, Pause, Erholung, übriger Teil; sich ausruhen
result Resultat, Folge, Ergebnis; folgen
return Rückkehr, Gewinn, Ertrag; zurückgeben, -senden
reverse rückgängig machen, umkehren
rewrite umschreiben, neu schreiben
rich reich, wohlhabend
right rechts, in Ordnung, richtig; rechte Seite, Recht
right (on the ~) auf der rechten Seite
right away sofort
ring through durchrufen
ring up anrufen
risk Risiko; riskieren
risky riskant
role Rolle
role play Rollenspiel
room Zimmer, Raum, Platz
round the clock rund um die Uhr
run laufen, rennen, fahren, leiten, betreiben
run out ausgehen, zu Ende gehen
safe Safe, Tresor; sicher, heil, wohlbehalten
same gleiche(r,s), der-, die-, dasselbe
Saturday Sonnabend, Samstag
say sagen, aussprechen
scene Szene
school Schule
screen Bildschirm
search Suche, Durchsuchung; (durch)suchen
seat (Sitz-)Platz, Sitz; setzen
second zweite(r,s); Sekunde
second-hand gebraucht, aus zweiter Hand
secretary Sekretär/in
see sehen, besuchen, verstehen
seek suchen
seem (er)scheinen
seldom selten
sell (sich) verkaufen, führen
selling price Verkaufspreis
send senden, schicken
send off abschicken
sender Absender
sense Sinn, Gefühl, Empfindung
sentence Satz, Strafe; verurteilen
September September
several etliche, einige, mehrere
shock Schock, Schlag; erschüttern
shoe shop Schuhgeschäft
shop Laden, Geschäft, Einkauf; einkaufen
shopper Käufer/in
shopping Einkauf(en)
shopping centre Einkaufszentrum
short kurz, klein, knapp
should solle/n, sollte/n
show zeigen
shut schließen, zumachen; (ab)geschlossen, zu
side Seite, Rand
simple einfach
simply einfach
since da, weil, seit
sit sitzen, sich hinsetzen
sit down sich setzen
situation Situation, Lage
sleep schlafen; Schlaf
slow langsam
small klein
smuggle schmuggeln
so also, damit
so do I ich auch
so that damit
some einige, etwas
somebody jemand
somehow irgendwie
someone jemand
something etwas
sometimes manchmal
somewhere irgendwo(hin)
son Sohn
soon bald
sooner or later früher oder später
sorry traurig, tut mir Leid
sort Art, Sorte, Typ; sortieren
sound Geräusch, Klang, Laut; (sich) anhören, klingen

space Raum, Platz, Abstand, Weltall
speak sprechen, reden
speaker Redner/in, Sprecher/in, Lautsprecher
special besondere(r,s)
specialist Spezialist/in, Fachmann/frau
speech Rede, Vortrag
spell buchstabieren
spend ausgeben, verbringen
stand for stehen für
standard Norm, Maßstab, Niveau; üblich, durchschnittlich
stare starren
start anfangen, beginnen; (Schul-, Arbeits- usw.)Beginn, Anfang
starting point Ausgangspunkt
station Bahnhof
stay bleiben, übernachten; Aufenthalt
stay on (noch) bleiben
steal stehlen
step Schritt, Stufe
still still; trotzdem, (immer) noch, immerhin
store Laden, Geschäft, Vorrat, Lager; speichern, aufbewahren
street Straße
strong stark, kräftig (gebaut), streng
strongly stark
stuff Material, Stoff, Zeug
style Stil
such as wie zum Beispiel
suitcase Koffer
sum Summe, Betrag
summer Sommer
supermarket Supermarkt
sure sicher, freilich
swim schwimmen
swimming pool Schwimmbad
symbol Symbol, Zeichen
system System
table Tisch, Tabelle
take nehmen, bringen, dauern
take a look at ansehen, betrachten
take notes (sich) Notizen machen
take out ausführen, abschließen, herausnehmen
take over übernehmen, sich entwickeln (zu)
take place stattfinden
talk Gespräch, Vortrag, Ansprache; sprechen, reden
teach unterrichten, beibringen
teacher Lehrer/in
technological technologisch
telephone Telefon; telefonieren (mit), anrufen
telephone banking Telefonbanking
telephone bill Telefonrechnung
television Fernsehen, Fernseher
tell sagen, erzählen, wissen, erkennen
terrible schrecklich, fürchterlich, furchtbar
text Text
than als
thanks Dank; danke
thank you danke
that dies, der, die, das, dass, jene/r/s
that doesn't matter das macht nichts
theatre Theater
then dann
there da, dort(hin)
therefore deshalb
these diese
thief Dieb/in
thing Sache, Ding
think denken, meinen, finden, glauben
think up (sich) ausdenken
third dritte/r/s; Drittel
through durch
Thursday Donnerstag
ticket (Fahr-, Eintritts-)Karte, Fahr-, Flugschein
time Zeit, Mal
today heute
together zusammen
tomorrow morgen
ton Tonne
tonight heute Abend/Nacht
too zu, auch
top Oberteil, obere Seite, Spitze, Gipfel; Spitzen-
top (at the ~) oben
top line Kopfzeile
tour Tour, Rundgang, -fahrt, Führung, Tournee
tourist Tourist/in
towards auf ... zu, in Richtung auf
town Stadt
traditional traditionell
train ausbilden, trainieren, sich ausbilden lassen; Zug
transaction Geschäft, Vertrag
transport Transport; transportieren
transportation Transport(wesen), Beförderung, Verkehr
travel Reisen; reisen, fahren
trend Trend, Anzeichen
trip Ausflug, Reise, Besuch
trouble Schwierigkeiten, Ärger, Problem/e; beunruhigen, stören
true richtig, wahr
truth Wahrheit
try probieren, kosten, versuchen
turn (sich) drehen, wenden, ein-, abbiegen; Runde
twice zweimal
type erfassen, tippen; Art, Typ, Sorte
unable unfähig, nicht in der Lage
uncle Onkel
under unter
underneath darunter
understand verstehen, begreifen
understanding Verständnis
unexpected unerwartet
unit Lektion, Einheit
university Universität
unless wenn nicht, es sei denn
unnecessary unnötig
unpaid unbezahlt
until bis
untrue unwahr, untreu
up (nach) oben, hin-, herauf
up to bis zu
use Gebrauch; gebrauchen
use up verbrauchen
useful nützlich
usual gewöhnlich, normal
usually normalerweise, gewöhnlich, meistens
various verschiedene(r)
varying wechselnd, unterschiedlich
very sehr, genau
visit Besuch; besuchen, besichtigen
visitor Besucher/in, Gast
vocabulary Vokabular, Wortschatz
wait warten
want wollen
war Krieg
warm warm
warn warnen, darauf hinweisen
washroom Waschraum
watch zusehen, beobachten; (Armband-)Uhr
water Wasser; bewässern, gießen
way Weg, Methode, Art (und Weise)
weak schwach
wear tragen, anhaben
weather Wetter
week Woche
well gesund
west Westen; nach Westen
what was, welche(r,s)
when wenn, als, wann
whenever immer wenn, wann auch immer
where (wo)hin
whether ob
which welche(r,s)
while während, wohingegen; Weile
who wer, der/die/das, welche(r/s)
whole ganze/r/s; Ganze/r/s
whose wessen, dessen, deren
why warum
why on earth warum um Himmels willen
wide breit, weit
widely weit
wife (Ehe-)Frau
win gewinnen, siegen
window Fenster
winter Winter
wish Wunsch; wünschen
with mit, bei

within innerhalb (von), in
without ohne
woman, women Frau, Frauen
wonder sich fragen, sich wundern; Wunder
word Wort
work Arbeit, Werk; funktionieren, bedienen, arbeiten
work out ausrechnen, kalkulieren, funktionieren
worker Arbeiter/in
workplace Arbeitsplatz
world Welt
world class Weltklasse
worry Sorge; sich Sorgen machen
write schreiben
wrong falsch
year Jahr
yearly jährlich, Jahres-
yesterday gestern
yet schon, bereits, doch
young jung

Banking word list: German–English

Die folgende Liste enthält ca. 430 Fachbegriffe aus dem Bankwesen.

abbuchen debit
Abbuchung debit (entry)
Abfindung indemnity
abheben withdraw
Abhebung withdrawal
ablösen redeem
Abteilung department
abtreten assign
Abtretung assignment
abzahlen pay off
abziehen deduct
Adressat consignee
Akkreditiv letter of credit
Aktie share, stock (AE)
Aktiengesellschaft, AG plc (public limited company)
Aktienhandel share-dealing
Aktienkapital share capital
Aktienkurs share price
Aktionär/in shareholder
Aktiva assets
Allgemeine Geschäftsbedingungen General Business Conditions
an der Börse notiert listed on the stock exchange
an die Börse gehen go public
anfängliche Gebühr initial charge
Anfrage inquiry
Angebot offer
Angebot und Nachfrage supply and demand
Angestellte/r clerk, employee
Anlage investment
Anlageberater/in investment consultant
Anlagevermögen fixed assets
anlegen invest
Anleihe(papier) bond
Anleihen bonds, stocks
Anteil share
Antragsformular application form
Antragsteller/in applicant
Arbeitgeber/in employer
Arbeitnehmer/in employee
auf eigene Rechnung handeln act on one's own account
Aufenthaltserlaubnis residence permit
Aufenthaltsnachweis proof of legal residence
Ausbildung(sverhältnis) traineeship
Ausgabe issue
Ausgabe(n) expense
Ausgaben expenditure (no pl.)
ausgeben issue
ausgeübter Beruf occupation
Außenstände receivables
außerhalb der Öffnungszeiten outside banking hours
Aussteller/in drawer
Ausstellungsdatum date of issue
auszahlen pay off
Auszubildende/r trainee
Bankleitzahl bank sort code, bank sorting code
Bankrott bankruptcy
Banktresor strongroom
Bargeld cash, currency
Bargeldautomat cash dispenser
Barscheck open cheque
Barvorschuss cash advance
Bausparkasse building society
Bausparvertrag building society policy
beantragen apply (for)
Bearbeitungsgebühr handling charge
Begleichung settlement
beisteuern contribute
Beitrag contribution
belasten debit
Beleg receipt
berechnen charge
Beruf profession
Berufsschule vocational school
bestätigen confirm, endorse
Betrag amount
Betriebskosten running costs
beurteilen assess
bevollmächtigen authorize (auch authorise)
bewilligen grant
bezahlen pay, honour
Bezahlung payment, settlement
Bezogene/r drawee
Bezugsrechtsemission rights issue
Bilanz balance (sheet)
Börse stock exchange, stock market
Börseneinführung listing
Börsengang flotation, IPO (initial public offering)
Broschüre brochure
brutto gross
Bruttoinlandsprodukt (BIP) GDP (gross domestic product)
Bürge guarantor
Bürgschaft guarantee
Darlehen loan
Dauerauftrag standing order
Debitoren accounts receivable
Depot portfolio
Depot (im ~ der Bank) in the custody of the bank
Depotkonto safe custody account
Devisen foreign currency, foreign exchange (forex)
Dienst(leistung) service
Dispositionskredit overdraft facility
Dividende dividend
Dokumente gegen bar/Zahlung documents against payment
echt genuine
Effekten securities (plural only)
Effektendepot safe custody account
effektiver Jahreszins APR (annual percentage rate), true APR
Eigenkapital equity (capital)
eine Hypothek aufnehmen take out a mortgage
Einkommen income
einlösen cash, honour, redeem
einschätzen assess
Eintrag entry
Einwohnermeldeamt residents' registration office
einzahlen pay in, pay into
Einzahler/in payer
Einzelhändler/in retailer
einziehen claim
Einzugsermächtigung direct debit authorization
Einzugsverfahren direct debit
Emission flotation, issue
Emissionsbank issuing house
Emittent issuer
emittieren issue
Empfänger/in recipient
Entschädigung indemnity
entsprechend equivalent
Entsprechung equivalent
erben inherit
Ersatz replacement
ersetzen replace
erstatten reimburse, refund
Erstattung refund
Ertrag yield
Erwerb acquisition
Europäische Zentralbank European Central Bank (ECB)
fällig werden fall due, mature
fällige Zahlungen payables
Fälligkeit maturity
Fälligkeit(sdatum) redemption date, maturity date
Familienname surname
Familienstand marital status
feindliche Übernahme hostile takeover
Festgeldkonto term deposit account
Filiale branch

Finanzierung financing
Firmendarlehen corporate loan
Firmenkunde corporate client
Firmenkunden corporate business
Forderungen receivables, trade debts
Frachtgut consignment, freight (no pl.)
Fremdkapital creditors
Fremdwährung(en) forex = foreign exchange
führen (Konten) keep (accounts)
Fusion merger
fusionieren merge
Gebühr charge, fee
gebührenfrei free of charge
Geburtsdatum date of birth
Geburtsname name at birth
Geburtsort place of birth
Gegenstück equivalent
Gegenwert equivalent
gegenzeichnen countersign
Gehalt salary
Gehaltskonto current account, checking account (AE)
Geldautomat ATM, cash dispenser
Geldwäschegesetz Money Laundering Act
Gemeinschaftskonto joint account
genehmigen approve
Geschäftsanteil share
geschäftsführende/r Direktor/in chief executive (officer)
Gesellschaftssatzung articles of association
gewähren grant
Gewinn profit
Gewinn- und Verlustrechnung profit and loss account
Girokonto checking account (US), current account
Gläubiger creditors
Gläubiger/in creditor
Grundschuld eintragen register a land-charge
gültig valid
günstig favourable
Güterstand system of marital property
Guthaben credit balance
gutheißen approve
gutschreiben credit
Habensaldo credit balance
haftbar liable
halbjährlich half-yearly
Handelsrechnung commercial invoice
Handlungsvollmacht power of attorney
Hauptgeschäftsführer/in chief executive (officer)
hochriskante Schuldverschreibungen junk bonds
Hypothek aufnehmen take out a mortgage
im Gewahrsam von in the custody of
im Rückstand in arrears
im Wert von ... Dollar ... dollars' worth of
immaterielle(s) Vermögen(swerte) intangible assets
Immobilien real estate
in Umlauf in circulation
in Verzug in arrears
in Zahlungsverzug geraten default
Indossament endorsement
indossieren endorse
Inkassoauftrag erteilen place a collection order
Insolvenz insolvency
institutionelle/r Fondsmanager/in institutional fund manager
Inventar inventory
investieren invest
Investition investment
Investmentanteile units
Investmentfonds unit trust, mutual fund
Investor/in investor
Jahreshauptversammlung annual general meeting (AGM)
Jahresumsatz annual turnover
jährlich annual(ly)
Kapital aufbringen raise capital
Kapitalanleger/in investor
Kapitalbrief certificate of deposit
Kapitalgewinnsteuer capital gains tax
Kapitalversicherung life assurance, endowment insurance
Kassa gegen Dokumente documents against payment
Kasse till
Kassierer/in cashier
Kleinanleger/in retail investor
Kleinkredit personal loan
Kleinkreditberater/in personal loan adviser
Kollege/Kollegin colleague
Konkurs bankruptcy
Konkurs (in ~ gehen) go bankrupt
Konnossement bill of lading
Konsortium syndicate
Konto account
Konto mit Kündigung(sfrist) notice account
Kontoauszug bank statement
Kontoauszugsdrucker statement printer
Kontoinhaber/in account holder
Kontokorrentkonto current account
Kontokorrentschuldner trade debtors
Kontostand balance
Kontoüberziehung overdraft
Kontovollmacht authority for per pro signatory
Kosten charge, expenditure
kostenlos free of charge
Kostenvoranschlag estimate
Kredit credit (no plural)
Kreditgeber lender
Kreditkarte credit card
Kreditnehmer/in borrower
Kreditoren accounts payable
Kreditsicherheiten collateral (security), security (no pl.)
Kunde/Kundin customer
Kundenberater/in customer service officer
Kundenberatung customer service
kündigen give notice
Kündigungsfrist period of notice
Kursspanne spread
Ladenkasse till
Ladung shipment
Lager(bestand) stocks
Lager(haus) warehouse
Lagerbestände inventory
Lagerschein warrant
langfristig long-term
Lastschrift debit, direct debit
Lebensversicherung life assurance, life insurance
Legitimation proof of identity
Leiter/in manager
Lieferung consignment, shipment, delivery
Lieferverbindlichkeiten trade creditors
Lohn salary, wage
Mädchenname maiden name
Mahnung reminder
Miete; mieten rent
Missbrauch misuse
Mitantragsteller/in co-applicant
Münze coin
Nachforschung inquiry
Nachfrage demand
Nachname surname
Nennwert denomination, nominal value
netto net
nominal nominal
Obligation bond, debenture
Orderscheck order cheque
Passiva liabilities
Pension pension
Pensionierung retirement
Personal staff
Personalausweis proof of identity, identity card
Pfand pledge
Pfandrecht lien
Portefeuille portfolio
Praktikant/in trainee
Präsentation presentation
Preisfindung bookbuilding
Privatkunde, -kundin personal customer
Profit profit
Prospekt brochure
Provision commission
prüfen examine

Quittung receipt
realisieren realise
Rechnung invoice, bill
reingezeichnet, clean on board clean on board
Reisescheck traveller's cheque
Rendite return, yield
Rente pension
Rentenpapier bond
Reserven reserves
Risikokapital venture capital
Risikokapitalismus venture capitalism
Risikokapitalist venture capitalist
rückgängig machen revoke
Rücklagen reserves
Rückstellungen für Verbindlichkeiten und Forderungen provisions for liabilities and charges
rückvergüten pay back
Rückzahlung repayment
Ruhestand retirement
Sach(anlage)vermögen tangible assets
Saldo balance
Schadensersatz indemnity
Scheck cheque
Scheckkonto checking account (US Eng)
Schiff vessel
Schiffsladung shipment
schriftlich in writing
SCHUFA German banks' credit reference agency
SCHUFA-Klausel SCHUFA declaration
Schuld(en) debt
schulden owe
Schuldner debtor
Schuldschein promissory note
Schuldverschreibung debenture
schwanken fluctuate
Schwankung fluctuation
selbständig self-employed
Selbstauskunft voluntary disclosure of confidential information
Sendung consignment, shipment
Seriennummer serial number
sich zusammenschließen merge
Sicherheit(en) collateral, security
Sicherheitsvorkehrung safety precaution
Sicherungsübereignung assignment by bill of sale
Soll debit
Soll(saldo) debit balance
Sorten foreign currency
Sparbrief certificate of deposit
sparen save
Sparkasse savings bank
Sparkonto deposit account, savings account
Spekulationssteuer capital gains tax
sperren stop
Staatsanleihen government bonds
Stahlkammer strongroom
Stammaktie equity, ordinary share
Stammaktien equities, ordinary shares
Standardwert blue chip
Steueraufkommen, -einnahmen tax revenue
Steuerbehörde tax authority
Strafe penalty
Strafgebühr penalty fee
Strafzinsen penalty interest
Stückelung denominations
Stundung der Zahlung deferred payment
subventionieren subsidize
Summe amount, total
Tabelle chart
Tätigkeit occupation
Teilverschiffung partial shipment
Termin appointment
tilgen pay back, pay off, repay
Tilgung repayment
Traditionspapier title document
Trassat drawee
Tresor strongroom
Überbringerscheck bearer cheque
übersteigen exceed
übertragen assign
überweisen transfer
Überweisung credit transfer, remittance
überziehen overdraw
Überziehungskredit overdraft
Umladung, Umladegeschäft transshipment
Umlaufvermögen, -kapital current assets
Umsatz turnover
umtauschen change
Umtauschkurs exchange rate
unbefugt unauthorized
unbeständig volatile
ungesicherte Schuldverschreibungen junk bonds
Unterhaltskosten running costs
Unternehmer/in entrepreneur
unterschätzen underestimate
unterschreiben sign
Unterschrift signature
Unterschriftsprobe specimen signature
untersuchen examine
Untersuchung inquiry
unwiderruflich irrevocable
Ursprungszeugnis certificate of origin
Verbindlichkeiten liabilities
Verfallsdatum expiry date
verfügbares Einkommen disposable income
Verladehafen port of loading
Verladung loading
Vermögen(swerte) assets
Vermögensberater/in investment consultant
Vermögensverwaltung asset management
verpfänden pledge
Verrechnungsscheck crossed cheque
Versicherung(spolice) insurance (policy)
Vertrag contract
Verwendungszweck purpose
vierteljährlich quarterly
Vollmacht power of attorney, authority for per pro signatory
Voranschlag estimate
Vorlage presentation
vorlegen present
Vorname first name
vorrätig in stock
Vorstand board of directors
Vorstandsvorsitzende/r chief executive (officer), chairman of the board
Vorzugsaktien preference shares
Währung currency
Wechsel bill of exchange
Wechselkurs exchange rate, rate of exchange
wechseln change
Werktag working day
Wertbezeichnung denomination
Wertpapierbestand Portfolio
Wertpapierbörse stock market, stock exchange
Wertpapiere securities (plural only), stocks and shares
wertvoll valuable
wieder erhalten recover
widerrufen revoke
Wohnverhältnisse residential status
Zahlung settlement, payment
Zahlung bei Sicht payment at sight
Zahlung gegen Rechnung (mit offenem Zahlungsziel) payment on open account
Zahlungsempfänger/in beneficiary, payee
Zahlungsmittel means of payment
Zahlungsunfähigkeit insolvency, default
Zahlungsweise method of payment
zeichnen subscribe to
Zeichnungsfrist subscription period
Zins(en) interest (no plural)
Zinssatz rate of interest, interest rate
Zukauf acquisition
Zulassung listing
zurückbekommen recover
zurückverfolgen trace
zurückzahlen pay back, pay off, repay
zurückziehen revoke
Zusammenschluss merger
Zweck purpose
Zweig(stelle) branch

Acknowledgements

Fotos
Titel: The Stock Market/Photomorgana
action press: S. 59/P. Horree (2)/M. Ulmer;
COMSTOCK: S. 10 (4); S. 15; S. 24 (2); S. 59; S. 60; S. 62; S. 81;
Das Fotoarchiv: S. 59/J. Tack/B. Nimtsch; S. 81/T. Mayer
Sally & Richard Greenhill: S. 15; S. 60;
The Image Bank: S. 10/De Lossy; S. 60/De Lossy;
M. Jüschke: S. 26;
Helga Lade Bildagentur: S. 10/BAV; S. 81/M. Laemmerer;
Lloyds TSB Image Bank: S. 36;
Premium: S. 81 (2);
THE STOCKMARKET: S. 15/T&D.A. McCarthy; S. 24/R. Lewine; S. 29/J. Feingersh; S. 59/J. Feingersh/P. Steel; S. 60/C. Savage; S. 63/Mug Shots; S. 75/J. Feingersh/M. Keller;
TIME Magazine: S. 49/J. Certola;
John Walmsley: S. 24;

Grafik
Oxford Designers & Illustrators
S. 84: The Financial Times Survey; 2.12.1999
S. 87: Beale, Financial Times;
S. 107: Jim Beaker, Financial Times;

Texte
S. 14: *Put yourself in contact,* National Westminster Bank plc;
S. 16: *The Bank,* Financial World, Roger Issott;
S. 22: *Barclays 60 Days Saving Account,* Barclays Bank plc;
S. 37: *World class...,* Lloyds TSB plc;
S. 48: *Beenz Counters,* Lev Grossmann, TIME Inc., 5.6.00;
S. 61: *Paying for online purchases* und S. 62: *Security on the web:* Amaya Guillermo, *Show me the money, Connectis*/Juli 2000;
S. 73: *Sliding Down the Slippery Slope of Consumer Credit,* Rod Usher, TIME inc., 17.1.2000;
S. 82: *Small Businesses Hang onto Credit Lifeline,* Naoko Nakamae, *Financial Times,* 15.12.1999;
S. 83: *Germany embraces venture capitalism,* Bertrand Benoit, *Financial Times,* 7.1.2000;
S. 88: *Offering could value Infineon at €20bn-plus,* Tony Barber, *Financial Times,* 22.2.2000;
S. 91: *Capital & Counties makes £182 million rights issue,* Cliff Feltham, *The Times,* 2000;
S. 96: *Crowded pipeline after dizzy launch,* Tony Barber, *Financial Times,* 25.10.1999;
S. 123: *What drives globalisation?, Financial Times Survey,* 1999;

SPÉCIALITÉ

SVT 1re

Objectif BAC

Laëtitia LEFÈVRE
Professeure agrégée de SVT

hachette
ÉDUCATION

MODE D'EMPLOI

Ce livre reprend à la base toutes les notions du programme de l'enseignement de spécialité de SVT de Première, et les met en œuvre à travers des exercices simples qu'il est indispensable de maîtriser. Il vous permettra ainsi d'assimiler parfaitement le cours et de savoir l'appliquer dans des exercices de difficulté variée. Un **lexique** des termes signalés par un astérisque complète utilement cet ouvrage (voir p. 261).

Chacun des seize chapitres comporte quatre grandes parties :

LE COURS

Un cours clair et structuré, avec tout ce qu'il faut savoir

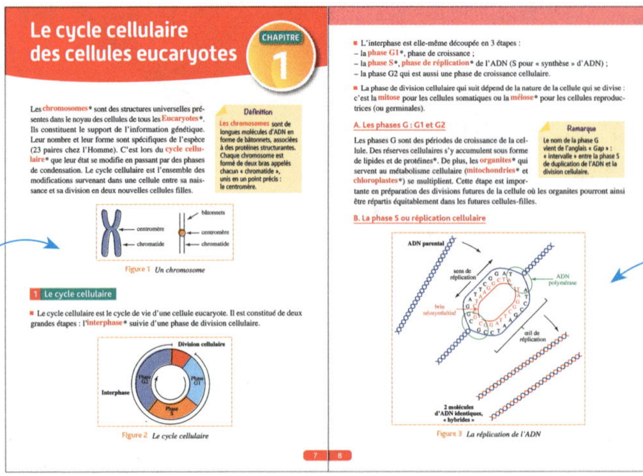

De nombreux schémas pour illustrer chaque thème

LES EXERCICES

Des exercices pour vérifier vos connaissances ou préparer la première partie de l'épreuve de contrôle continu : « maîtrise des connaissances »

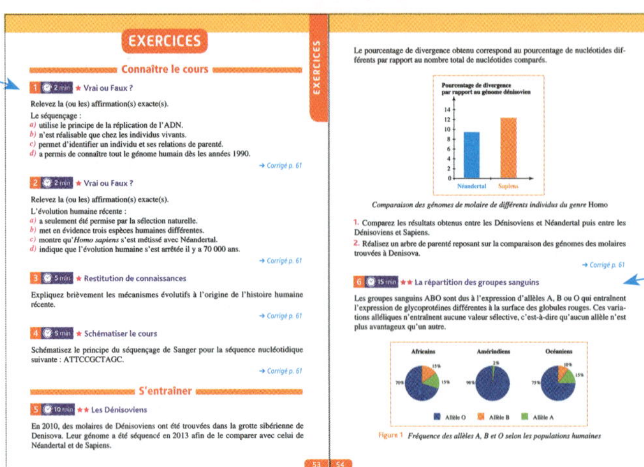

Des exercices progressifs (3 niveaux de difficulté) et minutés pour bien s'entraîner

LE CONTRÔLE CONTINU POUR LE BAC

Cette rubrique vous propose un exercice typique de la seconde partie de l'épreuve de contrôle continu : « pratique du raisonnement scientifique »

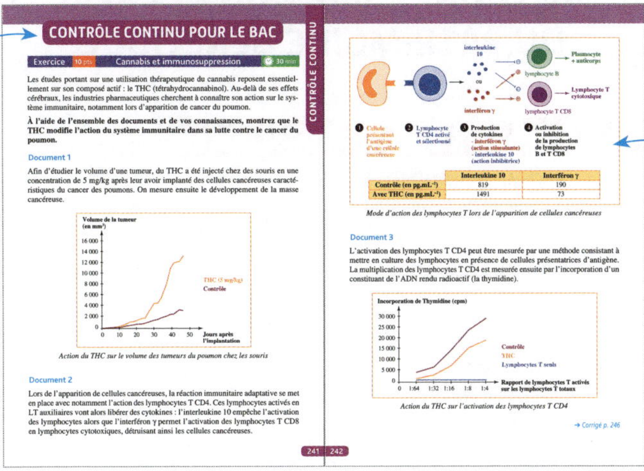

CONTRÔLE CONTINU POUR LE BAC

CONTRÔLE CONTINU

Exercice 10 pts — Cannabis et immunosuppression — 30 min

Les études portant sur une utilisation thérapeutique du cannabis reposent essentiellement sur son composé actif : le THC (tétrahydrocannabinol). Au-delà de ses effets cérébraux, les industries pharmaceutiques cherchent à connaître son action sur le système immunitaire, notamment lors d'apparition de cancer du poumon.

À l'aide de l'ensemble des documents et de vos connaissances, montrez que le THC modifie l'action du système immunitaire dans sa lutte contre le cancer du poumon.

Document 1

Afin d'étudier le volume d'une tumeur, du THC a été injecté chez des souris en une concentration de 5 mg/kg après leur avoir implanté des cellules cancéreuses caractéristiques du cancer des poumons. On mesure ensuite le développement de la masse cancéreuse.

Action du THC sur le volume des tumeurs du poumon chez les souris

Document 2

Lors de l'apparition de cellules cancéreuses, la réaction immunitaire adaptative se met en place avec notamment l'action des lymphocytes T CD4. Ces lymphocytes activés en LT auxiliaires vont alors libérer des cytokines : l'interleukine 10 empêche l'activation des lymphocytes alors que l'interféron γ permet l'activation des lymphocytes T CD8 en lymphocytes cytotoxiques, détruisant ainsi les cellules cancéreuses.

	Interleukine 10	Interféron γ
Contrôle (en pg.mL⁻¹)	819	190
Avec THC (en pg.mL⁻¹)	1491	73

Mode d'action des lymphocytes T lors de l'apparition de cellules cancéreuses

Document 3

L'activation des lymphocytes T CD4 peut être mesurée par une méthode consistant à mettre en culture des lymphocytes en présence de cellules présentatrices d'antigène. La multiplication des lymphocytes T CD4 est mesurée ensuite par l'incorporation d'un constituant de l'ADN rendu radioactif (la thymidine).

Action du THC sur l'activation des lymphocytes T CD4

→ Corrigé p. 246

241 242

Le problème scientifique posé s'appuie sur un ou plusieurs documents. Il amène l'élève à choisir et exposer sa démarche, à élaborer son argumentation et à préparer une conclusion

TOUS LES CORRIGÉS

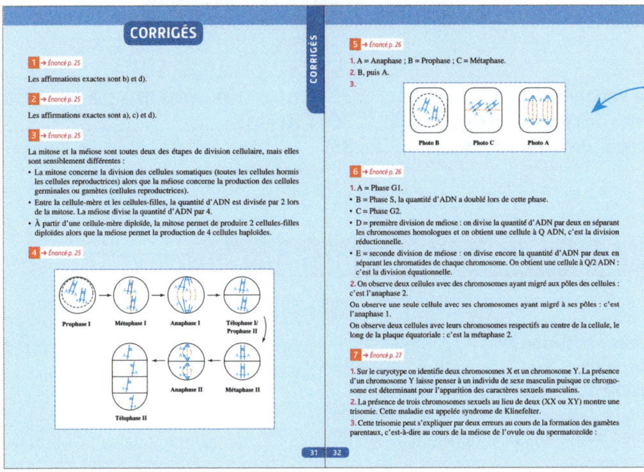

CORRIGÉS

CORRIGÉS

1 → Énoncé p. 25

Les affirmations exactes sont b) et d).

2 → Énoncé p. 25

Les affirmations exactes sont a), c) et d).

3 → Énoncé p. 25

La mitose et la méiose sont toutes deux des étapes de division cellulaire, mais elles sont sensiblement différentes :
- La mitose concerne la division des cellules somatiques (toutes les cellules hormis les cellules reproductrices) alors que la méiose concerne la production des cellules germinales ou gamètes (cellules reproductrices).
- Entre la cellule-mère et les cellules-filles, la quantité d'ADN est divisée par 2 lors de la mitose. La méiose divise la quantité d'ADN par 4.
- À partir d'une cellule-mère diploïde, la mitose permet de produire 2 cellules-filles diploïdes alors que la méiose permet la production de 4 cellules haploïdes.

4 → Énoncé p. 25

5 → Énoncé p. 26

1. A = Anaphase ; B = Prophase ; C = Métaphase.
2. B, puis A.
3.

6 → Énoncé p. 26

1. A = Phase G1.
- B = Phase S, la quantité d'ADN a doublé lors de cette phase.
- C = Phase G2.
- D = première division de méiose : on divise la quantité d'ADN par deux en séparant les chromosomes homologues et on obtient une cellule à Q ADN, c'est la division réductionnelle.
- E = seconde division de méiose : on divise encore la quantité d'ADN par deux en séparant les chromatides de chaque chromosome. On obtient une cellule à Q/2 ADN : c'est la division équationnelle.

2. On observe deux cellules avec des chromosomes ayant migré aux pôles des cellules : c'est l'anaphase 2.

On observe une seule cellule avec ses chromosomes ayant migré à ses pôles : c'est l'anaphase 1.

On observe deux cellules avec leurs chromosomes respectifs au centre de la cellule, le long de la plaque équatoriale : c'est la métaphase 2.

7 → Énoncé p. 27

1. Sur le caryotype on identifie deux chromosomes X et un chromosome Y. La présence d'un chromosome Y laisse penser à un individu de sexe masculin puisque ce chromosome est déterminant pour l'apparition des caractères sexuels masculins.
2. La présence de trois chromosomes sexuels au lieu de deux (XX ou XY) montre une trisomie. Cette maladie est appelée syndrome de Klinefelter.
3. Cette trisomie peut s'expliquer par deux erreurs au cours de la formation des gamètes parentaux, c'est-à-dire au cours de la méiose de l'ovule ou du spermatozoïde :

31 32

Les corrigés détaillés permettent de s'auto-évaluer tout au long de l'année

Conception graphique

Couverture : Stéphanie Benoit
Intérieur : Alicia Dassonville

Composition, schémas et mise en pages : Soft Office
Édition : Jeanne Mauboussin

I.S.B.N. 978-2-01-708183-8

Achevé d'imprimer en Slovaquie par Polygraf
Dépôt légal : Juin 2019 - Édition : 01
12/3021/7

SOMMAIRE

TRANSMISSION, VARIATION ET EXPRESSION DU PATRIMOINE GÉNÉTIQUE

LA DYNAMIQUE INTERNE DE LA TERRE

ENJEUX PLANÉTAIRES CONTEMPORAINS DE LA PLANÈTE

CORPS HUMAIN ET SANTÉ

Le cycle cellulaire des cellules eucaryotes

CHAPITRE 1

Les **chromosomes*** sont des structures universelles présentes dans le noyau des cellules de tous les **Eucaryotes***. Ils constituent le support de l'information génétique. Leur nombre et leur forme sont spécifiques de l'espèce (23 paires chez l'Homme). C'est lors du **cycle cellulaire*** que leur état se modifie en passant par des phases de condensation. Le cycle cellulaire est l'ensemble des modifications survenant dans une cellule entre sa naissance et sa division en deux nouvelles cellules filles.

Définition

Les chromosomes sont de longues molécules d'ADN en forme de bâtonnets, associées à des protéines structurantes. Chaque chromosome est formé de deux bras appelés chacun « chromatide », unis en un point précis : le centromère.

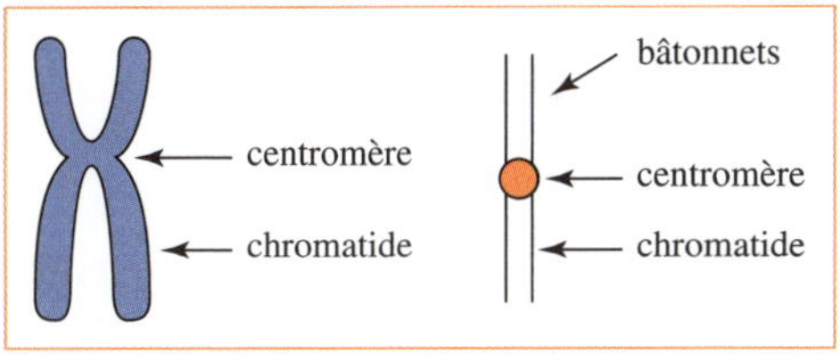

Figure 1 *Un chromosome*

1 Le cycle cellulaire

■ Le cycle cellulaire est le cycle de vie d'une cellule eucaryote. Il est constitué de deux grandes étapes : l'**interphase*** suivie d'une phase de division cellulaire.

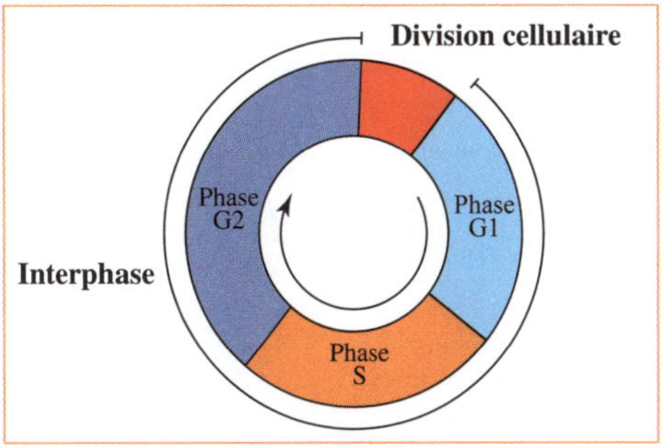

Figure 2 *Le cycle cellulaire*

■ L'interphase est elle-même découpée en 3 étapes :
– la **phase G1***, phase de croissance ;
– la **phase S***, **phase de réplication*** de l'ADN (S pour « synthèse » d'ADN) ;
– la phase G2 qui est aussi une phase de croissance cellulaire.

■ La phase de division cellulaire qui suit dépend de la nature de la cellule qui se divise : c'est la **mitose** pour les cellules somatiques ou la **méiose*** pour les cellules reproductrices (ou germinales).

A. Les phases G : G1 et G2

Les phases G sont des périodes de croissance de la cellule. Des réserves cellulaires s'y accumulent sous forme de lipides et de protéines*. De plus, les **organites*** qui servent au métabolisme cellulaire (**mitochondries*** et **chloroplastes***) se multiplient. Cette étape est importante en préparation des divisions futures de la cellule où les organites pourront ainsi être répartis équitablement dans les futures cellules-filles.

> **Remarque**
> Le nom de la phase G vient de l'anglais « *Gap* » : « intervalle » entre la phase S de duplication de l'ADN et la division cellulaire.

B. La phase S ou réplication cellulaire

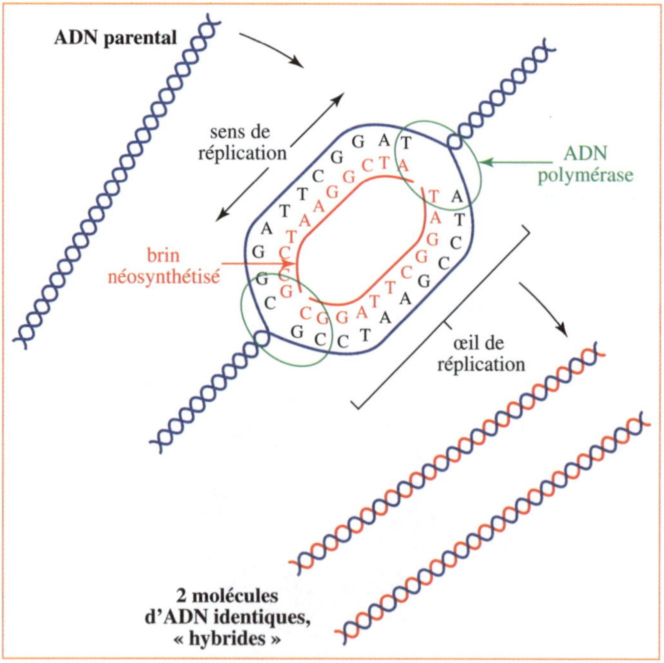

Figure 3 *La réplication de l'ADN*

■ Lors de la phase S, la quantité d'ADN double : c'est la **réplication de l'ADN** pendant laquelle les deux brins d'ADN sont séparés en un endroit précis pour former un œil de réplication. Chaque brin sert de modèle à la synthèse d'un nouveau brin d'ADN : cette réplication est donc semi-conservative.

■ Cette synthèse est effectuée par l'enzyme ADN polymérase, qui permet d'associer un nouveau nucléotide complémentaire à chaque nucléotide du brin parental : le nucléotide A (Adénine) s'associe toujours au nucléotide T (Thymine). De la même façon, le nucléotide C (Cytosine) est associé au nucléotide G (Guanine).

A-C-G-A-T-C ⊢ 1 chaîne
T-G-C-T-A-G ⊢ 1 chaîne

Figure 4 *Les deux chaînes complémentaires de l'ADN*

■ La réplication de la molécule d'ADN initiale permet d'obtenir deux molécules d'ADN filles de séquence nucléotidique identique à celle de la molécule d'ADN mère.

Ex. : Une molécule d'ADN parentale va donner deux molécules d'ADN de séquence identique.

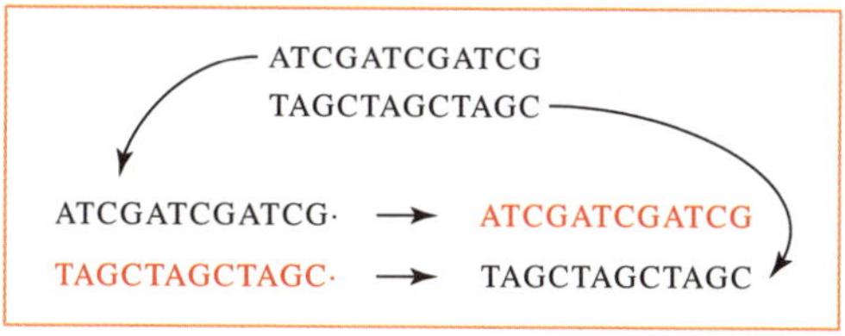

Figure 5 *Résultats théoriques de la réplication semi-conservative*

C. Les divisions cellulaires

■ Les divisions cellulaires chez les Eucaryotes sont différentes selon la nature de la cellule qui se divise. Pour les cellules germinales (ou reproductrices), la quantité d'ADN est divisée par quatre : c'est la méiose.

■ Pour les cellules somatiques (toutes les cellules non reproductrices), la quantité d'ADN est divisée par deux : c'est la mitose (voir *Chapitre* 2, p. 21).

2 L'état des chromosomes au cours du cycle cellulaire

A. Au cours de l'interphase

■ Durant toute l'interphase, les chromosomes subissent une décondensation pour former des amas diffus : la **chromatine***.

■ Lors de la phase G1, les chromosomes ne sont donc plus constitués que d'une seule chromatide.

■ La réplication (duplication du matériel génétique) qui a lieu au cours de la phase S permet de dupliquer chaque chromatide et donc de reconstituer le chromosome à deux chromatides identiques entre elles.

■ La phase G2 se poursuit pour les chromosomes à deux chromatides, chacune possédant la même information génétique.

B. Au cours des divisions cellulaires

■ Lors de la mitose ou de la méiose, les chromosomes s'enroulent sur eux-mêmes : ils se condensent.

■ Le chromosome représenté sous forme de deux bâtonnets n'existe réellement qu'au cours de l'étape de division cellulaire. Il s'agit de la forme condensée. Pour plus de rigueur, on le représentera comme ci-dessous :

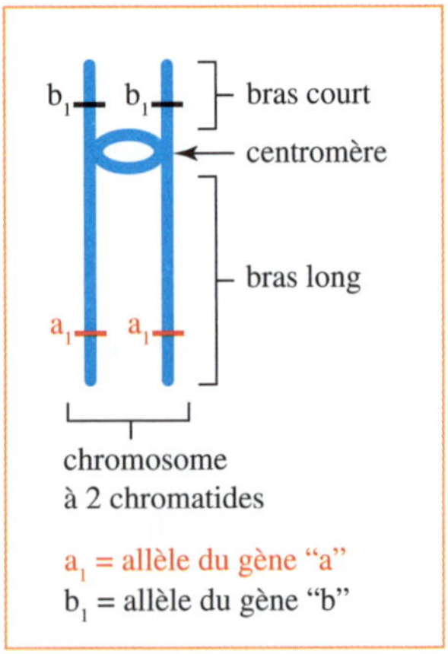

Figure 6 *Un chromosome*

EXERCICES

Connaître le cours

1 2 min ★ Vrai ou Faux ?

Relevez la (ou les) affirmation(s) exacte(s) :
a) Les chromosomes sont décondensés au cours de l'interphase.
b) La réplication de l'ADN est semi-conservative car elle conserve la moitié de l'information génétique.
c) L'interphase est la seule phase qui permet la stabilité du caryotype.
d) Les chromosomes sont toujours constitués de deux chromatides.

→ *Corrigé p. 17*

2 2 min ★ Vrai ou Faux ?

Relevez la (ou les) affirmation(s) exacte(s) :
a) Les chromosomes se condensent lors de la réplication.
b) La réplication a lieu tout au long de l'interphase.
c) La chromatine est visible durant l'interphase.
d) Les phases G du cycle cellulaire sont des phases de croissance de la cellule.

→ *Corrigé p. 17*

3 5 min ★ Restitution de connaissances

Expliquez brièvement les grands événements ayant lieu lors de l'interphase du cycle cellulaire.

→ *Corrigé p. 17*

4 5 min ★ Schématiser le cours

1. Schématisez simplement une molécule d'ADN à 2 brins, la séquence d'un brin étant : ACTGGATTCAG.
2. Schématisez les 2 molécules d'ADN obtenues après un cycle de réplication semi-conservative de l'ADN (représenter les brins d'origine en bleu et les brins nouveaux en rouge).

→ *Corrigé p. 17*

S'entraîner

5 10 min ★★ Les étapes du cycle cellulaire

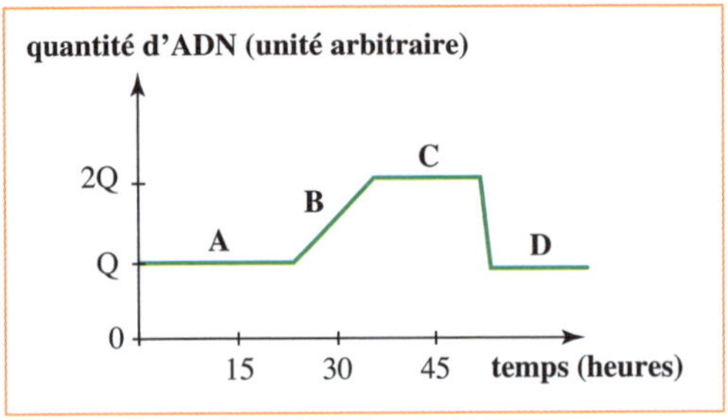

Figure 1 *Évolution de la quantité d'ADN*

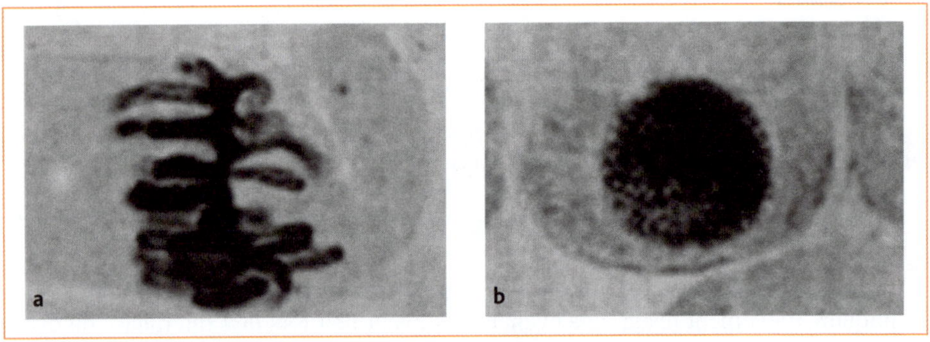

Figure 2 *Condensation des chromosomes*

1. Sur le graphique de la figure 1, identifiez les différentes phases du cycle cellulaire A, B, C, D.

2. Décrivez l'état des chromosomes pour chaque cellule représentée sur les deux photographies de la figure 2. En déduire pour chacune l'étape du cycle cellulaire dans laquelle elles sont.

→ Corrigé p. 17

6 15 min ★★ La cytométrie de flux

Lorsqu'on cultive des cellules humaines, les cellules peuvent être à des étapes différentes du cycle cellulaire.

On veut visualiser graphiquement le nombre de cellules bloquées dans chaque étape du cycle et ainsi en déduire la durée de chaque étape du cycle cellulaire : par exemple, plus les cellules sont nombreuses en phase G1, plus cette étape est longue dans le cycle cellulaire.

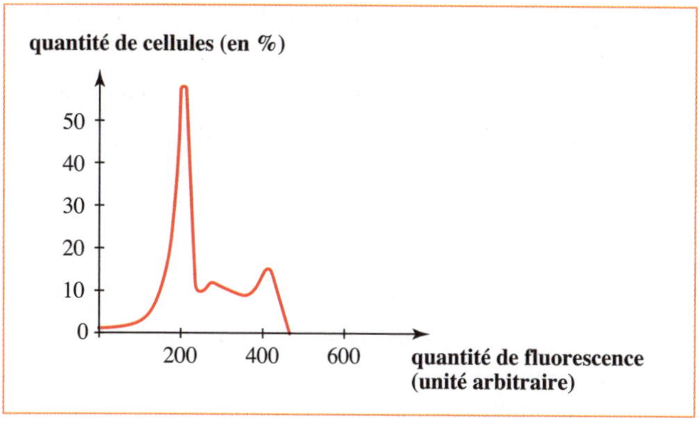

Résultats de cytométrie de flux

Pour cela, on intercale un agent fluorescent dans l'ADN. On mesure ensuite la fluorescence qui est ainsi proportionnelle à la quantité d'ADN contenue dans la cellule. Cette technique s'appelle la cytométrie de flux.

1. En vous aidant essentiellement de la quantité de fluorescence et donc d'ADN, identifiez les différentes étapes du cycle cellulaire.

2. Quelle est l'étape la plus longue du cycle cellulaire ?

→ *Corrigé p. 17*

7 20 min ★★ Taille de l'ADN

La molécule d'ADN qui constitue le chromosome n° 1 possède 246 millions de paires de nucléotides. L'ensemble du génome humain est quant à lui constitué de 3,2 milliards de paires de nucléotides.

Données :

- 1 paire de nucléotides mesure 0,33 nm de longueur
- 1 nm = 10^{-9} m
- 1 µm = 10^{-6} m
- Le corps est composé d'environ 75 milliards de cellules
- Le diamètre moyen d'une cellule humaine est de 20 µm

1. Calculez la longueur réelle de l'ADN contenu dans le chromosome n° 1.

2. Sachant que chaque cellule contient l'ensemble du génome, calculez ensuite la longueur totale des molécules d'ADN dans une cellule diploïde, c'est-à-dire possédant ses chromosomes en paire (en mètres).

3. L'analyse de vos résultats permet-elle de conclure que l'ensemble de l'ADN peut être contenu dans une cellule ?

4. Quelle hypothèse pouvez-vous formuler sur l'état de l'ADN dans les cellules ?

5. Calculez la taille globale de toutes les molécules d'ADN contenues chez un être humain.

→ *Corrigé p. 18*

8 20 min ★★ Les vitesses de réplication

On veut mesurer la vitesse de réplication dans différents types de cellules. Pour cela, on réalise l'expérience suivante : des cellules humaines et bactériennes sont cultivées en présence d'un nucléotide fluorescent durant 40 minutes. Les nucléotides fluorescents s'incorporent dans l'ADN nouvellement synthétisé et sont observables en microscopie où l'on pourra les compter.

	Espèce humaine	***Escherichia coli* (bactérie)**
Nombre de paires de nucléotides fluorescents incorporés en 40 min	240.10^3	$2\,400.10^3$
Taille des génomes (en paires de nucléotides)	$3,2.10^9$	$4,4.10^6$

Comparaison de différentes caractéristiques génétiques chez l'Homme et chez une bactérie

1. Calculez la vitesse de réplication dans les deux types de cellules.

2. Calculez la durée de la réplication de l'ensemble des génomes humain et bactérien.

3. La durée moyenne de réplication lors de la phase S chez l'Homme est de 8 heures et celle d'*E. coli* de 40 minutes environ. Calculez le nombre d'origines de réplication nécessaires pour répliquer respectivement tout le génome humain puis tout le génome bactérien.

→ *Corrigé p. 18*

CONTRÔLE CONTINU POUR LE BAC

Exercice 10 pts — L'expérience de Meselson et Stahl — 30 min

Deux chercheurs anglais, Meselson et Stahl, ont mis en évidence le mécanisme de la réplication de l'ADN. Leurs travaux ont été récompensés par le prix Nobel en 1958. Pour cela, ils avaient émis trois hypothèses.

Après avoir schématisé les trois hypothèses formulées par Meselson et Stahl, vous analyserez leurs résultats (p. 16) afin de déduire le modèle le plus juste de la réplication de l'ADN.

Document 1 : Les hypothèses de Meselson et Stahl

- Hypothèse 1 : les deux brins d'ADN initiaux restent ensemble après avoir servis de modèle. C'est la réplication conservative.
- Hypothèse 2 : chaque nouvelle molécule d'ADN contient un brin initial d'ADN et un brin nouvellement répliqué. C'est la réplication semi-conservative.
- Hypothèse 3 : les deux molécules filles d'ADN comportent des fragments d'ADN initial et des fragments d'ADN nouvellement répliqué. C'est la réplication dispersive.

Document 2 : Le principe de l'expérience

- Pour tester leurs hypothèses, Meselson et Stahl réalisèrent une expérience permettant de différencier les brins d'ADN « parentaux » et les brins d'ADN nouvellement répliqués.
- Pour cela, ils cultivèrent des bactéries dans un milieu riche en azote lourd ^{15}N. Cet azote rentre dans la composition des nucléotides de l'ADN.
- Les bactéries sont ensuite placées dans un milieu riche en azote léger ^{14}N où elles font l'objet de plusieurs cycles cellulaires. Les nouveaux brins d'ADN seront donc riches en azote léger ^{14}N et pourront être distingués des brins d'ADN « anciens » riches en azote lourd ^{15}N.
- L'ADN extrait est ensuite centrifugé de telle sorte que les molécules d'ADN se disposent dans les tubes selon leurs densités, proportionnelles à leurs richesses en ^{14}N ou en ^{15}N.

Document 3 : Les résultats de l'expérience

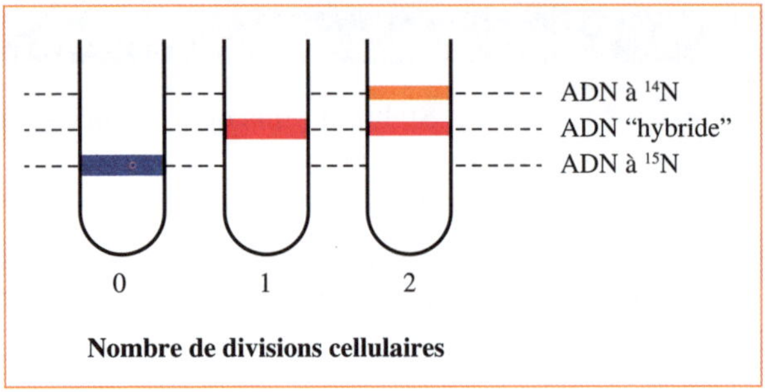

Résultats de l'expérience de Meselson et Stahl

→ *Corrigé p. 19*

CORRIGÉS

1 → Énoncé p. 11

L'affirmation exacte est a).

2 → Énoncé p. 11

Les affirmations exactes sont c) et d).

3 → Énoncé p. 11

Lors de l'interphase ont lieu des étapes de croissance cellulaire : ce sont les phases G (G1 et G2). Durant ces étapes, la cellule grossit et grandit grâce à l'accumulation de réserves de graisses (lipides) et de protéines. De plus, les organites se multiplient et la quantité de mitochondries et de chloroplastes est doublée en vue de la division cellulaire suivante.

Une étape existe entre la phase G1 et la phase G2 : c'est la phase S. Durant cette étape a lieu la réplication de l'ADN où la quantité d'ADN double.

4 → Énoncé p. 11

1. ACTGGATTCAG
   TGACCTAAGTC
2. ACTGGATTCAG ACTGGATTCAG
   TGACCTAAGTC TGACCTAAGTC

5 → Énoncé p. 12

1. **A :** Phase G1.

B : Phase S : la quantité d'ADN a doublé.

C : Phase G2.

D : Divisions cellulaires : la quantité d'ADN est divisée par deux.

2. Sur la photo a, les chromosomes sont condensés alors qu'ils sont sous forme de chromatine (décondensés) sur la photo b. On peut en déduire que la cellule de la photo a est en division cellulaire alors que celle de la photo b est en interphase.

6 → Énoncé p. 12

1. On observe deux pics importants du nombre de cellules : l'un pour une fluorescence de 200 unités arbitraires et l'autre pour une fluorescence de 400 unités arbitraires. Or,

on sait que la fluorescence reflète la quantité d'ADN. On peut donc supposer qu'entre ces deux pics, la quantité d'ADN a doublé.

Le premier pic à 200 unités arbitraires correspond donc à la phase G1 et le second pic à 400 unités arbitraires correspond à la phase G2. Ils sont séparés par la phase S pendant laquelle a eu lieu la réplication de l'ADN.

2. La quantité de cellules en phase G1 est beaucoup plus importante que celles en phase G2 : elles représentent plus de 50 % des cellules de la culture. Or, la quantité de cellules reflète la durée des phases du cycle cellulaire. On peut en déduire ici que la phase G1 est la phase la plus longue du cycle cellulaire.

7 → *Énoncé p. 13*

1. $246 \times 10^6 \times 0{,}33 = 81 \times 10^6$ nm soit environ 8 cm d'ADN contenu dans le chromosome n° 1.

2. $3{,}2 \times 10^9 \times 0{,}33 = 1{,}06 \times 10^9$ nm soit environ 1 m d'ADN contenu dans chaque cellule. Attention, il faut multiplier par deux pour une cellule diploïde (nos cellules possèdent chaque chromosome en deux exemplaires). Chaque cellule contient donc 2 m d'ADN.

3. La cellule, mesurant en moyenne 20 µm, est plus petite que la taille de l'ADN calculé précédemment.

4. On peut supposer que la molécule d'ADN est enroulée sur elle-même pour pouvoir être contenue dans les noyaux des cellules eucaryotes : l'ADN est condensé.

5. $2 \times 75 \times 10^9 = 150 \times 10^9$ m soit 150 millions de km (environ la distance Terre-Soleil).

8 → *Énoncé p. 14*

1. Pour l'Homme : $v = \frac{d}{t} = \frac{240 \times 10^3}{40} = 6 \times 10^3$ paires de nucléotides/min soit 100 paires de nucléotides/seconde.

Pour *E. coli* : $v = \frac{d}{t} = \frac{2\,400 \times 10^3}{40} = 6 \times 10^4$ paires de nucléotides/min soit 1 000 paires de nucléotides/seconde.

2. Pour l'Homme : $t = \frac{d}{v} = \frac{3{,}2 \times 10^9}{6 \times 10^3} = 5{,}3 \times 10^5$ min soit 8 833 heures.

Pour *E. coli* : $t = \frac{d}{v} = \frac{4{,}4 \times 10^6}{6 \times 10^4} = 73$ min.

3. Pour l'Homme : $\frac{8\,833}{8} = 1104$ origines de réplications.

Pour *E. coli* : $\frac{73}{40} = 1{,}8$; soit environ 2 origines de réplications.

CONTRÔLE CONTINU POUR LE BAC

Exercice → Énoncé p. 15

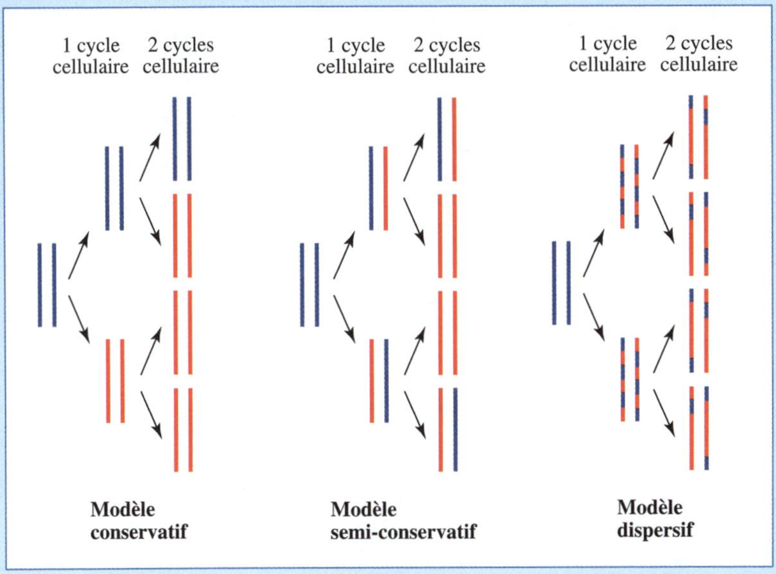

Initialement, on observe que l'ADN cultivé est constitué essentiellement d'azote lourd ^{15}N : c'est l'ADN initial.

Au bout d'un cycle cellulaire, les molécules d'ADN produites ont toutes un poids intermédiaire, c'est-à-dire qu'elles ont intégré 50 % d'ADN lourd à ^{15}N et 50 % d'ADN léger à ^{14}N. Seules les hypothèses d'un modèle semi-conservatif et d'un modèle dispersif sont compatibles avec ces résultats. En effet le modèle conservatif est à éliminer puisque l'une des molécules d'ADN produite aurait été intégralement imprégné d'azote ^{15}N et l'autre d'azote léger ^{14}N soit 50 % des molécules à ^{15}N et 50 % des molécules à ^{14}N.

Après un deuxième cycle cellulaire, on obtient 50 % d'ADN « hybrides » et 50 % d'ADN léger ^{14}N. Ces résultats ne peuvent qu'être corrélés au modèle semi-conservatif. On peut donc en déduire que c'est le modèle valable pour la réplication de l'ADN.

Les divisions cellulaires

CHAPITRE 2

La multiplication cellulaire fait intervenir deux divisions différentes selon le type de cellules : la **mitose*** concerne la division des cellules somatiques (toutes les cellules autres que reproductrices) et la **méiose** concerne la production de cellules reproductrices (gamètes).

Dans l'espèce humaine, les cellules somatiques sont diploïdes ; cela veut dire qu'elles possèdent 23 paires de chromosomes (soit $2n = 46$ chromosomes, n étant le nombre de chromosomes). Les gamètes sont haploïdes* et possèdent $n = 23$ chromosomes.

1 Une première division cellulaire : la mitose

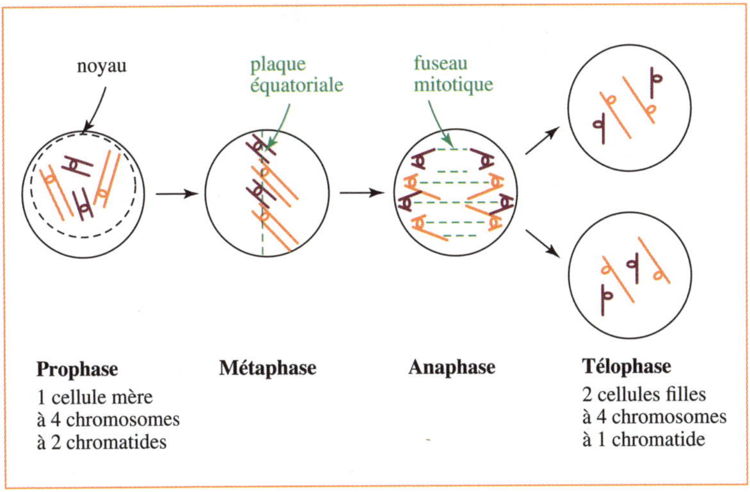

Figure 1 *La mitose*

A. Les différentes étapes de la mitose

■ La mitose se réalise en 4 étapes :

– La **prophase*** : les chromosomes se condensent et on voit apparaître leur forme à 2 chromatides reliées par le centromère. Le noyau disparaît progressivement.

– La **métaphase*** : les chromosomes migrent au centre de la cellule et constituent ainsi la plaque équatoriale.

– L'**anaphase*** : le centromère de chaque chromosome se rompt permettant à chacune des chromatides de migrer vers un pôle opposé de la cellule.
– La **télophase*** : les deux cellules-filles s'individualisent, leur noyau contient des chromosomes à une seule chromatide.

Remarque

Les mouvements chromosomiques sont assurés par un « squelette » cellulaire appelé fuseau mitotique.

B. Les conséquences sur la stabilité du caryotype

■ Un chromosome possède, sur chaque chromatide, un allèle de chaque gène. Les chromatides d'un même chromosome étant identiques entre elles, elles possèdent la même information génétique.

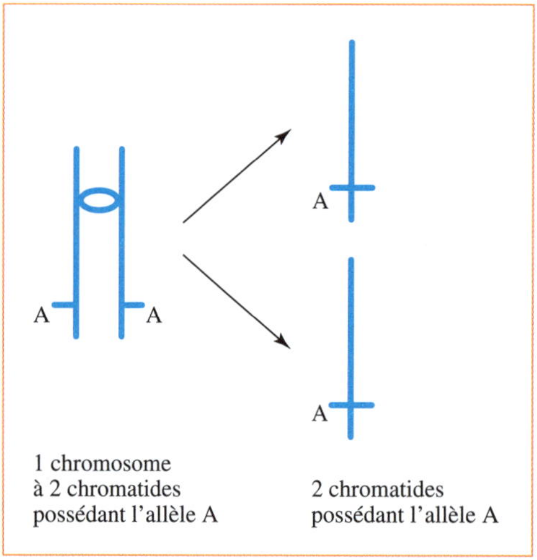

Figure 2 *Les allèles d'un chromosome*

■ Au cours de la mitose, les cellules filles reçoivent la même information génétique. La mitose permet la reproduction conforme d'une cellule-mère en deux cellules-filles possédant le même nombre de chromosomes et la même information génétique : elle est donc garante de la stabilité du **caryotype***. Un caryotype est une carte de l'ensemble des chromosomes d'une cellule, réalisée grâce à des photographies de microscopies électroniques. Les chromosomes sont classés et rangés par taille afin d'identifier d'éventuelles anomalies. Un caryotype humain d'une cellule diploïde possède 23 paires de chromosomes homologues.

2 Une seconde division cellulaire : la méiose

A. Les étapes de la méiose

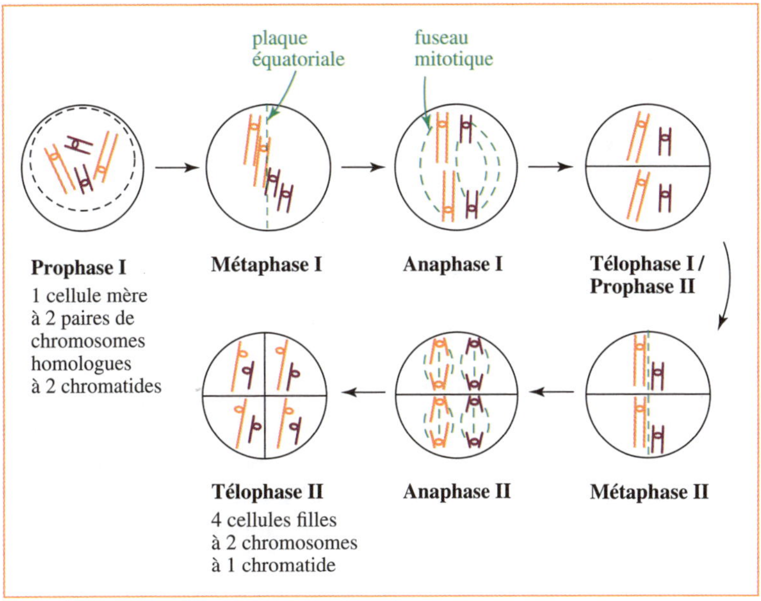

Figure 3 *La méiose*

■ Au cours de la méiose, une cellule-mère se divise pour donner quatre cellules-filles en deux étapes :

– la première division méiotique ou **division réductionnelle*** : prophase I, métaphase I, anaphase I et télophase I. Chaque chromosome d'une paire de chromosomes, appelés **chromosomes homologues**, migre vers un pôle différent de la cellule. On obtient 2 cellules-filles avec n chromosomes à 2 chromatides. Cette première division permet de transformer une cellule diploïde en cellule haploïde.

– la deuxième division méiotique ou **division équationnelle*** : prophase II, métaphase II, anaphase II et télophase II. Le centromère se rompt et chaque chromatide d'un chromosome migre vers un pôle différent de la cellule. On obtient en tout 4 cellules-filles composées de n chromosomes à 1 chromatide. Cette étape est une mitose ; elle permet de doubler le nombre de cellules haploïdes.

B. Les conséquences sur la stabilité du génotype

■ La cellule-mère est une **cellule diploïde***. Elle possède ses chromosomes par paire, ce sont des chromosomes homologues : on les note $2n$ chromosomes à 2 chromatides.

■ Pour chacun des chromosomes formant une paire, plusieurs combinaisons alléliques existent : soit les 2 allèles sont identiques et la cellule est dite **homozygote***, soit les 2 allèles sont différents et la cellule est **hétérozygote***.

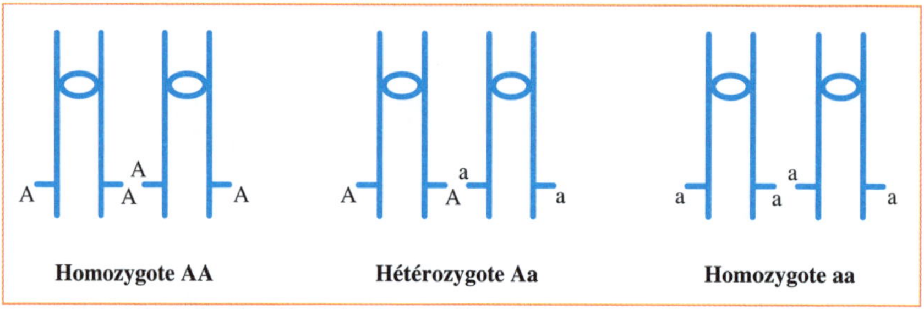

Figure 4 *Combinaisons alléliques des chromosomes homologues*

■ Les cellules reproductrices ou gamètes étant **haploïdes** (elles possèdent un seul lot de chromosomes ou *n* chromosomes), la méiose permet donc de passer d'une cellule mère diploïde à 4 cellules-filles haploïdes lors de la production de cellules reproductrices. Toutefois chaque chromosome homologue* possède les mêmes gènes. Ainsi la méiose est une division cellulaire conservant aussi l'information génétique.

EXERCICES

Connaître le cours

1 2 min ★ Vrai ou Faux ?

Relevez la (ou les) affirmation(s) exacte(s).

La mitose :

a) divise par deux le nombre de chromosomes dans chaque cellule-fille.
b) est une étape commune à tous les Eucaryotes.
c) est constituée de 4 phases : l'interphase, la métaphase, l'anaphase et la télophase.
d) transmet la totalité de l'information génétique d'une cellule-mère à deux cellules-filles.

→ *Corrigé p. 31*

2 2 min ★ Vrai ou Faux ?

Relevez la (ou les) affirmation(s) exacte(s).

La méiose :

a) est précédée d'une réplication de l'ADN.
b) produit des cellules somatiques.
c) permet la production de quatre cellules haploïdes.
d) permet le maintien de l'information génétique.

→ *Corrigé p. 31*

3 5 min ★ Restitution de connaissances

Expliquez brièvement les différences entre la mitose et la méiose.

→ *Corrigé p. 31*

4 5 min ★ Schématiser le cours

Schématisez la méiose d'une cellule diploïde hétérozygote pour un gène A et possédant une seule paire de chromosomes homologues.

→ *Corrigé p. 31*

S'entraîner

5 10 min ★★ Les étapes de la mitose

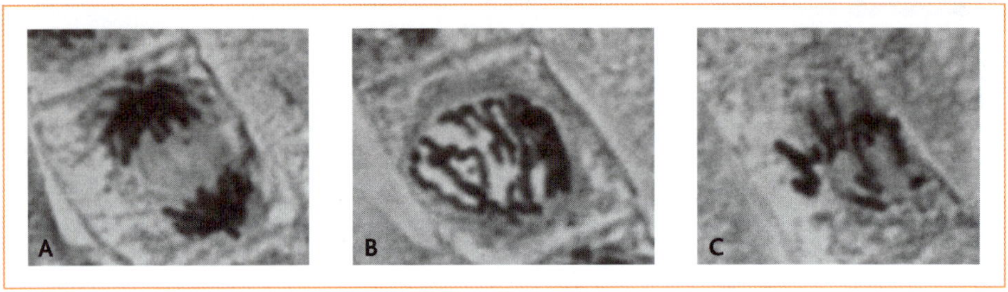

Microscopies de cellules mitotiques

1. Identifiez chacune des phases A, B et C de la mitose présentées sur la figure.
2. Classez ces photos dans l'ordre chronologique.
3. Schématisez chacune de ces phases pour une cellule-mère possédant une paire de chromosomes hétérozygotes pour un gène A.

→ *Corrigé p. 32*

6 10 min ★★ Les étapes de la méiose

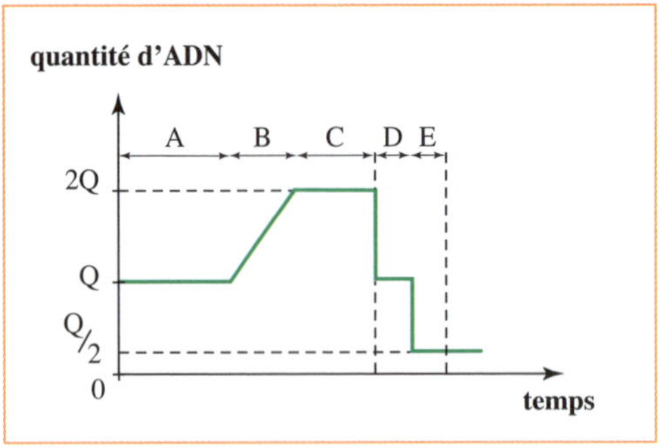

Figure 1 *Évolution de la quantité d'ADN au cours de la méiose*

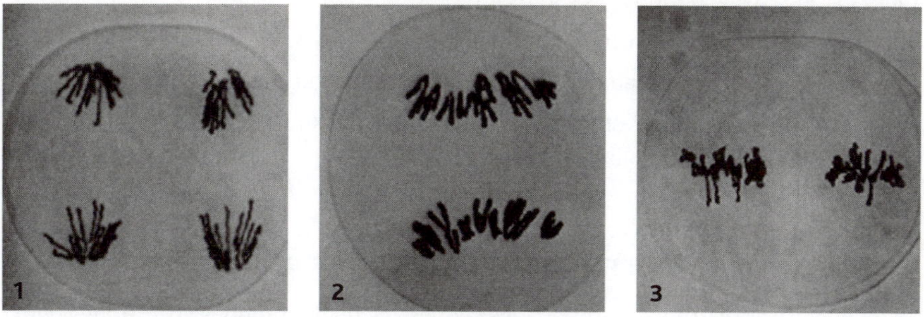

Figure 2 *Cellules germinales en formation (microscopie électronique)*

1. Identifiez les différentes phases du cycle cellulaire d'une cellule germinale, à partir du graphique de la figure 1.

2. Observez les trois photos de la figure 2 puis décrivez l'état des chromosomes pour chaque cellule et déduisez-en à quelles étapes du cycle cellulaire elles correspondent.

→ *Corrigé p. 32*

7 15 min ★★ Les anomalies du caryotype

Un caryotype est une carte de l'ensemble des chromosomes d'une cellule, réalisée grâce à des photographies de microscopies électroniques.

Le caryotype d'un individu est réalisé en vue de diagnostiquer une anomalie chromosomique.

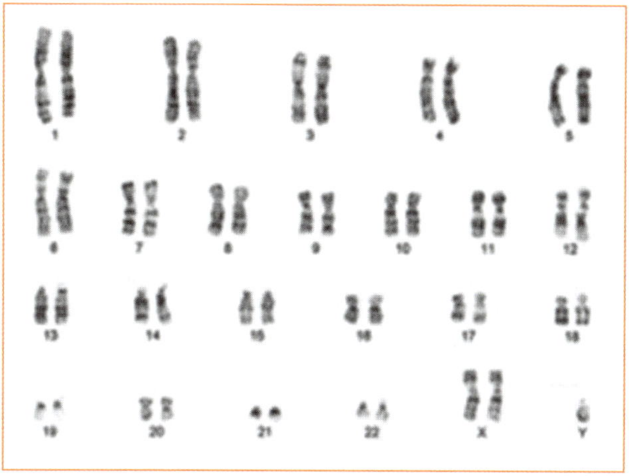

Caryotype de l'individu

1. Quel est le sexe génétique de l'individu étudié ?

2. Identifiez l'anomalie chromosomique de son caryotype.

3. Quelle(s) erreur(s) intervenue(s) lors de la méiose pourrai(en)t expliquer cette anomalie.

4. Réalisez un schéma de l'étape de la méiose en vous basant sur l'hypothèse d'une erreur en anaphase I lors de la formation de l'ovule.

→ *Corrigé p. 32*

8 15 min ★★ La composition génétique des chromosomes

Lors de la réalisation d'un caryotype, des séquences nucléotidiques spécifiques peuvent être révélées sur des chromosomes. Pour cela, on utilise la technique FISH (hybridation *in situ* en fluorescence), qui consiste à placer des marqueurs fluorescents spécifiques d'une séquence nucléotidique en présence des chromosomes. La fluorescence révèle alors la présence de cette séquence et sa localisation.

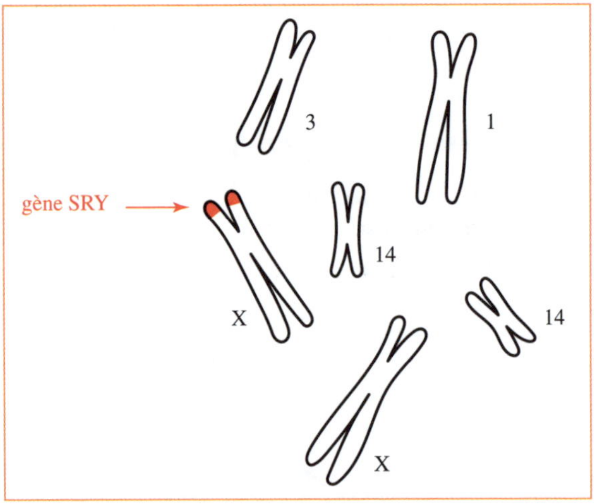

Caryotype FISH

1. Observez les chromosomes puis émettez une hypothèse sur le sexe de l'individu.

2. La présence du gène SRY (normalement localisé sur le chromosome Y) suffit à former un appareil génital masculin. En vous basant sur cette connaissance supplémentaire, localisez le chromosome sur lequel est situé le gène SRY de la personne dont on étudie ici le caryotype.

3. Déduisez-en si votre hypothèse est juste quant au sexe biologique de la personne étudiée.

→ *Corrigé p. 33*

CONTRÔLE CONTINU POUR LE BAC

Exercice 10 pts — Les traitements anti-cancéreux — 30 min

Le cancer est une maladie due à la multiplication incontrôlée d'une cellule formant des clones de cellules, ou tumeurs. La chimiothérapie, qui est un traitement du cancer, peut reposer sur l'utilisation d'une molécule : le taxol.

Expliquez comment le taxol permet de limiter la multiplication cellulaire et donc quel est son mode d'action pour traiter les cellules cancéreuses.

Document 1 : Évolution de la quantité d'ADN au cours du cycle cellulaire

La cytométrie de flux permet de mesurer la quantité d'ADN grâce à un agent fluorescent. On évalue la quantité d'ADN de cellules saines et de cellules chez une personne traitée par le taxol.

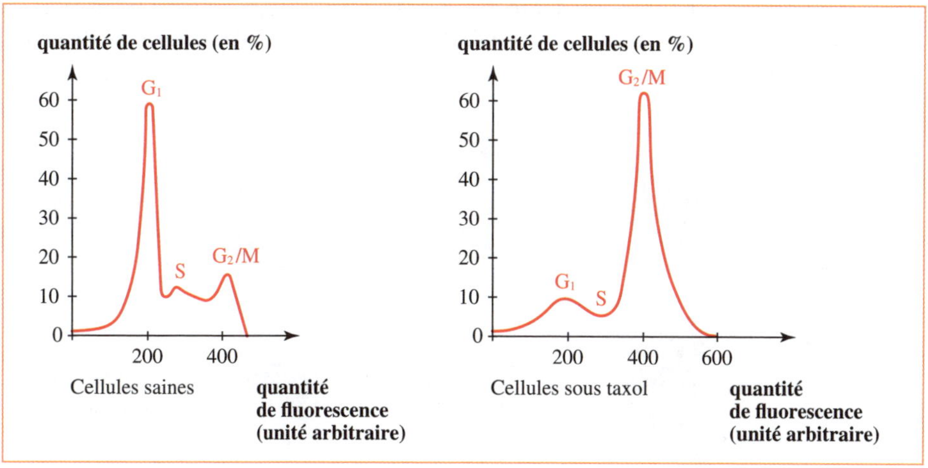

Quantité d'ADN de cellules saines et de cellules sous taxol

Document 2 : Les mouvements chromosomiques au cours de la mitose

La présence d'un squelette cellulaire (fuseau mitotique) permet le déplacement des chromosomes lors de la division cellulaire.

Le fuseau mitotique est relié aux chromosomes et aux pôles de la cellule. Il peut s'allonger ou se raccourcir.

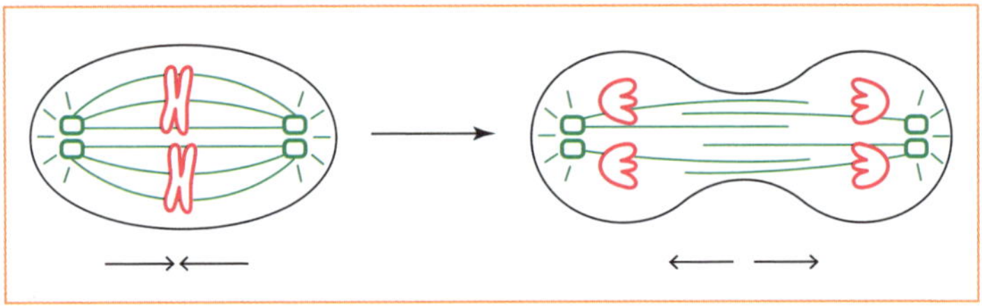

Mouvements du fuseau mitotique lors des étapes de métaphase et d'anaphase de la mitose

Document 3 : L'effet du taxol

On peut observer l'effet du taxol sur le déplacement des chromosomes : pour cela, on synchronise le cycle cellulaire de deux cellules. L'une sera mise en présence de taxol, l'autre non. On observe les cellules durant leurs divisions cellulaires.

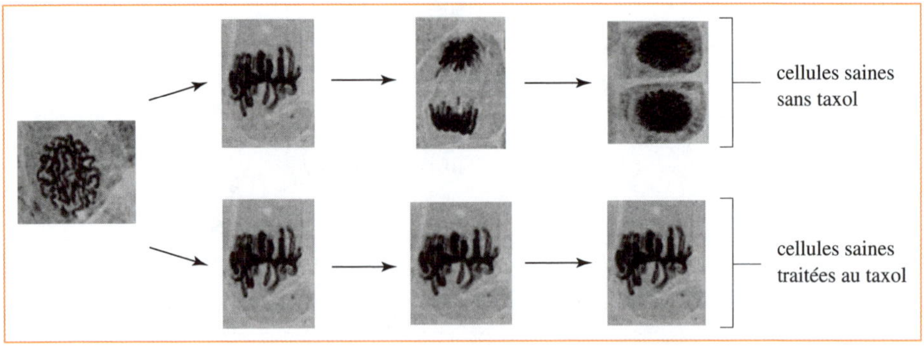

Effet du taxol sur la division cellulaire

→ Corrigé p. 33

1 → *Énoncé p. 25*

Les affirmations exactes sont b) et d).

2 → *Énoncé p. 25*

Les affirmations exactes sont a), c) et d).

3 → *Énoncé p. 25*

La mitose et la méiose sont toutes deux des étapes de division cellulaire, mais elles sont sensiblement différentes :

- La mitose concerne la division des cellules somatiques (toutes les cellules hormis les cellules reproductrices) alors que la méiose concerne la production des cellules germinales ou gamètes (cellules reproductrices).
- Entre la cellule-mère et les cellules-filles, la quantité d'ADN est divisée par 2 lors de la mitose. La méiose divise la quantité d'ADN par 4.
- À partir d'une cellule-mère diploïde, la mitose permet de produire 2 cellules-filles diploïdes alors que la méiose permet la production de 4 cellules haploïdes.

4 → *Énoncé p. 25*

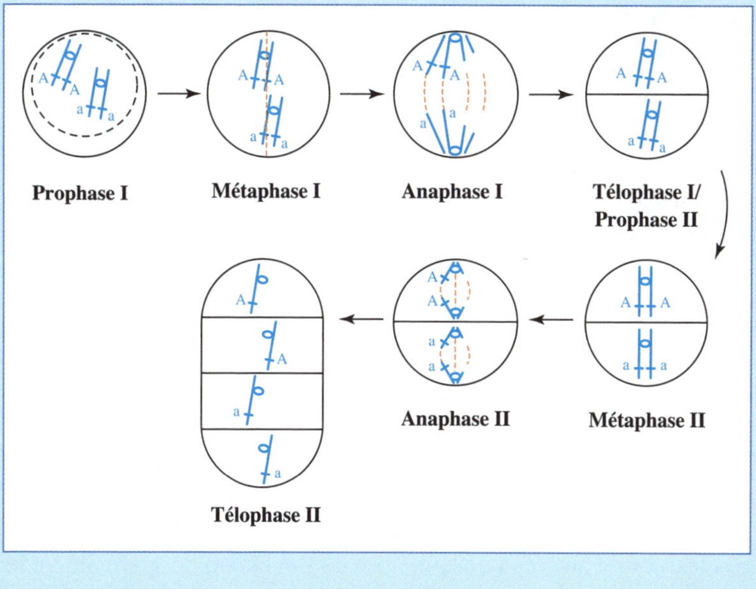

5 → *Énoncé p. 26*

1. A = Anaphase ; B = Prophase ; C = Métaphase.

2. B, puis C puis A.

3.

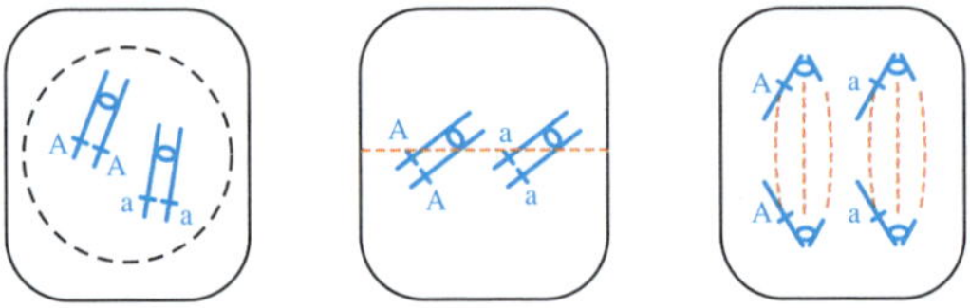

Photo B — Photo C — Photo A

6 → *Énoncé p. 26*

1. A = Phase G1 de l'interphase.

- B = Phase S de l'interphase, la quantité d'ADN a doublé lors de cette phase.
- C = Phase G2 de l'interphase.
- D = première division de méiose : on divise la quantité d'ADN par deux en séparant les chromosomes homologues et on obtient une cellule à Q ADN, c'est la division réductionnelle.
- E = seconde division de méiose : on divise encore la quantité d'ADN par deux en séparant les chromatides de chaque chromosome. On obtient une cellule à Q/2 ADN : c'est la division équationnelle.

2. On observe deux cellules avec des chromosomes ayant migré aux pôles des cellules : c'est l'anaphase II.

On observe une seule cellule avec ses chromosomes ayant migré à ses pôles : c'est l'anaphase I.

On observe deux cellules avec leurs chromosomes respectifs au centre de la cellule, le long de la plaque équatoriale : c'est la métaphase II.

7 → *Énoncé p. 27*

1. Sur le caryotype on identifie deux chromosomes X et un chromosome Y. La présence d'un chromosome Y laisse penser à un individu de sexe masculin puisque ce chromosome est déterminant pour l'apparition des caractères sexuels masculins.

2. La présence de trois chromosomes sexuels au lieu de deux (XX ou XY) montre une trisomie. Cette maladie est appelée syndrome de Klinefelter.

3. Cette trisomie peut s'expliquer par deux erreurs au cours de la formation des gamètes parentaux, c'est-à-dire au cours de la méiose de l'ovule ou du spermatozoïde :

- une non-séparation des chromosomes homologues lors de la première division de méiose ;
- une non-séparation des chromatides sœurs lors de la seconde division de méiose.

4.

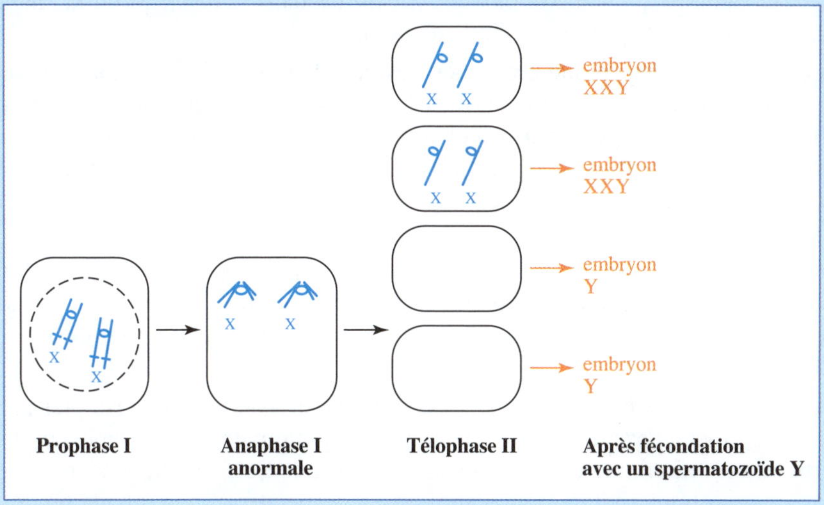

8 → Énoncé p. 28

1. L'individu possède deux chromosomes X : il est donc de sexe féminin.

2. Grâce au marquage fluorescent, on observe la présence du gène SRY sur l'un des chromosomes X.

3. La présence du gène SRY suffit à différencier un sexe masculin. Or ce gène est situé sur le chromosome X chez cette personne : il y a une incohérence entre son génome et son caryotype. C'est un homme XX.

CONTRÔLE CONTINU POUR LE BAC

Exercice → Énoncé p. 29

La chimiothérapie repose sur l'utilisation de substances bloquant les divisions cellulaires. Les cellules cancéreuses étant des cellules se divisant de façon incontrôlée, on veut donc utiliser ces substances pour arrêter leurs divisions cellulaires.

Comment le taxol peut-il bloquer la mitose et donc la propagation des cancers ?

D'après les résultats de la cytométrie de flux sur des cellules exposées au taxol, on observe que presque toutes les cellules sont en phase G2 et M (60 % des cellules) alors que les cellules non exposées au taxol sont majoritairement en phase G1. En effet, lors du cycle cellulaire, la phase G1 est la plus longue alors que la mitose est beaucoup plus brève.

On peut en déduire que le taxol bloque les cellules dans la phase M ou la phase G2. On cherche donc à connaître son mode d'action.

D'après les microscopies électroniques des cellules exposées ou non au taxol, on observe que la mitose se déroule normalement sans taxol. Mais après ajout de taxol, les chromosomes ne migrent plus vers l'équateur de la cellule lors de la métaphase, ce qui empêche aussi la séparation des chromatides et leur migration lors de l'anaphase. Ainsi la télophase ne permet pas de produire deux cellules-filles et le cycle cellulaire est bloqué en métaphase.

Or, on sait que les mouvements des chromosomes sont permis par le fuseau mitotique. On peut donc supposer que le taxol agit sur ce fuseau empêchant ainsi la métaphase de la mitose en bloquant tout mouvement chromosomique. Il arrête ainsi le cycle cellulaire.

On peut conclure que le taxol bloque les cellules en division cellulaire et plus particulièrement en métaphase de mitose, en stoppant les mouvements chromosomiques le long du fuseau mitotique. C'est la raison qui explique l'utilisation de cette molécule dans certaines chimiothérapies anticancéreuses. Cependant l'administration de taxol n'est pas sans effets secondaires car il bloque aussi la division d'autres cellules de l'organisme comme les cellules capillaires et les cellules intestinales, entraînant ainsi de nombreux effets secondaires.

Mutations de l'ADN et variabilité génétique

CHAPITRE 3

Si les divisions cellulaires et la réplication de l'ADN permettent d'assurer le maintien de l'information génétique, d'autres processus vont permettre sa diversité : les **mutations*** de l'ADN.

1 L'origine de la variabilité génétique

A. Des erreurs spontanées

■ Pendant la réplication de l'ADN, l'ADN polymérase peut effectuer des erreurs d'appariement des nucléotides.

■ Une séquence d'ADN peut ainsi être modifiée de plusieurs façons :
- Par **substitution*** : un (ou plusieurs) nucléotide(s) est(sont) remplacé(s) par un autre.
- Par **insertion*** : un (ou plusieurs) nucléotide est (sont) ajouté(s) à la séquence d'ADN.
- Par **délétion*** : un (ou plusieurs) nucléotides manque(nt) à la séquence d'ADN.

> **Remarque**
> **L'ADN polymérase humaine**, enzyme responsable de la duplication de l'ADN, est responsable d'un taux de mutation de 10^{-6} par gène et par génération (elle se trompe d'un nucléotide tous les millions répliqués).

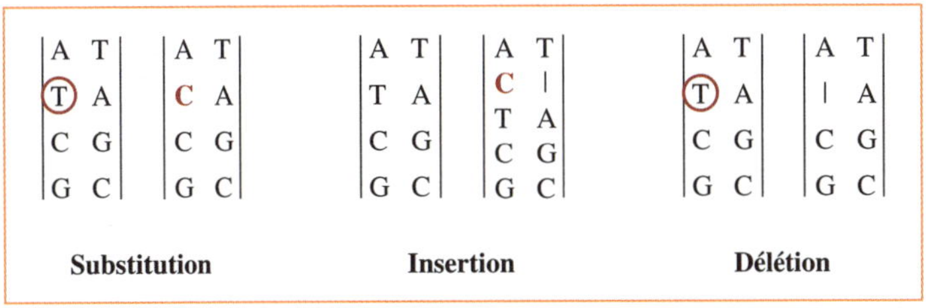

Figure 1 *Les différentes lésions de l'ADN*

■ Les erreurs causées par le « travail » de l'ADN polymérase créent des lésions spontanées et rares de l'ADN.

■ L'ADN peut aussi être endommagé lors des autres étapes du cycle cellulaire, comme lors des divisions cellulaires (erreur de séparation des chromosomes), ou lors des phases G par l'action d'**agents mutagènes***.

B. Des erreurs induites

■ Durant tout le cycle cellulaire, des lésions de l'ADN peuvent être induites par des **agents mutagènes**, comme les UV, la radioactivité et certains produits chimiques.

■ Ces lésions ont toutes différents effets sur l'ADN : de l'insertion de nucléotides au blocage complet de la réplication.

■ Ces agents mutagènes augmentent ainsi la fréquence des altérations de l'ADN.

Ex. : Les UV entraînent l'apparition de dimères de thymine (liaison covalente entre deux nucléotides T successifs). L'ADN polymérase va ainsi effectuer une erreur d'appariement lors de la réplication et créer une substitution d'un nucléotide A en un nucléotide C.

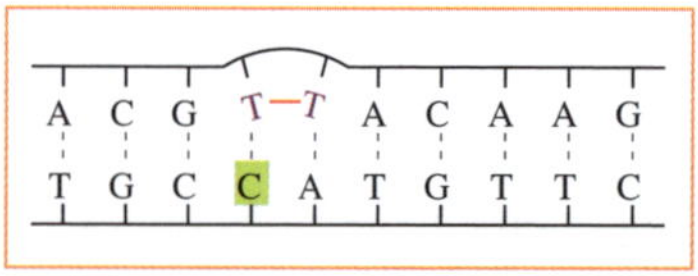

■ D'autres modifications de l'ADN peuvent être provoquées volontairement par l'Homme. C'est notamment le cas de la **transgénèse***. Son principe est de transférer un gène d'une espèce à une autre, permettant ainsi la production d'organismes génétiquement modifiés, ou **OGM**.

■ Cette technique se réalise sur les embryons mais la recherche a pour but de l'utiliser sur des adultes afin de guérir certaines maladies génétiques. On cherche donc à transférer certains allèles d'un individu sain à un individu malade grâce à des virus : c'est la **thérapie génique***.

2 Les mécanismes de réparation des erreurs

A. Les dispositifs de réparation

■ Le plus souvent les erreurs de réplication et les altérations de l'ADN (substitution, délétion et insertion) sont réparées par des mécanismes spécialisés impliquant des **enzymes*** (voir *chapitre* 5, p. 65). Ces enzymes peuvent reconnaître l'erreur, puis l'exciser et synthétiser les nucléotides manquants (voir *figure* 2, p. 37).

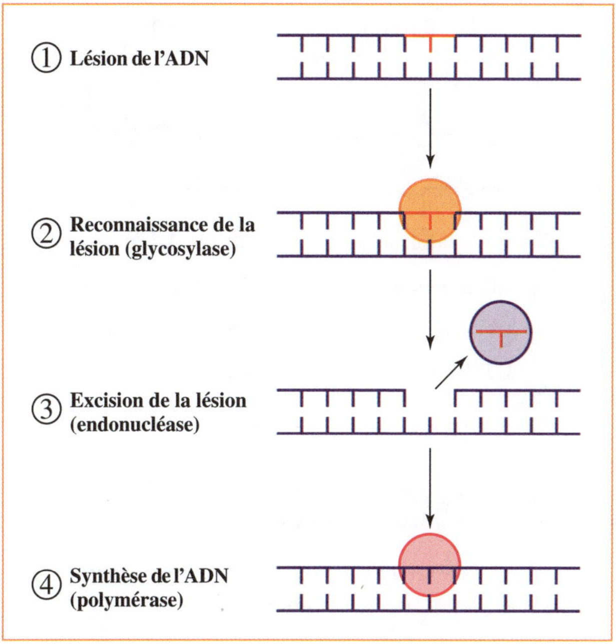

Figure 2 *La réparation de l'ADN par des enzymes*

B. La transmission des mutations

■ Quand l'erreur n'est pas réparée et que les modifications n'empêchent pas la survie de la cellule, la mutation est effective et sera transmise aux cellules-filles lors de la division cellulaire.

■ Une mutation peut survenir dans les différents types cellulaires. Dans les cellules somatiques, elle est transmise seulement aux cellules-filles, autrement dit aux clones de la cellule-mère mutée, et peut former une tumeur.

■ Dans le cas des cellules germinales, la mutation peut devenir héréditaire et être transmise d'une génération à une autre.

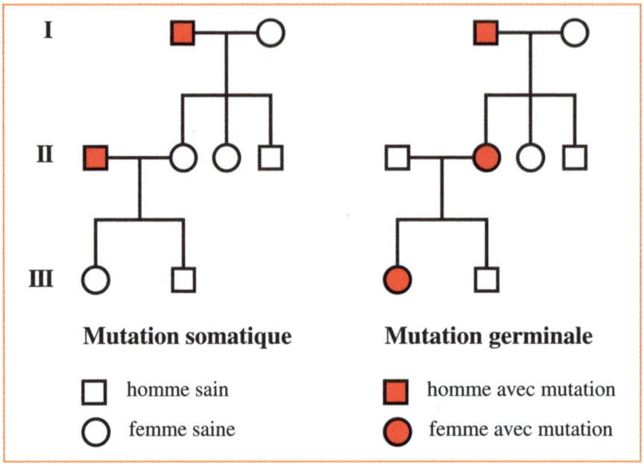

Figure 3 *Arbre généalogique de différentes mutations*

3 Les conséquences des mutations

■ Les mutations dans l'ADN sont à l'origine de l'apparition de nouvelles versions d'un même gène, autrement dit de nouveaux allèles.

Ex. : Dans une population de bactéries, une mutation peut apparaître et créer un allèle de résistance à un antibiotique. L'utilisation de cet antibiotique peut ensuite sélectionner ces bactéries nouvellement résistantes (elles survivent mieux et se reproduisent davantage).

■ Le **phénotype*** est l'ensemble des caractères observables d'un individu.

■ Un nouvel allèle en conséquence d'une mutation peut ainsi faire apparaître un nouveau phénotype dans une population.

■ Ces mutations augmentent la diversité allélique et donc la **biodiversité***.

EXERCICES

Connaître le cours

1 2 min ★ Vrai ou Faux ?

Relevez la (ou les) affirmation(s) exacte(s).

Les mutations :
a) ne touchent que les cellules germinales.
b) peuvent survenir de façon aléatoire.
c) ont lieu tout au long du cycle cellulaire.
d) sont provoquées essentiellement par des agents mutagènes.

→ *Corrigé p. 45*

2 2 min ★ Vrai ou Faux ?

Relevez la (ou les) affirmation(s) exacte(s).

Les lésions de l'ADN :
a) entraînent forcément une mutation héréditaire.
b) sont de 3 types : délétion, insertion et substitution.
c) sont réparées par des enzymes.
d) peuvent être augmentées par les UV.

→ *Corrigé p. 45*

3 5 min ★ Restitution de connaissances

Expliquez brièvement les conséquences des mutations de l'ADN.

→ *Corrigé p. 45*

4 5 min ★ Schématiser le cours

Schématisez les conséquences d'une lésion de l'ADN de type substitution d'un nucléotide A en T sur deux générations, pour la séquence initiale suivante :

TTCGAGCGGTCG.

→ *Corrigé p. 45*

S'entraîner

5 10 min ★★ Les taux de mutation

Le taux de mutation d'une espèce correspond à la fréquence d'apparition d'un nouveau caractère.

Un taux de mutation de 1/150 signifie qu'il faut 150 cycles cellulaires pour observer une modification d'un nucléotide dans le génome.

Espèce	Taille du génome (nombre de nucléotides)	Taux de mutations spontanées par cycle cellulaire
Homo sapiens (mammifère)	$3{,}3.10^9$	1/150
Drosophile (insecte)	$1{,}7.10^8$	1/200

Tableau comparatif des génomes de différentes espèces

1. Au bout de combien de nucléotides répliqués une mutation peut-elle survenir chez ces deux espèces ?

2. Ces taux de mutations spontanées vous paraissent-ils élevés ?

3. Quels facteurs peuvent les augmenter ?

→ Corrigé p. 45

6 10 min ★★ Les différentes mutations

Les bêta-thalassémies sont des maladies dues à une altération de la synthèse de la chaîne bêta de l'hémoglobine, molécule indispensable au transport de l'O_2 dans le sang. Les individus atteints produisent moins ou aucune chaîne bêta, ce qui a des incidences sur l'hémoglobine produite. Cette maladie peut entraîner des anémies graves.

	30 35 40 45 50
Allèle Hbβ	A G _ T C T G C C G T T A C T G C C C T G T G G G G C A A
Allèle thalassémie 3	- - _ - A - - - - - -
Allèle thalassémie 6	- - _ - _ - -
Allèle thalassémie 7	- - C -

Séquences nucléotidiques des différents allèles responsables de la thalassémie

1. Identifiez les différentes mutations pour chaque thalassémie : la thalassémie 3, la thalassémie 6 et la thalassémie 7.

2. D'après l'énoncé, détaillez les différentes conséquences de la thalassémie à l'échelle de l'individu suite à ces mutations de l'ADN.

→ Corrigé p. 46

7 15 min ★★ L'action des UV sur les levures

On veut étudier l'effet des UV sur l'apparition de mutations. Pour cela, on applique des doses croissantes d'UV sur une population de levures.

Les levures forment des colonies naturellement rouges. Lorsque leur ADN est endommagé, les colonies deviennent blanches, on peut ainsi compter la fréquence des mutations.

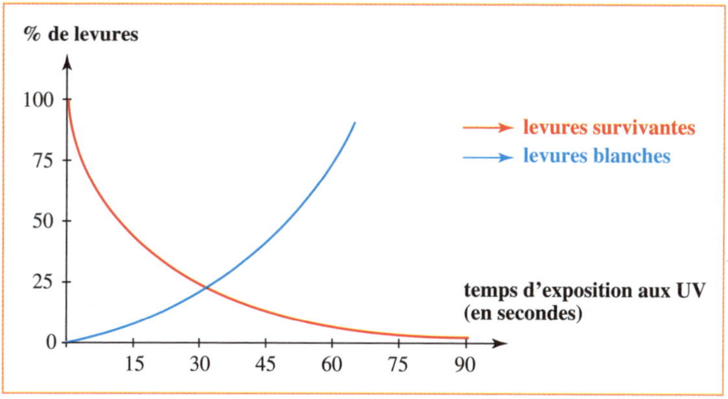

Figure 1 *Évolution de la survie et des mutations des levures*

	95					100					105	
Allèle Ade2 blanc	T	A	G	A	T	G	C	T	G	A	A	A
Allèle Ade2 rouge	T	A	G	A	T	G	C	T	T	A	A	A

Figure 2 *Comparaison des allèles Ade2 blanche et Ade2 rouge des levures*

1. D'après la figure 1, quels sont les deux effets des UV sur les levures ?

2. À l'aide de la figure 2, déterminez le type de mutation induit par les UV.

3. Quels comportements chez l'Homme pourraient augmenter les risques de mutations causées par les UV et donc l'apparition de cancer de la peau ?

→ Corrigé p. 46

8 15 min ★★ La résistance bactérienne

Escherichia coli est une espèce de bactéries intestinales qui facilitent notre digestion. Elles sont inoffensives, sauf certaines souches mutantes comme celles impliquées, en 2011, lors de l'épidémie du « concombre tueur » qui provoqua des diarrhées sanguinolentes chez les personnes atteintes.

On cherche à déterminer quels antibiotiques peuvent éliminer *E. coli.*

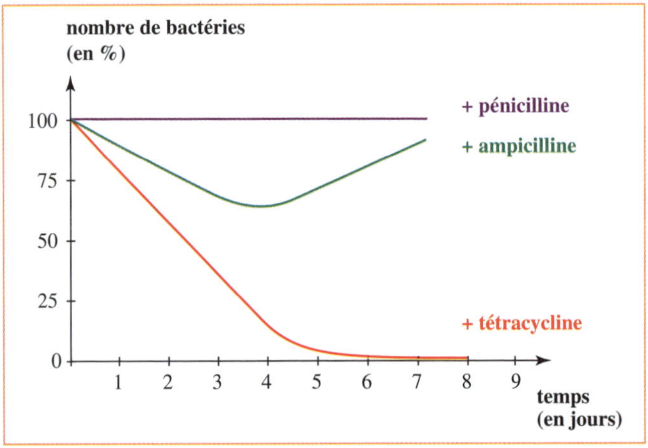

Croissance bactérienne en fonction de l'exposition aux antibiotiques

1. Déterminez si *E. coli* est résistante ou sensible aux trois antibiotiques.

2. Quel mécanisme évolutif pourrait expliquer l'évolution du nombre d'*E. coli* exposées à l'ampicilline ?

→ *Corrigé p. 46*

CONTRÔLE CONTINU POUR LE BAC

Exercice 10 pts — La réparation de l'ADN — 40 min

Xeroderma pigmentosum est une maladie provoquant l'apparition de cancers de la peau et de taches brunes à chaque exposition aux UV. Les enfants atteints doivent se protéger continuellement contre les UV : on les appelle « enfants Lune ».

Identifiez l'origine génétique de la maladie *Xeroderma pigmentosum* et ses conséquences sur l'individu atteint.

Document 1 : Taux de mutation de la peau après exposition répétée aux UV

On expose des fragments de peau d'une personne malade et d'une personne saine aux UV. On étudie ensuite la quantité d'ADN lésée au cours du temps.

	Avant exposition	10 min après exposition	1 semaine après exposition
Peau d'un individu sain	0 % de cellules mutées	5 % de cellules mutées	0 % de cellules mutées
Peau d'un individu atteint de *Xeroderma pigmentosum*	0 % de cellules mutées	15 % de cellules mutées	15 % de cellules mutées

Taux de mutation au cours du temps

Document 2 : Action des UV sur l'ADN

Les UV créent des dimères de thymine, c'est-à-dire des liaisons fortes entre deux thymines successives.

Cette liaison empêche l'ADN polymérase de répliquer correctement l'ADN et provoque ainsi des erreurs d'appariement transmises de cellules-filles en cellules-filles.

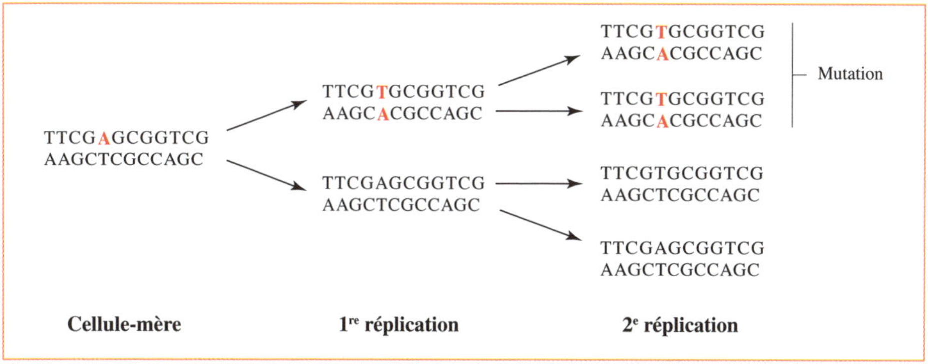

Action des UV au niveau de la duplication de l'ADN

Document 3 : Comparaison des allèles responsables de la production d'une enzyme XPA

L'enzyme XPA est une enzyme qui permet la reconnaissance des mutations de l'ADN. Elle est codée par le gène *xpa* localisé sur le chromosome 9.

Noms des allèles	Nature et position de la mutation	Conséquences phénotypiques	Incidence sur la protéine XPA
Allèle normal *xpa*		Pas d'hypersensibilité aux UV	Reconnaissance des dimères de thymine
Xpa_mut3	C → T (457)	Forte sensibilité aux UV	Protéine XPA écourtée
Xpa_mut5	T → A (174)	Forte sensibilité aux UV	Protéine XPA écourtée
Xpa_mut10	Délétion du 172e au 177e nucléotide	Forte sensibilité aux UV	Séquence protéique modifiée

Quelques mutations du gène xpa

→ *Corrigé p. 47*

CORRIGÉS

1 → Énoncé p. 39

Les affirmations exactes sont b) et c).

2 → Énoncé p. 39

Les affirmations exactes sont b), c) et d).

3 → Énoncé p. 39

Les lésions de l'ADN, si elles ne sont pas réparées, peuvent provoquer des mutations.

Ces mutations peuvent affecter les cellules somatiques et seront transmises de cellules-filles en cellules-filles (les générations suivantes de cellules germinales) et peuvent ainsi être transmises de génération en génération.

Une mutation peut affecter un gène et créer l'apparition d'un nouvel allèle. En conséquence, le phénotype peut être touché à tous ses niveaux (macroscopique, cellulaire, moléculaire) et augmenter ainsi la biodiversité.

4 → Énoncé p. 39

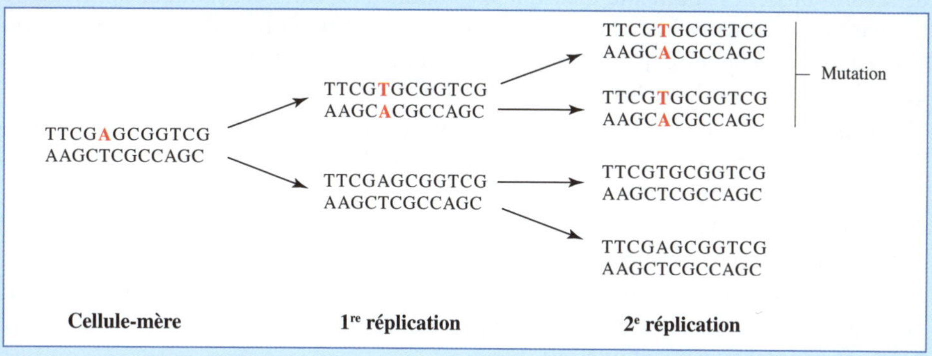

5 → Énoncé p. 40

1. Homo sapiens :

$3,3.10^9 \times 150 = 4,95.10^{11}$ soit un nucléotide muté tous les 5.10^{11} nucléotides répliqués.

Drosophile :

$1,7.10^8 \times 200 = 3,4.10^{10}$ soit un nucléotide muté tous les $3,4.10^{10}$ nucléotides répliqués.

2. Ces taux de mutations spontanées sont particulièrement faibles quelle que soit l'espèce étudiée.

3. Il doit donc exister des facteurs augmentant les mutations : les agents mutagènes. Ce sont les facteurs de l'environnement qui augmentent les taux de mutation comme la radioactivité, les UV, les agents chimiques…

6 → *Énoncé p. 40*

1. On observe que la thalassémie 3 est causée par une substitution du 48ᵉ nucléotide : un A à la place d'un G.

La thalassémie 6 est provoquée par une délétion du 52ᵉ nucléotide, le nucléotide C.

Enfin la thalassémie 7 trouve son origine dans une insertion d'un nucléotide C en 28ᵉ position.

2. Ces mutations de l'ADN entraînent des anémies sévères chez un individu : c'est le phénotype macroscopique. Ce manque d'oxygénation de l'organisme est causé par des globules rouges transportant moins bien le dioxygène sanguin (phénotype cellulaire) à cause de l'hémoglobine qui les constitue : cette hémoglobine est « altérée » au niveau de sa chaîne bêta, ce qui l'empêche de fixer efficacement le dioxygène (phénotype moléculaire).

7 → *Énoncé p. 41*

1. Suite à une exposition aux UV de plus en plus longue, on observe que la proportion de levures blanches augmente mais que la quantité de levures survivantes diminue. Or l'apparition de levures blanches signifie qu'il y a eu mutation de l'ADN de la levure. On peut donc en déduire que les UV ont un effet mutagène mais aussi létal (en provoquant la mort des cellules lorsque l'ADN est trop endommagé).

2. En comparant l'allèle responsable de la couleur rouge des colonies de levures avec l'allèle responsable de leur couleur blanche, on observe un nucléotide T (pour les levures rouges) à la place du nucléotide G (pour les levures blanches) en 103ᵉ position : c'est une substitution.

3. Une partie des UV est naturellement bloquée par la couche d'ozone. Cependant des comportements peuvent favoriser leur concentration et entraîner des mutations comme une exposition trop fréquente, entraînant des coups de soleils sur une peau claire, et l'utilisation intensive de cabines à UV.

8 → *Énoncé p. 42*

1. Après une exposition de plusieurs colonies d'*E. coli* à des antibiotiques différents, on observe que le nombre de ces bactéries reste constant en présence de pénicilline : cet antibiotique ne semble pas affecter la bactérie. On peut donc supposer que cette souche bactérienne est résistante à la pénicilline.

À l'opposé, la tétracycline permet une grande diminution de la quantité de bactéries. La bactérie est donc sensible à la tétracycline.

Enfin, l'ampicilline a un effet « intermédiaire » : dans un premier temps elle entraîne la diminution des bactéries, puis leur quantité augmente subitement. On peut supposer que la bactérie est passée de sensible à l'antibiotique, à résistante.

2. L'apparition d'une résistance de la bactérie à l'ampicilline peut trouver son origine dans l'apparition d'une mutation spontanée de l'ADN lui permettant d'être résistante à cet antibiotique. L'ajout d'ampicilline a ensuite sélectionné les quelques bactéries résistantes qui se sont multipliées : c'est un exemple de sélection naturelle.

CONTRÔLE CONTINU POUR LE BAC

Exercice → *Énoncé p. 43*

Les patients atteints de *Xeroderma pigmentosum* sont plus fréquemment touchés par l'apparition de taches brunes ainsi que par les cancers de la peau. Le phénotype macroscopique est donc lié directement à l'exposition aux UV.

Par ailleurs, au niveau du phénotype cellulaire, l'exposition aux UV des cellules de peau chez ces patients provoque davantage de mutations (15 % contre 5 % pour des cellules normales). Le plus important reste cependant une absence de réparation de l'ADN lorsque les cellules ne sont plus exposées aux UV. On peut ainsi supposer que la maladie trouve son origine dans un dysfonctionnement des systèmes de réparation des lésions de l'ADN.

En effet, les UV provoquent la formation de dimères de thymine, ce qui perturbe l'action de l'ADN polymérase et crée des problèmes d'appariement des nucléotides. Or, on sait que ces lésions de l'ADN chez une personne saine sont réparées par un système qui reconnaît la lésion, l'excise puis synthétise un nouveau fragment d'ADN. L'une de ces étapes semble donc être impossible chez les « enfants Lune ».

On observe, en effet, que l'enzyme XPA, responsable de la reconnaissance des dimères de thymine, peut être écourtée et peu fonctionnelle chez les individus malades. C'est le phénotype moléculaire.

Ces différents phénotypes trouvent leur origine dans la mutation du gène *xpa* (soit par des substitutions soit par des délétions de nucléotides). C'est donc une maladie génétique.

On peut en conclure que la maladie *Xeroderma pigmentosum* est causée par une mutation du gène *xpa* responsable de la production d'une enzyme XPA dysfonctionnelle. N'assurant plus sa fonction de réparation des lésions de l'ADN causées par les UV, les mutations s'accumulent et provoquent l'apparition de taches brunes, voire de cancers de la peau.

L'histoire humaine lue dans son génome

CHAPITRE 4

L'ADN a été découvert en 1952. En 2003, le génome humain a pu être séquencé. Depuis, il est possible d'étudier le génome d'un être humain, afin de connaître l'histoire de sa propre évolution. Cette étude est toutefois interdite en France, sauf dans le cadre d'enquêtes criminelles ou d'études médicales.

1 Méthodes de reconstitution des génomes humains

A. Les méthodes de séquençage

■ Connaître l'ensemble du **génome***, notamment humain, repose sur une technique appelée **séquençage***. L'objectif est de déterminer l'ordre de l'enchaînement des nucléotides de tout le génome.

■ La méthode la plus utilisée est le séquençage de Sanger. Cette technique est réalisée en plusieurs étapes. On ajoute au brin à étudier :
– quatre nucléotides A, T, C et G, et de l'ADN polymérase ;
– des nucléotides modifiés, les didésoxynucléotides ddATP, ddCTP, ddGTP et ddTTP, afin d'arrêter la réplication du brin dès leur incorporation.

Ex. : Quand on ajoute du ddGTP, la synthèse des brins s'arrête au niveau des nucléotides G. Il en résulte un mélange de fragments de tailles différentes qui se terminent tous au niveau d'un G. Ces fragments sont ensuite séparés par électrophorèse, ce qui permet de repérer la position des G dans la séquence.

■ On obtient des fragments d'ADN de différentes tailles qui sont soumis à une électrophorèse afin de les séparer grâce à un courant électrique (l'ADN étant chargé négativement, les fragments vont migrer selon leur poids moléculaire et donc leur longueur). Chaque fragment reflète la position du nucléotide modifié incorporé.

■ D'autres méthodes plus récentes et plus efficaces existent aujourd'hui. Elles permettent un séquençage à moindre coût.

Remarque

Les premiers séquençages complets du génome :
– 2003 : le génome humain : 3,2 milliards de nucléotides (21 000 gènes).
– 2010 : le génome néandertalien : 3,2 milliards de nucléotides.

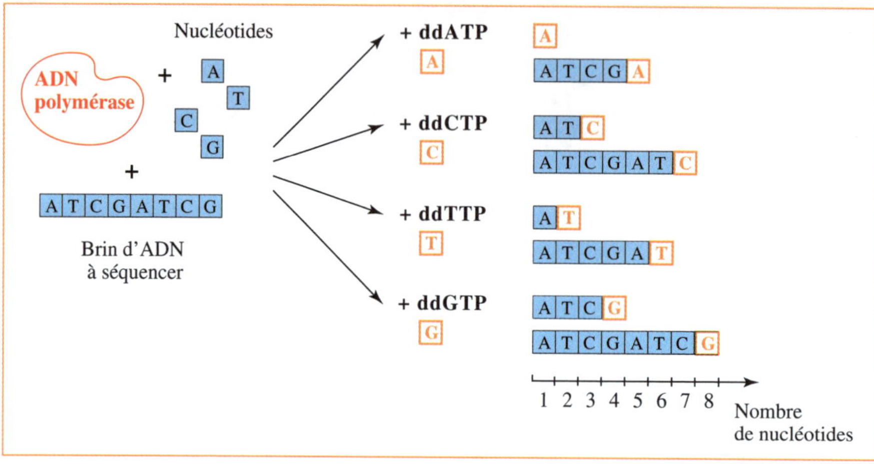

Figure 1 *La méthode de Sanger*

B. Les différents génomes humains étudiés

■ Chez les Eucaryotes en général, il existe deux types de génome : l'ADN nucléaire (contenu dans le noyau) et l'ADN mitochondrial (contenu dans les mitochondries).

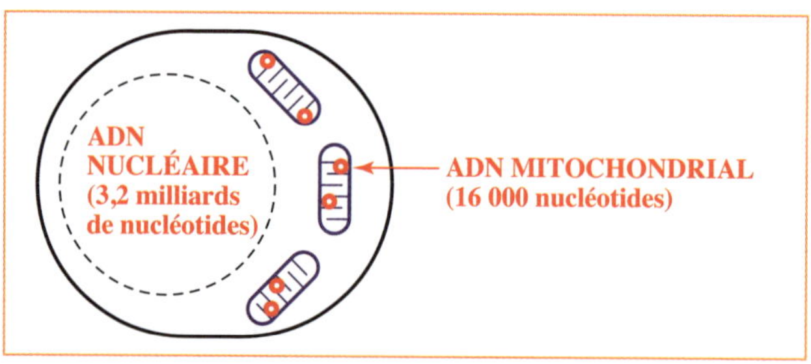

Figure 2 *Les deux types de génome des cellules eucaryotes*

■ Le génome humain peut être étudié à partir de cellules d'individus vivants, c'est le génome actuel, mais aussi à partir de fossiles humains, c'est le génome ancien. La principale difficulté pour étudier l'ADN de fossiles est son état car celui-ci a généralement été endommagé par la putréfaction : l'ADN se dégrade vite, entraînant notamment la délétion des nucléotides A et G et la substitution des nucléotides C en T.

■ Pour que la molécule d'ADN soit préservée, il faut de bonnes conditions de conservation comme le froid. Le génome humain le plus ancien est ainsi daté de 70 000 ans car il a été conservé dans le permafrost, un sol gelé en permanence.

2 La reconstitution des histoires individuelles et humaines

A. Génome et identification des individus actuels

■ L'analyse génétique d'un individu permet de dresser son **empreinte génétique***, c'est-à-dire de caractériser les séquences de son ADN qui lui sont propres. En effet, entre les gènes, il existe des portions d'ADN qui ne codent aucune protéine et qui sont très variables entre les individus. On les appelle « séquences répétées ».

■ Deux échantillons présentant la même empreinte génétique sont donc issus du même individu ou de son jumeau homozygote.

■ En étudiant les génomes, on peut donc identifier les individus et reconstituer leurs relations de parenté.

B. Génome et histoire humaine récente

■ Après séquençage des génomes actuels et fossiles, on compte le nombre de différences nucléotidiques et on dresse des arbres de parenté entre espèces fossiles et actuelles afin de reconstituer les principales étapes de l'histoire humaine récente.

■ On distingue trois lignées différentes récentes du genre *Homo* : les Sapiens, les Néandertaliens et les Dénisoviens.

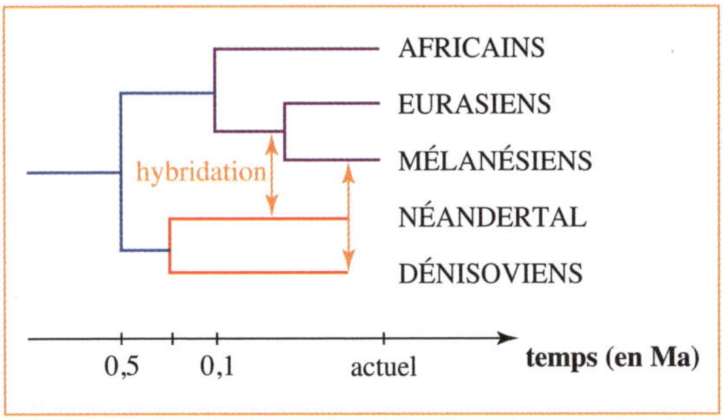

Figure 3 *Arbre de parenté récent du genre* Homo

■ Les Homo sapiens africains sont plus éloignés de l'homme de Néandertal que les Homo sapiens non africains (européens et asiatiques). Il y a donc eu un métissage avec Néandertal en Europe et en Asie qui daterait de 47 000 à 60 000 ans. Ce métissage aurait eu lieu plutôt au Proche-Orient. Ainsi, 1 à 2 % du génome des *Homo sapiens* européens et asiatiques a été hérité de Néandertal.

■ Les gènes d'origine néandertalienne chez Homo sapiens ont été favorables à la survie et ont permis une meilleure résistance dans un environnement défavorable. Ce sont notamment les gènes responsables de la couleur de la peau, de la réponse immunitaire et du catabolisme des lipides. Dans un environnement peu sélectif, comme l'environnement actuel, ces gènes sont à l'origine de problèmes d'allergie et d'obésité.

3 Les mécanismes de l'évolution humaine

A. La sélection naturelle

■ Certaines caractéristiques génétiques résultent d'une **sélection naturelle*** comme la tolérance au lactose, la résistance aux hautes altitudes et la résistance à la peste.

Ex. : La grande épidémie de peste noire qui frappa l'Europe en 1347 extermina un tiers des européens en 5 ans. Elle a permis la sélection dans les populations humaines d'un allèle « TLR » permettant une réponse immunitaire plus efficace contre les bactéries.

■ Dans une population humaine possédant une variabilité allélique, une pression de sélection exercée par l'environnement peut favoriser certains individus qui possèdent un allèle particulier dit « allèle favorable » ou « avantageux » (au détriment des individus possédant des allèles désavantageux).

■ Les individus favorisés vont alors survivre plus longtemps et davantage se reproduire, augmentant ainsi la fréquence de l'allèle avantageux dans la population.

B. La dérive génétique

■ Chez Néandertal, la **dérive génétique*** a été forte et a eu pour conséquence une accumulation des allèles délétères. La disparition de l'homme de Néandertal est donc probablement due à cette force évolutive qui s'est exercée sur des populations déjà réduites et a entraîné une forte mortalité infantile, des décès de femmes en couche (et donc une baisse des naissances) ainsi qu'une forte consanguinité.

■ Chez Homo sapiens, le hasard a également modifié les populations en agissant d'autant plus fortement que les populations étaient petites. Un cas particulier est l'**effet fondateur*** : il concerne l'isolement d'une petite population dont les fréquences alléliques seront différentes de la population initiale. C'est le cas des colons canadiens : dans la région québécoise de Saguenay-Lac-Saint-Jean, colonisée au XVIIe siècle, dont les individus présentent de nombreuses anomalies génétiques. C'est par hasard que les colons possédant plus d'allèles délétères se sont retrouvés dans cette région et que la consanguinité a accentué leur fréquence.

EXERCICES

Connaître le cours

1 2 min ★ Vrai ou Faux ?

Relevez la (ou les) affirmation(s) exacte(s).

Le séquençage :
a) utilise le principe de la réplication de l'ADN.
b) n'est réalisable que chez les individus vivants.
c) permet d'identifier un individu et ses relations de parenté.
d) a permis de connaître tout le génome humain dès les années 1990.

→ Corrigé p. 61

2 2 min ★ Vrai ou Faux ?

Relevez la (ou les) affirmation(s) exacte(s).

L'évolution humaine récente :
a) a seulement été permise par la sélection naturelle.
b) met en évidence trois espèces humaines différentes.
c) montre qu'*Homo sapiens* s'est métissé avec Néandertal.
d) indique que l'évolution humaine s'est arrêtée il y a 70 000 ans.

→ Corrigé p. 61

3 5 min ★ Restitution de connaissances

Expliquez brièvement les mécanismes évolutifs à l'origine de l'histoire humaine récente.

→ Corrigé p. 61

4 5 min ★ Schématiser le cours

Schématisez le principe du séquençage de Sanger pour la séquence nucléotidique suivante : ATTCCGCTAGC.

→ Corrigé p. 61

S'entraîner

5 10 min ★★ Les Dénisoviens

En 2010, des molaires de Dénisoviens ont été trouvées dans la grotte sibérienne de Denisova. Leur génome a été séquencé en 2013 afin de le comparer avec celui de Néandertal et de Sapiens.

Le pourcentage de divergence obtenu correspond au pourcentage de nucléotides différents par rapport au nombre total de nucléotides comparés.

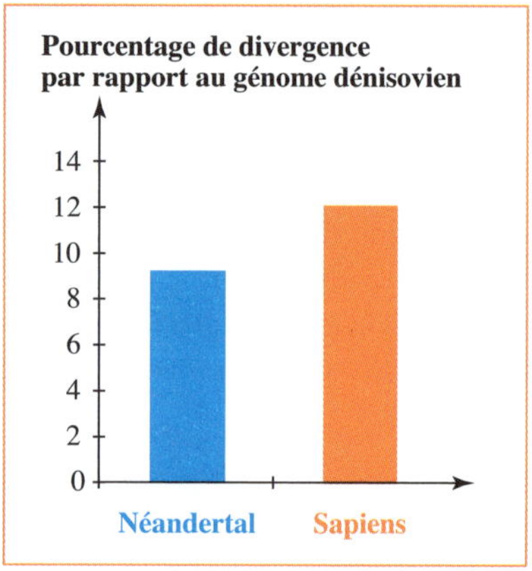

Comparaison des génomes de molaire de différents individus du genre Homo

1. Comparez les résultats obtenus entre les Dénisoviens et Néandertal puis entre les Dénisoviens et Sapiens.

2. Réalisez un arbre de parenté reposant sur la comparaison des génomes des molaires trouvées à Denisova.

→ *Corrigé p. 61*

6 15 min ★★ La répartition des groupes sanguins

Les groupes sanguins ABO sont dus à l'expression d'allèles A, B ou O qui entraînent l'expression de glycoprotéines différentes à la surface des globules rouges. Ces variations alléliques n'entraînent aucune valeur sélective, c'est-à-dire qu'aucun allèle n'est plus avantageux qu'un autre.

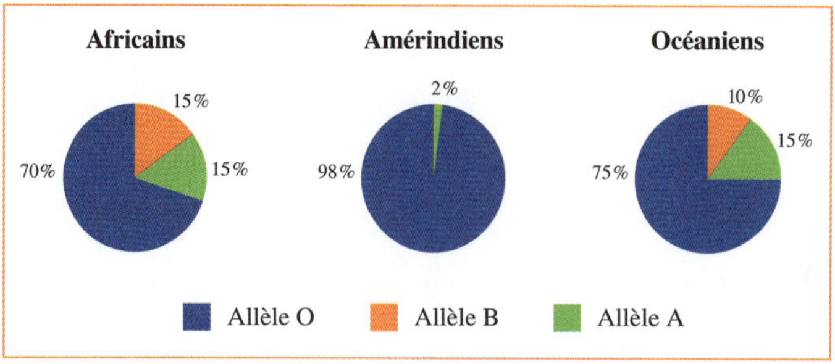

Figure 1 *Fréquence des allèles A, B et O selon les populations humaines*

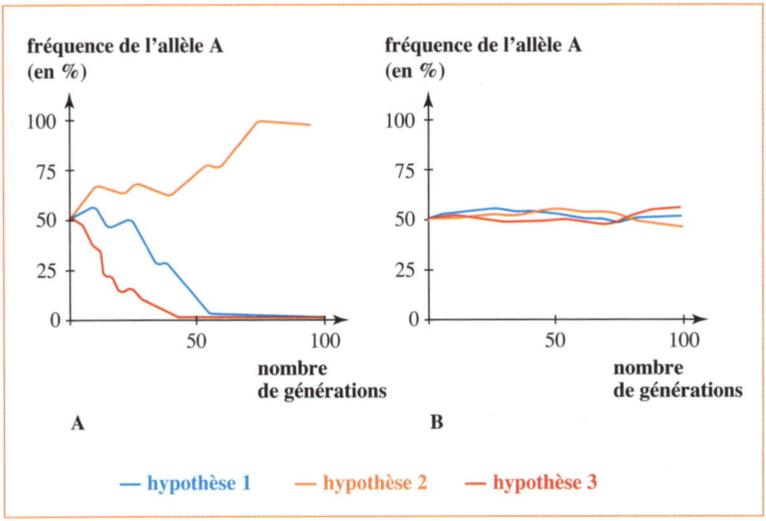

Figure 2 *Modélisation de la relation hasard et fréquence de l'allèle A de deux populations sur 100 générations : une petite population (A) et une grande population (B)*

1. À partir de la figure 1, mettez en évidence l'inégale répartition des allèles responsables des groupes sanguins selon les populations.

2. À l'aide de la figure 2 et de vos connaissances, expliquez la force évolutive ayant permis cette répartition inégale, notamment pour les populations amérindiennes.

→ *Corrigé p. 62*

7 20 min ★★ La drépanocytose

La drépanocytose est une maladie génétique qui modifie la structure de l'hémoglobine, protéine constitutive des globules rouges et qui permet le transport du dioxygène dans le sang. La mutation du 6e acide aminé de la chaîne bêta (le glutamate est remplacé par une valine) produit une hémoglobine HbS rigide, donnant aux globules rouges une forme de « faucille » qui peut boucher les vaisseaux sanguins.

Autrefois, les individus homozygotes HbS/HbS souffraient d'une anémie grave par destruction des globules rouges et mouraient précocement. Les individus hétérozygotes HbA/HbS, eux, survivent sans crises.

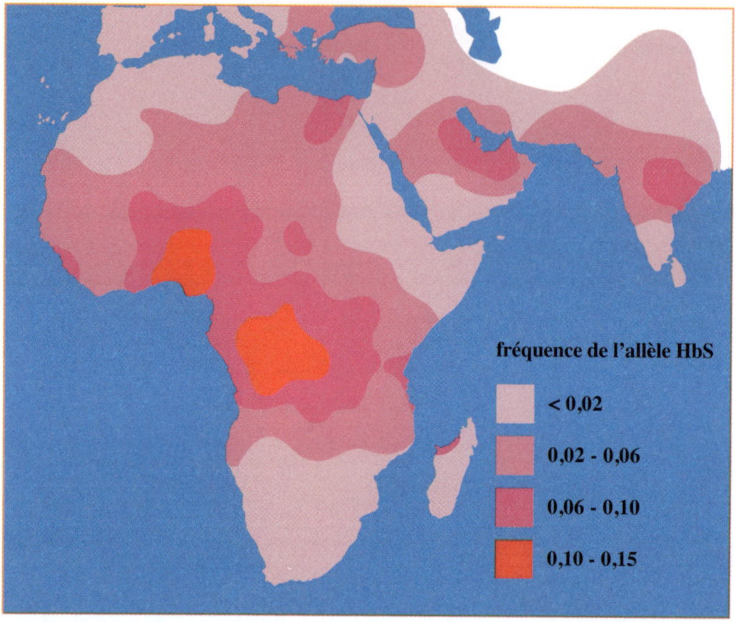

Figure 1 *Fréquence de l'allèle HbS en Afrique*

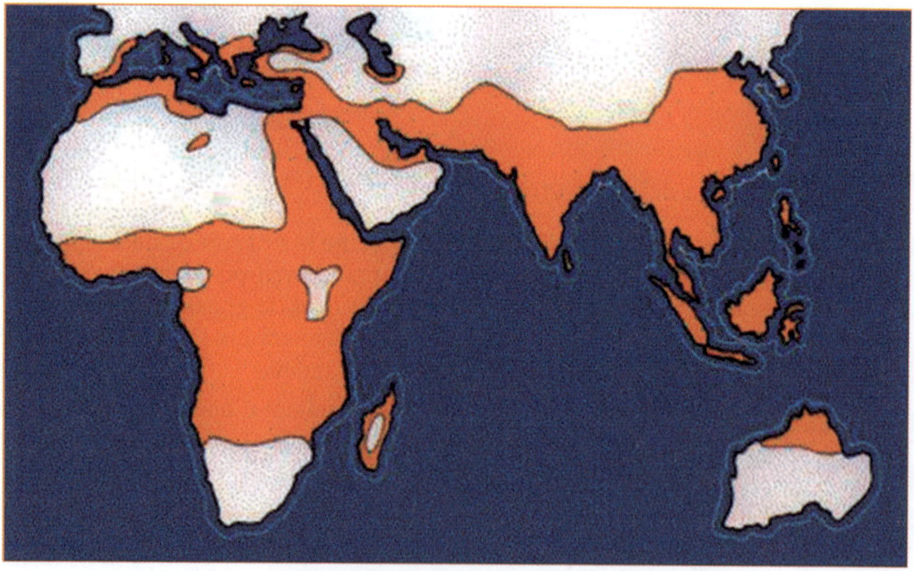

Figure 2 *Répartition du paludisme dans le monde*

	Nombre d'individus morts du paludisme	Pourcentage d'hétérozygotes HbA/HbS	Nombre théorique d'hétérozygotes tués par le paludisme	Nombre réel d'hétérozygotes morts du paludisme
République démocratique du Congo (villes de Kinshasa et Kananga)	44	27,5 %	12	1
Nigéria (ville de Ibadan)	27	24 %	6,5	0

Figure 3 *Comparaison de la répartition des allèles HbS réelle et théorique en Afrique centrale (en 1964)*

1. Quelles sont les conséquences phénotypiques de la drépanocytose ?
2. D'après la figure 1, décrivez la répartition de l'allèle HbS dans la population africaine. Cette fréquence de la drépanocytose en Afrique est-elle en accord avec les symptômes de la maladie et sa valeur sélective décrits dans la question 1 ?
3. D'après la figure 2, établissez un parallèle entre la fréquence de l'allèle HbS et la répartition du paludisme.
4. À l'aide de vos connaissances et de la figure 3, expliquez la forte concentration d'allèle HbS en Afrique centrale.

→ *Corrigé p. 62*

8 20 min ★★ La tolérance au lactose

Pour pouvoir être absorbé par les intestins, le lactose, principal constituant du lait, nécessite d'être hydrolysé. Cette réaction enzymatique est réalisée par une enzyme, la lactase.

Il existe deux catégories d'êtres humains dans la population humaine : les individus LP (lactase persistante) qui digèrent le lactose toute leur vie et les individus LNP (lactase non persistante) qui ont des douleurs abdominales ou encore des diarrhées après ingestion de lait à partir de l'âge de 5 ans.

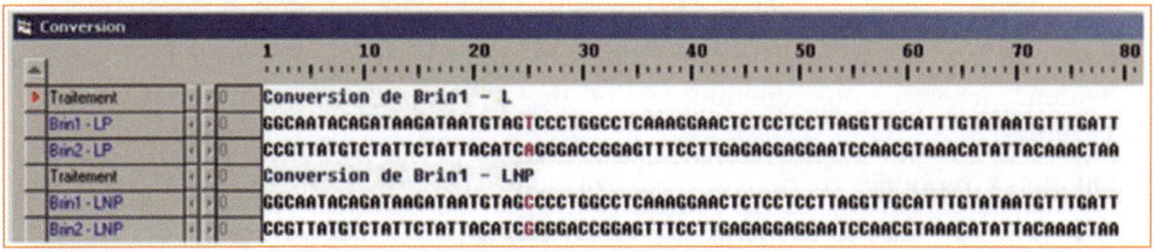

Figure 1 *Répartition des individus LP*

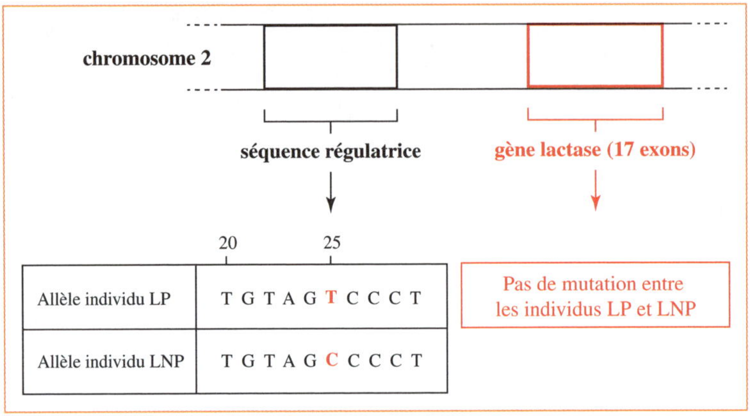

Figure 2 *Expression du gène de la lactase*

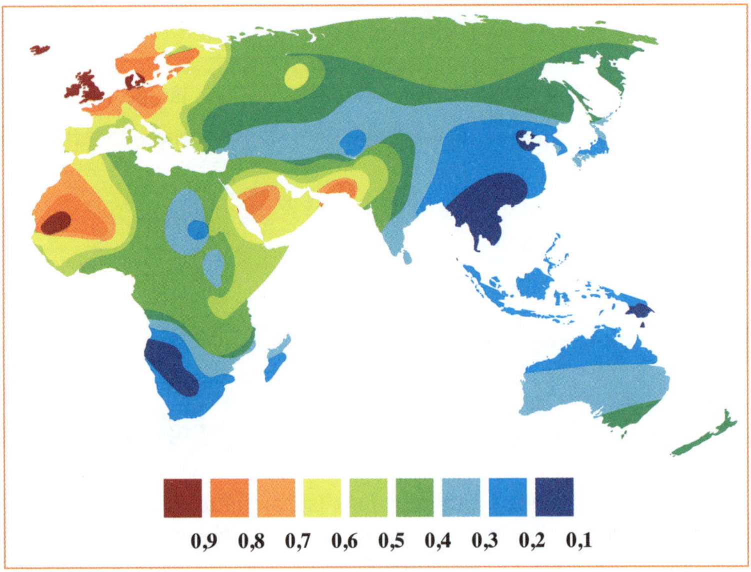

Figure 3 *Répartition des individus LP*

1. À l'aide de la figure 3, décrivez la répartition mondiale des individus LNP et LP.

2. La production d'ARN_m de lactase étant inexistante chez les personnes LNP, mettez en évidence les variations génétiques à l'origine de l'apparition d'individus LP à l'aide de la figure 2.

3. Quelle(s) hypothèse(s) pouvez-vous formuler sur le mécanisme à l'origine d'une plus grande fréquence de l'allèle LP en Europe ?

→ *Corrigé p. 63*

CONTRÔLE CONTINU POUR LE BAC

Exercice 10 pts La résistance à l'altitude des Tibétains 30 min

Lors d'une montée rapide en altitude, certains symptômes peuvent survenir : maux de tête, vomissements, vertiges, fatigue générale. On les regroupe communément sous le nom de « mal des montagnes ». Cependant, certaines populations ne sont pas affectées par les hautes altitudes. C'est le cas des Tibétains.

À l'aide des documents et de vos connaissances, décrivez les effets de l'altitude chez les Tibétains et le mécanisme évolutif à l'origine de leur résistance.

Document 1 : Étude allélique des Tibétains

On compare les fréquences des allèles dans les populations de Tibétains et de Hans (ethnie principale de Chine vivant à basse altitude) :

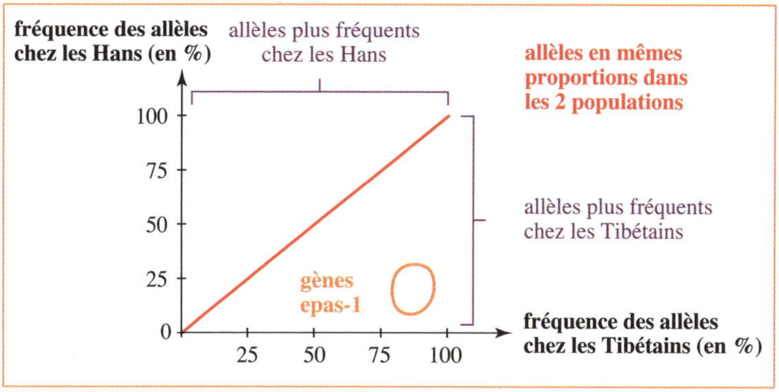

Comparaison de la fréquence allélique des Tibétains et des Hans

Le gène *epas-1* est impliqué dans une cascade d'expression de gènes permettant la production d'une hormone, l'érythropoïétine (EPO) qui permet une meilleure oxygénation des tissus.

Dans certains cas, l'augmentation de globules rouges due à la meilleure oxygénation se fait de façon trop importante et trop rapide (polyglobulie), entraînant les symptômes du mal des montagnes.

Chez les Tibétains, on n'observe jamais l'apparition de ces symptômes quelle que soit l'altitude.

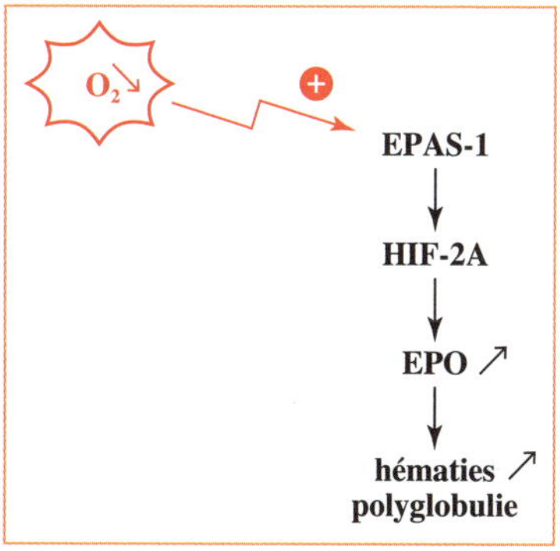

Document 2 : Effets de l'altitude sur l'expression des gènes

Les chercheurs ont déterminé le nombre d'hématies et la concentration d'hémoglobine chez les Tibétains et les Hans après les avoir placés à des altitudes supérieures à 4 000 m.

	Concentration moyenne en hémoglobine (g/L)	**Nombre moyen d'hématies**
Hans	178	5,3
Tibétains résistants à l'altitude	167,5	5,2

Comparaison des caractéristiques sanguines après un séjour prolongé à 4 000 m d'altitude

Document 3 : Origine évolutive de l'adaptation à l'altitude

Depuis 2012, on dispose du séquençage génomique des Néandertaliens et des Dénisoviens, ce qui a permis de dresser des arbres de parenté.

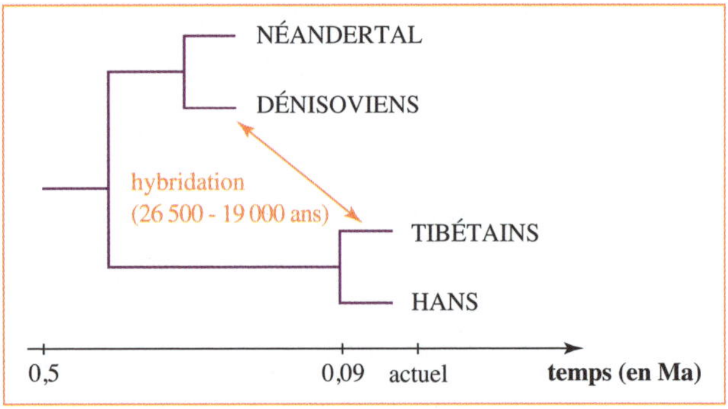

Arbre de parenté des populations asiatiques

L'allèle EPAS-1 est retrouvé chez plusieurs espèces humaines, notamment les Dénisoviens qui devaient donc posséder des capacités d'adaptation à la haute altitude. L'hybridation entre Sapiens et Dénisoviens a dû avoir lieu avant la séparation de ce groupe humain en deux groupes, celui des Hans et celui des Tibétains, il y a 20 000 ans environ.

L'allèle EPAS-1 devait être peu fréquent au début dans la population de Tibétains mais, lorsque ceux-ci se sont établis à de hautes altitudes, il s'est répandu au fil des générations.

→ Corrigé p. 63

CORRIGÉS

1 → Énoncé p. 53

Les affirmations exactes sont a) et c).

2 → Énoncé p. 53

Les affirmations exactes sont b) et c).

3 → Énoncé p. 53

La variabilité allélique présente dans la population humaine actuelle peut varier selon deux forces évolutives : la sélection naturelle liée à l'environnement et la dérive génétique, indépendante de l'environnement.

La sélection naturelle est liée à une pression environnementale qui favorise les individus possédant un allèle favorable, qui va donc augmenter dans la population au fur et à mesure des générations (grâce à une meilleure survie et une meilleure reproduction).

La dérive génétique est l'effet du hasard sur les fréquences alléliques. Elle est d'autant plus rapide et forte que la population est petite.

4 → Énoncé p. 53

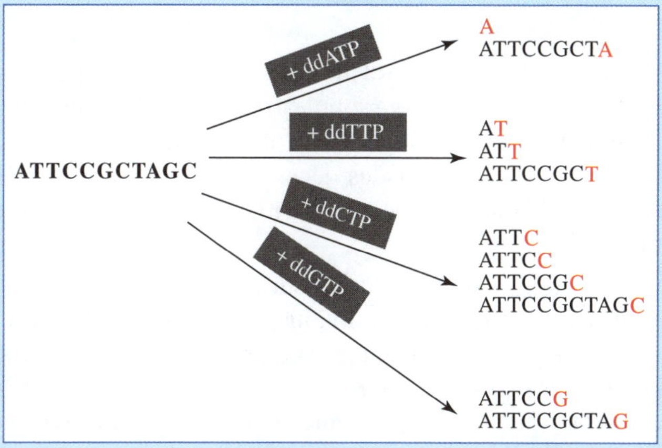

On obtient des fragments de tailles différentes.

5 → Énoncé p. 53

1. On observe que le génome des molaires de Dénisoviens possède seulement 9 % de divergence avec celui de Néandertal mais davantage avec celui de Sapiens (12 %).

Ceci nous permet de supposer l'existence d'un ancêtre commun plus récent entre Dénisoviens et Néandertal qu'avec Sapiens ou encore des hybridations entre ces deux espèces.

2.

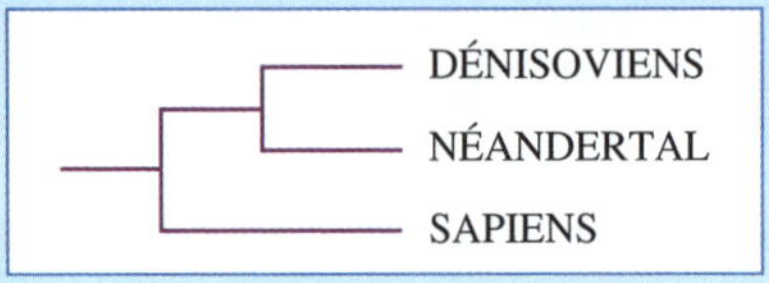

6 → *Énoncé p. 54*

1. Les allèles responsables des groupes sanguins ne sont pas répartis de façon équitable entre les différentes populations humaines. L'allèle O est le plus fréquent et l'allèle B est très peu répandu. Cependant un cas très particulier est observé : celui des populations amérindiennes qui possèdent l'allèle O à 98 %.

2. Les allèles responsables des groupes sanguins n'ont pas de valeur sélective. On n'explique donc pas cette répartition particulière par la sélection naturelle. Par ailleurs la modélisation par l'effet du hasard montre que les fréquences alléliques varient peu dans une grande population mais varient rapidement dans les petites populations. On peut donc supposer que les populations amérindiennes, plus isolées et en petit effectif, ont subi une dérive génétique expliquant qu'elles ne possèdent plus que les allèles O et A.

7 → *Énoncé p. 55*

1. Autrefois les individus homozygotes HbS/HbS avaient des chances de survie faibles en raison de la déformation de leurs globules rouges (phénotype cellulaire) causée par la mutation touchant leur hémoglobine (phénotype moléculaire). Leurs crises d'anémie sévère pouvaient entraîner des décès (phénotype macroscopique), et donc peu de chances de se reproduire et de transmettre ces allèles. Cet allèle HbS semble donc désavantageux.

2. On observe que l'allèle HbS est très fréquent en Afrique centrale avec une proportion s'élevant à plus de 10 à 15 % des individus le possédant. Or cet allèle confère des modifications de l'hémoglobine pouvant provoquer la mort des individus homozygotes et des handicaps pour les personnes hétérozygotes. C'est donc un allèle désavantageux, qui diminue la valeur sélective des personnes le possédant. Sa fréquence en Afrique centrale est donc trop élevée.

3. On remarque que le maintien de cet allèle à une fréquence élevée coïncide avec le fait que ces populations vivent dans des régions où le paludisme est très répandu.

4. On constate que la mortalité réelle des individus atteints de drépanocytose dans les pays où règne le paludisme est inférieure à la mortalité théorique (par rapport au reste de la population).

On peut donc supposer que l'allèle HbS, en déformant les globules rouges, confère un avantage sélectif aux individus drépanocytaires face au paludisme. La pression de sélection que constitue le paludisme favorise donc les allèles HbS. Les individus hétérozygotes vont alors transmettre cet allèle de génération en génération.

8 → *Énoncé p. 57*

1. Les individus LP sont plus nombreux en Europe du Nord (entre 80 et 95 %) et en Afrique occidentale. Dans le reste du monde, leur fréquence reste faible. Plus généralement les individus LP représentent 35 % de la population mondiale contre 65 % pour les individus LNP.

2. Il n'y a aucune production d'ARNm de lactase à partir de 5 ans chez les individus LNP. Pourtant on n'observe aucune mutation du gène responsable de la production de lactase. La différence doit donc se situer au niveau de la région régulatrice située en amont du gène. Chez les individus LP, on observe une mutation de cette région qui permet donc la transcription du gène tout au long de la vie des individus.

3. L'allèle qui permet la production de lactase tout au long de la vie doit conférer un avantage sélectif aux personnes LP. On peut supposer que le lait constitue un apport énergétique non négligeable dans certaines régions en période de disette. Une deuxième hypothèse réside en un avantage sélectif grâce à un meilleur apport en vitamine D dans les régions peu ensoleillées. Et enfin on peut supposer aussi que le lait a pu présenter une source d'eau non polluée.

CONTRÔLE CONTINU POUR LE BAC

Exercice → *Énoncé p. 59*

Le mal des montagnes touche la majorité des êtres humains mais les Tibétains semblent être les rares individus non affectés. **Comment les caractéristiques biologiques et évolutives des Tibétains leur permettent-elles de vivre en haute altitude ?**

Quand on compare le génome des Tibétains avec celui des Hans, on observe que la majorité des allèles est présent en même proportion dans les deux populations. Ces deux ethnies sont donc très apparentées. Pourtant on observe que le gène *epas-1* est plus fréquent chez les Tibétains que chez les Hans. Ce gène pourrait être à l'origine de leur adaptation à l'altitude.

Chez les Hans et les autres *Homo sapiens*, ce gène permet de produire davantage de globules rouges dans les cas de pénurie en dioxygène, ce qui est le cas lorsque l'altitude est élevée. Or, un effet secondaire de cette polyglobulie est le mal des montagnes. On sait cependant que chez les Tibétains, les quantités d'hémoglobine produite et de globules rouges sont plus faibles quelle que soit l'altitude. On peut en déduire que ce faible taux d'hémoglobine leur permet d'éviter d'avoir le mal des montagnes et de supporter une faible oxygénation.

Les Tibétains doivent donc posséder une variation allélique d'*epas-1* qui leur permet de produire moins de globules rouges et d'hémoglobine.

Cet allèle semble issu d'une hybridation avec une autre espèce humaine asiatique : les Dénisoviens. Tous les Hans devaient posséder cet allèle mais la vie en altitude des Tibétains leur a conféré un avantage sélectif qui a permis d'augmenter la fréquence de l'allèle EPAS-1 dans la population.

L'expression du patrimoine génétique

CHAPITRE 5

Couleur de la peau, couleur des cheveux… chaque être humain vivant sur Terre est unique. Ses différents caractères héréditaires sont déterminés par le patrimoine génétique.

1 Les étapes de la synthèse des protéines

A. 1re étape : la transcription de l'ADN en ARN

■ Dans la cellule eucaryote, l'ADN est protégé par le noyau. Pour que l'information génétique puisse être transmise du noyau vers le cytoplasme, il faut un intermédiaire : c'est l'**ARN pré-messager** dont la synthèse, appelée **transcription***, se passe dans le noyau.

	ADN ou désoxyribonucléotide	ARN ou ribonucléotide
Nucléotides	Adénine Cytosine Guanine Thymine	Adénine Cytosine Guanine Uracile
Glucides	Désoxyribose	Ribose
Taille de la molécule (nombre de nucléotides)	10^6 à 10^8 nucléotides (longue)	10^2 à 10^3 nucléotides (courte)
Nombre de chaînes (brin)	2 chaînes en hélice (1 double brin)	1 chaîne en hélice (1 simple brin)

Figure 1 *Comparaison des compositions de l'ADN et de l'ARN*

■ Comme l'ADN, l'ARN pré-messager est un **acide nucléique*** composé de nucléotides. Trois caractéristiques le différencient de l'ADN :
– le nucléotide thymine **T** est remplacé par le nucléotide « uracile » **U** ;
– le sucre est un ribose (au lieu d'un désoxyribose) ;
– ses nucléotides s'assemblent sous forme d'une seule chaîne.

Rappel

Un nucléotide est le constituant élémentaire des acides nucléiques, formé par un nucléoside associé à un phosphate. Un nucléotide est composé :
– d'une base azotée A, T, C ou G ;
– d'un sucre ;
– d'un phosphate.

■ Le brin de l'ADN qui est copié en ARN pré-messager est appelé « **brin transcrit*** ».
La transcription respecte la complémentarité des bases :
- un nucléotide A (adénine) est toujours apparié à un nucléotide U, uracile ;
- un nucléotide T (thymine) est toujours apparié à un nucléotide A ;
- un nucléotide G (guanine) est toujours apparié à un nucléotide C (cytosine) ;
- un nucléotide C est toujours apparié à un nucléotide G.

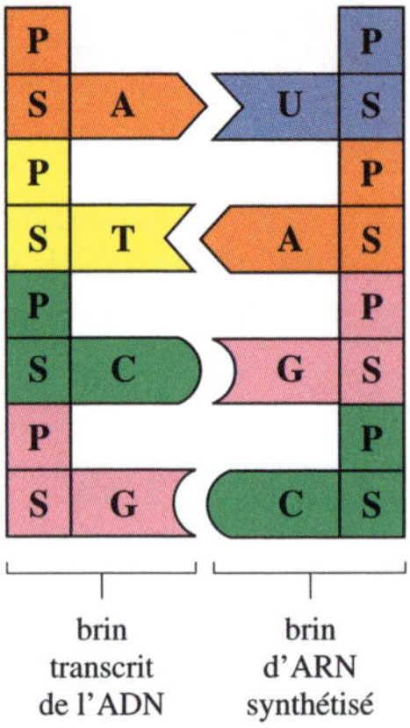

■ La transcription est réalisée par une enzyme, l'**ARN polymérase*** dont le travail est de transformer l'information génétique de l'ADN en une succession de nucléotides qui formera l'ARN. Cette étape permet de conserver l'ordre de succession des nucléotides de l'ADN à l'ARN pré-messager et donc de conserver l'information génétique.

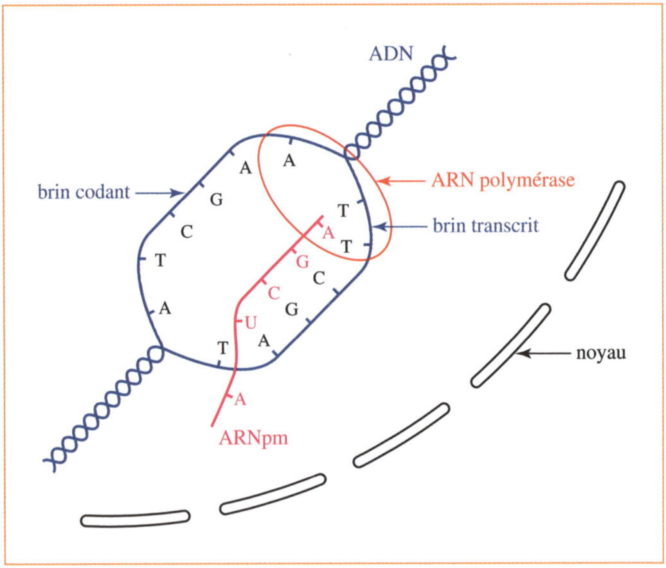

Figure 2 *La transcription*

B. 2e étape : l'épissage de l'ARN

■ Chez les Eucaryotes, les gènes sont morcelés en parties codantes (**exons***) et en parties non codantes (**introns***). Avant de migrer dans le cytoplasme, l'ARN pré-messager subit des modifications dans le noyau, une sorte de découpage : ses introns sont éliminés et les exons restants sont réunis bout à bout. On parle de maturation ou **épissage***. On obtient ainsi un **ARN messager***.

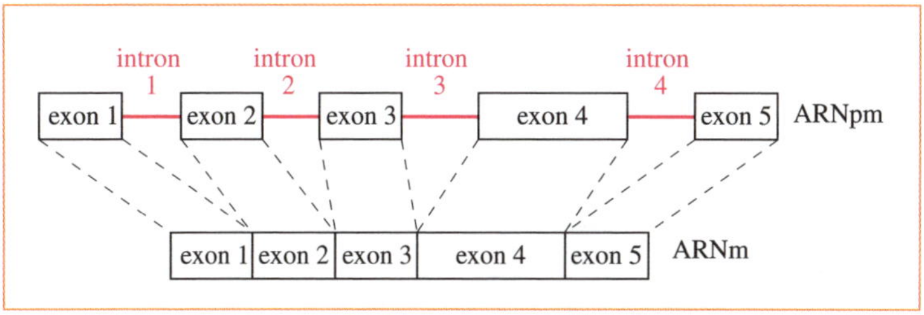

Figure 3 *L'épissage*

■ Différentes associations d'exons sont possibles. On peut donc obtenir des ARNm différents et donc des protéines différentes à partir d'un même gène : c'est l'**épissage alternatif***.

> **Remarque**
>
> Dans l'espèce humaine, il existe 90 000 protéines pour « seulement » 21 000 gènes. Cette différence s'explique par l'épissage alternatif : un même gène peut être à l'origine de la production de plusieurs protéines.

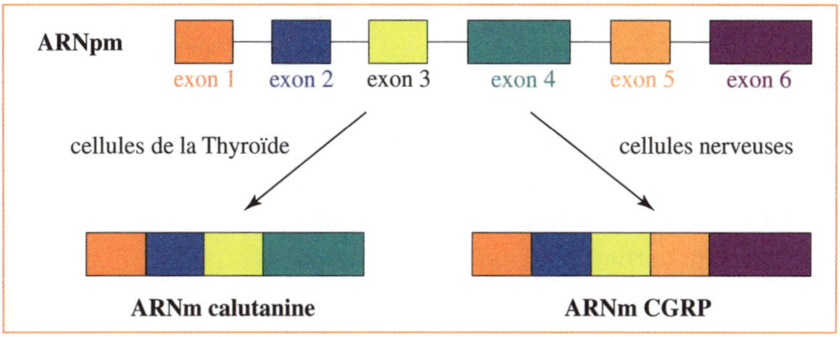

Figure 4 *L'épissage alternatif*

C. 3e étape : la traduction de l'ARN en protéines

■ Les **protéines** sont des molécules organiques constituées d'une succession d'**acides aminés**. Certaines protéines permettent l'expression des caractères héréditaires.

Ex. : Chez l'Homme, la protéine « mélanine » est responsable des caractères « couleur des cheveux », « couleur des yeux » ou encore « couleur de la peau ».

La production d'une protéine à partir d'un ARN messager permet de transformer sa séquence de nucléotides en une séquence d'acides aminés : cette étape est appelée **traduction*** et se déroule dans le cytoplasme.

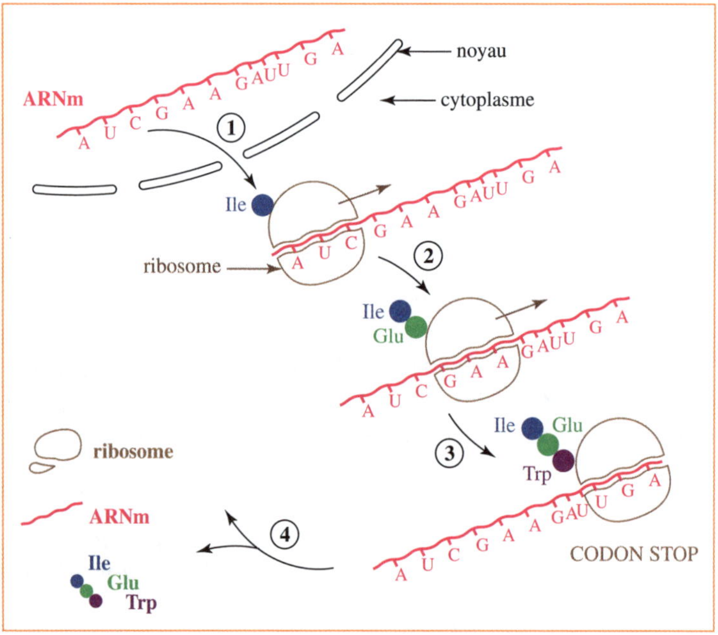

Figure 5 *La traduction*

■ L'ARN messager est composé d'une longue séquence de nucléotides. Sa traduction consiste en la lecture d'une succession de trois nucléotides consécutifs de cette séquence. Chaque triplet est appelé **codon***. Chaque codon correspond à un acide aminé spécifique : c'est le **code génétique*** (voir *figure 6* p. 69). Cette lecture est réalisée par une petite particule du cytoplasme, un **ribosome***.

Première lettre	Deuxième lettre U	Deuxième lettre C	Deuxième lettre A	Deuxième lettre G	Troisième lettre
U	UUU Phe	UCU Ser	UAU Tyr	UGU Cys	U
U	UUC Phe	UCC Ser	UAC Tyr	UGC Cys	C
U	UUA Leu	UCA Ser	**UAA Stop**	**UGA Stop**	A
U	UUG Leu	UCG Ser	**UAG Stop**	UGG Trp	G
C	CUU Leu	CCU Pro	CAU His	CGU Arg	U
C	CUC Leu	CCC Pro	CAC His	CGC Arg	C
C	CUA Leu	CCA Pro	CAA Gln	CGA Arg	A
C	CUG Leu	CCG Pro	CAG Gln	CGG Arg	G
A	AUU Ile	ACU Thr	AAU Asn	AGU Ser	U
A	AUC Ile	ACC Thr	AAC Asn	AGC Ser	C
A	AUA Ile	ACA Thr	AAA Lys	AGA Arg	A
A	**AUG Met**	ACG Thr	AAG Lys	AGG Arg	G
G	GUU Val	GCU Ala	GAU Asp	GGU Gly	U
G	GUC Val	GCC Ala	GAC Asp	GGC Gly	C
G	GUA Val	GCA Ala	GAA Glu	GGA Gly	A
G	GUG Val	GCG Ala	GAG Glu	GGG Gly	G

codon d'initiation **codon de terminaison**

Figure 6 *Le code génétique*

■ Le code génétique est :
- universel : valable pour presque tous les êtres vivants ;
- redondant : plusieurs codons correspondent à un même acide aminé ;
- non chevauchant : la lecture d'un codon étant effectuée, aucun des nucléotides de ce codon n'est utilisé pour former le codon suivant.

Remarque

Il existe trois codons qui ne sont associés à aucune acide aminé : ce sont des codons « STOP », responsables de l'arrêt de la synthèse de la protéine. En les « lisant », le ribosome s'arrête.

L'information portée par une molécule d'ARN (message génétique) est donc convertie en une information fonctionnelle (la séquence des acides aminés d'une protéine).

2 Les liens entre le génotype et le phénotype

A. L'origine génétique du phénotype

■ Le **phénotype** est l'ensemble des caractères observables d'un individu. On le définit à différents niveaux :
- le phénotype macroscopique, à l'échelle de l'individu ;
- le phénotype cellulaire, à l'échelle des cellules ;
- le phénotype moléculaire, à l'échelle des protéines ;

Le phénotype macroscopique dépend du phénotype cellulaire, lui-même dépendant du phénotype moléculaire.

■ Un nouvel allèle résultant d'une mutation peut être à l'origine d'une modification protéique ou de l'absence de synthèse de la protéine et ainsi faire apparaître un nouveau phénotype dans une population. D'après le code génétique, la mutation d'un nucléotide peut :

– Passer inaperçue grâce à la redondance du code génétique : un même acide aminé est produit malgré le changement de nucléotide. On parle de mutation silencieuse.
– Faire apparaître un codon STOP précoce et ainsi arrêter la synthèse de la protéine : cette dernière sera alors plus courte et peu fonctionnelle. C'est une mutation non-sens.
– Faire apparaître un acide aminé différent dans la protéine : c'est une mutation faux-sens.

B. L'origine environnementale du phénotype

■ L'expression des gènes de la cellule est régulée par l'action de facteurs internes à l'organisme comme l'apparition de mutations lors du développement embryonnaire.

Elle peut aussi être influencée par des conditions de l'environnement. En effet, des facteurs environnementaux peuvent modifier l'aspect de la chromatine et ainsi modifier l'expression de certains gènes. On appelle ce phénomène l'**épigénétique***.

Ex. : Si un œuf de drosophile (la mouche du vinaigre) est chauffé à 37 °C alors la mouche qui éclot a les yeux rouges (au lieu de noirs). Ce nouveau caractère est transmis à toute sa descendance. La température peut donc influencer l'expression des gènes chez la drosophile.

EXERCICES

Connaître le cours

1 2 min ★ Vrai ou Faux ?

Relevez la (ou les) affirmation(s) exacte(s).

L'épissage :

a) est une modification de l'ADN en ARN pré-messager.
b) permet de sélectionner quelques exons afin d'obtenir des ARN messagers différents.
c) se déroule dans le cytoplasme.
d) est une maturation de l'ARN pré-messager.

→ Corrigé p. 77

2 2 min ★ Vrai ou Faux ?

Relevez la (ou les) affirmation(s) exacte(s).

La traduction :

a) se déroule dans le cytoplasme grâce aux ribosomes.
b) permet la synthèse d'une protéine à partir de la lecture du brin transcrit de l'ARN.
c) respecte le code génétique.
d) n'existe que chez les Eucaryotes.

→ Corrigé p. 77

3 5 min ★ Restitution de connaissances

Expliquez brièvement comment il est possible d'obtenir plusieurs protéines à partir d'un même ARN pré-messager.

→ Corrigé p. 77

4 5 min ★ Schématiser le cours

Schématisez la transcription d'un brin transcrit de l'ADN de séquence nucléotidique suivante : ATTGGCCAAGCAT.

→ Corrigé p. 77

S'entraîner

5 10 min ★★ Le code génétique

On cherche à calculer le nombre de nucléotides nécessaires pour coder un acide aminé. On réalise donc un raisonnement par hypothèses.

1. Si on suppose qu'il ne faut qu'un seul nucléotide (A, T, C ou G) pour coder un seul acide aminé, combien d'acides aminés sont alors produits ?

2. Si on suppose qu'il faut deux nucléotides pour coder un acide aminé, quelles combinaisons de nucléotides obtient-on et combien d'acides aminés différents sont produits ?

3. Si on suppose qu'il faut trois nucléotides pour coder un acide aminé, quelles combinaisons de nucléotides obtient-on et combien d'acides aminés différents sont produits ?

4. Sachant qu'il existe 20 acides aminés, quelle hypothèse est la plus vraisemblable ?

5. Quelles propriétés du code génétique permettent d'expliquer la différence entre le nombre de combinaisons calculées et le nombre réel d'acides aminés ?

→ Corrigé p. 77

6 10 min ★★ La transcription

On prépare des extraits de chromatine pour les observer en microscopie électronique. On observe ce genre de structures en « sapin de Noël » :

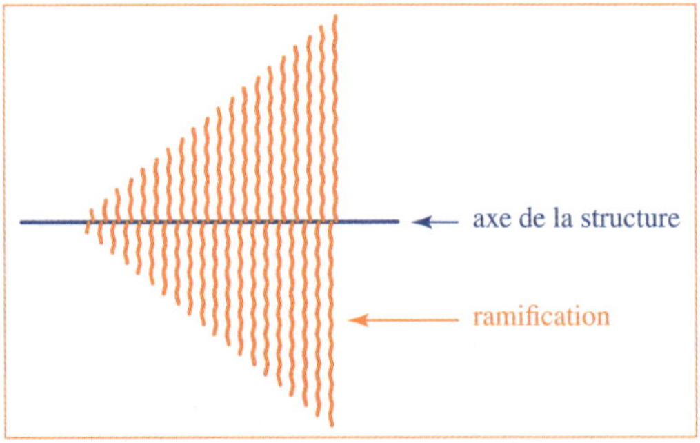

Les structures en « sapin de Noël »

Si on ajoute une DNase (enzyme détruisant l'ADN), à ces extraits, l'axe est détruit. Cependant si on ajoute des RNases (enzymes détruisant les ARN), ce sont les ramifications qui sont détruites.

1. D'après les expériences enzymologiques, déduisez-en quelles sont les molécules qui constituent l'axe et les ramifications de la structure de la figure.

2. Schématisez cette structure en la légendant et en indiquant le sens de la transcription.

→ Corrigé p. 78

7 10 min ★★ Conséquences des mutations

Numéro de nucléotide	1				5					10					15			
Brin transcrit	G	G	G	G	G	G	T	G	T	A	A	C	C	A	G	T	A	A

Séquence nucléotidique aléatoire

1. Donnez la séquence nucléotidique de l'ARNm du brin transcrit présenté.

2. Donnez la séquence en acides aminés de l'ARNm obtenu en vous aidant du code génétique fourni.

3. Expliquez les conséquences sur les protéines des mutations génétiques suivantes :
a. Substitution en position 3 par un nucléotide T.
b. Substitution en position 11 par un nucléotide T.

→ *Corrigé p. 78*

8 15 min ★★ Rôle de l'ARN

Afin de démontrer que l'ARN assure bien le rôle d'intermédiaire entre l'ADN contenu dans le noyau et les protéines contenues dans le cytoplasme, on utilise un marquage radioactif. Pour cela, on incorpore, dans la cellule, des éléments radioactifs qui entreront dans la composition de l'ARN lors de sa synthèse (le nucléotide d'uracile par exemple).

On étudie ensuite l'évolution de la radioactivité à différents temps. C'est la technique du *pulse-chase* (« pulse » = marquage radioactif ; « chase » = « chasse », on chasse la radioactivité).

On observe les résultats par autoradiographie : la radioactivité apparaît en noir sur les photographies.

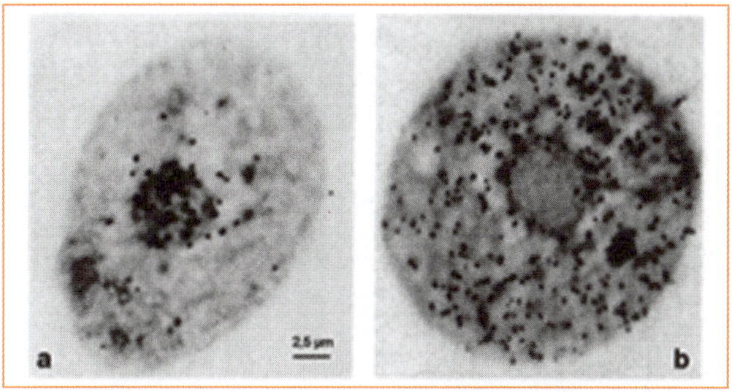

Résultats du pulse-chase
(a : 15 secondes d'incubation ; b : 90 secondes après la chasse)

1. Décrivez la localisation de la radioactivité sur les deux photographies.

2. Déduisez-en comment cette expérience permet de mettre en évidence que l'ARN est le « bon » intermédiaire entre l'ADN du noyau et les protéines contenues dans le cytoplasme.

→ Corrigé p. 79

9 20 min ★★ L'épissage

On étudie le gène responsable de la production de l'ovalbumine dans l'œuf de poulet. Pour cela, on dénature l'ADN, c'est-à-dire que l'on sépare des deux brins, puis on hybride le brin transcrit de l'ADN avec l'ARN messager correspondant. On obtient la structure suivante caractérisée par des séquences communes ADN/ARNm notées de 1 à 7 alors que les séquences propres à l'ADN sont identifiées par des lettres de 1 à G.

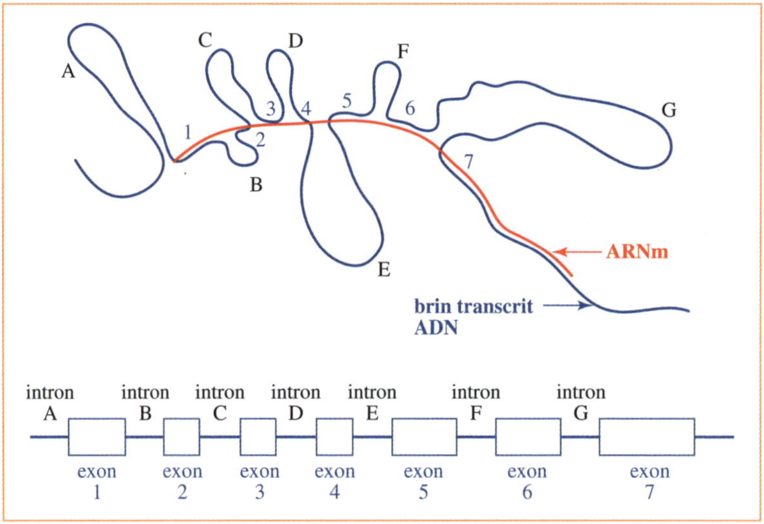

Hybridation ADN/ARNm d'ovalbumine

1. D'après vos connaissances, nommez les séquences communes entre l'ADN et l'ARNm et les séquences propres à l'ADN.

2. Quelle étape de la synthèse des protéines permet d'expliquer ces différences ?

3. Schématisez le passage entre le gène de l'ovalbumine et sa transcription en ARNm.

→ Corrigé p. 79

CONTRÔLE CONTINU POUR LE BAC

Exercice 10 pts — Les échelles du phénotype — 30 min

La mucoviscidose est la maladie génétique la plus fréquente chez les individus d'origine européenne (200 naissances par an en France).

Identifiez l'origine génétique de la mucoviscidose et ses différentes conséquences phénotypiques.

Document 1 : Étude moléculaire de la maladie

On étudie le gène CFTR responsable de la production d'une protéine CFTR en forme de canal, située dans la membrane plasmique des cellules épithéliales (pulmonaires, intestinales…).

intitulé	1485 — 1490 — 1495 — 1500 — 1505 — 1510 — 1515 — 1520 — 1525 — 1530
Allèle CFTR malade	TTCCTGGATTATGCCTGGCACCATTAAAGAAAATATCATC- - -GGTGTTT
Allèle CFTR sain	TTCCTGGATTATGCCTGGCACCATTAAAGAAAATATCATCTTTGGTGTTT

Figure 1 *Comparaison entre l'allèle CFTR sain et l'allèle DF508 (muté)*

intitulé		1505		1510		1515		1520	1525
Protéine CFTR saine	Thr	Ile	Lys	Glu	Asn	Ile	Ile	Phe	Gly
Protéine CFTR malade	Thr	Ile	Lys	Glu	Asn	Ile	Ile	-	Gly

Figure 2 *Comparaison entre la protéine CFTR saine et la protéine CFTR du malade*

Document 2 : Caractéristiques cellulaires de la maladie

Au niveau pulmonaire, les bronches et les alvéoles sont recouvertes d'un mucus.

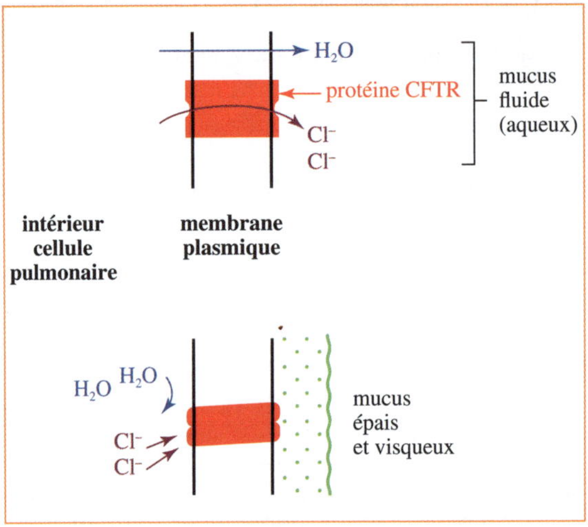

Chez un individu sain, le canal CFTR est ouvert et permet des échanges normaux de chlore et d'eau entre l'intérieur et l'extérieur de la cellule épithéliale. Le mucus est ainsi fluide et peut être évacué.

Chez un individu atteint de mucoviscidose, le canal CFTR est obstrué. Il n'y a plus d'échanges moléculaires et le mucus s'épaissit. Ceci entraîne une accumulation de bactéries et donc augmente les risques d'infection et les difficultés respiratoires.

Document 3 : Symptômes et traitements

La mucoviscidose affecte les cellules épithéliales, et a donc des conséquences sur le fonctionnement de trois organes principaux : les poumons, l'intestin et l'appareil reproducteur.

Chez les individus atteints par la maladie, les bronches peuvent s'obstruer et ainsi favoriser les infections pulmonaires et entraîner des difficultés respiratoires.

Au niveau digestif, les canaux pancréatiques sont eux aussi obstrués, ce qui empêche la libération des enzymes digestives et provoque des difficultés à assimiler les graisses.

D'un point de vue reproducteur, la mucoviscidose peut entraîner des problèmes de fertilité.

→ *Corrigé p. 79*

CORRIGÉS

1 → *Énoncé p. 71*

Les affirmations exactes sont b) et d).

2 → *Énoncé p. 71*

Les affirmations exactes sont a) et c).

3 → *Énoncé p. 71*

Après sa transcription, l'ARN pré-messager va subir une maturation. C'est l'épissage. Durant cette étape, les exons de l'ARN pré-messager sont conservés et les introns vont être excisés et supprimés. On obtient ainsi un ARN messager. Les exons conservés peuvent varier d'un ARN messager à un autre : à partir d'un même ARN pré-messager on peut donc aboutir à différents ARN messagers et donc différentes protéines après traduction. Cette étape particulière est appelée l'épissage alternatif.

4 → *Énoncé p. 71*

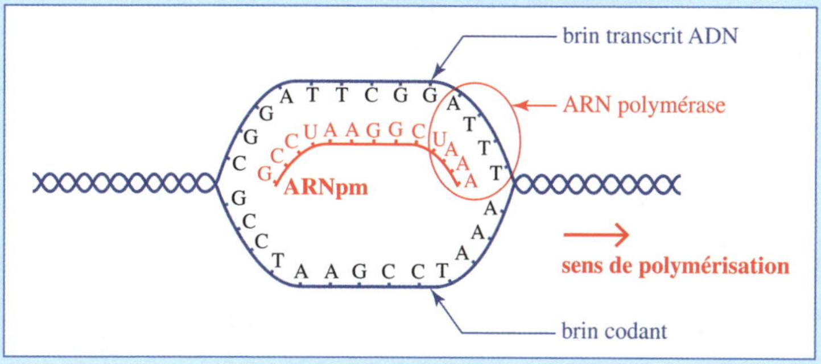

5 → *Énoncé p. 72*

1. Si 1 nucléotide code pour 1 acide aminé, il y a seulement 4 combinaisons possibles (A, C, G et U) et donc la production de 4 acides aminés.

2. Si 1 nucléotide code pour 2 acides aminés, il y a 16 combinaisons possibles :

AA AC AG AU CC CA CG CU GG GA GC GU UU UA UC UG

3. Si 1 nucléotide code pour 3 acides aminés, il y a 64 combinaisons possibles :

UUU UUC UUA UUG UCU UCC UCA UCG UAU UAC UAA UAG UGU UGC UGA UGG CUU CUC CUA CUG CCU CCC CCA CCG CAU CAC CAA CAG CGU CGC CGA CGG AUU AUC AUA AUG ACU ACC ACA ACG AAU AAC AAA

AAG AGU AGC AGA AGG GUU GUC GUA GUG GCU GCC GCA GCG GAU GAC GAA GAG GGU GGC GGA GGG

4. La dernière hypothèse incluant 64 possibilités de combinaisons est la seule qui soit suffisante pour produire les 20 acides aminés.

5. Dans cette dernière hypothèse, il y a 44 combinaisons en trop, ce qui peut s'expliquer par la redondance du code génétique (plusieurs codons permettent de produire un même acide aminé) et par l'existence des codons STOP.

6 → Énoncé p. 72

1. Les DNases détruisent l'axe de la structure. Or les DNases sont des enzymes qui dégradent l'ADN. On peut en déduire que l'axe de la figure est la molécule d'ADN à transcrire. De la même façon, les RNases détruisent les ramifications de la structure, ainsi ces ramifications sont constituées d'ARN pré-messager.

2.

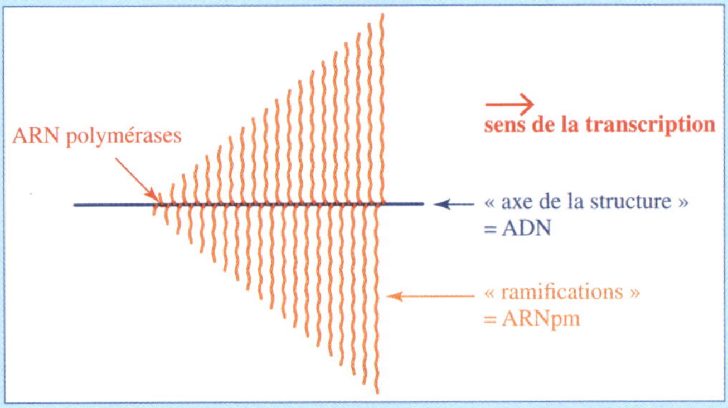

7 → Énoncé p. 73

1. GGG GGG TGT AAC CAG (ADN, brin transcrit) à CCC CCC ACA UUG GUC (ARNm)

2. Pro – Pro – Thr – Leu – Val

3. *a.* La première mutation a pour résultat la transcription du brin suivant :

GGA GGG TGT AAC CAG.

L'ARNm produit est donc le suivant : CCU CCC ACA UUG GUC.

Ainsi le premier codon est responsable d'un acide aminé « Pro ». La séquence en acides aminés est donc identique à la protéine qui n'est pas le résultat d'un gène muté : cette mutation était donc silencieuse.

b. Pour la seconde mutation, l'ARNm produit est : CCC CCC ACA UAG GUC. Or le 3e codon UAG est un codon STOP. La protéine traduite sera donc plus courte que la protéine initiale : Pro – Pro – Thr. C'est une mutation non-sens.

8 → Énoncé p. 73

1. Après marquage radioactif, on observe que la radioactivité est localisée dans le noyau. Or la molécule marquée est de l'ARN. On peut en déduire que l'ARN est produit dans le noyau.

Après la chasse, on observe que la radioactivité s'est déplacée dans le cytoplasme. L'ARN est donc produit dans le noyau et migre ensuite dans le cytoplasme de la cellule.

2. L'ADN qui reste dans le noyau permet donc la production de l'ARN : c'est la traduction. Cet ARN sort ensuite du noyau pour migrer dans le cytoplasme et produire les protéines : c'est la traduction.

9 → Énoncé p. 74

1. Les séquences s'hybridant entre l'ADN et l'ARNm sont des séquences de nucléotides complémentaires : par exemple, les nucléotides A de l'ADN s'associent aux nucléotides U de l'ARNm. Ces séquences sont donc identiques entre l'ADN et l'ARNm : ce sont les exons. Les séquences de l'ADN en « surplus », que l'on ne retrouve donc pas dans l'ARNm, sont les introns.

2. Cette étape de maturation de l'ARN qui consiste à mettre les exons bout à bout et à éliminer les introns est l'épissage.

3.

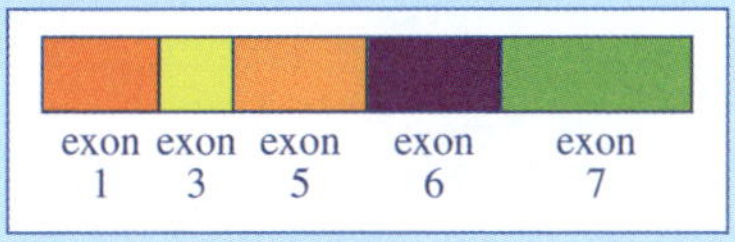

CONTRÔLE CONTINU POUR LE BAC

Exercice → Énoncé p. 75

La mucoviscidose est la maladie la plus fréquente chez les individus d'origine européenne.

Quelle est l'origine génétique de la maladie et ses conséquences sur le phénotype ?

On observe que les individus affectés par la mucoviscidose possèdent une mutation de trois nucléotides par délétion (les n° 1522, 1523 et 1524) : trois nucléotides T ont été supprimés au niveau de leur allèle DF508.

La mutation de l'allèle muté a pour conséquence la formation d'une protéine CFTR anormale. En effet on observe que la séquence en acides aminées est modifiée : le 508e acide aminé, « Phe », n'est plus présent. Cette mutation entraîne une déformation de la protéine qui n'assure plus son rôle. En effet la protéine CFTR est une protéine en forme de canal insérée dans la membrane plasmique des cellules épithéliales, notamment pulmonaires. À l'état physiologique, la protéine CFTR laisse passer les ions chlore et l'eau vers l'extérieur de la cellule : le mucus est donc hydraté et fluide. Chez l'individu atteint par la maladie, cette protéine est déformée et ne laisse plus passer les ions chlore. L'eau n'hydrate donc plus le mucus qui devient visqueux. C'est l'échelle moléculaire du phénotype (mutation de la protéine CFTR) qui affecte donc l'échelle cellulaire (le mucus s'épaissit car l'eau ne sort plus de la cellule).

Le phénotype macroscopique se manifeste par une accumulation du mucus dans les poumons, les voies génitales et les intestins ; ce qui entraîne des difficultés respiratoires, des infections, une infertilité et des troubles digestifs.

Les enzymes, des biocatalyseurs

CHAPITRE 6

Certains nutriments doivent être dégradés par les sucs digestifs pour pouvoir être assimilés par l'organisme. C'est un exemple d'action d'une catégorie de protéines spécifiques appelées les **enzymes***.

1 Les caractéristiques des enzymes

A. Définition

■ Les enzymes sont des protéines dont le rôle est d'accélérer les réactions chimiques de l'organisme, pour transformer une molécule initiale (appelée substrat) en un produit nouveau. Elles sont notamment impliquées dans les réactions chimiques du métabolisme. On les appelle donc des **biocatalyseurs***.

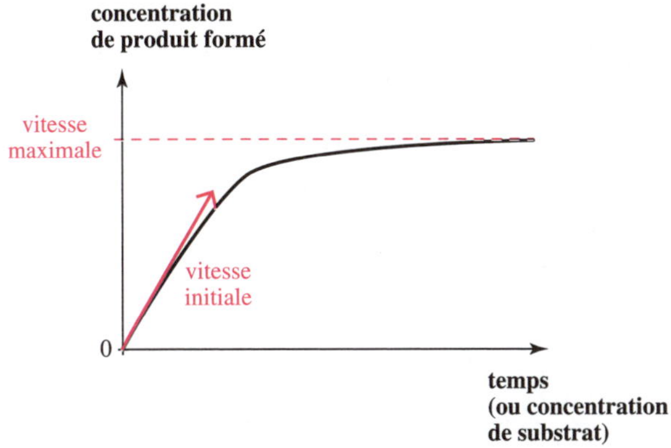

Figure 1 *La catalyse enzymatique*

Ex. : L'hydrolyse est une réaction enzymatique qui permet de catalyser une molécule en présence d'eau. C'est le cas de la transformation de l'amidon en maltose et glucose, une hydrolyse réalisée par l'amylase présente dans la salive et les cellules intestinales (voir *figure 2* p. 82).

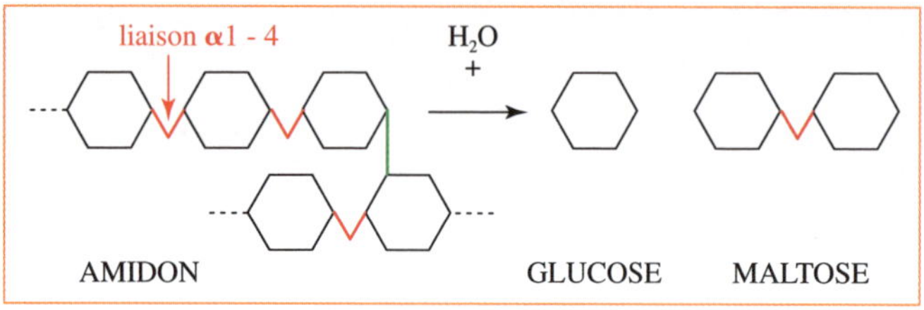

Figure 2 *L'hydrolyse*

■ L'activité enzymatique est caractérisée par la vitesse initiale de réaction (V_i), qui correspond à la quantité de produit formé (ou de substrat transformé) par unité de temps, en début de réaction. Déterminer cette vitesse initiale revient à calculer la pente de la tangente du début de la réaction de catalyse. Plus le coefficient directeur de la tangente est grand, plus la vitesse initiale de la réaction est forte.

$$\text{cœfficient directeur de la tangente} = V_i = \frac{yA - yB}{xA - xB}$$

■ V_i augmente en fonction de la concentration en substrat ou d'enzyme, jusqu'à atteindre une vitesse maximale (V_{max}) lorsque tous les complexes ES sont formés (saturation de toutes les molécules d'enzymes).

B. Le mode d'action des enzymes

■ Les enzymes possèdent une sorte de cavité au niveau de laquelle le substrat se fixe pour y être transformé : c'est le **site actif*** de l'enzyme.

■ Le site actif et le substrat doivent avoir une complémentarité de forme et de liaison pour qu'ils s'assemblent et forment un **complexe Enzyme – Substrat** (ES).

■ Le complexe ainsi formé, le substrat est transformé en produits sans que la structure de l'enzyme ne soit modifiée.

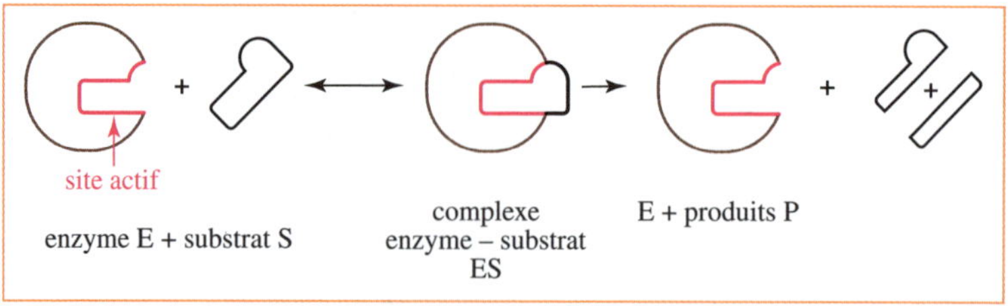

Figure 3 *Modèle « clé-serrure » de l'activité enzymatique*

C. La spécificité des enzymes

■ Les enzymes ne catalysent qu'un substrat donné : on dit qu'elles sont spécifiques à un substrat.

■ De plus, chaque enzyme ne réalise qu'une seule réaction métabolique à partir d'un substrat : c'est leur spécificité d'action.

■ Les enzymes sont donc des biocatalyseurs à double spécificité.

> **Remarque**
> **L'amylase** peut hydrolyser l'amidon mais aussi le glycogène. En effet, ces deux molécules possèdent une liaison commune entre leurs glucoses constitutifs : la liaison α1-4. Cette enzyme est ainsi spécifique à une liaison plus qu'à un substrat.

2 Les modifications de l'activité enzymatique

A. Les modifications dues à l'environnement

■ Certaines variations des conditions physico-chimiques régnant dans la cellule peuvent modifier la conformation du site actif de l'enzyme et ainsi modifier son activité catalytique qui est optimale à un pH et une température donnés. Ceci permet une spécificité de l'enzyme en fonction de son environnement : par exemple, les enzymes digestives sont actives à 37 °C mais à des pH différents (l'amylase à pH 7 comme dans la salive et les intestins, et la pepsine à pH 2 dans l'estomac).

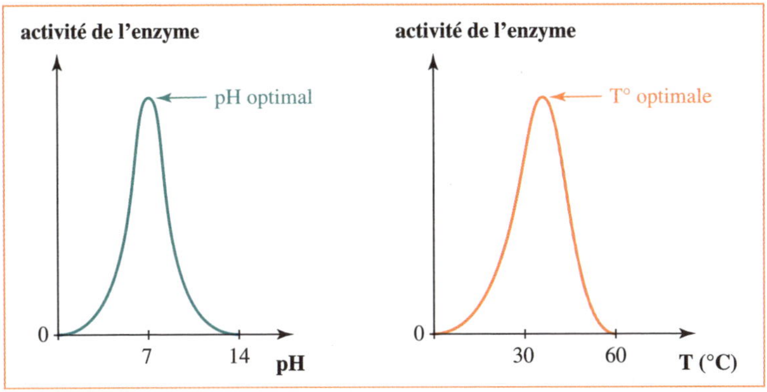

Figure 4 *Variations environnementales de la catalyse enzymatique*

B. Les inhibiteurs

■ Des substances peuvent interagir avec une enzyme et modifier sa vitesse de réaction. Ce sont des **inhibiteurs**. On en distingue principalement deux catégories selon leur mode d'action :

– les **inhibiteurs compétitifs*** : ils se fixent sur le site actif de l'enzyme à la place du substrat grâce à une certaine analogie de structure avec ce dernier. Ils empêchent ainsi la formation du complexe enzyme-substrat* et ralentissent la vitesse de réaction enzymatique.
– les **inhibiteurs non compétitifs*** : ils se fixent sur l'enzyme et non sur son site actif. Ils modifient la conformation 3D de l'enzyme, qui ne peut donc pas former de produits.

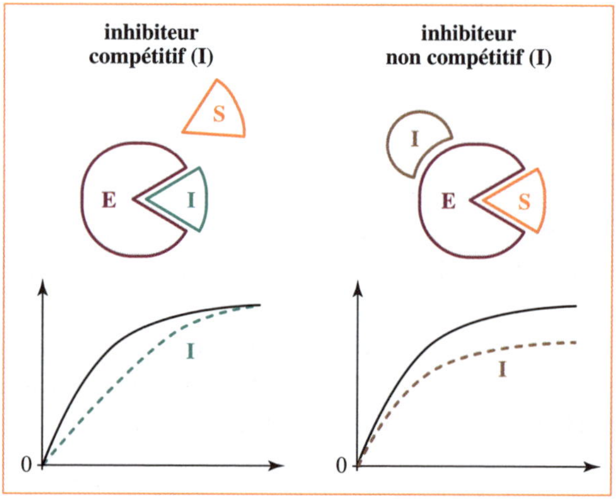

Figure 5 *Les deux types d'inhibiteurs*

C. Les modifications génétiques

■ D'autres facteurs, comme des facteurs internes à l'organisme, peuvent modifier la conformation du site actif d'une enzyme : ce sont des facteurs génétiques.

■ Toute mutation de la séquence d'un gène codant une enzyme modifiera la séquence en acides aminés de l'enzyme. Cette modification, si elle affecte le site actif notamment, ralentira la vitesse de la réaction catalytique ou modifiera l'affinité de l'enzyme avec son substrat.

EXERCICES

Connaître le cours

1 2 min ★ Vrai ou Faux ?

Relevez la (ou les) affirmation(s) exacte(s).

Les enzymes :
a) accélèrent les réactions métaboliques.
b) réalisent toutes des hydrolyses.
c) peuvent voir leurs activités catalytiques modifiées.
d) sont seulement présentes dans les sucs digestifs.

→ *Corrigé p. 93*

2 2 min ★ Vrai ou Faux ?

Relevez la (ou les) affirmation(s) exacte(s).

Toute modification de l'activité enzymatique peut :
a) ralentir les réactions métaboliques.
b) être obligatoirement due à une modification de son site actif.
c) être causée par des facteurs environnementaux et génétiques.
d) modifier la nature du substrat.

→ *Corrigé p. 93*

3 5 min ★ Restitution de connaissances

Expliquez brièvement comment les enzymes peuvent accélérer les réactions métaboliques de l'organisme (à une température de 37 °C et un pH 7).

→ *Corrigé p. 93*

4 5 min ★ Schématiser le cours

Schématisez le mode d'action des inhibiteurs compétitifs et leurs conséquences sur la vitesse de la catalyse enzymatique.

→ *Corrigé p. 93*

5 10 min ★★ La digestion du lactose

Le lactose n'est pas un sucre directement assimilable par l'organisme : il doit être dégradé dans les intestins, en deux sucres plus petits : le glucose et le galactose. On place une solution de lactose en présence de deux enzymes : la lactase et la β-galactosidase.

	Tube 1	Tube 2	Tube 3
Solution de lactase	10 mL	0 mL	8 mL
Solution de β-galactosidase	0 mL	10 mL	2 mL
Test de présence de glucose	Négatif	Négatif	Positif

Figure 1 *Mise en évidence des étapes de la digestion du lactose*

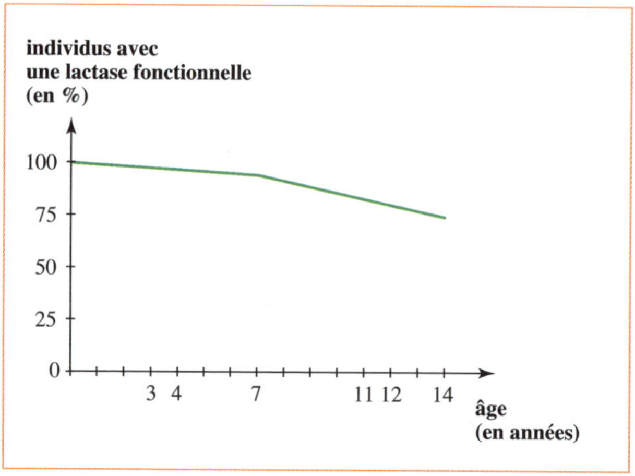

Figure 2 *Évolution de l'activité de la lactase au cours du temps chez les Européens*

1. D'après la figure 1, déterminez quelle enzyme est nécessaire pour digérer le lactose.
2. À l'aide de la figure 2, expliquez l'intolérance au lactose existante chez une partie des Européens.

→ *Corrigé p. 94*

6 15 min ★★ La spécificité de substrat

On cherche à déterminer si l'amylase peut hydrolyser des glucides de nature différente. Pour cela, on place une amylase en présence de deux substrats, l'amidon et le lactose, à 37 °C durant 20 minutes. On révèle la présence de glucose grâce à la liqueur de Fehling qui se colore en rouge brique en présence de sucres réducteurs.

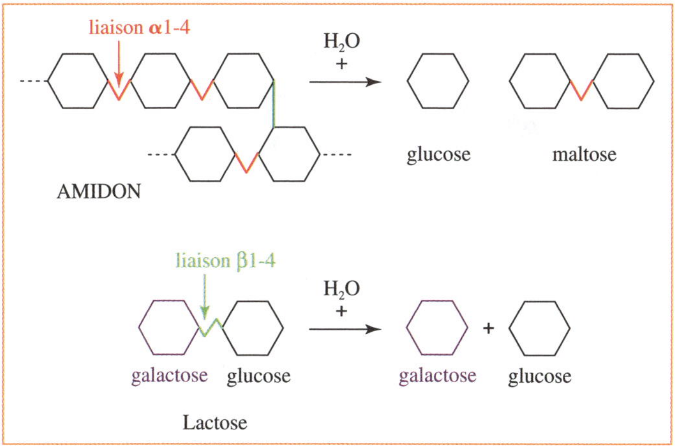

Figure 1 *Réactions d'hydrolyse de l'amidon et du lactose*

	Tube 1	Tube 2	Tube 3	Tube 4	Tube 5	Tube 6
Composition du tube	Amylase + amidon	Amylase + lactose	Amylase bouillie + amidon	Amylase bouillie + lactose	Amidon + eau	Lactose + eau
Résultats à la liqueur de Fehling	Rouge brique	Bleu	Bleu	Bleu	Bleu	Bleu

Figure 2 *Résultats de l'expérience*

1. Quelle est l'utilité de faire bouillir l'amylase dans cette expérience ?
2. Analysez les résultats de l'expérience pour mettre en évidence la spécificité de l'amylase.

→ Corrigé p. 94

7 15 min ★★ Les variations environnementales

Certaines personnes présentent des douleurs à l'estomac causées par un excès de sécrétion acide. Si cet excès d'acidité n'est pas pris en charge, les douleurs peuvent entraîner une inflammation (gastrite) puis dégénérer en ulcère (perforation de la paroi de l'estomac). Avant de diminuer l'acidité gastrique par un traitement adapté, on veut savoir si cela affectera la digestion des patients. La pepsine est une enzyme du suc gastrique qui permet de dégrader les protéines.

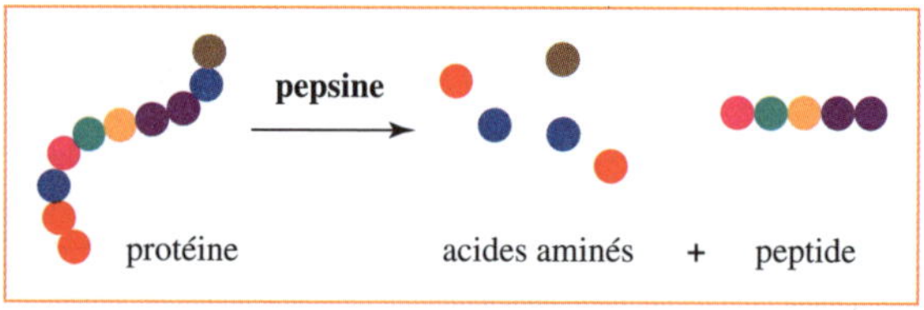

Figure 1 *Activité de la pepsine*

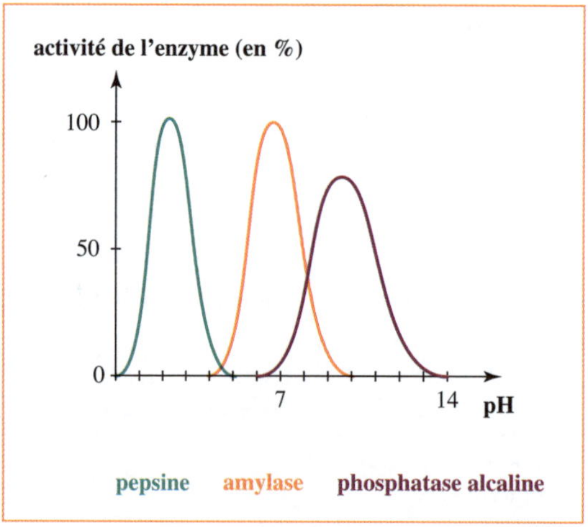

Figure 2 *Effet du pH sur certaines enzymes*

1. Déterminez l'effet du pH sur l'activité de la pepsine.

2. Expliquez pourquoi une forte diminution de l'acidité de l'estomac peut avoir des conséquences sur la digestion des patients.

→ *Corrigé p. 94*

8 20 min ★★ Les vitesses catalytiques

On veut déterminer quelle variété de tomate est la plus sucrée entre les tomates cœurs de bœuf et les tomates cerises. On prend un échantillon de jus de tomate de chaque variété.

Pour évaluer la concentration de glucose du jus de tomate, on peut utiliser une enzyme, la glucose oxydase (GOx) qui catalyse la réaction suivante :

$$C_6H_{12}O_6 \text{ (glucose)} + O_2 + H_2O \rightarrow C_6H_{12}O_7 + H_2O_2$$

Une molécule de glucose est transformée à la même vitesse qu'une molécule de dioxygène.

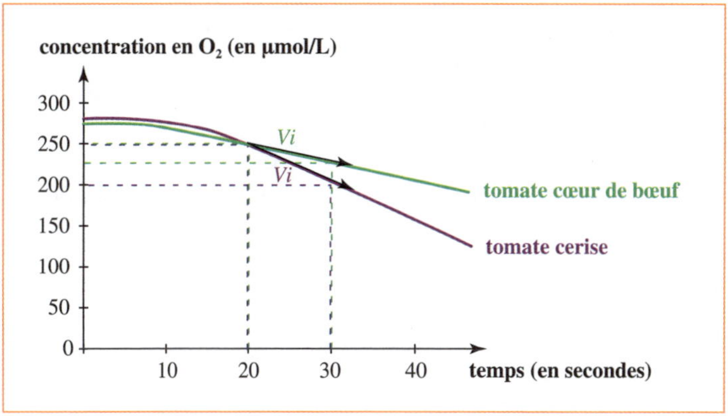

Consommation d'O_2 par la GOx des deux variétés de tomates

1. Calculez la vitesse initiale de la réaction pour chaque variété de tomates.
2. Sachant que la disparition d'une molécule d'O_2 se fait à la même vitesse que la disparition d'une molécule de glucose, déterminez quelle variété de tomate est la plus sucrée.

→ Corrigé p. 94

9 25 min ★★ L'origine de l'albinisme

L'albinisme est une maladie due à un défaut de production de mélanine au niveau des yeux (l'iris est clair voire rouge), de la peau (peau blanche) et des poils (poils et cheveux blancs). La mélanine est une protéine produite par les mélanocytes (cellules pigmentaires de la peau), responsables de la coloration des tissus.

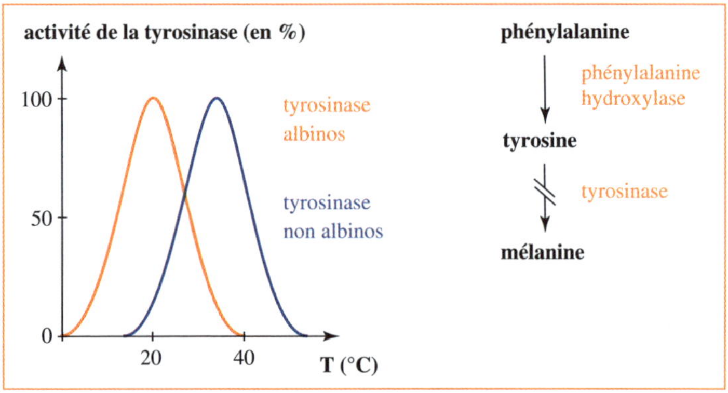

Figure 1 *Rôle de la tyrosinase dans la production de mélanine*

	525						530					
allèle Tyr^+ (sain)	C	T	C	T	T	T	G	T	C	T	G	G
allèle Tyr^- (albinos)	C	T	C	T	T	T	G	T	C	T	A	G

	175	176	177	178	
tyrosinase	Leu -	Phe -	Val -	Trp	... 529 acides aminés
tyrosinase albinos	Leu -	Phe -	Val		

Figure 2 *Comparaison des allèles* Tyr^+ / Tyr^- *et des tyrosinases produites*

1. D'après la figure 1, expliquez comment les enzymes peuvent être à l'origine des différences de phénotype chez l'Homme.

2. Comment expliquer que chez certains Mammifères, comme les lapins himalayens et les chats siamois, les extrémités des pattes, du museau et des oreilles sont pigmentées malgré leur albinisme ?

3. À l'aide de la figure 2, faire le lien entre la mutation génétique et le dysfonctionnement de la tyrosinase.

→ *Corrigé p. 95*

CONTRÔLE CONTINU POUR LE BAC

Exercice 10 pts Les effets du pamplemousse 30 min

La félodipine est une substance active (médicament) permettant de diminuer la pression artérielle en dilatant les vaisseaux sanguins.

Sur les notices d'utilisation de ce médicament, il est indiqué qu'il est fortement déconseillé de la prendre avec un verre de pamplemousse.

Montrez comment le jus de pamplemousse peut interférer avec la prise médicamenteuse et entraîner une hypotension sévère.

Document 1 : Concentration de la félodipine

La félodipine est un médicament naturellement dégradé par le foie grâce à une enzyme, le cytochrome P450.

On détermine la concentration sanguine (plus précisément plasmatique) en félodipine d'un patient traité pour sa tension artérielle, à différents intervalles de temps. Le dosage de la concentration se fait avec et sans absorption d'un verre de jus de pamplemousse.

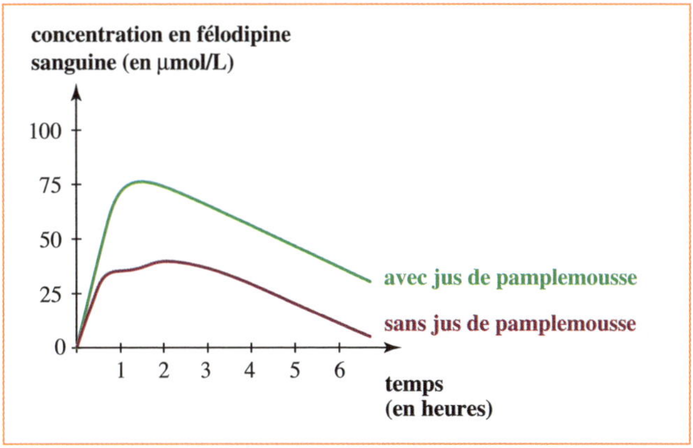

Variations de la concentration sanguine de félodipine avec ou sans absorption de pamplemousse

Document 2 : Action du jus de pamplemousse sur le cytochrome P450

Le cytochrome P450 permet la dégradation de certaines substances, notamment médicamenteuses.

On schématise l'activité de ce cytochrome P450 avec ou sans jus de pamplemousse sur la dégradation de la félodipine.

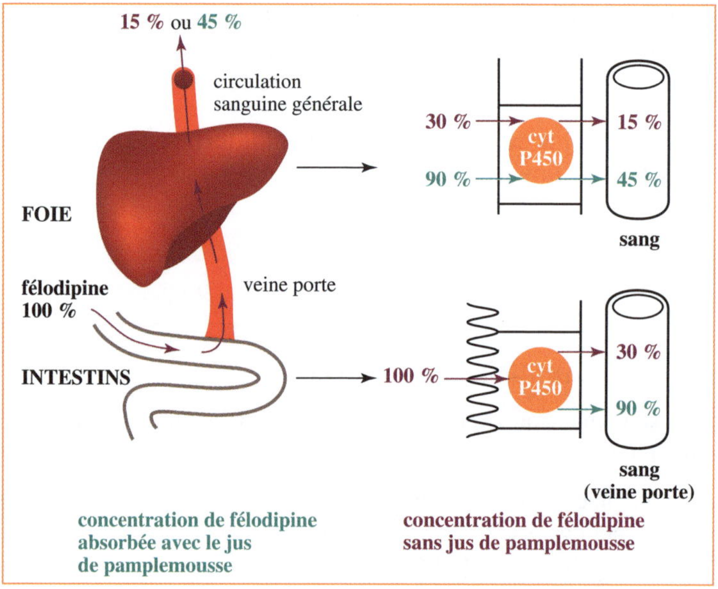

Absorption intestinale et hépatique de la félodipine

Document 3 : Représentation 3D du cytochrome P450

Grâce à des logiciels de modélisation, on peut représenter les interactions entre les molécules. Le cytochrome P450 est représenté ici en interaction avec la félodipine et avec une molécule spécifique présente dans le jus de pamplemousse.

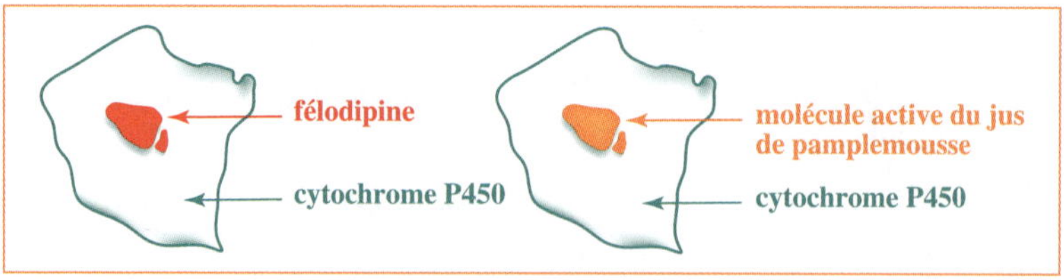

Modélisation 3D du cytochrome P450

→ Corrigé p. 95

CORRIGÉS

1 → Énoncé p. 85

Les affirmations exactes sont a) et c).

2 → Énoncé p. 85

Les affirmations exactes sont a) et c).

3 → Énoncé p. 85

Dans les conditions physiologiques de l'organisme, c'est-à-dire à 37 °C et pH 7, les enzymes doivent être actives pour réaliser les réactions métaboliques.

La catalyse enzymatique est la vitesse de dégradation du substrat par les enzymes. Cette vitesse peut être modulée par les facteurs de l'environnement comme le pH et la température. En effet, la catalyse enzymatique présente une vitesse optimale à un pH et une température précis. En dessous de ces valeurs, l'enzyme est peu active. Au-delà de ces valeurs, l'enzyme peut être dénaturée et son site actif modifié. La vitesse optimale est donc à 37 °C et à pH 7 pour la majorité des enzymes du corps humain.

4 → Énoncé p. 85

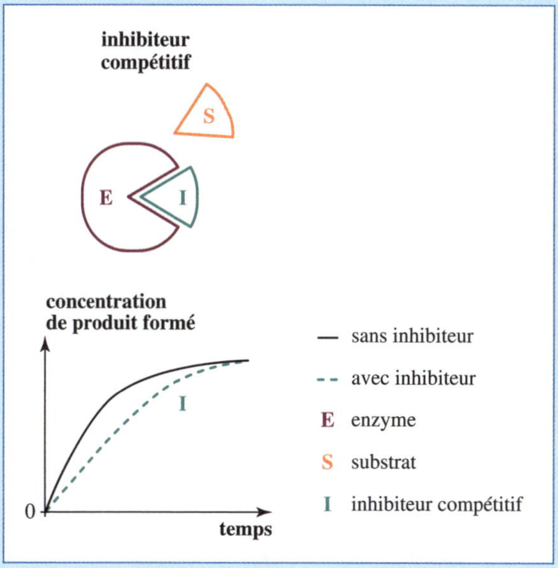

5 → *Énoncé p. 86*

1. Suite aux expériences de catalyse du lactose par différentes enzymes, on observe que la présence de lactase ou de β-galactosidase, seules, ne permet pas de formation de glucose. Il faut ajouter ces deux enzymes ensemble pour que la digestion du lactose en glucose se réalise.

2. On observe qu'avant l'âge de 7 ans, tous les européens sont capables de digérer le lait. Au-delà de cet âge, la digestion du lactose devient impossible pour environ 20 % des enfants européens. Ce phénomène coïncide avec le changement d'alimentation et l'arrêt de la lactation depuis quelques années. Les enfants, contrairement aux bébés, sont sevrés et trouvent une source d'énergie ailleurs que dans le lactose.

6 → *Énoncé p. 87*

1. Faire bouillir une protéine, en particulier une enzyme, permet de la déformer. La conformation 3D d'une enzyme est importante pour interagir avec le substrat grâce au site actif de l'enzyme. Une fois bouillie, l'enzyme n'est plus fonctionnelle : ceci constitue une expérience témoin.

2. L'amylase fonctionnelle (donc non bouillie) entraîne la formation de glucose seulement en présence d'amidon. Or on sait que l'amidon est une molécule possédant une liaison α 1-4 entre deux molécules de glucose, alors que le lactose possède une liaison β 1-4. On peut donc en déduire que l'amylase est spécifique à un substrat : l'amidon, et plus particulièrement à la liaison α 1-4.

7 → *Énoncé p. 88*

1. On observe que le maximum d'activité de la pepsine se situe à un pH de 2, soit très acide. D'autres enzymes voient leurs activités varier selon le pH : c'est le cas de l'amylase (pH optimal d'activité : 6-7) et de la phosphatase alcaline (pH optimal d'activité : 9).

2. La pepsine permet la digestion des protéines en rompant les liaisons entre les acides aminés. Elle permet ainsi la production d'acides aminés et de peptides (protéines plus petites). Si le pH augmente et devient plus alcalin, la pepsine sera moins fonctionnelle. Cela peut entraîner des difficultés pour digérer les protéines au niveau de l'estomac. Il faudra donc faire appel à d'autres enzymes dégradant les protéines situées au niveau des intestins.

8 → *Énoncé p. 89*

1. On peut calculer la vitesse initiale de la réaction grâce à une lecture graphique :

Pour la tomate cerise :

$$\text{cœfficient directeur de la tangente} = v_i = \frac{y_A - y_B}{x_A - x_B} = \frac{200 - 250}{30 - 20} = |-5| = 5\ \mu\text{mol/L/sec}$$

Pour la tomate cœur de bœuf :

$$\text{cœfficient directeur de la tangente} = v_i = \frac{y_A - y_B}{x_A - x_B} = \frac{250 - 275}{30 - 20} = |-2{,}5| = 2{,}5\ \mu\text{mol/L/sec}$$

2. Sachant que plus la vitesse initiale de dégradation de l'O_2 par la GOx est élevée, plus la quantité de glucose initiale était forte, on peut en déduire que la tomate cerise est plus riche en sucre que la tomate cœur de bœuf.

9 → *Énoncé p. 90*

1. L'albinisme est une maladie qui trouve son origine dans un défaut de production de mélanine (phénotype moléculaire). Or la synthèse de cette protéine est permise grâce à plusieurs enzymes, la principale étant la tyrosinase. Toute modification du fonctionnement de cette enzyme peut donc provoquer la maladie et l'absence de synthèse de mélanine.

2. On observe que l'activité de la tyrosinase, chez les individus albinos, est maximale à 20 °C (contre 37 °C chez les personnes non atteintes par la maladie). Or le corps des Mammifères est maintenu à une température constante de 37 °C, sauf pour les extrémités (les doigts, les oreilles, le nez…). Chez les chats siamois et les lapins himalayens, la tyrosinase est donc fonctionnelle au niveau de ces extrémités mais non fonctionnelle au niveau du tronc.

3. Si on compare l'allèle permettant la production d'une tyrosinase fonctionne (*Tyr^+*) et l'allèle des albinos, on observe une mutation au niveau du 533e nucléotide : un nucléotide G a été remplacé par un nucléotide A.

D'un point de vue moléculaire, cette mutation entraîne l'action précoce d'un codon STOP ayant pour conséquence la formation d'une tyrosinase plus courte : 177 acides aminés au lieu de 529 pour une tyrosinase fonctionnelle.

Toute mutation du gène codant une enzyme peut donc modifier son activité et affecter le phénotype.

CONTRÔLE CONTINU POUR LE BAC

Exercice → *Énoncé p. 91*

La félodipine est un médicament permettant de diminuer la pression artérielle. Comment le pamplemousse majore-t-il l'effet de ce médicament ?

On observe que la concentration en félodipine dans le plasma sanguin diminue naturellement après une prise. La félodipine est presque entièrement métabolisée au bout de 6 heures en raison de sa dégradation par une enzyme présente dans le foie : le cytochrome P450.

Si le patient boit un jus de pamplemousse, on observe que la concentration en félodipine est beaucoup plus importante dans le sang : il existe donc un paramètre qui diminue sa capacité à être métabolisée.

On peut donc supposer que le jus de pamplemousse diminue la catalyse de la félodipine par une action sur l'enzyme responsable de sa dégradation, le cytochrome P450. En effet, si on mesure l'activité du cytochrome P450, c'est-à-dire l'efficacité de la dégradation du médicament, on observe qu'avec du jus de pamplemousse, la félodipine absorbée oralement se retrouve à 45 % dans la circulation sanguine générale contre 15 % seulement de la dose initiale sans jus de pamplemousse. On peut donc en déduire que le jus de pamplemousse inhibe l'activité du cytochrome P450 et donc la dégradation de la félodipine.

Il existe en effet, dans le jus de pamplemousse, une molécule active qui se fixe sur le site actif de l'enzyme et empêche la fixation de son substrat, ici la félodipine, et donc son métabolisme. Cette molécule est un inhibiteur compétitif.

La structure du globe terrestre

CHAPITRE 7

La tectonique des plaques est la théorie actuelle de l'existence d'une mobilité horizontale des plaques tectoniques. Elle repose sur la connaissance de l'intérieur de la Terre.

1 Les contrastes des croûtes océanique et continentale

A. La bimodalité des altitudes

- Les altitudes se répartissent selon deux pics de fréquences différentes : l'altitude moyenne élevée (840 m) correspond aux continents et l'altitude moyenne basse (–3 800 m) aux océans. C'est la **bimodalité des altitudes***.

Cette différence d'altitudes des continents et des océans serait causée par des caractéristiques distinctes de ces deux croûtes liées aux natures différentes des roches qui les composent.

Remarque

En 1912, Alfred Wegener est le premier scientifique à formuler l'hypothèse d'une mobilité horizontale des continents avec sa théorie de la « dérive des continents ».
L'un des arguments repose sur l'hypothèse d'une bimodalité des altitudes et donc d'océans et de continents de natures différentes.

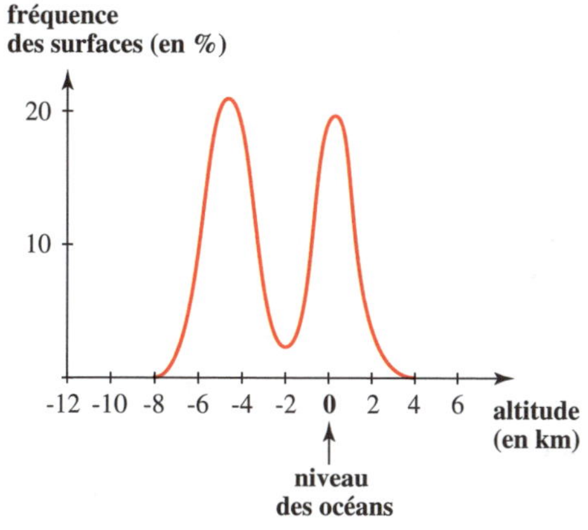

Figure 1 *Répartition des altitudes*

B. Des natures de roches différentes

■ L'étude des échantillons de surface, ou étude pétrographique*, permet de définir 2 types de croûtes :
– la croûte océanique formée de **basalte*** et de **gabbro*** ;
– la croûte continentale, elle-même constituée d'une grande variété de types de roches :
- sédimentaires*, provenant de l'accumulation de sédiments ;
- métamorphiques*, ayant subi des changements minéralogiques à cause de variations de pression et de température ;
- magmatiques*, issues de la minéralisation d'un magma.

■ Des études en profondeur révèlent néanmoins que le **granite*** est la roche principale qui constitue la croûte continentale. Le granite est une roche magmatique* **plutonique***, c'est-à-dire que le magma a refroidi lentement en profondeur, lui donnant une structure entièrement cristallisée ou une **texture grenue***.

■ Les propriétés physiques différentes de ces roches expliquent la distribution bimodale des altitudes : la croûte océanique est plus dense (2,9) et s'enfonce davantage dans le manteau alors que la croûte continentale, moins dense de 2,7 à 2,8), présente une altitude plus faible.

	Croûte océanique		**Croûte continentale**
	Basalte	**Gabbro**	**Granite**
Structure de la roche	Microlitique	Grenue	Grenue
Densité	2,7	3,2	2,7
Composition minéralogique	Feldspaths plagioclases Pyroxènes Olivine	Feldspaths plagioclases Pyroxènes	Feldspaths potassiques Biotite (mica noir) Quartz

Figure 2 *Comparaison des roches océaniques et continentales*

2 La structure interne de la Terre

A. Les apports de la connaissance des séismes

■ Au sein d'un bloc de roche, des **contraintes*** peuvent s'exercer et entraîner des ruptures brutales libérant une grande quantité d'énergie : c'est un **séisme***. Les blocs de roches peuvent alors glisser l'un par rapport à l'autre le long de **failles***.

■ Lors d'un séisme, les stations sismiques, localisées à de nombreux endroits dans le monde enregistrent des sismogrammes. Ces enregistrements sont caractérisés par trois types d'ondes sismiques : les ondes P, les ondes S et les ondes de surface. Les ondes S sont des ondes particulières qui ne se propagent pas dans les liquides.

Définition

Les ondes P sont les ondes « primaires », les premières enregistrées sur un sismogramme, alors que **les ondes S** sont les ondes « secondaires », les secondes mesurées.
Ces ondes se propagent dans toutes les directions à partir du foyer sismique. À chaque surface entre deux milieux de natures différentes, ou discontinuité, les ondes sont réfléchies et réfractées.

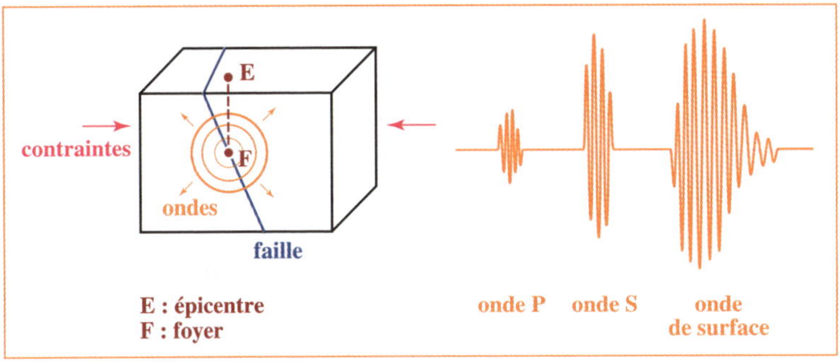

Figure 3 *Caractéristiques d'un séisme et tracé d'un sismogramme*

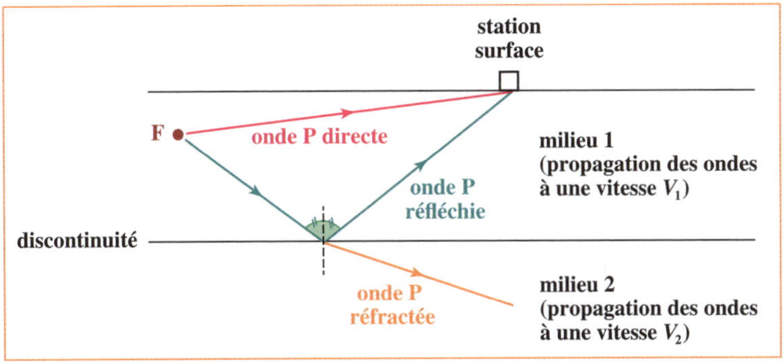

Figure 4 *Réflexion et réfraction des ondes sismiques*

■ Après un séisme, les stations sismiques mondiales situées entre 98° et 145° du foyer n'enregistrent aucun enregistrement d'ondes P directes : c'est une zone d'ombre*. On peut supposer que cette absence d'ondes est causée par la réfraction des ondes P en profondeur par une surface de discontinuité : on met ainsi en évidence la présence du noyau externe à 2 900 km de profondeur.

■ Ainsi, l'étude de la vitesse de propagation des ondes et de leur trajectoire a permis de mettre en évidence des discontinuités et la présence d'enveloppes à l'intérieur de la Terre : cette compréhension de la structure interne de la Terre a permis de construire un modèle, le PREM pour *Preliminary Reference Earth Model*.

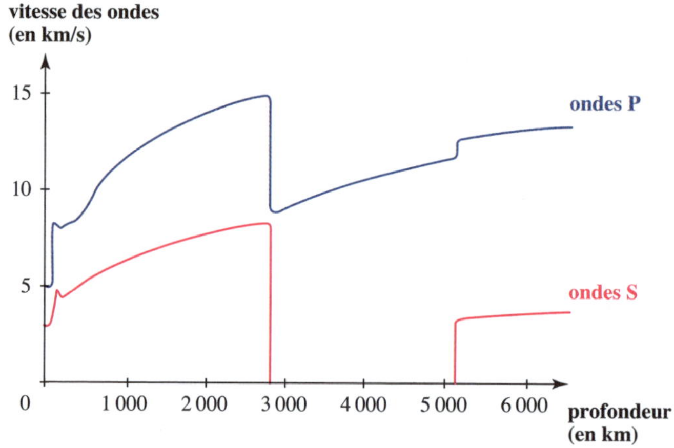

Figure 5 *Le modèle PREM*

■ On distingue trois couches principales : la croûte (océanique ou continentale), le manteau et le noyau.

■ Quand on étudie la vitesse de propagation des ondes en profondeur, on observe un ralentissement des ondes sismiques entre 100 et 200 km de profondeur : il indique la présence d'une couche visqueuse (mais pas liquide), la *Low Velocity Zone* ou **LVZ***. Ce changement de comportement du manteau qui, de solide devient visqueux au niveau de la LVZ, délimite la frontière entre la **lithosphère*** rigide et cassante (de 0 à 100 km) et l'**asthénosphère*** ductile* (de 100 à 670 km).

Définition

La **LVZ** présente 3 propriétés :
– sismique : elle ralentit les ondes sismiques ;
– thermique : elle est délimitée par l'isotherme 1 300 °C ;
– mécanique : par sa viscosité, elle démarque la base de la lithosphère rigide.

B. Les apports de la connaissance des modes de transferts thermiques

■ Il n'existe aucune mesure directe de la température interne de la Terre. Les géologues utilisent des indices pour déterminer le **gradient géothermique***, c'est-à-dire l'évolution des températures en fonction de la profondeur. On estime ainsi que dans la lithosphère, le géotherme moyen est de 10 à 30 °C/km, dans l'asthénosphère de 0,3 °C/km et dans le noyau de 0,55 °C/km (voir *figure 6* p. 101).

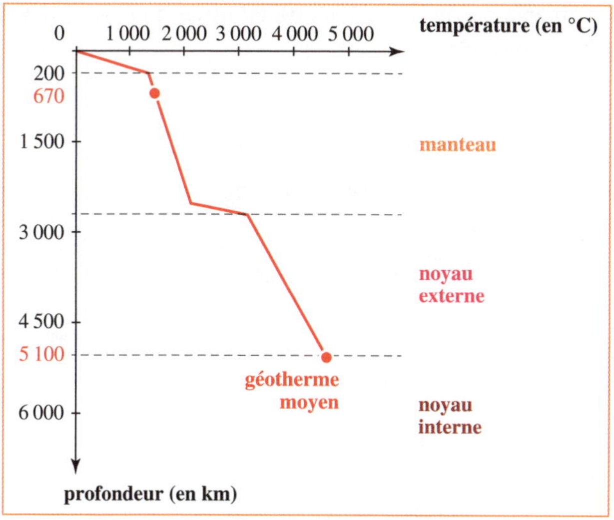

Figure 6 *Le gradient géothermique terrestre*

■ Les **isothermes*** sont des lignes fictives d'égales températures au sein du manteau et de la croûte terrestre. Elles délimitent la lithosphère et l'asthénosphère : la LVZ est représentée par l'isotherme 1 300 °C.

■ Plus on s'éloigne de la dorsale, plus la LVZ s'enfonce : ainsi, la lithosphère océanique a une épaisseur variable (de 0 à 100 km de profondeur) mais qui reste plus fine que l'épaisseur de la lithosphère continentale, qui atteint 150 km en moyenne.

C. Une structure interne dynamique

■ Le manteau terrestre n'est pas homogène et il fait l'objet de variations de température. Cette hétérogénéité thermique du manteau crée des anomalies de vitesse des ondes sismiques par rapport au modèle PREM : leur étude constitue la **tomographie sismique***.

■ Si les vitesses enregistrées sont plus rapides que les vitesses théoriques du modèle PREM, alors l'anomalie est négative et on peut supposer l'existence d'un matériel mantellique plus dense. À l'inverse, si les vitesses enregistrées sont plus lentes que les vitesses théoriques, alors l'anomalie est positive et on peut supposer l'existence d'un matériel mantellique moins dense.

■ La tomographie révèle l'existence de mouvements mantelliques : le manteau « chaud » en profondeur est moins dense et « monte » alors que le manteau « froid », plus dense, « tombe ». Ces mouvements de matière permettent d'homogénéiser les températures internes : c'est la **convection mantellique***.

■ D'autres mouvements thermiques, sans transfert de matière, existent au sein de la lithosphère, c'est la **conduction***.

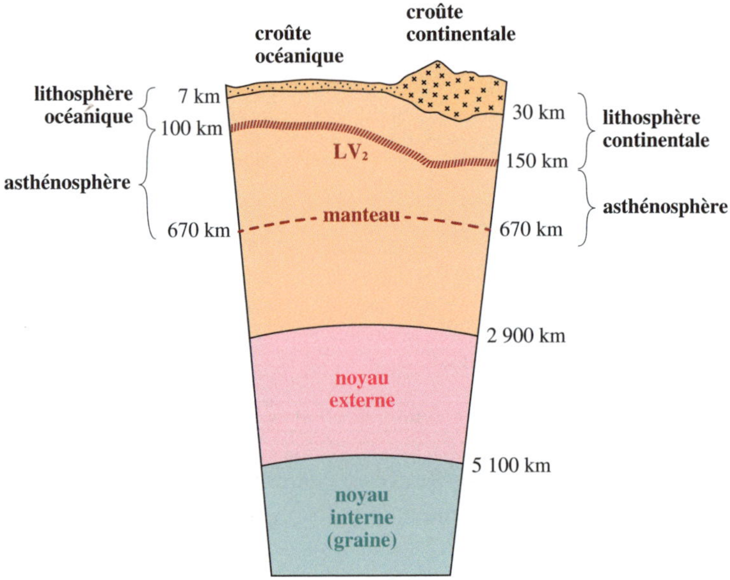

Figure 7 *Schématisation de la structure interne de la Terre*

EXERCICES

Connaître le cours

1 2 min ★ Vrai ou Faux ?

Relevez la (ou les) information(s) exacte(s).

La LVZ :

a) est caractérisée par une température de 1 300 °C.
b) a une épaisseur constante de 100 km.
c) délimite la partie supérieure de l'asthénosphère.
d) est caractérisée par une accélération des ondes P.

→ *Corrigé p. 110*

2 2 min ★ Vrai ou Faux ?

Relevez la (ou les) information(s) exacte(s).

La bimodalité des altitudes :

a) est caractérisée par deux pics de fréquences différentes : l'altitude des océans et l'altitude des continents.
b) trouve son origine dans les différences de densité entre croûtes océanique et continentale.
c) permet d'expliquer directement la théorie de la dérive des continents de Wegener.
d) est liée à la convection du manteau.

→ *Corrigé p. 110*

3 5 min ★ Restitution de connaissances

Expliquez brièvement comment les données sismiques ont permis de mettre en évidence le noyau externe liquide.

→ *Corrigé p. 110*

4 5 min ★ Schématiser le cours

Schématisez la structure interne de la Terre de 0 à 670 km de profondeur.

→ *Corrigé p. 110*

S'entraîner

5 10 min ★ Étude minéralogique

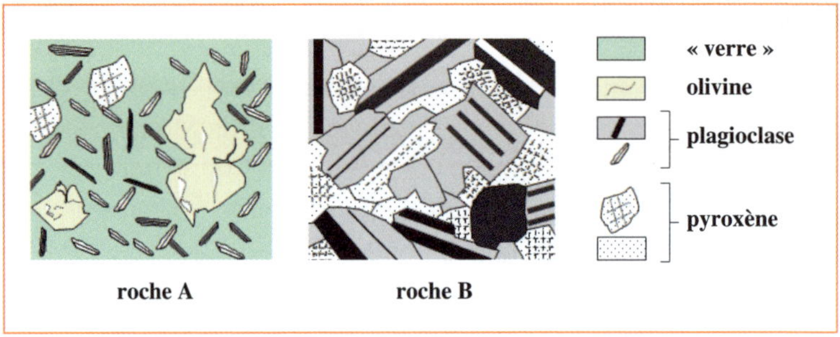

Observations microscopiques des roches A et B

1. Identifiez les structures des roches A et B.
2. D'après leur assemblage minéralogique, identifiez les roches.
3. De quelle lithosphère ces roches sont-elles constitutives ?

→ Corrigé p. 110

6 10 min ★★ Les enveloppes terrestres

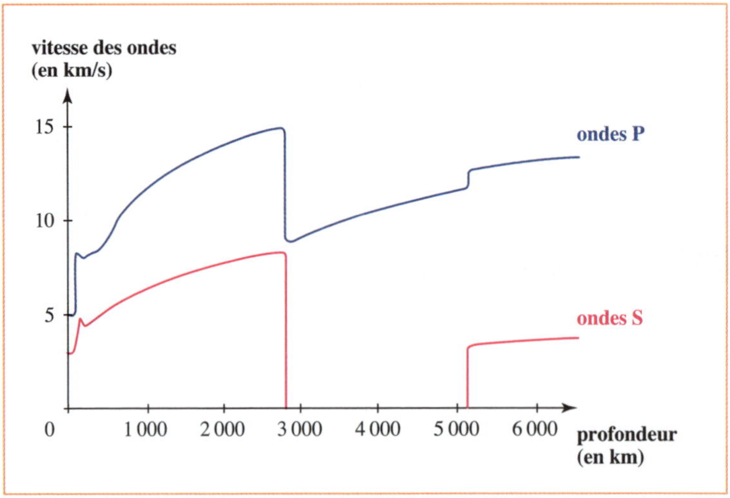

Le modèle PREM

1. D'après le modèle PREM présenté, identifiez les différentes enveloppes terrestres.

2. D'après les vitesses de propagation des ondes P et S, identifiez le comportement solide ou liquide de ces enveloppes.

→ *Corrigé p. 111*

7 20 min ★★ Calcul de l'épaisseur de la croûte continentale

L'existence d'une discontinuité entre le manteau et la croûte a été identifiée pour la première fois en Croatie, en 1909, par le géologue Andrija Mohorovičić. Cette discontinuité porte son nom et l'abréviation en est « Moho ». En se reposant sur la même méthode d'étude d'arrivée des ondes sismiques, on veut calculer la profondeur du Moho sous les Alpes au niveau de deux stations d'enregistrement sismique. Pour cela, il suffit de connaître le temps d'arrivée des ondes P directes ainsi que celui des ondes P s'étant réfléchies sur le Moho et d'utiliser la méthode de calcul suivante, reposant sur le théorème de Pythagore (sachant que $V_p = 6{,}5$ km.s^{-1}) :

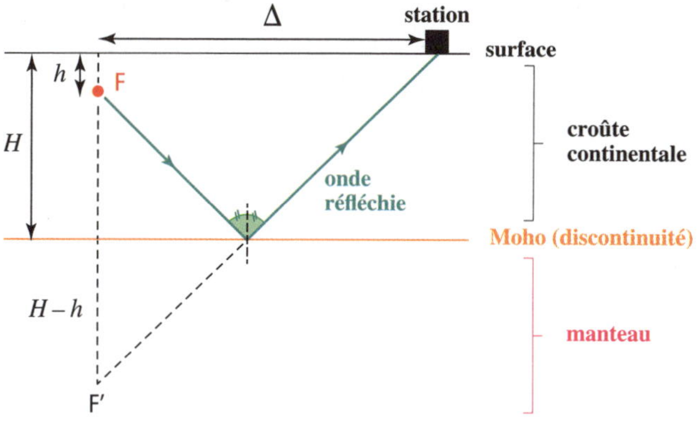

Données :
– Δ = distance à l'épicentre de la station
– H = profondeur du Moho (ou épaisseur de la croûte)
– V_p = vitesse des ondes P dans la croûte
– δt = différence entre le temps d'arrivée des ondes directes et des ondes réfléchies sur le Moho

$$H = \frac{1}{2}\left[h + \sqrt{\left(V \times \delta t + \sqrt{h^2 + \Delta^2}\right)^2 - \Delta^2}\right]$$

Figure 1 *Méthode de calcul de la profondeur du Moho*

	h = profondeur du foyer	**Δ = distance à l'épicentre**	**Temps d'arrivée des ondes P**	**Temps d'arrivée des ondes P réfléchies (PmP)**
Station OG02 (Annemasse)	11 km	63,3 km	3 h 12 min 15,580 s	3 h 12 min 18,540 s
Station RSL (Roselend)	10 km	135,8 km	5 h 23 min 5,325 s	5 h 53 min 2,005 s

Figure 2 *Données sismiques de deux stations alpines*

1. D'après les données de la figure 2, calculez le δt, soit le retard entre le temps d'enregistrement des ondes P directes et celui des ondes P réfléchies pour chacune des stations.

2. Calculez la profondeur du Moho entre les deux stations à l'aide de la méthode de calcul présenté en figure 1.

→ *Corrigé p. 111*

8 20 min ★★ La température au centre de la Terre

Grâce aux données sismiques et à des études de roches en laboratoire, les scientifiques calculent deux points pour lesquels les coordonnées profondeur et température sont connues : ce sont des points d'ancrage. Ainsi, à la limite noyau interne/noyau externe (5 150 km), la température serait de 4 700 °C alors qu'à 670 km de profondeur, la température serait de 1 600 °C.

1. Calculez le géotherme moyen terrestre (en $°C.km^{-1}$) entre ces deux points d'ancrage.

2. On estime que le gradient géothermique du manteau est de 0,3 $°C.km^{-1}$ et de 0,55 $°C.km^{-1}$ pour le noyau. Vos calculs précédents vous paraissent-ils cohérents ?

3. Sachant que le rayon de la Terre est de 6 371 km, calculez la température théorique du centre de la Terre.

4. Comment homogénéiser le contraste de températures important entre la base du manteau et son sommet ?

→ *Corrigé p. 111*

9 20 min ★★ La LVZ

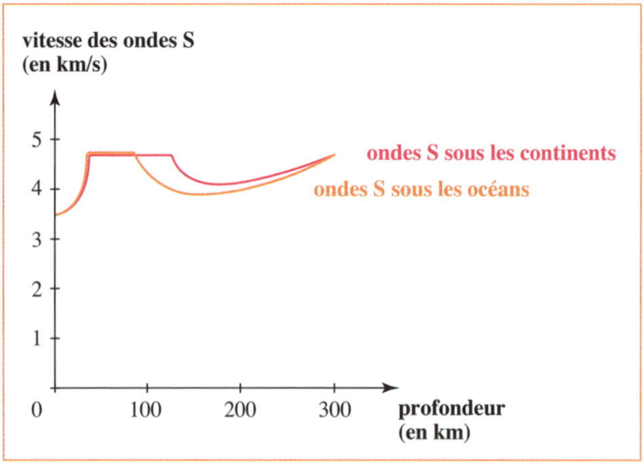

Figure 1 *Étude de la vitesse des ondes S sous les océans et les continents*

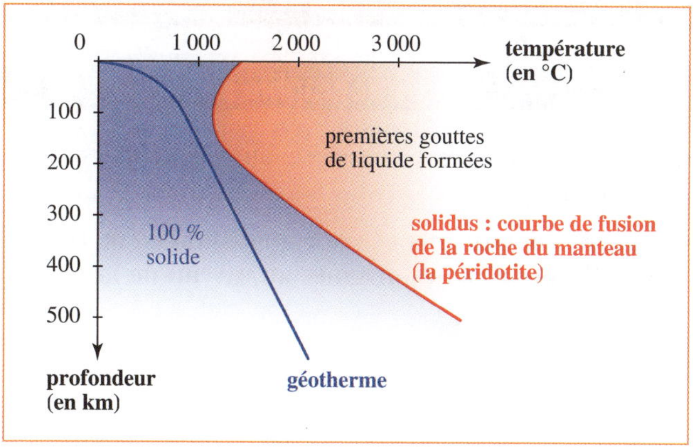

Figure 2 *Gradient géothermique et solidus du manteau*

1. À l'aide de vos connaissances et de la figure 1, identifiez la couche qui cause le ralentissement des ondes S observé entre 100 et 200 km de profondeur.

2. L'épaisseur de la lithosphère est-elle la même entre les continents et les océans ?

3. À l'aide de la figure 2, expliquez l'origine du ralentissement de la vitesse des ondes.

→ *Corrigé p. 111*

Exercice 10 pts **La tomographie sismique** 30 min

Lors de séismes au Japon, on observe une accélération des ondes sismiques reçues par rapport au modèle PREM.

D'après l'ensemble des documents et vos connaissances, mettez en évidence les mouvements mantelliques et leurs origines au niveau de la croûte terrestre du Japon.

Document 1 : Tomographie sismique japonaise

On étudie les anomalies de vitesse sous la fosse océanique du Japon par rapport au modèle PREM et on dresse une coupe d'ouest en est, jusqu'à la limite manteau/noyau.

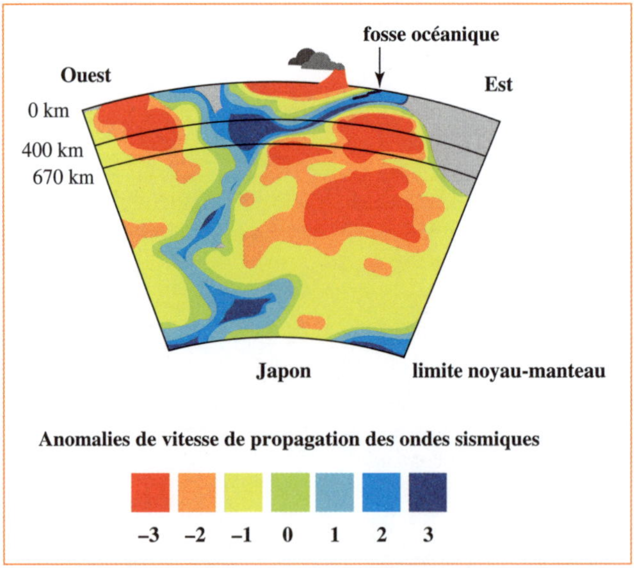

Tomographie sismique de la fosse océanique du Japon

Document 2 : Répartition des isothermes sous la fosse océanique japonaise

On représente la répartition des isothermes (lignes d'égales températures) sous la fosse japonaise.

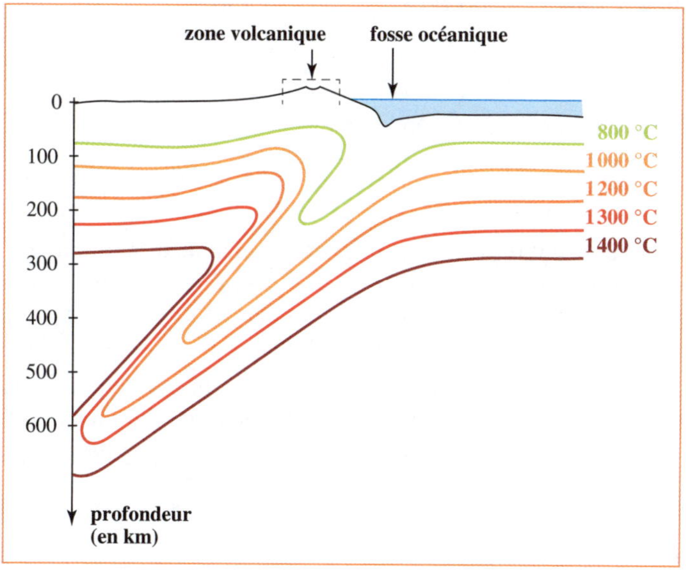

Isothermes sous la fosse océanique japonaise

Document 3 : La convection mantellique

En classe, un modèle de convection peut être réalisé en plaçant une bougie chauffe-plat sous un bécher contenant une huile rouge dans le fond et une huile jaune surnageante. Les résultats sont présentés ci-dessous :

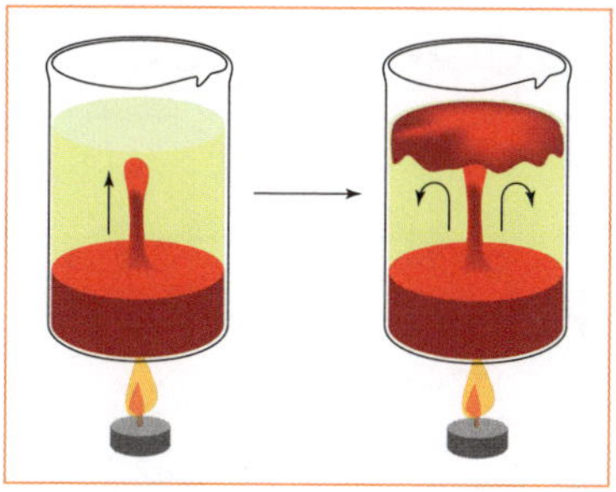

Modèle de convection

→ Corrigé p. 112

CORRIGÉS

1 → *Énoncé p. 103*

Les affirmations exactes sont a) et c).

2 → *Énoncé p. 103*

Les affirmations exactes sont a) et b).

3 → *Énoncé p. 103*

Les ondes sismiques sont réfléchies et réfractées à chaque discontinuité. Or, à la suite d'un séisme, on observe une zone d'ombre, c'est-à-dire que l'on enregistre aucune onde P directe entre 98° et 145° du foyer. Ceci permet de mettre en évidence la présence d'une discontinuité à 2 900 km de profondeur.

Par ailleurs la disparition des ondes S à partir de cette profondeur indique l'existence d'une enveloppe liquide car ces ondes ne se propagent pas dans les liquides.

Ainsi le noyau externe liquide est mis en évidence par l'étude de la propagation des ondes sismiques.

4 → *Énoncé p. 103*

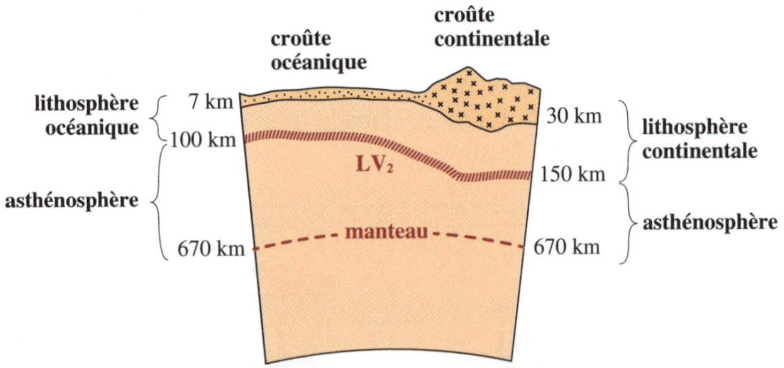

5 → *Énoncé p. 104*

1. La roche A est composée de petits minéraux englobés dans une pâte appelée « verre ». C'est une structure microlitique. La roche B présente de grands minéraux cohésifs : sa structure est grenue.

2. Les deux roches sont constituées de feldspaths plagioclases et de pyroxènes : la roche A, microlitique, est donc du basalte alors que la roche B, grenue, est du gabbro.
3. Ces deux roches sont caractéristiques de la croûte océanique.

6 → Énoncé p. 104

1. Jusqu'à 2 900 km de profondeur, la vitesse des ondes P et S augmente : c'est le manteau. À 2 900 km, la vitesse des ondes P diminue fortement, ce qui indique une discontinuité : le noyau externe. À 5 100 km, les ondes P accélèrent légèrement, ce qui indique la présence de la discontinuité de Lehmann et l'apparition du noyau interne.
2. Par ailleurs l'enregistrement des ondes S disparaît entre 2 900 km et 5 100 km : le noyau externe est donc liquide. Les ondes se propagent dans les autres enveloppes : le manteau et le noyau interne sont donc entièrement solides.

7 → Énoncé p. 105

1. Station Annemasse : retard des ondes PmP = 2,96 s
Station Roselend : retard des ondes PmP = 3,32 s
2. Station Annemasse : $H = 32{,}7$ km
Station Roselend : $H = 45{,}1$ km

8 → Énoncé p. 106

1. La distance entre les deux points d'ancrage est de 4 480 km et l'écart de température est de 3 100 °C. Le géotherme moyen entre ces deux points est donc de 3 100/4 480 = 0,7 $°C.km^{-1}$.
2. Le géotherme moyen dans le manteau est de 0,3 $°C.km^{-1}$ et de 0,55 $°C.km^{-1}$ dans le noyau ; Ces nombres sont inférieur au résultat du calcul théorique précédent. On en déduit qu'il doit exister des sauts de température. au sein du manteau.
3. À partir de 5 100 km, la température est de 4 700 °C. Or le géotherme moyen du noyau est de 0,55 $°C.km^{-1}$. On peut donc en déduire que pour atteindre le centre de la Terre, situé à 1 221 km à partir de la discontinuité de Lehmann, il faut donc $0{,}55 \times 1\,221 = 672$ °C. La température au centre de la Terre serait donc de $4\,700 + 672 = 5\,372$ °C.
Ceci est une valeur théorique. Des expériences ont été réalisées en laboratoire sur l'état du fer au sein du noyau qui suggéreraient une température plus élevée (6 000 °C).
4. Les différences de température entre la base du manteau et son sommet entraînent des mouvements de convection permettant une homogénéisation des températures.

9 → Énoncé p. 106

1. À partir de 130 km de profondeur sous les continents et 100 km de profondeur sous les océans, les ondes S ralentissent dans le manteau. On peut donc supposer que le

manteau est visqueux à cette profondeur (ralentissement des ondes) mais pas liquide (sinon les ondes S ne passeraient pas).

2. Cette couche visqueuse est la LVZ qui délimite la lithosphère de l'asthénosphère. On peut donc en déduire que la lithosphère océanique mesure en moyenne 100 km d'épaisseur alors que la lithosphère continentale est ici de 130 km d'épaisseur : la lithosphère n'a donc pas une épaisseur constante.

3. On observe que le géotherme se rapproche du solidus de la péridotite vers 100 km de profondeur : on peut donc penser que la péridotite, roche du manteau, ne fond pas mais devient plus visqueuse à cette profondeur

CONTRÔLE CONTINU POUR LE BAC

Exercice → *Énoncé p. 108*

On observe une anomalie positive des vitesses sismiques de +3 sous la fosse japonaise qui semble « tomber » vers l'ouest jusqu'à 670 km de profondeur. Or, une anomalie positive reflète une accélération des ondes sismiques dans cette zone par rapport au modèle théorique PREM. Cette accélération peut être causée par une lithosphère plus dense : la lithosphère océanique japonaise.

On peut en déduire que sous la fosse japonaise, la lithosphère océanique plonge vers l'ouest.

À quoi est dû ce mouvement vertical de la lithosphère ?

On observe que les isothermes fléchissent sous la fosse océanique japonaise. Par exemple, l'isotherme 1 300 °C qui délimite la base de la lithosphère passe de 250 km de profondeur à 600 km. Ceci correspond bien à la tomographie précédente : la lithosphère océanique, froide et donc plus dense, tombe dans le manteau environnant, plus chaud et moins dense.

Ces mouvements verticaux et horizontaux de la lithosphère peuvent être modélisés par une expérience avec de l'huile colorée. On observe que si on crée un gradient thermique à l'aide d'une bougie chauffe-plat, l'huile chaude, moins dense, monte. Lorsqu'elle se refroidit en surface, elle devient plus dense et retombe. Ce phénomène permet d'homogénéiser les températures par des mouvements de matière : c'est la convection. On modélise ainsi la convection mantellique qui permet de transférer la température par des mouvements du manteau et de la lithosphère.

Sous le Japon, la lithosphère océanique plonge donc dans le manteau, sous la lithosphère continentale japonaise.

La dynamique de la lithosphère

CHAPITRE 8

La lithosphère est découpée en plaques qui sont animées de mouvements. La tectonique des plaques est un modèle scientifique permettant de les étudier.

1 La mobilité horizontale de la lithosphère

A. Les méthodes d'observation

■ La tectonique des plaques repose sur plusieurs méthodes permettant de visualiser le déplacement des plaques lithosphériques.

1. Les anomalies magnétiques et l'âge des sédiments

■ Lors du refroidissement du basalte, certains minéraux vont enregistrer les caractéristiques du champ magnétique terrestre de l'époque de leur formation.

Remarque

Les basaltes enregistrent le sens et l'intensité du champ magnétique de l'époque de leur formation, grâce à leur composition minérale de magnétite et d'hématite. Ainsi lorsqu'on rapproche une boussole d'un basalte, celle-ci est déviée et n'indique plus le nord : c'est la mémoire magnétique.

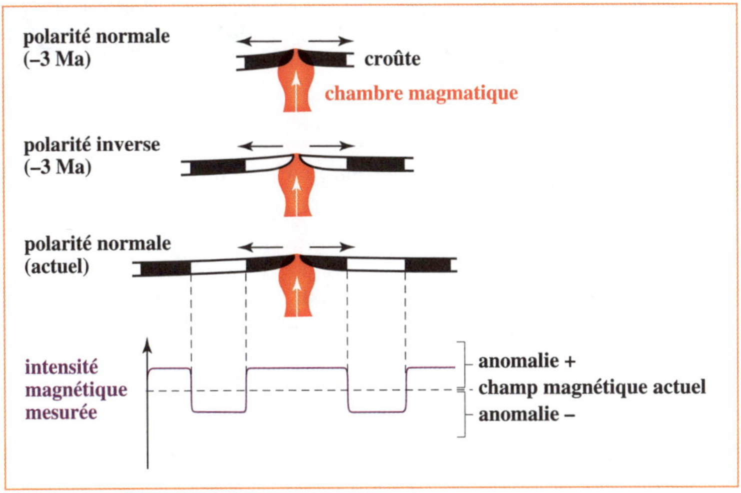

Figure 1 *La mémoire magmatique*

■ Les **anomalies magnétiques*** correspondent à un écart entre le champ magnétique mesuré dans les roches et le champ magnétique terrestre qui règne actuellement. Ces anomalies peuvent être datées car elles suivent la même alternance que les époques d'inversion du champ magnétique. On peut en conclure que la croûte océanique est d'autant plus âgée qu'elle s'éloigne de la dorsale. Au niveau d'une dorsale a donc lieu la formation de la croûte océanique qui est en expansion : les basaltes se mettent en place à l'axe de la dorsale puis s'en écartent.

■ De la même façon, on peut étudier l'âge des sédiments au contact des basaltes. Plus on s'éloigne de l'axe de la dorsale, plus les basaltes sont âgés. En connaissant l'âge de ces roches, on peut calculer la vitesse d'accrétion de la dorsale.

2. Le volcanisme intraplaque

■ Le volcanisme intraplaque est défini par la présence d'alignements de volcans au milieu d'une plaque lithosphérique océanique ou continentale, et non pas aux frontières des plaques. Ces volcans sont créés par la remontée du manteau sous forme de panache mantellique. Ce phénomène, appelé « **point chaud*** », est considéré « fixe » dans le manteau. Le déplacement de la plaque lithosphérique au-dessus de ce point chaud va donc créer un alignement des volcans. On peut ainsi déterminer la direction, le sens et la vitesse de déplacement de la plaque.

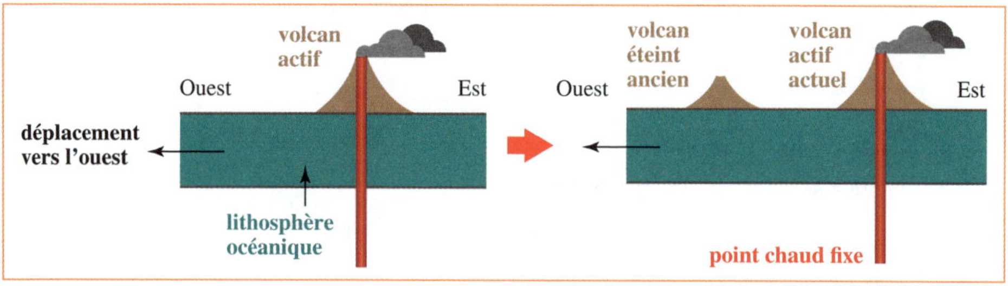

Figure 2 *Mouvement des plaques et points chauds*

3. Le GPS

■ Des techniques modernes de positionnement par satellite permettent de visualiser de façon immédiate le déplacement et la vitesse des plaques lithosphériques les unes par rapport aux autres.

■ Les satellites envoient un signal aux stations GPS et mesurent ensuite le temps de trajet de l'onde. La méthode **GPS*** (*Global Positioning System*) permet, selon le principe de la triangulation, de déterminer en temps réel des vecteurs de vitesse de déplacement des plaques lithosphériques.

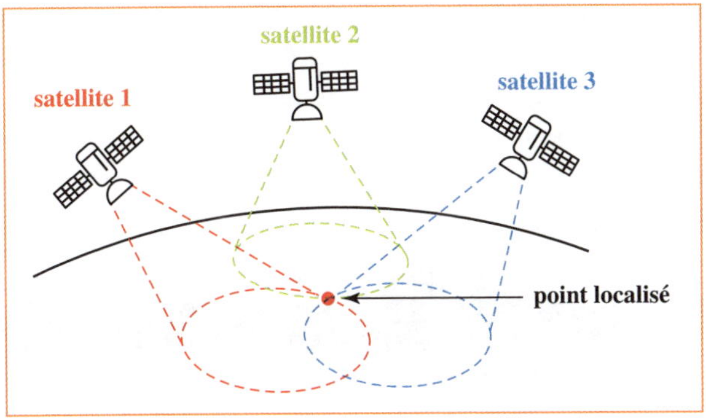

Figure 3 *Le principe de triangulation*

Ex. : Selon les vitesses d'accrétion des dorsales, c'est-à-dire la vitesse à laquelle elles produisent de la lithosphère océanique, on distingue les dorsales rapides (17 cm pour la dorsale Pacifique) et les dorsales lentes (2 cm pour la dorsale Atlantique nord).

B. Les principaux mouvements des plaques lithosphériques

■ Les mouvements de plaques lithosphériques mis en évidence par les méthodes décrites précédemment sont principalement des mouvements de **divergence*** et de **convergence***. L'étude de la **topographie*** des océans, des variations du **flux thermique*** terrestre et des séismes permet de différencier ces deux mouvements lithosphériques (voir *figure 4*, p. 116).

■ Au niveau des zones de divergence, les dorsales sont caractérisées par un relief positif : ce sont des chaînes de montagnes sous-marines dans lesquelles le flux thermique est élevé. Il y a donc une libération de chaleur qui correspond à une remontée du manteau profond et à un volcanisme associé.

Ex. : Les dorsales culminent à 2,5 km sous le niveau de la mer alors que les fosses océaniques peuvent atteindre 11 km comme la fosse des Mariannes bordant le Nord-Ouest de l'océan Pacifique.

■ À l'opposé, au niveau des zones de convergence, les fosses océaniques sont caractérisées par un relief négatif et un flux thermique faible. La distribution spatiale des foyers des séismes en fonction de leur profondeur s'établit selon un plan incliné : le **plan de Wadati-Benioff*** ; ce sont des **marges actives***.

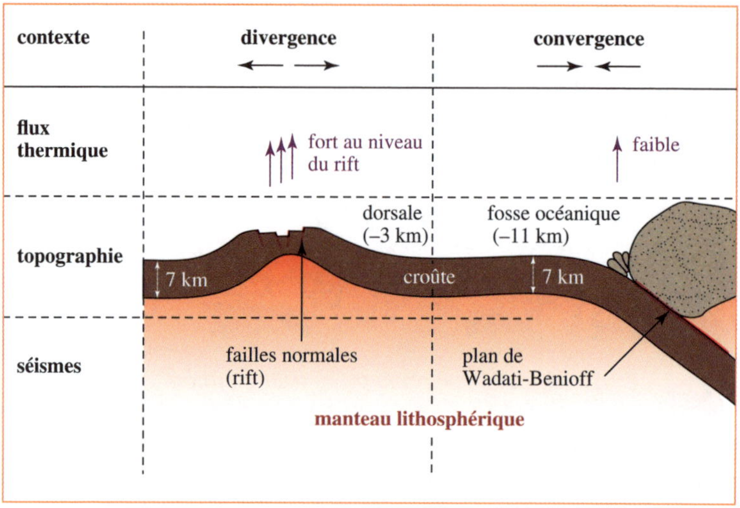

Figure 4 *Les mouvements des plaques lithosphériques*

2 Les mouvements de divergence : les dorsales océaniques

A. La formation de la lithosphère océanique

■ La divergence des plaques lithosphériques de part et d'autre de la dorsale permet la mise en place d'une nouvelle lithosphère océanique à partir du manteau asthénosphérique. En effet, celui-ci subit une décompression : il remonte sous la dorsale et sa pression diminue en perdant peu de chaleur. Cette **décompression adiabatique*** permet aux péridotites de franchir le **solidus***, c'est-à-dire de former les premières gouttes de magma.

■ La péridotite ne fond pas entièrement : on dit que la fusion du manteau est partielle (voir *figure 5* p. 117). Ce phénomène permet de former un magma de composition différente de la péridotite d'origine, plus riche en pyroxène et plagioclase : un magma basaltique qui va refroidir lors de sa remontée. S'il refroidit rapidement, en surface, il forme du basalte, roche volcanique*, alors que s'il refroidit en profondeur (bloqué sous les basaltes), il forme des gabbros, roches plutoniques.

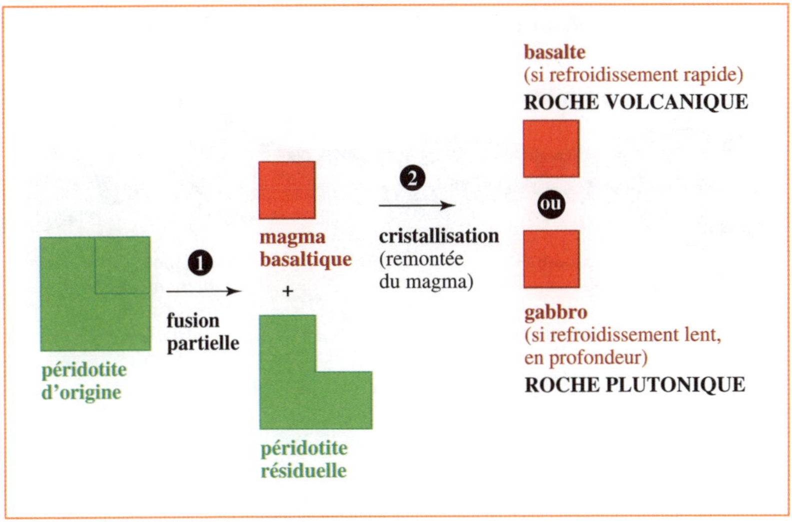

Figure 5 *Fusion partielle et cristallisation*

B. Variété des dorsales

■ Le taux de fusion partielle de la péridotite varie en fonction du type de dorsale (voir *figure 6* p. 118).

Au niveau des dorsales lentes (2 à 3 cm par an), on observe une production de magma discontinue (faible fusion partielle de la péridotite) avec une vallée centrale appelée « **rift axial*** » bordé de **failles normales***. La croûte océanique et les niveaux superficiels du manteau sont alors le siège d'une circulation d'eau qui s'infiltre par les failles, qui va modifier les minéraux : c'est l'hydrothermalisme. L'hydratation des roches de la lithosphère océanique peut donner naissance à des minéraux hydroxylés modifiant ainsi l'aspect des roches : la péridotite devient de la **serpentinite*** alors que le gabbro devient un gabbro à hornblende (minéral hydroxylé).

■ Les dorsales rapides (6 à 16 cm par an) sont caractérisées par une production importante de magma (fusion partielle forte de la péridotite) et une forme en dôme, haut de plusieurs centaines de mètres.

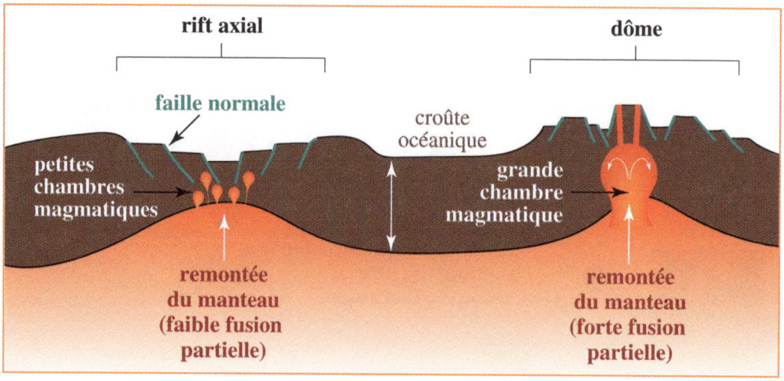

Figure 6 *Diversité des dorsales*

3 Les mouvements de convergence

A. La subduction

1. Le magmatisme de subduction

■ Plus la lithosphère océanique s'éloigne de la dorsale, plus elle refroidit. L'isotherme 1 300 °C devient de plus en plus profond et la lithosphère est donc de plus en plus épaisse. Ainsi, sa densité augmente et la lithosphère océanique s'enfonce davantage dans le manteau asthénosphérique.

■ Lorsque la lithosphère océanique devient plus dense que le manteau asthénosphérique environnant, celle-ci plonge dans l'asthénosphère : c'est la **subduction*** (voir *figure 7* p. 119).

■ Au niveau de la plaque chevauchante sont échantillonnées des roches magmatiques hydratées : des granodiorites (roches plutoniques issues d'une cristallisation en profondeur) et des andésites (roches volcaniques issues d'une cristallisation en surface). Ces deux roches sont riches en minéraux hydroxylés comme les **amphiboles***.

■ Cette hydratation trouve son origine dans la cristallisation d'un magma hydraté visqueux. La viscosité du magma permet l'apparition d'un **volcanisme explosif.** Lors de son ascension, ce magma peut être contaminé par les roches continentales environnantes, ce qui explique la grande diversité de roches observées.

■ Ce magma s'est formé grâce à la fusion partielle des péridotites du manteau chevauchant dont l'hydratation a permis le franchissement du solidus.

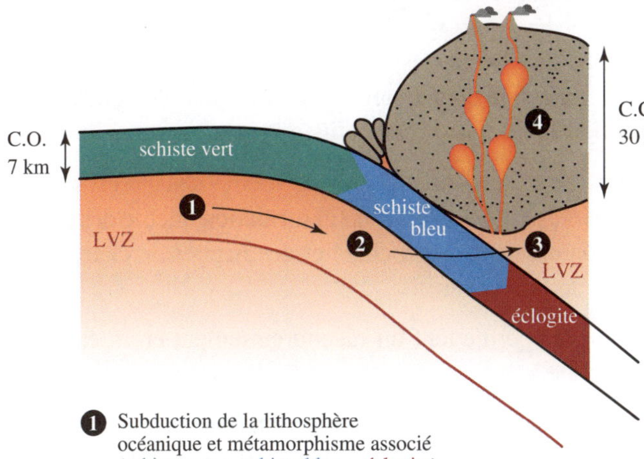

❶ Subduction de la lithosphère océanique et métamorphisme associé (schiste vert > schiste bleu > éclogite)

❷ Déshydratation de la lithosphère océanique et l'eau migre dans le manteau chevauchant

❸ Abaissement du solidus grâce à l'hydratation des péridotites > fusion partielle

❹ Remontée du magma hydraté et visqueux : cristallisation en profondeur ou en surface et contamination possible par la croûte continentale

Figure 7 *Subduction et fusion des péridotites*

2. Le métamorphisme de subduction

■ Les fluides hydratant le manteau sont apportés par la déshydratation de la lithosphère océanique tombant en subduction. En effet, au cours de la subduction, la lithosphère océanique est entraînée en profondeur et subit du **métamorphisme*** : les minéraux deviennent instables, réagissent entre eux entraînant la formation de nouveaux minéraux.

■ L'apparition de certains minéraux métamorphiques comme le **glaucophane*** (caractéristique du faciès schiste bleu) et la **coésite*** (caractéristique du faciès éclogitique à très haute pression) indique que la lithosphère océanique a subi des conditions de forte pression et de faible température.

■ Par ailleurs, ces minéraux métamorphiques sont de plus en plus denses, ce qui entretient la subduction. Cette augmentation de la densité de la lithosphère constitue un facteur important contrôlant la subduction et les mouvements descendants de la convection.

B. La collision

■ Lorsque la lithosphère océanique est entièrement tombée en subduction, c'est au tour de la lithosphère continentale de débuter son mouvement descendant. Ce phénomène est appelé **subduction continentale** ou **collision***.

■ Cet affrontement entre deux lithosphères de même densité est caractérisé par des marqueurs tectoniques assimilés à des plis (déformation ductile des roches), des failles inverses (déformation cassante des roches) et des nappes de charriage (déplacement de grands lambeaux de lithosphère).

■ Ces trois phénomènes permettent un raccourcissement et un épaississement de la lithosphère continentale.

■ Les conditions de pression et de température vont donc varier lorsque les roches sont enfouies en profondeur : le gradient de moyenne pression et de moyenne température permet un métamorphisme marqué par la présence d'un minéral, la **sillimanite***, ainsi que la formation d'une roche particulière appelée **migmatite***. Celle-ci est caractéristique d'une fusion partielle de la croûte continentale : c'est un mélange de zones claires, leucosomes, ressemblant au granite (partie étant entrée en fusion) et de zones foncées, mélanosomes, ressemblant au gneiss (roche métamorphique n'ayant pas franchi le solidus).

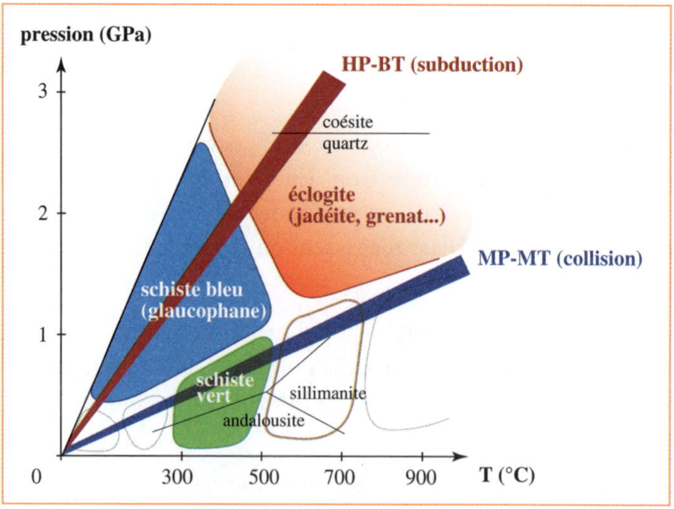

Figure 8 *Les métamorphismes*

EXERCICES

Connaître le cours

1 2 min ★ Vrai ou Faux ?

Relevez la (ou les) information(s) exacte(s).

Les dorsales sont caractérisées par :
a) un flux thermique élevé.
b) une zone de convergence.
c) une décompression du manteau.
d) des failles normales formant un rift axial.

→ Corrigé p. 128

2 2 min ★ Vrai ou Faux ?

Relevez la (ou les) information(s) exacte(s).

Les zones de subduction sont définies par :
a) un relief négatif, appelé fosse océanique.
b) des marqueurs métamorphiques de basse pression et haute température.
c) une déshydratation du manteau chevauchant.
d) une grande diversité de roches magmatiques formées sur la plaque chevauchante.

→ Corrigé p. 128

3 5 min ★ Restitution de connaissances

Expliquez brièvement comment les anomalies magnétiques constituent un indice d'une expansion océanique au niveau des dorsales.

→ Corrigé p. 128

4 5 min ★ Schématiser le cours

Schématisez l'organisation et la diversité des dorsales océaniques.

→ Corrigé p. 128

S'entraîner

5 10 min ★★ Étude d'une roche

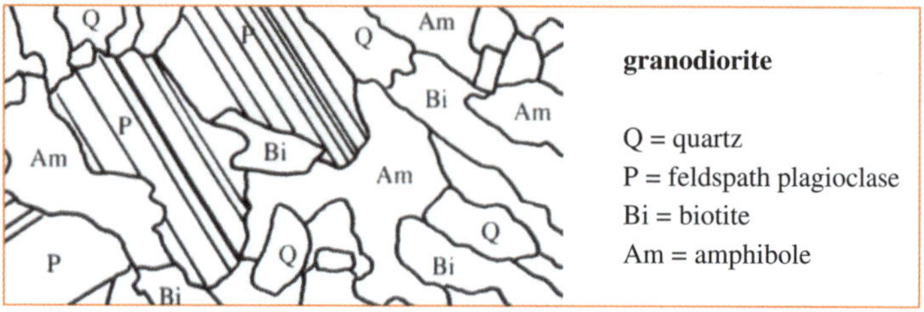

Schématisation de l'observation microscopique de granodiorite

1. À partir de l'observation microscopique de la roche, indiquez son contexte de cristallisation.

2. À partir de sa composition minéralogique, expliquez si elle s'est formée dans un contexte de divergence ou de convergence.

3. À l'aide de vos connaissances, expliquez le mécanisme à l'origine de la formation du magma dont est issue cette roche.

→ *Corrigé p. 128*

6 15 min ★★ Diversité des dorsales

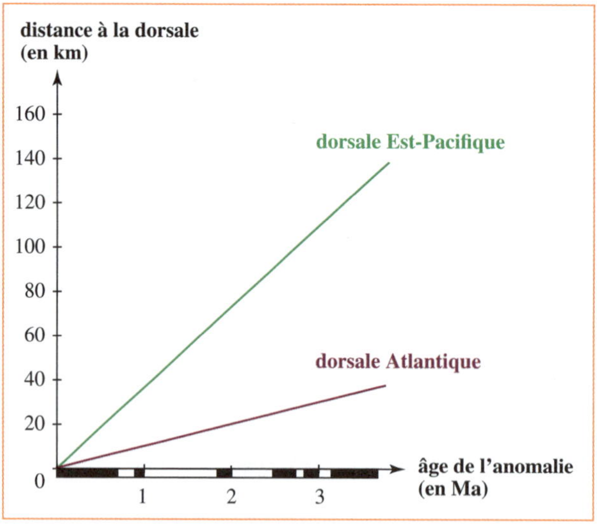

Anomalies magnétiques et vitesse des dorsales

1. Calculez les vitesses d'accrétion des dorsales Est-Pacifique et Atlantique.
2. D'après vos connaissances, déterminez si elles sont rapides ou lentes, ainsi que leurs caractéristiques.
3. Calculez de combien de centimètres New York et Paris se sont éloignés depuis 1789 et la prise de la Bastille.

→ *Corrigé p. 129*

7 15 min ★★ Profil sismique

Le 25 avril 2015 eu lieu un séisme destructeur au Népal. Des études sismiques ont été réalisées pour trouver son origine. Les réflecteurs observés sur la figure ci-dessous montrent des surfaces de discontinuité qui réfléchissent les ondes sismiques.

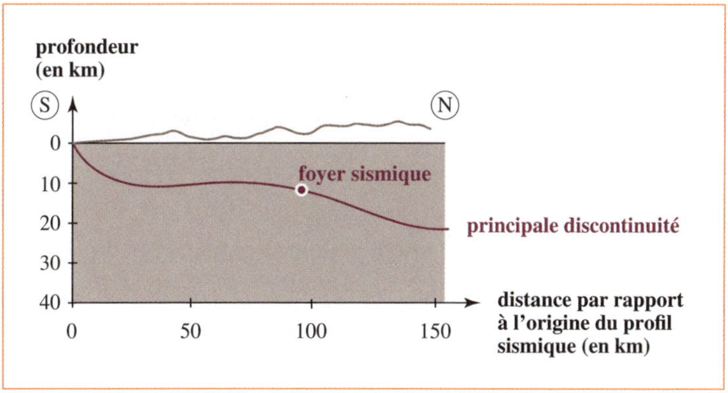

Profil sismique sous la chaîne Himalayenne

1. Localisez le foyer sismique ayant causé le séisme de 2015.
2. Précisez le type de figure tectonique à l'origine du séisme.
3. Quel contexte a pu créer cette figure tectonique ?

→ *Corrigé p. 129*

8 15 min ★★ La fusion de la péridotite

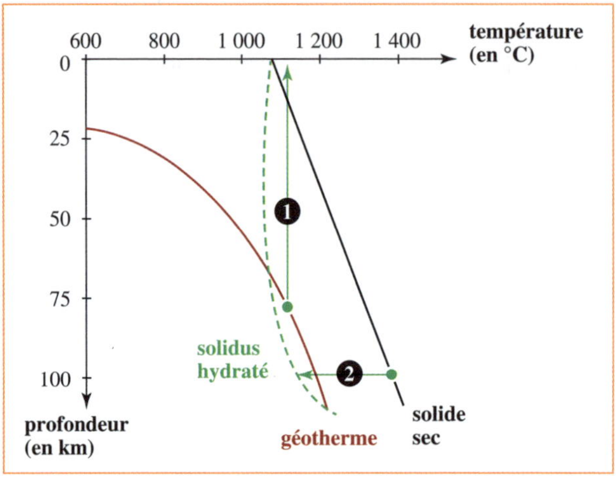

Géotherme et solidus de la péridotite

1. Expliquez les 2 mécanismes permettant la fusion de la péridotite et la formation de magmas.

2. Quels contextes tectoniques permettent cette diversité magmatique ?

→ *Corrigé p. 129*

9 20 min ★★ Volcanisme intraplaque

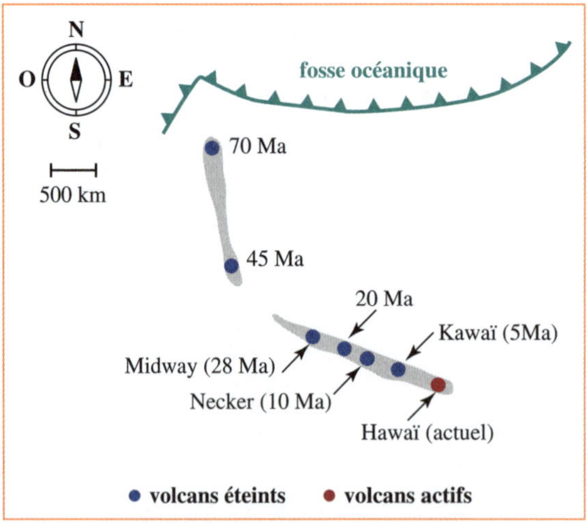

Alignement volcanique d'Hawaï

1. Déterminez le sens et la direction du mouvement de la plaque Pacifique de 70 à 45 Ma puis de 28 Ma à nos jours.

2. Calculez la vitesse de déplacement de la plaque Pacifique sur les 5 derniers millions d'années.

→ Corrigé p. 130

10 30 min ★★★ GPS

Stations	Latitude (°)	Longitude (°)	Vitesse de déplacement en latitude ($cm.an^{-1}$)	Vitesse de déplacement en longitude ($cm.an^{-1}$)	Vitesse globale ($cm.an^{-1}$)
HAWAI	19,53 N	–155,68 W	+3,07	–6,03	69,61
TOKYO	40 N	+140 E	–1,4	+1,2	27,28

Figure 1 *Coordonnées de deux stations GPS*

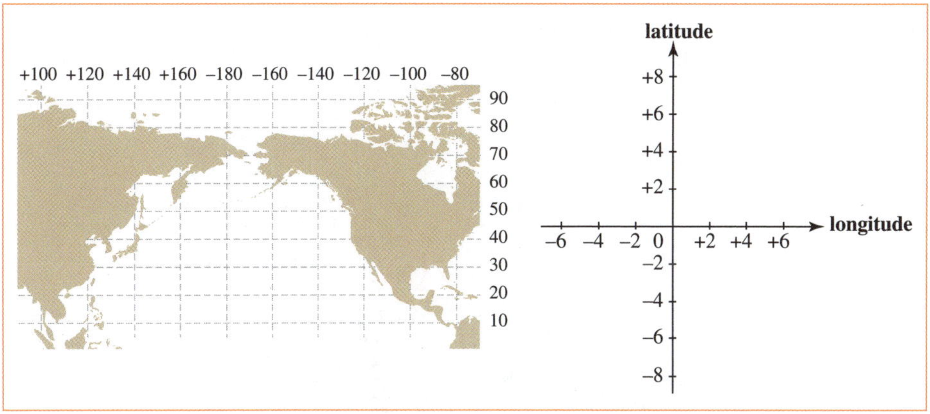

Figure 2 *Carte de l'océan Pacifique et graphique de coordonnées GPS*

1. Placez les stations GPS de Tokyo et d'Hawaï sur la carte de la figure 2 grâce à leurs coordonnées de latitude et de longitude.

2. Tracez les vecteurs GPS des deux stations de Tokyo et d'Hawaï sur la figure 2 à l'aide des vitesses de déplacement en latitude et longitude. Reportez-les sur la carte.

3. Déduisez-en le mouvement réalisé par les plaques lithosphériques pacifique et japonaise.

→ Corrigé p. 130

CONTRÔLE CONTINU POUR LE BAC

Exercice 10 pts Évolution de la lithosphère océanique 30 min

On étudie le mécanisme à l'origine de la tombée en subduction de la lithosphère océanique. On prend l'exemple de la plaque lithosphérique Juan de Fuca au large de la Californie.

À l'aide de l'ensemble des documents et de vos connaissances, expliquez l'évolution de la lithosphère océanique, de sa création à sa disparition, en prenant l'exemple de la plaque Juan de Fuca.

Document 1

En 1965, des expéditions sondent le fond des océans et dressent des cartes des anomalies magnétiques le long de la plaque Juan de Fuca.

Les anomalies positives, représentées par des bandes colorées, se sont formées à une époque où le champ magnétique était dans la même polarité qu'à l'actuel, alors que les anomalies négatives, figurées par des bandes blanches, correspondent à une époque où le champ magnétique était dans une polarité inverse à l'actuel.

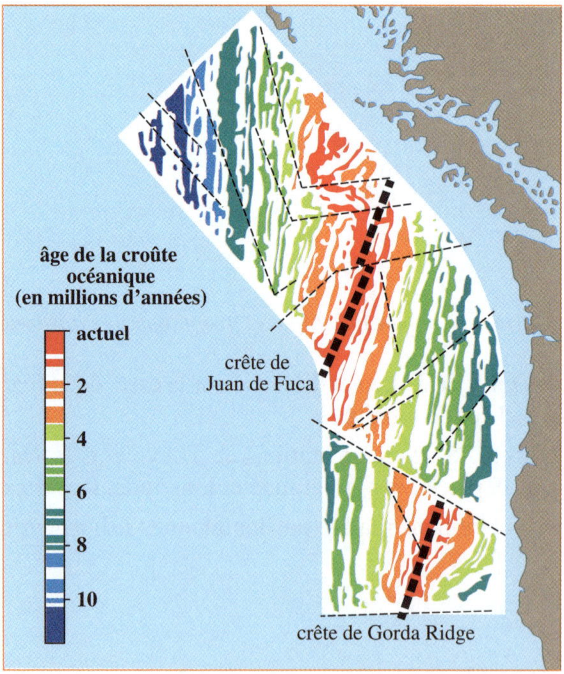

Figure en peau de zèbre de la plaque Juan de Fuca

Document 2

Le flux de chaleur correspond à l'énergie thermique libérée par unité de surface. On peut la mesurer tout le long de la lithosphère océanique.

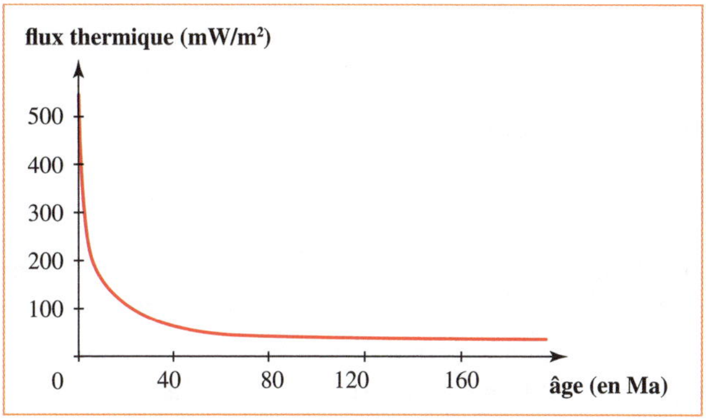

Flux de chaleur de la lithosphère océanique en fonction de son âge

Document 3

Des relevés bathymétriques permettent de mesurer la profondeur des fonds océaniques. On fait le parallèle avec l'âge de la lithosphère océanique.

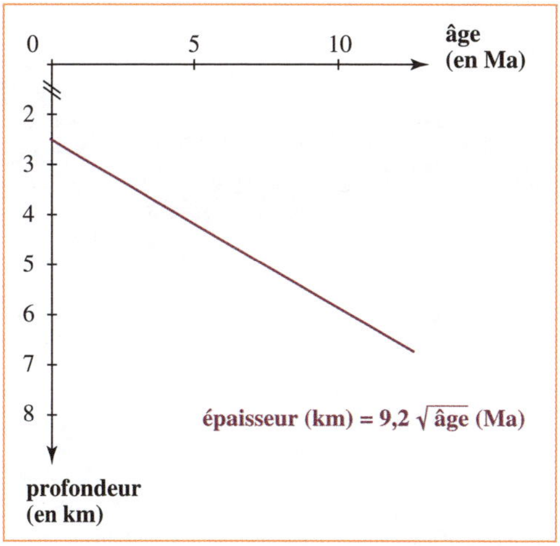

Évolution de la profondeur et de l'épaisseur de la lithosphère océanique en fonction de son âge

→ Corrigé p. 131

CORRIGÉS

1 → *Énoncé p. 121*

Les affirmations exactes sont a), c) et d).

2 → *Énoncé p. 121*

Les affirmations exactes sont a) et d).

3 → *Énoncé p. 121*

Les basaltes, lors de leur refroidissement, enregistrent le champ magnétique et les caractéristiques de l'époque de leur formation : c'est la mémoire magnétique.

On enregistre ainsi des anomalies qui coïncident avec l'échelle des inversions du champ magnétique. Les anomalies sont d'autant plus âgées qu'elles s'éloignent de l'axe de la dorsale de façon symétrique. On peut donc en déduire que la dorsale est le lieu de production des basaltes et que les nouveaux basaltes formés « poussent » les anciens : c'est l'expansion océanique.

4 → *Énoncé p. 121*

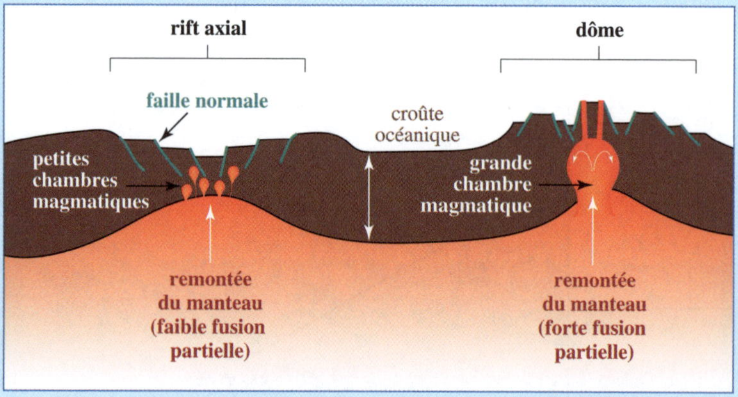

5 → *Énoncé p. 122*

1. La granodiorite est entièrement cristallisée : les minéraux sont cohésifs entre eux et il n'y a pas de verre volcanique (pâte volcanique sans minéraux cristallisés). La roche s'est donc formée en profondeur grâce à un refroidissement lent : c'est une roche plutonique.

2. Dans cette roche sont présents des minéraux hydroxylés comme les amphiboles. C'est donc une roche plutonique issue de la minéralisation d'un magma hydraté caractéristique d'une zone de subduction : c'est donc un contexte de convergence.

3. Au niveau d'une zone de subduction, la lithosphère océanique hydratée lors de l'hydrothermalisme subit des transformations minéralogiques : les minéraux métamorphiques se déshydratent et l'eau libérée migre dans la lithosphère chevauchante, abaissant le point de fusion de la péridotite. Le magma se forme alors et remonte dans la croûte, car moins dense.

6 → *Énoncé p. 122*

1. Océan Atlantique-Nord : $v = \frac{d}{t} = \frac{(30 - 10) \times 10^5}{(3 - 1) \times 10^6} = 1$ cm.an soit pour la dorsale complète qui produit des basaltes des deux côtés (vers l'ouest et l'est) : $v = 2$ cm.an.

Océan Est-Pacifique : $v = \frac{d}{t} = \frac{(110 - 40) \times 10^5}{(3 - 1) \times 10^6} = 3{,}5$ cm.an soit pour la dorsale complète $v = 7$ cm.an.

2. La dorsale Est-Pacifique présente une vitesse d'accrétion supérieure à 6 cm/an, c'est donc une dorsale rapide alors que la dorsale Atlantique est lente.

3. New-York et Paris sont séparés par la dorsale Atlantique qui présente une vitesse de 2 cm/an. En 1789, il y a 230 ans, les deux villes étaient plus proches de : $230 \times 2 = 460$ cm soit 4,6 mètres.

7 → *Énoncé p. 123*

1. Le foyer du séisme de 2015 est situé à 10 km de profondeur et à 100 km depuis l'origine du profil sismique.

2. Ce séisme se situe sur une faille presque horizontale et longue de plus de 150 km. Le bloc rocheux nord « monte » sur celui du dessous, situé plus au sud : c'est une nappe de charriage.

3. Ce chevauchement se forme en contexte de convergence et plus particulièrement lors de la subduction continentale ou collision. Dans le cas de l'Himalaya, ce chevauchement s'appelle le MCT.

8 → *Énoncé p. 124*

1. Pour provoquer la fusion de la péridotite, il faut que le géotherme franchisse son solidus. Pour cela, on observe deux possibilités : soit le géotherme est élevé grâce à une décompression du manteau (cas ①), soit le solidus de la péridotite est rabaissé grâce à son hydratation (cas ②).

2. La décompression du manteau est caractéristique d'une remontée mantellique rapide dans un contexte de divergence, au niveau des dorsales. L'hydratation de la péridotite est, elle, caractéristique des zones de subduction et donc d'un contexte de convergence.

9 → *Énoncé p. 124*

1. D'après l'alignement volcanique, on observe que, de 70 à 45 Ma, la plaque Pacifique s'est déplacée vers le Nord-Ouest puis à partir de 28 Ma, elle se déplace davantage vers l'Ouest. Elle a donc subi un changement de direction entre 45 et 28 Ma.

2. $v = \dfrac{d}{t} = \dfrac{(0{,}5 \times 500/0{,}6) \times 10^5}{5 \times 10^6} = 8{,}3\ \text{cm.an}^{-1}$

10 → *Énoncé p. 125*

1 et **2.**

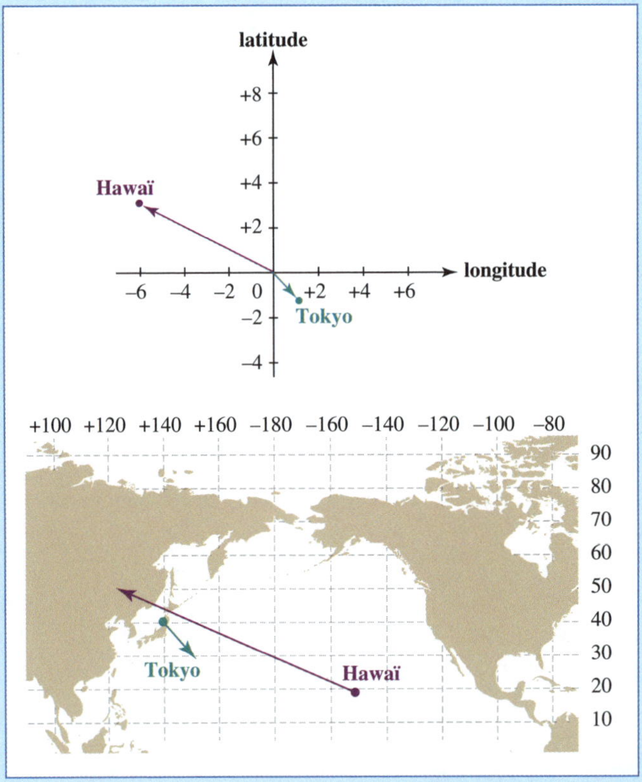

3. On observe que les vecteurs GPS convergent l'un vers l'autre : celui de la station de Tokyo est dirigé vers le sud-est alors que celui de la plaque Pacifique Nord est dirigé vers le nord-est. C'est donc un contexte de convergence.

CONTRÔLE CONTINU POUR LE BAC

Exercice → Énoncé p. 126

La lithosphère océanique au large de la Californie est étudiée en raison de son activité sismique importante et de la recherche d'hydrocarbures. **Comment se forme et vieillit une lithosphère océanique ?**

Au niveau de l'axe de la dorsale Juan de Fuca, on observe que les basaltes les plus récents se forment. Plus on s'éloigne vers l'ouest ou l'est, plus les basaltes sont âgés et se répartissent de façon symétrique de part et d'autre de la dorsale. La lithosphère océanique est donc produite au niveau de l'axe des dorsales : c'est l'accrétion océanique.

En s'éloignant de cet axe, la lithosphère océanique se refroidit. En effet, on observe une décroissance exponentielle du flux thermique en fonction de l'âge de la lithosphère : la lithosphère océanique refroidit donc plus elle vieillit. Or la plaque lithosphérique de Juan de Fuca est âgée de 10 Ma vers l'Ouest : peut-elle entrer en subduction ?

Cet âge correspond à un flux thermique d'environ 150 $mW.m^{-2}$ ce qui semble assez élevé.

De plus, plus la lithosphère est âgée, plus sa profondeur est importante. En effet, le refroidissement de la lithosphère océanique approfondit la LVZ et donc augmente l'épaisseur de la lithosphère. Ceci entraîne son enfoncement dans le manteau asthénosphérique. Pour la plaque de Juan de Fuca, âgée de 10 Ma sur son flanc Ouest, la profondeur de la lithosphère est de 6 km pour une épaisseur totale de 29 km d'après la formule donnée dans l'énoncé.

La plaque Juan de Fuca n'est donc pas entrée en subduction : la lithosphère est surement trop jeune et pas assez dense ou alors il existe des forces qui empêchent sa tombée en subduction.

Les écosystèmes : des interactions dynamiques

CHAPITRE 9

La biodiversité, ou diversité du vivant, présente différents aspects : la diversité allélique au sein d'une population d'individus de même espèce, la diversité spécifique (des espèces) et la diversité des écosystèmes.

1 Structure des écosystèmes

A. La définition d'un écosystème

■ Un **écosystème*** est un ensemble d'êtres vivants, la **biocénose***, en interaction entre eux et avec leur milieu, le **biotope***.

> **Remarque**
> Le mot écosystème vient du grec « oîkos » qui signifie « maison ».

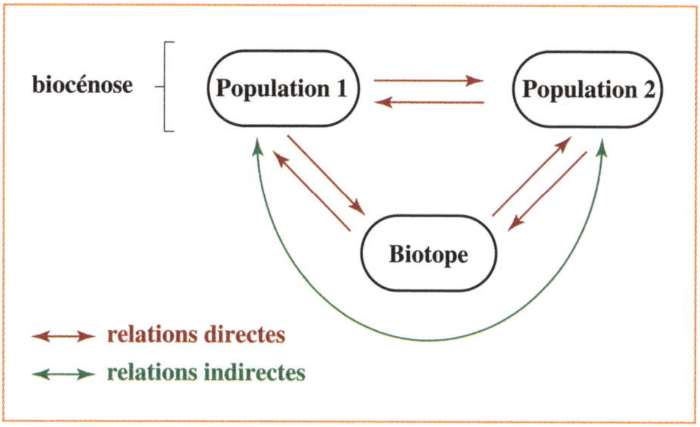

Figure 1 *Les composants d'un écosystème*

■ Les conditions physico-chimiques (**conditions abiotiques***) du milieu constituent les caractéristiques du biotope : ce sont l'humidité, la luminosité, le pH…

■ Les espèces se répartissent selon ces conditions du milieu. Par exemple, une forêt présente certaines conditions abiotiques (humidité, pH, température, ensoleillement) qui permettent à un ensemble d'êtres vivants particuliers de coexister. Ceux-ci interagissent entre eux au sein de **relations interspécifiques*** (entre espèces différentes).

Dans cette forêt, un arbre constitue lui aussi un écosystème à part entière : le tronc et les racines notamment peuvent être le refuge d'oiseaux, de larves d'insectes, de mammifères, etc. Si on augmente encore le grossissement, un mammifère vivant dans cet arbre abrite une flore intestinale très diversifiée (bactéries, virus, ciliés, levures). Un écosystème présente donc une grande diversité d'échelles.

■ Il existe une grande **diversité des écosystèmes**, au-delà des différences d'échelles, lorsqu'on fait varier les conditions abiotiques. On trouve par exemple l'écosystème montagnard qui est caractérisé par une altitude élevée avec présence d'une température faible et de vent desséchant ; l'écosystème urbain, influencé par les constructions humaines ; l'écosystème récifal, dont les exigences de pH et de température des coraux le rendent très fragile au changement climatique, etc.

B. Les interactions au sein d'un écosystème

■ Les relations interspécifiques sont les interactions qui ont lieu entre les espèces présentes au sein d'un écosystème. Elles sont diverses et peuvent évoluer au fil du temps.

Type d'interaction	Espèce A	Espèce B
Compétition	–	–
Prédation	+	–
Mutualisme	+	+
Parasitisme	+	–

Figure 2 *Tableau comparatif des différentes relations interspécifiques*

■ On différencie les relations interspécifiques par leurs effets sur la **valeur sélective*** (ou **fitness**) des individus impliqués. En effet, tout comportement adopté par un individu ou tout allèle qu'il possède peuvent lui conférer un avantage sélectif et augmenter ses chances relatives de survie et de reproduction dans un environnement donné. Certaines relations augmentent la valeur sélective de l'un des partenaires mais diminuent celle de l'autre : c'est le cas des **relations par exploitation**, reposant souvent sur la recherche de nourriture :
- la **prédation*** constitue ainsi le fait de se nourrir d'un autre être vivant ;
- le **parasitisme*** ressemble à la prédation en ceci qu'elle bénéficie à l'un des partenaires mais est néfaste à l'autre : la différence réside dans la durée du lien entre les espèces (plus durable et obligatoire dans le cas du parasitisme) ;

– la **compétition*** repose sur la lutte indirecte (par exploitation) ou directe (par interférence) pour les mêmes ressources. Deux espèces ne peuvent ainsi pas coexister dans la même **niche écologique*** (ensemble des conditions biologique et physicochimique dans lesquelles vit une espèce) : elles s'excluent par définition.

■ D'autres interactions permettent d'augmenter la valeur sélective des deux partenaires : le **mutualisme*** constitue ainsi l'ensemble des relations à bénéfices réciproques. Dans le cas particulier où cette association est obligatoire (les espèces ne peuvent vivre l'une sans l'autre), le mutualisme est appelé **symbiose***.

2 L'équilibre dynamique des écosystèmes

A. Le fonctionnement d'un écosystème

■ Un écosystème reçoit de l'énergie externe (solaire dans la majorité des cas) et de la matière (eau par les racines, gaz atmosphériques…). À partir de ces entrées d'énergie et de matière, les **producteurs primaires*** vont produire de la matière organique grâce à la **photosynthèse***. Ils transforment donc une énergie physique (énergie lumineuse) en énergie chimique (molécules organiques) et produisent de la **biomasse***. Cette matière va ensuite être transformée tout au long de la chaîne alimentaire par les **consommateurs*** (primaires puis secondaires) qui réalisent notamment la **respiration*** : il y a ainsi des **flux de matière*** dans les écosystèmes. C'est le **réseau trophique***.

Rappel

Les molécules organiques sont des molécules produites par les êtres vivants. Elles sont constituées majoritairement de carbone, d'hydrogène, d'oxygène et d'azote.

■ Des sorties de matière et d'énergie ont lieu tout au long de ce réseau trophique par évapotranspiration (perte en eau des végétaux au niveau de leurs parties aériennes et souterraines), excrétion (formation d'urine) et déjections.

■ Une partie de la matière organique morte est ensuite recyclée, notamment grâce au sol et aux **décomposeurs***. Les micro-organismes du sol transforment la matière organique morte en matière minérale (voir *figure 3*, p. 136).

■ Un écosystème naturel est donc un cycle géochimique équilibré : il est caractérisé par autant d'entrées que de sorties.

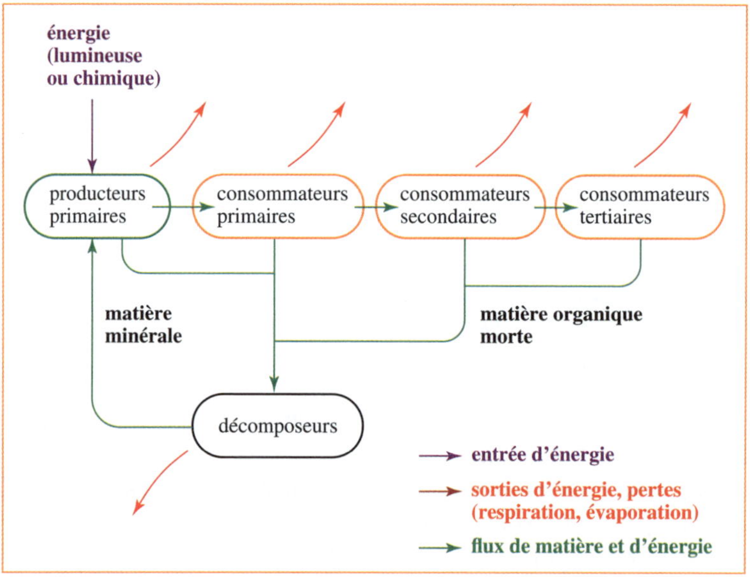

Figure 3 *Fonctionnement d'un écosystème*

B. L'évolution dynamique des écosystèmes

■ L'Homme peut perturber le fonctionnement des écosystèmes en modifiant les habitats des espèces animales ou en polluant l'environnement.

■ Un exemple de modification des habitats est la transformation des écosystèmes dans un but agricole : ce sont les **agrosystèmes***. La biocénose y est réduite à une seule espèce et c'est l'Homme qui contrôle le biotope en modifiant les entrées de matière (irrigation et engrais) et les sorties (récoltes de la matière organique).

■ Cependant, même sans action de l'Homme, les écosystèmes peuvent être perturbés. C'est le cas des incendies et des maladies qui peuvent affecter les populations.

■ Plus un écosystème possède une biocénose complexe et diverse, plus sa capacité à retrouver son état initial après la perturbation est forte : c'est la **résilience*** (voir *figure 4* p. 137).

■ Un écosystème se caractérise donc par un équilibre dynamique susceptible d'être bousculé par des perturbations internes et externes. Il évoluera ensuite de façon prévisible et ordonnée jusqu'à l'installation d'une biocénose finale.

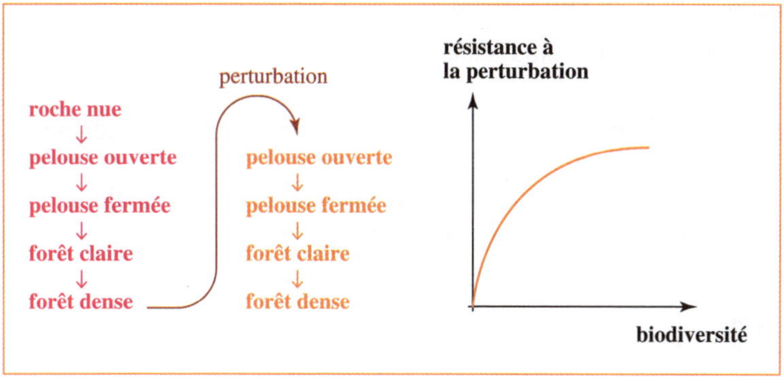

Figure 4 *Résilience des écosystèmes*

EXERCICES

Connaître le cours

1 2 min ★ Vrai ou Faux ?

Relevez la (ou les) affirmation(s) exacte(s).

Un écosystème :

a) est un ensemble d'êtres vivants en interactions entre eux et avec leur environnement.
b) évolue peu au cours du temps.
c) repose sur la diversité des espèces mais aussi leur diversité allélique.
d) est perturbé essentiellement par l'Homme.

→ *Corrigé p. 147*

2 2 min ★ Vrai ou Faux ?

Relevez la (ou les) affirmation(s) exacte(s).

Les relations interspécifiques :

a) reposent sur des interactions alimentaires uniquement.
b) peuvent être à bénéfices réciproques ou néfastes pour les partenaires.
c) n'évoluent pas au cours du temps.

→ *Corrigé p. 147*

3 5 min ★ Restitution de connaissances

Expliquez brièvement comment les relations à bénéfices réciproques permettent d'améliorer les valeurs sélectives des espèces.

→ *Corrigé p. 147*

4 5 min ★ Schématiser le cours

Schématisez les flux d'énergie et de matière dans un écosystème.

→ *Corrigé p. 147*

S'entraîner

5 10 min ★★ Pyramide des biomasses

La biomasse est la quantité de matière vivant à un moment donné. On la calcule en « poids frais ».

Niveau trophique	Exemple d'espèce	Biomasse produite (en tonnes par an)
Producteur primaire	Phytoplancton	4 200 000 000
Consommateur primaire	Zooplancton	64 000 000 000
Consommateur secondaire	Poissons planctoniques	1 000 000 000
Consommateur tertiaire	Poissons carnivores	150 000 000
Superprédateur	Thon	20 000 000

Biomasse produite par niveau trophique dans un écosystème aquatique

1. Représentez une pyramide des biomasses à partir du tableau ci-dessus.

2. Calculez le rendement entre les deux derniers niveaux trophiques (consommateur tertiaire et superprédateur), c'est-à-dire la production d'un niveau trophique divisée par la production du niveau trophique inférieur.

→ Corrigé p. 148

6 10 min ★★ Le cycle court du carbone

Réservoirs de carbone à replacer (Gt)	Formes du carbone à replacer	Flux de carbone à replacer
Atmosphère (770) Hydrosphère (39 000) Biosphère (610) Lithosphère (50 005 000)	CO_2 HCO_3^- molécules organiques (2 fois sur le schéma)	photosynthèse décomposition partielle volcanisme et combustion érosion respiration

Les différents réservoirs de carbone

1. Reproduisez le schéma de la page suivante et représentez les différents réservoirs de carbone dans ce cycle court ainsi que la quantité de carbone qu'ils renferment.

2. Indiquez sur ce même schéma, dans chaque réservoir, sous quelle forme est présent le carbone.

3. Légendez (au niveau des flèches) les différents flux de carbone entre ces réservoirs.

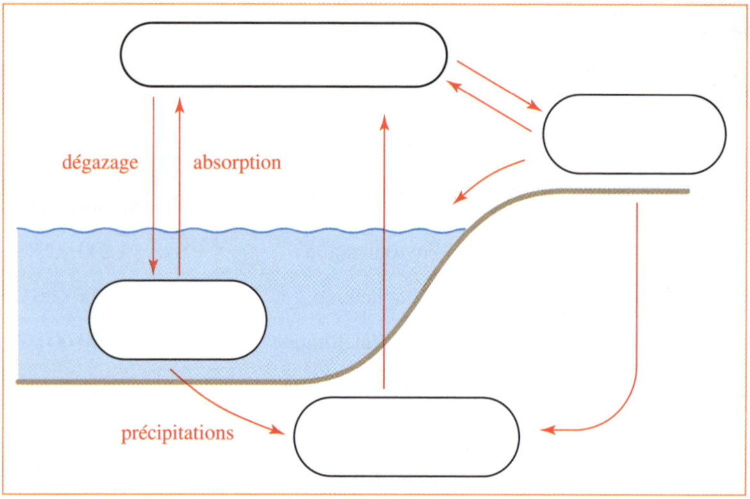

→ *Corrigé p. 148*

7 15 min ★★ La pollution des sols

Lors d'étés chauds, certaines plages de Bretagne sont envahies d'algues vertes dont le pourrissement laisse échapper une odeur d'œuf pourri et des gaz toxiques. Certains scientifiques suspectent les élevages porcins des environs ainsi que l'épandage de nitrates dans les champs d'être responsables de cette marée verte.

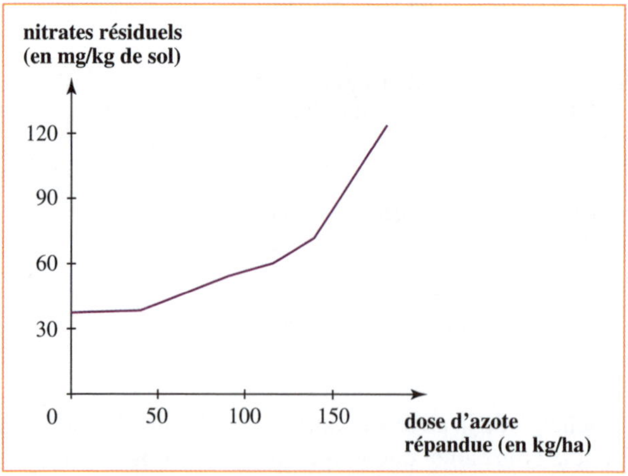

Figure 1 *Quantité de nitrates résiduels en fonction de la dose répandue dans les champs de pomme de terre*

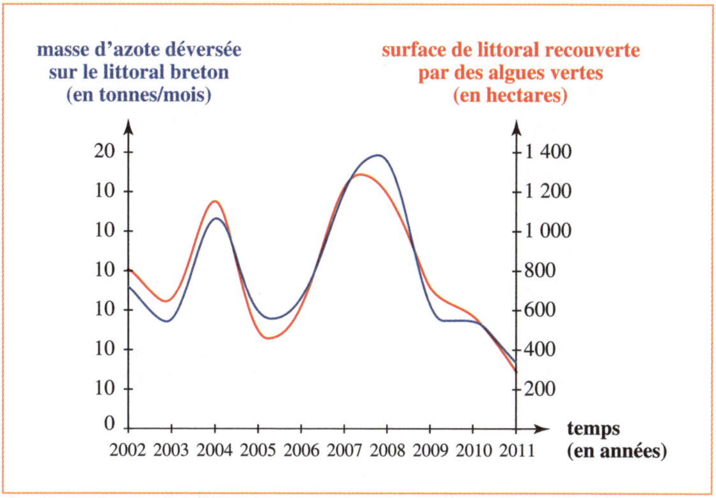

Figure 2 *Lien entre la concentration de nitrates déversés et la quantité d'algues vertes*

1. D'après la figure 1, montrez comment l'apport d'azote par les agriculteurs dans leurs champs de pomme de terre pourrait se retrouver dans les sols puis les nappes phréatiques.

2. Faites le lien entre les marées vertes et la quantité d'azote déversée sur le littoral d'après la figure 2.

→ *Corrigé p. 148*

8 15 min ★★ Les lapins australiens

En 1859, six lapins d'Europe furent introduits par un amateur de chasse en Australie. En 1909, ils étaient 600 millions à ravager les prairies australiennes.

En 1950, le virus de la myxomatose fut introduit par les scientifiques australiens et décima 80 % des lapins. À cause de la sélection naturelle, les lapins sont devenus peu sensibles à ce virus et le sont toujours actuellement.

Les scientifiques ont donc pensé à une alternative et cherchent à introduire dans l'environnement un prédateur naturel du lapin : le renard.

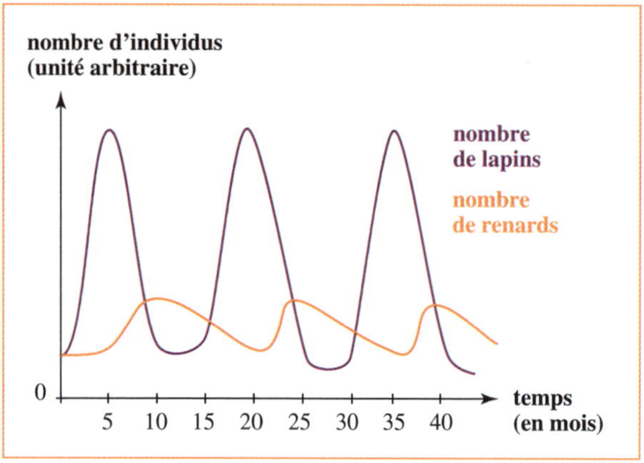

Dynamique des populations de lapins et de renards

1. D'après le graphique modélisant l'évolution des populations de lapin et de renard, expliquez si l'introduction de ces derniers en Australie serait judicieuse pour réguler la population de lapins.

2. Sachant que des marsupiaux comme les wallabies sont aussi des proies du renard, prévoyez les effets secondaires de l'introduction des renards en Australie.

→ *Corrigé p. 149*

9 15 min ★★ Les relations interspécifiques

Certaines fourmis vivent en étroite collaboration avec les pucerons : elles leur caressent le dos et extraient ainsi une goutte de miellat (substance sucrée produite par les intestins des pucerons) aussitôt aspirée.

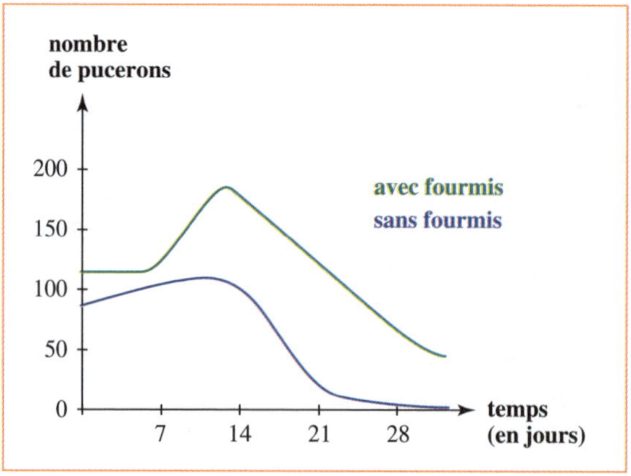

Figure 1 *Évolution des populations de pucerons en présence ou non de fourmis*

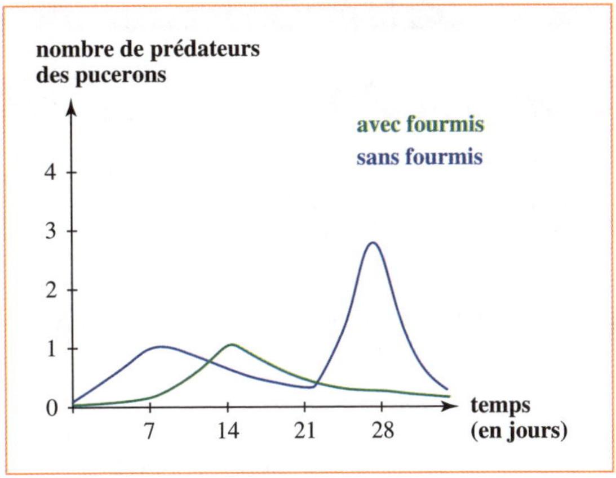

Figure 2 *Évolution des prédateurs des pucerons en présence ou en l'absence de fourmis*

1. D'après le graphique de la figure 1, montrez que la présence de fourmis est bénéfique pour la population de pucerons. Quel est le type de relation interspécifique présentée ici ?

2. D'après la figure 2, expliquez quels bénéfices les pucerons tirent de leur relation avec les fourmis.

3. Schématisez les échanges réalisés entre les fourmis et les pucerons.

→ *Corrigé p. 149*

CONTRÔLE CONTINU POUR LE BAC

Exercice 10 pts **Symbiose Rhizobium/Fabacées** 30 min

La permaculture et la rotation des cultures sont des techniques consistant à associer différents végétaux dans l'espace (permaculture) ou dans le temps (rotation) afin de limiter l'ajout d'engrais et de pesticides dans les écosystèmes.

À l'aide de l'ensemble des documents, expliquez l'importance de planter des Fabacées (petits pois, haricots…) lors de la rotation des cultures.

Document 1

Certaines plantes, comme les Fabacées (petits pois, trèfle, luzerne…), possèdent au niveau de leurs racines une structure particulière : les nodosités. À l'intérieur de ces nodosités, vivent des bactéries du genre Rhizobium incorporées dans leurs cellules. Le lien entre les Fabacées et les bactéries type Rhizobium est appelé « mycorhize ».On veut connaître la nature de la relation entre ces bactéries et les Fabacées.

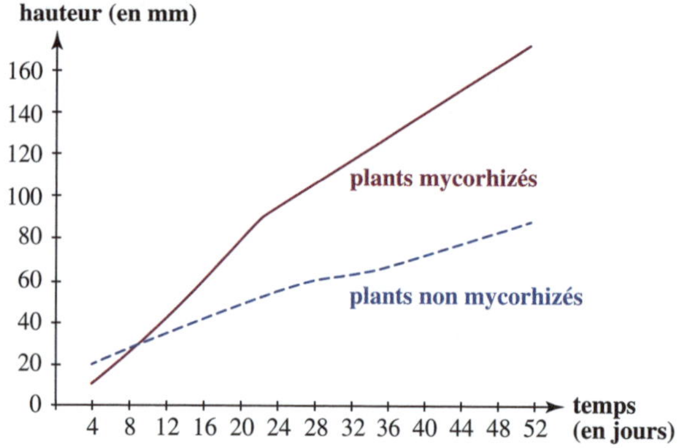

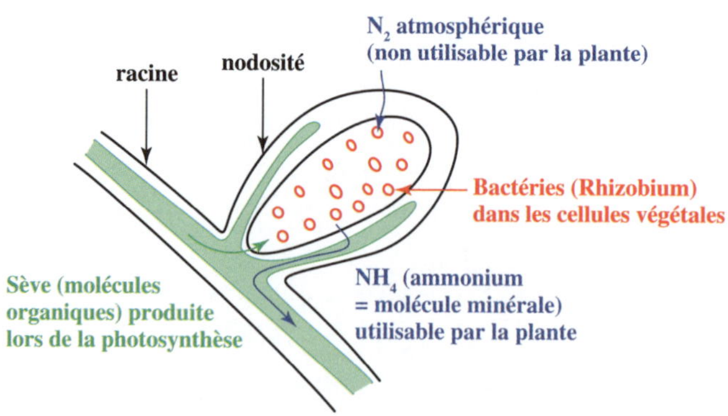

Symbiose Rhizobium/Fabacées

Document 2

L'azote est le quatrième élément le plus important dans la biomasse. Il est constitutif des protéines, des acides aminés, ainsi que des nucléotides. Comme tout élément minéral, il subit des transformations entre des réservoirs de stockage au cours d'un cycle.

La fixation de l'azote atmosphérique, N_2, en azote minéral utilisable pour les plantes ne se fait pas spontanément. Elle nécessite la présence d'êtres vivants. Certains sont les bactéries du genre Rhizobium, présents dans les nodosités des Fabacées. Ces bactéries réalisent la réaction suivante grâce à une enzyme, la nitrogénase :

$$N_2 + 6\ e^-(\text{électrons}) + 8\ H^+ + \text{énergie} \rightarrow 2\ NH_4^+$$

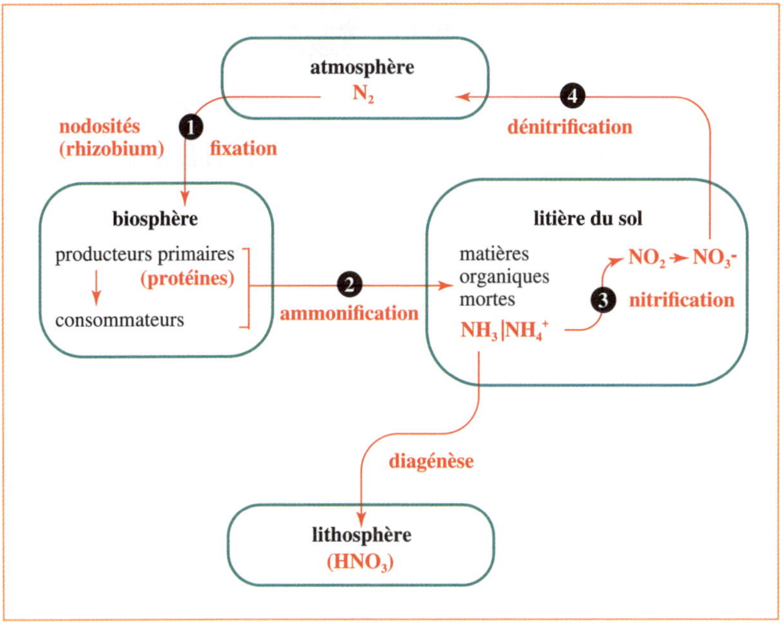

Cycle court de l'azote

Document 3

L'azote sous forme ammonium NH_4+ est assimilable par les plantes pour produire leur matière organique (protéines par exemple). Cependant, on se demande si l'azote atmosphérique fixé par les nodosités des Fabacées est bénéfique pour le sol (est-il produit en excès par Rhizobium ?).

On calcule donc le rendement d'un même champ de blé en regardant le type de culture qui l'a précédé sur le même emplacement. Si la croissance est forte, cela signifie que le sol a été enrichi naturellement en éléments minéraux, notamment l'ammonium.

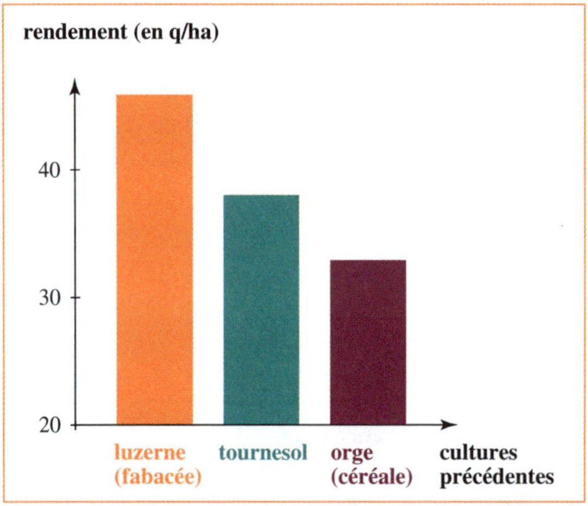

Rendement du blé en fonction de la précédente culture utilisée

→ *Corrigé p. 150*

CORRIGÉS

1 → *Énoncé p. 138*

Les affirmations exactes sont a) et c).

2 → *Énoncé p. 138*

Les affirmations exactes sont b) et c).

3 → *Énoncé p. 138*

Les relations de mutualisme permettent à chaque partenaire d'améliorer leurs valeurs sélectives. En effet, elles reposent sur des échanges à bénéfices réciproques. Prenons l'exemple du poisson clown vivant dans les anémones : l'anémone fournit protection au poisson clown contre des prédateurs alors que celui-ci lui fournit les restes de ses repas. Il peut aussi, en se frottant à la base de l'anémone, s'enduire d'une substance lui permettant d'éviter les cellules urticantes. Ainsi les deux partenaires présentent une meilleure survie et donc un meilleur taux de reproduction que s'ils vivaient séparément.

4 → *Énoncé p. 138*

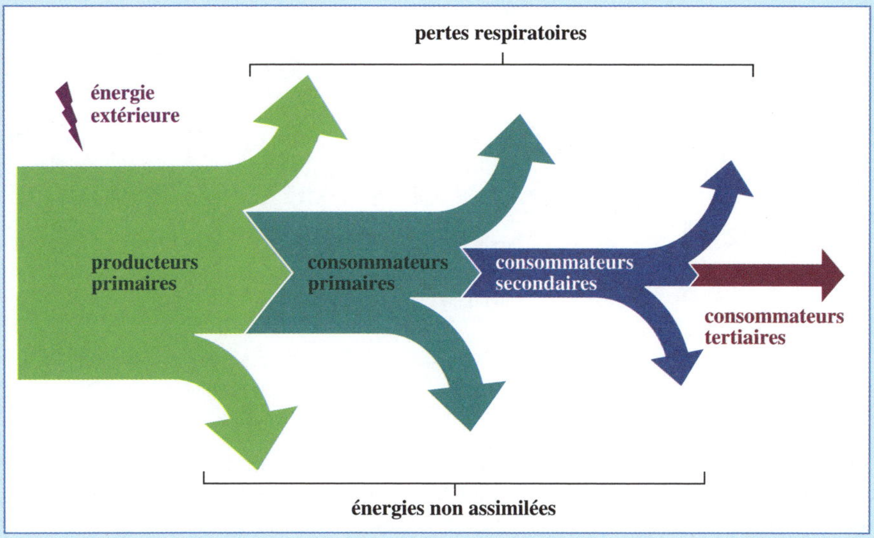

5 → *Énoncé p. 139*

1.

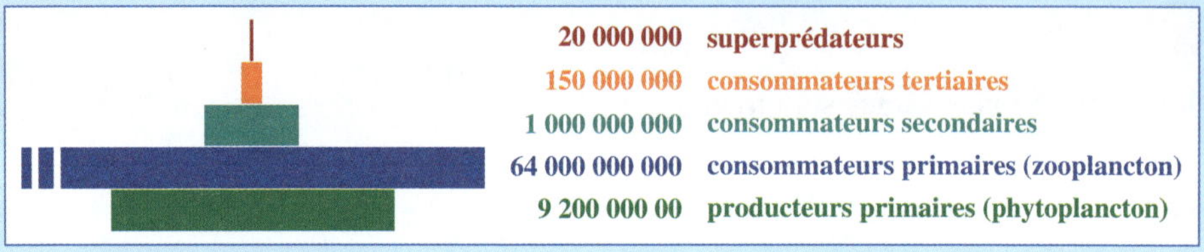

2. $R = \dfrac{20\,000\,000}{150\,000\,000} = 0{,}13$

Le rendement entre le niveau des consommateurs tertiaires et des superprédateurs est de 13 %. Il y a donc eu une perte de matière d'environ 67 %. Cette perte s'explique par l'excrétion, les déjections et la respiration.

6 → *Énoncé p. 139*

1., **2.** et **3.**

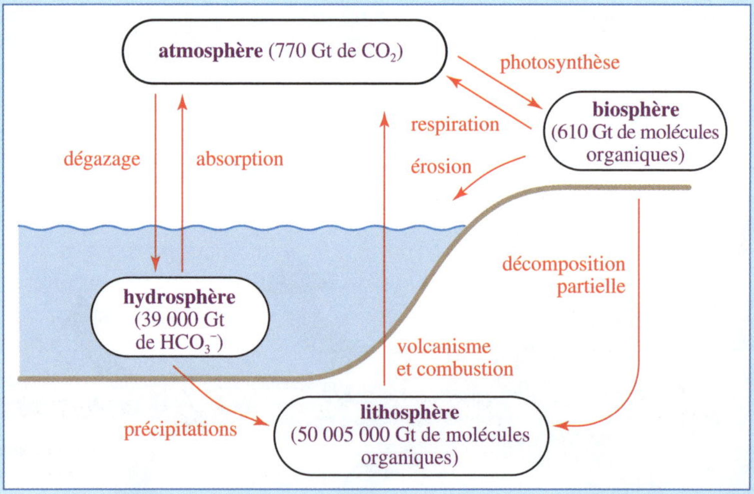

7 → *Énoncé p. 140*

1. On observe que plus la dose d'azote répandue est importante, plus la quantité de nitrates résiduels retrouvés dans les sols augmente. En effet, les végétaux absorbent l'azote des engrais par leurs racines. Cependant si l'azote est apporté en trop grande quantité, les végétaux cultivés ne l'assimilent plus et il reste dans le sol. Par lessivage on peut supposer que ce nitrate va se retrouver dans les nappes phréatiques et les rivières.

2. On observe une corrélation entre la dose de nitrate déversée et la surface recouverte par les algues vertes sur le littoral breton. En effet, en 2004 et 2008, entre 25 et

35 tonnes d'azote ont été déversées et en parallèle on observe un pic de la quantité d'algues vertes entre 1 100 et 1 300 hectares de littoral recouverts.

On peut donc supposer qu'il existe un lien entre l'agriculture et l'épandage important d'engrais à base de nitrates. L'excès de nitrate du sol est lessivé jusqu'au littoral où d'autres végétaux vont l'utiliser pour réaliser leur photosynthèse et donc proliférer : les algues vertes.

8 → *Énoncé p. 141*

1. D'après le graphique, on observe que l'évolution des populations de renards et de lapins est cyclique : quand les renards voient leur nombre diminuer, la population de lapin augmente (il y a moins de prédateurs, ils se reproduisent donc davantage). Or, quand la population de renards augmente, celle des lapins, davantage chassés, diminue. C'est un cycle proie-prédateur. On peut donc supposer qu'introduire des renards dans les prairies australiennes pour réguler les populations de lapins pourrait diminuer cycliquement et temporairement leur prolifération.

2. Les renards chassent aussi les wallabies. On peut donc supposer que l'introduction d'espèces non australiennes comme le renard pourrait déséquilibrer l'écosystème et entraîner une diminution de la biodiversité locale en affectant les populations de wallabies.

9 → *Énoncé p. 142*

1. On observe que les pucerons sont globalement plus nombreux quand ils sont mis en présence de fourmis (une centaine d'individus en plus au 14e jour). Les fourmis pourraient donc permettre aux pucerons d'augmenter leurs valeurs sélectives en échange de leur don de miellat. Cette situation ressemble donc à une relation interspécifique de type mutualisme.

2. Sans fourmis, le nombre de prédateurs des pucerons est plus élevé que lorsque les fourmis sont présentes. On peut supposer que les fourmis défendent les pucerons contre les prédateurs et permettent ainsi aux pucerons une meilleure survie.

3.

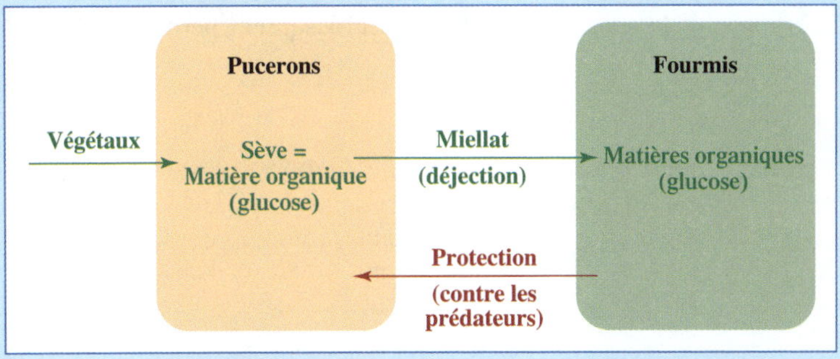

Exercice → Énoncé p. 144

Comment l'implantation de Fabacées dans les champs peut-il être bénéfique aux cultures suivantes ?

Les plantes de type Fabacées possédant des nodosités où vivent les bactéries Rhizobium ont une meilleure croissance : au bout de 50 jours, la hauteur de ces plants a doublé par rapport à un plant qui n'est pas en interaction avec les bactéries.

On peut donc supposer que l'association de ces deux espèces permet d'augmenter la valeur sélective des Fabacées.

Par ailleurs, on observe que Rhizobium vit dans les cellules racinaires des Fabacées, au contact de la sève et donc des matières organiques produites par la photosynthèse du végétal. Rhizobium tire donc un bénéfice de cette relation en absorbant de la matière organique nécessaire à sa respiration.

De plus, Rhizobium est capable de fixer l'azote atmosphérique et donc de produire des éléments minéraux pour la Fabacée. On peut donc dire que cette relation est à bénéfices réciproques entre les deux protagonistes : c'est une symbiose.

Cette symbiose constitue une part importante du cycle de l'azote car les nodosités permettent la fixation de l'azote atmosphérique et la production de matière minérale de type ammonium. Cela est permis par la présence d'une enzyme chez Rhizobium : la nitrogénase. Cette étape permet le transfert de l'azote entre deux réservoirs : l'atmosphère et la biosphère.

De plus, on observe que cette symbiose permet au sol de s'enrichir en azote : elle n'est pas bénéfique qu'à la Fabacée. L'ammonium produit en excès par cette symbiose est retrouvé dans le sol et il sera utilisé par les plantations suivantes comme le blé. Celui-ci connait ainsi 12 % à 15 % de rendement supplémentaire lors d'une rotation des cultures faisant suite à un champ de Fabacées symbiotiques plutôt qu'à d'autres plantations.

On peut donc conclure que la symbiose entre le Rhizobium et les Fabacées permet de fixer l'azote atmosphérique en ammonium, ce qui permet aux végétaux une meilleure croissance et enrichit le sol en azote. Cet enrichissement permet de limiter l'apport d'engrais.

L'humanité et les écosystèmes

CHAPITRE 10

La biodiversité, définie par la conférence de Rio en 1992, subit actuellement un déclin important affectant le fonctionnement des écosystèmes. La cause principale en est l'activité humaine.

1 L'action de l'Homme sur les écosystèmes

A. La place de l'Homme dans les écosystèmes

■ L'espèce humaine est un élément parmi d'autres de tous les écosystèmes qu'elle a colonisés. Elle fait partie de la biocénose et y interagit avec d'autres espèces.

■ En effet, l'Homme est impliqué dans des relations interspécifiques comme le **parasitisme** et le **commensalisme**, mais il peut aussi influencer le reste de la biocénose en exploitant les autres espèces ou en les modifiant par la **domestication**.

■ Au sein d'un écosystème, l'Homme se situe au niveau des consommateurs primaires (régime végétarien) ou secondaires (régime omnivore), voire des superprédateurs. Il peut cependant subir aussi des relations diminuant sa valeur sélective comme le parasitisme et prendre alors la place d'un hôte parasité.

Ex. : Le *Taenia* (ou ver solitaire) se nourrit des nutriments intestinaux et peut entraîner une perte de poids chez l'homme parasité. Les œufs produits dans les excréments vont alors contaminer un hôte intermédiaire, le porc, où des kystes se logeront dans ses muscles. En cas d'ingestion de viande contaminée, les kystes libéreront le parasite et le cycle parasitaire reprendra.

■ Dans certains cas, les espèces retirent un bénéfice de leur interaction avec l'Homme mais sans affecter sa valeur sélective : c'est le **commensalisme***. La présence de blattes, de rats, de pigeons et de goélands dans l'écosystème urbain en est un exemple.

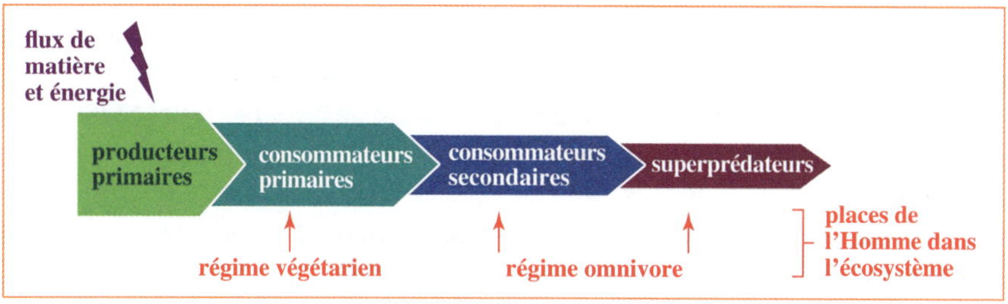

Figure 1 *Place de l'Homme dans les écosystèmes*

B. Les conséquences des activités humaines

■ L'espèce humaine peut aussi affecter le fonctionnement des écosystèmes en modifiant la biocénose ou le biotope.

■ Les modifications de la biocénose sont nombreuses comme la création d'**espèces domestiquées**, leur exploitation ou l'introduction d'**espèces invasives***.

■ Depuis l'apparition de l'agriculture il y a 10 000 ans, l'Homme a modifié les espèces en les sélectionnant (il sélectionne les individus les plus productifs et les plus résistants afin de les faire se reproduire entre eux et que la population obtenue possède ces nouveaux caractères), en les hybridant (on croise des individus possédant chacun un caractère d'intérêt et on obtient un individu hybride possédant ces deux caractères : c'est la **vigueur hybride***) ou encore en modifiant leur génome (création d'organismes génétiquement modifiés ou OGM par **transgénèse**).

■ D'autres modifications de la biocénose, plus néfastes, peuvent diminuer la biodiversité : c'est l'introduction d'espèces invasives. Une espèce exotique introduite par l'Homme peut devenir nuisible à la biodiversité locale et à son écosystème.

Ex. : La perruche à collier est une espèce invasive : originaire du Pakistan, elle a été libérée par des particuliers dans les années 1960. On dénombre actuellement 6 000 individus en Île-de-France. Sans prédateurs et grâce à une reproduction efficace en milieu urbain, la perruche affecte les autres espèces comme les écureuils roux et les étourneaux, par compétition, et endommage aussi directement les cultures locales à cause de son régime granivore et frugivore.

■ L'espèce humaine peut aussi affecter le fonctionnement des écosystèmes en exploitant des ressources et le biotope local. C'est le cas de l'exploitation des forêts. Ainsi, l'Homme agit sur le développement des forêts dans le but d'exploiter le bois à des fins économiques (chauffage, ameublement, construction et papeterie) ou durables (en limitant l'impact sur les sols ou la biodiversité et en permettant une meilleure résilience face aux perturbations). Les différents aménagements forestiers sont :

- la **futaie*** (les arbres ont un tronc unique) qui consiste à couper les espèces préexistantes afin de rajeunir le couvert végétal et d'obtenir du bois d'œuvre (ameublement et construction) ;
- le **taillis*** (plusieurs tiges partent d'une même base) qui consiste à produire du bois de faible diamètre destiné au chauffage.

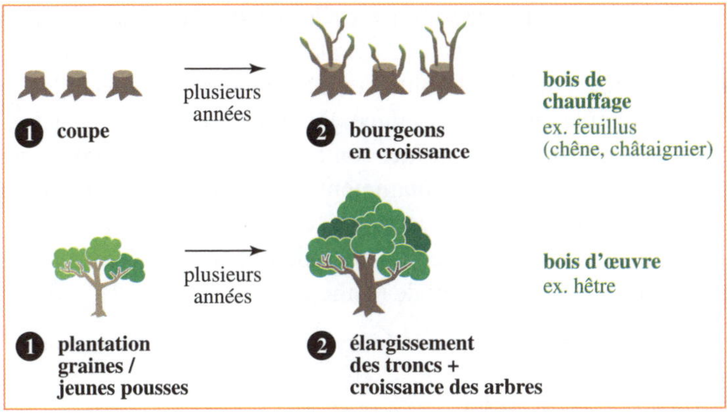

Figure 2 *La futaie et le taillis*

■ Une autre action humaine néfaste aux écosystèmes consiste à modifier le biotope mondial : c'est le changement climatique.

■ Beaucoup d'écosystèmes mondiaux sont impactés, avec une perte mondiale de la biodiversité (c'est la 6e extinction de masse) et des conséquences néfastes pour les activités humaines (diminution de la production, pollution des eaux, développement de maladies).

Modifications de la biocénose		Modifications du biotope		
Domestication	**Espèces invasives**	**Exploitation**	**Érosion des sols**	**Changement climatique**
chien (– 100 000 ans), bœuf (8 000 ans), blé, maïs…	perruche à collier, caulerpe, frelon asiatique, écrevisse de Louisiane…	sylviculture	déforestation, agrosystèmes	acidification des océans, fonte de la calotte polaire, désertification…

Figure 3 *Exemples de modifications anthropiques des écosystèmes*

2 Les bénéfices des écosystèmes

A. Les services écosystémiques

■ L'humanité tire un grand bénéfice de fonctions assurées gratuitement par les écosystèmes : ce sont les **services écosystémiques***.

■ On distingue :
– les **services d'approvisionnement*** : c'est la valeur économique des écosystèmes qui représentent des sources de nourriture (champignons, fruits, graines) et des outils de construction (production du bois) ;

Remarque
Le blé, le maïs et le riz fournissent la moitié de la ration énergétique de la population humaine.

– les **services de régulation*** : ce sont les services écologiques comme la dépollution de l'eau par des plantes qui piègent le nitrate, l'épuration de l'air et la fixation du CO_2 grâce à la photosynthèse, la lutte contre l'érosion des sols grâce aux racines des végétaux (exemple de l'oyat des dunes), la lutte contre les ravageurs de culture (introduction des coccinelles pour lutter contre les pucerons), la production de médicaments (pénicilline et morphine notamment) ou encore la pollinisation des plantes cultivées (par les abeilles, les chauve-souris, etc.).
– les **services culturels*** : la biodiversité possède une valeur récréative (randonnées, plongée…) et une valeur patrimoniale (esthétique).

■ Notre santé dépend ainsi de celle des écosystèmes qui nous environnent.

B. La gestion des écosystèmes

■ La connaissance scientifique des écosystèmes peut permettre une gestion rationnelle des ressources exploitables, assurant à la fois l'activité économique et un maintien des services écosystémiques.

■ L'**ingénierie écologique*** est l'ensemble des techniques qui visent à manipuler, modifier, exploiter ou réparer les écosystèmes afin d'en tirer durablement le maximum de bénéfices.

■ Différentes techniques de gestion des écosystèmes existent :
– la **protection des espèces** (exemple du loup des Alpes protégé en Europe en 1989 et dont la population augmente de nouveau actuellement) ;
– la protection des milieux par une création de **réserves biologiques** ;

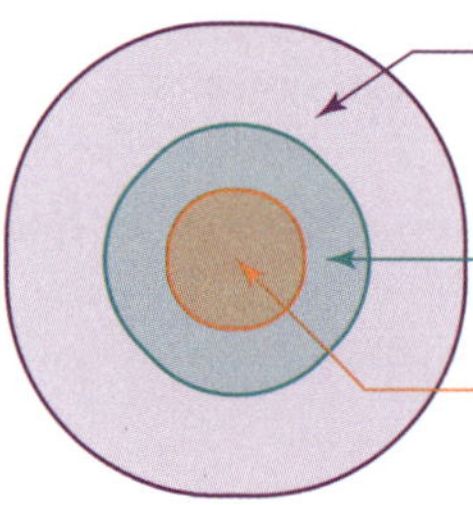

Figure 4 *L'organisation des réserves naturelles**

– la **réintroduction des espèces** à partir d'individus captifs (exemple du vautour fauve des Pyrénées réintroduit en 1990, 140 individus actuellement) ;
– le **renforcement** des populations où des individus extérieurs sont introduits afin d'augmenter les effets de l'espèce menacée (exemple de l'ours des Pyrénées avec une population de seulement 5 individus en 1990, renforcée en 1997 par un plan de réintroduction des ours slovènes proches génétiquement).

EXERCICES

Connaître le cours

1 2 min ★ Vrai ou Faux ?

Relevez la (ou les) affirmation(s) exacte(s).

Dans les écosystèmes, l'espèce humaine :
a) occupe une place de consommateur primaire essentiellement.
b) modifie seulement la biocénose.
c) fait évoluer les espèces grâce à la domestication notamment.
d) peut être parasitée.

→ Corrigé p. 164

2 2 min ★ Vrai ou Faux ?

Relevez la (ou les) affirmation(s) exacte(s).

Les services écosystémiques :
a) sont essentiellement éthiques et esthétiques.
b) permettent à l'Homme de concevoir des médicaments notamment.
c) peuvent être protégés par une gestion durable des écosystèmes.
d) sont menacés par la perte de la biodiversité.

→ Corrigé p. 164

3 5 min ★ Restitution de connaissances

Expliquez brièvement comment l'ingénierie écologique permet de mieux gérer les écosystèmes et de maintenir leurs services écosystémiques.

→ Corrigé p. 164

4 5 min ★ Schématiser le cours

Schématisez l'organisation générale d'une réserve naturelle.

→ Corrigé p. 164

S'entraîner

5 10 min ★★ La place de l'Homme dans les écosystèmes

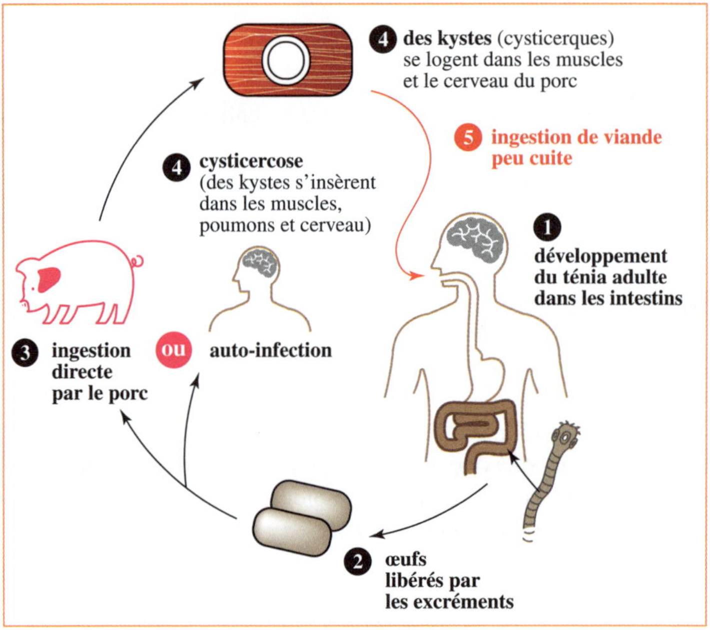

Le cycle de vie du Taenia solum

1. Expliquez le type de la relation interspécifique entre le ver solitaire et l'Homme.

2. Mettez en évidence que la position de l'Homme dans l'écosystème en tant que consommateur primaire ou secondaire peut modifier la gravité de cette infection parasite.

→ *Corrigé p. 164*

6 10 min ★★ La domestication du blé

À partir du Moyen Âge, le moissonnage s'effectue à la faucille. Il est suivi du battage qui sépare les épillets des épis. Aujourd'hui, des machines comme la moissonneuse-batteuse, remplacent ce travail fastidieux.

Comparaison des épis	Comparaison des grains
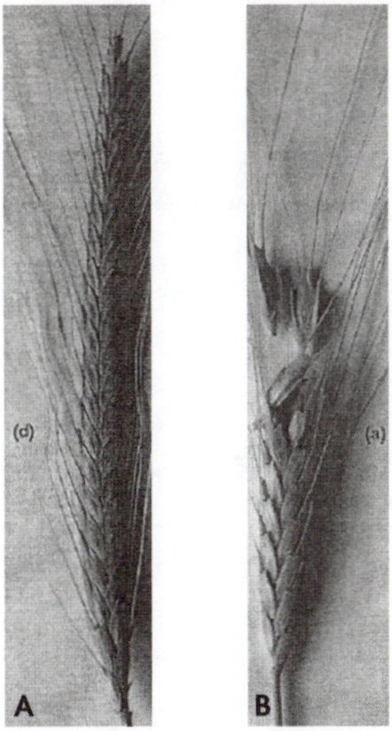 Chaque épi de blé est formé d'un axe portant des épillets qui se détachent à maturité chez le blé ancestral (A) mais restent fixés chez le blé cultivé (B).	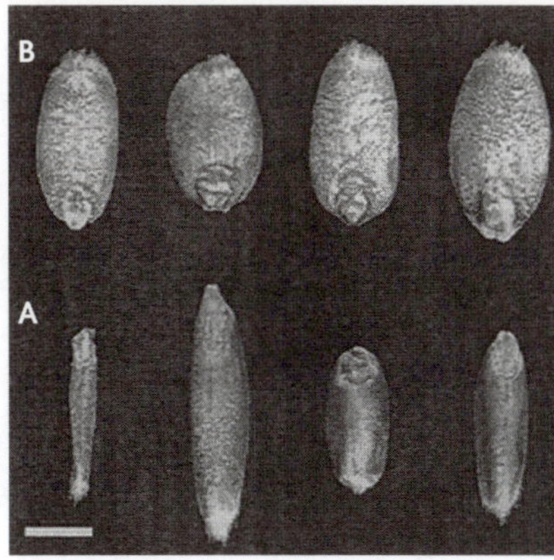 Les grains sont contenus dans les épillets. (échelle = 1 mm)

Comparaison entre le blé ancestral (A) et le blé cultivé (B)

1. Mettez en évidence les caractères morphologiques sélectionnés pour créer la variété de blé actuelle.

2. Expliquez le lien entre ces caractères sélectionnés et les techniques agricoles utilisées.

→ *Corrigé p. 165*

7 15 min ★★ Les espèces invasives

Au XXe siècle, des rats surmulots ont été introduits accidentellement à la suite du naufrage d'un cargo sur des îles bretonnes comme l'île de Trielen. En 1992, l'île devient une réserve naturelle et en 1996 le rat surmulot est éradiqué. On observe les conséquences sur les populations d'oiseaux nicheurs : la corneille noire (*Corvus cerone*) nichant dans les troncs d'arbre et le troglodyte mignon nichant dans les murs et les rochers.

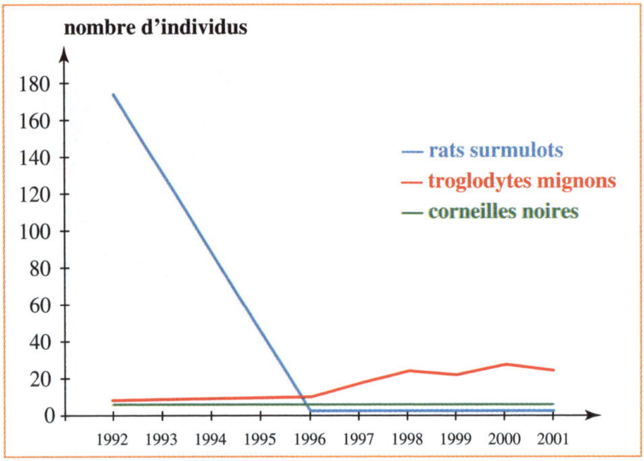

Évolution des populations de rats surmulots et d'oiseaux nicheurs

1. Décrivez et expliquez les conséquences de l'arrivée du rat surmulot sur les populations d'oiseaux nicheurs.

2. Comment peut-on qualifier l'espèce de rat surmulot sur l'île de Trielen ?

3. Expliquez comment l'action de l'Homme a pu limiter ensuite l'impact du surmulot sur l'écosystème de l'île de Trielen.

→ *Corrigé p. 165*

8 15 min ★★ Le cabillaud de Terre-Neuve

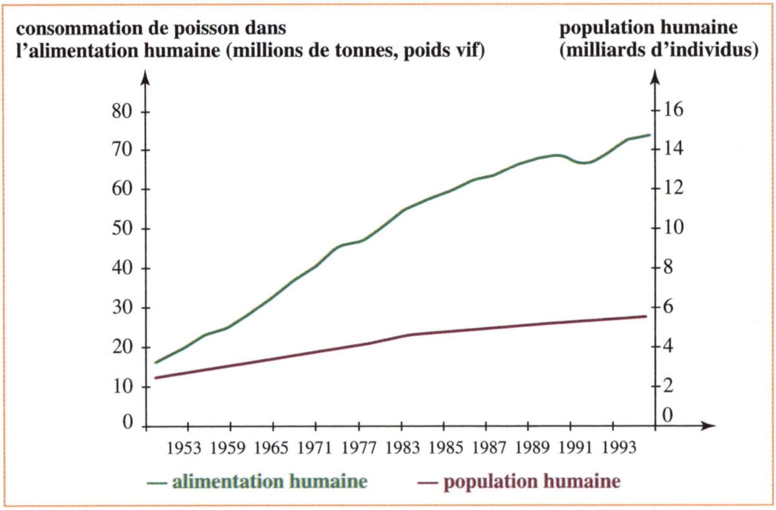

Figure 1 *Consommation des poissons dans l'alimentation humaine*

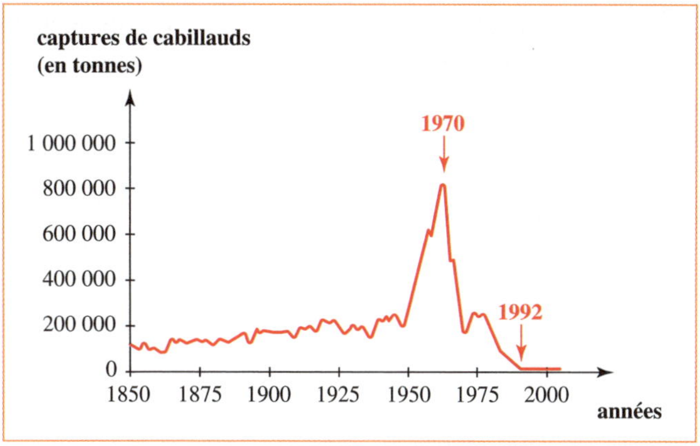

Figure 2 *Évolution du nombre de cabillauds (morues) au Canada dans la région de Terre-Neuve*

1. Décrivez l'évolution de la consommation mondiale de poissons à partir de la figure 1.

2. Quelle place l'Homme occupe-t-il au sein de l'écosystème dans cet exemple ?

3. Expliquez les conséquences sur l'écosystème de la surpêche humaine à partir de la figure 2.

→ *Corrigé p. 165*

9 20 min ★★ La protection des éléphants

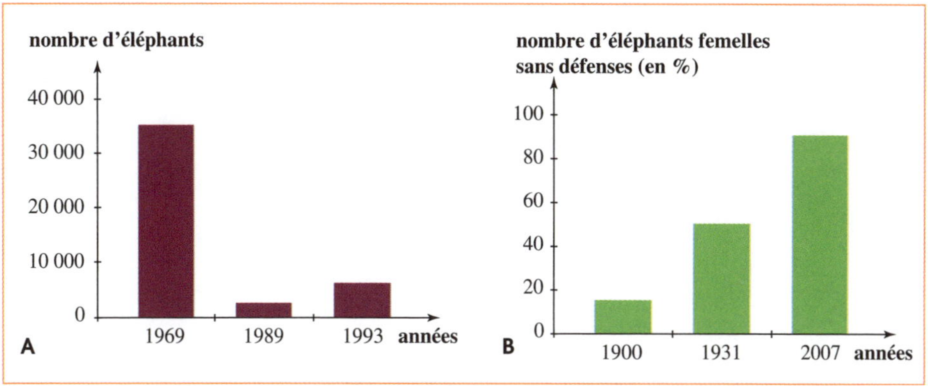

Évolution du nombre d'éléphants (A) et du nombre d'éléphants femelles sans défenses (B) en Zambie

1. Décrivez l'évolution de la population des éléphants à l'aide du graphique A. Quelle action humaine peut ainsi être mise en évidence ?

2. D'après l'analyse du graphique B, expliquez le mécanisme à l'origine de la perte de leurs défenses chez certains éléphants.

3. Quelles mesures de gestion écologique l'Homme pourrait-il mettre en place afin de limiter la disparition des éléphants ?

→ *Corrigé p. 166*

Exercice 10 pts L'évolution des populations d'abeilles 30 min

Le syndrome d'effondrement des colonies d'abeilles est un phénomène de disparition des colonies d'abeilles domestiques depuis 1998. Il se manifeste par une disparition des abeilles dans les ruches. Les chercheurs estiment que les abeilles domestiques et sauvages permettent de polliniser 80 % des cultures, soit 3 000 $ par hectare de production agricole.

Montrez que la disparition des abeilles et de leurs services écosystémiques est causée par l'action humaine.

Document 1

Une étude de 2010 a recensé les causes de mortalité des abeilles à travers toute l'Europe en interrogeant les apiculteurs.

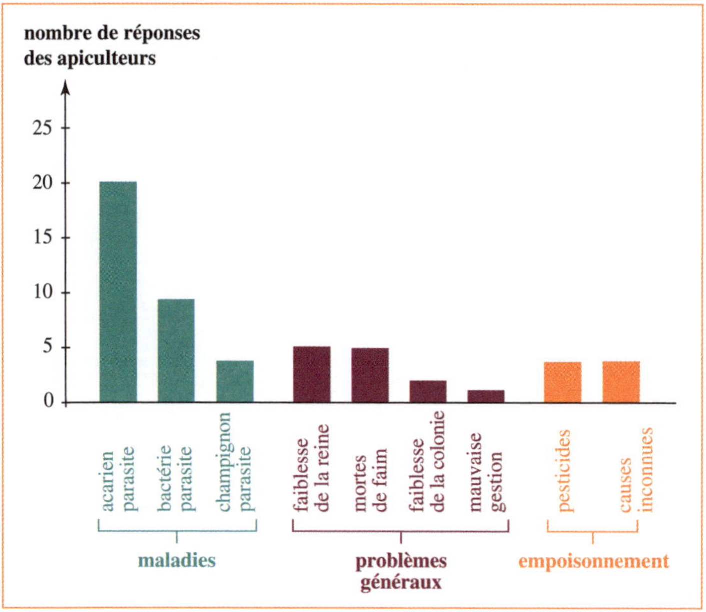

Principales causes de décès des abeilles selon les apiculteurs européens

Document 2

Les néocotinoïdes sont des pesticides utilisés dans les champs cultivés afin de s'attaquer au système nerveux des insectes. Ils sont notamment utilisés dans les champs de maïs et de colza, espèces butinées par les abeilles.

Les reines sont les seules femelles reproductrices dans les ruches. Elles pondent des larves toute la journée ; on en trouve qu'une seule par ruche.

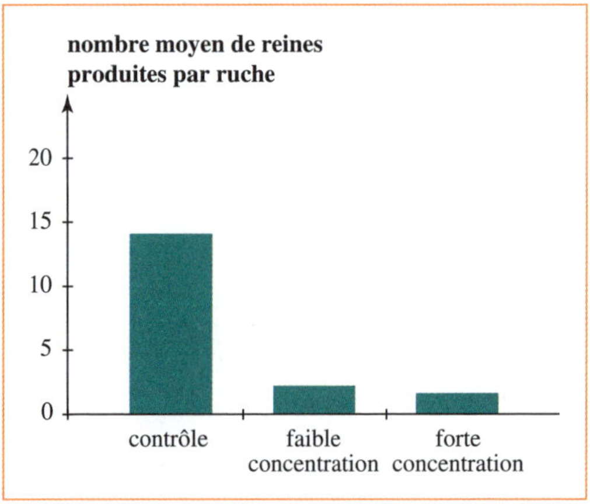

Évolution du nombre de reines en fonction de la concentration en néocotinoïdes de l'environnement

Document 3

Vespa velutina, ou frelon asiatique, est une espèce originaire de Corée arrivée en Europe, et plus particulièrement en France, en 2004. C'est un prédateur d'Hyménoptères comme les abeilles et les guêpes.

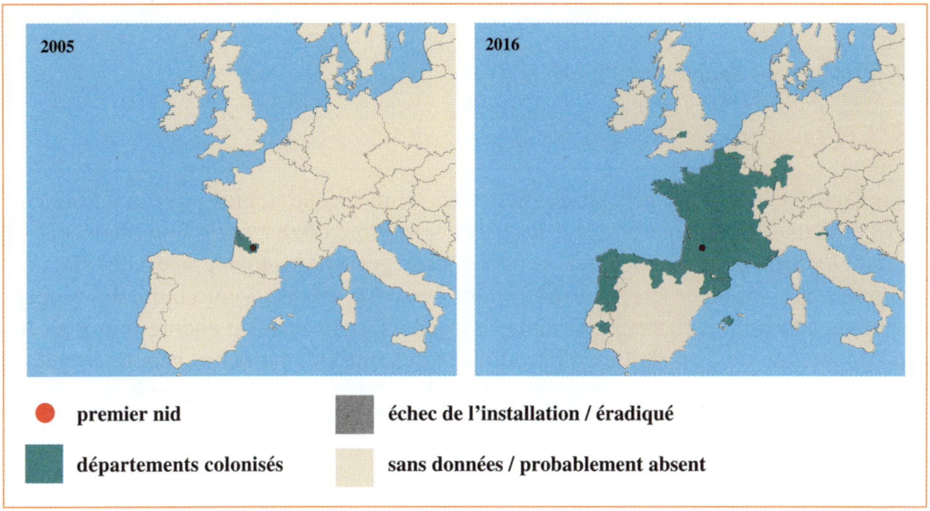

Figure 1 *Évolution géographique de la présence des frelons asiatiques en Europe entre 2005 et 2016*

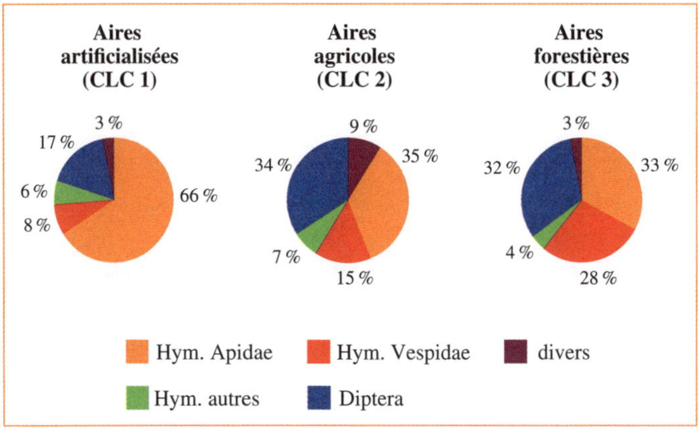

Figure 2 *Principales proies des frelons asiatiques en fonction de l'écosystème*

→ Corrigé p. 166

CORRIGÉS

1 → *Énoncé p. 155*

Les affirmations exactes sont c) et d).

2 → *Énoncé p. 155*

Les affirmations exactes sont b), c) et d).

3 → *Énoncé p. 155*

L'ingénierie écologique permet de mettre au point des stratégies pour améliorer les services écosystémiques : protéger les espèces en voie de disparition ou menacées en limitant l'action de la chasse ou de la pêche, protéger leur biotope grâce à des réserves naturelles où l'action de l'Homme est limitée voire inexistante, réintroduire des espèces disparues naturellement mais existantes encore à l'état captif ou encore renforcer les espèces en voie de disparition en introduisant des individus proches génétiquement.

4 → *Énoncé p. 155*

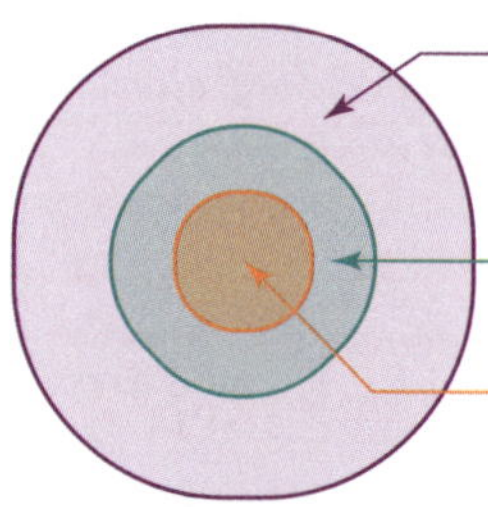

5 → *Énoncé p. 156*

1. On observe que le ver solitaire se loge dans les intestins de l'Homme ou ses muscles et son cerveau dans le cas des cysticercoses. Le ver solitaire peut alors détourner les nutriments de l'organisme humain et diminuer ainsi sa valeur sélective. De même, quand les cysticerques se logent dans le cerveau ou les muscles, cela peut entraîner des effets secondaires importants. L'Homme ne retire aucun avantage à cette relation : c'est donc une relation interspécifique de type parasitisme.

2. Lorsque l'Homme se nourrit de la viande de porc (consommateur secondaire), il peut être contaminé par le ver adulte et présenter un amaigrissement. Or, quand il se nourrit de végétaux souillés par les œufs du ver solitaire (consommateur primaire), des cysticerques se développent dans ses muscles et son cerveau, ce qui peut être létal : les effets du parasitisme sont donc plus graves lorsque l'Homme prend la place du porc en tant que consommateur primaire.

6 → *Énoncé p. 156*

1. On observe que le blé cultivé possède un épi plus court avec des épillets qui y restent fixés. De plus les grains du blé cultivé sont plus gros et surement plus nutritifs que ceux du blé ancestral.

2. On peut supposer que le blé sauvage, avec ses épillets plus fragiles, pouvait se disséminer facilement par le vent. Le blé cultivé, dont les épillets restent fixés sur les épis, nécessite un battage pour libérer les épillets. Le blé cultivé dont les épillets restent fixés sur les épis, nécessite un battage pour libérer les épillets.

7 → *Énoncé p. 157*

1. Lorsque le surmulot est présent sur l'île, la quantité d'oiseaux nicheurs est faible. Cependant, à partir de 1996, lorsque le surmulot est éradiqué, on observe une augmentation de la quantité de troglodytes mignons de 5 à 25 individus. La corneille n'est pas affectée par les variations d'effectifs du surmulot. On peut donc supposer que la façon de nicher des deux espèces d'oiseaux a influencé l'action du surmulot : en effet, le troglodyte mignon niche plus bas que la corneille, ses œufs peuvent donc être attaqués par le rat surmulot.

2. Le rat surmulot étant une espèce allochtone (n'existant pas sur l'île) introduite par l'Homme au XXe siècle et ayant entraîné une diminution de la biodiversité locale (les troglodytes mignons notamment), on peut le considérer comme une espèce invasive.

3. L'Homme a exercé deux actions de gestion de l'écosystème : protéger l'île en la classant comme réserve naturelle en 1992 mais, surtout, éradiquer le rat surmulot en 1996.

8 → *Énoncé p. 158*

1. On observe que la consommation en poissons passe de 20 millions de tonnes de poissons pêchés en 1953 à 75 millions de tonnes quarante ans plus tard, parallèlement à l'augmentation de la population humaine. Les humains consomment de plus en plus de poissons dans leur alimentation quotidienne.

2. L'Homme, en consommant des poissons, consommateurs primaires, occupe la place de consommateur secondaire, voire tertiaire si le poisson consommé est un prédateur de petits poissons.

3. On observe que de 1850 à 1950, le nombre de cabillauds capturés est relativement constant (entre 100 000 et 250 000 individus). À partir de 1950, on observe une augmentation brutale de la capture de cabillauds, avec plus de 800 000 individus capturés. Cette évolution est liée à l'augmentation de notre consommation et donc de la demande mondiale en poissons. En conséquence, à partir de 1992, peu de cabillauds sont capturés dans leur milieu sauvage : le cas des cabillauds est un exemple de surpêche ayant appauvri la biocénose et donc fragilisé l'écosystème marin.

9 → *Énoncé p. 159*

1. Le nombre d'éléphants est passé de 35 000 en 1969 à 5 000 en 1993 soit une diminution d'un facteur 7. Cependant on observe une légère amélioration des effectifs entre 1989 et 1993. La chute du nombre d'éléphants est causée par une chasse intensive voire du braconnage.

2. En parallèle à la diminution du nombre d'éléphants, on observe une augmentation du nombre de femelles ne possédant plus de défenses. On peut supposer que les individus naissant sans défenses ont mieux survécu, échappant au braconnage pour l'ivoire, et se sont donc plus reproduits. C'est la sélection naturelle. De plus, les petits effectifs peuvent aussi être soumis à la dérive génétique.

3. Afin de limiter la disparition des éléphants, l'Homme peut protéger cette espèce en la plaçant sur la liste des espèces en voie de disparition, mais aussi en créant des réserves naturelles pour protéger son environnement.

CONTRÔLE CONTINU POUR LE BAC

Exercice → *Énoncé p. 161*

Les abeilles sont les principaux pollinisateurs de nos écosystèmes agricoles ; elles rendent ainsi de nombreux services écosystémiques à l'Homme. Pourtant, on observe actuellement un effondrement de la population des abeilles domestiques et sauvages.

Cette perte de la diversité des abeilles est-elle causée par l'Homme ?

On observe que les apiculteurs européens désignent principalement les maladies comme responsables de l'effondrement des cultures d'abeilles (32 apiculteurs). Ces maladies sont diverses : infections bactériennes et fongiques ou causées par des acariens. Pourtant, on dénombre aussi quelques cas de disparition des abeilles dans les ruches provoquées par les pesticides (4 apiculteurs). Les pesticides sont, par exemple, des insecticides aspergés sur les champs par l'Homme.

Les néocotinoïdes sont un exemple d'insecticides. On observe qu'ils provoquent une diminution de la quantité de reines dans les ruches. Or les reines sont les seules abeilles capables d'assurer la reproduction de la ruche. On peut donc supposer qu'en attaquant le système nerveux des insectes, les néocotinoïdes empêchent la reproduction des abeilles et donc le développement des ruches.

Par ailleurs, l'Homme est aussi responsable de l'introduction d'une espèce invasive en Europe : le frelon asiatique (via l'importation depuis l'Asie, en 2004, de vases qui auraient contenu des nids de frelon). Depuis 2005, où il n'était présent que dans deux départements français du Sud-Ouest, il s'est propagé : en 2016, on le retrouve partout en France ainsi que dans une partie de l'Espagne, du Portugal, de la Belgique et de l'Allemagne. Ce frelon se nourrit d'Hyménoptères mais on remarque qu'il privilégie davantage les abeilles dans un écosystème agricole.

On peut donc en conclure que l'Homme contribue à la disparition actuelle des abeilles par des actions funestes comme le traitement des champs par des insecticides mais aussi l'introduction d'espèces invasives. Par ailleurs les virus, les bactéries et les champignons sont des espèces qui se propagent davantage en Europe en raison du changement climatique.

Patrimoine génétique, mutations et santé

CHAPITRE 11

1 Les maladies d'origine génétique

A. La transmission des maladies génétiques

■ Certaines mutations de l'ADN, responsables de la modification d'un allèle, peuvent affecter les gènes (dont les séquences de nucléotides codent une protéine). Les mutations empêchent la production de la protéine ou en modifient sa structure : il en résulte une absence de la protéine, ou bien quand elle produite, une protéine non fonctionnelle ou peu efficace.

■ L'expression modifiée du gène est responsable de maladies caractérisées par des modifications :
– du phénotype macroscopique ;
– du phénotype cellulaire ;
– du phénotype moléculaire.

■ Une mutation peut être héritée d'un ou des deux parents, on dit alors qu'elles sont **héréditaires**, ou bien apparaître spontanément chez l'embryon.

■ L'étude des arbres généalogiques familiaux permet de connaître les modes de transmission des maladies :
– Elles peuvent être causées par la mutation d'un gène (maladie **monogénique***) ou de plusieurs gènes (maladie **multigénique***).
– Elles sont **dominantes** si un allèle touché sur les deux suffit à faire apparaître la maladie, ou **récessives** s'il faut posséder les deux allèles mutés pour développer les symptômes.
– Elles sont **gonosomiques*** lorsque la mutation touche un gène situé sur les chromosomes sexuels et **autosomiques*** si la mutation touche les autres chromosomes.

■ Ainsi, dans le cas d'une maladie monogénique à transmission autosomique récessive, seuls les homozygotes pour l'allèle muté sont atteints. Les hétérozygotes sont donc des porteurs sains qui ne développent aucun symptôme mais peuvent transmettre l'allèle muté à leur descendance (voir *figure 1* p. 170).

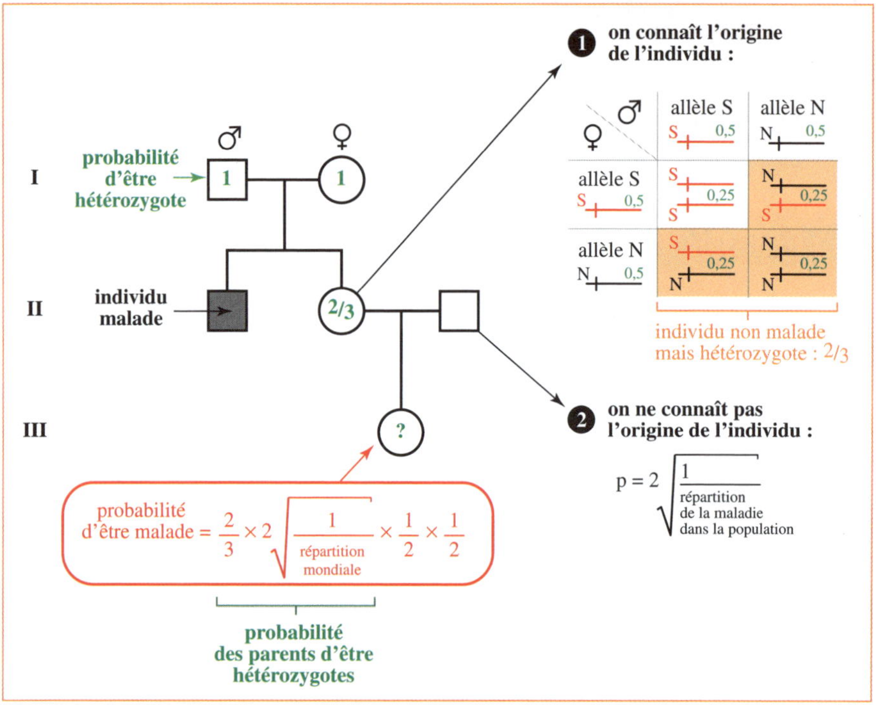

Figure 1 *Arbre généalogique d'une maladie monogénique autosomique récessive et les probabilités de transmission de l'allèle atteint*

B. Les traitements envisagés

■ Selon les cas, des médicaments vont compenser la fonction altérée en remplaçant le rôle de la protéine dont l'action a été affectée par la mutation du gène.

■ Les médicaments peuvent aussi traiter les symptômes pour soulager les malades sans pour autant traiter l'origine génétique de la maladie. Ce sont des **traitements symptomatiques***.

■ Les **thérapies géniques*** sont les seuls **traitements curatifs*** qui pourraient à terme guérir certaines maladies monogéniques. Cette technique consiste à remplacer l'allèle muté par l'allèle sain dans les cellules du tissu atteint. L'incorporation de l'allèle à remplacer se fait grâce à l'utilisation de vecteurs notamment viraux (voir *figure 2* p. 171).

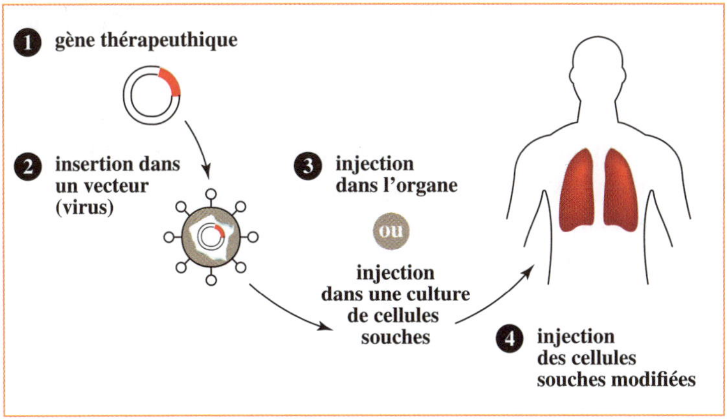

Figure 2 *Principe de la thérapie génique*

2 Les maladies multifactorielles

A. L'origine multigénique des maladies

■ La plupart des pathologies d'origine génétique sont dues à l'interaction de nombreux gènes qui ne sont pas tous connus : ce sont les **maladies multigéniques**. Certains allèles de certains gènes augmentent la probabilité d'apparition d'une pathologie : ce sont des **gènes de prédisposition***.

■ Le profil génétique individuel intervient donc dans la santé de l'individu.

B. L'influence des facteurs environnementaux

■ D'autres facteurs, autres que génétiques, peuvent affecter la santé d'une personne : ce sont les facteurs environnementaux. Certains modes de vie comme le tabagisme, l'exposition aux UV, l'exposition à certaines substances chimiques peuvent ainsi augmenter la probabilité d'apparition d'une pathologie.

■ Les maladies causées à la fois par des mutations génétiques et des facteurs environnementaux sont **multifactorielles***.

■ Pour identifier le ou les gènes causant une maladie, on étudie les génomes de grandes populations de patients. L'**épidémiologie*** est l'étude de la répartition et des facteurs de risque des maladies humaines. On distingue deux domaines différents :

– l'**épidémiologie descriptive*** : c'est la description des fréquences et de la répartition des maladies en répondant à trois questions : « Chez qui ? », « Où ? » et « Quand ? ». On calcule ainsi des taux de prévalence, c'est-à-dire des statistiques de répartition de la maladie dans différentes populations à différentes époques.

– l'**épidémiologie analytique*** : c'est l'estimation du lien entre l'exposition à des facteurs et l'apparition de la maladie. On étudie de grands groupes d'individus malades ou non, en fonction de leurs expositions à des facteurs de risque et on estime ainsi une probabilité de développer la maladie associée à ce facteur : c'est le **risque relatif***.

Définition

Un facteur de risque, c'est le facteur par lequel on peut multiplier la probabilité de développer une maladie chez les sujets exposés à un facteur particulier.

EXERCICES

Connaître le cours

1 2 min ★ Vrai ou Faux ?

Relevez la (ou les) affirmation(s) exacte(s).

Une pathologie d'origine génétique :

a) est guérie par les médicaments remplaçant le rôle de la protéine affectée par la mutation.

b) peut être étudiée par des arbres généalogiques et l'étude du génome de nombreux individus.

c) est uniquement monogénique.

d) peut trouver son origine dans la mutation d'un gène situé sur les chromosomes non sexuels.

→ *Corrigé p. 181*

2 2 min ★ Vrai ou Faux ?

Relevez la (ou les) affirmation(s) exacte(s).

La thérapie génique :

a) traite les maladies multifactorielles.

b) doit être appliquée sur l'embryon pour affecter toutes les cellules.

c) utilise des vecteurs viraux pour insérer l'allèle sain.

d) est encore en cours d'élaboration.

→ *Corrigé p. 181*

3 5 min ★ Restitution de connaissances

Expliquez brièvement comment l'épidémiologie étudie les maladies humaines.

→ *Corrigé p. 181*

4 5 min ★ Schématiser le cours

Schématisez un arbre généalogique d'une maladie monogénique autosomique récessive sur trois générations.

→ *Corrigé p. 181*

S'entraîner

5 10 min ★★ La drépanocytose

La drépanocytose est une maladie provoquant une forme grave d'anémie chronique. Elle trouve son origine dans la mutation du gène codant pour la β-globine, chaîne β de l'hémoglobine, ce qui entraîne une production d'une hémoglobine anormale et des globules rouges déformés (hématie falciforme, en forme de faucille).

Un patient de 13 ans suivi à l'hôpital Necker à Paris a été le premier patient à être guéri de la maladie en octobre 2014 après avoir bénéficié d'un nouveau traitement : la thérapie génique.

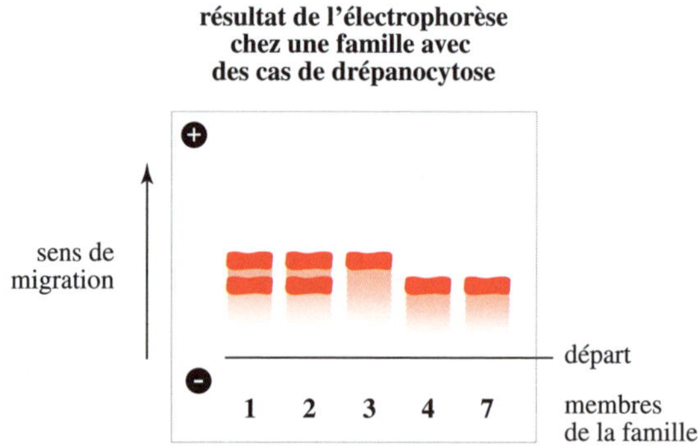

L'électrophorèse est une technique de séparation puis de migration des protéines selon leurs tailles. Dans le cas de la drépanocytose, l'hémoglobine S du malade migre moins loin que l'hémoglobine β d'un individu sain.

Figure 1 *Électrophorèse de l'hémoglobine de plusieurs individus*

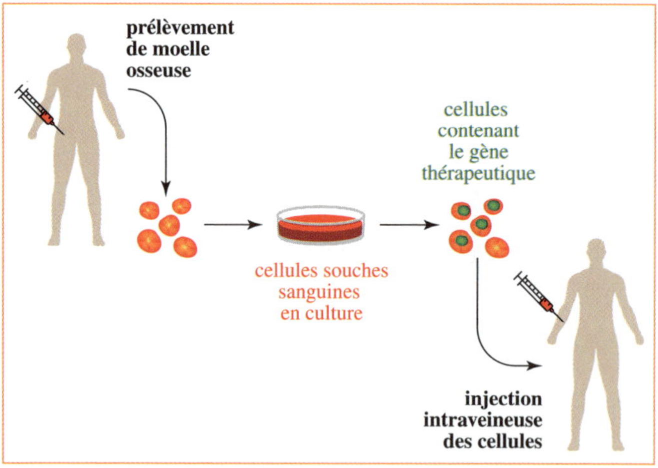

Figure 2 *Technique utilisée pour le patient de l'hôpital Necker*

1. À l'aide des résultats de l'électrophorèse de la figure 1, déterminez quels individus sont hétérozygotes ou homozygotes pour la maladie.

2. Expliquez quelle méthode a permis le traitement définif du patient de l'hôpital Necker.

→ *Corrigé p. 181*

6 10 min ★★ L'hémophilie

L'hémophilie est une maladie caractérisée par un trouble de la coagulation du sang. Elle est causée par l'absence de production de certains facteurs plaquettaires : pour l'hémophilie A, c'est le facteur VIII qui est absent. Cette maladie a particulièrement concerné certains membres des familles royale anglaise et russe aux XIXe et XXe siècles.

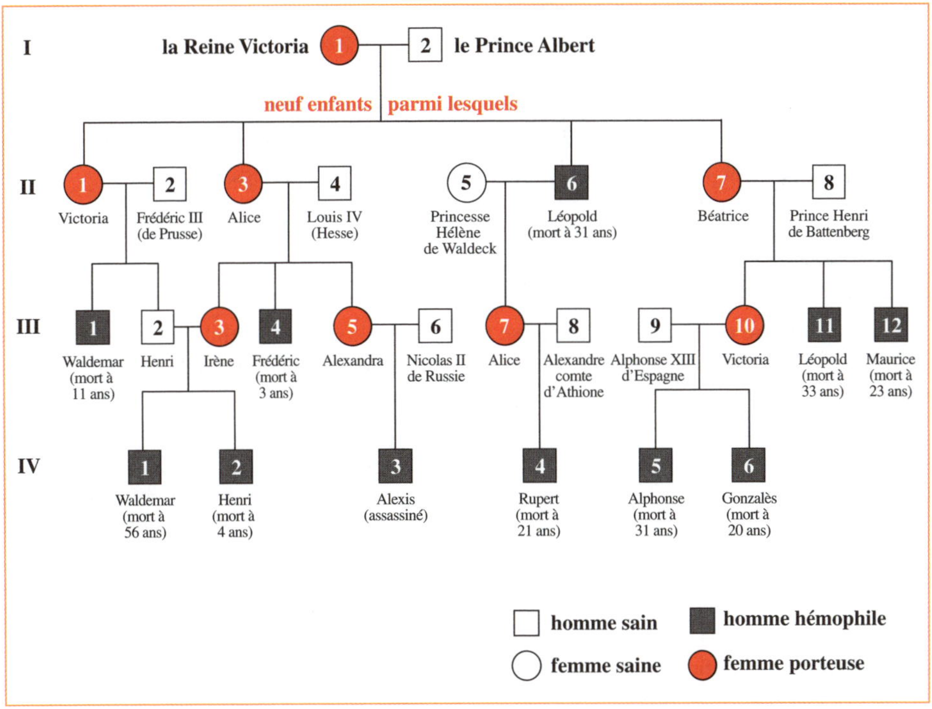

Les cas d'hémophilie dans l'arbre généalogique de la famille royale anglaise

1. À partir de l'arbre généalogique, déterminez si le gène de l'hémophilie est porté par un chromosome sexuel.

2. Expliquez si l'allèle de la maladie est récessif ou dominant.

→ *Corrigé p. 182*

7 10 min ★★ La mucoviscidose

La mucoviscidose touche, en France, 7 000 individus.

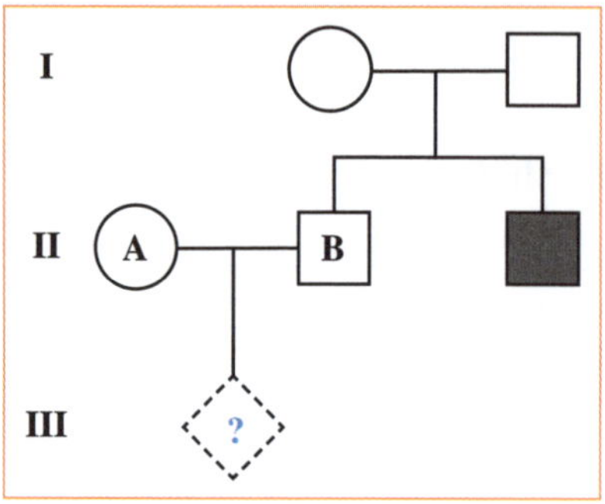

Arbre généalogique d'une famille touchée par la mucoviscidose

1. Déterminez la probabilité pour la mère A d'être hétérozygote pour la mucoviscidose.
2. Déterminez la probabilité pour le père B d'être hétérozygote pour la mucoviscidose.
3. Calculez la probabilité pour l'enfant III de développer la pathologie.

→ *Corrigé p. 182*

8 15 min ★★ La thrombophilie

La thrombophilie est une maladie qui se manifeste par une coagulation du sang excessive et peut provoquer des accidents cardio-vasculaires par formation d'un caillot sanguin.

		Prévalence dans la population générale	**Risque relatif d'un premier accident cardio-vasculaire**
Facteurs génétiques	Mutation du facteur V (coagulant)	3 – 7 %	5 – 7
	Mutation de la prothrombine (coagulant)	0,7 – 4 %	2 – 3
	Déficit en antithrombine (anticoagulant)	0,002 %	15 – 20
	Déficit en protéine C (anticoagulant)	0,2 %	15 – 20
	Déficit en protéine S (anticoagulant)	0,003 – 0,13 %	15 – 20
Facteur environnemental	Prise d'un contraceptif hormonal (pilule, patch ou implant)	Non renseigné	4

Données épidémiologiques sur le risque relatif de la thrombophilie

1. D'après les données épidémiologiques présentées, déterminez l'origine monogénique, multigénique, environnementale ou multifactorielle de la maladie.
2. Calculez le risque relatif de développer un premier accident cardio-vasculaire pour une femme possédant la mutation du facteur V et prenant un contraceptif hormonal.

→ Corrigé p. 183

9 15 min ★★ Le diabète de type 2

Certaines populations comme les Indiens Pimas des États-Unis, originaires du Mexique, possèdent le record mondial de diabète de type II. Ce diabète est une maladie caractérisée par une hyperglycémie tardive apparaissant à partir de 40 ans.

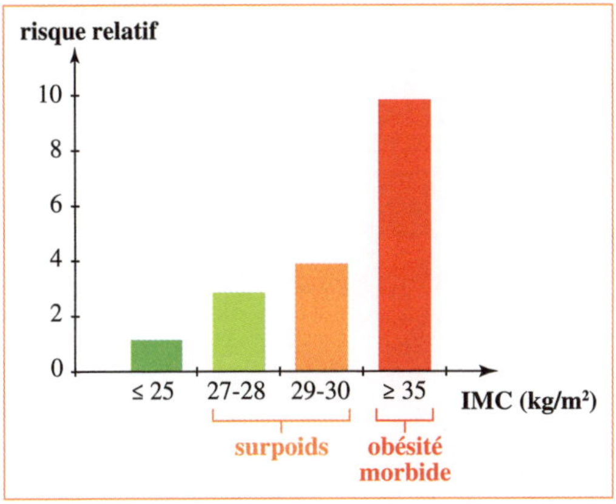

Figure 1 *Risque relatif du diabète de type II en fonction de l'IMC (IMC = poids/taille² = indice de masse corporelle pouvant être utilisé comme indice sur la charge pondérale)*

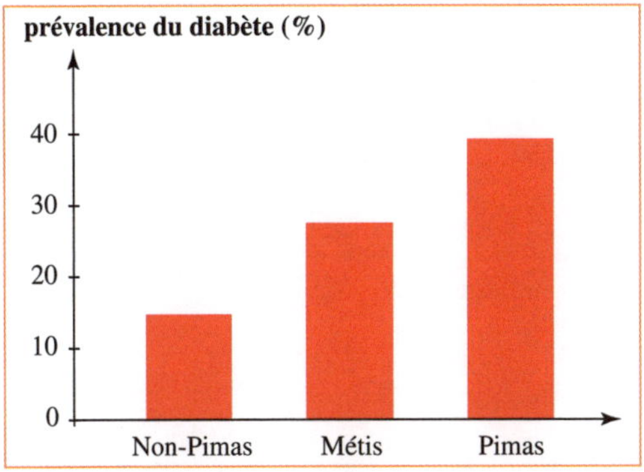

Figure 2 *Prévalence du diabète de type II pour des individus de même IMC mais d'origine ethnologique variée*

1. À partir de la figure 1, déterminez quel facteur environnemental favorise l'apparition d'un diabète de type II.

2. Expliquez pourquoi les Indiens Pimas sont plus fréquemment diabétiques que les autres populations d'Américains.

3. Déduisez-en l'origine de la maladie (génétique, environnementale, multifactorielle).

→ *Corrigé p. 183*

CONTRÔLE CONTINU POUR LE BAC

Exercice 10 pts La myopathie de Duchenne 30 min

La myopathie de Duchenne est une maladie touchant majoritairement les garçons, liée à la modification d'une protéine : la dystrophine. C'est une maladie évolutive caractérisée par une dégénérescence progressive des muscles de l'organisme.

Effectuez une analyse épidémiologique de la myopathie de Duchenne en étudiant sa répartition mondiale, son mode de transmission ainsi que les pistes thérapeutiques actuelles.

Document 1

Une étude épidémiologique est réalisée au Canada et notamment dans sa partie Est, la province de Saguenay-Lac-Saint-Jean. Par dérive génétique, les individus présentent une diversité génétique différente du reste du Canada.

Prévalence mondiale (pour 100 000 habitants)	Prévalence au Canada (pour 100 000 habitants)	Prévalence à Saguenay-Lac-Saint-Jean (province canadienne) (pour 100 000 habitants)
16,1	106,8	189

Données épidémiologiques sur la myopathie de Duchenne au Canada

Document 2

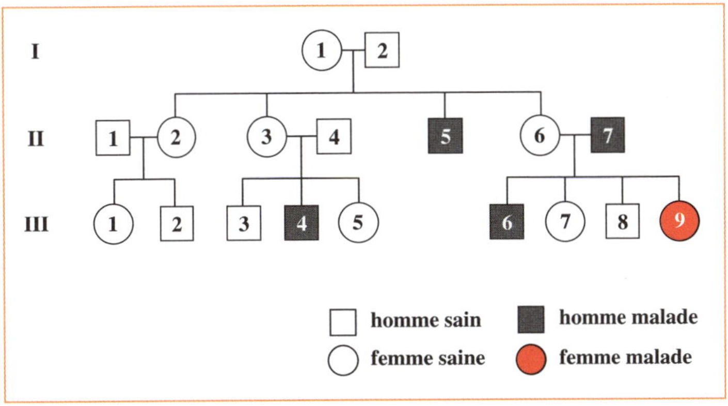

Arbre généralogique d'une famille canadienne atteinte de myopathie de Duchenne

Document 3

Pour traiter la myopathie de Duchenne, la thérapie génique fut envisagée en introduisant un allèle sain dans l'ADN des cellules musculaires. Le saut d'exon est une autre technique mise sur le marché depuis 2014 pour traiter les myopathies de Duchenne chez les patients de plus de 5 ans.

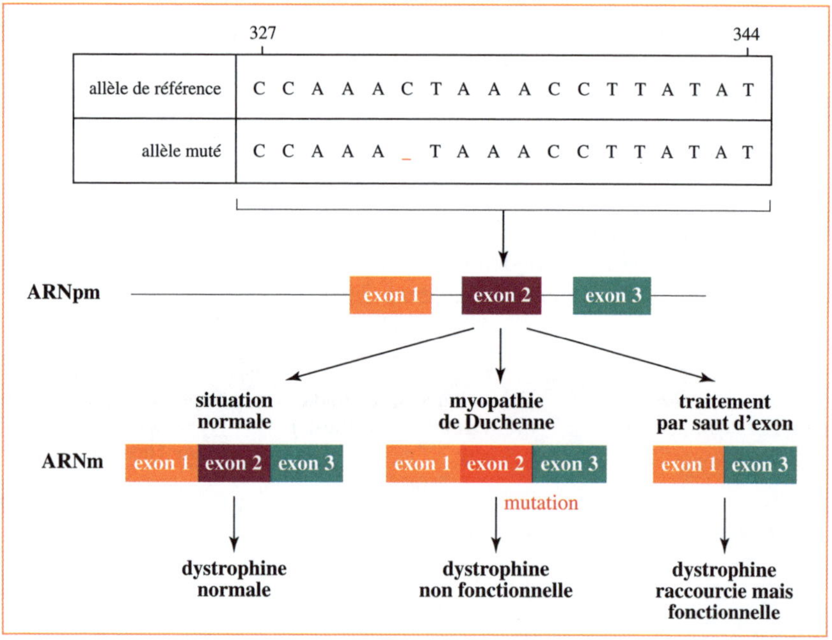

Allèle responsable de la myopathie de Duchenne et technique du saut d'exon

→ Corrigé p. 183

CORRIGÉS

1 → *Énoncé p. 173*

Les affirmations exactes sont : b) et d).

2 → *Énoncé p. 173*

Les affirmations exactes sont : a), c) et d).

3 → *Énoncé p. 173*

L'épidémiologie est la science permettant d'étudier la répartition spatiale et temporelle des maladies humaines. Elle repose sur l'étude de grandes populations d'individus atteints ou non par une maladie et réalise ensuite des statistiques pour étudier la prévalence (pourcentages d'individus atteints) et le risque relatif (probabilité de développer la maladie en fonction d'une exposition à un facteur).

4 → *Énoncé p. 173*

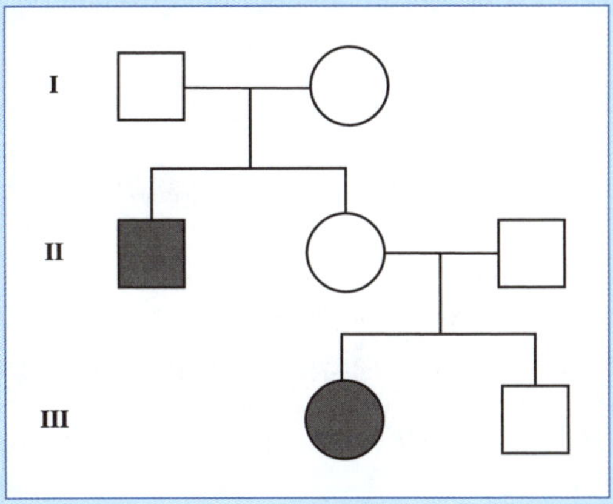

5 → *Énoncé p. 174*

1. Dans le cas de la drépanocytose, l'électrophorèse consiste à faire migrer, selon leurs poids, les hémoglobines de plusieurs individus au sein d'une famille. On observe que les individus 1 et 2 possèdent deux hémoglobines différentes : l'une qui a migré plus loin, plus petite, c'est l'hémoglobine β. L'autre migre moins loin, c'est l'hémoglobine responsable de la maladie : l'hémoglobine S. Ces deux individus sont hétérozygotes (ou porteurs sains). L'individu 3 possède une hémoglobine qui migre plus loin : c'est l'hémoglobine saine. Il est donc homozygote pour l'allèle normal. Les individus 4 et

7 possèdent essentiellement une hémoglobine migrant peu : ils sont homozygotes pour l'allèle S et sont donc atteints de la forme sévère de la maladie.

2. La méthode utilisée pour soigner cet enfant de 13 ans souffrant de drépanocytose consiste à injecter un allèle sain dans un virus puis d'infecter les cellules souches sanguines de l'enfant avant de les lui réinjecter. Ainsi, toutes ses cellules sanguines produites posséderont l'allèle sain à la place de l'allèle muté : ses globules rouges ne seront donc plus en forme de faucille et il ne présentera plus de symptômes. Cet enfant a donc bénéficié de la thérapie génique.

6 → *Énoncé p. 175*

1. Quelle que soit la génération étudiée, on observe que seuls les hommes souffrent d'hémophilie alors que les femmes sont des porteuses saines, autrement dit hétérozygotes pour l'allèle muté. On peut donc supposer que la mutation est présente sur le chromosome X, transmis par la mère à son fils (1 risque sur 2) : la maladie est gonosomique.

2. Pour la 2e génération, Léopold souffre d'hémophilie alors que ses deux parents n'en souffraient pas : il a donc hérité du chromosome X muté de sa mère Victoria. De plus, ses sœurs porteuses saines, et donc hétérozygotes pour la maladie, ne souffrent d'aucun symptôme. On peut donc supposer qu'il faut posséder l'allèle muté en deux exemplaires (ou un seul si on est un homme) pour déclarer la maladie : c'est une maladie récessive.

7 → *Énoncé p. 176*

1. Pour la mère A dont on ne connaît pas les origines : $p = 2 \times \sqrt{\dfrac{1}{7\,000}} = 0{,}024$.

Elle possède donc 2,4 % de risques d'être hétérozygote pour la maladie.

2. Pour le père B dont on connaît les origines :

Ne présentant pas les symptômes, on sait qu'il n'est pas homozygote pour la mucoviscidose. Il reste donc 3 possibilités dont seulement 2 sont des cas d'hétérozygotie : le père possède donc 2/3 = 0,67 soit 67 % de risques d'être hétérozygote pour la maladie.

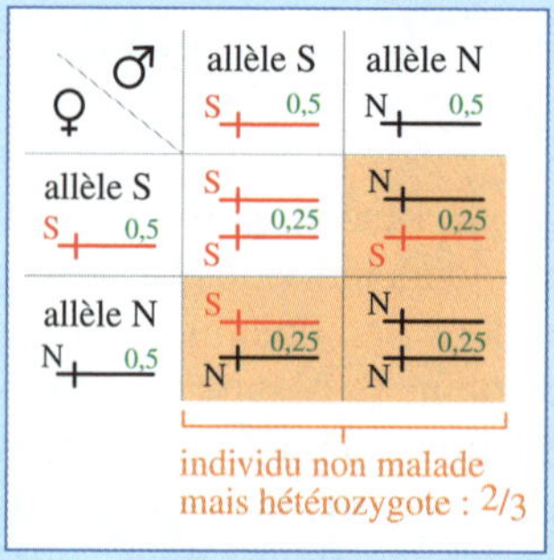

3. $p = 0{,}67 \times 0{,}024 \times 0{,}5 \times 0{,}5 = 0{,}004$

L'enfant a 0,4 % de risques d'être atteint par la mucoviscidose.

8 → *Énoncé p. 176*

1. On observe que la prévalence de la thrombophilie augmente selon plusieurs facteurs : des facteurs génétiques comme les mutations touchant les gènes régulant la coagulation (facteur V, protéine C et S, prothrombine et antithrombine) ce qui entraîne une hypercoagulation. La mutation la plus répandue dans la population est celle du facteur V (avec entre 3 et 7 % de la population atteinte). De plus, d'autres facteurs environnementaux semblent fréquemment liés à la thrombophilie notamment la prise d'un contraceptif hormonal. La thrombophilie est donc multifactorielle (provoquée par des facteurs génétiques et environnementaux) et multigénique (plusieurs gènes sont responsables de la maladie).

2. Une femme possédant la mutation du facteur V et étant sous un contraceptif hormonal augmente de ($7 \times 4 =$) 24 fois le risque de développer la maladie.

9 → *Énoncé p. 177*

1. On observe que plus l'IMC est élevé, plus le risque relatif de développer un diabète de type II augmente. Par exemple, une personne en forte obésité (IMC supérieur à 35) a 10 fois plus de risque de développer un diabète de type II qu'une autre dont l'IMC est inférieure à 25.

2. De plus on observe que l'origine génétique des individus compte : en effet, les Indiens Pimas ont une plus forte prévalence au diabète de type II (40 % de la population est atteinte) que les Américains non indiens (15 %) et les métis ont une prévalence intermédiaire.

3. On peut en déduire que le diabète de type II est une maladie multifactorielle liée à la masse graisseuse mais aussi à des facteurs génétiques.

CONTRÔLE CONTINU POUR LE BAC

Exercice → *Énoncé p. 179*

La myopathie de Duchenne, maladie génétique répandue au Canada, touche principalement les hommes.

On se demande donc comment se transmet cette maladie, quelle est son origine ainsi que les différents moyens de traitements curatifs actuels.

On observe que la myopathie de Duchenne est une maladie génétique rare dans le monde avec 0,016 % de la population touchée. Or, au Canada, elle est plus répandue, touchant 0,1 % de la population et 0,19 % à Saguenay-Lac-Saint-Jean. Ceci s'explique par le phénomène de dérive génétique sur des petites populations d'individus. Comment cette maladie est-elle transmise génétiquement ?

D'après l'arbre généalogique, on observe que la maladie touche les hommes et les femmes, il s'agit donc d'une maladie autosomique. De plus, au sein d'une famille, les parents peuvent être sains (I.1 et I.2) mais un enfant (II.5) peut déclarer la myopathie. On peut donc supposer qu'il a hérité d'un allèle muté de chacun de ses parents, hétérozygotes donc porteurs sains : il faut donc être homozygote pour être malade. C'est une maladie récessive. Quel allèle est touché et comment espérer le soigner ?

On observe que le gène permettant de produire une protéine musculaire, la dystrophine, est muté chez les individus malades. Ceux-ci possèdent effectivement un allèle muté avec une délétion du 332e nucléotide C qui est situé sur l'exon 2 du gène.

La thérapie génique pourrait constituer un espoir de traitement de la maladie en remplaçant l'allèle muté par l'allèle sain à l'aide d'un vecteur viral. Une autre technique est en cours d'élaboration : le saut d'exon. On veut ainsi enlever l'exon 2 qui possède l'allèle muté. Cela est permis grâce à la stimulation de l'épissage alternatif qui pourra produire une dystrophine raccourcie mais fonctionnelle au lieu d'une dystrophine non fonctionnelle dans le cas d'un exon 2 muté.

En conclusion, la myopathie est une maladie génétique autosomique récessive particulièrement fréquente au Canada mais des techniques se développent pour espérer la soigner, en particulier la thérapie génique et le saut d'exon.

Altération du génome et cancérisation

CHAPITRE 12

Le cancer représente la première cause de mortalité en France, devant les pathologies cardiovasculaires.

1 L'origine de la cancérisation

A. Les facteurs génétiques

■ Des lésions de l'ADN peuvent se produire dans les cellules somatiques et se transmettre aux cellules-filles lors des mitoses successives. Les cellules-filles obtenues sont donc des clones cellulaires de la cellule initiale dont le génome a été modifié.

■ Si les gènes mutés sont impliqués dans les processus de contrôle de la division cellulaire, alors les cellules peuvent se multiplier de façon incontrôlée et former des **tumeurs***. Les gènes favorisant la division cellulaire sont appelés **oncogènes*** et ceux inhibant la mitose sont des **anti-oncogènes***.

■ D'autres critères que la mitose incontrôlée sont caractéristiques des cellules cancéreuses : leur immortalité, leur dédifférenciation (elles n'assurent plus leur rôle biologique) et leur mobilité (elles peuvent coloniser d'autres organes et devenir des **métastases*** ou tumeurs secondaires).

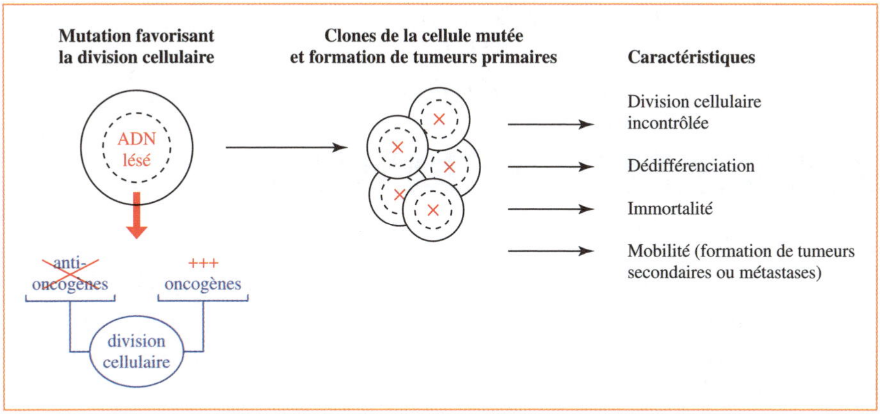

Figure 1 *Caractéristiques et origine des cellules cancéreuses*

■ Néanmoins les cellules immortelles et à prolifération incontrôlée ne deviennent pas toutes des cancers. Celles qui ne provoquent pas de métastases et restent immobiles sont appelées des **tumeurs bénignes*** (par opposition aux **tumeurs malignes***).

B. Les facteurs environnementaux

■ Des mutations somatiques peuvent survenir spontanément et créer ainsi des **gènes de prédisposition**. D'autres mutations peuvent être favorisées par des facteurs environnementaux : ce sont des **agents mutagènes***. Le tabagisme, l'alcool, la pollution, les UV, l'alimentation ou encore les infections virales peuvent constituer des agents mutagènes.

■ Connaître ces facteurs de risque génétiques et/ou environnementaux permet la mise en place de mesures de protection.

Facteurs de risque			Exemples de cancers associés
Génétiques	Gènes de prédisposition (mutation de l'anti-oncogène p53)		60 % des cancers (côlon, poumons, œsophage, estomac, foie, sein, vessie…)
Environnementaux	Tabagisme		Cancer des poumons, de la vessie, de la cavité buccale…
	Alcoolisme		Cancer de l'estomac, du foie, de la cavité buccale…
	Radiations		Lymphomes et cancer de la thyroïde
	Alimentation riche en graisse et sucre		Hépatocarcinome (tumeur du foie), cancer du pancréas, du côlon et de la prostate
	UV		Mélanome (cancer de la peau)
	Virus	papillomavirus	Cancer du col de l'utérus
		virus de l'hépatite B (VHB)	Cancer du foie

Figure 2 *Facteurs de risque et cancers*

2 Les moyens de protection contre les cancers

A. La prévention

■ Pour éviter l'apparition d'un cancer, des mesures de protection existent :

– Limiter l'exposition aux facteurs mutagènes : les études épidémiologiques permettent de calculer les risques relatifs en fonction de l'exposition à différents facteurs environnementaux. On peut ainsi empêcher leur action avec des campagnes de prévention ou la prise de mesures dissuasives (c'est le cas du tabagisme, de l'alcoolisme ou encore de l'exposition aux UV).

– Mettre en place un suivi régulier en fonction de l'âge : on surveille l'apparition des premières cellules cancéreuses par des mesures préventives de détection avec des examens de type mammographies, frottis et certaines prises de sang.
– Vacciner : c'est l'exemple du vaccin contre le papillomavirus qui est un virus favorisant l'apparition de certains cancers du col de l'utérus.

B. Les traitements

■ Quand le cancer est développé, certains traitements existent comme la **chimiothérapie***, la **radiothérapie***, la chirurgie ou la **thérapie génique**.

■ La chimiothérapie consiste à injecter au patient des substances antimitotiques. Les effets secondaires comme la chute des cheveux et des poils ainsi que des troubles intestinaux s'expliquent par l'action générale de la chimiothérapie qui affecte aussi les autres cellules à division rapide de l'organisme, comme les cellules de la peau ou des follicules pileux et les cellules intestinales.

■ La chirurgie permet d'enlever tout ou partie de la tumeur alors que la radiothérapie permet de traiter les tumeurs par leur exposition à des radiations localisées (radioactivité).

■ Ces techniques peuvent être utilisées seules ou combinées.

■ La thérapie génique peut être utilisée pour espérer guérir des cancers selon plusieurs méthodes :
– en stimulant les défenses immunitaires, en injectant dans les lymphocytes un gène permettant de produire une substance détruisant les cellules cancéreuses ;
– en injectant un gène dans la cellule tumorale, la rendant sensible à un agent toxique que l'on administrera ensuite ;
– en injectant un gène antimitotique dans les cellules tumorales comme le gène p53.

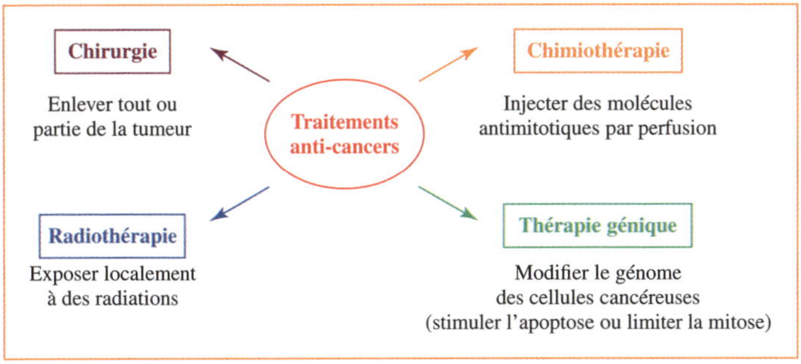

Figure 3 *Traitements contre les cancers*

EXERCICES

Connaître le cours

1 2 min ★ Vrai ou Faux ?

Relevez la (ou les) affirmation(s) exacte(s).

Les cellules cancéreuses :
a) sont des cellules immortelles.
b) sont des clones d'une cellule-mère mutée.
c) créent des tumeurs malignes ou bénignes.
d) sont favorisées par des gènes de prédisposition seulement.

→ *Corrigé p. 197*

2 2 min ★ Vrai ou Faux ?

Relevez la (ou les) affirmation(s) exacte(s).

Les traitements contre les cellules cancéreuses :
a) n'ont aucun effet secondaire.
b) sont encore tous en cours de développement.
c) peuvent reposer sur des transferts de gène stimulant la destruction des cellules cancéreuses.
d) peuvent être associées pour détruire les tumeurs.

→ *Corrigé p. 197*

3 5 min ★ Restitution de connaissances

Expliquez brièvement comment les facteurs environnementaux peuvent favoriser l'apparition de cancers.

→ *Corrigé p. 197*

4 5 min ★ Schématiser le cours

Schématisez l'ensemble des caractéristiques des cellules cancéreuses.

→ *Corrigé p. 197*

S'entraîner

5 10 min ★★ Risques relatifs du cancer de l'œsophage

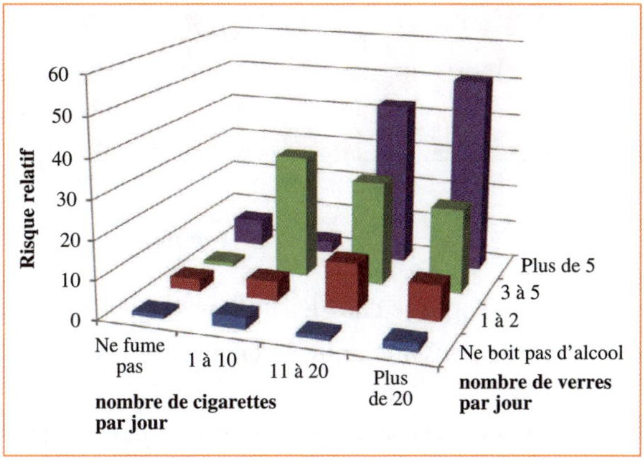

Risque relatif de développer un cancer de l'œsophage en fonction de la dose d'alcool et du nombre de cigarettes consommées

1. Déterminez les facteurs de risques environnementaux du cancer de l'œsophage.
2. Relevez le risque relatif de développer un cancer de l'œsophage pour un homme qui consommerait 3 à 5 verres d'alcool tout en fumant 1 à 10 cigarettes par jour.

➔ *Corrigé p. 197*

6 15 min ★★ Tabagisme et prévention des cancers

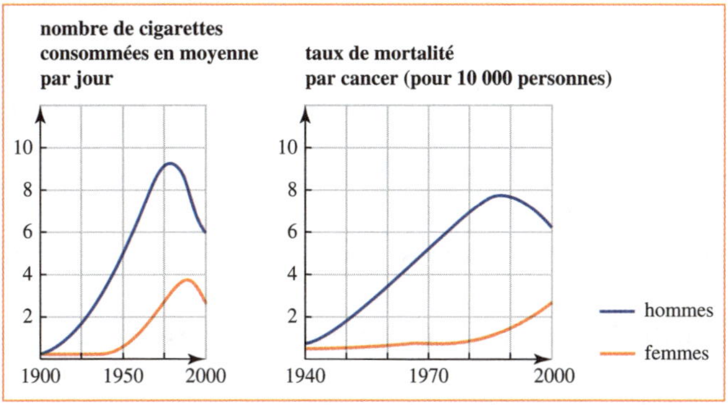

Figure 1 *Évolution de la consommation de cigarettes et des décès par cancer chez les hommes et les femmes*

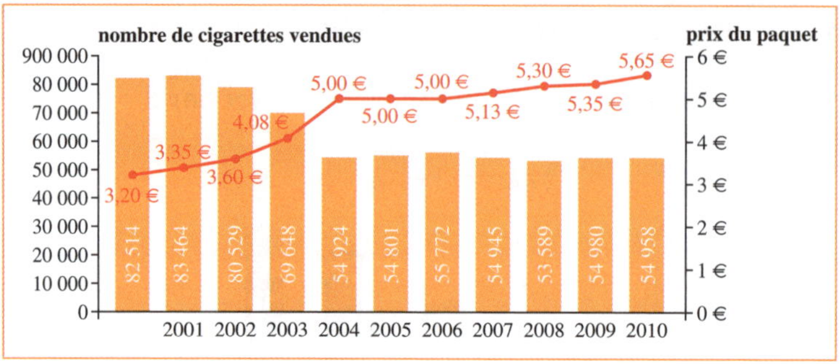

Figure 2 *Vente de cigarettes et prix annuel du paquet*

1. Décrivez l'évolution du tabagisme chez les hommes et les femmes depuis 1900.

2. Établissez une relation de causalité entre le tabagisme observé et la mortalité par cancer.

3. Quelle méthode de prévention est actuellement mise en place pour limiter l'épidémie de cancer lié au tabagisme ?

→ *Corrigé p. 198*

7 15 min ★★ Les UV

Une souche de levures, les Ade2, forme des colonies rouges. Toute mutation dans la chaîne de synthèse de cette pigmentation peut faire apparaître des colonies de couleur crème. On expose ces levures à des doses croissantes d'UV.

Durée d'exposition aux UV (secondes)	Nombre de clones	Nombre total de clones couleur crème
0	200	20
30	22	3
45	12	2
80	7	2

Nombre de levures mutantes en fonction de la durée d'exposition aux UV

1. À partir du tableau, calculez le taux de mutations spontanées lorsque les levures ne sont pas exposées aux UV.

2. Calculez ensuite le taux de mutations provoquées par les UV en fonction de la dose reçue.

3. Déduisez-en enfin les différentes actions des UV sur les levures.

→ *Corrigé p. 198*

8 20 min ★★ Les hépatocarcinomes

Le cancer du foie, ou hépatocarcinome, est le cinquième le plus fréquent chez l'homme. Il est en augmentation de 80 % dans les pays en voie de développement, en lien avec l'augmentation de l'hépatite C.

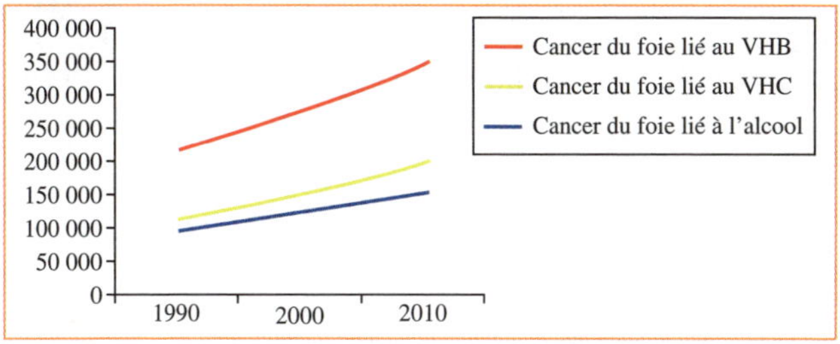

Figure 1 *Prévalence mondiale des cancers du foie provoqués par l'alcool, le virus de l'hépatite B (VHB) et le virus de l'hépatite C (VHC)*

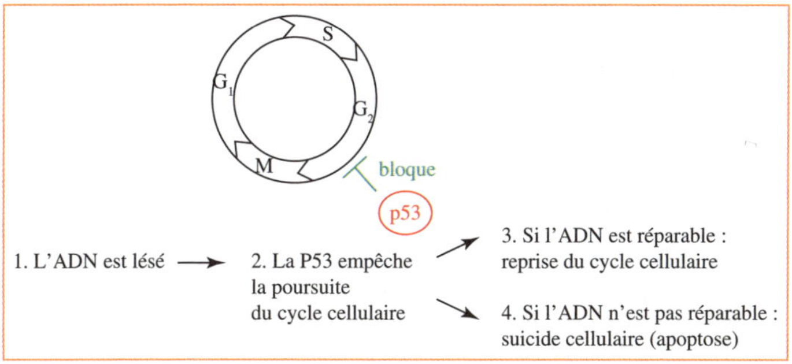

Figure 2 *Rôle de la p53 dans le cycle cellulaire*

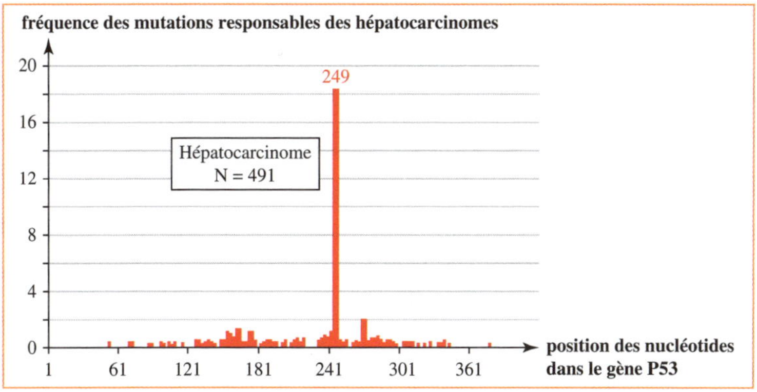

Figure 3 *Fréquence de mutations des codons dans les hépatocarcinomes*

1. À partir de la figure 1, montrez que le cancer du foie a une origine environnementale.
2. À partir de la figure 2 et 3, expliquez l'origine génétique du cancer du foie.

→ Corrigé p. 198

9 20 min ★★ Hépatite B et vaccination

L'hépatite B est provoquée par une contamination par le virus VHB par voie sanguine ou sexuelle. Ce virus infecte les cellules hépatiques (du foie).

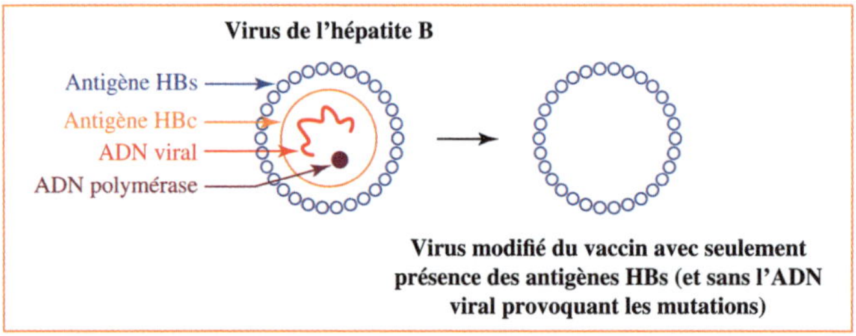

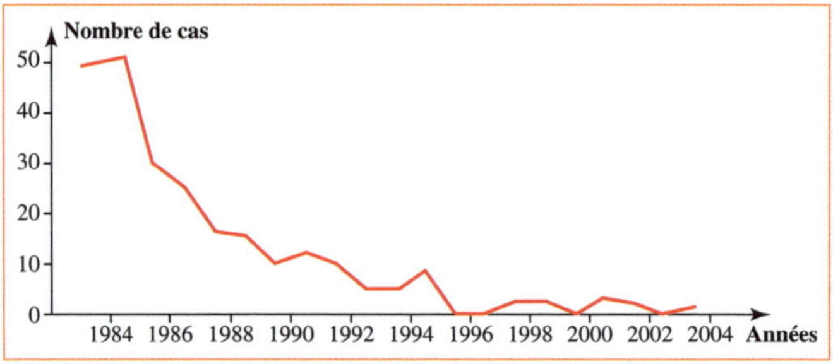

Figure 1 *Nombre de cas de nouvelles contaminations par le virus de l'hépatite B en France*

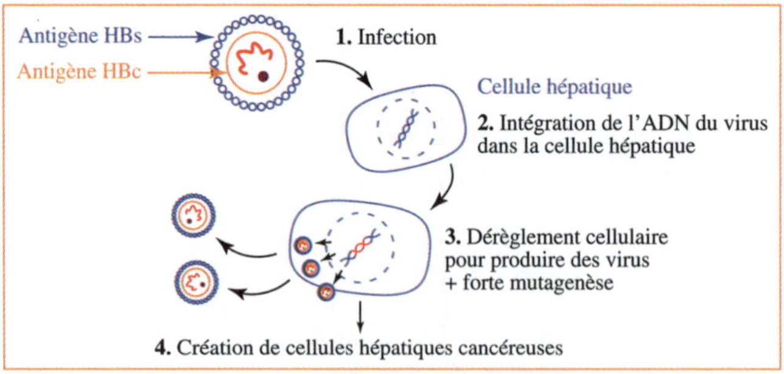

Figure 2 *Lien entre le VHB et le développement d'un hépatocarcinome*

1. D'après la figure 1, décrivez l'évolution du nombre de contaminations par le virus de l'hépatite B suite à la mise sur le marché du vaccin anti-VHB en 1981.

2. D'après la figure 2, expliquez le lien entre l'hépatite B et l'apparition d'un cancer du foie.

3. Déduisez-en l'intérêt de l'obligation de vaccination contre l'hépatite B depuis janvier 2018.

→ *Corrigé p. 199*

10 20 min ★★ L'immortalité des cellules cancéreuses

L'immortalité des cellules cancéreuses est causée par la mutation d'une enzyme : la télomérase.

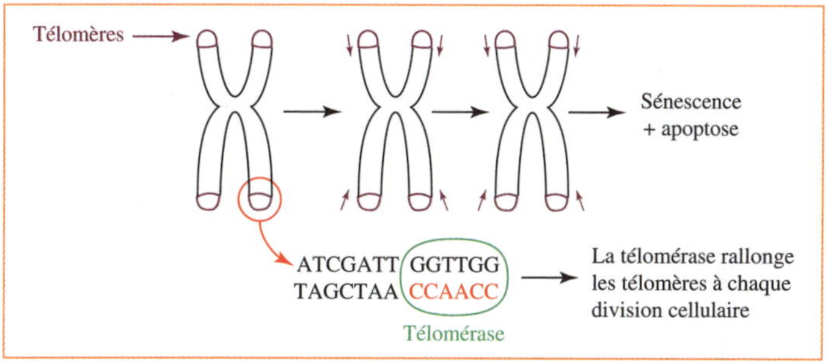

Figure 1 *Organisation des télomères et rôle de la télomérase*

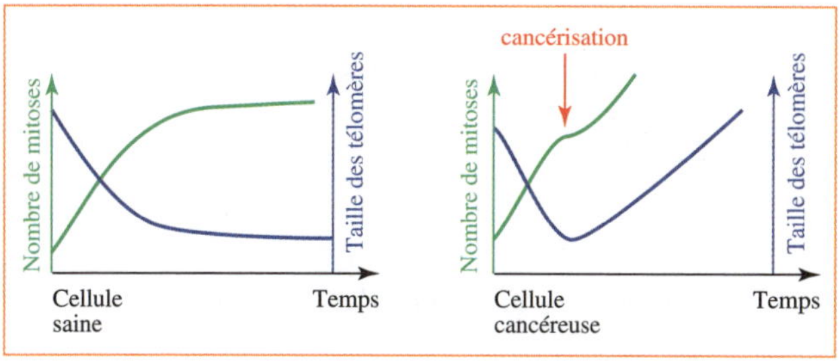

Figure 2 *Taille des télomères et nombre de mitoses chez des cellules saines et des cellules cancéreuses*

1. D'après la figure 1, décrivez le rôle de la télomérase dans le cycle de vie d'une cellule.

2. D'après la figure 2, expliquez pourquoi les cellules cancéreuses deviennent immortelles.

→ *Corrigé p. 199*

CONTRÔLE CONTINU POUR LE BAC

Exercice 10 pts — **Le cancer du col de l'utérus** — 30 min

Le cancer du col de l'utérus est responsable de 1 100 décès par an en France. C'est la 12e cause de cancer. Le taux d'incidence en France est de 6,1 pour 100 000 femmes en 2018 alors que l'Australie a le taux d'incidence le plus faible dans le monde.

À l'aide de l'ensemble des documents, expliquez les différentes causes à l'origine du cancer du col de l'utérus ainsi que les moyens de traitement qui ont notamment permis aux Australiens de diminuer les risques de développer cette maladie.

Document 1 : L'incidence et la mortalité du cancer du col de l'utérus

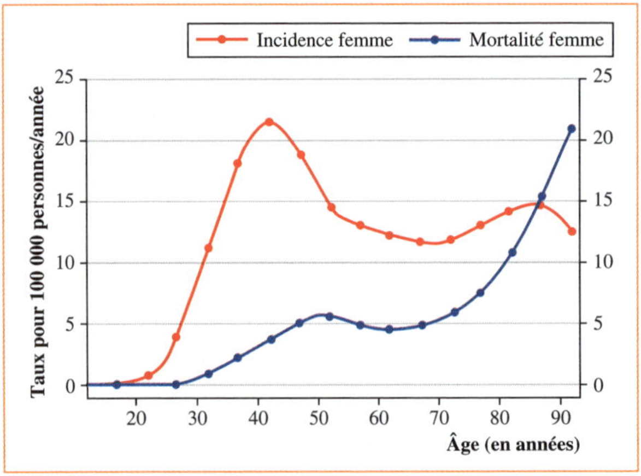

Incidence et mortalité du cancer du col de l'utérus en France en 2005

Document 2 : Les facteurs de risques du cancer du col de l'utérus

Une quarantaine de papillomavirus affectent le tractus anogénital et peuvent provoquer un cancer.

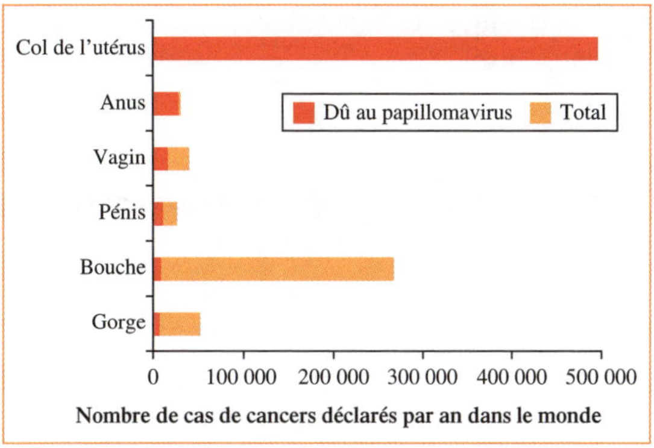

Figures 1 *Lien entre le papillomavirus et différents cancers*

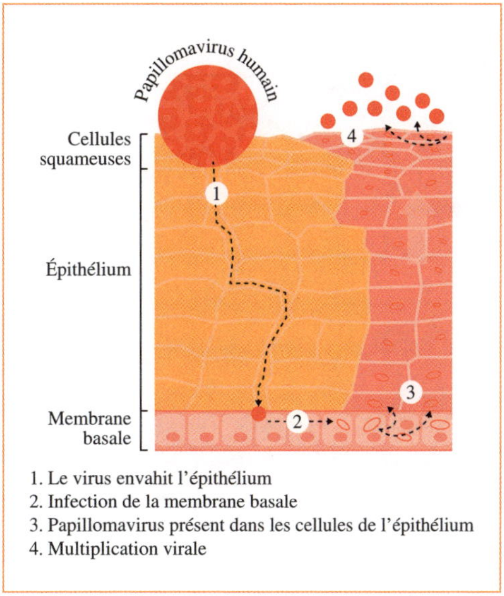

Figure 2 *Action du papillomavirus*

Document 3 : Les traitements

En 2007, le vaccin anti-papillomavirus est devenu obligatoire en Australie pour les femmes entre 12 et 29 ans. Il traite contre certaines variétés du VHP (n° 16 et 18).

D'autres méthodes de prévention existent comme les frottis du col de l'utérus. Le frottis consiste à prélever quelques cellules du col et à les analyser afin de détecter la présence de cellules cancéreuses.

Vaccins	Efficacité contre les cancers du col de l'utérus
Cervarix	71 %
Gardasil	71 %

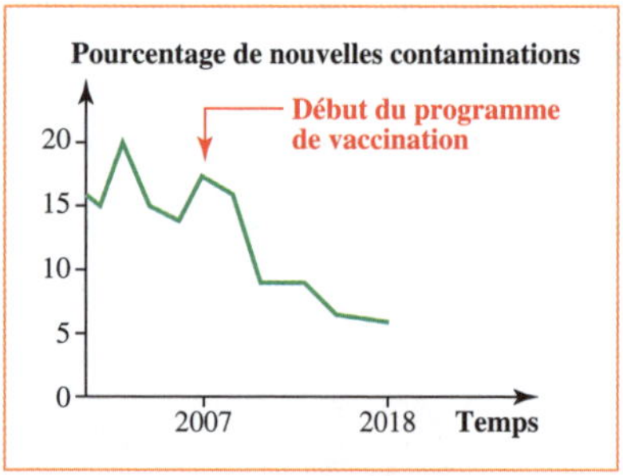

Pourcentage de nouvelles contaminations en Australie

→ *Corrigé p. 199*

CORRIGÉS

1 → *Énoncé p. 188*

Les affirmations exactes sont a), b) et c).

2 → *Énoncé p. 188*

Les affirmations exactes sont c) et d).

3 → *Énoncé p. 188*

Des mutations de l'ADN peuvent être induites par des facteurs environnementaux : ce sont des agents mutagènes. Le tabagisme, l'alcool, la pollution, les UV, l'alimentation ou encore les infections virales peuvent provoquer des lésions de l'ADN et ainsi l'apparition de certains cancers comme les cancers des poumons, du foie, du col de l'utérus…

Connaître les facteurs de risque lorsque l'on est exposé à ces facteurs environnementaux permet de mettre au point des traitement curatifs et préventifs adaptés.

4 → *Énoncé p. 188*

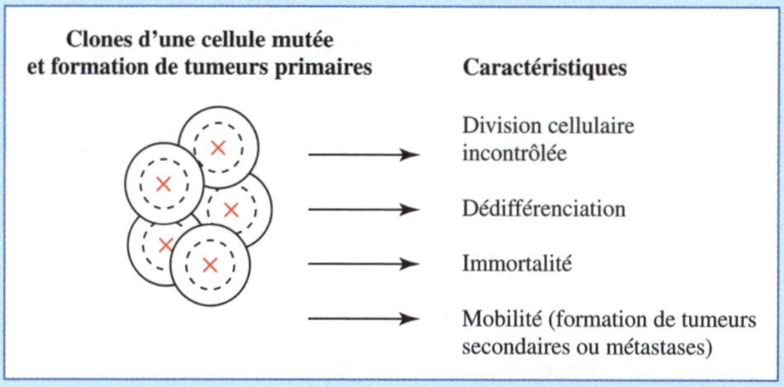

5 → *Énoncé p. 189*

1. On observe que la consommation de cigarettes augmente le risque relatif de développer un cancer de l'œsophage. Ainsi on passe d'un risque relatif de 1 à 3 en consommant 1 à 10 cigarettes par jour. Cependant, ce risque est décuplé par la consommation d'alcool. On observe, en effet, que les deux comportements combinés augmentent d'autant plus le risque relatif de cancer. Ainsi, fumer plus de 20 cigarettes par jour et boire plus de 5 verres d'alcool augmente le risque relatif d'avoir un cancer de l'œsophage de 50. C'est donc une maladie multifactorielle.

2. Un homme buvant 3 à 5 verres d'alcool et fumant 1 à 10 cigarettes par jour augmente son risque relatif de souffrir d'un cancer de l'œsophage de 28.

6 → Énoncé p. 189

1. On observe que jusqu'en 1975 pour les hommes et 1990 pour les femmes, la consommation de cigarettes augmente puis diminue. On peut mettre en relation ces observations avec l'augmentation des cas de cancer du poumon avec un pic dans les années 1985 chez les hommes et une augmentation à partir des années 1980 chez les femmes.

2. Cette augmentation de la consommation de cigarettes est suivie par celle de cas de mortalité par cancer des poumons 10 ans plus tard. On peut donc supposer un lien entre ces deux événements : la consommation de cigarettes augmenterait les risques de développer un cancer des poumons avec une latence de 10 ans. Cependant, cette corrélation doit encore être vérifiée par une étude épidémiologique.

3. Depuis 2000, on observe une diminution de la consommation de cigarettes en parallèle de l'augmentation du prix du tabac. Il s'agit d'une technique de prévention : on dissuade la consommation de cigarettes en augmentant le prix des paquets afin d'éviter l'exposition au facteur de risque qu'est le tabagisme et donc de diminuer l'épidémie de cancer des poumons.

7 → Énoncé p. 190

1. Sans exposition aux UV, on observe 20 colonies blanches sur les 200 comptabilisées. Or on sait que les colonies blanches de levures sont caractéristiques d'une mutation de l'ADN. On peut donc calculer le taux de mutations spontanées : 20/200 = 0,1, soit 10 % de mutations spontanées.

2. Au bout de 30 secondes d'exposition aux UV, le taux de mutation est de 3/22 = 14 %. Au bout de 45 secondes 2/12 = 17 % et au bout de 80 secondes 2/7 = 28,6 %. Globalement, plus l'exposition aux UV est forte, plus le taux de mutations induites est élevé. C'est l'effet mutagène des UV.

3. De plus, on observe une diminution du nombre de clones de levures plus l'exposition aux UV est forte. Les UV ont donc une action létale sur les levures. S'il y a trop de mutations dans l'ADN, les cellules meurent. Les UV sont donc des agents mutagènes et létaux.

8 → Énoncé p. 191

1. Entre 1990 et 2010, on observe une augmentation des cas de cancer du foie liés aux virus de l'hépatite B et C ainsi qu'à l'alcoolisme. L'hépatocarcinome est donc provoqué par des facteurs environnementaux.

2. On observe qu'une protéine, la p53, est responsable normalement d'un blocage du cycle cellulaire en cas de lésions de l'ADN. L'ADN est ensuite réparé (le cycle cellulaire reprend) ou non (la cellule part en apoptose). Dans le cas du cancer du foie, on observe que le gène codant la p53 est muté dans 18 % des cas au niveau du codon 249.

Si p53 n'est pas fonctionnelle, l'arrêt du cycle cellulaire n'est pas possible en cas de mutation et la cellule peut devenir cancéreuse en se divisant incessamment. C'est un anti-oncogène. L'hépatocarcinome est donc un cancer génétique et environnemental : il est multifactoriel.

9 → Énoncé p. 192

1. À partir de 1984, on observe une diminution des nouvelles contaminations d'individus par le virus de l'hépatite B de 50 à presque 0 actuellement.

2. Ce virus de l'hépatite B infecte les hépatocytes en y injectant son ADN afin de détourner la synthèse de la cellule hôte pour que celle-ci produise des nouveaux virus. Ceci est permis notamment par un grand nombre de mutations. Ceci peut favoriser l'apparition, quelques années après la contamination par le VHB, de cellules cancéreuses.

3. L'obligation vaccinale repose sur le lien entre le VHB et l'apparition de cancer du foie. En permettant au système immunitaire de se protéger contre le VHB, on évite le développement d'un cancer du foie. Pour cela, on modifie le VHB en injectant seulement les antigènes qui permettent au virus d'infecter les cellules : le virus est donc inoffensif.

10 → Énoncé p. 193

1. Au cours des divisions cellulaires, le chromosome répliqué diminue en taille. Lorsqu'il est trop court, la cellule vieillit et meurt. Pour limiter le vieillissement cellulaire, la télomérase sert à rallonger l'extrémité des chromosomes. Elle perd en activité au cours de la vie : les cellules vieillissent donc.

2. Dans les cellules cancéreuses, la télomérase est suractivée, ce qui empêche le vieillissement cellulaire et l'apoptose de la cellule. On observe que les télomères deviennent beaucoup plus grands et les divisions cellulaires nombreuses : la cellule est donc devenue immortelle.

CONTRÔLE CONTINU POUR LE BAC

Exercice → Énoncé p. 194

Le cancer du col de l'utérus est en voie de disparition en Australie grâce à une campagne de vaccination sur les femmes.

Comment les traitements vaccinaux et les frottis utérins on-ils permis une diminution des cas de cancers du col de l'utérus ?

L'incidence du cancer du col de l'utérus est forte vers 40 ans chez la femme puis diminue de 50 à 80 ans. Parallèlement, la mortalité augmente seulement à partir de 70 ans.

On peut alors supposer que le cancer du col de l'utérus met du temps à se développer et à provoquer un décès. Ou bien qu'il est difficile à détecter. Il doit donc exister des méthodes curatives et de prévention de son apparition.

On observe que le cancer du col de l'utérus est le cancer le plus induit par le papillomavirus avec près de 500 000 nouveaux cas dans le monde par an. Presque 100 % de ces cancers du col de l'utérus sont attribuables à l'une des variétés du papillomavirus. Ce virus provoque le cancer du col de l'utérus en pénétrant des cellules de l'épithélium du col via une lésion. Il infecte ces cellules et se multiplie, provoquant l'apparition progressive de cellules cancéreuses sur plusieurs mois, voire années.

Pour le prévenir, une vaccination existe : elle est efficace à 71 % des cas de cancers du col de l'utérus et permet d'éviter toute nouvelle contamination (en Suisse, par exemple, le pourcentage de nouveaux cas a diminué de 16 % à 6 % depuis la mise en place du programme de vaccination). Dans tous les cas, cela n'évite pas la réalisation de frottis utérins qui permettent de surveiller l'apparition de nouvelles cellules cancéreuses régulièrement. Ces deux méthodes permettent de faire diminuer l'incidence du cancer du col de l'utérus, notamment en Australie.

Variation génétique bactérienne et résistance aux antibiotiques

CHAPITRE 13

Les bactéries sont des micro-organismes qui peuvent provoquer des infections dangereuses. Le traitement médical des infections bactériennes repose sur l'utilisation d'antibiotiques.

1 La variabilité génétique des bactéries

■ Le génome bactérien peut être soumis à des mutations spontanées ou induites.

■ Les mutations spontanées chez les bactéries sont des phénomènes rares : elles affectent peu de bactéries au sein d'une grande population. La probabilité qu'une bactérie mute sur un temps donné s'appelle un **taux de mutation***.

■ Ces mutations sont aléatoires et peuvent conférer des résistances aux antibiotiques.

■ D'autres mutations peuvent être provoquées par l'exposition des bactéries à des agents mutagènes. C'est le cas des expositions aux UV ou à des substances chimiques.

■ Par ailleurs, une particularité des bactéries est la possibilité de transférer du matériel génétique entre plusieurs cellules (transfert horizontal de gène) : c'est la **conjugaison bactérienne***.

Remarque

Les bactéries sont des cellules procaryotes, dont l'ADN est directement dans le cytoplasme, sans être protégé par un noyau. Leur génome est circulaire (et non linéaire comme chez les Eucaryotes).

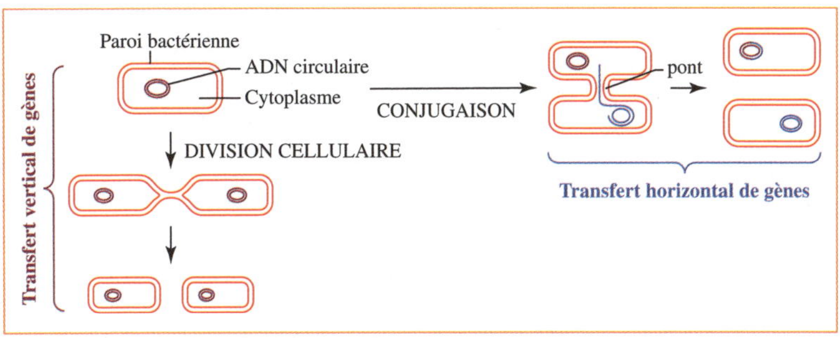

Figure 1 *Les transferts d'ADN chez les bactéries*

2 Les conséquences de l'utilisation des antibiotiques

A. La sélection naturelle induite par les antibiotiques

■ L'application d'un antibiotique sur une population bactérienne tue les bactéries dites « sensibles » à cet antibiotique. Les antibiotiques bloquent la croissance bactérienne ou tuent les bactéries en agissant de différentes façons :
– destruction de la paroi de la bactérie ;
– destruction de la membrane plasmique ;
– blocage de la traduction des protéines ;
– blocage de la transcription de l'ADN en ARN.

Remarque

Le premier antibiotique a été découvert par inadvertance en 1928 par Alexander Fleming : au retour de vacances, ses boîtes de Petri ensemencées par des staphylocoques furent contaminées par une souche de champignon (*Pénicillium notatum*). Il remarqua alors qu'autour du champignon la bactérie n'avait pas poussé : ainsi fut découverte la pénicilline.

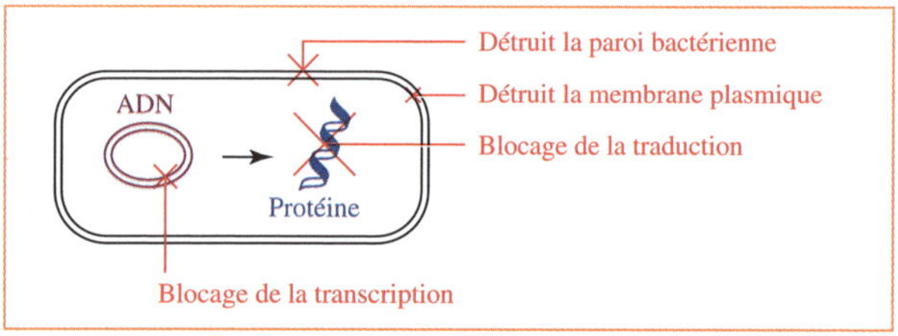

Figure 2 *Le mode d'action de différents antibiotiques*

■ On peut déterminer l'efficacité d'un antibiotique par l'utilisation d'un antibiogramme. On étale les bactéries sur une boîte de Petri et on y applique des pastilles de différents antibiotiques. L'antibiotique diffuse sur la gélose et, plus il est efficace, plus le halo de destruction sera grand. Cette méthode est qualitative.

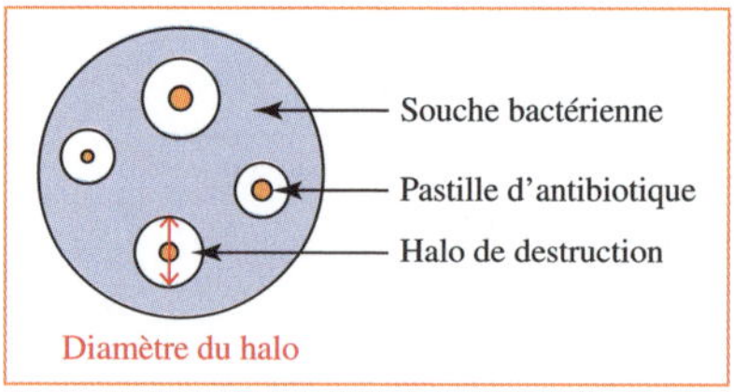

Figure 3 *Antibiogramme et efficacité des antibiotiques*

■ On peut aussi mesurer la CMI (pour concentration minimale inhibitrice). C'est la concentration d'antibiotique minimale à appliquer pour bloquer efficacement la croissance bactérienne.

■ Certains antibiotiques se révèlent inefficaces contre certaines bactéries : ces dernières sont devenues **résistantes***. L'antibiotique tue les bactéries sensibles mais n'affecte pas les bactéries résistantes qui sont apparues par des mutations spontanées dans la population initiale. Les bactéries résistantes vont alors mieux survivre et davantage se reproduire : leur fréquence va augmenter au fur et à mesure des générations. C'est le phénomène de **sélection naturelle***.

Définition

Le taux de mutation d'apparition des résistances aux antibiotiques se calcule de la façon suivante :

$$Tm = \frac{\text{Nombre de mutants}}{\text{Nombre de bactéries initiales}}$$

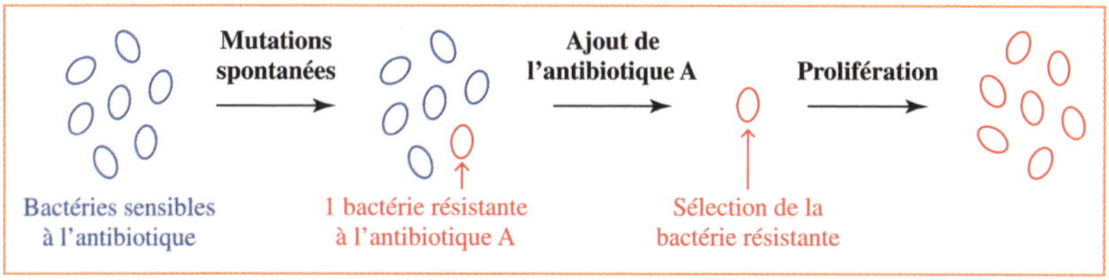

Figure 4 *Sélection naturelle des bactéries par l'ajout des antibiotiques*

B. La résistance multiple aux antibiotiques

■ L'utilisation systématique de traitements antibiotiques en santé humaine comme en usage agronomique ou vétérinaire conduit à augmenter la fréquence des formes résistantes dans les populations naturelles de bactéries. Cela peut aboutir à la sélection de formes simultanément résistantes à plusieurs antibiotiques.

■ On appelle ainsi **résistance naturelle*** les résistances à un antibiotique apparues de manière spontanée chez les bactéries. À l'opposé, on appelle **résistance acquise*** l'apparition de mutations induites par des transferts de gène d'une bactérie résistante à une bactérie sensible. Ce phénomène est provoqué par la conjugaison bactérienne.

■ Cette **résistance multiple*** constitue un important problème de santé publique car le nombre de familles d'antibiotiques disponibles est limité. Une utilisation des antibiotiques plus raisonné et responsable doit donc être recherchée. D'autres méthodes sont en cours d'élaboration comme l'utilisation de virus à bactéries : les **phages***.

EXERCICES

Connaître le cours

1 2 min ★ Vrai ou Faux ?

Relevez la (ou les) affirmation(s) exacte(s).

Les antibiotiques :
a) peuvent être testés grâce à des antibiogrammes.
b) sont utilisables contre les bactéries et les virus.
c) peuvent être produits de façon naturelle par certains champignons.
d) perdent en efficacité à cause de leur utilisation systématique.

→ *Corrigé p. 211*

2 2 min ★ Vrai ou Faux ?

Relevez la (ou les) affirmation(s) exacte(s).

Les bactéries :
a) sont des Eucaryotes.
a) possèdent un génome linéaire.
c) peuvent transférer une partie de leur ADN à d'autres bactéries.
d) possèdent un ADN qui peut muter spontanément ou par des facteurs environnementaux.

→ *Corrigé p. 211*

3 5 min ★ Restitution de connaissances

Expliquez brièvement comment les antibiotiques peuvent traiter les infections bactériennes.

→ *Corrigé p. 211*

4 5 min ★ Schématiser le cours

Schématisez la sélection des bactéries résistantes par les antibiotiques.

→ *Corrigé p. 211*

S'entraîner

5 10 min ★★ La résistance bactérienne

Entre 2000 et 2015, le nombre d'antibiotiques disponibles en France a diminué de plus de 20 %. Lors d'un séjour hospitalier, des infections peuvent être contractées : ce sont les infections nosocomiales (par exemple *Streptococcus pneumoniae*).

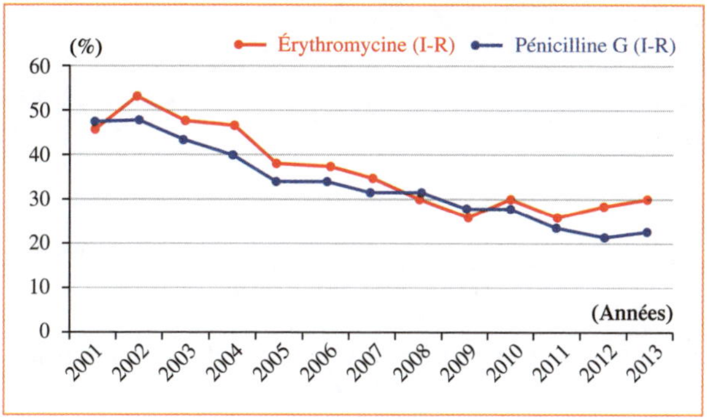

Figure 1 *Évolution de la résistance de* Streptococcus pneumoniae *à deux antibiotiques*

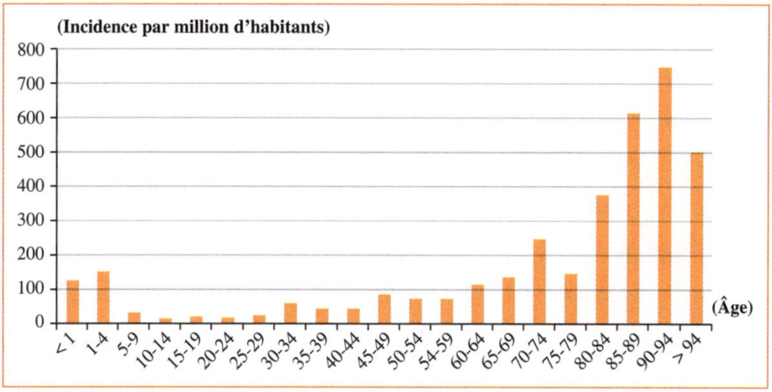

Figure 2 *Incidence estimée par classe d'âges des infections par* Streptococcus pneumoniae

1. D'après la figure 1, montrez que *Streptococcus pneumoniae* est une souche de bactérie résistante à plusieurs antibiotiques.

2. Grâce à la figure 2, indiquez quelles personnes sont particulièrement touchées par cette infection.

→ *Corrigé p. 211*

6 10 min ★★ L'impact des élevages agricoles

Certains élevages agricoles utilisent des antibiotiques de façon systématique pour prévenir les risques d'infection en cas de blessures des animaux d'élevage.

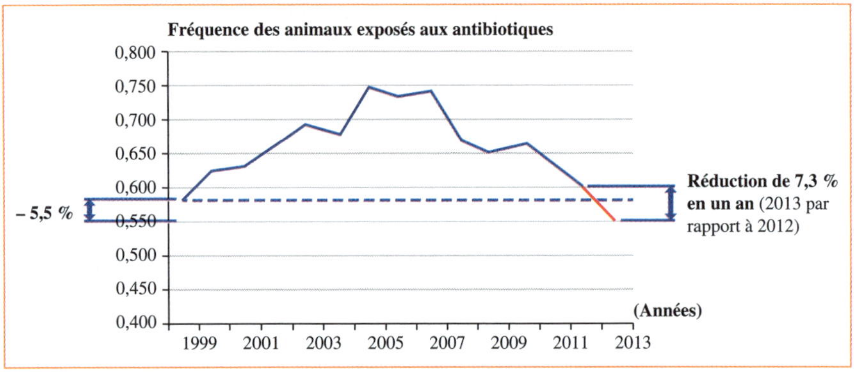

Figure 1 *Évolution de l'exposition des animaux d'élevage aux antibiotiques entre 1999 et 2013*

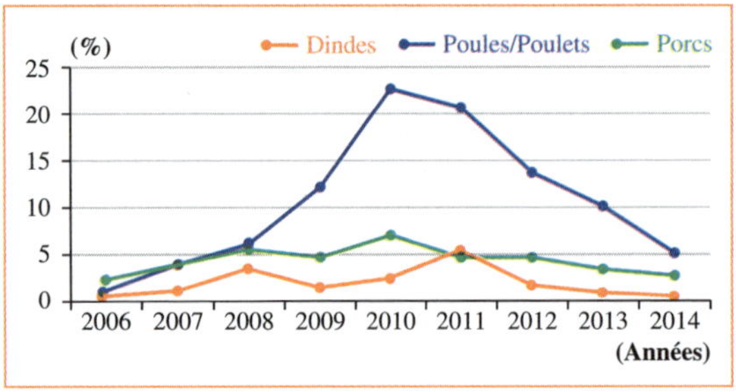

Figure 2 *Évolution des proportions d'*Escherichia coli *résistantes chez les porcs, les poules et les dindes entre 2006 et 2014*

1. Décrivez l'évolution de l'utilisation des antibiotiques entre 1999 et 2013 sur les animaux d'élevage.

2. Expliquez l'origine de la résistance d'*Escherichia coli* chez les poulets d'élevage en 2011.

→ Corrigé p. 212

7 15 min ★★ Les taux de mutation

Soit une culture de bactéries *E. coli* normalement sensibles à la streptomycine. On cultive ces bactéries sur un milieu gélosé en présence de streptomycine. Après incubation, on dénombre 4 colonies sur une quantité initiale de bactéries étalées de 10^8 UFC (unité formant des colonies). On effectue ensuite la même expérience mais après avoir exposé les bactéries à un agent mutagène : la nitrosoguanidine. On dénombre alors 40 colonies bactériennes.

1. Quelle est la caractéristique principale des bactéries composant les 4 colonies après la première culture ?

2. Calculez le taux de mutation des résistants à la streptomycine.

3. Calculez le taux de mutation des résistants à la streptomycine après exposition à la nitrosoguanidine.

4. Quel est le rôle de la nitrosoguanidine et quelles sont ses conséquences sur le génome des bactéries ?

→ *Corrigé p. 212*

8 15 min ★★ Antibiogramme et CMI

Pour déterminer la concentration d'antibiotique à donner à un patient souffrant d'une infection bactérienne, on effectue des antibiogrammes avec des pastilles d'antibiotiques de concentration croissante et on mesure le diamètre des halos de destruction obtenus.

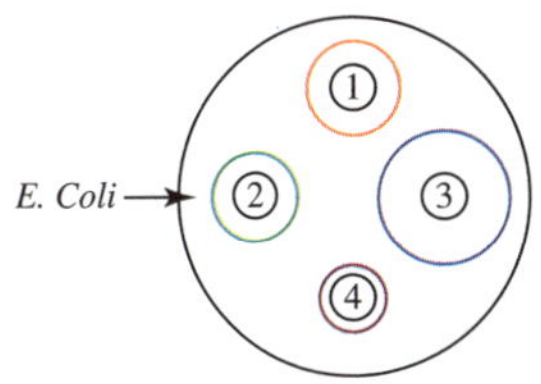

Antibiotiques	Diamètre du halo
① ampicilline	1,5 cm
② acide nalidixique	1,75 cm
③ tétracycline	3 cm
④ pénicilline	0,5 cm

Figure 1 *Antibiogramme réalisé sur* E. coli

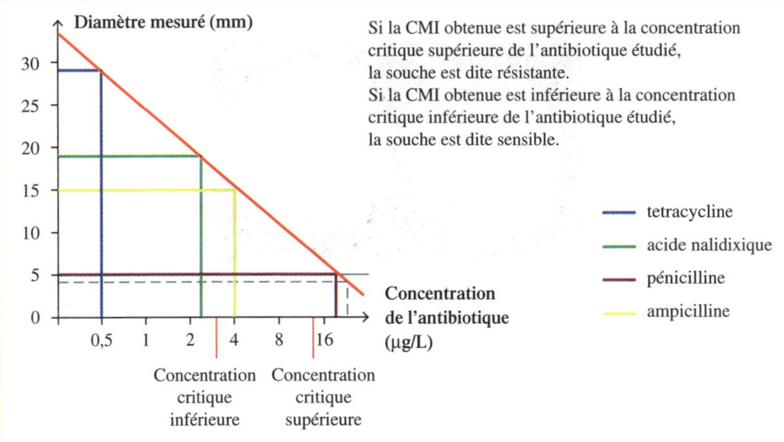

Figure 2 *Concentration minimale inhibitrice (CMI)*

1. Déterminez l'antibiotique le plus efficace d'après l'antibiogramme testant *E. coli*.
2. À l'aide d'une lecture graphique de la figure 2, déterminez la CMI de chaque antibiotique.
3. *E. coli* est-elle sensible ou résistante à ces différents antibiotiques ?

→ Corrigé p. 212

9 15 min ★★ Les nouveaux traitements antibactériens

Aux Hospices civils de Lyon, en septembre 2017, un patient atteint d'une infection sévère aux os et aux articulations a été guéri grâce à un nouveau traitement : la phagothérapie. Il souffrait d'une infection causée par le staphylocoque doré, à la suite de la greffe d'une prothèse articulaire.

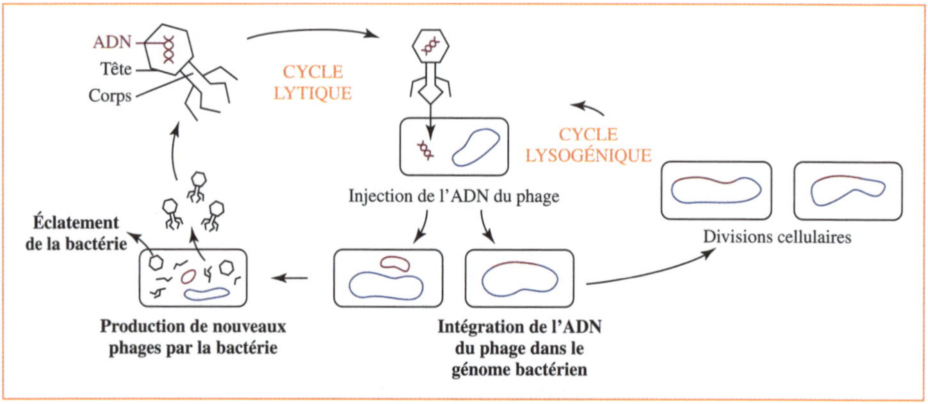

Figure 1 *Cycle de vie d'un phage*

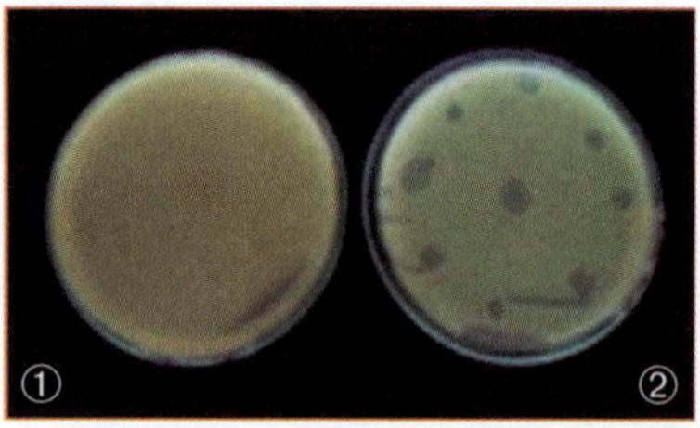

Figure 2 *Résultats d'une phagothérapie sur la bactérie* E. coli

1. À l'aide de la figure 1, décrivez le principe de la phagothérapie et son intérêt pour détruire les bactéries.
2. À l'aide de la figure 2, montrez l'efficacité d'une phagothérapie sur *E. coli*.

→ Corrigé p. 213

Exercice 10 pts Les résistances multiples bactériennes 30 min

Les bactéries *E. coli*, présentes naturellement dans les intestins, peuvent muter et devenir pathogènes, provoquant ainsi 80 % des infections urinaires féminines. La souche sauvage n'est pas pathogène, tandis que les souches mutantes ΔcyaA et ΔptsI le sont.

À l'aide de l'ensemble des documents et de vos connaissances, mettez en évidence que la diversité génétique d'*E. coli* lui a permis de résister à plusieurs antibiotiques, et expliquez les traitements possibles.

Document 1

Différentes souches d'*E. coli* sont cultivées dans un milieu enrichi en urine pour se rapprocher des conditions de l'organisme, en présence de fosfomycine. On observe leur croissance au cours du temps.

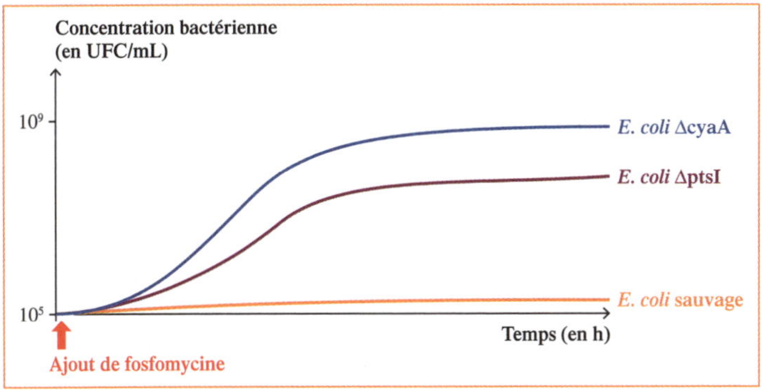

*Croissance de différentes souches d'*E. coli *dans un milieu enrichi en antibiotique*

Document 2

La CMI de la fosfomycine est déterminée pour les souches sauvages d'*E. coli* et quelques souches mutantes.

Souche d'*E. coli*	CMI après culture dans un milieu riche en urine ($\mu g.mL^{-1}$)
Sauvage	0,38
ΔptsI	1,5
ΔcyaA	2

*CMI de la fosfomycine sur différentes variétés d'*E. coli

Document 3

On étudie la variation de la résistance d'*E. coli* à différents antibiotiques chez les femmes françaises ayant souffert d'infection urinaire.

Antibiotique	**Nombre d'*E. coli* sensibles**	**Pourcentage d'*E. coli* sensibles dans la population**	**Pourcentage d'*E. coli* résistantes dans la population**
fosfomycine	331	100	0
acide nalidixique	311	94,7	5,3
céfotaxime	323	98,1	1,9
amoxicilline	215	62	38

Proportion de bactéries E. coli *sensibles ou résistantes chez les femmes françaises traitées à différents antibiotiques*

→ *Corrigé p. 213*

CORRIGÉS

1 → *Énoncé p. 204*

Les affirmations exactes sont a), c) et d).

2 → *Énoncé p. 204*

Les affirmations exactes sont c) et d).

3 → *Énoncé p. 204*

Les antibiotiques ont pour but de limiter la croissance bactérienne ou de tuer les bactéries en détruisant leur paroi, ou en affectant la production de la membrane plasmique, en empêchant la traduction des protéines ou bien encore en arrêtant la transcription de l'ADN en ARN.

On peut tester l'efficacité des antibiotiques à l'aide d'antibiogrammes en déterminant la Concentration minimal efficace afin de choisir les antibiotiques les plus efficaces et limiter la sélection de bactéries résistantes.

4 → *Énoncé p. 204*

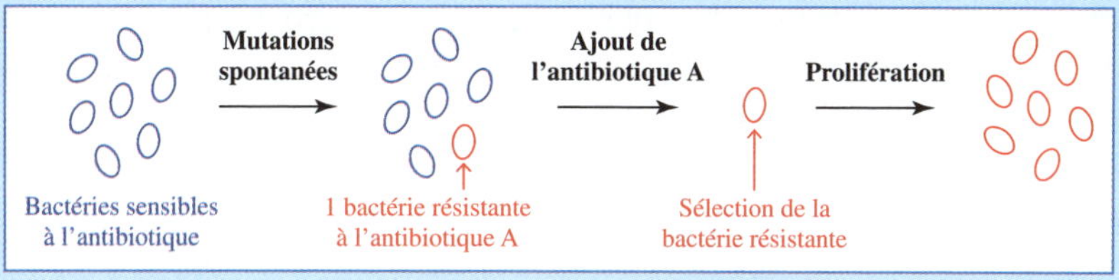

5 → *Énoncé p. 205*

1. On observe que *Streptococcus pneumoniae* était résistante à 50 % à la pénicilline et à l'érythromycine en 2001. Douze ans plus tard, sa résistance diminue à 30 % pour l'érythromycine et à 20 % pour la pénicilline mais reste très élevée. Cette souche bactérienne possède donc une résistance multiple aux antibiotiques.

2. On observe que les infections invasives à *Streptococcus pneumoniae* touchent les personnes dont le système immunitaire est le plus faible : les enfants en bas âge (de 0 à 4 ans) et les personnes âgées (de 70 à plus de 94 ans).

6 → *Énoncé p. 206*

1. On observe une augmentation de l'utilisation des antibiotiques de 1999 à 2007 dans les élevages agricoles puis une baisse de cette utilisation jusqu'à revenir à un taux inférieur à 1999, en 2013. Les élevages sont donc une source d'utilisation d'antibiotiques.

2. En conséquence, en 2011 a eu lieu un pic de résistance d'*E. coli* aux antibiotiques chez les poules. Ceci peut être lié à l'utilisation massive des antibiotiques en 2007. Utiliser des antibiotiques de façon massive peut donc avoir un impact sur l'apparition de bactéries résistantes à plusieurs antibiotiques et donc affecter la santé humaine.

7 → *Énoncé p. 206*

1. Naturellement sensible à l'antibiotique, *E. coli* va tout de même se développer dans un milieu avec de la streptomycine à raison de 4 colonies. On peut donc en déduire que 4 cellules initiales étaient résistantes à la streptomycine sur les 10^8 étalées et qu'elles ont donc survécu. Ce sont des mutations qui sont apparues spontanément chez *E. coli*.

2. $Tm = \frac{\text{Nombre de mutants}}{\text{Nombre de bactéries initiales}} = \frac{4}{10^8} = 4.10^{-8}$

3. $Tm = \frac{\text{Nombre de mutants}}{\text{Nombre de bactéries initiales}} = \frac{40}{10^8} = 4.10^{-7}$

4. On observe ainsi que le taux de mutation après exposition à la nitrosoguanidine est plus élevé que celui provoqué par des mutations spontanées : c'est un agent mutagène qui favorise l'émergence de résistance à l'antibiotique.

8 → *Énoncé p. 207*

1. D'après l'antibiogramme réalisé sur *E. coli*, on observe que la tétracycline est l'antibiotique donnant le plus grand halo de destruction. Or, on sait que plus le halo de destruction est grand, plus l'antibiotique est efficace. On peut donc supposer qu'*E. coli* est plus sensible à la tétracycline qu'à la pénicilline (dont le halo de destruction est le plus faible).

2. D'après le graphique de la CMI, pour inhiber la croissance bactérienne, il faudrait :

– 4 $\mu g.L^{-1}$ d'ampicilline

– 3 $\mu g.L^{-1}$ d'acide nalidixique

– 0,3 $\mu g.L^{-1}$ de tétracycline

– plus de 16 $\mu g.L^{-1}$ de péniciline

On peut donc en déduire que seules la tétracycline et l'acide nalidixique se situent sous la concentration critique inférieure d'antibiotique. Ce sont donc les antibiotiques les plus efficaces contre *E. coli*.

3. D'après l'ensemble de ces observations, on peut supposer qu'*E. coli* est sensible à la tétracycline, à l'ampicilline et l'acide nalidixique mais résistante à la pénicilline.

9 → *Énoncé p. 208*

1. Lors de la phagothérapie, on utilise un virus à bactérie : les phages. Ces phages vont pénétrer et injecter leur ADN dans les bactéries infectées. Deux possibilités s'offrent ici : le cycle lysogénique où l'ADN du phage intègre celui de la bactérie et subira les divisions cellulaires sans affecter la vie de la bactérie. L'autre possibilité est le cycle lytique où l'ADN du phage détourne le matériel génétique de la bactérie pour se reproduire et entraîne son éclatement. Lors de la phagothérapie, le but recherché est donc le cycle lytique du phage afin de détruire la bactérie.

2. Après ajout de phages sur une culture d'*E. coli*, on observe l'apparition de halos de destructions, comme c'est le cas sur les antibiogrammes. On peut donc en déduire que cette phagothérapie permet la destruction des bactéries.

CONTRÔLE CONTINU POUR LE BAC

Exercice → *Énoncé p. 209*

E. coli est une bactérie non pathogène, sauf dans certains cas d'apparition de variétés mutantes pouvant provoquer des infections urinaires ou des diarrhées.

On se demande donc comment les mutations peuvent permettre l'apparition de variétés mutantes chez *E. coli* et comment les traiter.

On observe qu'il existe des souches d'*E. coli* répondant différemment à un antibiotique, la fosfomycine. En effet, la croissance de la souche sauvage est fortement ralentie par l'action de la fosfomycine. En revanche, d'autres formes comme la ΔptsI et la ΔcyaA possèdent une croissance toujours aussi efficace malgré l'ajout de l'antibiotique. L'antibiotique est-il inefficace sur ces souches bactériennes ?

Après réalisation d'antibiogramme, on réalise une comparaison des CMI de la fosfomycine sur ces différentes variétés d'*E. coli*. On observe que les variétés ΔptsI et ΔcyaA nécessitent plus d'antibiotique pour être détruites alors que la souche sauvage y est très sensible. On peut donc en déduire qu'il existe une variété génétique importante chez *E. coli* due à des mutations spontanées et ayant provoqué l'apparition de mutants résistants à la fosfomycine. Pourtant, cet antibiotique est toujours utilisé en France pour traiter les infections urinaires.

En effet, on observe que les femmes françaises ayant souffert d'infection urinaire sévère ne possédent pas ces souches mutantes. La souche sauvage est donc bien sensible à la fosfomycine et a pu être traitée grâce à la prescription de cet antibiotique.

Il faut veiller à ne pas fournir d'autres antibiotiques notamment de l'amoxicilline car même la souche sauvage y est très résistante.

Pour conclure, l'utilisation parcimonieuse d'antibiotique peut permettre de traiter contre la souche sauvage d'*E. coli* provoquant des infections urinaires. Cependant certaines mutations ayant entraîné l'apparition de variétés résistantes, il faudra faire attention à l'utiliser de façon minutieuse pour ne pas sélectionner ces bactéries mutantes.

L'immunité innée

CHAPITRE 14

Les micro-organismes sont des organismes microscopiques (bactéries, virus, parasites…) présents dans l'environnement. Certains d'entre eux peuvent provoquer des maladies, ils sont alors dits « pathogènes ».

Lorsque les barrières naturelles (muqueuses, peau, mucus) de l'organisme sont franchies, une première réaction immunitaire se déclenche : la réaction immunitaire innée.

1 Les caractéristiques de l'immunité innée

A. L'origine évolutive de l'immunité innée

■ Le système immunitaire des Vertébrés est composé de cellules présentes dans les liquides circulants (le sang et la lymphe) et d'organes spécialisés : les **ganglions lymphatiques*** et les **organes lymphoïdes** (moelle osseuse et rate).

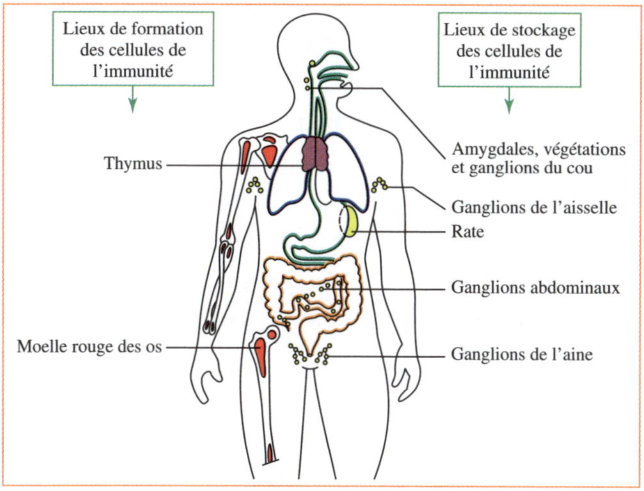

Figure 1 *Le système immunitaire*

■ La première réponse immunitaire, la réaction immunitaire innée, est présente chez 95 % des espèces animales. Elle est liée à une origine génétique et est présente dès la naissance, sans apprentissage nécessaire : c'est donc une réaction génétiquement **héritée** ou **innée**.

■ Elle permet la protection de l'organisme contre des situations variées : une lésion des tissus, une infection ou encore l'apparition de cellules cancéreuses.

> **Remarque**
> L'étude de la réponse immunitaire innée par Jules Hoffmann et son équipe fut récompensée par un Prix Nobel de médecine en 2011… grâce à la Drosophile (mouche des fruits) !

B. Les symptômes de l'immunité innée

■ Suite à la lésion d'un tissu et à l'entrée de micro-organismes, la réponse innée s'enclenche rapidement. Les symptômes sont la rougeur, la douleur, le gonflement et la sensation de chaleur. On appelle cette réaction **réponse inflammatoire aiguë***.

■ La rougeur et la chaleur s'expliquent par l'augmentation du diamètre des vaisseaux sanguin qui augmentent le débit sanguin. Ceci permet d'apporter davantage de cellules immunitaires au niveau du lieu de l'infection : les **granulocytes*** et les **monocytes***.

> **Remarque**
> Les cellules de l'immunité innée chez la Drosophile sont appelées hémocytes.

■ De plus, les fibres nerveuses responsables de la sensation de douleur sont activées.

2 Les étapes de l'immunité innée

A. La reconnaissance des agents infectieux

■ La réaction immunitaire innée repose sur l'action de cellules et de molécules de l'immunité. Le mécanisme d'action est très conservé au cours de l'évolution.

■ Les cellules de l'immunité innée, grâce à des récepteurs spécifiques, les **PRR*** (Pattern Recognition Receptor), reconnaissent des molécules de surface des pathogènes, les **PAMP*** (Pathogen Associated Molecular Patterns), qui sont communes entre les différentes catégories de micro-organismes.

■ La fixation des récepteurs des cellules de l'immunité est la première étape avant la réalisation de la **phagocytose*** ou la libération de **médiateurs chimiques de l'inflammation***.

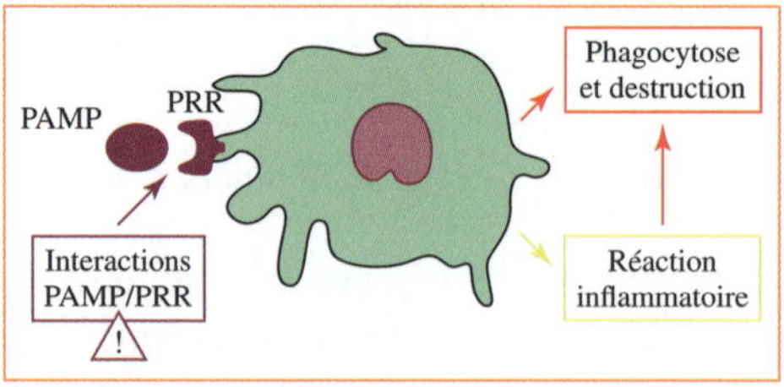

Figure 2 *La reconnaissance des agents infectieux*

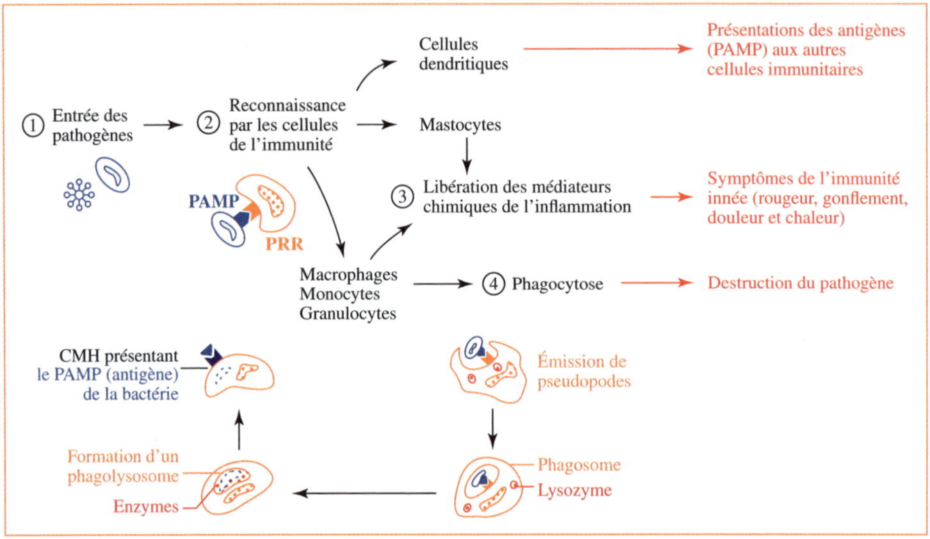

Figure 4 *Schéma de la réaction immunitaire innée*

C. Le mode d'action des anti-inflammatoires

■ Les **médicaments anti-inflammatoires*** agissent en bloquant la synthèse de certains médiateurs chimiques de l'inflammation.

■ Par exemple, l'aspirine et l'ibuprofène se fixent sur le site actif d'une enzyme : la COX. Celle-ci permet normalement la production de prostaglandine dans les mastocytes. L'aspirine et l'ibuprofène sont donc des inhibiteurs compétitifs de l'enzyme et vont limiter son activité : la prostaglandine n'est donc plus produite et les symptômes de l'inflammation disparaissent. Ce sont des molécules anti-inflammatoires.

B. Les agents de l'inflammation

■ Deux grandes catégories de cellules de l'immunité innée existent :
- les **cellules phagocytaires*** : **macrophages*** (ou **monocytes** si elles circulent dans le sang) et **granulocytes** ;
- les cellules libérant les médiateurs chimiques de l'inflammation : les **mastocytes*** libèrent de l'histamine par exemple.

Macrophage/Monocyte	Granulocyte	Mastocyte
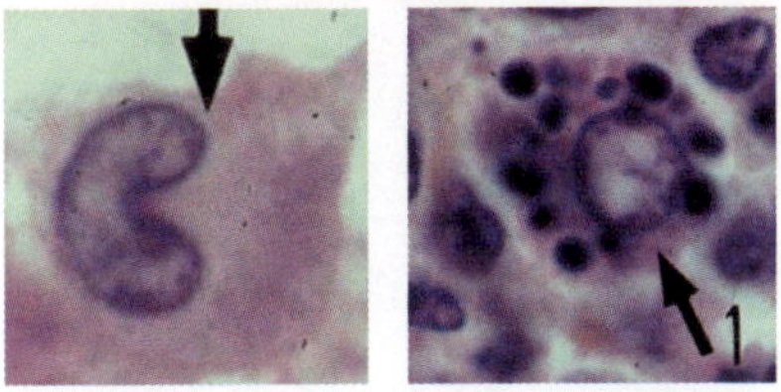	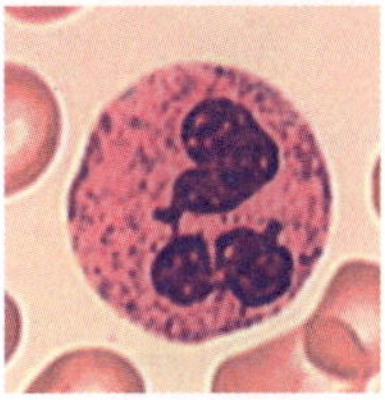	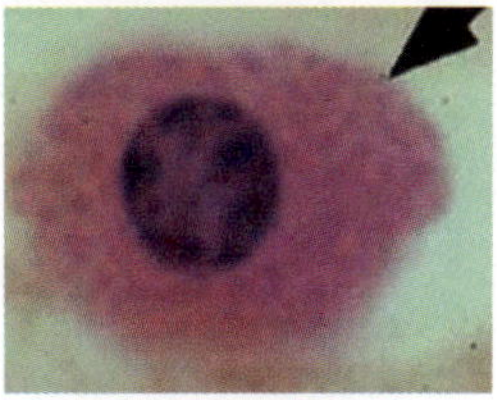
Gros noyau parfois en forme de haricot Peut présenter des phagosomes visibles en microscopie	Noyau plurilobé	Noyau rond Nombreux granules contenant les médiateurs de l'inflammation

Figure 3 *Différentes caractéristiques des cellules de l'immunité innée*

■ Les macrophages et les granulocytes réalisent donc la phagocytose qui consiste en l'ingestion et l'élimination des agents infectieux. Tout d'abord, la cellule phagocytaire reconnaît des PAMP présents sur le micro-organisme, puis elle émet des pseudopodes qui vont entourer le pathogène et enfin elle l'ingère dans un **phagosome** qui fusionne avec un **lysosome** contenant des enzymes et qui permet donc la destruction du micro-organisme.

■ Les mastocytes sont des cellules qui libèrent des molécules de l'immunité : les médiateurs chimiques de l'inflammation. Ces molécules permettent de coordonner la réponse immunitaire et l'action des cellules de l'immunité.

■ L'histamine et les prostaglandines, libérées par les mastocytes, permettent d'augmenter le recrutement des cellules immunitaires dans les tissus infectés en augmentant le débit sanguin (provoquent une vasodilatation) et en augmentant la perméabilité des vaisseaux. D'autres molécules, comme les **interleukines*** 1 produites par les macrophages, vont activer les cellules de la seconde réaction immunitaire et provoquer les fièvres. Ces médiateurs chimiques de l'inflammation sont ainsi à l'origine des symptômes observés : rougeur, chaleur et gonflement (voir *figure* 4 p. 218).

EXERCICES

Connaître le cours

1 2 min ★ Vrai ou Faux ?

Relevez la (ou les) affirmation(s) exacte(s).

La réaction immunitaire innée :
a) est aussi appelée réaction inflammatoire aiguë.
b) n'a lieu qu'au début d'une infection.
c) fait intervenir seulement des cellules phagocytaires.
d) peut être atténuée par la prise d'anti-inflammatoires.

→ *Corrigé p. 225*

2 2 min ★ Vrai ou Faux ?

Relevez la (ou les) affirmation(s) exacte(s).

Les macrophages :
a) sont des globules blancs ou leucocytes.
b) circulent dans le sang.
c) sont des cellules phagocytaires.
d) produisent des médiateurs chimiques de l'inflammation.

→ *Corrigé p. 225*

3 5 min ★ Restitution de connaissances

Expliquez brièvement comment les médiateurs chimiques de l'inflammation provoquent les symptômes caractéristiques de l'immunité innée.

→ *Corrigé p. 225*

4 5 min ★ Schématiser le cours

Schématisez les actions d'un macrophage suite à une infection bactérienne.

→ *Corrigé p. 225*

S'entraîner

5 10 min ★★ Les cellules de l'immunité innée

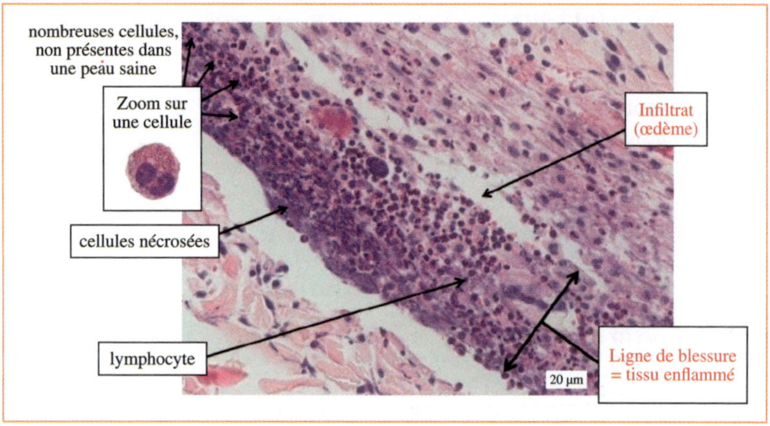

Coupe de peau de souris suite à une blessure

1. Observez la coupe microscopique d'une peau suite à une blessure et identifiez les symptômes de l'inflammation.
2. À l'aide de vos connaissances, identifiez la cellule responsable de cette inflammation sur le zoom.

→ Corrigé p. 225

6 15 min ★★ Les médiateurs de l'inflammation

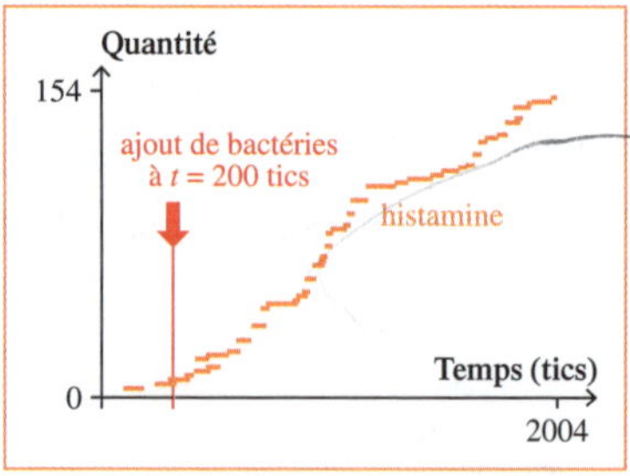

Figure 1 *Quantité d'histamine après ajout de bactéries*

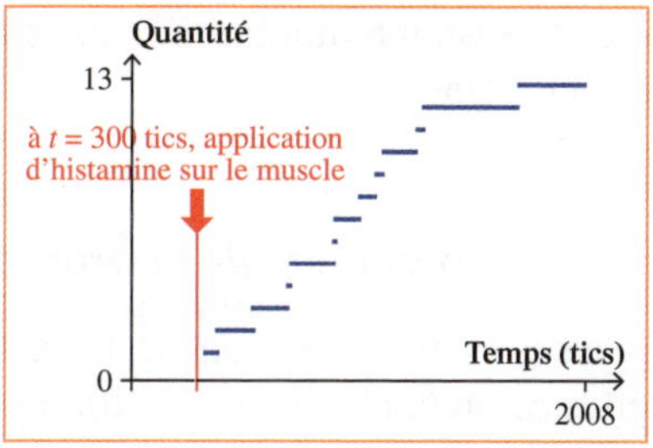

Figure 2 *Injection plasmatique de molécules fluorescentes dans le muscle et suivi de la quantité de cette fluorescence après ajout d'histamine*

1. À l'aide de vos connaissances et de la figure 1, décrivez l'effet de l'injection de bactéries sur la quantité de médiateurs de l'inflammation.

2. À l'aide de la figure 2, expliquez l'action de l'histamine et ses conséquences dans la réalisation de la réaction inflammatoire.

→ *Corrigé p. 225*

7 15 min ★★ Origine évolutive de la réponse immunitaire innée

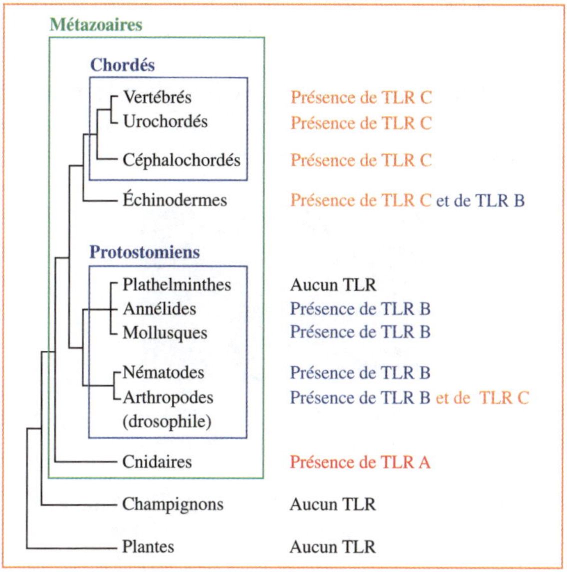

Arbre de parenté de quelques êtres vivants et présence de récepteurs PRR (exemple des TLR A, B et C)

1. Mettez en évidence que tous les animaux (Métazoaires) possèdent une réaction immunitaire innée.

2. Expliquez en quoi l'étude du système immunitaire de la drosophile peut nous renseigner sur celui de l'espèce humaine.

→ *Corrigé p. 226*

8 15 min ★★ Le système immunitaire de la Drosophile

Le syndrome des taches blanches est une infection virale par le virus WSSV qui touche certaines variétés de crevettes. Cette maladie est très fortement létale et contagieuse.

On incube des cellules S2 de Drosophile avec le virus WSSV. Le virus est marqué par une fluorescence verte afin de suivre son devenir.

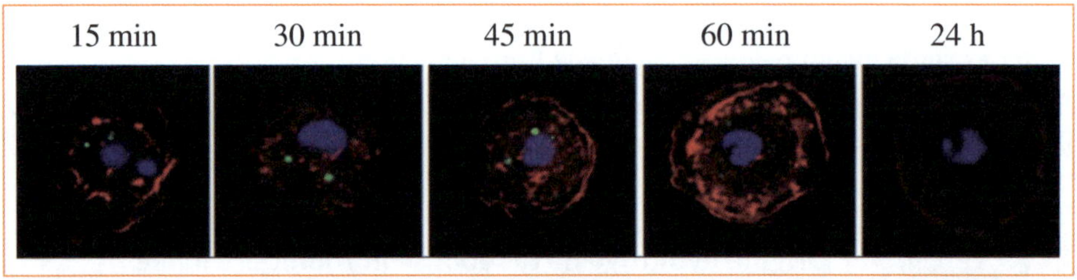

Figure 1 *Cellules S2 de Drosophile (rouge) en présence de virus WSSV (vert) observées au microscope*

Lors d'une deuxième expérience, on cherche à déterminer le mécanisme d'attaque des cellules S2. Ainsi on marque les virus avec un fluorochrome rouge dépendant du pH : sa couleur rouge s'active seulement en pH acide.

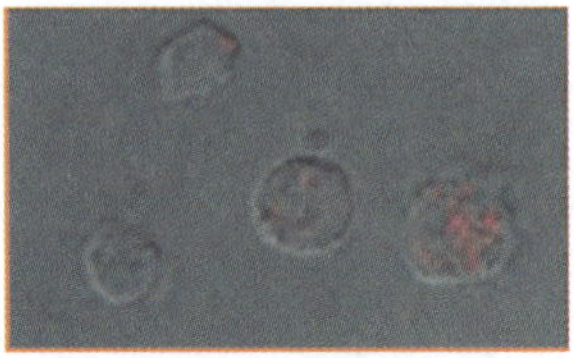

Figure 2 *Cellules S2 de Drosophile en présence de virus et d'un marqueur rouge d'acidité, observées au microscope*

1. D'après l'expérience de la figure 1, déterminez quelle catégorie de cellule de l'immunité est la cellule S2 de la Drosophile.

2. D'après les cellules observées sur la figure 2, mettez en évidence les étapes du mécanisme à l'origine de la disparition du virus WSSV.

→ *Corrigé p. 226*

Exercice 10 pts — Les anti-inflammatoires — 30 min

L'aspirine est l'un des médicaments les plus prescrits au monde pour traiter la fièvre, les douleurs modérées ainsi que l'hyper-coagulation.

À l'aide de vos connaissances et des documents, expliquez le mode d'action de l'aspirine afin de limiter les effets de la réaction immunitaire innée.

Document 1

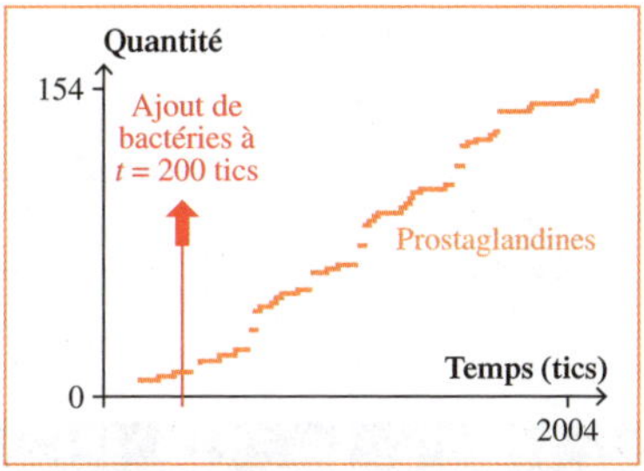

Quantité de prostaglandines produites après l'ajout de bactéries

Document 2

La prostaglandine est produite par les mastocytes à partir de molécules de leurs propres membranes. Pour qu'elle soit synthétisée une chaîne de synthèse permise par l'action de différentes enzymes a lieu.

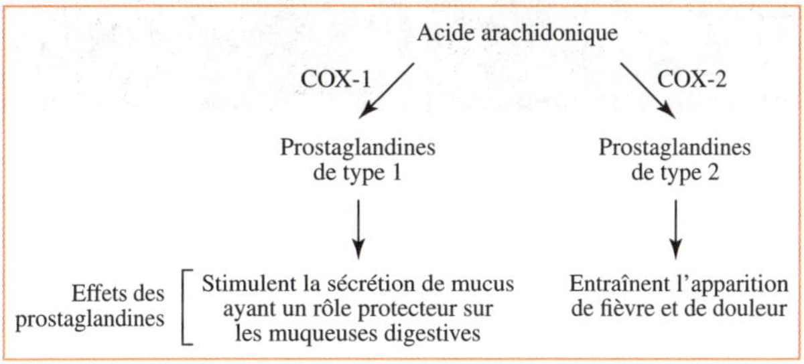

Chaîne de synthèse des prostaglandines

Document 3

On mesure la quantité de prostaglandines sanguines après absorption d'aspirine puis on modélise l'action de l'aspirine à l'aide d'un logiciel de visualisation de molécules en 3D.

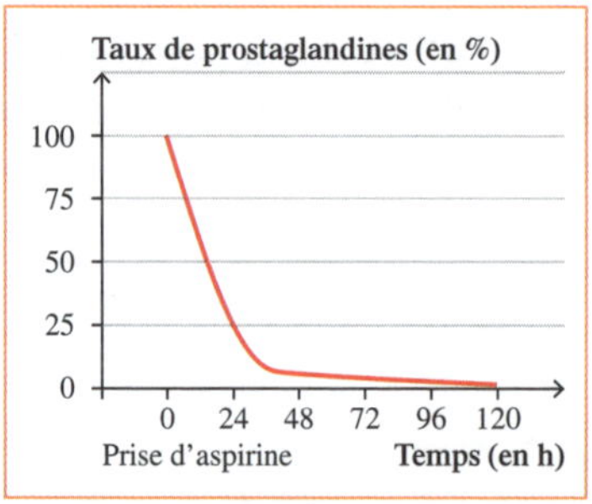

Figure 1 *Effet de l'aspirine sur la quantité de prostaglandines plasmatiques*

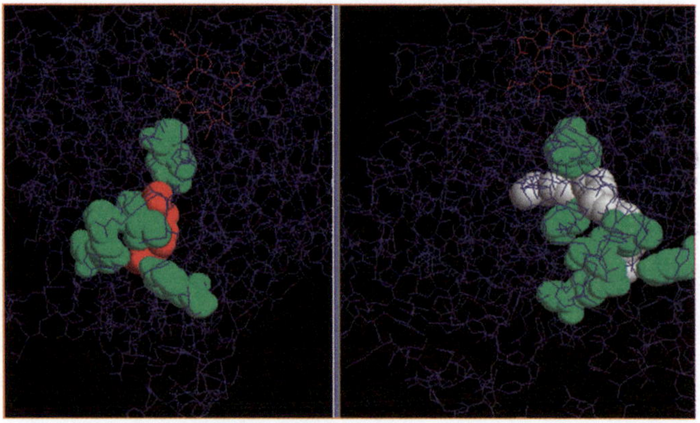

Figure 2 *Visualisation par un logiciel de modélisation moléculaire de l'enzyme COX (en bleu), de son site actif (en vert) et de son interaction avec l'aspirine (en rouge) et l'acide arachidonique (en blanc)*

→ Corrigé p. 226

CORRIGÉS

1 → Énoncé p. 219

Les affirmations exactes sont a) et d).

2 → Énoncé p. 219

Les affirmations exactes sont a), c) et d).

3 → Énoncé p. 219

Les macrophages et les mastocytes sont des cellules qui libèrent des molécules de l'immunité : les médiateurs chimiques de l'inflammation.

Les macrophages libèrent des interleukines qui provoquent des fièvres.

Les mastocytes libèrent des histamines et des prostaglandines qui augmentent le débit sanguin et la perméabilité des vaisseaux : cela permet de recruter les cellules immunitaires et provoque aussi la sensation de chaleur ainsi que les rougeurs et les gonflements.

4 → Énoncé p. 219

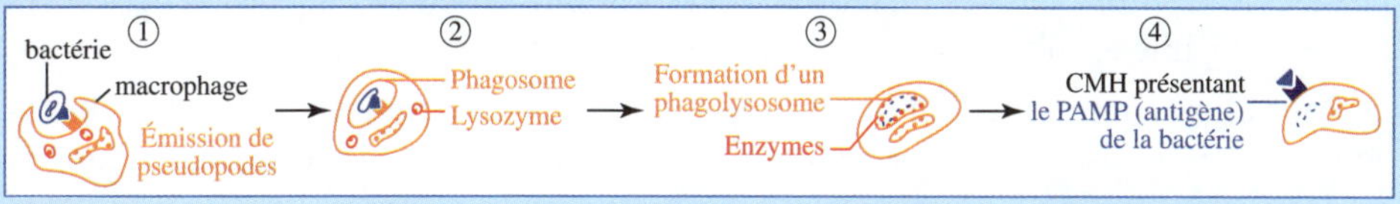

5 → Énoncé p. 220

1. Au niveau de la coupe microscopique d'une peau blessée, il y a présence d'un œdème (liquide), de cellules nécrosées (mortes) et de tissu enflammé. Par ailleurs on observe une grande quantité de cellules dont les noyaux sont importants et très denses : les cellules de l'immunité.

2. La cellule dans le grossissement présente un noyau plurilobé : c'est donc un granulocyte.

6 → Énoncé p. 220

1. Après ajout de bactéries, on observe une augmentation importante de la quantité d'histamine dans le plasma. Or cette histamine est un médiateur chimique de l'inflammation libéré par les mastocytes suite à la reconnaissance par les récepteurs PRR des marqueurs bactériens PAMP.

2. On injecte des molécules fluorescentes dans le plasma. La fluorescence est alors de plus en plus concentrée au niveau musculaire suite à l'injection d'histamine dans les muscles : l'histamine a donc permis une augmentation de la quantité de fluorescence et donc de plasma. C'est un vasodilatateur et facilitateur de la perméabilité des vaisseaux sanguins, le tout permettant d'augmenter le débit sanguin au niveau du tissu lésé.

7 → *Énoncé p. 221*

1. On observe que les animaux (ou Métazoaires) possèdent des récepteurs TLR qui sont une catégorie de PRR. Leur ancêtre commun a donc acquis ce caractère lui ayant permis de développer une réaction immunitaire innée.

2. Il existe cependant une certaine diversité au sein des TLR. En effet, l'espèce humaine possède le TLR de type C comme les autres Chordés mais aussi comme les Drosophiles. Ces insectes peuvent donc être étudiés afin de comprendre une partie du système immunitaire inné de l'Homme.

8 → *Énoncé p. 222*

1. On observe qu'en présence du virus, la cellule S2 « l'absorbe » à l'intérieur d'elle-même puisqu'on y retrouve la fluorescence verte propre au virus. Par ailleurs, le virus tend à disparaître au fur et à mesure du temps : on peut supposer que la cellule S2 a phagocyté le virus dans ses phagosomes et l'élimine progressivement. La cellule S2 de la drosophile est donc une cellule phagocytaire appelée hémocyte.

2. Pour éliminer ce virus, on observe que l'hémocyte l'a enfermé dans des phagosomes. Or ce virus devient fluorescent rouge en présence d'un milieu acide. On peut en déduire que la cellule phagocytaire a fusionné ses phagosomes avec des lysosomes acides contenant des enzymes, afin de le détruire.

CONTRÔLE CONTINU POUR LE BAC

Exercice → *Énoncé p. 223*

L'aspirine, ou acide salicylique, appartient au groupe des médicaments anti-inflammatoires contrairement au paracétamol.

On se demande quel est son mode d'action lui permettant de limiter la réaction immunitaire innée.

La prostaglandine est une molécule produite lors d'une infection par une bactérie par exemple. C'est un médiateur de l'inflammation de la réponse immunitaire innée. Comment est-elle produite et quels sont ses effets ?

On observe que la prostaglandine est produite par les mastocytes grâce à la transformation des molécules membranaires et de l'acide arachidonique. Cette transformation est réalisée au cours d'une chaîne de réactions permises par plusieurs enzymes dont la COX. Une fois produite, la prostaglandine permet ainsi la production de mucus par les cellules digestives ainsi que l'apparition de fièvre et la sensation de douleur. Elle permet donc d'expliquer une partie des symptômes liés à la réaction inflammatoire aiguë. Comment l'aspirine agit-elle pour limiter l'action de la prostaglandine et donc diminuer la réaction immunitaire innée ?

On observe que l'aspirine diminue la quantité plasmatique de prostaglandine et donc diminue son effet et donc la sensation de fièvre et de douleur. La COX est une enzyme permettant la transformation de l'acide arachidonique en prostaglandine grâce à la fixation de l'acide arachidonique (le substrat) sur son site actif. Or l'aspirine se fixe sur ce même site actif et empêche le substrat d'être transformé en prostaglandine. C'est un inhibiteur compétitif.

On peut donc conclure que l'aspirine est un inhibiteur compétitif d'une enzyme, la COX, permettant la production de prostaglandine par les mastocytes et provoquant de la fièvre et une sensation douloureuse. L'aspirine est donc un anti-inflammatoire et atténue la réponse immunitaire innée.

L'immunité adaptative

CHAPITRE 15

Alors que l'immunité innée existe chez la majorité des animaux, l'immunité adaptative est caractéristique des Vertébrés.

1 Les effecteurs de la réponse immunitaire adaptative

■ Si l'infection se prolonge après la réaction inflammatoire, on observe une augmentation d'autres cellules de l'immunité : les **lymphocytes***. Ces lymphocytes se distinguent par leurs récepteurs membranaires : les récepteurs B ou T. Les lymphocytes T possèdent en plus des récepteurs CD4 ou CD8 qui permettent de distinguer les lymphocytes T4 et les lymphocytes T8. Des molécules sont aussi caractéristiques de cette réaction immunitaire : les **anticorps*** ou **immunoglobulines***.

Remarque

Les noms des lymphocytes B et T trouvent leur origine dans les organes qui les produisent : les lymphocytes B (B pour *bone*, « os » en anglais) sont produits dans la moelle osseuse et les lymphocytes T dans le thymus.

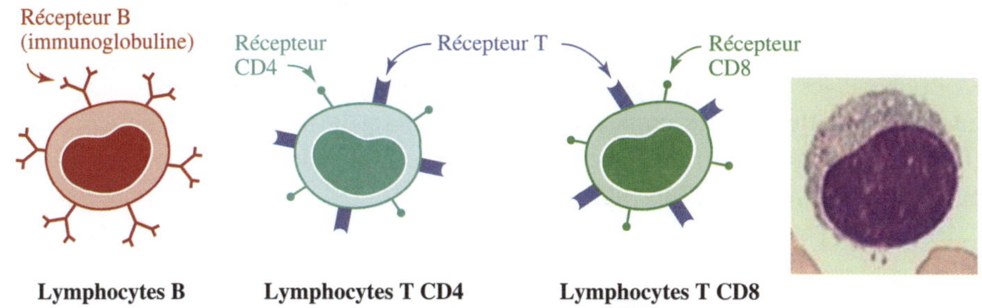

Figure 1 *Les différents types de lymphocytes*

■ Cette seconde réaction immunitaire complète la réaction immunitaire innée : c'est la **réponse immunitaire adaptative***. Son objectif est d'éliminer la cause du déclenchement de la réaction immunitaire comme l'intrusion d'agents infectieux ou la présence de cellules anormales (comme les cellules cancéreuses), en collaboration avec la réaction inflammatoire.

■ Les virus et les autres micro-organismes possèdent sur leur surface des molécules qui ne sont pas présentes chez l'Homme mais déclenchent une réaction immunitaire : ce sont des **antigènes***. Les cellules et les molécules de l'immunité vont donc reconnaître ces motifs moléculaires et déclencher la réaction immunitaire adaptative.

Ex. : Le terme « antigène » vient de l'anglais « *anticorps generator* » ou molécule qui déclenche la production des anticorps. Dans l'exemple du virus de la grippe, les antigènes sont les hémagglutinines H et les neuraminidases (d'où le nom des virus comme H5N1 ou H1N1).

■ On distingue donc la **réponse adaptative cellulaire*** (intervention des lymphocytes) et la **réponse adaptative humorale*** (intervention des anticorps).

2 La réponse adaptative humorale

A. La structure d'un anticorps

■ Une immunoglobuline est une protéine en forme de Y insérée dans la membrane des lymphocytes B. Une fois libérée dans le plasma sanguin, on l'appelle anticorps. Les anticorps sont formés de 4 chaînes d'acides aminés identiques entre elles deux à deux : 2 chaînes lourdes et 2 chaînes légères. Les chaînes lourdes et les chaînes légères d'un même anticorps n'ont pas la même séquence : elles sont différentes l'une par rapport à l'autre. Les extrémités des chaînes lourdes et légères de l'anticorps sont très variables d'un anticorps à un autre. Elles reconnaissent ainsi de façon spécifique les antigènes et s'y fixent : c'est le site de fixation à l'antigène.

■ À l'opposé, les parties basales des chaînes lourdes et légères sont de séquence identique : ce sont des parties constantes qui permettent la fixation de l'anticorps aux cellules phagocytaires. Un anticorps possède donc 2 sites de fixation aux antigènes et un site de fixation aux cellules phagocytaires.

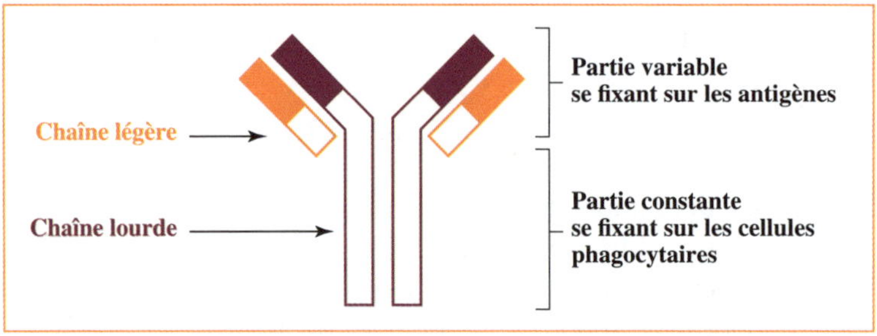

Figure 2 *Structure d'un anticorps*

B. La production et le mode d'action des anticorps

■ Les anticorps présents dans le sang vont reconnaître les antigènes et s'agglomérer grâce à leur partie variable : ces liaisons anticorps-antigènes forment un **complexe immun***.

■ Les sites de fixation des anticorps ne reconnaissent qu'un seul antigène (chaque anticorps est donc spécialisé dans la reconnaissance d'un antigène donné) : la réponse adaptative est une réponse immunitaire spécifique.

■ Ce complexe immun est ensuite reconnu par les granulocytes et les macrophages qui se fixeront à la partie constante des anticorps puis phagocyteront le complexe immun.

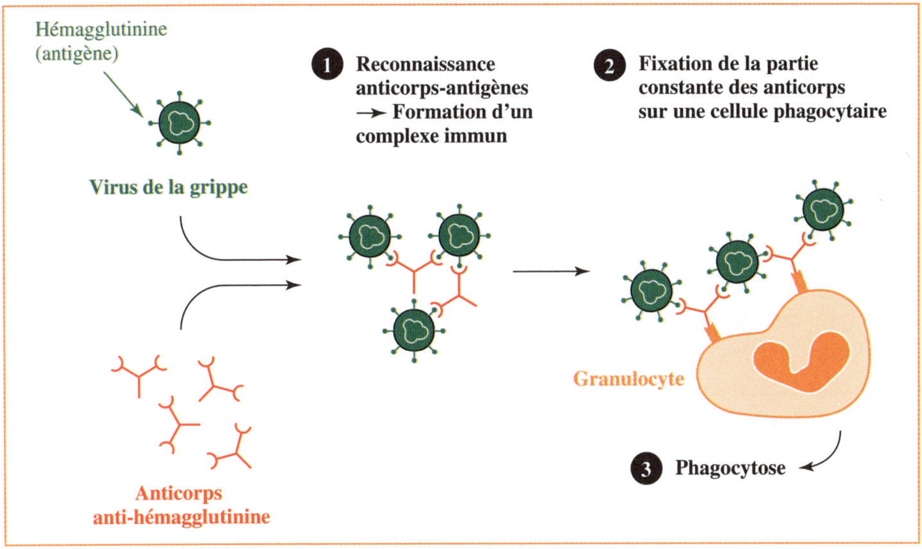

Figure 3 *Le mode d'action des anticorps*

■ Pour mettre en évidence la présence d'un anticorps donné dans le plasma sanguin ou pour révéler la présence d'un antigène précis dans une solution, on réalise un **test d'Ouchterlony*** : les solutions de plasma et d'antigènes sont déposées dans des puits créés dans la gélose puis vont diffuser dans toutes les directions. S'il existe des anticorps ciblés contre les antigènes étudiés, un complexe immun va alors se former et être visible grâce à un arc de précipitation (voir *figure 4* p. 232).

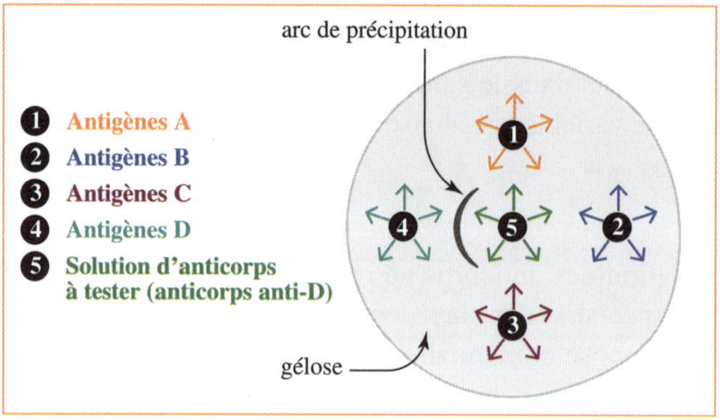

Figure 4 *Principe du test d'Ouchterlony*

3 La réponse adaptative cellulaire

A. Les étapes de la réponse adaptative cellulaire

- Dans un premier temps, les cellules phagocytaires (comme les cellules dendritiques) phagocytent les pathogènes ou les cellules anormales puis migrent vers les ganglions lymphatiques. Elles exposent les antigènes du pathogène sur leur propre CMH (complexe membranaire humain) et présentent ainsi cet antigène aux lymphocytes : ce sont des cellules présentatrices d'antigène.

- Les lymphocytes vont alors subir des étapes communes grâce à la production d'interleukine 2 par les cellules présentatrices d'antigène : les lymphocytes les plus spécifiques sont sélectionnés, se multiplient et s'activent. C'est l'étape de **sélection et de multiplication clonales***.

- Les lymphocytes vont alors assurer des rôles différents :
  - les LT CD4 se différencient en LT auxiliaires qui vont stimuler la sélection, l'activation et la multiplication des autres lymphocytes ;
  - les LT B vont se différencier en **plasmocytes*** sécréteurs d'anticorps ;
  - les LT CD8 s'activent en LT cytotoxiques qui vont ensuite reconnaître l'antigène sur les cellules infectées et libérer des protéines, les porines et les granzymes, permettant la destruction (ou lyse) des cellules infectées.

Remarque

Les LT4, grâce à leur rôle d'auxiliaires, constituent l'une des pièces centrales de la réponse immunitaire adaptative. Ce sont ces cellules qui sont infectées par le virus du VIH, provoquant, sans traitement adapté, une destruction du système immunitaire et l'apparition d'un syndrome d'immunodéficience humaine : le SIDA.

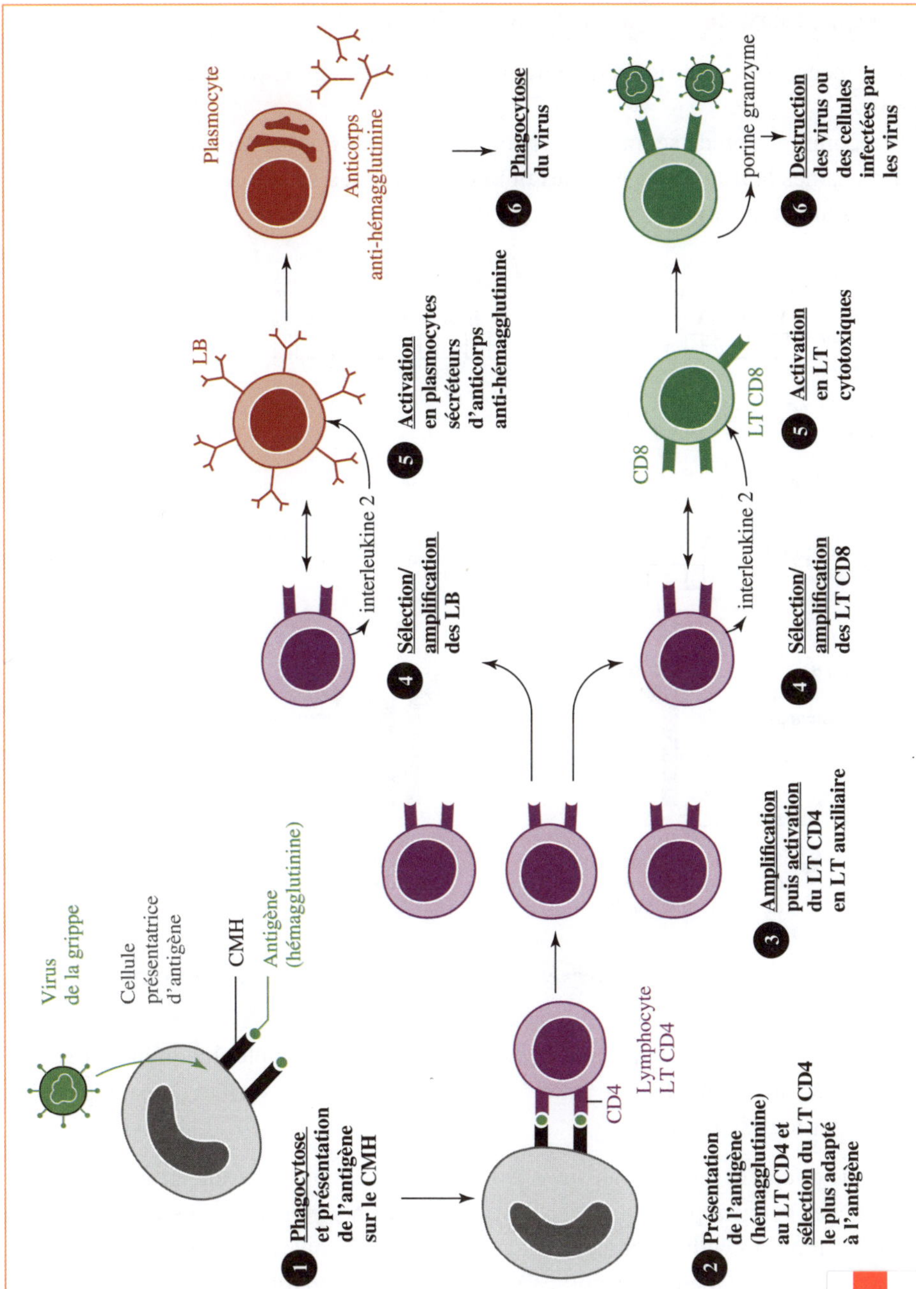

Figure 5 *La réponse immunitaire adaptative*

B. La spécificité de la réponse immunitaire adaptative

■ Des mécanismes particuliers entrent en jeu pour augmenter la diversité des anticorps :

– la recombinaison de segments de gène exprimant les parties constantes et variables des chaînes lourdes et légères des immunoglobulines ;

– un assemblage varié des chaînes lourdes et légères.

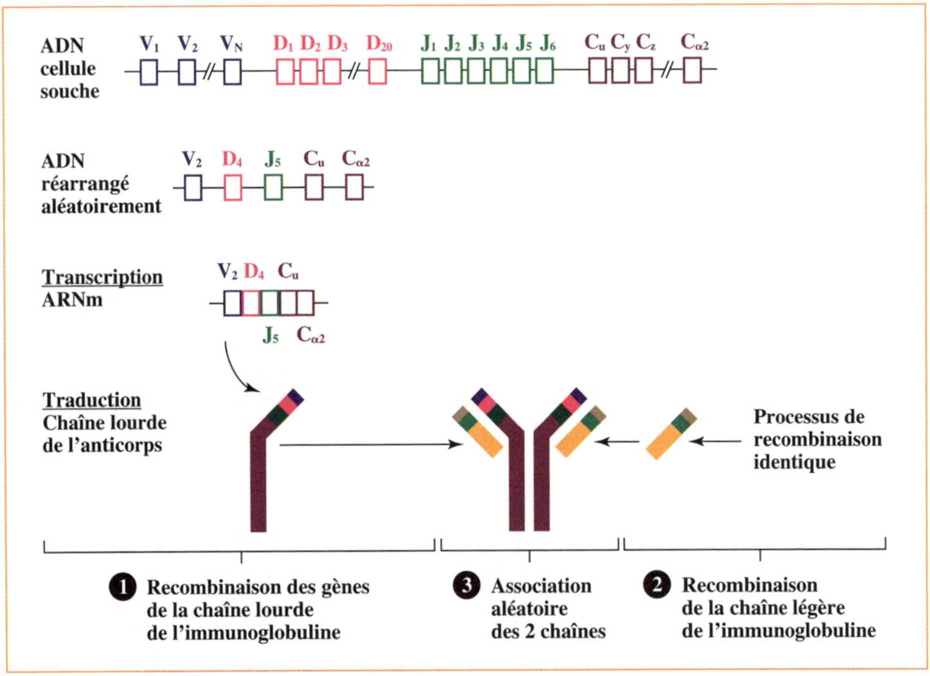

Figure 6 *Les mécanismes à l'origine de la diversité des anticorps*

■ Cette réponse immunitaire adaptative prend donc en compte une grande diversité d'antigènes, lui permettant de lutter contre une importante variété de pathogènes et d'anticiper leur évolution.

■ Paradoxalement, ces mécanismes permettant de reconnaître une grande diversité d'antigènes peuvent provoquer l'apparition de lymphocytes reconnaissant les cellules du soi comme des cellules étrangères : cela provoque l'apparition d'une **maladie auto-immune***. Une étape de sélection va alors limiter l'apparition de ces **lymphocytes auto-réactifs*** grâce aux cellules présentatrices d'antigène qui vont déclencher la destruction des lymphocytes reconnaissant le soi.

■ La maturation des lymphocytes se déroule ainsi en deux étapes :
- une première étape de sélection qui élimine ce qui est incompatible avec le soi afin d'éviter la production de lymphocytes auto-réactifs qui se déclencheraient contre des parties saines de l'organisme ;
- une deuxième sélection lors de la circulation des lymphocytes dans la lymphe et le sang : les lymphocytes vont alors rencontrer pour la première fois un antigène particulier et subir les étapes de sélection (pour sélectionner le lymphocyte le plus adapté au pathogène), d'amplification et de différenciation clonale.

■ Ces étapes expliquent un délai de réaction de plusieurs jours pour la réaction immunitaire adaptative.

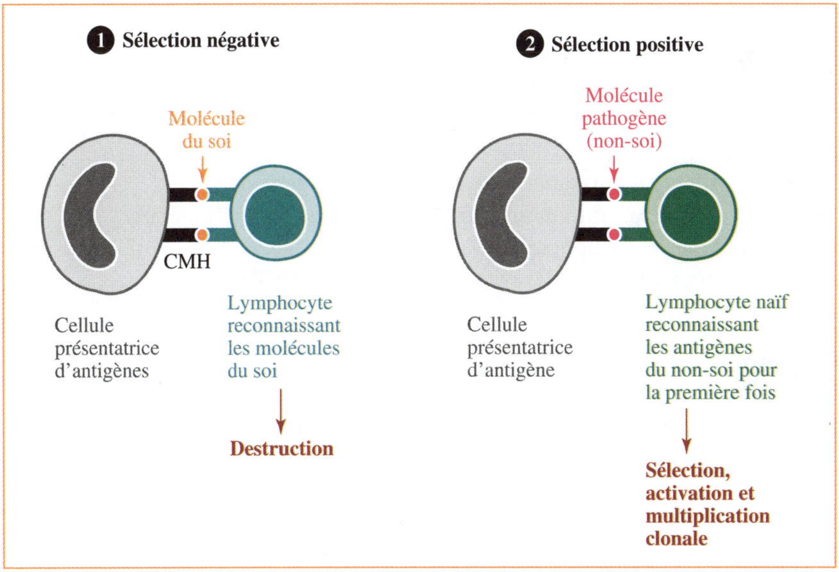

Figure 7 *La maturation des lymphocytes*

EXERCICES

Connaître le cours

1 2 min ★ Vrai ou Faux ?

Relevez la (ou les) affirmation(s) exacte(s).

La réaction immunitaire adaptative :
a) remplace la réaction immunitaire innée.
b) se décompose en une réponse humorale et une réponse cellulaire.
c) reconnaît une grande variété d'antigènes.
d) est présente chez tous les animaux.

→ Corrigé p. 243

2 2 min ★ Vrai ou Faux ?

Relevez la (ou les) information(s) exacte(s).

Les anticorps :
a) permettent une reconnaissance spécifique des antigènes.
b) forment un complexe immun en s'agglutinant avec les pathogènes.
c) sont produits par les lymphocytes T CD4.
d) peuvent être reconnus et se fixer sur les lymphocytes T CD8.

→ Corrigé p. 243

3 2 min ★ Vrai ou Faux ?

Expliquez brièvement comment les lymphocytes T CD8 peuvent éliminer les virus et les cellules infectées par eux.

→ Corrigé p. 243

4 5 min ★ Schématiser le cours

Schématisez l'organisation d'un anticorps.

→ Corrigé p. 243

S'entraîner

5 15 min ★★ Les cellules de l'immunité adaptative

Le diabète de type I est une maladie d'origine essentiellement génétique. L'hyperglycémie apparaît tôt dans la vie des individus : on l'appelle aussi diabète précoce.

Les îlots de Langerhans sont des amas de cellules situés dans le pancréas et produisant les hormones de régulation de la glycémie, notamment l'insuline (hypoglycémiante).

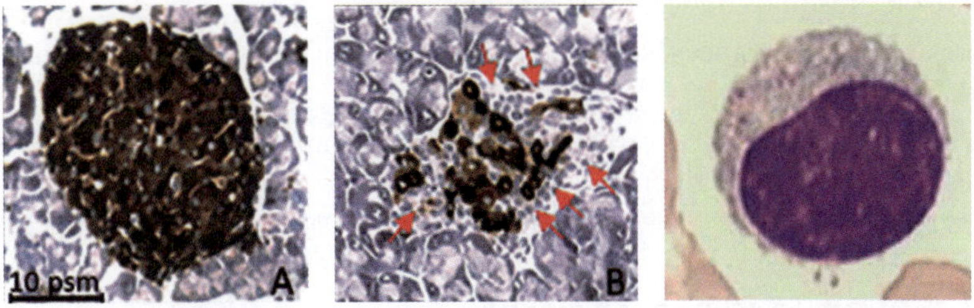

grossissement au niveau d'une flèche rouge

Évolution des îlots de Langerhans chez un individu sain (A) et une personne diabétique (B)

1. Montrez que le diabète de type I est provoqué par la disparition des îlots de Langerhans.

2. Mettez en évidence l'origine auto-immune de la maladie à l'aide du grossissement réalisé sur les cellules observées dans la microscopie B.

→ *Corrigé p. 243*

6 15 min ★★ Test d'Ouchterlony

On cherche à commercialiser un sérum constitué d'anticorps anti-venins de vipères françaises. Ce sérum doit donc protéger contre les venins de trois variétés de vipères aspic françaises : la commune, celle des Alpes et celle des Pyrénées. Pour cela on réalise un test d'Ouchterlony pour vérifier son efficacité.

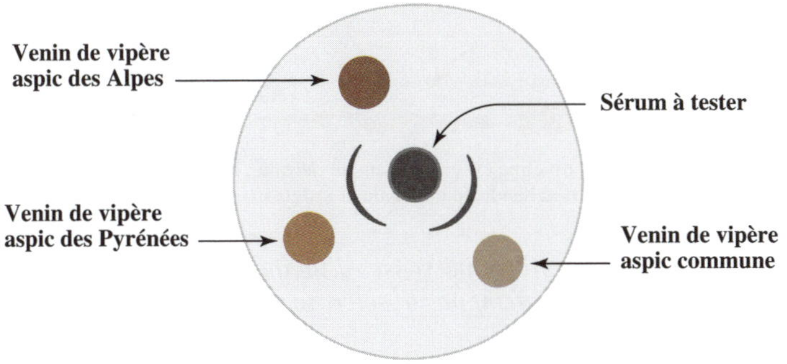

Résultats du test d'Ouchterlony pour le sérum anti-venins de vipères

1. Décrivez les résultats du test d'Ouchterlony.

2. D'après vos connaissances, schématisez l'événement cellulaire mis en évidence par un arc de précipitation.

3. Déduisez-en si le sérum est efficace et peut être commercialisé pour traiter les morsures des trois espèces de vipères.

→ Corrigé p. 244

7 15 min ★★ La sclérose en plaques

La sclérose en plaques (SEP) est une maladie évolutive provoquant l'apparition de symptômes progressifs comme une faiblesse musculaire et parfois une baisse de l'acuité visuelle ainsi qu'une perte de sensation (fourmillements).

Les cellules sanguines comme les lymphocytes ne franchissent normalement pas la paroi des vaisseaux sanguins situés au niveau du cerveau : on parle de barrière hémato-encéphalique.

La myéline est une substance biologique riche en lipides qui s'enroule autour des neurones, qui les protège et permet une augmentation de la vitesse du message nerveux.

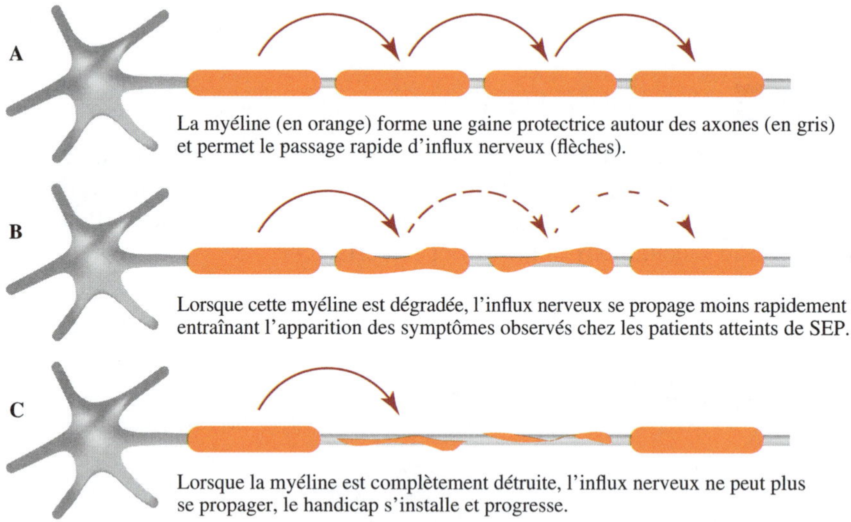

Figure 1 *Les fibres nerveuses d'un individu sain (A) et d'un individu atteint par la sclérose en plaques (B et C)*

	Individu non atteint		Individu atteint	
	Sang	Système nerveux central (cerveau et moelle épinière)	Sang	Système nerveux central (cerveau et moelle épinière)
Lymphocytes T CD4 et CD8 auto-réactifs anti-myéline	Rares	Absents	Rares mais activés et réactifs	Abondants, très réactifs
Lymphocytes B auto-réactifs anti-myéline	Rares	Absents	Rares	Abondants, activés et producteurs d'anticorps anti-myéline

Figure 2 *État et abondance des cellules de l'immunité selon leur localisation chez un individu non atteint et un individu atteint par la sclérose en plaques*

1. D'après la figure 1, expliquez l'origine des symptômes de la sclérose en plaques.
2. D'après les données du tableau de la figure 2, montrez que la sclérose en plaques est une maladie auto-immune.

→ *Corrigé p. 244*

8 15 min ★★ Le virus du VIH

Les personnes contaminées par le VIH (ou virus de l'immunodéficience humaine), si elles ne sont pas traitées, peuvent voir leur maladie évoluer en 3 étapes : une phase de primo-infection, une phase asymptomatique (pas de symptômes visibles) et l'étape SIDA (syndrome d'immunodéficience acquise) où le malade souffre de maladies opportunistes, comme la tuberculose ou le syndrome de Kaposi qui n'apparaissent que lorsque le système immunitaire est déjà très affaibli.

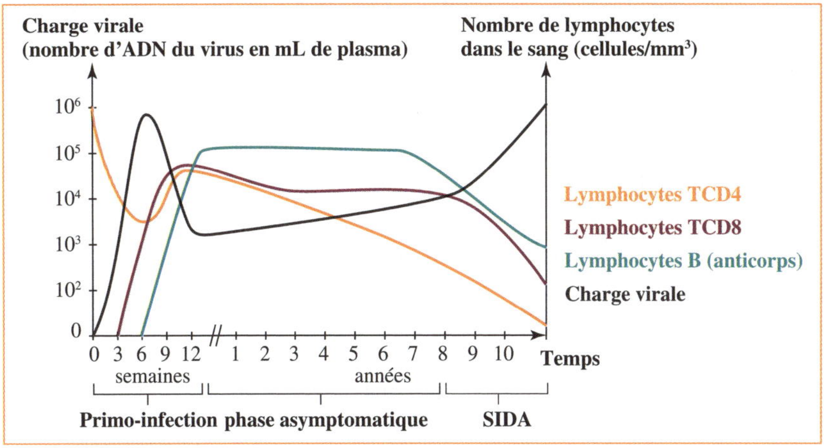

Évolution de la quantité des cellules de l'immunité adaptative et de la quantité de virus (charge virale) au cours de la vie d'une personne contaminée par le VIH (sans traitement)

1. Expliquez le lien entre les différentes étapes de la maladie et la concentration des lymphocytes LT CD8 et des anticorps ainsi que de la charge virale.

2. Décrivez l'évolution des LT CD4 au cours de l'infection.

3. Sachant que le VIH s'attaque au LT CD4, mettez en évidence l'action majeure de ces cellules dans la réponse immunitaire adaptative.

→ Corrigé p. 245

9 15 min ★★ Les tests de grossesse

Le principe des tests de grossesse est de mettre en évidence la présence d'une hormone produite seulement par les femmes enceintes : l'hCG ou hormone chorionique Gonadotrope. Celle-ci est en effet sécrétée par l'embryon puis par le placenta.

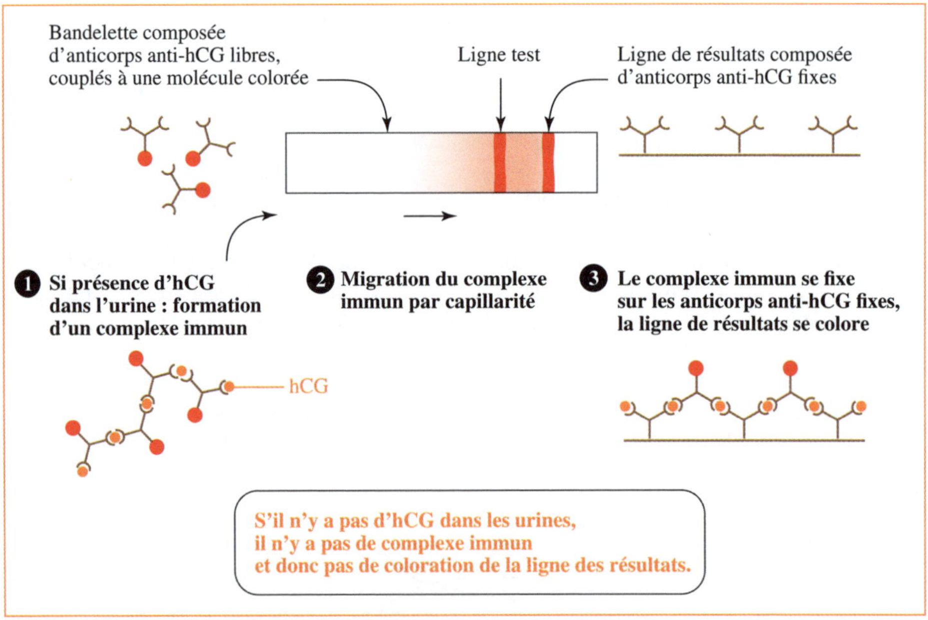

Mécanisme d'action du test de grossesse

1. Expliquez en quoi les interactions anticorps-antigènes permettent de mettre en évidence une grossesse.

2. Décrivez et expliquez les résultats d'une bandelette mettant en évidence l'absence d'hormone hCG.

→ Corrigé p. 245

Exercice 10 pts Cannabis et immunosuppression 30 min

Les études portant sur une utilisation thérapeutique du cannabis reposent essentiellement sur son composé actif : le THC (tétrahydrocannabinol). Au-delà de ses effets cérébraux, les industries pharmaceutiques cherchent à connaître son action sur le système immunitaire, notamment lors d'apparition de cancer du poumon.

À l'aide de l'ensemble des documents et de vos connaissances, montrez que le THC modifie l'action du système immunitaire dans sa lutte contre le cancer du poumon.

Document 1

Afin d'étudier le volume d'une tumeur, du THC a été injecté chez des souris en une concentration de 5 mg/kg après leur avoir implanté des cellules cancéreuses caractéristiques du cancer des poumons. On mesure ensuite le développement de la masse cancéreuse.

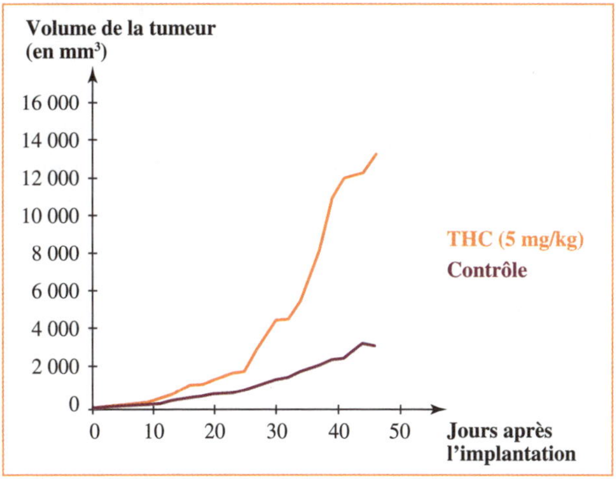

Action du THC sur le volume des tumeurs du poumon chez les souris

Document 2

Lors de l'apparition de cellules cancéreuses, la réaction immunitaire adaptative se met en place avec notamment l'action des lymphocytes T CD4. Ces lymphocytes activés en LT auxiliaires vont alors libérer des cytokines : l'interleukine 10 empêche l'activation des lymphocytes alors que l'interféron γ permet l'activation des lymphocytes T CD8 en lymphocytes cytotoxiques, détruisant ainsi les cellules cancéreuses.

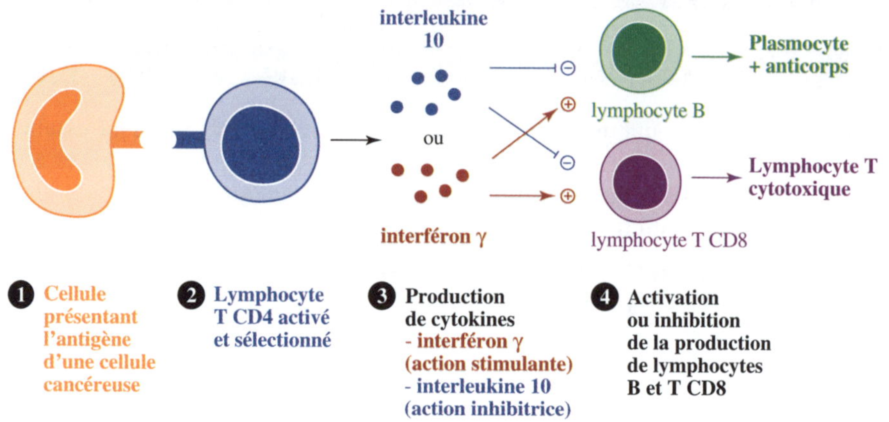

	Interleukine 10	Interféron γ
Contrôle (en $pg.mL^{-1}$)	819	190
Avec THC (en $pg.mL^{-1}$)	1491	73

Mode d'action des lymphocytes T lors de l'apparition de cellules cancéreuses

Document 3

L'activation des lymphocytes T CD4 peut être mesurée par une méthode consistant à mettre en culture des lymphocytes en présence de cellules présentatrices d'antigène. La multiplication des lymphocytes T CD4 est mesurée ensuite par l'incorporation d'un constituant de l'ADN rendu radioactif (la thymidine).

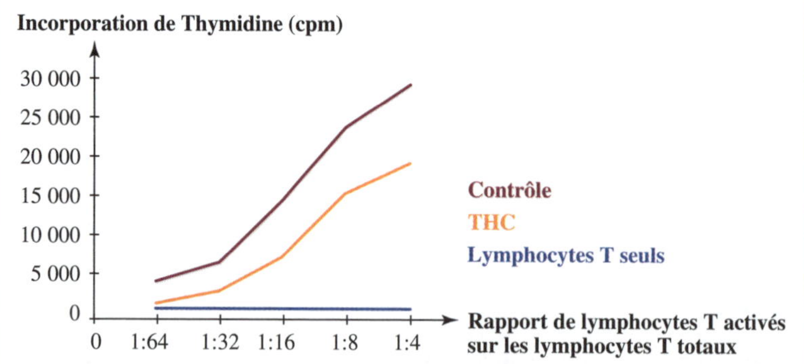

Action du THC sur l'activation des lymphocytes T CD4

→ Corrigé p. 246

CORRIGÉS

1 → *Énoncé p. 236*

Les affirmations exactes sont b) et c).

2 → *Énoncé p. 236*

Les affirmations exactes sont a) et b).

3 → *Énoncé p. 236*

Lors d'une infection virale, le virus peut être retrouvé dans le sang mais aussi infecter les cellules hôtes qui vont alors exprimer ses antigènes.

Les LT CD8 peuvent reconnaître directement ces antigènes viraux (du virus ou des cellules infectées) ou bien les antigènes peuvent leur être présentés par les lymphocytes T auxiliaires. Le LT CD8 le plus spécifique à l'antigène viral va alors être sélectionné puis être amplifié et activé grâce à la production de molécules par le lymphocyte T CD4 (les interleukines 2). Le LT CD8 s'active en LT cytotoxique qui va ensuite reconnaître l'antigène sur les cellules infectées et libérer des protéines, les porines et les granzymes, permettant la destruction (ou lyse) des cellules infectées.

4 → *Énoncé p. 236*

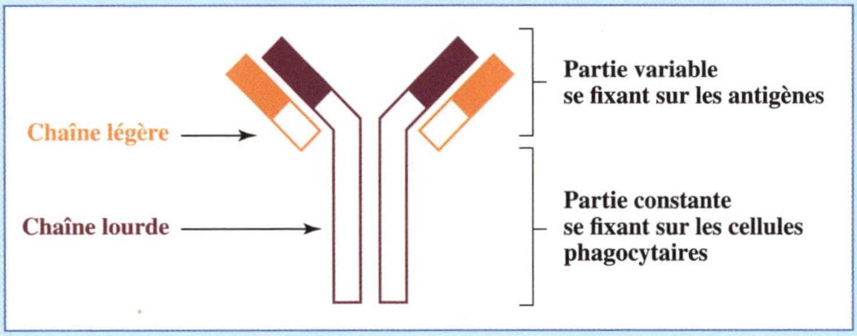

5 → *Énoncé p. 236*

1. D'après les microscopies de pancréas, on observe que le pancréas d'un individu sain possède des îlots de Langerhans intacts avec donc des cellules permettant la production d'insuline et permettant ainsi de diminuer la glycémie. Or chez un individu diabétique de type 1, on observe une destruction des îlots de Langerhans et donc des cellules produisant l'insuline : le manque d'insuline provoque une hyperglycémie et donc le diabète.

2. Les îlots de Langerhans d'une personne diabétique de type I sont riches en cellules particulières. Celles-ci possèdent un noyau volumineux caractéristique des lymphocytes. On peut donc supposer que le diabète de type I est provoqué par l'attaque des lymphocytes contre les cellules des îlots de Langerhans produisant l'insuline : ce sont des lymphocytes auto-réactifs. Il s'agit donc d'une maladie auto-immune.

6 → *Énoncé p. 237*

1. D'après le test d'Ouchterlony, on observe la présence de deux arcs de précipitation : entre le sérum à étudier et les antigènes présents dans les venins des vipères aspics communes et des Pyrénées.

2.

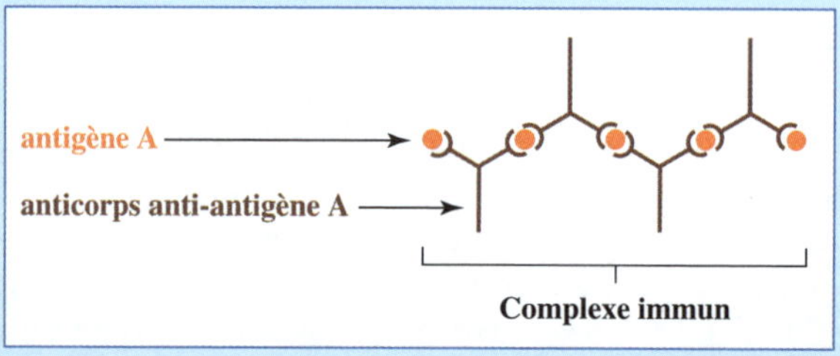

3. Ces arcs de précipitation sont des visualisations des complexes immuns formés entre les antigènes des venins des vipères aspics communes et des Pyrénées et les anticorps correspondants. Le sérum est donc composé des anticorps anti-venin de la vipère aspic commune et de celle des Pyrénées, mais pas des anticorps s'agglutinant contre le venin de vipère des Alpes. Il n'est pas donc pas commercialisable car il ne remplit pas les objectifs fixés.

7 → *Énoncé p. 238*

1. On observe que la sclérose en plaque se traduit par des zones de dégradation de la myéline autour des cellules nerveuses du cerveau et de la moelle épinière, faisant apparaître des plaques. Or on sait que la myéline est une couche de lipides entourant les prolongements des cellules nerveuses permettant de les protéger et d'accélérer la transmission du message nerveux. Le message nerveux est donc ralenti, voire disparaît dans certains cas, entraînant les symptômes décrits comme les paralysies si la maladie touche les nerfs moteurs.

2. Chez les individus atteints de sclérose en plaques on observe la présence de lymphocytes T CD4, CD8 et B anti-myéline. Leur présence est particulièrement abondante au niveau du système nerveux central, ce qui explique la disparition de la myéline décrite précédemment. Dans le cas de cette maladie, les lymphocytes auto-réactifs anti-myéline franchissent donc la barrière hémato-encéphalique et provoquent cette maladie auto-immune.

8 → *Énoncé p. 239*

1. Lors de la primo-infection, on observe une forte augmentation de la charge virale en parallèle à une augmentation des lymphocytes T CD8 et des anticorps produits : ceci entraîne des symptômes légers comme une infection virale quelconque. Dans un premier temps, la production des lymphocytes T CD8 et des anticorps compense la charge virale et la contient à un niveau faible : il n'y a donc aucun symptôme lors de la phase asymptomatique. À partir d'un certain temps, la quantité de lymphocytes T CD8 et d'anticorps chute, la charge virale augmente donc. La disparition des cellules de l'immunité adaptative provoque l'apparition de maladies opportunistes : c'est la phase SIDA.

2. Lors de la primo-infection, on observe une diminution des lymphocytes T CD4 car ce sont les cellules cibles du VIH. Ils sont donc détruits par les lymphocytes T CD8 qui reconnaissent en eux des cellules infectées. Par la suite, la production forte des lymphocytes T CD4 coïncide avec la diminution de la charge virale. Durant toute la phase asymptomatique, la quantité de lymphocytes T CD4 diminue jusqu'à atteindre un seuil trop bas et leur disparition : c'est la phase SIDA.

3. La diminution de la quantité de lymphocytes T CD4 produits déclenche une chute des taux de lymphocytes B et T CD8. En se retournant contre les lymphocytes T CD4 infectés par les virus, les lymphocytes T CD8 détruisent les lymphocytes auxiliaires jusqu'à un seuil : lorsque leur quantité devient trop faible, la réaction immunitaire adaptative s'effondre et ne produit plus de lymphocytes B (et donc d'anticorps) ni de lymphocytes T CD8. Les maladies opportunistes peuvent se développer.

9 → *Énoncé p. 240*

1. Lors d'un test de grossesse, les anticorps anti-hCG sont couplés à des marqueurs colorés. Si l'hCG est présente, alors il se forme un complexe immun qui va migrer le long de la bandelette. Ce complexe immun est ensuite capté par des anticorps anti-hCG fixes sur la ligne des résultats. La molécule d'hCG est donc en « sandwich » entre deux anticorps. Les tests de grossesse reposent donc sur la formation d'un complexe immun et donc sur le principe de la réponse immunitaire adaptative humorale.

2. Si la femme n'est pas enceinte, elle ne produira pas d'hCG dans ses urines. Les anticorps anti-hCG couplés à une molécule colorée vont donc migrer seuls dans la bandelette et ne seront pas captés par les anticorps anti-hCG fixés sur les lignes de résultats. La coloration n'apparaîtra donc pas.

Exercice → Énoncé p. 241

Le THC, molécule active du cannabis, possède des effets neurologiques mais peut aussi modifier le système immunitaire. **On se demande donc quels sont les effets du THC sur le système immunitaire lors de l'apparition d'un cancer des poumons.**

On observe que l'injection de THC à des souris qui possèdent des cellules cancéreuses augmente fortement la taille des tumeurs pulmonaires. On peut donc supposer que le THC est une molécule qui favorise, dans cet exemple, le développement des tumeurs pulmonaires : c'est un effet tumorigène. Cette augmentation de la tumeur est-elle due à une activité du THC sur le système immunitaire ?

Lors de l'apparition de cellules cancéreuses, les lymphocytes T CD4 jouent un rôle primordial : ils s'activent en lymphocytes auxiliaires et libèrent alors deux types de cytokines en fonction des besoins. L'interféron γ favorise l'activation des autres lymphocytes et donc la disparition des cellules cancéreuses, alors que l'interleukine 10 empêche cette activation.

On observe que l'ajout de THC entraîne l'augmentation de l'interleukine 10 et la diminution de la production d'interféron γ. Le THC a donc bien un effet favorisant le développement des tumeurs pulmonaires en modifiant la production de cytokines libérées par les lymphocytes T CD4.

On observe qu'en absence de THC, les lymphocytes T sont activés. À la suite d'un traitement des souris au THC, on peut observer que l'activation des lymphocytes T est réduite.

On peut donc en déduire que le THC empêche l'activation des lymphocytes T CD4 en lymphocytes auxiliaires et donc la libération de certaines cytokines.

Pour conclure, le THC empêche l'activation des lymphocytes T CD4 et modifie ainsi la production de cytokines dans le sens d'une inactivation de la réaction anti-tumorale. Le THC a donc un effet immunosuppresseur.

L'utilisation de l'immunité adaptative en santé humaine

CHAPITRE 16

Dès la naissance, nous possédons nos propres lymphocytes, ce qui constitue notre phénotype immunitaire. Lors de contacts avec des pathogènes ou par l'injection de vaccins, ce phénotype immunitaire peut évoluer : nous produisons alors d'autres lymphocytes, spécifiques aux antigènes rencontrés.

1 La mémoire immunitaire

■ Lors d'une première rencontre avec un antigène, la réponse immunitaire adaptative est lente et faible : la production des lymphocytes T4 et T8 ainsi que la production des anticorps permettent juste d'éliminer le pathogène. Toutefois, il y a production de lymphocytes mémoires spécifiques à l'antigène rencontré. Ces cellules ont une durée de vie longue et sont conservées dans le système immunitaire. On obtient donc des lymphocytes T mémoires, des lymphocytes B mémoires et des plasmocytes mémoires.

■ La deuxième rencontre avec l'antigène va ainsi déclencher une réponse beaucoup plus rapide et quantitativement plus importante : les lymphocytes B et T spécifiques à l'antigène ont déjà été sélectionnés lors de la première exposition et se multiplient donc directement. Cette **mémoire immunitaire** permet une protection à long terme de l'organisme contre les antigènes. C'est sur ce principe que repose la **vaccination***.

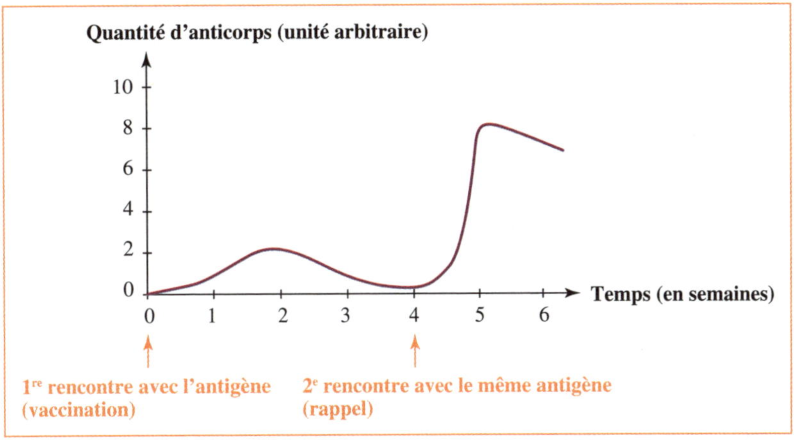

Figure 1 *Production d'anticorps lors des différentes rencontres avec un même antigène*

2 Les modifications du phénotype immunitaire

A. La vaccination préventive

■ La **vaccination préventive** consiste à activer la mémoire immunitaire dirigée contre certains agents infectieux afin de prévenir l'apparition de la maladie. Pour cela, on injecte des antigènes non virulents mais à effet **immunogène**, c'est-à-dire qu'ils provoquent la réaction immunitaire adaptative et donc la production de lymphocytes et de plasmocytes mémoires.

■ Les vaccins peuvent contenir différents antigènes :
- le pathogène est injecté **vivant** mais sa virulence est atténuée. C'est le cas du vaccin contre la tuberculose. La limite de ce type de vaccin est le cas où l'on injecte des pathogènes qui n'auraient pas tous été atténués lorsque ce pathogène est létal (cas du VIH par exemple) ;
- les pathogènes sont **inertes**, c'est-à-dire injectés après avoir été tués ou **purifiés** (on injecte seulement une partie des antigènes comme des particules virales). C'est le cas des vaccins contre le choléra, le tétanos et les hépatites. La limite de ce type de vaccin est qu'il provoque une plus faible immunité et nécessite donc des rappels.

Remarque

Le premier vaccin a été mis au point par Edward Jenner en 1796. Il observa que les fermiers en contact avec le virus bovin de la vaccine n'étaient pas atteints par la variole, maladie mortelle chez l'Homme. Il décida donc d'injecter le virus de la vaccine par scarification afin d'immuniser contre la variole.

■ Les vaccins possèdent, en plus de l'antigène, des **adjuvants***. Ce sont des substances ajoutées en plus des antigènes qui vont provoquer une réponse immunitaire innée afin d'amplifier la réponse immunitaire adaptative produite et donc de renforcer la production de cellules mémoires. Cette vaccination préventive améliore ainsi la défense de l'organisme et modifie son phénotype immunitaire selon les vaccins et donc les antigènes inoculés. Pour qu'elle protège efficacement une population, elle doit dépasser un certain taux de **couverture vaccinale***, c'est-à-dire un certain pourcentage d'individus vaccinés dans une population à un instant donné.

■ Dans une population, on définit différents paramètres :
- ρ, le nombre moyen d'individus qu'une personne malade infectera dans une population non immunisée (dans le cas d'une épidémie, ρ est supérieur à 1) ;
- S, la proportion de la population non immunisée ;
- q, la proportion de la population immunisée.

L'épidémie a lieu si : $\rho \times S > 1$ soit si $q < 1 - \dfrac{1}{\rho}$

L'éradication de la maladie a lieu si : $\rho \times S < 1$ soit si $q > 1 - \dfrac{1}{\rho}$

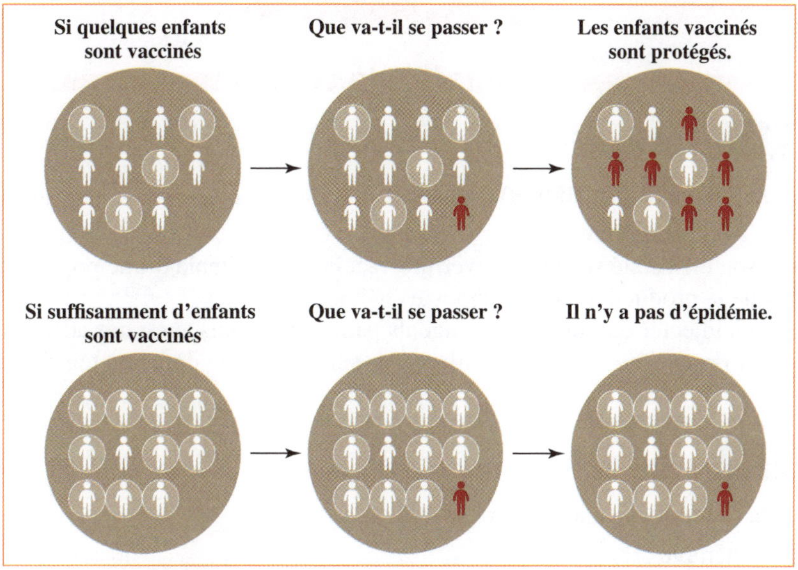

Figure 2 *Intérêt de la couverture vaccinale*

■ Il faut donc une couverture maximale q supérieure à $1 - \frac{1}{\rho}$ pour protéger efficacement une population.

■ La vaccination est donc une démarche où le bénéfice collectif est largement supérieur au risque vaccinal individuel.

B. L'immunothérapie

■ L'**immunothérapie*** est un traitement général visant à stimuler le système immunitaire. Il repose notamment sur deux méthodes :

– Les **vaccins thérapeutiques*** consistent à injecter des cytokines (interleukine 2, interférons…) produites normalement par les lymphocytes T CD4 : ces molécules de l'immunité adaptative permettent de stimuler la production des lymphocytes.

– Les **anticorps monoclonaux*** : ce sont des anticorps issus de la multiplication d'un lymphocyte spécifique à un antigène. On utilise des injections d'anticorps monoclonaux dirigés contre des antigènes spécifiques des cellules cancéreuses (comme l'antigène HER-2 des cellules du cancer du sein).

■ L'immunothérapie a pour objectif de lutter contre certains cancers, particulièrement les cancers du sang et les maladies neurodégénératives. C'est un champ de recherche aux implications sociétales importantes.

Remarque

Le prix Nobel de médecine 2018 fut attribué aux chercheurs James P. Allison et Tasuku Honjo pour leurs travaux sur les différentes méthodes d'immunothérapie dans la lutte contre les cancers.

EXERCICES

Connaître le cours

1 2 min ★ Vrai ou Faux ?

Relevez la (ou les) affirmation(s) exacte(s).

La vaccination préventive :

a) repose son efficacité sur une couverture vaccinale maximale d'une population.
b) provoque la production de lymphocytes mémoires.
c) consiste à injecter des antigènes d'agents pathogènes mais aussi des adjuvants.
d) protège l'organisme contre des pathogènes sur une courte durée de temps.

→ *Corrigé p. 258*

2 2 min ★ Vrai ou Faux ?

Relevez la (ou les) affirmation(s) exacte(s).

L'immunothérapie :

a) repose essentiellement sur la vaccination thérapeutique.
b) peut consister en l'injection d'anticorps monoclonaux.
c) permet de traiter actuellement tous les cancers existants.
d) est encore une voie de recherche thérapeutique.

→ *Corrigé p. 258*

3 5 min ★ Restitution de connaissances

Expliquez brièvement comment les rappels de vaccins permettent d'améliorer la mémoire immunitaire.

→ *Corrigé p. 258*

4 5 min ★ Schématiser le cours

Schématisez la propagation d'une maladie dans une population où 50 % des individus sont immunisés et 50 % sont sensibles.

→ *Corrigé p. 258*

S'entraîner

5 10 min ★★ Couverture vaccinale et rougeole

Le 18 février 2019, une famille française est suspectée d'avoir réintroduit la rougeole au Costa Rica où le dernier cas remontait à 2014. L'enfant de 5 ans, non vacciné, souffrait des premiers symptômes de la maladie : forte fièvre, écoulement nasal, conjonctivite, toux et éruptions cutanées.

On estime qu'une personne contaminée par la rougeole peut infecter 12 à 18 personnes, soit $\rho = 12\text{-}18$.

1. D'après vos connaissances, donnez la formule faisant le lien entre ρ et la couverture vaccinale maximale.

2. Calculez la couverture vaccinale maximale permettant de protéger efficacement contre la rougeole.

→ Corrigé p. 259

6 15 min ★★ L'immunothérapie

Le récepteur CTLA-4 agit comme un frein pour les lymphocytes : la cellule présentatrice d'antigène (CPA) se fixe sur ce récepteur, ce qui empêche l'activation des lymphocytes T et donc la destruction des cellules cancéreuses, normalement reconnues par les lymphocytes T.

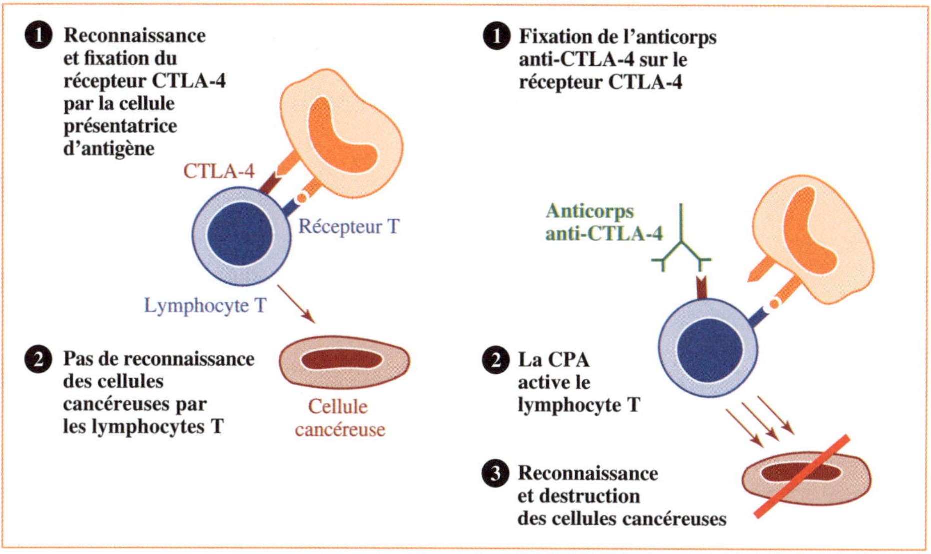

Figure 1 *Mode d'action des anticorps anti-CTLA-4*

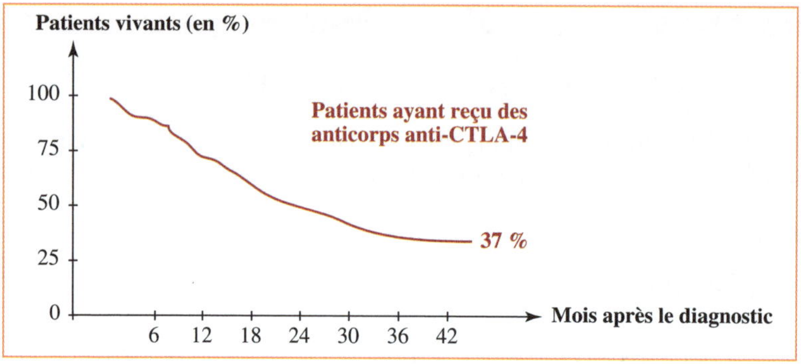

Figure 2 *Efficacité du traitement par immunothérapie contre les mélanomes*

1. D'après la figure 1, expliquez le principe de l'immunothérapie à base d'anticorps monoclonaux dirigés contre les récepteurs CTLA-4 dans la lutte contre le cancer.

2. D'après la figure 2, discutez de l'efficacité de ce traitement par immunothérapie sur les cancers de la peau (ou mélanome).

→ *Corrigé p. 259*

7 15 min ★★ La poliomyélite

La poliomyélite est une maladie causée par un virus. Celui-ci est retrouvé dans les excréments et la contamination s'effectue par ingestion d'eau ou d'aliments souillés. Le virus provoque alors une inflammation de la moelle épinière, ce qui entraîne de la fièvre, des courbatures, des vomissements, des douleurs dans le dos et, dans certains cas, des paralysies des jambes. C'est donc une maladie invalidante qui toucha notamment le président américain Franklin Delano Roosevelt et l'artiste Frida Kahlo.

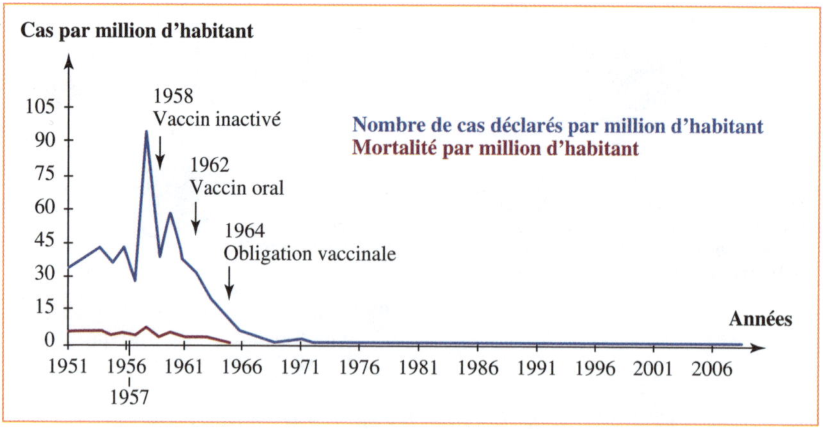

Évolution des cas de poliomyélite en France depuis 1951

1. Décrivez l'évolution des cas de poliomyélite en France depuis 1951.
2. Expliquez quel type de vaccin est utilisé dans le cas de la poliomyélite.
3. Mettez en évidence les conséquences de l'obligation vaccinale en 1964 sur la propagation de la poliomyélite en France.

→ Corrigé p. 259

8 15 min ★★ Les adjuvants

Certains adjuvants servent à amplifier la réponse immunitaire mémoire en activant les lymphocytes T CD4. Pour lutter contre le papillomavirus HPV 16 ou 18, deux adjuvants sont étudiés pour maximiser la réponse vaccinale et empêcher efficacement le développement d'un cancer du col de l'utérus :

- l'$AlSO_4$ active les lymphocytes T CD4 produisant des cytokines provoquant la réaction immunitaire inflammatoire et donc l'activation des cellules présentatrices d'antigènes ;
- l'$Al(OH)_2$ oriente la différenciation des lymphocytes T CD4 permettant l'activation des lymphocytes B mémoires et des plasmocytes mémoires.

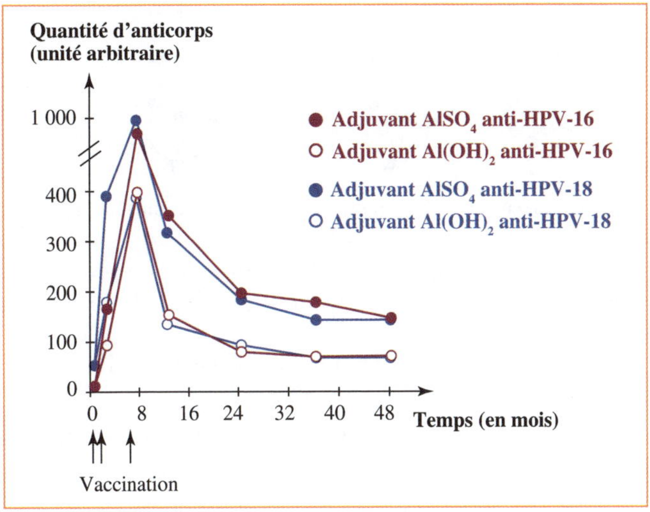

Quantité d'anticorps anti-HPV produits suite à l'injection de vaccins composés de différents adjuvants

1. Décrivez l'effet de la vaccination sur la production d'anticorps anti-HPV 16 et 18.
2. Comparez les deux adjuvants et déduisez-en lequel serait plus efficace pour induire une mémoire immunitaire forte et durable.

→ Corrigé p. 259

9 15 min ★★ Spécificité de l'immunité adaptative

Un individu est atteint par le virus de la grippe trois fois au cours de sa vie : on mesure sa production d'anticorps à chaque contamination en fonction de la variété virale par laquelle il a été atteint.

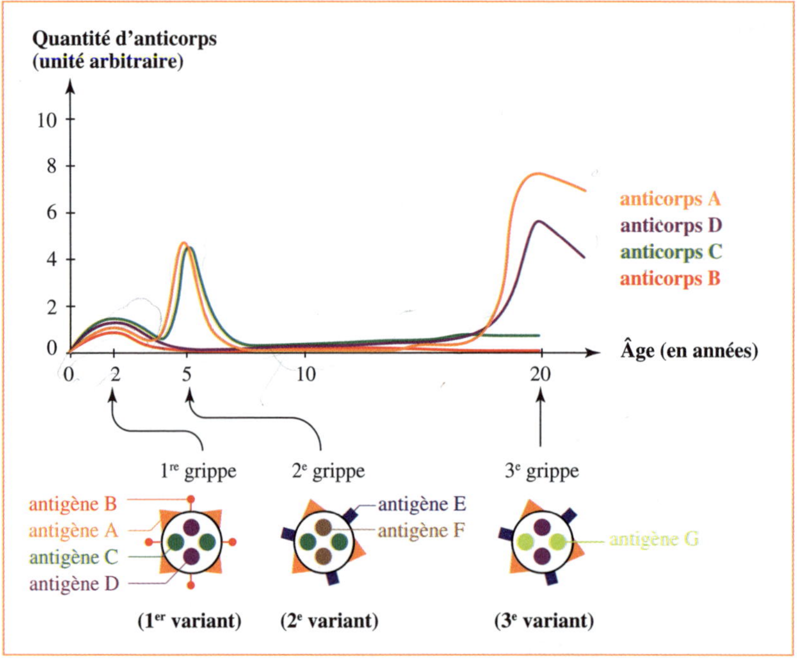

Évolution de la quantité de différents anticorps produits en fonction des virus grippaux infectant le même individu au cours de sa vie

1. Décrivez l'évolution de la production d'anticorps de cet individu au cours de sa vie en fonction du type de virus de la grippe qui l'a infecté.

2. D'après vos connaissances, expliquez l'augmentation de la quantité d'anticorps A produits à chaque nouvelle infection.

→ Corrigé p. 260

CONTRÔLE CONTINU POUR LE BAC

Exercice 10 pts **Cancer du sein et immunothérapie** 30 min

Le trastuzumab, anticorps monoclonal, est commercialisé sous le nom d'Herceptin®, aux États-Unis depuis septembre 1998, et en Europe depuis 2000. Il est utilisé dans le traitement du cancer du sein.

À l'aide de vos connaissances et des documents fournis, mettez en évidence les modes d'action et l'intérêt de l'immunothérapie dans la lutte contre le cancer du sein.

Document 1

Des études sur 10 000 femmes souffrant d'un cancer du sein ont été réalisées en 2008.

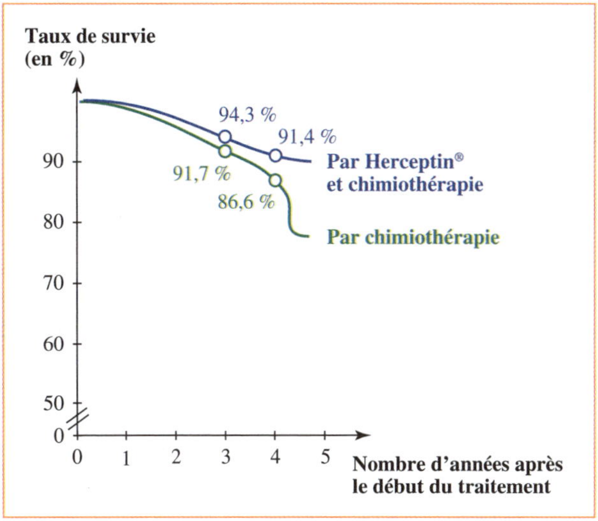

Proportion de survie après un cancer du sein traité par chimiothérapie et par Herceptin®

Document 2

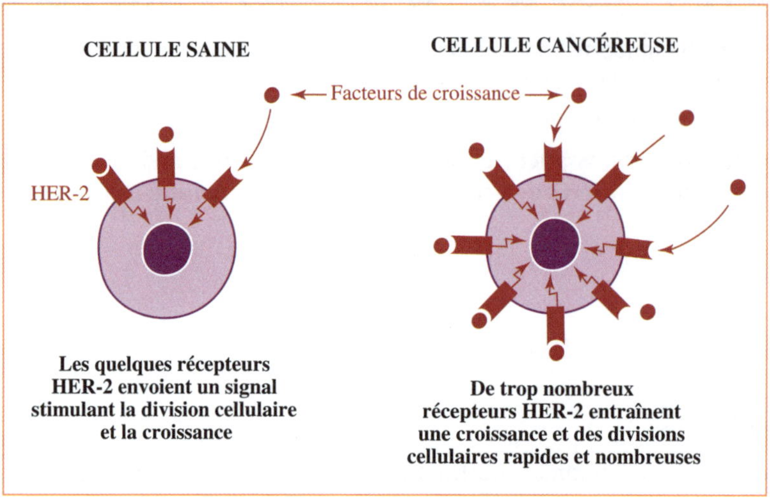

Rôle des protéines HER-2 dans la multiplication cellulaire et l'apparition de cellules cancéreuses

Chez 20 à 30 % des femmes atteintes d'un cancer du sein, le gène permettant la production de la protéine HER-2 est surexprimé.

Cette surexpression est provoquée par certaines mutations et s'accompagne alors d'une prolifération des cellules cancéreuses qui vont produire trop de récepteurs HER-2 (1,5 million de récepteurs HER-2 pour une cellule cancéreuse contre 20 000 pour une cellule saine).

Ces récepteurs HER-2 sont des protéines reconnaissant des facteurs de croissance et déclenchant ainsi la multiplication des cellules.

Document 3

L'Herceptin® est un médicament composé d'un anticorps monoclonal, le trastuzumab, dont l'action est dirigée contre les récepteurs HER-2 des cellules cancéreuses. On étudie son mode d'action ainsi que ses effets sur le nombre de cellules cancéreuses.

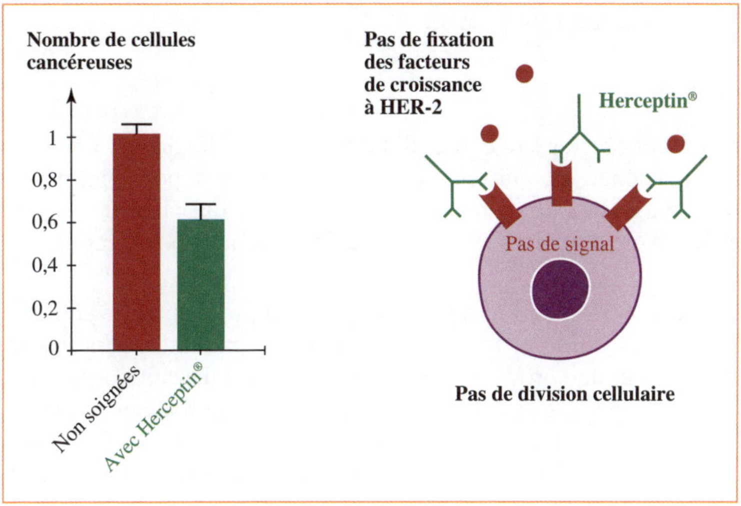

Mode d'action d'Herceptin®

→ Corrigé p. 260

CORRIGÉS

1 → *Énoncé p. 250*

Les affirmations exactes sont a), b) et c).

2 → *Énoncé p. 250*

Les affirmations exactes sont b) et d).

3 → *Énoncé p. 250*

La vaccination repose sur l'injection d'antigènes de pathogènes : soit le pathogène est entier mais atténué (ce qui provoque une très bonne réponse immunitaire), soit on injecte des fragments du pathogène avec l'antigène qui présente l'effet immunogène (mais le vaccin doit alors être associé à des adjuvants pour amplifier la réponse immunitaire).

La première rencontre avec l'antigène entraîne une production de cellules et molécules immunitaires faible et lente. Les rencontres suivantes, lors des rappels de vaccins, provoquent une production très rapide et forte des anticorps et autres lymphocytes. Ceci est permis grâce à la production de lymphocytes mémoires lors de la première rencontre, qui ont été sélectionnés pour répondre de façon spécifique à l'antigène. Lors des rencontres suivantes, les lymphocytes mémoires se multiplient directement et rapidement.

4 → *Énoncé p. 250*

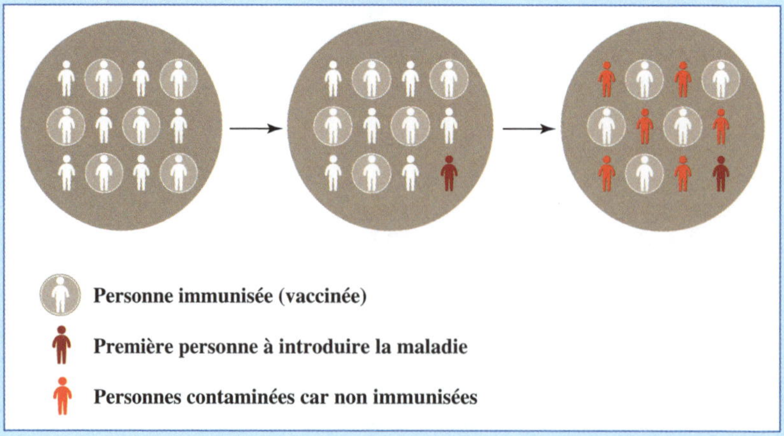

5 → Énoncé p. 251

1. Il faut une couverture maximale q supérieure à $1 - \frac{1}{\rho}$ pour protéger efficacement une population.

2. Dans le cas de la rougeole, on a donc $1 - \frac{1}{18} = 0{,}95$. La couverture vaccinale doit donc être de 95 % de la population pour protéger contre la rougeole et l'éradiquer.

6 → Énoncé p. 251

1. La fixation d'un anticorps anti-CTLA-4 empêche la reconnaissance du récepteur CTLA-4 par les cellules présentatrices d'antigènes. Le lymphocyte T peut alors être sélectionné et activé car le récepteur CTLA-4 n'a plus d'action « frein » sur le lymphocyte. Il reconnaît alors les cellules cancéreuses et permet leur destruction.

2. On observe que 37 % des patients traités par immunothérapie ont survécu à leur mélanome au bout de 42 mois de traitement. Ce traitement présente donc une certaine efficacité mais peut encore être associé à d'autres traitements anti-cancer comme les chimiothérapies et les traitements par rayonnement.

7 → Énoncé p. 252

1. On observe que les cas de poliomyélite étaient élevés avant 1956, entre 30 à 45 cas par million d'habitants, jusqu'à un pic en 1957 avec plus de 90 cas par million d'habitants. Depuis 1958, et la création d'un vaccin anti-poliomyélite, le nombre de cas chute jusqu'à disparaître à partir de 1971.

2. Le vaccin anti-poliomyélite est un vaccin inoculant un virus atténué, c'est-à-dire que le virus est injecté dans son ensemble mais avec une virulence rendue faible (par une augmentation de chaleur, une exposition aux UV, des cultures successives, etc.).

3. À partir de l'obligation vaccinale en 1964, on observe que les cas de poliomyélite ont disparu en France depuis 1971. Cette mesure a permis d'augmenter la couverture vaccinale française et donc d'arrêter la propagation de la maladie.

8 → Énoncé p. 253

1. On observe après l'injection des vaccins, que la quantité d'anticorps produit augmente fortement de 0 à 400 ou 1 000 UA selon le type d'adjuvant utilisé puis reste à un taux constant de 100 ou 200 UA. Il permet donc d'induire une protection contre les virus HPV 16 et 18.

2. Le vaccin formulé avec l'adjuvant $AlSO_4$ induit une réponse plus importante et durable que le vaccin formulé avec de l'$Al(OH)_2$. Cet adjuvant est donc plus efficace et sera utilisé lors des campagnes de vaccination anti-papillomavirus.

9 → Énoncé p. 254

1. Lors d'une première infection par la première variété du virus de la grippe, l'enfant de 2 ans a produit peu d'anticorps A, B, C et D. Trois années plus tard, au contact d'une deuxième variété de virus de la grippe, présentant cette fois-ci des antigènes A, C, E et F, l'enfant produit davantage d'anticorps A et C mais aucun anticorps B et D. Enfin, 15 ans après, une troisième contamination par la grippe a lieu avec une variété présentant les antigènes A, D, E et G, on observe une très forte production d'anticorps A et D.

2. On observe donc qu'à chaque nouvelle rencontre avec l'antigène A, l'organisme a produit davantage d'anticorps anti-A (1 UA lors de la première infection, 5 UA lors de la deuxième et enfin 8 UA lors de la dernière). On peut donc en déduire que la réponse immunitaire adaptative est de plus en plus efficace lors d'une rencontre répétée à un même antigène et plus rapide.

CONTRÔLE CONTINU POUR LE BAC

Exercice → Énoncé p. 255

Le trastuzumab est un anticorps monoclonal utilisé lors de traitements contre les cancers du sein. **Comment ces anticorps peuvent-ils limiter les cancers du sein ?**

On observe qu'au bout de 5 ans 91,4 % des femmes atteintes d'un cancer du sein survivent après traitement par injection de trastuzumab en plus d'une chimiothérapie, contre 86,6 % pour les femmes ayant suivi seulement une chimiothérapie. On peut donc supposer que ces anticorps permettent de mieux lutter contre les cancers du sein. Il nous reste à savoir quel est leur mode d'action.

Les cellules cancéreuses présentent des mutations sur le gène codant une protéine : HER-2. Ce gène est alors surexprimé et la cellule va posséder de nombreux récepteurs protéiques HER-2. Celle-ci reconnaît des facteurs de croissance et va alors déclencher la division de la cellule. Les cellules cancéreuses ayant trop de récepteurs HER-2, elles vont trop se multiplier.

Or, on observe qu'en présence de trastuzumab on obtient seulement 66 % de cellules cancéreuses soit 34 % de moins qu'en absence de traitement. Les anticorps trastuzumab permettent donc de diminuer le nombre de cellules cancéreuses et donc la taille des tumeurs du sein. Ces anticorps agissent en bloquant les récepteurs HER-2, qui ne vont donc plus stimuler la division cellulaire.

On peut donc conclure que les anticorps monoclonaux de trastuzumab permettent de diminuer les tumeurs lors d'un cancer du sein en bloquant les récepteurs HER-2, empêchant ainsi les divisions cellulaires nombreuses des cellules cancéreuses.

LEXIQUE

A

Acide nucléique
Molécule constituée de nucléotides (ADN et ARN par exemple).

Agents mutagènes
Facteurs environnementaux favorisant l'apparition de mutations.

Agrosystèmes
Écosystème modifié et contrôlé par l'Homme dans un but agricole.

Amphiboles
Minéraux hydroxylés caractéristiques des roches cristallisées à partir d'un magma hydraté ou des roches métamorphisées.

Anaphase
Étape de division cellulaire où le centromère de chaque chromosome se rompt et où chacune des chromatides migre vers un pôle opposé de la cellule. Lors de l'anaphase I de la méiose, ce sont les chromosomes homologues qui se séparent et migrent.

Anomalie magnétique
Différence calculée entre le champ magnétique mesuré par les roches et le champ magnétique actuel.

Anticorps
Molécule de l'immunité adaptative produite par les lymphocytes B activés en plasmocytes. Elle est spécifique à un antigène donné grâce à sa partie variable et permet la formation d'un complexe immun qui sera phagocyté grâce à sa partie constante.

Antigène
Molécule de surface des pathogènes déclenchant la réaction immunitaire.

Anti-inflammatoire
Médicament permettant de diminuer les symptômes de l'immunité innée en bloquant la synthèse de certains médiateurs chimiques de l'inflammation (par exemple l'aspirine et l'ibuprofène).

Anti-oncogène
Gène limitant la division cellulaire.

ARN messager
Acide nucléique synthétisé à partir de l'ADN lors de la transcription et l'épissage. Il assure l'intermédiaire entre l'ADN contenu dans le noyau et la synthèse de protéines dans le cytoplasme.

ARN polymérase
Enzyme permettant la synthèse de l'ARN pré-messager lors de la transcription.

Asthénosphère
Couche mantellique ductile délimitée dans sa partie supérieure par la LVZ.

B

Basalte
Roche magmatique volcanique de la croûte océanique. Sa composition est riche en feldspaths plagioclases et en pyroxènes.

Bimodalité des altitudes
Différence entre l'altitude moyenne des continents (+ 840 m) et l'altitude moyenne des océans (– 3,8 km) permettant de supposer l'existence de deux croûtes aux compositions et aux propriétés différentes.

Biocatalyseur
Propriété des enzymes qui consiste à accélérer les réactions métaboliques.

Biocénose
Ensemble des êtres vivants composant un écosystème.

Biodiversité
Diversité du vivant définie à trois niveaux : la diversité allélique, la diversité des espèces et la diversité des écosystèmes.

Biomasse
Quantité de matière organique produite dans un écosystème.

Biotope
Ensemble des conditions du milieu, caractéristiques d'un écosystème.

Brin transcrit
Chaîne de l'ADN qui sert de modèle à la transcription de l'ARN pré-messager par l'ARN polymérase.

C

Caryotype
Carte des chromosomes d'une cellule, caractéristique d'une espèce.

Cellules phagocytaires
Cellules de l'immunité innée qui réalisent la phagocytose. Ce sont les monocytes, les macrophages et les granulocytes.

Chimiothérapie
Traitement qui consiste à injecter au patient des substances antimitotiques.

Chloroplaste
Organite permettant la réalisation de la photosynthèse.

Chromatine
État diffus des chromosomes lors de l'interphase.

Chromosome
Complexe d'ADN et de protéines. C'est le support de l'information génétique dont la forme peut varier au cours du cycle cellulaire : diffuse lors de l'interphase (chromatine) et condensée lors des divisions cellulaires.

Chromosomes homologues
Paire de chromosomes présentant les mêmes gènes chez une cellule diploïde (mais des versions pouvant être différentes : les allèles).

Code génétique
Ensemble de règles permettant de connaître la correspondance entre les codons et les acides aminés lors de la traduction. Il est universel, redondant et non chevauchant.

Codon
Trois nucléotides de l'ARN messager lus par le ribosome et correspondant à un acide aminé précis.

Coésite
Minéral métamorphique caractéristique du faciès « éclogite », de très forte pression, des zones de subduction.

Collision
Subduction continentale d'une lithosphère continentale sous une autre.

Commensalisme
Relation interspécifique caractérisée par une espèce qui tire profit de sa relation avec une autre espèce sans effet néfaste sur cette dernière.

Compétition
Relation interspécifique entre plusieurs individus qui luttent pour les mêmes ressources.

Complexe enzyme-substrat
Complexe reposant sur l'interaction physique entre le substrat et l'enzyme au niveau du site actif.

Complexe immun
Complexe moléculaire d'antigènes et d'anticorps spécifiques à cet antigène. On peut les mettre en évidence par le test d'Ouchterlony.

Conditions abiotiques
Ensemble des conditions du milieu (température, pH, pluviométrie...).

Conduction
Mécanisme de transfert thermique par contact.

Conjugaison bactérienne
Transfert du matériel génétique entre plusieurs bactéries (transfert horizontal de gène).

Consommateurs
Êtres vivants transformant la matière organique des producteurs en leur propre matière organique.

Contraintes
Ensemble de forces s'exerçant sur la surface d'une roche.

Convection mantellique
Mécanisme de transfert thermique par mouvement de matière.

Convergence
Mouvement de rapprochement des plaques lithosphériques l'une par rapport à l'autre, caractéristique des zones de subduction.

Cycle cellulaire
Cycle de vie des cellules, composé d'une alternance d'interphase et de division cellulaire.

D

Décomposeurs
Êtres vivants permettant le recyclage de la matière organique morte en matière minérale.

Décompression adiabatique
Diminution rapide de la pression mantellique avec peu de perte de chaleur. Ce phénomène a lieu lors de la divergence des plaques au niveau des dorsales et entraîne la fusion partielle du manteau.

Délétion
Lésion de l'ADN consistant à enlever un nucléotide.

Dérive génétique
Mécanisme modifiant les fréquences alléliques d'une population par l'action du hasard.

Diploïde
Cellule possédant ses chromosomes par paires : les chromosomes homologues.

Divergence
Mouvement d'éloignement des plaques lithosphériques l'une par rapport à l'autre, caractéristique des dorsales océaniques.

Division équationnelle
Étape de la méiose où les chromosomes voient leur centromère se rompre et où chaque chromatide migre vers les 4 cellules-filles : on obtient des cellules haploïdes.

Division réductionnelle
Étape de la méiose où les chromosomes homologues de la cellule-mère diploïde se séparent et migrent dans les deux cellules-filles.

E

Écosystème
Ensemble d'êtres vivants, la biocénose, en interaction entre eux et avec leur milieu, le biotope.

Effet fondateur
Cas particulier de dérive génétique. Le hasard a modifié fortement la diversité

allélique d'un petit groupe d'individus fondateurs d'une nouvelle population.

Empreinte génétique
Technique de caractérisation des séquences génétiques propres à un individu.

Enzyme
Molécule permettant d'accélérer les réactions biologiques, notamment métaboliques. Ce sont des biocatalyseurs.

Épidémiologie
Étude de la répartition et des facteurs de risque des maladies humaines.

Épidémiologie analytique
Étude du lien entre l'exposition à des facteurs et l'apparition de la maladie.

Épidémiologie descriptive
Étude de la fréquence et de la répartition des maladies.

Épigénétique
Étude des modifications de l'expression des gènes, et donc du phénotype, sans lésions de l'ADN.

Épissage
Étape de maturation de l'ARN pré-messager en ARN messager qui consiste notamment à ôter les introns et à recoller les exons bout à bout.

Espèce invasive
Espèce exotique introduite dans un écosystème par l'Homme et qui peut devenir nuisible pour la biodiversité locale.

Eucaryotes
Cellules possédant un noyau et des organites (ex. : les cellules animales, végétales et les champignons).

Exon
Séquence nucléotidique codante de l'ADN conservée lors de l'épissage de l'ARN pré-messager en ARN messager.

F

Faille
Plan de glissement de deux blocs de roches les uns par rapport aux autres pouvant provoquer des séismes.

Faille normale
Faille le long de laquelle le bloc rocheux du dessus « tombe » sur le bloc du dessous.

Flux de matière
Ensemble des transferts de matière et d'énergie entre les niveaux trophiques d'un écosystème.

Flux thermique
Quantité d'énergie thermique libérée par surface et sur un temps donné.

Futaie
Aménagement forestier qui consiste à couper les espèces préexistantes afin de rajeunir le couvert végétal et d'obtenir du bois d'œuvre (ameublement et construction).

G

Gabbro
Roche magmatique plutonique de la croûte océanique. Sa composition est riche en feldspaths plagioclases et en pyroxènes.

Gène de prédisposition
Allèle augmentant la probabilité d'apparition d'une pathologie.

Génome
Ensemble des gènes d'un individu (ou d'une espèce).

Glaucophane
Minéral métamorphique caractéristique du faciès « schiste bleu », de forte pression et basse température, des zones de subduction.

GPS
Technique de positionnement par satellites permettant de visualiser instantanément la vitesse et la direction de déplacement des plaques lithosphériques.

Gradient géothermique
Évolution de la température terrestre en fonction de la profondeur.

Granite
Roche magmatique plutonique de la croûte continentale. Sa composition est riche en quartz, feldspaths et biotite.

Granulocyte
Cellule de l'immunité innée caractérisée par des « granules » dans son cytoplasme et un noyau plurilobé. Elle assure la phagocytose.

H

Haploïde
Cellule possédant ses chromosomes en un unique exemplaire.

Hétérozygote
Individu, ou cellule diploïde, possédant des allèles différents pour un gène donné.

Homozygote
Individu, ou cellule diploïde, possédant les mêmes allèles pour un gène donné.

I

Ingénierie écologique
Ensemble des techniques qui visent à manipuler, modifier, exploiter ou réparer les écosystèmes afin d'en tirer durablement le maximum de bénéfices.

Inhibiteur compétitif
Molécule se fixant sur le site actif de l'enzyme à la place du substrat et ralentissant ainsi sa vitesse de réaction.

Inhibiteur non compétitif
Molécule se fixant sur une autre région de l'enzyme que son site actif et diminuant ainsi son affinité avec le substrat.

Insertion
Lésion de l'ADN consistant à ajouter un nucléotide.

Interleukine
Médiateur de l'inflammation produit par les mastocytes qui permet le recrutement des cellules de l'immunité innée sur le lieu de l'infection.

Interphase
Phase du cycle cellulaire où se déroulent les étapes de croissance de la cellule (phases G1 et G2) et de doublement du matériel génétique (phase S).

Intron
Séquence nucléotidique non codante de l'ADN éliminée lors de l'épissage de l'ARN pré-messager en ARN messager.

Isotherme
Ligne fictive d'égales températures.

L

Lithosphère
Ensemble de croûte continentale ou océanique et du manteau supérieur. Elle est entièrement rigide et est délimitée dans sa partie basse par la LVZ.

LVZ (*Low Velocity Zone*)
Couche mantellique visqueuse qui délimite la lithosphère rigide de l'asthénosphère ductile. Elle est caractérisée par sa

température (1 300 °C) et sa profondeur moyenne (entre 100 et 150 km).

Lymphocyte
Cellule de l'immunité adaptative caractérisée par son grand noyau et la présence de récepteurs B ou T (lymphocyte B et lymphocyte T).

Lymphocyte auto-réactif
Lymphocyte reconnaissant le soi comme un pathogène et provoquant ainsi une maladie auto-immune.

M

Macrophage
Cellule de l'immunité innée présente dans les tissus. Elle dérive des monocytes et assure la phagocytose.

Maladie auto-immune
Maladie causée par l'apparition de lymphocytes reconnaissant les cellules de soi comme des cellules étrangères.

Maladie autosomique
Maladie dont la mutation est liée aux chromosomes non sexuels.

Maladie gonosomique
Maladie dont la mutation est liée aux chromosomes sexuels.

Maladie monogénique
Maladie génétique causée par la mutation d'un seul gène.

Maladie multifactorielle
Maladie causée à la fois par des mutations génétiques et des facteurs environnementaux.

Maladie multigénique
Maladie génétique causée par la mutation de plusieurs gènes appelés gènes de prédisposition.

Marges active et passive
- Bordure continentale fortement sismiques (ex. : les zones de subduction).
- Bordure continentale faiblement sismique.

Mastocyte
Cellule de l'immunité innée libérant des médiateurs de l'inflammation comme l'histamine et les prostaglandines.

Médiateurs chimiques de l'inflammation
Molécules produites par les mastocytes permettant d'augmenter le recrutement des cellules de l'immunité sur le lieu d'infection et ainsi de créer les symptômes de l'immunité innée.

Méiose
Division cellulaire caractéristique des cellules reproductrices. Il y a production de 4 cellules-filles haploïdes à partir d'une seule cellule-mère diploïde.

Métamorphisme
Variation des conditions de température et de pression d'une roche entraînant une modification de son assemblage minéralogique.

Métaphase
Étape de division cellulaire où les chromosomes migrent au centre de la cellule au niveau de la plaque équatoriale.

Métastase
Tumeur secondaire formée par la migration de cellules cancéreuses issues d'une tumeur primaire.

Migmatite
Roche « hybride » formée par le début de fusion partielle de la croûte continentale (couches claires de la roche ou leucosomes) et par son métamorphisme (couches sombres ou mélanosomes).

Mitochondrie
Organite permettant la réalisation de la respiration cellulaire.

Mitose
Division cellulaire permettant la production de deux cellules-filles diploïdes à partir d'une cellule-mère diploïde en 4 étapes : la prophase, la métaphase, l'anaphase et la télophase.

Monocyte
Cellule de l'immunité innée assurant la phagocytose. C'est une cellule circulatoire (dans le sang ou la lymphe) qui peut franchir les vaisseaux sanguins pour se localiser dans les tissus et devenir alors un macrophage.

Mutation
Changement, non réparé, dans la séquence en nucléotides d'un allèle et transmis de cellules-mères en cellules-filles.

Mutualisme
Relation interspécifique à bénéfices réciproques entre les individus.

N

Niche écologique
Ensemble des conditions biologiques et physico-chimiques dans lesquelles vit une espèce.

O

Oncogène
Gène favorisant la division cellulaire.

Organite
Élément intracellulaire permettant notamment les réactions métaboliques. Ce sont les mitochondries, les chloroplastes, les vacuoles…

P

PAMP (*Pathogen Associated Molecular Patterns*)
Molécules de surface communes à de nombreux micro-organismes et reconnues par les récepteurs PRR des cellules de l'immunité.

Parasitisme
Relation interspécifique entre un individu qui parasite un autre (la relation est bénéfique seulement pour l'un des individus et durable).

Phage
Virus à bactéries.

Phagocytose
Réaction de destruction des pathogènes par « digestion » grâce aux cellules phagocytaires (monocytes, macrophages et granulocytes).

Phases G1 et G2
Étapes de croissance de la cellule et de doublement de ses organites lors de l'interphase.

Phase S
Étape de doublement du matériel génétique lors de l'interphase. C'est lors de la phase S qu'a lieu la réplication semi-conservative de l'ADN.

Phénotype
Ensemble des caractères observables d'un individu à plusieurs échelles : moléculaire, cellulaire et macroscopique.

Photosynthèse
Réaction métabolique permettant la transformation de l'énergie lumineuse en énergie chimique (matière organique).

Plasmocyte
Cellule de l'immunité adaptative produisant des anticorps et issus de l'activation des lymphocytes B.

Point chaud
Remontée d'un panache mantellique considéré comme fixe. Le déplacement des plaques lithosphériques au-dessus de ce point chaud entraîne la création d'un alignement de volcans.

Prédation
Relation interspécifique entre un individu qui se nourrit d'un autre être vivant.

Producteurs primaires
Êtres vivants à la base des écosystèmes qui permettent la production de matière organique.

Prophase
Étape de division cellulaire où les chromosomes se condensent faisant apparaître leur forme à 2 chromatides reliées par un centromère. Le noyau disparaît progressivement.

Protéine
Molécule organique constituée d'un assemblage d'acides aminés. On peut les nommer peptides lorsque la séquence en acides aminés est réduite et polypeptides lorsque l'assemblage en acides aminés est grand.

PRR (*Pattern Recognition Receptor*)
Récepteurs des cellules immunitaires permettant la reconnaissance des PAMP des pathogènes.

R

Radiothérapie
Traitement des tumeurs à l'aide de l'exposition à des radiations localisées (radioactivité).

Réponse adaptative cellulaire
Réaction immunitaire adaptative faisant intervenir les cellules de type lymphocytes B et T.

Réponse adaptative humorale
Réaction immunitaire adaptative faisant intervenir les molécules de type anticorps.

Réponse immunitaire adaptative
Réaction immunitaire se déclenchant suite à la réaction immunitaire innée et la complétant. Elle fait intervenir des lymphocytes B et T, ainsi que des anticorps.

Réponse inflammatoire aiguë
Première réponse immunitaire mise en place suite à l'intrusion d'un pathogène ou la lésion d'un tissu. Elle est très conservée au cours de l'évolution (tous les Vertébrés la possèdent) et se caractérise par des symptômes d'inflammation : rougeur, gonflement, douleur et chaleur.

Relations interspécifiques
Différentes interactions possibles entre espèces d'un écosystème.

Réplication
Étape de doublement du matériel génétique lors de la phase S. Elle se réalise selon un modèle semi-conservatif permettant un assemblage complémentaire des nucléotides entre les deux brins d'ADN.

Réseau trophique
Ensemble des chaînes alimentaires d'un écosystème.

Réserve naturelle
Type d'ingénierie écologique reposant sur la protection des milieux.

Résilience
Capacité d'un écosystème à retrouver son état initial suite à une perturbation.

Résistance acquise
Résistance bactérienne apparue par des mutations induites par des transferts de gène d'une bactérie résistante à une bactérie sensible.

Résistance bactérienne
Phénomène de survie de certaines bactéries à l'application d'antibiotique.

Résistance multiple
Résistance bactérienne à plusieurs antibiotiques.

Résistance naturelle
Résistance bactérienne apparue de manière spontanée.

Respiration
Réaction métabolique aérobie permettant la transformation d'une énergie chimique (matière organique : les glucides) en une autre énergie chimique (ATP).

Ribosome
Complexe moléculaire permettant la traduction de l'ARN messager en protéine, en respectant le code génétique.

Rift axial
Vallée centrale d'une dorsale bordée par des blocs basculés, délimités par des failles normales.

Risque relatif
Probabilité de développer la maladie associée à un facteur.

Roche magmatique
Catégorie de roches cristallisées à partir du refroidissement d'un magma.

Roche métamorphique
Catégorie de roches issues de modifications minéralogiques causées par des variations de température et/ou de pression.

Roche plutonique
Catégorie de roches magmatiques, issues du refroidissement lent, en profondeur, d'un magma.

Roche sédimentaire
Catégorie de roches issues de la compaction de sédiments.

Roche volcanique
Catégorie de roches magmatiques, issues du refroidissement rapide, en surface, d'un magma.

S

Séisme
Rupture brutale d'une roche, libérant une grande quantité d'énergie.

Sélection, activation et multiplication clonales
Étapes de sélection des lymphocytes les plus spécifiques à un antigène par les cellules présentatrices d'antigène puis activation de ces lymphocytes en LT auxiliaires, LT cytotoxiques ou en plasmocytes et enfin amplification.

Sélection naturelle
Mécanisme modifiant les fréquences alléliques d'une population par l'action de l'environnement.

Séquençage
Techniques permettant de reconstituer l'enchaînement des nucléotides de l'ensemble du génome d'un individu (ou d'une espèce).

Serpentinite
Roche métamorphique issue de l'hydratation de la péridotite.

Services culturels
Valeur récréative et patrimoniale de la biodiversité.

Services d'approvisionnement
Valeur économique des écosystèmes.

Services de régulation
Services écologiques des écosystèmes.

Services écosystémiques
Bénéfices apportés par les écosystèmes à l'Homme.

Sillimanite
Minéral métamorphique caractéristique des zones de collision.

Site actif
Région de l'enzyme où le substrat se fixe et subit sa transformation en produit.

Solidus
Conditions de température et de pression au-delà desquelles la péridotite commence à fondre et à former les premières gouttes de magma.

Subduction
Contexte tectonique de convergence des plaques lithosphériques entraînant la tombée d'une lithosphère sous une autre le long d'un plan sismique de Wadati-Benioff.

Substitution
Lésion de l'ADN consistant à changer un nucléotide par un autre.

Symbiose
Relation interspécifique à bénéfices réciproques et obligatoires entre les individus.

Système lymphatique
Système circulatoire de la lymphe (liquide contenant les cellules de l'immunité) et les organes lymphatiques correspondants (moelle osseuse qui produit les lymphocytes B, thymus qui produit les lymphocytes T, la rate, les ganglions...).

T

Taillis
Aménagement forestier qui consiste à produire du bois de faible diamètre destiné au chauffage.

Taux de mutation
Probabilité qu'une bactérie mute sur un temps donné.

Télophase
Étape de division cellulaire où les deux cellules-filles s'individualisent.

Test d'Ouchterlony
Test de mise en évidence de la présence d'anticorps spécifiques à un antigène donné par la visualisation d'arcs de précipitation correspondant à la formation de complexes immuns.

Texture grenue
Assemblage minéralogique d'une roche caractéristique des roches magmatiques plutoniques. Les minéraux sont de taille importante et cohésifs.

Thérapie génique
Technique permettant de transférer un allèle sain aux cellules d'un individu atteint par une maladie génétique afin de remplacer l'allèle défectueux.

Tomographie sismique
Méthode d'étude de la vitesse de propagation des ondes sismiques par rapport au modèle PREM.

Topographie
Étude du relief terrestre.

Traduction
Dernière étape de la synthèse de protéines dans le cytoplasme. Elle consiste à produire des protéines à partir de la lecture de l'ARN

messager par les ribosomes, en respectant le code génétique.

Traitement curatif
Médicament permettant de guérir une maladie en traitant son origine génétique (ex. : la thérapie génétique).

Traitement symptomatique
Médicament compensant la fonction altérée de la protéine dont l'action a été affectée par la mutation du gène. Il traite donc les symptômes de la maladie mais pas son origine.

Transcription
Première étape de la production de protéines. L'ARN polymérase permet la production d'un ARN pré-messager à partir de l'ADN en associant les nucléotides de façon complémentaire.

Transgénèse
Méthode de modification du génome. Elle consiste à transférer l'allèle d'un organisme à un autre et à créer ainsi un OGM (organisme génétiquement modifié).

Tumeur
Amas de cellules cancéreuses issues des divisions cellulaires anarchiques d'une même cellule-mère mutée.

Tumeur bénigne
Tumeurs ne se propageant pas dans l'organisme.

Tumeur maligne
Tumeur irrégulière se propageant sur d'autres organes et formant des métastases.

V

Valeur sélective
Capacité d'un individu à se reproduire relativement au reste de la population.

Vigueur hybride
Technique de croisement d'individus aux caractères d'intérêt pour l'Homme afin d'obtenir des descendants plus performants.

Z

Zone d'ombre
Zone d'absence d'enregistrement d'ondes P directes par les sismographes suite à un séisme. Elle met en évidence la présence d'un noyau liquide.

biblio BAC 2020 lycée

Découvrez les œuvres au programme du Bac de français 2020, avec les titres de notre collection Bibliolycée

Toutes les clés pour réussir votre BAC 2020

- **Le texte de l'œuvre** clarifié grâce à de nombreuses notes explicatives.
- **La biographie** de l'auteur.
- **Le contexte historique, artistique et culturel** d'écriture de l'œuvre.
- **La genèse et la réception** de l'œuvre.
- **Le genre** de l'œuvre.
- **Des prolongements artistiques et culturels,** richement illustrés.
- **Un dossier SPÉCIAL BAC** proposant un groupement de textes et des sujets d'écrit sur le parcours littéraire associé à l'œuvre.

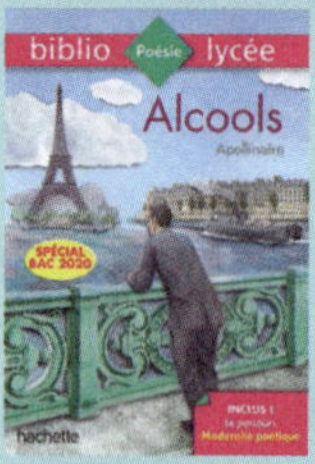

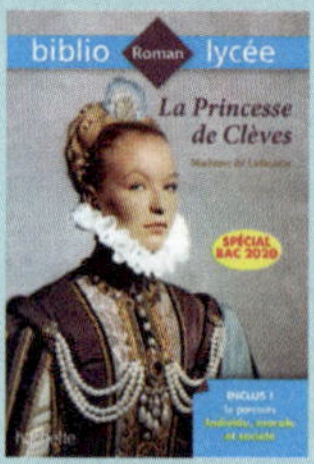

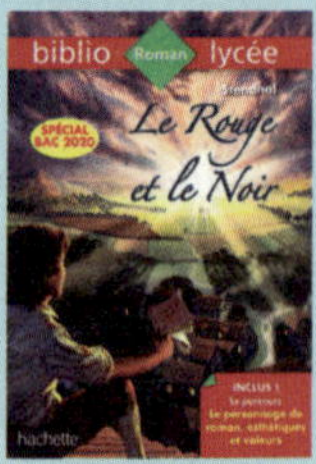

hachette
ÉDUCATION